Cambridge International AS and A Level

Psychology

Coursebook

Julia Russell, Fiona Lintern, Jamie Davies and Lizzie Gauntlett

CAMBRIDGE
UNIVERSITY PRESS

CAMBRIDGE
UNIVERSITY PRESS

University Printing House, Cambridge CB2 8BS, United Kingdom

One Liberty Plaza, 20th Floor, New York, NY 10006, USA

477 Williamstown Road, Port Melbourne, VIC 3207, Australia

314–321, 3rd Floor, Plot 3, Splendor Forum, Jasola District Centre, New Delhi – 110025, India

103 Penang Road, #05-06/07, Visioncrest Commercial, Singapore 238467

Cambridge University Press is part of the University of Cambridge.

It furthers the University's mission by disseminating knowledge in the pursuit of education, learning and research at the highest international levels of excellence.

www.cambridge.org
Information on this title: www.cambridge.org/9781316605691

First published 2016

20 19 18 17 16 15 14 13 12 11 10

Printed in India by Multivista Global Pvt Ltd.

A catalogue record for this publication is available from the British Library

ISBN 978-1-316-60569-1 Paperback

Contents

iii

How to use this book

Introduction – A brief overview of each chapter to set the scene and help with navigation through the book.

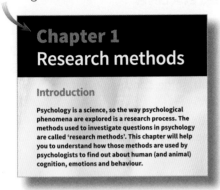

Chapter 1
Research methods

Introduction

Psychology is a science, so the way psychological phenomena are explored is a research process. The methods used to investigate questions in psychology are called 'research methods'. This chapter will help you to understand how those methods are used by psychologists to find out about human (and animal) cognition, emotions and behaviour.

Opening discussion – An engaging discussion to bring each chapter topic to life, encouraging students to read around the topic and sparking discussion in class.

Why do psychologists do research?

As students, you may be bombarded with 'facts' about how to improve your learning. Perhaps you have heard of different learning styles, or the benefits of repetition or mind maps to help you to revise. Each of these methods should have been tested to see if they actually work (although many haven't!). The process of research allows scientists such as psychologists to test ideas in order to discover whether there is evidence to support them. This is how we decide which drugs or therapies work best for mental illnesses, whether different displays or music help

1.1 Where do we focus when we concentrate on a problem?

Key terms – Clear and straightforward explanations of the most important terms in each topic.

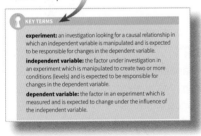

KEY TERMS

experiment: an investigation looking for a causal relationship in which an independent variable is manipulated and is expected to be responsible for changes in the dependent variable.

independent variable: the factor under investigation in an experiment which is manipulated to create two or more conditions (levels) and is expected to be responsible for changes in the dependent variable.

dependent variable: the factor in an experiment which is measured and is expected to change under the influence of the independent variable.

Core studies – Clear outlines of the studies mentioned in the syllabus discussing the aims, methodology, outcomes and evaluation.

2.1 Core study 1:
Canli et al. (2000)

Canli, T., Zhao, Z., Brewer, J., Gabrieli, J. D. E., & Cahill, L. (2000). Event-related activation in the human amygdala associates with later memory for individual emotional experience. *Journal of Neuroscience, 20*, 1–5.

Aim

Canli et al. aimed to show that emotive images will be remembered better than those that have little emotional impact on an individual.

The central questions addressed by this study were whether the amygdala is sensitive to varying degrees of emotional intensity to external stimuli and whether the level of intensity enhances memory for the stimuli.

Research methods – Specific aspects of research methods that relate to key points in each chapter.

RESEARCH METHODS IN PRACTICE

Dr Splash is conducting a laboratory experiment to test whether older adults detect emotions as quickly as younger people. He has two groups of participants, older and younger ones. This is his IV. He tests them by comparing how quickly they press a button to say that they have recognised the emotion on a face of a screen. This is the DV. Each participant sits at the same distance from the screen. This is one aspect of the **standardisation** of the procedure. In a pilot study, Dr Splash had shown the participants pictures and used a stopwatch to time their reactions himself, but he found he was not very consistent in his ability to stop timing exactly when the participant responded. He therefore changed to the computerised system to improve **reliability**. The pictures of faces included both younger and older people to ensure it was a **valid** test.

Reflections – Short prompts for students to reflect on their own experiences and to consider the psychological implications of those experiences.

Reflections: Look at the Research methods in practice box above.

- Define the independent variable.
- Define the dependent variable.
- Name and explain the experimental design being used in this study.
- Suggest why the use of faces of a range of ages would have improved validity.

Issues and debates – Areas of each topic that relate to current issues and debates in psychology are highlighted throughout each chapter, providing extra opportunities for discussion in class.

ISSUES AND DEBATES

The management of conflict is obviously extremely important for all organisations. Riggio offers a starting point in identifying that conflict may have individual or situational causes. Situational causes will be something to do with the organisation, the working conditions, salary levels, expectations and so on and being able to identify the causes may help in identifying a solution. However conflict may not be situational. It may simply be between two individuals and obviously very different strategies will be needed to manage this.

However it is also useful to recognise that conflict can also be positive and organisations need to recognise the potential positive outcomes from allowing some conflict to continue. Disagreement is not conflict and one problem

for organisations may be to establish the level of conflict that ensures good decision making (all aspects of the argument have been considered) and reduces the chances of groupthink while at the same time does not lead to the breakdown of good working relationships.

Having a range of strategies for managing conflict is obviously important for all organisations. When is it appropriate to allow the individuals concerned to continue to fight until one of them wins and when it is appropriate to step in and offer some sort of compromise solution? Strategies based on collaboration or the pursuit of a superordinate goal have their roots in the social psychology of prejudice and discrimination and the application of this understanding to the workplace is invaluable.

Self-assessment questions – Students can check their knowledge and track their progress by answering questions throughout each chapter.

SELF-ASSESSMENT QUESTIONS

6   A student is designing an experiment which aims to test whether dogs are more intelligent than cats. He has three dogs and two cats which he plans to use as his sample. To find out which is most intelligent, he is going to hide their food bowl inside a box and time how long it takes the animal to get to the food.
   a   Identify and operationalise the independent variable in this experiment.
   b   Identify and operationalise the dependent variable in this experiment.
   c   Write a non-directional hypothesis for this experiment.
   d   Write a null hypothesis for this experiment.
   e   Identify and outline the sampling technique used in this study.

Summary – A brief summary is included at the end of each chapter, providing a clear reminder of the key themes discussed.

Summary

Psychologists can use several different **research methods**; **experiments (laboratory, field and natural)**, **self-reports (questionnaires and interviews)**, **case studies** (detailed investigations of a single instance, e.g. one person), **observations** and **correlations**.

In experiments there is an **independent variable** (IV), which is manipulated, changed or (in natural experiments) used to create different conditions and a measured **dependent variable** (DV). By imposing **controls**, the experimenter can be more certain that changes in the IV are the cause of changes in the DV. There are three **experimental designs**. In an **independent measures design** there are different participants in each level of the IV, in a **repeated measures design** the same participants are used in all levels of the IV and in a **matched pairs design** the participants are paired up with one member of each pair in each level of the IV. In a repeated measures design **counterbalancing**

from the **population**. This can be done by **opportunity sampling** (choosing people who are available), **random sampling** (selecting participants so that each individual has an equal chance of being chosen) or **volunteer** (self-selecting) **sampling** (inviting participants, e.g. by advertising).

Studies can collect different types of data. **Quantitative data** is numerical and **qualitative data** is descriptive. **Data analysis** of quantitative data includes using various **measures of central tendency** (the **mean, median and mode**) and **measures of spread** (the **range** and **standard deviation**). Data can be displayed graphically using **bar charts, histograms** or **scatter graphs**.

The **normal distribution** is a pattern which can be seen on a frequency histogram which shows that the results have an even (symmetrical) spread around the mean, median and mode.

Exam-style questions – Students can use the questions at the end of each chapter to check their knowledge and understanding of the whole topic and to practise answering questions similar to those they will encounter in their exams.

Exam-style questions

1   A hypothesis in a study says 'Greater emotions will be experienced after an adrenalin injection than after a saline injection'.
   a   Is this a directional (one-tailed) hypothesis or a non-directional (two-tailed) hypothesis? Include a reason for your answer. [1 mark]
   b   Write a null hypothesis that could be used with the hypothesis given above. [2 marks]

2   Declan is conducting a self-report study about attitudes to people with phobias. He cannot decide whether to use a questionnaire or an interview.
   a   Suggest **one** advantage and **one** disadvantage of using a questionnaire for Declan's study. [4 marks]
   b   Write **one** open and **one** closed question that Declan could ask. [2 marks]
   c   Declan is concerned that his interpretation of the responses to questions might not be consistent. Is this mainly a reliability or a validity issue? Explain your answer. [2 marks]

Extension – Material that goes beyond the syllabus and encourages broader understanding of a topic, discussion and engagement.

Kahneman and Tversky (1979) have done a great deal of research into the consequences of System 1 thinking, which they claim is the way most people think, most of the time. This does not mean that we are incapable of System 2 thought but that we use this rarely and this may be why predictions of decision making are so difficult to get right.

One of their best known experiments asked Americans to respond to this statement: 'Steve is very shy and withdrawn, invariably helpful but with very little interest in people or in the world of reality. A meek and tidy soul, he has a need for order and structure, and a passion for detail.' Is Steve more likely to be a librarian or a farmer?

Not surprisingly, most Americans respond that Steve is more likely to be a librarian than a farmer. Steve sounds more like a librarian than a farmer. We do not consider the fact that there are at least five times as many farmers in the USA as there are librarians and that male librarians

Kahneman calls this the anchoring heuristic. Imagi[ne] wheel of fortune marked from 0 to 100. It has been the experimenters to stop at either number 10 or n[umber] When it stops, students are asked to write down th[e] at which it stops and they are then asked two quest[ions]

•   Is the percentage of African nations in the Unite[d] larger or smaller than the number you just wrot[e]
•   What is your best guess of the percentage of Afr[ican] nations in the United Nations?

Remember that the number the student has just w[ritten] down has absolutely nothing to do with the quest[ions] that have been asked. Despite this, students who [saw the] wheel stop at 10 gave an average guess for the se[cond] question of 25%. Those who saw the wheel stop a[t 65] gave an average guess of 45%. There are many st[udies like] this which show how the first question (the ir[relevant] material) anchors the answer to the second quest[ion]

Issues and debates at AS Level

Psychology can be defined as 'the science of mind and behaviour'. The topics explored in psychology include ways to understand, explain and predict the behaviour, thinking and emotions of humans and animals. Two of the key concepts on the syllabus describe the breadth of psychology as a subject. Most topics in psychology can be explored from a number of different approaches (e.g. biological, cognitive, learning and social). This means that explanations or theories used to understand a topic could be based on one of several different perspectives. The range of core studies illustrates a variety of approaches, and each approach has strengths and weaknesses. There are therefore debates both within and between approaches. However, the different approaches should not necessarily be seen as being in competition, but as alternative ways of thinking about and explaining topics, ideas or observations. These topics are the content of psychology and include ways to understand the behaviour, thinking and emotions of humans and animals.

In addition to debates based on the approaches, psychologists have a range of research methods they can use to test their explanations or theories and these also have strengths and weaknesses. The alternative methods can therefore be considered in terms of their relative usefulness and limitations. In particular, the role of ethics and the use of children and animals are issues that should be considered in the discussion of methods. Another difference between methods relates to the type of data they collect and whether it is numerical (quantitative) or descriptive (qualitative). For all psychological investigations, both those you learn about and those you design yourself, it is important to consider how well the research could be or has been done. In addition to ethics, two other key ideas here are validity (whether the research is really testing what it claims to) and reliability (the consistency of the measures used).

Psychological research and explanations aim to improve our understanding. Research which helps us to understand psychological phenomena may or may not have practical applications to everyday life. The extent to which the findings of research, or psychological theories, can be effectively applied to day-to-day problems is another important debate.

Finally, there are two specific debates you need to understand at AS Level. One is the nature versus nurture argument. This is about whether behaviour, feelings or thinking processes could result from nature (innate, genetic factors) or from nurture (can be explained in terms of the environmental influences). Again, these two sides of the debate are not necessarily in opposition. Contemporary psychology considers the relative contributions of each influence. The second debate is about the relative importance of individual versus situational influences in explanations. This means the role played by factors such as the person's personality or physiology that are unique to them (individual) and by factors in the setting, such as the people or the place (situational). Again, such factors may be present simultaneously and may interact, rather than being the influences working in isolation in a way which would be 'one or the other'.

Chapter 1
Research methods

Introduction

Psychology is a science, so the way psychological phenomena are explored is a research process. The methods used to investigate questions in psychology are called 'research methods'. This chapter will help you to understand how those methods are used by psychologists to find out about human (and animal) cognition, emotions and behaviour.

The chapter is divided into several sections, covering the basic research methods that you need to understand: experiments, self-reports, case studies, observations and correlations.

In addition, you will learn about features of the research process (hypotheses, variables, designs and sampling) and data and data analysis. There are also two further topics, which you will also consider within issues and debates: ethical and methodological issues. Together, these will help you to understand and be able to evaluate all aspects of research methods and to be able to apply your knowledge of research methods to novel research situations.

Why do psychologists do research?

As students, you may be bombarded with 'facts' about how to improve your learning. Perhaps you have heard of different learning styles, or the benefits of repetition or mind maps to help you to revise. Each of these methods should have been tested to see if they actually work (although many haven't!). The process of research allows scientists such as psychologists to test ideas in order to discover whether there is evidence to support them. This is how we decide which drugs or therapies work best for mental illnesses, whether different displays or music help to sell products in shops, and how we should organise work schedules to help factory workers to be efficient and healthy.

To be trustworthy, research needs to be planned well and conducted effectively. Imagine an investigation into new classroom techniques. If the researcher didn't know how hard the children worked, and compared the new techniques on a lazy class and a highly motivated class, this would produce false results. Consider a study into consumer psychology that compared how many goods were sold with and without music playing in the store. The researcher only played music at the weekends and played no music on weekdays. Would you believe the findings of studies such as these?

1.1 Where do we focus when we concentrate on a problem?

Reflections: Next time you see someone thinking really hard, perhaps trying to remember a name or work out the answer to a question, watch their eyes. It has been suggested that in such situations our eyes tend to look upwards and to the left (Figure 1.1). Consider how you might test whether this is true. Would you wait for people to get confused and then look at what they do, or would you give them a puzzle to make them think? How would you decide where they are looking? What would you do to be sure that they aren't just looking around the room for clues? Being able to decide on the answers to questions such as these is the basis of designing experiments in psychology.

1.1 Experiments

An **experiment** is an investigation which is looking for a cause-and-effect relationship. The researcher investigates the way one variable, called the **independent variable**, is responsible for the effect in another, the **dependent variable**. To test this, the researcher manipulates the independent variable (IV) to produce two or more conditions, such as 'high' or 'low' light levels or 'early' and 'late' in the day. The effect of these conditions on the dependent variable (DV) is measured. For example, an IV of light level might affect attention, with people being better at paying attention when the light levels are high. How well people pay attention would be the DV. If there is a big difference in the DV between the conditions, the researcher would conclude that the IV has caused the difference in the DV, i.e. that light levels affect attention (Figure 1.2).

> ### KEY TERMS
>
> **experiment:** an investigation looking for a causal relationship in which an independent variable is manipulated and is expected to be responsible for changes in the dependent variable.
>
> **independent variable:** the factor under investigation in an experiment which is manipulated to create two or more conditions (levels) and is expected to be responsible for changes in the dependent variable.
>
> **dependent variable:** the factor in an experiment which is measured and is expected to change under the influence of the independent variable.

1.2 An experiment can investigate whether the light level affects how well we concentrate

2

In order to be more certain that the difference between the conditions is caused by the IV, the researcher needs to control any other variables that might affect the DV. For example, people might find it harder to be attentive if they have eaten, exercised or sat through a very dull class. Such **extraneous variables** should therefore be controlled, i.e. kept the same in each condition (or 'level of the IV').

The levels of the IV being compared may be two or more **experimental conditions** (such as bright and dull artificial lights) or there may be one or more experimental conditions which are compared to a **control condition** (for example, artificial light compared to daylight). The control condition is simply the absence of the experimental variable. For example, in a comparison of the effect of eating chocolate on paying attention, we might compare either the effect of eating one bar or two bars (two experimental conditions) or the effect of eating one bar to no chocolate at all (one experimental and one control condition).

KEY TERMS

extraneous variable: a variable which either acts randomly, affecting the DV in all levels of the IV or systematically, i.e. on one level of the IV (called a confounding variable) so can obscure the effect of the IV, making the results difficult to interpret.

experimental condition: one or more of the situations in an experiment which represent different levels of the IV and are compared (or compared to a control condition).

control condition: a level of the IV in an experiment from which the IV is absent. It is compared to one or more experimental conditions.

laboratory experiment: a research method in which there is an IV, a DV and strict controls. It looks for a causal relationship and is conducted in a setting that is not in the usual environment for the participants with regard to the behaviour they are performing.

RESEARCH METHODS IN PRACTICE

A researcher might conduct a laboratory experiment to test the effect of the **independent variable** of time of day on the **dependent variable** of happiness of students. They might choose to control **extraneous variables** such as which lessons the students were in and whether they had recently eaten since these might affect happiness too. This would be a comparison between two **experimental conditions**.

Reflections: Look at the Research methods in practice box. Can you suggest:

- two different times of day to use as the levels of the *independent variable*
- how the *dependent variable* might be measured
- one other *extraneous variable* that it would be important to control?

Experimental design

The way that participants are used in different levels of the IV is called the **experimental design**. They may be allocated to all, or only one, of the levels of the IV.

The three experimental designs are:

- independent measures design
- repeated measures design
- matched pairs design.

Independent measures design

In an **independent measures design**, a separate group of participants is used for each experimental condition or level of the IV. This means that the data for each level of the IV is 'independent' because it is not related to any other data – it has come from different people. Note that this is a different use of the word 'independent' from that in the 'independent variable'.

If we wanted to know whether seeing aggressive models on television had long-term effects, we could (rather unethically) expose a group of young people to aggressive television and then wait for them to grow older. However, it would much quicker to compare two groups of adults, one group who had been allowed to watch aggressive TV as children and one group who had not been allowed to. This second example would be an independent measures design.

This design is good because the participants only encounter the experimental setting once. They are therefore unlikely

KEY TERMS

experimental design: the way in which participants are allocated to levels of the IV.

independent measures design: an experimental design in which a different group of participants is used for each level of the IV (condition).

3

to notice or respond to clues that might tell them the aims of the experiment (**demand characteristics**). One problem is that there might be individual differences between participants that could influence the findings. For example, in a study on the effect of noise on dreams, all the people who normally remember their dreams well might end up in the 'no noise' group. If so, it might look as though noise prevented dream recall when in fact it had little effect. This risk can be reduced by the **random allocation** of participants to different conditions. This spreads possible differences between individuals across the levels of the IV. To randomly allocate participants, each person is given a number, and the numbers are then randomly divided into two groups. This can be done by telling each participant a number, putting numbers into a hat and drawing out two sets, or using a random number generator (e.g. on a computer) to do the same thing.

Repeated measures design

In a **repeated measures design** the same group of people participate in every level of the IV. To help you to remember, think of the participants 'repeating' their performance under different conditions. For example, in a study looking at the effects of doodling on learning, we could count the number of words recalled in the same group of people when they did doodle and when they did not.

The main advantage of a repeated measures design is that each person acts as their own baseline. Any differences between participants that could influence their performance and therefore the DV will affect both levels of the IV in the same way. Individual differences are therefore unlikely to bias the findings. Imagine that in our experiment on doodling, one person was generally very quick to learn and another quite slow. In an independent measures design this might cause a problem if they were in different groups, but using a repeated measures design makes the differences between them less important, as both could show an improvement with doodling. Individual differences between participants are called **participant variables**. These variables, such as age, gender, personality or intelligence, can affect scores on the DV. It is therefore important to make sure that these variables do not hide, or exaggerate, differences between levels of the IV.

As each individual participates in every level of the IV they will perform the same or similar tasks two or more times. This can lead to a problem called the **order effect**. Repeated performance could cause participants to improve because they have encountered the task before – a **practice effect**. This matters because participants who

were tested on a condition second would perform better than those who did it first. Alternatively, repetition might make performance worse, perhaps if they were bored or tired – a **fatigue effect**. In addition, the participants see both levels of the IV and have more opportunity to work out what is being tested, so are more likely to respond to demand characteristics.

Order effects can be solved in two ways: by randomisation or counterbalancing. Imagine an experiment with two conditions: learning while listening to music (M) and learning with no music (N). In randomisation, participants are randomly allocated to do either condition M followed by N, or vice versa. As some will do each order, any advantage of doing one of the conditions first will probably be evened out in the results. To be more certain that possible effects are evened out, **counterbalancing** can be used. Here, the group of participants is divided into two and one half will

KEY TERMS

demand characteristics: features of the experimental situation which give away the aims. They can cause participants to try to change their behaviour, e.g. to match their beliefs about what is supposed to happen, which reduces the validity of the study.

random allocation: a way to reduce the effect of confounding variables such as individual differences. Participants are put in each level of the IV such that each person has an equal chance of being in any condition.

repeated measures design: an experimental design in which each participant performs in every level of the IV.

participant variables: individual differences between participants (such as age, personality and intelligence) that could affect their behaviour in a study. They could hide or exaggerate differences between levels of the IV.

order effects: practice and fatigue effects are the consequences of participating in a study more than once, e.g. in a repeated measures design. They cause changes in performance between conditions that are not due to the IV, so can obscure the effect on the DV.

practice effect: a situation where participants' performance improves because they experience the experimental task more than once, e.g. due to familiarity or learning the task.

fatigue effect: a situation where participants' performance declines because they have experienced an experimental task more than once, e.g. due to boredom or tiredness.

randomisation:

counterbalancing: counterbalancing is used to overcome order effects in a repeated measures design. Each possible order of levels of the IV is performed by a different sub-group of participants. This can be described as an ABBA design, as half the participants do condition A then B, and half do B then A.

do M followed by N, the other half N followed by M. If on the second test there was a risk of participants accidentally including items learned in the first test, this would be a problem for exactly half the participants in the 'music' condition, and exactly half in the 'no music' condition. Alternatively, a different design could be used.

The problems associated with both independent measures and repeated measures designs are overcome in a **matched pairs design**. Participants are matched into pairs who are similar in ways that are important to the experiment, such as age, gender, intelligence or personality (Figure 1.3). This matching is done on variables relevant to the study, so in a study on the effects of playing a violent computer game, participants might be matched on their existing level of aggression. Identical twins make ideal

matched pairs as they are both genetically the same and are likely to have had very similar experiences. Different groups of participants are then used for each level of the IV, with one participant from each pair being in each level of the IV. By using different participants in each group order effects are avoided and the matching of participants minimises the influence of individual differences.

1.3 Identical twins are perfect participants for a matched pairs design

> **KEY TERM**
>
> **matched pairs design:** an experimental design in which participants are arranged into pairs. Each pair is similar in ways that are important to the study and one member of each pair performs in a different level of the IV.

Experimental design			
	Independent measures	**Repeated measures**	**Matched pairs**
Strengths	Different participants are used in each level of the IV so there are no order effects Participants see only one level of the IV, reducing the effect of demand characteristics Random allocation to levels of the IV can reduce the effects of individual differences	Participant variables are unlikely to distort the effect of the IV, as each participant does all levels Counterbalancing reduces order effects Uses fewer participants than repeated measures so is good when participants are hard to find or if participants are at risk	Participants see only one level of the IV, reducing the effect of demand characteristics Participant variables are less likely to distort the effect of the IV than in an independent measures design as individual differences are matched No order effects
Weaknesses	Participant variables can distort results if there are important individual differences between participants in different levels of the IV More participants are needed than in a repeated measures design so the study may be less ethical if participants are harmed and less effective if there is a small sample because participants are hard to find	Order effect could distort the results As participants see the experimental task more than once, they have greater exposure to demand characteristics	The similarity between pairs is limited by the matching process, so the right matching criteria must be chosen in advance for this to be effective Availability of matching pairs may be limited, making the sample size small (although some studies conducted on twins use very large numbers of pairs)

Table 1.1 Strengths and weaknesses of experimental designs

RESEARCH METHODS IN PRACTICE

A child psychologist conducted an experiment to look at the effect of violent computer games (Figure 1.4). There were two experimental conditions (violent and non-violent). The **dependent variable** was the children's subsequent violent behaviour. The **experimental design** chosen was an **independent measures design**, with different children in each of the experimental conditions. If a **repeated measures design** had been used, in which the same children played each type of game, there could be **order effects**. For example, aggression caused by playing the violent game could still affect children in the non-violent game condition if they did this second. If this were the case, the problem could be reduced by using **counterbalancing**.

1.4 Are children more violent after they have played a violent computer game than before?

However, the use of an independent measures design risks **participant variables**, such as the original level of violence of each child, affecting the results. This could be reduced by either using **random allocation** of participants to each condition or by using a **matched pairs design**. In this case, children with similar aggression levels would be put in the different conditions. To avoid **demand characteristics**, the children would ideally be unaware that they are in an experiment, perhaps by telling them that they are in a computer games competition.

Reflections: Look at the Research methods in practice box. Think about the following:

- It would be a good idea to have another level of the IV that did not use a computer game but did use a computer, such as looking at non-violent pictures. Would this be a control condition or another experimental condition?

- One potential order effect that could arise if a repeated measures design was used for this experiment is that the children might get fed up with playing computer games by the second condition. Is this a practice effect or a fatigue effect?

- Suggest a *participant variable* other than initial level of violence that could affect the results of this study.

Types of experiments
Laboratory experiments

Many experiments in psychology are conducted in artificial surroundings, such as a laboratory. Experiments conducted in this way are called laboratory experiments; the participants are not in their usual environment for the behaviour they are performing, and there are strict controls over the situation. For example, a laboratory experiment on the attention of schoolchildren in high and low light levels could be conducted. It might be investigated by testing the children on a computerised attention task conducted in a psychology room in a university.

Evaluating laboratory experiments

Laboratory experiments use many controls. In addition, researchers in laboratory experiments can use **standardisation**, which means that the procedure for each participant can be kept exactly the same. Both controls and standardisation help to make the findings of the experiment **reliable**, that is the researchers would be more certain that the procedures and measures they are using are consistent. Controlling variables also improves **validity** – how certain the researcher can be that they are testing what they claim to be testing. By keeping the situation the same, the researcher can be more certain that any differences in the DV really are due to the differences between levels of the IV rather than due to any extraneous variables.

RESEARCH METHODS IN PRACTICE

Dr Splash is conducting a laboratory experiment to test whether older adults detect emotions as quickly as younger people. He has two groups of participants, older and younger ones. This is his IV. He tests them by comparing how quickly they press a button to say that they have recognised the emotion on a face of a screen. This is the DV. Each participant sits at the same distance from the screen. This is one aspect of the **standardisation** of the procedure. In a pilot study, Dr Splash had shown the participants pictures and used a stopwatch to time their reactions himself, but he found he was not very consistent in his ability to stop timing exactly when the participant responded. He therefore changed to the computerised system to improve **reliability**. The pictures of faces included both younger and older people to ensure it was a **valid** test.

Reflections: Look at the Research methods in practice box above.

- Define the independent variable.
- Define the dependent variable.
- Name and explain the experimental design being used in this study.
- Suggest why the use of faces of a range of ages would have improved validity.

Field experiments

Returning to the idea at the beginning of this section of the effect of light levels, the schoolchildren could be tested by altering the number of lights turned on in their normal classroom. Light level would still be the IV and the levels of the IV could be 'all the lights on' and 'half the lights on'. The DV of attention could then be measured by looking at their scores on a class test they were due to take that day. This is still an experiment because it has an IV and a DV (and there will still be some controls, such as the amount of time they spend studying for the test). However, it would be a **field experiment** because the children are being tested on a usual behaviour (the topic test) in their normal environment (the classroom).

Evaluating field experiments

It is a little harder to control variables and standardise procedures in a field experiment than a laboratory experiment. Reliability and validity may therefore be lower. However, validity might be improved because the

participants are performing a task that seems normal in a familiar environment. School students taken into a university laboratory might concentrate really hard because they are nervous or interested, which might cover up any differences between the different light level conditions. This means the findings from the laboratory would not **generalise** to other settings as well as those from the classroom. This is a problem of **ecological validity**, and field experiments often have better ecological validity than laboratory experiments (but not always).

Another advantage, if the participants are unaware that they are in an experiment, is that there may be fewer demand characteristics than there would be in a laboratory experiment. These are any features of the experiment that give away the aims and cause participants' behaviour to change, for example to try to 'make the experiment work'.

Natural experiments

A third type of experiment is the **natural experiment**. This is not a true experiment because the researcher cannot manipulate the levels of the IV. The differences or changes in the IV exist, or would occur, even in the absence of the experiment. For example, children's attention could be measured on very dull and very bright days, when the amount of light in the classroom differed (even with the lights turned on). The DV could again be measured with a class test.

 KEY TERMS

field experiment: an investigation looking for a causal relationship in which an independent variable is manipulated and is expected to be responsible for changes in the dependent variable. It is conducted in the normal environment for the participants for the behaviour being investigated.

generalise: apply the findings of a study more widely, e.g. to other settings and populations.

ecological validity: the extent to which the findings of research in one situation would generalise to other situations. This is influenced by whether the situation (e.g. a laboratory) represents the real world effectively and whether the task is relevant to real life (has **mundane realism**).

natural experiment: an investigation looking for a causal relationship in which the independent variable cannot be directly manipulated by the experimenter. Instead they study the effect of an existing difference or change. Since the researcher cannot manipulate the levels of the IV it is not a true experiment.

7

Evaluating natural experiments

Using this method there is less opportunity to control and standardise the situation. There may be **uncontrolled variables**, such as how warm the classroom is. It might be much warmer on sunny days for example. This could matter because the warmth might make the children sleepy and less able to concentrate. This would lower the validity of the findings, although this is countered by the

familiarity of the task and setting, which would increase ecological validity.

KEY TERM

uncontrolled variable: a confounding variable that may not have been identified and eliminated in an experiment, which can confuse the results. It may be a feature of the participants or the situation.

Types of experiment		
	Laboratory experiment	**Field experiment**	**Natural experiment**
Strengths	Good control of extraneous variables, raising validity Causal relationships can be determined Standardised procedures raise reliability and allow replication	As participants are in their normal situation for the activity being studied they are likely to behave naturally, making the results representative If participants are unaware that they are in a study, the problem of demand characteristics is less than in laboratory experiments	They can be used to study real-world issues If participants are in their normal situation, their behaviour is likely to be representative If participants are unaware that they are in a study, demand characteristics will be less problematic They enable researchers to investigate variables that it would not be practical or ethical to manipulate
Weaknesses	The artificial situation could make participants' behaviour unrepresentative Participants could respond to demand characteristics and alter their behaviour	Control of extraneous variables is harder than in laboratory experiments, lowering reliability and making replication difficult The researcher will be less sure that changes in the DV have been caused by changes in the IV than in a laboratory experiment Participants may be unaware that they are in a study, raising ethical issues	They are possible only when differences arise naturally Control over extraneous variables is often very difficult As the researcher is not manipulating the IV, they will be less sure of the cause of changes in the DV, so a causal relationship cannot necessarily be established They are often hard to replicate, as controls and standardisation are hard to implement, so the reliability may be low

Table 1.2 Strengths and weaknesses of experimental methods

RESEARCH METHODS IN PRACTICE
A research team is deciding how to test the effect of watching television on children's pro-social behaviour, that is, how nice children are to each other. They will measure pro-social behaviour by observing how often the children hold hands. They are considering two methods. One is a **field experiment**, in which parents either do or do not allow their child to watch television. Alternatively, they could observe the children in a remote place that has no television and then observe them again after the area has begun to receive satellite transmissions. This would be a **natural experiment**. Both of these studies would have more **ecological validity** than a laboratory experiment in which children were shown additional television, because in a laboratory the children would in an unfamiliar environment so may not pay attention to the television if they were nervous or distracted. In both situations there may be **uncontrolled variables**, such as which exact programmes were watched, and for how long. These factors could affect later pro-social behaviour. If the children are aware that their television viewing is being manipulated (in the field experiment) or their pro-social behaviour is being observed (in either experiment) they may try to alter their behaviour to meet the research team's expectations, for example being extra nice to each other (or especially nasty!).

Reflections: Look at the Research methods in practice box above. Which of the following can you identify?

- Independent variable
- Dependent variable.

Is there a *control condition*?

Can you suggest one *extraneous variable* that it would be important to control?

What effect might *demand characteristics* have in this study?

Suggest **one** strength and **one** weakness of conducting the study as a natural experiment in terms of *generalisability*.

Ethics in experiments

The role of ethics in psychology is discussed in detail in Section 1.10. Here we will briefly consider ethics in experiments (Figure 1.5). A participant in a laboratory experiment is likely to know that they are participating in a study and can readily be asked for their **informed consent**. However, it may be necessary to deceive them

in order to avoid them working out the aim of the study and altering their behaviour, i.e. to reduce demand characteristics. There is therefore a balance between good ethics and good science. In field and natural experiments, in contrast, it may not be possible to gain consent as the participants may be unaware that they are even in a study. This is an ethical problem because participants should have the right to know what they are entering into and to agree to participate or not. They should also have the **right to withdraw**, which they cannot do if they do not even know that they are in a study, and they should be protected from possible harm.

1.5 Researchers must achieve a balance between good ethics and good science

In all experiments, privacy and confidentiality are important. **Privacy** can be respected in laboratory experiments because the tests or questions used are pre-planned. In the natural settings of field and natural experiments, however, there is a risk of invading privacy so researchers must be more careful of this. **Confidentiality** can be respected in all experiments by keeping the participants' data secure and anonymous, although if the participants are unaware that data has been collected, as in a field experiment, it is important to ensure that they cannot be individually identified, for example by their place of work.

 KEY TERMS

informed consent: knowing enough about a study to decide whether you want to agree to participate.

right to withdraw: a participant should know that they can remove themselves, and their data, from the study at any time.

privacy: participants' emotions and physical space should not be invaded, for example they should not be observed in situations or places where they would not expect to be seen.

confidentiality: participants' results and personal information should be kept safely and not released to anyone outside the study.

RESEARCH METHODS IN PRACTICE

A psychology department ethical committee is looking at a research proposal for a study about the effect of cognitions on a therapy designed to help people to relax. The researchers only plan to ask for **consent** about the procedure they will use – listening to an imagery-based relaxation tape – and not their aim. They intend to deceive the participants about the independent variable, which will be either to tell them what will really happen – their pulse rate should fall – or to give them false information by telling them that some people see disturbing flashing lights. When the participants are given the limited information at the start of the study, they will also be told that they can leave at any time, giving them the **right to withdraw**. The instructions on the tape tell the participants to imagine relaxing, intimate thoughts. However, they will also be told that they will not be asked about these thoughts, which ensures their **privacy** is protected. When the participants join the study, each will be given a number, which will be used to identify their data so that their names do not have to be used, ensuring their **confidentiality**.

Reflections: Look at the Research methods in practice box above. Which of the following can you identify?

- The type of *experiment* being planned
- The independent variable
- The dependent variable
- The experimental design

Can you suggest one way in which possible harm to participants could arise as a result of this study?

Suggest why participants may want to withdraw from the study.

Why might it be necessary for the researchers to *deceive* the participants?

Applying your knowledge of experiments to novel research situations

You should be able to recognise experiments (including the IV and DV – and be able to operationalise them, i.e. define them in detail) to decide whether an experiment is a laboratory, field or natural experiment and to comment on controls, standardisation, ethics and reliability and validity. In addition, you should be able to plan an experiment, deciding on an IV and a DV, the type of experiment and how to implement suitable controls and to avoid ethical issues.

SELF-ASSESSMENT QUESTIONS

1 Barry and Anouk are deciding how to test whether gender affects artistic ability. Barry suggests doing a study in the psychology department where they ask students to come in for a study about memory in which they must redraw a complicated image. Barry and Anouk can then see how well they do it. Anouk thinks it would be better to persuade the art teacher to use an art class and set a lesson where students have to copy the same complicated image.

   a Explain the type of experiment that is being suggested:

      i by Barry

      ii by Anouk.

   b The independent variable is the same in Barry and Anouk's studies, as is the dependent variable.

      i Describe the independent variable (IV).

      ii Describe the dependent variable (DV).

   c Explain **one** ethical issue that is clear from the procedure they have suggested.

   d Suggest **one other** ethical issue and how they could avoid problems with this issue.

1.2 Self-reports

In a **self-report**, the participant gives the researcher information about themselves directly. This is different from experimental tests or observations where the researcher finds the data out from the participant. There are two techniques, questionnaires and interviews, both of which ask the participant questions.

Questionnaires

In a **questionnaire**, the questions are presented to the participant in written form. This may be on paper or as an online survey. There are several different types of questions. The two most important are **closed questions**, which have

KEY TERMS

self-report: a research method, such as a questionnaire or interview, which obtains data by asking participants to provide information about themselves.

questionnaire: a research method that uses written questions.

closed questions: questionnaire, interview or test items that produce quantitative data. They have only a few, stated alternative responses and no opportunity to expand on answers.

a fixed set of possible responses, and **open questions**, which ask for descriptive answers in the participant's own words. Closed questions can take the form of simple choices, such as those asking for yes/no answers or items from a list. Other forms of closed questions include rating scales (where a number is chosen, e.g. between 0 and 5) and Likert scales, which ask the respondent to say how much they agree with a statement such as 'Obesity is not important' or 'Exercise is a necessity' using the choices 'strongly agree / agree / don't know / disagree / strongly disagree'. Some examples of closed questions are as follows:

- What is your gender: male or female?
- How do you travel to school? walk / bicycle / bus / train / car
- Indicate which animal(s) scare you: dog, spider, cat, rat, fish, rabbit, bird. [You may tick as many as you like]
- How much do you like psychology on a scale of 0–4? (0 = not at all, 4 = very much)

Open questions prompt the respondent to give detailed answers, which may be quite long. They contain more depth than the answers to closed questions and are more likely to be able to explore the reasons behind behaviours, emotions or reasoning. They typically ask 'Why…' or simply 'Describe…'. Some examples of open questions are as follows:

- What do you think about children having access to the internet?
- Why do you believe it is important to help people who suffer from phobias?
- How would you suggest parents should discipline their children?
- When do you feel it is important to allow young people the freedom to control their own TV viewing?
- Describe your views on the use of social media sites with regard to encouraging helping behaviour.
- Explain how you would respond if you were told to hurt another person.

KEY TERMS

open questions: questionnaire, interview or test items that produce qualitative data. Participants give full and detailed answers in their own words, i.e. no categories or choices are given.

inter-rater reliability: the extent to which two researchers interpreting qualitative responses in a questionnaire (or interview) will produce the same records from the same raw data.

social desirability bias: trying to present oneself in the best light by determining what a test is asking.

filler questions: items put into a questionnaire, interview or test to disguise the aim of the study by hiding the important questions among irrelevant ones so that participants are less likely to alter their behaviour by working out the aims.

Evaluating questionnaires

Questionnaires using mainly closed questions are easier to analyse than interviews (using more open questions) as they can be used to produce totals of each category of answers so making it simple to summarise the findings. It is also possible to work out averages, which can help to describe the patterns in the results. Where qualitative data is gathered from questionnaires, it produces more detailed, in-depth information. This is an advantage, although it also leads to a problem. Answers to open questions have to be interpreted, and this can lead to a lack of reliability as the researcher may not be consistent in their interpretation. If more than one researcher is involved, there may also be differences between them. This would be a lack of **inter-rater reliability**.

One problem with questionnaires is that it is easy for participants to ignore them, which means the return rate may be very low. Importantly, the people who do reply to a questionnaire may all be quite similar, for example have time to spend because they are unemployed or retired. This would mean all the people who filled out the questionnaire would be quite similar.

1.6 People may lie in questionnaires, lowering validity, for example giving socially desirable responses to questionnaires about eating habits

Another problem with questionnaires is that participants may lie. They may do this because they want to look more acceptable; this is called a **social desirability bias** (Figure 1.6). Participants may also lie if they believe they have worked out the aim of the study. To avoid this, researchers sometimes include **filler questions** among the real questions. The answers to filler questions are not analysed in the research since they serve only to hide the real purpose of the study.

RESEARCH METHODS IN PRACTICE

Dr Blot is a psychology teacher. She wanted to know how her students were progressing on the course. She decided to use the **self-report** method and used an online **questionnaire** that the students did in their free time to collect data. This included several **closed questions** (1–4), which collected quantitative data, and some **open questions** (5 and 6) which collected qualitative data. She asked her colleague to help her to interpret the responses to the open questions and to help to ensure that they had good **inter-rater reliability**, she devised a list to help them to interpret questions 5 and 6. For question 5 it included looking for comments about:

reading up notes
copying up notes
reading the textbook
looking things up online
asking friends
checking with the teacher

For question 6 it included looking for comments about:

copying out notes
making summary notes
making mind maps
using past paper questions
making test cards

Some of the questions on the questionnaire were:

1   How often do you do the homework set?

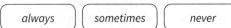

| always | sometimes | never |

2   Have you written yourself a research methods glossary?

| yes | no |

3   'Psychology is a difficult subject'. Do you:

| strongly agree | agree | don't know | disagree | strongly disagree |

4   Rate from 0 to 6 how well you understand the topic we have just completed:

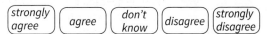

| 0 = don't understand at all |

| 6 = completely understand |

5   Explain what you do after each lesson to help you to remember what you have learned.

6   Describe how you will plan your revision for the next test.

Reflections: Look at the Research methods in practice box.

- Explain the difference between the *open* and *closed questions.*
- Suggest one more open question.
- Suggest one more closed question.
- Suggest why Dr Blot may have chosen to use an online questionnaire rather than one the students did on paper in the classroom.
- Explain why it was important that Dr Blot took steps to raise *inter-rater reliability*.

Interviews

In an **interview**, the researcher is typically face-to-face with the participant. Interviews can, however, be conducted through any medium that allows real-time interaction, such as by telephone or through a chat facility. The same kinds of questions can be asked in interviews as in questionnaires, although more open questions may be used.

The schedule of questions, that is the range of questions that are asked and the order of them, differs between different types of interviews. In a **structured interview**, the questions asked are the same for every participant and the order is fixed. There may even be instructions for the interviewer about how to sit or dress in order that the procedure is standardised each time data is collected. In an **unstructured interview**, in contrast, the questions asked depend on what the participant says, so the questions may be different for each participant. This is a very flexible technique but it may be hard to compare data collected from different participants or by different researchers. A compromise is a **semi-structured interview**. Here, there

KEY TERMS

interview: a research method using verbal questions asked directly, e.g. face-to-face or on the telephone.

structured interview: an interview with questions in a fixed order which may be scripted. Consistency might also be required for the interviewer's posture, voice, etc. so they are standardised.

unstructured interview: an interview in which most questions (after the first one) depend on the respondent's answers. A list of topics may be given to the interviewer.

semi-structured interview: an interview with a fixed list of open and closed questions. The interviewer can add more questions if necessary.

are some fixed questions, which make sure that there is some similar information from every participant. This means that comparisons can be made between them, and averages can be calculated if this is appropriate. In addition, it is possible to ask some questions that are specific to individual participants. This allows the researcher to develop ideas and explore issues that are particular to that person.

Evaluating interviews

As with questionnaires, interviewees may lie either because they want to seem more acceptable (a social desirability bias) or because they think they know the aim of the study, and are either trying to help the researcher by giving the answers they need, or to disrupt the research by doing the opposite. Interviewing is often time consuming and this can be a problem if it restricts the types of participants who volunteer for the research because it would give a narrow representation of feelings, beliefs or experiences.

When interpreting participants' responses to questions in an interview, researchers must be careful not to be **subjective**, that is, to produce findings which are based on a personal perspective. Instead, they should aim for **objectivity**, i.e. taking a view that is not led by one's own feelings or beliefs. To achieve this, the interviewer may ask other researchers, who are experienced but unaware of the aims of their research, to interpret the findings.

KEY TERMS

subjectivity: a personal viewpoint, which may be biased by one's feelings, beliefs or experiences, so may differ between individual researchers. It is not independent of the situation.

objectivity: an unbiased external viewpoint that is not affected by an individual's feelings, beliefs or experiences, so should be consistent between different researchers.

Applying your knowledge of self-reports to novel research situations

You should be able to recognise self-report studies, and decide whether they are questionnaires or interviews. You should also be able to choose which of these to use in a new situation. In addition, you should be able to recognise and write different types of questions (open and closed) and to identify and design different interview schedules (structured, semi-structured and unstructured). When doing this, it is important to consider how the

method used affects the availability of different types of participants and their honesty, as this affects the validity of the findings.

You should also think about the kinds of data that are produced, and the way it will be used. Although numerical data from closed questions can be analysed mathematically, data from open questions provides more in-depth information which may be more valid. For example, a closed question might not have a response close to a person's view, so an open question would allow that person to express views that they could not do in the choices available in the closed question.

Finally, the reliability of self-report data is important. Questionnaires and structured interviews may be higher in reliability because they are likely to be administered in a consistent way and because they generate numerical results which do not need interpretation. Responses to open questions, in contrast, have to be interpreted by the researcher and since they may differ in their opinions there is the possibility that they will be subjective.

RESEARCH METHODS IN PRACTICE

Dr Splash is planning an **interview**-based study because he wants to confirm that a new shopping centre is making people more helpful to each other. He wants to collect objective data about the number of times people are altruistic so has devised a **structured interview** with a list of specific questions such as 'How many times has someone held a door open for you?', 'Have you helped anyone carry their shopping?' and 'Have you seen anyone assisting a parent with a buggy?'. However, he is worried that this may produce very limited data so has an alternative plan to use an **unstructured interview**. This would begin with the question 'Please can you describe how friendly or helpful you have found people to be at the new shopping centre', after which he would base his questions on what they said. A colleague suggests that both methods have limitations. Interpreting the responses to the unstructured interview might lead to very **subjective** data, especially as Dr Splash already believes that the participants will be finding the shopping centre encourages helpfulness. Although the data from the closed questions in the structured interview might produce more objective measures, this would limit opportunities for asking participants to expand on their answers. The colleague suggests that a **semi-structured interview** might be better.

Reflections: Look at the previous Research methods in practice box.

- Why is the first of Dr Splash's suggestions a structured interview?
- Why would the data from these questions be more objective?
- Why is the second plan an unstructured interview?
- What is the problem with subjective interpretations of the participants' responses in the unstructured interview?
- Suggest why a semi-structured interview would be better in this case.

SELF-ASSESSMENT QUESTIONS

2 Shareen and Judith are investigating people's phobias. They have decided to use self-reports. Shareen is suggesting using a questionnaire and Judith wants to interview people instead.

   a Suggest **one** closed question and **one** open question that Shareen could use.

   b Suggest **one** reason why Judith might want to conduct an unstructured interview.

   c Describe **one** ethical problem that might arise in **either** Shareen's **or** Judith's version of the study.

1.3 Case studies

A case study is a detailed investigation of a single instance, usually just one person, although it could, for example, be a single family or institution. The data collected is detailed and in-depth and may be obtained using a variety of different techniques. For example, the participant may be interviewed, observed, given tests or asked to fill in questionnaires. Case studies are particularly useful for looking at rare cases where a detailed description is useful, and for following developmental changes, where the progress of a child, or a person with a disorder can be tracked through their improvement or decline. Case studies are therefore sometimes linked to therapy but it is important to remember that when the case study as a research method is being discussed, the therapeutic purpose is not the main aim.

Evaluating case studies

In some ways, the findings from case studies are highly valid, as the individual is explored in great depth and within a genuine context such as their work or family. Validity may be improved further using triangulation, where the use of different techniques should produce similar findings, for example observations and interviews with the participant and questionnaires for their family should all lead to similar conclusions. The research includes details such as their past as well as their present situation, their social interactions, their thinking and their emotions as well as their behaviours. Such detail, however, carries risks. One potential problem is the development of a close relationship with the researcher. This may make the researcher subjective in their outlook, which would reduce the validity of the study. The level of detail can also be an ethical threat, as the questions asked may intrude into the participant's private life and they may feel unable to refuse to answer them. The detail about the individual may make it hard to disguise their identity, even if they are not referred to by name, which would risk breaking the guideline of confidentiality.

Reliability is also an issue, as there is a single participant and perhaps one or only a few researchers. This, and their involvement with the case, means that they may find it hard to be objective, that is to take an external, unbiased view of the findings, for example when they interpret what the participant has said. This means that the findings may be limited to only this case, or to very few others.

Applying your knowledge of case studies to novel research situations

You should be able to recognise case studies, and when it is appropriate to use one. You should also be able to suggest possible techniques that could be used in a case study. When making these decisions, it is important to consider the validity and reliability of the findings. One way that the validity can be improved is though triangulation, where different methods are used within the case study to obtain the same information: for example, finding out about the participant's behaviour by observing them, interviewing them and asking their relatives to fill out a questionnaire. If the same results are obtained by all the methods, this suggests that the results are valid. Another consideration in planning case studies is an ethical one. Participants should be aware of their commitment, so that they can give their informed consent, and particular attention should be paid to ensuring their privacy is not invaded and that confidentiality is maintained.

RESEARCH METHODS IN PRACTICE

A psychologist in a sleep clinic has been conducting a **case study** on a patient, SL, who has had very bad dreams for several years. The psychologist uses an EEG to follow SL's sleep cycles and to detect when the patient is dreaming. The patient is then woken up and asked what the dream is about. SL has also been asked to keep a dream diary to record when the bad dreams occur. Members of SL's family have been interviewed to find out when the problems with nightmares started and how often they occur.

Reflections: Look at the Research methods in practice box above.

- How many different methods can you identify?
- Give two reasons why this is a case study.
- The psychologist is concerned that if the patient SL wanted to *withdraw* from the study, this might be quite difficult. Explain why this might be so.
- Explain the *ethical* reason for the researcher referring to the patient as SL.
- Suggest one **other** ethical issue that might be a problem in this study.
- Suggest **one** practical issue that might be a problem in this study.

SELF-ASSESSMENT QUESTIONS

3   Damon and Inka are planning a case study to investigate responses to emotional situations.

   a   Suggest **three** techniques that Damon and Inka might use in their case study.

   b   i   Describe **two** ethical problems that might arise in the study that Damon and Inka are planning.

      ii   For **one** of these problems, suggest a possible solution.

   c   Explain whether the results from Damon and Inka's study would be typical of the way everyone would respond to emotional situations.

1.4 Observations

Observations involve watching human or animal participants. This can be done in two overall ways. A **naturalistic observation** is conducted in the participants' normal environment, without interference from the

researchers in either the social or physical environment. A **controlled observation** is conducted in a situation which has been manipulated by the researchers. This may be in terms of the social or physical environment. Controlled observations can be done in either the participants' normal environment or in an artificial situation such as a laboratory.

At the beginning of a study, observations may be non-focused, that is, the whole range of possible behaviours are considered. If this continues throughout the study, it is called an **unstructured observation**. Usually, however, the range of behaviours studied is narrowed to a set of behaviours, and this technique is called a **structured observation**. The specific activities to be recorded are clearly defined in **behavioural categories**. This helps the observers to be consistent, i.e. it improves **inter-observer reliability**.

Another decision to be made is the role of the observer in the social setting. This may be participant or non-participant. A **participant observer** is part of the social setting, whereas a **non-participant observer** does not become involved in the situation being studied. This can be

KEY TERMS

naturalistic observation: a study conducted by watching the participants' behaviour in their normal environment without interference from the researchers in either the social or physical environment.

controlled observation: a study conducted by watching the participants' behaviour in a situation in which the social or physical environment has been manipulated by the researchers. It can be conducted in either the participants' normal environment or in an artificial situation.

unstructured observation: a study in which the observer records the whole range of possible behaviours, which is usually confined to a pilot stage at the beginning of a study to refine the behavioural categories to be observed.

structured observation: a study in which the observer records only a limited range of behaviours.

behavioural categories: the activities recorded in an observation. They should be operationalised (clearly defined) and should break a continuous stream of activity into discrete recordable events. They must be observable actions rather than inferred states.

inter-observer reliability: the consistency between two researchers watching the same event, i.e. whether they will produce the same records.

participant observer: a researcher who watches from the perspective of being part of the social setting.

non-participant observer: a researcher who does not become involved in the situation being studied, e.g. by watching through one-way glass or by keeping apart from the social group of the participants.

15

> **KEY TERMS**
>
> **overt observer:** the role of the observer is obvious to the participants.
>
> **covert observer:** the role of the observer is not obvious, e.g. because they are hidden or disguised.

achieved by watching through one-way glass or by keeping apart from the social group of the participants.

The role played by the observer may be either **overt** (it is obvious that they are an observer) or **covert** (they are hidden or disguised so the participants do not know the individual is an observer). Participant observers are overt, for example, if the researcher is holding a clipboard. When a participant observer is disguised as a member of the social group (Figure 1.7), or when a non-participant observer is physically hidden (e.g. by using CCTV), they are covert. Participants cannot be aware that they are being watched if the observer is covert. This increases validity as it is unlikely that participants would be affected by being observed, so demand characteristics and the effects of social desirability are reduced. However, covert observations raise practical issues, as the observer must be either hidden, far away or disguised in their role. This may make data collection more difficult, potentially reducing validity and reliability. Furthermore, covert participant observation raises ethical issues as the participants cannot give informed consent, and if they work out the observer's role this can cause distress.

1.7 A covert participant observer is disguised by being part of the social group: which one is the observer?

Evaluating observations

Naturalistic observations have the advantage that the behaviours seen are true to life. They are more likely to reflect the way the individuals really behave than if there is interference in the situation from researchers, as is the case in controlled observations. However, there is no guarantee

that the behaviours being studied will actually occur in a naturalistic situation, so it may be necessary to use a controlled observation.

Using an unstructured observation ensures that any important behaviours are recognised, but it may be very difficult to record all the activities accurately and many may be irrelevant. It is therefore likely, especially when only specific activities are of interest, that a structured observation will produce more reliable data.

The role played by the observer, and the participants' awareness of this, affect validity. If participants are unaware of the observer, or can ignore them, their activities are more likely to reflect their normal behaviour. This means that covert observers would produce more valid results than overt ones. However, in the case of covert participant observers there is an ethical issue of deception. The participants may interact with the observer in ways that they might have chosen not to if they had been aware that the individual was a researcher. This could invade their privacy and cause distress. However, an overt observer is likely to alter the behaviour of the participants as they are aware that they are being watched. This would reduce the validity of the findings as the activities being recorded are less likely to reflect real-world behaviour.

Applying your knowledge of observations to novel research situations

Observations can be used either as a research method or as a means to collect data in other research methods such as case studies, experiments or correlations. You should be able to distinguish between these two situations. Observation is being used as a research method in itself when the study consists solely of a means to collect data by watching participants and recording their behaviour directly to provide data. Observations are used as a technique to collect data about variables in other research methods when they are used to measure the dependent variable in an experiment or one or both variables in a correlation. In a case study, observations can be used alongside other techniques to explore a single instance in detail.

You will need to be able to decide when it is appropriate to use observations as a method, or as a technique within other methods. You should be able to recognise and justify choices about naturalistic versus controlled, structured versus unstructured, participant versus non-participant and covert versus overt observations. You will also need to be able to suggest ways of achieving these, such as how to make an observer participant or covert.

RESEARCH METHODS IN PRACTICE

Dr Blot is interested in whether her students detect each other's emotions and plans a **controlled observation**. She asks three students to act as confederates. They are told to take it in turns to appear quite sad in the common room at lunchtime. Dr Blot is on lunch duty with a colleague so they can act as **non-participant**, **overt** observers as they walk through the common room. The students will take no notice of them as they are used to them being there. Dr Blot suggests that she and her colleague use a list of specific behaviours to record, so they are doing a **structured observation**. This will also help to raise **inter-observer reliability** as they will be working from the same definitions, such as recording 'shows concern without action' if people look at the confederate without moving towards them, 'verbalises concern' if someone goes up to the confederate and asks them if they are OK and 'takes action' if they engage in a behaviour such as putting their arm round the confederate or buying them a drink.

Reflections: Look at the Research methods in practice box above.

- Suggest **one** other *behavioural category* that might have been included in the structured observation and define it.
- If Dr Blot had conducted an *unstructured observation*, how would the method have differed?
- An alternative plan would have been to have conducted a *naturalistic observation* and watched to see if any students appeared to be sad and how others responded. Outline **one** way it would have been ethically more acceptable and **one** way in which it would have been ethically less acceptable.
- Suggest how Dr Blot could have used a *participant, covert observer* rather than being an overt observer.

SELF-ASSESSMENT QUESTIONS

4   Debra and Jin want to use observations to find out about the behaviour of animals. Debra wants to go to the park and hide in a tree to observe the animals that live there. Jin thinks it would be better to set up an artificial situation and watch laboratory rats interacting with objects they would put in a special box.
   a   Who is suggesting a naturalistic observation and who is suggesting a controlled observation?
   b   Explain whether the observers in Debra's study would be overt or covert.
   c   For either Debra's or Jin's suggestion, decide whether it should be conducted as an unstructured or a structured observation and justify your choice.

1.5 Correlations

A correlational analysis is a technique used to investigate a link between two measured variables. **Correlations** are useful when it is possible only to measure variables, rather than manipulate them, i.e. when an experiment cannot be conducted. This may be because changing the variables would not be practical or would be unethical. For example, it would not be practical to conduct an experiment which controlled children's long-term exposure to television and it would not be ethical to increase real-life exposure to violent television programmes. Both of these could, however, be investigated using correlations. It is important to recognise that any link found between two variables in a correlation cannot be assumed to be a **causal relationship**, that is, we cannot know whether the change in one variable is *responsible* for the change in the other variable (Figure 1.8).

1.8 A bizarre positive correlation has been reported between ice cream consumption and murder rates. This relationship is a correlation, however, so we cannot conclude that eating ice cream causes people to commit murder

To look for a correlation between two variables, each variable must exist over a range and it must be possible to measure them numerically. Several techniques can be used to collect data for correlations, such as self-reports, observations and different kinds of tests.

We cannot say from one correlation that an increase in one variable has caused an increase (or decrease) in the other, because it is possible that the changes in both variables could be the result of another factor. Imagine that two variables are being measured: attention in class and score

KEY TERM

correlation: a research method which looks for a causal relationship between two measured variables. A change in one variable is related to a change in the other (although these changes cannot be assumed to be causal).

on a test. If these two correlate it would be tempting to say that paying attention in class is responsible for good test results but we cannot be sure of this. It is possible that both of these factors depend on another variable, such as the dedication of the individual student. The sort of student who pays more attention in class might also study much harder for the test. All we can conclude is that the two factors we have measured vary together, not that there is a cause-and-effect or causal relationship between them. As a consequence, it is important that you refer to 'measured variables' or 'co-variables' in a correlation and not independent and dependent variables. To make judgements about causality, an experiment must be used, so that we can be more certain that it is the manipulation of one variable that is responsible for the change in the other. If, on the other hand, we conduct a correlational study and find that there is *no* link between two variables, then we can conclude that there is no causal relationship.

The nature of the relationship between the two variables in a correlation can be described in terms of its *direction*. In a **positive correlation**, the two variables increase together. The change is in the same direction, so higher scores on one variable correspond with higher scores on the other. For example, in a positive correlation between exposure to aggressive models and violent behaviour, greater exposure to models would be linked to higher levels of violence. When two variables are **negatively correlated**, higher scores on one variable correspond with low scores on the other. For example, a negative correlation might exist between number of years in education and level of obedience: people with fewer years of education are more obedient (see also Section 1.9 on how to draw a scatter graph and a discussion of the *strength* of a correlation).

Evaluating correlations

A correlational study can only be valid if the measures of both variables test real phenomena in effective ways. To achieve this, the variables must be clearly defined and relate directly to the relationship being investigated. The reliability of a correlation depends on the measures of both variables

being consistent. So, for some correlations, such as those using scientific scales (such as volume in cm³ or time in seconds), the measures will be highly reliable. In other cases, such as studies correlating variables measured using self-reports or observations, there is a risk that reliability will be lower. This is because results from these measures may be less objective than from scientific measurements.

The main issue with correlations, however, is to remember that the conclusions do *not* necessarily reflect a causal relationship.

Applying your knowledge of correlations to novel research situations

Correlations provide a good starting point for research. They can indicate whether a relationship exists that might be worth pursuing with other research methods, such as experiments. Correlations are also useful because they enable researchers to explore problems when it is not practically or ethically possible to conduct experiments. You should be able to distinguish between correlations (with two measured variables) and experiments (where there is one variable – the IV – that is manipulated by the researcher and only one that is measured – the DV). You should also be able to recognise the difference between positive and negative correlations.

You will need to be able to decide when it is appropriate to use a correlation rather than any other method, for example when it is impossible to manipulate variables for practical or ethical reasons. You should also be able to justify choices about ways to measure the variables in a correlation and to suggest whether you would expect a positive or a negative correlation in a study. Finally, you will need to understand how to display the results of a correlational study on a scatter graph. This is discussed in Section 1.9.

RESEARCH METHODS IN PRACTICE

Professor Smudge is studying phobias. She thinks that there may be a **correlation** between how long a phobia has lasted and how severe it is. She is asking her sample of participants with phobias to record how many years they have suffered with their fear and rate how much the phobia interferes with their life on a scale of 1 (hardly at all) to 10 (almost constantly and prevents me from functioning normally). If there is a link between the two measured variables, there are two possible outcomes. There may be a **positive correlation** – phobias that have lasted longer may be more severe. There may, however, be no relationship between the two variables. If so, when she plotted the results on a **scatter graph**, the points would appear randomly placed, rather than lying on a line.

KEY TERMS

positive correlation: a relationship between two variables in which an increase in one accompanies an increase in the other, i.e. the two variables increase together.

negative correlation: a relationship between two variables in which an increase in one accompanies a decrease in the other, i.e. higher scores on one variable correspond with lower scores on the other.

Reflections: Look at the Research methods in practice box above.

- An alternative outcome might have been that phobias that have lasted longer are less severe. Explain why this is a negative correlation.
- If Professor Smudge found a positive correlation, it would be tempting, but incorrect, to say that the passage of time makes phobias worse. Why would this conclusion be incorrect?

SELF-ASSESSMENT QUESTIONS

5 Ekua and Takis are going to find out if there is a correlation between the amount of coffee people drink and the number of dreams they recall.

   a Explain why this is a correlational study and not an experiment.

   b Suggest whether the results will show a positive correlation or a negative correlation.

   c i Suggest **one** way to measure the amount of coffee that people drink.

   ii Explain either **one** advantage or **one** disadvantage of the way you have suggested measuring this variable.

1.6 Research processes

We began this chapter with a discussion about the need for research to test different ways to help students to learn or different therapies to help people who are mentally ill. These are examples of real-world problems that psychologists try to solve through their research. In this section we will consider the steps a psychologist might take in developing research to investigate a question or problem. This research process can be thought of as having several steps, the:

- development of an aim and **hypothesis**
- selection of a research method and, in an experiment, the experimental design
- definition, manipulation, measurement and control of variables
- ethical considerations
- selection of participants
- analysis of data, including the drawing of conclusions
- evaluation of research.

We will consider each of these steps in turn, evaluating the alternatives where appropriate and illustrating how the ideas can be applied to novel research situations.

Aims and hypotheses

Aims

Consider the idea of different ways to help students to study, perhaps using mind maps or revision apps (see Figure 1.9). Imagine that a psychologist, Dr Blot, asks a few of her psychology students which method they prefer, and finds that both are quite popular. Dr Blot wants to know which is most effective. This is Dr Blot's aim – *to investigate whether mind maps or revision apps are more effective at helping students to learn*. So, the *aim* tells you the purpose of the investigation. It is generally expressed in terms of what the study intends to show.

In a correlation, the aim is to investigate a link or relationship between two measured variables, such as between the number of computer games a student plays and their final A Level grade.

1.9 Revision apps such as Quizlet and Gojimo may – or may not – help students to learn

Hypotheses

To make her research more exact, Dr Blot needs to present this aim as a hypothesis, that is, as a testable statement. A hypothesis should provide a little more detail about the

---

 KEY TERM

hypothesis (plural hypotheses): a testable statement predicting a difference between levels of the independent variable (in an experiment) or a relationship between variables (in a correlation).

variables being investigated than the aim. Importantly, a hypothesis should also be *falsifiable*, that is it should be possible for it to be shown to be wrong. The main hypothesis in a study (sometimes called the **alternative hypothesis**) can be written in several different ways. They differ in terms of the nature of the prediction they make about the results of an investigation.

Non-directional hypotheses

A **non-directional (two-tailed) hypothesis** predicts that there will be an effect, but not the direction of that effect (Figure 1.10). In an experiment, this means that the hypothesis will suggests that the IV will change the DV but not whether the effect will be an increase or a decrease. This type of hypothesis is chosen if the effect of the variable is being tested for the first time, so there are no previous results to suggest what the results might be. For example, Dr Blot's hypothesis could be: *There is a difference between the effectiveness of mind maps and revision apps in helping students to learn.* Note that it is predicting a difference, but not which condition will be better at helping with learning.

A non-directional hypothesis in a correlational study predicts that there will be a relationship between the two measured variables. For example, a directional hypothesis might be: *There will be a correlation between the number of computer games a student plays and their final A Level grade.*

Directional hypotheses

When most previous research or other evidence suggests the nature or 'direction' of an effect we can use a **directional (one-tailed) hypothesis**. In an experiment this means saying which condition will be 'best' (i.e. produce the 'highest' scores) and in a correlational study, whether there will be a positive or negative correlation.

1.10 Unlike with a one-tailed hypothofish, you can't see which way a two-tailed hypothofish will swim

Returning to Dr Blot's study, there might be evidence that revision apps are better than mind maps, perhaps because they are more 'active' and being actively engaged helps memory. This is a directional prediction so the hypothesis might be: *Students using revision apps will learn better than students using mind maps.* Note that the opposite prediction could also be expressed as a directional hypothesis. This

would be: *Students using mind maps will learn better than students using revision apps.* We might make this prediction if we believed that writing a mind map yourself was more effective than just reusing ready-made materials on revision apps.

A directional hypothesis for the correlational study about computer games and grades could say: *There will be a negative correlation between the number of computer games a student plays and their final A Level grade.* We might make this prediction if we believed that the time spent playing games might stop students working. However, a different directional hypothesis could be: *As the number of computer games a student has increases, their A Level grade increases.* We might make this prediction if we believed that students who engaged more with technology, even through games, were also more likely to benefit from technology-based learning aids. Remember that your hypothesis should not say that one factor *causes* the change in the other.

Null hypotheses

The alternative hypothesis is an alternative to the **null hypothesis**. In an experiment, the null hypothesis states that any difference in the DV between levels of the IV is so small that it is likely to have arisen by chance. For Dr Blot's study, the null hypothesis could be written either as: *There will be no difference between the effectiveness of mind maps and revision apps in helping students to learn* or *Any difference in effectiveness of mind maps and revision apps in helping students to learn is due to chance.*

KEY TERMS

alternative hypothesis: the testable statement which predicts a difference or relationship between variables in a particular investigation.

non-directional (two-tailed) hypothesis: a statement predicting only that one variable will be related to another, e.g. that there will be a difference in the DV between levels of the IV in an experiment or that there will be a relationship between the measured variables in a correlation.

directional (one-tailed) hypothesis: a statement predicting the direction of a relationship between variables, e.g. in an experiment whether the levels of the IV will produce an increase or a decrease in the DV or in a correlation whether an increase in one variable will be linked to an increase or a decrease in another variable.

null hypothesis: a testable statement saying that any difference or correlation in the results is due to chance, i.e. that no pattern in the results has arisen because of the variables being studied.

To help you to write null hypotheses for experiments, remember that they should say 'There will be no difference in the DV between *condition X* and *condition Y*' or that 'Any difference in the DV between *condition X* and *condition Y* is due to chance'. Make sure that you *always* state both of the levels of the IV and the DV otherwise your null hypothesis will not make sense. For example, the null hypothesis 'There is no difference between mind maps and revision apps' is meaningless.

Correlational studies also need a null hypothesis. These predict either no link or that any relationship could have occurred by chance. A general null hypothesis for a correlational study reads: *There will be no relationship between variable X and variable Y* (or *Any relationship between variable X and variable Y is due to chance*). For example: *There will be no relationship between the number*

of computer games a student has and their A Level grade (or *Any relationship between the number of computer games a student has and their A Level grade is due to chance*).

1.7 The definition, manipulation, measurement and control of variables

Variables are factors that change or can be changed. In experiments these are the independent and dependent variables as well as any extraneous factors that are or are not controlled. In correlations there are two measured variables (see Section 1.5).

Experiments look for changes or differences in the dependent variable (DV) between two or more levels of the independent variable (IV), which are set up by the experimenter. It is important that the IV is clearly defined, or **operationalised**, so that the manipulation of the conditions represents the intended differences. Consider

 KEY TERM

operationalisation: the definition of variables so that they can be accurately manipulated, measured or quantified and replicated. This includes the IV and DV in experiments and the two measured variables in correlations.

Reflections: Look at the Research methods in practice box.

- Which study is an experiment and which is a correlation?
- Can you suggest a different directional hypothesis for the correlation, one that proposes a negative correlation?
- What is wrong with the alternative hypothesis '*Soft chairs will be better than hard chairs*'?

RESEARCH METHODS IN PRACTICE

Dr Blot is thinking about buying new chairs for her classroom. Her **aim** is to explore whether hard or soft chairs help her students to work better (Figure 1.11). She wonders whether to predict a **non-directional (two-tailed) hypothesis**: *There is a difference in work rate of students sitting on comfortable and uncomfortable chairs.* Another psychology teacher says that students respond well to other comforts like access to a drinks machine or snack bar, and the soft chairs might make them happier, so they work harder. Dr Blot rewrites her prediction as a **directional (one-tailed) hypothesis**, saying: *Students on comfortable chairs will have a higher work rate than ones sitting on uncomfortable chairs.* A third teacher is not convinced and suggests that if the students are too comfortable they will become sleepy and lazy, so work less. The hypothesis would then be: *Students on comfortable chairs will have a lower work rate than ones sitting on uncomfortable chairs.* Her **null hypothesis** would be: *Any difference in work rate of students sitting on comfortable and uncomfortable chairs is due to chance.*

Now imagine a study which aims to look for a link between sleep and emotions. A non-directional hypothesis might be: *There will be a correlation between amount of sleep and*

1.11 Would you work harder in lessons if you had more comfortable classroom chairs?

emotional reactivity. The possible directional hypothesis could say: *There will be a positive correlation between amount of sleep and how emotional someone is.* Remember *not* to say that one factor causes the other to change. The null hypothesis here would be: *Any relationship between amount of sleep and emotional reactivity is due to chance.*

a study testing the effect of age on susceptibility to false memories. The IV would be age, with, for example, 'young', 'middle-aged' and 'old' groups. It is important to know *how* old the people in the groups are; this is operationalisation. You might operationalise 'young' as under 20 years old, 'middle aged' as 40–50 years old and 'old' as over 70. The DV must also be operationalised, so it can be measured effectively. We could operationalise the DV by counting the number of details 'remembered' about the false memory or how convinced the participants were that it was true.

Controlling variables and standardising procedures

Controlling of variables

Psychologists need to control variables in their studies in order to be more certain about their findings. In particular, in experiments, it is important to control any **extraneous variables** that might have a consistent effect. These are called **confounding variables** as they confound, i.e. confuse, the results. Confounding variables can either work against the effect of the IV or increase the apparent effect of the IV because they act on the DV selectively in one level of the IV. These variables are the most important to control. Other extraneous variables, which have a random effect on the DV across all levels of the IV, are not so problematic. The difficulty is to identify which variables it will be important to control before the experiment starts. This is one function of a **pilot study**, a preliminary test of the procedures of a study. However, if important extraneous variables are not identified in advance, they will become uncontrolled variables, which will affect the results, making them difficult to interpret because it will be hard to separate the effects of the IV from those of the other factors that may have influenced the DV systematically.

Consider Dr Blot's study of students and chairs (Section 1.6). Perhaps Dr Blot compares one class in a room with the new (soft) chairs and another class in a different room with the old (hard) chairs. If the room containing the new chairs happens to have better lighting, Dr Blot may find that the students in the 'soft chairs' condition perform better. However, this may be due to the confounding variable of brighter lighting rather than the comfort level of the chairs. This is an example of a **situational variable**, because lighting is an aspect of the environment. Another possible extraneous variable is how hard working the individual students are. We might expect normally hard-working students to be randomly distributed among the different classes, in which case this variable is not a problem. However, suppose that all the students in the 'soft chairs'

class do arts and humanities subjects and all the students in the 'hard chairs' class do maths and sciences. If Dr Blot happens to use a test of data analysis as her measure of the DV, she might find that the students in the 'hard chairs' level of the IV perform better. This would suggest that the soft chairs make students perform worse but could in fact be due to the extraneous variable of subject groups. This is an example of a participant variable, because the difference has been caused by a feature of the individuals, i.e. their ability in maths.

Standardisation

Controls make sure that the levels of the IV represent what they are supposed to, i.e. that the differences between them are going to create the intended situations to test the hypothesis. This helps to ensure validity (see Section 1.11). It is also important that every participant is treated in the same way. This is the process of standardisation. One way that this is achieved is by having standardised instructions, that give the same advice to every person in the study. Imagine a questionnaire testing attitudes to helping behaviour. All participants would need to have the same advice about how to fill it in, so that any effects of social desirability – the influence of needing to give answers that were acceptable to society – were equally likely.

1.12 Scientific instruments are likely to produce objective, reliable data

The procedure itself also needs to be standardised. This involves having equipment or tests that are consistent, i.e. that measure the same variable every time and always do so in the same way. Consider the questionnaire about attitudes to helping again. All the questions should focus on the same aspect of behaviour, i.e. helping, rather than some looking at a different but possibly

KEY TERM

situational variable: a confounding variable caused by an aspect of the environment, e.g. the amount of light or noise.

control: a way to keep a potential extraneous variable constant, e.g. between levels of the IV, to ensure measured differences in the DV are likely to be due to the IV, raising validity.

related factor, such as being friendly or happy. In laboratory experiments, standardisation is easier than in other studies, as equipment is likely to be consistent, for example stopwatches or brain scans. However, some of these measures, such as brain scans, may need to be interpreted and this must also be done in a standardised way (Figure 1.12).

Applying your knowledge of variables and controls to novel research situations

In experiments it is important to be able to decide how to operationalise the IV to produce the different conditions (to achieve validity) and to measure the DV in a consistent (reliable) way and to be able to justify these choices. You will also need to be able to decide what controls it is appropriate to use and to suggest how these can be implemented.

When writing hypotheses, you should ideally operationalise the variables you are referring to. For example, in the hypothesis 'Students using revision apps will learn better than students using mind maps', we do not know how 'better learning' will be measured, or which apps are being used because the variables are not operationalised. To be complete, the hypothesis needs more detail, such as 'Students using the Gojimo revision app will gain better test marks than students using mind maps'. Similarly, the hypothesis 'There will be a correlation between amount of sleep and emotional reactivity' does not operationalise either variable. This could be improved by saying 'There will be a correlation between the number of hours a person sleeps for and their emotional reactivity indicated by how loudly they cry during a sad film'.

RESEARCH METHODS IN PRACTICE

In Dr Blot's experiment about classroom chairs (see Section 1.6), the IV of hard and soft chairs must be operationalised. The text also referred to them as 'comfortable' and 'uncomfortable' chairs, but this still does not make clear what is meant by 'hard' and 'soft'. This could be done by saying *'chairs with wooden/plastic seats'* and *'chairs with padded seats'*. **Operationalisation** of the DV is also needed. The text referred to working 'better' and 'harder' but this is also incomplete. We need to expand on the idea of *work rate,* which was also used. This might be measured by counting the number of pieces of homework handed in late, or the time spent doing extra work. Either of these would indicate the amount of work being done. There are many **extraneous variables** that could be important in this study, for example, some of the students might work harder anyway or the rate of work might vary with the weather. If students worked harder

on sunny days, this would be a **situational variable**. The important variables to control are those that could confound the results. For example, if there was a choice of chairs, the students who chose to sit on comfy ones might be the laziest. If left as an **uncontrolled variable**, this could alter the results by making it look as if soft chairs made students work less.

In the description of the correlation on sleep and emotions (Section 1.6), the two measured variables were the *'amount of sleep'* and *'how emotional someone is'* or their *'emotional reactivity'*. It is important to operationalise variables in correlations too. To operationalise these variables we could measure *the amount of time* spent sleeping and ask the participant to fill in a questionnaire about their feelings to measure their emotions.

Reflections: Look at the Research methods in practice box.

For the experiment:

- Suggest **one other** way the IV could be operationalised.
- Suggest **one other** way the DV could be operationalised.
- Would a possible difference between how lazy students were be a *situational variable* or a *participant variable*?
- Suggest **one other** possible *extraneous variable*.

For the correlation:

- Suggest **one other** way the variable of 'emotions' could be operationalised.

1.8 Sampling of participants

A **population** is a group of people (or animals) with one or more characteristics in common. For example, the population of a country is all the people who live there, the population of internet users is everyone who can access the internet. A population could also be people who share a particular interest, such as 'all football supporters' or who have a particular feature, for example 'all left-handed people'. The **sample** is the group of people who participate in a study. They are taken from a population and should ideally be representative of that group so that the findings will be representative. Details about the sample, such as age, ethnicity and gender, are important in most investigations because these features affect many psychological differences.

23

Other characteristics of the sample, such as socio-economic status, education, employment, geographical location or occupation, may also be relevant. The size of the sample also matters. Small samples are less reliable and are likely to be less representative. The different **sampling techniques** described below produce samples which differ in terms of how well they represent the population. The extent to which they are representative of the population determines how effectively generalisations can be made.

Opportunity sampling

Studies are often conducted with the people who are around at the time. Selecting participants in this way is called **opportunity sampling**. An opportunity sample is unlikely to represent the population fairly because readily available people will tend to be alike so they are unlikely to include the variety that exists. For example, many studies are conducted using university students as they are convenient for the researchers. However, this means that the sample will be predominantly young, with a better than average education. This means that the results may not reflect the scores that people of different ages or educational opportunities might produce. Despite this potential problem, opportunity sampling is the most common method, even for professional psychologists, as for many investigations the results are unlikely to be affected by age or education.

Volunteer (self-selected) sampling

Rather than the researcher choosing individuals to ask, they may invite people to volunteer to take part in their

study. They might put up an advertisement, make an announcement or post a request on the internet. In this way, the people who respond and become participants choose to do so, i.e. are volunteers, so are described as a **volunteer sample** (Figure 1.13). As the individuals are self-selected, that is they choose whether to join in, this sampling technique is unlikely to be representative of the population. Volunteers may have more free time than average and, apart from being willing, often have other characteristics in common, such as being better educated. Nevertheless, it is a useful technique when looking for participants who are unusual in some way, for example in Baron-Cohen et al.'s study, where people on the autistic spectrum were needed.

Public Announcement

WE WILL PAY YOU $4.00 FOR ONE HOUR OF YOUR TIME

Persons Needed for a Study of Memory

• We will pay five hundred New Haven men to help us complete a scientific study of memory and learning. The study is being done at Yale University.
• Each person who participates will be paid $4.00 (plus 50c carfare) for approximately 1 hour's time. We need you for only one hour: there are no further obligations. You may choose the time you would like to come (evenings, weekdays, or weekends).

• No special training, education, or experience is needed. We want:

Factory workers	Businessmen	Construction workers
City employees	Clerks	Salespeople
Laborers	Professional people	White-collar workers
Barbers	Telephone workers	Others

All persons must be between the ages of 20 and 50. High school and college students cannot be used.
• If you meet these qualifications, fill out the coupon below and mail it now to Professor Stanley Milgram, Department of Psychology, Yale University, New Haven. You will be notified later of the specific time and place of the study. We reserve the right to decline any application.
• You will be paid $4.00 (plus 50c carfare) as soon as you arrive at the laboratory.

- -

TO:
PROF. STANLEY MILGRAM, DEPARTMENT OF PSYCHOLOGY, YALE UNIVERSITY, NEW HAVEN, CONN. I want to take part in this study of memory and learning. I am between the ages of 20 and 50. I will be paid $4.00 (plus 50c carfare) if I participate.

NAME (Please Print). . . . .

ADDRESS . . . .

TELEPHONE NO. . . . . Best time to call you . . . .

AGE. . . . . OCCUPATION. SEX . . . . . .
CAN YOU COME:

WEEKDAYS . . . . EVENINGS . . . . . . WEEKENDS. . . . .

1.13 Would you respond to this advert?

Random sampling

Opportunity and volunteer samples may be biased – they will probably contain very similar people so are unlikely to include the spread of characteristics in the population. In **random sampling** each person in the population has an equal chance of being chosen so the sample is much

KEY TERMS

population: the group, sharing one or more characteristics, from which a sample is drawn.

sample: the group of people selected to represent the population in a study.

sampling technique: the method used to obtain the participants for a study from the population.

opportunity sample: participants are chosen because they are available, e.g. university students are selected because they are present at the university where the research is taking place.

volunteer (self-selected) sample: participants are invited to participate, e.g. through advertisements via email or notices. Those who reply become the sample.

random sample: all members of the population (i.e. possible participants) are allocated numbers and a fixed amount of these are selected in a unbiased way, e.g. by taking numbers from a hat.

more likely to be representative. Imagine you are looking for a sample of students at your school and you put an advert for volunteers on the library notice board. Students who never go to the library cannot be included so your sample might be biased towards those who work the hardest. Similarly, if you took an opportunity sample from the common room, it would only include students who are relaxing. Now your sample might be biased towards the *least* hard working. To obtain a representative sample you could instead use a numbered list of all students and use a random number generator to choose the participants. This would be a random sample as any individual is equally likely to be chosen. If the population is small, such as all the members of your class, you can simply give each person a number, put pieces of paper with each number on in a hat, and draw out numbers until there are enough for the sample.

Applying your knowledge of sampling techniques to novel research situations

An early step in any research is to obtain an appropriate sample. The extent to which generalisations can be made from research depends in part on how representative the sample is. It is therefore important to get the best possible sample. However, practical constraints prevent researchers from using random samples most of the time and, for many psychological phenomena, it is reasonable to believe that processes happen in a fairly universal way so some sample bias is unproblematic. However, to assume there are no differences in emotional responses, cognitive processing or behaviour between populations would be misleading. Indeed, the psychology of individual differences, of developmental psychology and cross-cultural research are three areas specifically devoted to the study of such differences. It is therefore important that you can recognise limitations in the sampling technique used. This means that you should be able to identify possible differences between individuals or groups that might matter for the particular phenomena being explored in a study. Imagine two researchers at different universities are both studying obedience and both want samples from people nearby but not students. One university is near a police college and the other is next to a hospital and the researchers both obtain opportunity samples with the same age and gender spreads from these workplaces. Even though the samples are similar in age and gender, the difference in occupations may mean that the results of their studies will be different – because police officers tend to be more obedient than nurses.

You will need to be able to explain how you would use each sampling technique and to explain reasons for choosing each technique. For example, why it might be difficult to use a technique in practice or why generalisations could or could not be made from the sample obtained.

	Sampling technique		
	Opportunity sampling	**Volunteer (self-selected) sampling**	**Random sampling**
Strengths	Quicker and easier than other methods as the participants are readily available	Relatively easy because the participants come to the researcher. They are also likely to be committed, e.g. willing to return for repeat testing	Likely to be representative as all types of people in the population are equally likely to be chosen
Weaknesses	Likely to be non-representative as the variety of people available is likely to be limited, so they will tend to be similar and the sample could therefore be biased	Likely to be non-representative as people who respond to requests may be similar, e.g. all have free time	In reality everyone may not be equally likely to be chosen, e.g. if they cannot be accessed (if the original list is incomplete) or if mainly one type of participant, e.g. girls, happen to be selected. This is particularly important if the sample is small

Table 1.3 Strengths and weaknesses of sampling techniques

Your teacher has asked you to do a cognitive psychology investigation. You want it to work well so you want a **sample** of 30 people from which you can generalise. You think it would be easiest to take an **opportunity sample** from your classes at the college but you realise this might produce a biased sample as all your subjects are sciences. This might matter as the investigation is about using logic to solve problems and you think that science students might be especially good at the task. If so, their results might not be representative of the college **population** as a whole. A friend suggests making an announcement in the canteen asking for students studying all different subjects. This **volunteer sampling** technique might be better but there would be no guarantee of getting a range of people. You decide that the best sampling technique would be to choose individuals at random from a list of all the students in the college. You hope that this would mean you would be equally likely to get students taking each subject. You decide to use this **random sampling** technique based on the students' examination candidate numbers. You enter the candidate numbers into a random number generator and use the first 30 numbers that are generated.

Reflections: Look at the Research methods in practice box above. What problems would the following situations lead to?

- You revert to your idea of an *opportunity sample* but use your neighbours, who are mainly retired people.
- You followed your friend's advice about *volunteer sampling* but lots of the younger students were in detention at lunchtime that day.

Read the examples below. Which *sampling technique* is being used in each situation?

- Professor Smudge is doing some internet research and is recruiting participants by posting on Facebook asking for people to help with her study.
- Dr Splash is investigating the effects of ageing and is asking all the residents at two local care homes for their help.
- Dr Blot pulls student numbers on the college register from a hat to select a sample for a new study on homework and part time jobs.

1.9 Data and data analysis

Psychologists, like all scientists, often produce numerical results from their investigations. These results are called the 'raw data'. As it is difficult to interpret large amounts of figures, the results are often simplified mathematically and represented visually on graphs. We will discuss a range of methods in this section. Note that you are not required to perform calculations in examinations but you could be asked to count up scores, find the mode, median and range of a data set, make simple comparisons and interpret data from tables or graphs.

Types of data

As you may know from the core studies or from earlier parts of this chapter, psychologists use a variety of different research methods. These methods can produce a range of different types of data. The main types are discussed below.

Quantitative and qualitative data

When psychologists collect data they can collect either numerical results, called **quantitative data**, or **qualitative data**, which is detailed and descriptive. Quantitative data indicates the *quantity* of a psychological measure, such as the amount or strength of a response and tends to be measured on scales, such as time, or as numerical scores on tests such as IQ or personality. Quantitative data is associated with experiments and correlations which use numerical scales but it is also possible to obtain quantitative

KEY TERMS

quantitative data: numerical results about the *quantity* of a psychological measure such as pulse rate or a score on an intelligence test.

qualitative data: descriptive, in-depth results indicating the *quality* of a psychological characteristic, such as responses to open questions in self-reports or case studies and detailed observations.

Data type		
	Quantitative	**Qualitative**
Strengths	Typically uses objective measures Scales or questions often very reliable Data can be analysed using measures of central tendency and spread making it easy to compare	Data is often valid as participants can express themselves exactly rather than being limited by fixed choices Important but unusual responses are less likely to be ignored because of averaging
Weaknesses	Data collection method often limits responses so the data are less valid, e.g. if the participant wants to give a response that is not available	Data collection is often relatively subjective so findings may be invalid as data recording or interpretation may be biased by the researcher's opinions or feelings Detailed data from one or a few individuals may not generalise to the majority

Table 1.4 Quantitative versus qualitative data

data from observations, questionnaires or interviews. For example, a record of the number of times a behaviour is seen or the total of responses to a closed question in an interview would be quantitative data. The sources of quantitative data are typically highly objective, as the scales or questions used need little if any interpretation, making them high in validity. In addition, the measures used are generally highly reliable, as the measures are fixed quantities.

Qualitative data indicates the *quality* of a psychological characteristic. Such data is more in-depth than quantitative data and includes detailed observer accounts and responses to open questions in questionnaires, interviews or case studies. Although there is a risk of subjectivity in the interpretation of such data by the researcher, qualitative data may be more representative as the participant can express themselves fully, so in some senses qualitative data can also be valid.

RESEARCH METHODS IN PRACTICE

Dr Splash and Professor Smudge disagree over the best way to collect data about people's emotions when they are put in stressful situations. Dr Splash wants to collect **quantitative data** by measuring their pulse rate and give them scales of very / quite / not at all to rate how stressed they feel. Professor Smudge thinks it would be better to collect **qualitative data** by interviewing each participant and getting them to describe their feelings. She plans to ask questions such as *'How do you feel when you meet an important person for the first time?'* and *'Describe how you felt the last time you were late'*.

Reflections: Look at the Research methods in practice box above. What are the advantages and disadvantages of each suggested data collection method?

Are the questions suggested by Professor Smudge open or closed questions?

Using ethical ideas only, suggest two more questions that could be used in the *interview*, **one** *open question* and **one** *closed question*. State which type of question would collect *qualitative data* and which would collect *quantitative data*.

Data analysis

This section explores different ways that mathematics can be used to simplify and understand the data produced by studies in psychology.

Measures of central tendency

A set of quantitative results can be summarised to one number that represents the 'middle' or typical score, called a **measure of central tendency** or 'average'. There are three different measures of central tendency: the **mode**, **median** and **mean**.

The mode

The mode is the most frequent score in a data set. It can be used with numerical data (such as scores on a test) and also with data sets that are choices that can be counted (such as written responses to the question 'What is your favourite subject: maths, English or psychology?'). If two (or more) values are equally common there will be two (or more) modes. For example, the faces in Figure 1.14 could be used in a test to compare people on the autistic spectrum with a control group. The participants could be asked 'Which face looks the happiest?' The face which was chosen as the happiest by each group would be the mode for that group.

1.14 A facial expression test

A self-report in a school produced the data set in Table 1.5. The mode for subject choice is 'Psychology', because more people said this subject was their favourite – ten compared to four and six for the other subjects.

Subject		
	Maths	**English**	**Psychology**
Number of people	4	6	10

Table 1.5 Number of people choosing each subject as their favourite

Another question asked 'On which day of the week do you do most homework?' (see Table 1.6). The responses from girls and boys were compared.

In Table 1.6 more boys have 'Sunday' as their main homework night, so this is the mode for boys. Girls have said that 'Friday' and 'Sunday' are their main homework nights, but these two categories are the same, so there are two modes, each containing six girls. We could also combine the totals to work out an overall mode. Adding together the totals for each day shows that for all students, Sunday is the most popular homework night, with 17 students in total.

The median

Unlike the mode, the median cannot be used with data in discrete (separate) categories, it is only used with numerical data on a linear scale (i.e. points in a sequence). To find the median, all the scores in the data set are put in a list from smallest to largest (ranked). The middle one in the list is the median. If there are an even number of participants, so there are two numbers in the middle, these are added together and divided by 2 to find the median.

Another question in the school survey asked participants to rate how hard they thought they worked, from 1 to 10. Students in their AS and A Level years were asked.

AS student data:

8, 6, 9, 1, 5, 6, 2, 7, 3, 6, 9, 8, 5, 6, 3, 8, 5, 10, 2, 3

A Level student data:

7, 9, 6, 7, 9, 7, 10, 10, 7, 10, 9, 4, 9, 6, 10, 10, 7, 9, 7, 7

Putting these data into order for the two groups separately:

AS students:

1, 2, 2, 3, 3, 3, 5, 5, 5, 6, 6, 6, 6, 7, 8, 8, 8, 9, 9, 10

6 + 6 = 12, 12/2 = 6 so the median = 6

A Level students:

4, 6, 6, 7, 7, 7, 7, 7, 7, 7, 9, 9, 9, 9, 9, 10, 10, 10, 10, 10

7 + 9 = 16, 16/2 = 8 so the median = 8

Night of the week						
	Monday	**Tuesday**	**Wednesday**	**Thursday**	**Friday**	**Saturday**	**Sunday**
Number of boys	0	1	2	3	3	0	11
Number of girls	1	1	2	4	6	0	6

Table 1.6 Main homework night

The median for the A Level group, of 8, is higher than the median for AS students, which is 6. This suggests that A Level students believe they are working harder than AS students do.

The mean

The mean is the measure of central tendency that we usually call the 'average'. It can only be used with numerical data from linear scales. The mean is worked out by adding up all the scores in the data set and dividing by the total number of scores (including any that were zeros). It is the most informative measure of central tendency because it takes every score into account.

Looking back at the data used in the section on the median, mean could be calculated instead. There were 20 students in each group. For the AS students, the calculation is therefore all the scores added together, then divided by 20, i.e. 112/20 = 5.6, so the mean is 5.6. For the A Level students, the calculation is again all the scores added together, and divided by 20, i.e. 160/20 = 8, so the mean is 8. Like the median, this too shows that the A Level students believe they are working harder than the AS students do.

Measures of spread

A **measure of spread** is an indicator of how varied the results are within a data set: are they clustered together or widely dispersed? If two data sets are the same size, with the same average, they could still vary in terms of how close the majority of data points were to that average. Differences such as this are described by measures of spread: the **range** and the **standard deviation**.

The range

The range is the simplest measure of spread and is calculated in the following way:

1   Find the largest and smallest value in the data set.

2   Subtract the smallest value from the largest value, then add 1.

You may have learned to calculate the range without adding 1. In psychology we do this because the scales we use measure the gaps between points, not the points themselves. Consider a scale of student happiness from 1 (sad) to 8 (very happy). This can be represented on a line:

Number line   1   2   3   4   5   6   7   8

If we say someone's happiness is at level of 3, they could be anywhere between 2.5 and 3.5, and someone scoring 6 has a happiness level somewhere between 5.5 and 6.5. So, if 3 and 6 were the lowest and highest scores, the real spread extends to those limits, i.e. from 2.5 to 6.5, so this spread works out as 6.5 – 2.5 = 4. This figure is one bigger than the largest score (6) minus the smallest score (3) = 3.

The range for the two sets of data given in the section on the median would be calculated in the following way:

AS students:

1, 2, 2, 3, 3, 3, 5, 5, 5, 6, 6, 6, 7, 8, 8, 8, 9, 9, 10

10 – 1 = 9, 9 + 1 = 10 so the range = 10

A Level students:

4, 6, 6, 7, 7, 7, 7, 7, 7, 9, 9, 9, 9, 9, 10, 10, 10,10, 10

10 – 4 = 6, 6 + 1 = 7 so the range = 7

So, not only are the medians and means for these two data sets slightly different, the ranges are different too. This tells us that the diversity of opinion about how hard they are working is greater for AS students than A Level students. We could also say that although most A Level students think they are working very hard, AS student opinion varies from 'not working hard' to 'working very hard'.

One problem with the range is that it does not accurately reflect outliers. That is, it would not be clear from the range whether the most extreme scores, e.g. very large scores, were single odd scores or typical of the data set. Imagine that the least hard-working student in the A Level set had rated themselves as working at level 1 rather than 4. This would make very little difference to the mean (it would be 7.85 instead of 8), but would change the range from 7 to 10 (the same as the range for the AS group).

The standard deviation

In the same way that the mean can tell us more than the mode, a measure of spread called the standard deviation can tell us more than the range. Rather than looking only at the extremes of the data set, the standard deviation (given

KEY TERMS

measure of spread: a mathematical way to describe the variation or dispersion within a data set.

range: the difference between the biggest and smallest values in the data set plus one (a measure of spread).

standard deviation: a calculation of the average difference between each score in the data set and the mean. Bigger values indicate greater variation (a measure of spread).

the name s, SD or σ) considers the difference between each data point and the mean. This is called the *deviation*. These deviations are then squared, added together and the total is divided by the number of scores in the data set, minus 1. The final step is to find the square root. The standard deviation is represented by the formula:

$$s = \sqrt{\frac{\Sigma\,(x-\bar{x})^2}{n-1}}$$

The following symbols are used:

s = standard deviation

x = each score in the data set, i.e. a figure for the variable being measured

$\bar{x}$ = the mean of the data set (called the 'sample mean')

Σ = the Greek letter sigma means 'the sum of', i.e. 'add them all up'

n = the number of scores in the data set

$\sqrt{}$ = the square root.

The deviation, d, is sometimes used in place of the difference between each score in the data set and the mean $(x - \bar{x})$ in the formula above.

As the standard deviation tells us the spread of a group, groups with scores that are more spread out have larger standard deviations, groups with closely clustered scores have smaller standard deviations. When the standard deviations of two groups are similar, this means that they have a similar variation around the mean.

Returning to the data about how hard students believe they are working (from the section on the median) the standard deviations for the two sets of data would be:

AS students: SD = 2.62
A Level students: SD = 1.72

These figures show, as the range did, that there is greater variation in the opinions of the AS students (as the figure of 2.62 for the standard deviation for this group is larger than 1.72, the figure for the A Level group). Note that if the standard deviation is calculated for the A Level group with the opinion score of 4 for one student being replaced with a 1, the standard deviation increases, as this makes the group more varied. However, it still does not become as large as the figure for the AS group. This is different from

the effect of the change in this participant's score on the range. The range of the two year groups become the same (they would both be 10), whereas in fact *within* the groups, the AS students are more varied. This is reflected in the standard deviation however, which changes from 1.72 when the student has a score of 4 to 2.16 if they have a score of 1. So, the main advantage of the standard deviation over the range is that it takes every score into account and therefore provides a representation of variation *within* the data set. As it is not just considering the extremes is not distorted by outliers like the range would be.

RESEARCH METHODS IN PRACTICE

A new psychology teacher has tested a group of ten of his students on their recall of the aims, methods, results and conclusions of one of the core studies. The test was marked out of 15. Two students scored 0, and one student scored each of the marks 3–10. The teacher works out the **mode** and is horrified to find that the modal score is zero! A colleague recommends he works out the **median** instead, so he finds the two middle scores in the group (5 and 6), adds them together and divides by 2. This is 5.5, so he feels much better. He wonders if calculating the **mean** will make him feel better still, but it doesn't. When he adds up all the scores and divides by 10 (because he had 10 students), the mean is only 5.2. This is because the median does not consider the value of two zero scores, whereas the mean does. These three figures are different **measures** of **central tendency**. He wants to compare this group to his colleague's students, who scored 0, 1, 1, 2, 2, 2, 3, 4, 4, 5. He calculates two different **measures of spread**. The biggest and smallest values in her set are 0 and 5, so he subtracts 0 from 5 and adds 1, giving a **range** of 6. The **standard deviation** for her group is 1.58.

Reflections:

1 Look back at Figure 1.14. For the data set in the table below, which is the modal response?

	Face A	Face B	Face C	Face D
Number of participants selecting each face as the happiest	0	3	7	1

2 Look back at the data for AS and A Level students in the section on the median. What is the mode for each group?

3 Using the information about the teacher in the Research methods in practice box above answer the following questions:

- What is the mode for the colleague's group?
- Which group does this suggest performed better on the test?
- What is the median for his colleague's group?
- Which group does this suggest performed better on the test?
- The mean for his colleague's group was 2.4. Which group does this suggest performed better on the test?
- What is the range for the teacher's own group?
- When compared to the range for his colleague's group, what does this tell you?
- The standard deviation for his own group was 3.49. Does this tell you that his group was more varied or less varied than hers?

Graphs

A graph is a visual illustration of data. There are many different types of graph and in this section we will consider only bar charts, histograms and scatter graphs, each of which you should be able to name, recognise, draw and use to interpret data. In addition, you will need to be able to recognise, interpret and understand a normal distribution curve.

Bar charts

A **bar chart** is used when the data are in separate categories rather than on a continuous scale. Bar charts are therefore used for the totals of data collected in named categories and for all measures of central tendency (modes, medians or means). The bars on a bar chart must be separate. This is because the x-axis represents the distinct groups and not a linear scale. For a bar chart of the results

of an experiment, the levels of the IV go along the bottom (on the x-axis) and the DV goes on the y-axis. To help you to remember which is the x-axis and which is the y-axis, think 'X is a-*cross*' (Figure 1.15).

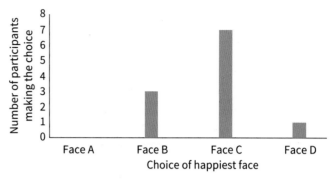

1.15 A bar chart showing the number of participants selecting each face as the happiest

Histograms

Histograms can be used to show the pattern in a whole data set, where this is continuous data, i.e. data measured on a scale rather than in separate categories. A histogram may be used to illustrate the distribution of a set of scores. In this case, the DV is plotted on the x-axis (across) and the frequency of each score plotted on the y-axis (up the side). The scores along the x-axis may be grouped into categories (e.g. if the DV is age, the data may be grouped into 0–5 years, 6–10 years, 11–15 years, etc.). As the scale represented on the x-axis is continuous the bars are drawn next to each other, unlike in a bar chart. This means that if there are no scores in a category, a gap must be left to show that the category is empty (see Figure 1.19, which shows 'empty' categories on the x-axis).

31

> **KEY TERMS**
>
> **bar chart:** a graph used for data in discrete categories and total or average scores. There are gaps between each bar that is plotted on the graph because the columns are not related in a linear way.
>
> **histogram:** a graph used to illustrate continuous data, e.g. to show the distribution of a set of scores. It has a bar for each score value, or group of scores, along the x-axis. The y-axis has frequency of each category.

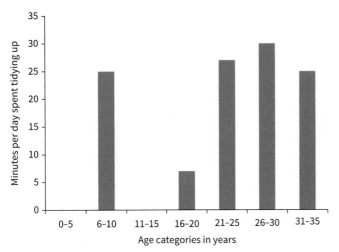

1.16 A histogram of the time spent tidying by people of different ages

Scatter graphs

Correlations were discussed in Section 1.5. The results from a correlational study are displayed on a scatter graph. To construct a **scatter graph**, a dot is marked at the point where an individual's scores on each variable cross. Sometimes you will see a 'line of best fit' drawn on a scatter graph. The position of this line is calculated and its line is drawn so that it comes close to as many points as possible (see Figure 1.17a-d). In a strong correlation all the data points lie close to the line, but in a weak correlation they are more spread out. Note that you will often see the strength of a correlation described as a number from +1 to –1. Values close to +1 are strong positive correlations and values close to –1 are strong negative correlations. Lower or 'smaller' values (closer to 0) are weaker correlations. Where there is no correlation, the points do not form a clear line (and this has a 'r' value of 0).

KEY TERMS

scatter graph: a way to display data from a correlational study. Each point on the graph represents the point where one participant's score on each scale for the two measured variables cross.

It is important to remember that you *cannot* draw a causal conclusion from a correlational study. Therefore, scatter graphs such as the ones in Figure 1.17 only tell you that there is a relationship between the variables but not which (if either) of them, is the cause of this link. An experiment could help to find this out.

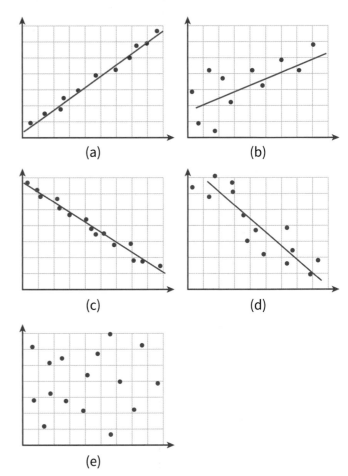

1.17 Scatter graphs showing (a) strong positive correlation, (b) weak positive correlation, (c) strong negative correlation, (d) weak negative correlation and (e) no correlation

The normal distribution curve

The graph in Figure 1.18 forms a 'bell-shape', which is typical of a **normal distribution**. This is a frequency distribution that:

- has the mode, median and mean together in the centre
- has 50% of the scores to the left and 50% to the right of the mean
- is symmetrical.

normal distribution: an even spread of a variable that is symmetrical about the mean, median and mode. The graph showing this distribution is sometimes called a 'bell curve' because of its shape. The graph of the frequency of each score or value rises gradually and symmetrically to a maximum at the point of the mean, median and mode.

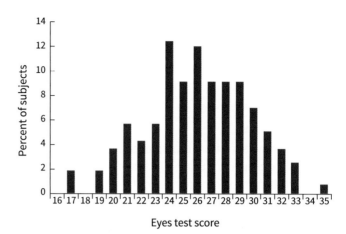

1.19 A normal distribution of the Eyes test scores

A histogram of the distribution of Eyes test scores for non-autistic participants is a normal distribution (see Figure 1.19).

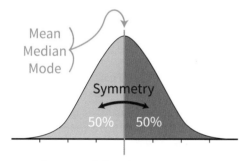

1.18 The normal distribution

Reflections: Look at the Research methods in practice box.

- Draw the four graphs suggested, one for each of the groups A–D using the data provided.
- Look at the graph you have drawn for the results from Group C. Do you think this has the general pattern of a normal distribution?

33

RESEARCH METHODS IN PRACTICE

Groups of students in Dr Blot's class are doing different psychological investigations into altruism. Group A is counting the number of times boys and girls in the class say 'thank you'. They find that on average, the boys said thank you six times and the girls said thank you seven times. They are going to plot a **bar chart** of these averages. Group B is asking everyone the question, 'Which of these situations have you ever helped in: a parent with a pram / a elderly person with their shopping / a child crossing the road / an injured person?' The totals for each group are 14,

7, 16, 3 respectively. They are also going to plot a bar chart. Group C is using an online computer game to test how many seconds it takes each student to respond to another player's request for help. They work out the percentage of students who took 0–5, 6–10, 11–15, 16–20 and 21–25 seconds. The results are 0%, 15%, 45%, 20% and 5%. They plot a **histogram** of their results. Group D asks every person to answer two questions 'How many times have you lent your notes to someone else?' and 'How likely on a scale of 1–10 are you to give away your lunch to somebody who is hungry?' Their results were:

Lend notes	5	3	9	4	2	6	9	7	3	4
Give lunch	7	2	7	10	1	8	8	7	4	5

They are correlating the two sets of scores and will draw a **scatter graph**.

1.10 Ethical considerations

You will encounter **ethical issues** in other chapters. Here we will look at the ethical dilemmas that psychologists face and how they can deal with them effectively.

Ethical issues

As you will have seen from examples of psychological research, investigations using humans or animals have the potential to cause concerns about the welfare of the participants. Such concerns are called ethical issues. Problems may arise through the nature of the study, such as the potential for psychological discomfort caused by a study about stress, or from aspects of the procedure, such as the need to hide the real aim of the study. Ethical issues may also arise from the implications of the research, for example the possibility for results having a negative impact on part of society.

To help psychologists to cope with potential ethical issues that could arise in their research, many countries have an organisation which produces a code of conduct. In addition, research that is being conducted at a university is likely to require approval from the institution's ethical committee. An ethical code provides advice, for example as a set of **ethical guidelines**, that helps psychologists to work in a way that satisfies the primary concern of the welfare of individuals involved in the research as well as the perception of psychology in society. Participants who are deceived or distressed may not want to participate again, may view psychology badly and pass this message on to others, and are less likely to trust the findings of psychological research. These are all outcomes that should be avoided.

Ethical guidelines relating to human participants

The discussion which follows is based on the British Psychological Society Code of Ethics and Conduct (2009), although there are many other similar ethical codes in use throughout the world.

Informed consent

Sometimes it is important in experiments to hide the aims from participants in order to reduce demand characteristics. However, participants have the right to know what will happen in a study so they can give their **informed consent**. The researcher's need to hide the aim makes it hard to get genuine consent. Ideally, full and informed consent should be obtained from participants before the study starts by giving them sufficient information

about the procedure to decide whether they want to participate. In some situations it is not even possible to ask for consent. This is often the case in naturalistic observations and field experiments. In such situations, a researcher may ask a group of people similar to those who will become participants whether they would find the study acceptable if they were involved. This is called **presumptive consent** because it allows the researcher to presume that the actual participants would also have agreed to participate if asked.

Especially when participants have not been fully informed, it is important to **debrief** them at the end of the study.

KEY TERMS

ethical issues: problems in research that raise concerns about the welfare of participants (or have the potential for a wider negative impact on society).

ethical guidelines: pieces of advice that guide psychologists to consider the welfare of participants and wider society.

debriefing: giving participants a full explanation of the aims and potential consequences of the study at the end of a study so that they leave in at least as positive a condition as they arrived.

protection of participants: participants should not be exposed to any greater physical or psychological risk than they would expect in their day-to-day life.

deception: participants should not be deliberately misinformed (lied to) about the aim or procedure of the study. If this is unavoidable, the study should be planned to minimise the risk of distress, and participants should be thoroughly debriefed.

Protection (physical and psychological)

A study may have the potential to cause participants psychological harm (e.g. embarrassment or stress) or physical harm (e.g. engaging in risky behaviours or receiving injections). Participants in such studies have the right to be **protected** and should not be exposed to any greater risk than they would be in their normal life. Care should be taken to eliminate such risks (e.g. by screening participants), experienced researchers should be used and studies should be stopped if unexpected risks arise.

Right to withdraw

Participants should be able to leave a study whenever they wish. This is their **right to withdraw** and it must be made clear to participants at the start of the study. Although participants can be offered incentives to join a study, these cannot be taken away if they leave. This prevents participants thinking that they have to continue. Researchers should not use their position of authority to encourage participants to remain in a study if they want to stop. So in practice, participants may need to be reminded of this right and researchers should follow this guideline even if data will be lost.

Deception

Participants should not be deliberately misinformed, i.e. **deception** should be avoided. When it is essential to deceive participants, they should be told the real aim as soon as possible and be allowed to remove their results if they want to. When participants have been deceived and they know they have been in a study, debriefing (see below) should follow immediately.

Confidentiality

All data should be stored separately from the participants' names and personal information held, and names should never be published unless the individuals have specifically agreed to this. Such information should be stored securely and should not be shared with anyone outside they study. These measures ensure **confidentiality**. The identity of participants should be protected by destroying personal information. However, where it is needed to re-contact participants or to pair up an individual's scores in each condition in a repeated measures design, each participant can be allocated a number which can be used to identify them.

When conducting a case study or field experiment with institutions, confidentiality is still important and identities must be hidden. For example, the names of schools or hospitals should be concealed.

Privacy

1.20 Privacy should still be maintained even if consent cannot be given by participants

Observations, self-reports which ask personal questions and any study which uses personal information risk invading **privacy**. This means that they may enter physical space or emotional territory that the individual would want to keep to themselves. A researcher should make clear to participants their right to ignore questions they do not want to answer. When completing a questionnaire in a laboratory situation, participants should be given an individual space. In observations, people should only be watched in situations where they would expect to be on public display.

The only exception to this is that personally identifiable information can be communicated or published when the participant gives their informed consent for this or in exceptional circumstances when the safety or interests of the individual or others may be at risk.

Debriefing

All participants who are aware that they have been in a study should be thanked and given the chance to ask questions. Debriefing participants provides them with an explanation at the end of the study that explains fully the aims of the study and ensures that they do not want to withdraw their data. If participants have been negatively affected by a study the researcher must return them to their previous condition. However, debriefing is not an alternative to designing an ethical study, so it is important to consider all the ways in which a study could cause distress and to minimise them.

Ethical guidelines relating to the use of animals

Animals are used in psychological research for a number of different reasons. Driscoll and Bateson (1988) suggested animals may be: convenient models (e.g. for processes such as learning), a way to carry out procedures that could not be done ethically on humans (e.g. isolation or brain surgery) or be good or interesting examples in their own right (e.g. communication in birds, bats or whales). As a consequence, much psychological research is conducted on animals and therefore their welfare needs protecting.

The discussion which follows is based on the British Psychological Society Guidelines for Psychologists Working with Animals (2012), although there are many other similar ethical codes in use throughout the world. Animals are also often protected by law, but these guidelines specifically consider the effects of research in which animals may be confined, harmed, stressed or in pain, so suffering should be minimised. Veterinary advice should be sought in any case of doubt.

Researchers must aim to ensure that in any research, the means justify the ends, i.e. that the animal suffering caused by the planned experiment is outweighed by the benefits. One way to consider this question is to use Bateson's (1986) cube (see Figure 1.21). When the certainty of benefit (e.g. to humans) is high, the research is good and the suffering is low, the research is worthwhile.

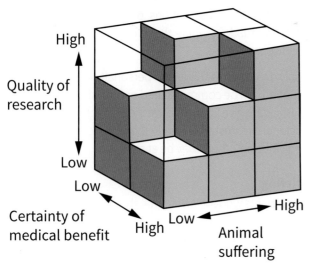

1.21 Bateson's cube (1986)

Replacement
Researchers should consider replacing animal experiments with alternatives, such as videos from previous studies or computer simulations.

Species and strain
The chosen species and strain should be the one least likely to suffer pain or distress. Other relevant factors include whether the animals were bred in captivity, their previous experience of experimentation and the sentience of the species (its ability to think and feel).

Number of animals
Only the minimum number of animals needed to produce valid and reliable results should be used. To minimise the number, pilot studies, reliable measures of the dependent variable, good experimental design and appropriate data analysis should all be used.

Procedures: pain and distress
Research causing death, disease, injury, physiological or psychological distress or discomfort should be avoided. Where possible, designs which improve rather than worsen the animals' experience should be used (e.g. studying the effect of early enrichment on development compared

to normal rather than early deprivation). Alternatively, naturally occurring instances may be used (e.g. where stress arises naturally in the animal's environment or lifetime). During research, attention should be paid to the animals' daily care and veterinary needs and any costs to the animals should be justified by the scientific benefit of the work (see Bateson's cube).

Housing
Isolation and crowding can cause animals distress. Caging conditions should depend on the social behaviour of the species (e.g. isolation will be more distressing for social animals than solitary ones). Overcrowding can cause distress and aggression (therefore also physical harm). The level of stress experienced by individuals should also be considered (e.g. the animal's age and gender). Between testing, animals should be housed with enough space to move freely and with sufficient food and water for their health and well-being, both in terms of their biological and ecological needs. However, the artificial environment only needs to recreate the aspects of the natural environment that are important to welfare and survival, e.g. warmth, space for exercise or somewhere to hide. Cage cleaning should balance cleanliness against avoiding stress.

Reward, deprivation and aversive stimuli
In planning studies using deprivation the normal feeding or drinking patterns of the animals should be considered so that their needs can be satisfied (e.g. carnivores eat less frequently than herbivores, young animals need greater access to food and water). The use of preferred food should be considered as an alternative to deprivation (e.g. for rewards in learning studies) and alternatives to aversive stimuli and deprivation should be used where possible.

Anaesthesia, analgesia and euthanasia
Animals should be protected from pain, e.g. relating to surgery using appropriate anaesthesia and analgesia, and killed (euthanised) if suffering lasting pain.

Evaluating studies based on ethical guidelines and applying your knowledge of ethical guidelines to novel research situations
All research with human participants should be ethical. Researchers should, for example, always follow the guideline of confidentiality. Although ethical guidelines should always be followed, sometimes it is necessary to accept some risks to participants in order for a study to achieve its objectives. When this is the case, the researchers

must consider whether the risks can be justified and, if so, how they can be minimised. Ethical issues may arise because of the nature of the topic being studied, such as stress, as this threatens participants' psychological well-being, or they may be at risk of physical harm. Alternatively, ethical issues may arise from the need to use controls which limit participants' knowledge or choices so threaten their privacy, informed consent or right to withdraw. This, in turn, has the potential to cause psychological harm. Although debriefing can help to reduce any harm that has been done, it is not a substitute for designing a more ethical study. Researchers must therefore consider all appropriate guidelines when planning a study, if necessary consulting with colleagues and following the advice of an ethical committee.

You will need to be able to make decisions based on ethical guidelines, and these can be applied to a study you already know about, a novel example that is presented to you or a study that you are asked to design. So, in relation to informed consent, protection (physical and psychological), right to withdraw, deception, confidentiality, privacy and debriefing, you will need to be able to explain why issues have arisen and how and why each guideline has been broken or has been followed.

All research with animals should be ethical. However, in order for any good research to be conducted a compromise must be reached between animal suffering and the good that will come out of the research. In evaluating studies it is important to remember that when the research is planned, decisions must be based on *expected* outcomes, i.e. the potential gains of the study. This is governed by the importance of the work, how certain it is that there will be a valuable benefit and this, in turn, is in part determined by the effectiveness of the research itself. So in deciding whether a piece of research is ethical, we must think about:

- how much the animals suffer (e.g. in terms of pain, deprivation, distress)
- what the positive outcomes might be (e.g. the benefits for people and whether these are worthwhile)
- whether the research is sufficiently well planned to achieve these possible benefits.

You can consider these three elements in terms of Bateson's cube, illustrating each one with examples relating to the particular study. The same ideas can be used whether you are considering a study you already know about, a novel example that is presented to you or a study that you are

asked to design. So, in relation to the three points, you will need to be able to explain or justify:

- choices about the animals and their care, such as the species and how they are housed, and the procedures chosen, e.g. the number of animals used and the design of the study in terms of the aspects of feeding, access to companions or pain and distress that arise as a consequence of the study
- why the study is being done, for example in terms of the need for new research or the ways in which humans (or animals) could benefit from the findings
- the strengths of the design of the study, e.g. in terms of controls and ways that good objectivity, validity and reliability have been achieved.

RESEARCH METHODS IN PRACTICE

Professor Smudge is planning an **experiment** on emotions in animals. She wants to see if, like us, they tend to approach things they like and avoid things they don't like. She considered *replacing* the use of animals with videos of animals in the wild responding to different stimuli but decided that she would not know for certain what they were reacting to so the findings might not be valid. She chose to use rats as the *species* is bred for laboratory use and rats can be *housed* alone without distressing them. She decided to use a repeated measures design as it would limit the *number of animals* used compared to an independent measures design. To reduce *pain and distress*, she used food they liked a lot (peanuts) in the 'approach' condition and food they did not like a lot (lettuce) in the 'avoidance' condition. Although the rats were tested before they were given fresh food in their cages, they were not *deprived* of food. As the rats had not been hurt by the procedure, there was no need for *anaesthesia*, *analgesia* or *euthanasia*.

Reflections: Look at the Research methods in practice box above.

- Professor Smudge considered using *aversive stimuli* such as loud noises or electric shocks in the 'avoid' condition but decided this was unethical. Why?
- Suggest **one** problem with Professor Smudge's decision to use a repeated measures design, and explain how this problem might be solved.

1.11 Evaluating research: methodological issues

As well as evaluating research in terms of ethics, it can also be considered in terms of whether it is 'good science', i.e. by looking at methodological issues. There are several key methodological issues that you have encountered elsewhere in the chapter: **reliability**, **validity** and **generalisability**. We will now explore these again, some in a little more depth, and see why they are important in the evaluation of research.

KEY TERMS

reliability: the extent to which a procedure, task or measure is consistent, for example that is would produce the same results with the same people on each occasion.

validity: the extent to which the researcher is testing what they claim to be testing.

generalisability: how widely findings apply, e.g. to other settings and populations.

test–retest: a way to measure the consistency of a test or task. The test is used twice and if the participants' two sets of scores are similar, i.e. correlate well, it has good reliability.

inter-rater reliability: the extent to which two researchers interpreting qualitative responses in a questionnaire (or interview) will produce the same records from the same raw data.

inter-observer reliability: the consistency between two researchers watching the same event, i.e. whether they will produce the same records.

demand characteristics: features of the experimental situation which give away the aims. They can cause participants to try to change their behaviour, e.g. to fit with their beliefs about what is supposed to happen, which reduces the validity of the study.

ecological validity: the extent to which the findings of research in one situation would generalise to other situations. This is influenced by whether the situation (e.g. a laboratory) represents the real world effectively and whether the task is relevant to real life (has *mundane realism*).

Reliability

Whenever research is conducted data is obtained. Researchers must attempt to ensure that the way in which these results are collected is the same each time, otherwise differences could occur (between participants, between conditions in an experiment or between the data obtained

by different researchers). Such inconsistencies would be problems of reliability.

The reliability of the measures used to collect data depends on the 'tool' used. A researcher collecting reaction times or pulse rates as data will probably have reliability as the machines used are likely to produce very consistent measures of time or rates. One way to check reliability is to use the **test–retest** procedure. This involves using a measure once, and then using it again in the same situation. If the reliability is high, the same results will be obtained on both occasions, i.e. there will be a high correlation between the two sets of scores. Imagine an experiment on euphoria and anger in which a researcher is not sure whether their questionnaire is a reliable measure of 'happiness'. They use a group of participants and give them the questionnaire on two separate occasions. All the participants would need to be tested at the same time of day and the same day of the week to ensure that their happiness levels were indeed the same. If the 'happiness scale' was reliable, this test–retest procedure would produce a high correlation between the scores on the first and second tests. If the reliability was low, the test would need to be redesigned.

Another reliability problem relates to subjective interpretations of data. For example, a researcher who is using a questionnaire or interview with open questions may find that the same answers could be interpreted in different ways, producing low reliability. If these differences arose between different researchers, this would be an **inter-rater reliability** problem. Similarly if, in an observation, researchers gave different interpretations of the same actions, this would be low **inter-observer reliability**. If the reliability was low, the researchers in either case would need to discuss why the differences arose and find ways to make their interpretations or observations more similar. This can be done by agreeing on operational definitions of the variables being measured and by looking at examples together. These steps would help to make the researchers more objective.

To minimise differences in the way research is conducted that could reduce reliability, standardisation can be used, that is, the procedure is kept the same. This could include instructions, materials and apparatus, although remember that there would be no reason to change many of these. Important aspects of standardisation are those factors which might differ, such as an experimenter's manner towards participants in different levels of the IV, an interviewer's posture or tone in asking questions or an observer's success at concealing their presence.

Validity

Many factors affect validity, including reliability – a test or task cannot measure what it intends to measure unless it is consistent. Objectivity also affects validity – if a researcher is subjective in their interpretation of data, their findings will not properly reflect the intended measure.

To have **face validity** a test or task must seem to test what it is supposed to. Imagine a test of helping behaviour that involved offering to assist people who were stuck in a bath full of spiders or worms. It might not be a valid test of helping because people who were frightened of spiders or worms would not help, even though they might otherwise be very altruistic. This would be a lack of face validity.

If participants think that they understand the aim of a study, their behaviour or responses are likely to be affected. This would also lower validity. In the design of a study, the researcher should aim to minimise **demand characteristics**, that is, those features which could indicate to the participants what is expected. For example, in a study about false memories, the researcher needs to hide the aim from the participants otherwise they will try to spot which memory is false. They might then try to remember this information particularly well, or might not report it at all if that is what they think the researcher expects.

Another problem for validity is whether the results obtained in one situation will apply to other situations, if not, then the test or task is too specific to be measuring the general phenomenon it was intended for. This is the problem of ecological validity, which applies more widely than considering just whether findings from the laboratory apply to the 'real world'. For example, a test of stress conducted in a laboratory may indeed not reflect the stress experienced in day-to-day life. But equally, a test of stress conducted at home might not reflect the stressful experiences people endure at work or during healthcare procedures. If so, the results may not generalise beyond the situation tested.

The task itself matters too. If a task participants are asked to do is similar to tasks in day-to-day life, it has mundane realism. This is important as the findings are more likely to have high ecological validity if the task is realistic. For example, in an experiment on emotions, responses to dangerous polar bears or dangerous insects could be used. As fewer people would encounter polar bears, responses to insects are likely to have higher mundane realism and therefore higher ecological validity.

Generalisability

Ecological validity contributes to the generalisability of the results. Another factor which affects the ability to generalise is the sample. If the sample is very small, or does not contain a wide range of the different types of people in the population, it is unlikely to be representative. Restricted samples like this are more likely to occur with opportunity or volunteer samples than with a random sample.

Evaluating studies based on methodological issues and applying your knowledge to novel research situations

You will need to be able to make evaluative decisions about methodology in relation to studies you already know about or a novel example of research or a study that you are asked to design yourself. In all of these cases, you need to ask yourself the following questions:

- Are the measures *reliable*? The study will collect data. Does the tool used to collect that data work consistently? Are the researchers using that tool in a consistent way? Is it *objective* or could they be **subjective** in their interpretation of the data?
- Is the study *valid*: Does it test what it is supposed to? This may depend on the reality of the task and the *generalisability* of setting (*ecological validity*) or of the sample. Might the participants have been affected by *demand characteristics*?

You will also need to be able to suggest ways to improve the methodology used. You can consider improving the:

- *method* (e.g. a field versus a laboratory experiment or a questionnaire versus an interview)
- *design* (independent measures will have fewer problems with order effects but repeated measures could overcome issues with individual differences)
- *sample* (using opportunity sampling might allow a larger sample to be collected, volunteer sampling could help to find particular types of participants and random sampling would give better generalisability)
- *tool* (measuring the inter-rater reliability or test–retest reliability and changing procedures to make improvements)
- *procedure* (to raise validity by reducing demand characteristics, making the task more realistic, etc.).

RESEARCH METHODS IN PRACTICE

Dr Splash is planning an experiment on obedience. He wants to test whether drivers are more obedient to traffic wardens wearing white clothing or black clothing. He wants the test to be **valid**, so he uses the same male traffic warden wearing different clothing in each condition. He has four observers, one watching cars approaching a junction from each direction. It is important that they are **reliable**, so he gives them operational definitions for the behavioural categories they are to observe:

- *Obedient behaviours*
  - slowing down: visibly reducing speed
  - stopping: coming to a halt before the line on the road.

- *Disobedient behaviours*
  - stopping late: coming to a halt past the line on the road
  - driving on: failing to stop when instructed to do so by the traffic warden.

These categories aimed to be very **objective**. He believes that it is unlikely that the participants (the drivers) will respond to **demand characteristics** as they would not know that they were in an experiment.

Finally, the drivers who stop past the line are given a note by a confederate while they are stationary. This debriefs them and asks if they would be happy to answer questions by telephone. Dr Splash's office number is given for them to call.

Reflections: Look at the Research methods in practice box above.

- Dr Splash is concerned about the generalisability of his findings. He has two ideas for changes to the procedure: conducting the same test in a village rather than a town and using a female traffic warden in both conditions. Explain how each idea would improve generalisability.
- The proposed study has high *ecological validity*. Explain why.
- Dr Splash thinks that of the observations in one of the behavioural categories, visibly reducing speed could be subjective. Explain why this is likely.
- Dr Splash wants to measure the *inter-observer reliability* of his four observers. Explain why this is important.
- In the final part of the study, some participants find out that they have been in a study. Suggest one ethical problem that could arise from this.
- By giving the drivers a number to call, rather than taking their number and calling them, Dr Splash is giving the participants their *right to withdraw*. Why is this important?
- Dr Splash asks the participants who do call him why they stopped and why they stopped over the line. He asks two of his colleagues to interpret the reasons they give but wants to ensure that they have high inter-rater reliability. He gives them a list of possible interpretations including a numerical scale to indicate how strongly the participant felt they may be punished. As both colleagues interpreted the responses from all the available drivers, Dr Splash can correlate the score given to each driver by the two colleagues to see if they are similar. What can he conclude if this produces a strong positive correlation?

SELF-ASSESSMENT QUESTIONS

6   A student is designing an experiment which aims to test whether dogs are more intelligent than cats. He has three dogs and two cats which he plans to use as his sample. To find out which is most intelligent, he is going to hide their food bowl inside a box and time how long it takes the animal to get to the food.
   a   Identify and operationalise the independent variable in this experiment.
   b   Identify and operationalise the dependent variable in this experiment.
   c   Write a non-directional hypothesis for this experiment.
   d   Write a null hypothesis for this experiment.
   e   Identify and outline the sampling technique used in this study.
   f   Which measure of central tendency would be best to find out the average time taken to find the food?
   g   A friend suggests that this is not a very valid test of intelligence because it might depend on how well the animal can smell the food. Explain this criticism.

7   A study into sleep obtained participants by placing advertisements in shops near to the university. The participants who responded were a sample of nine females and one male and were mainly retired people. The study was testing a new way to help people to fall asleep, using a recording of bubbling stream. Half the participants were told it would help them to sleep, the others were told it would keep them awake.
   a   Identify and outline the sampling technique used in this study.
   b   Explain **one** possible problem with generalisability in this study.
   c   Describe **one** ethical issue that would arise in this study.
   d   How well the participants slept was measured in two ways, by self-report and by how many minutes they stayed asleep for. Which of these measures is more reliable and why?

Summary

Psychologists can use several different **research methods**; experiments (**laboratory**, **field** and **natural**), **self-reports** (**questionnaires** and **interviews**), **case studies** (detailed investigations of a single instance, e.g. one person), **observations** and **correlations**.

In experiments there is an **independent variable** (IV), which is manipulated, changed or (in natural experiments) used to create different conditions and a measured **dependent variable** (DV). By imposing **controls**, the experimenter can be more certain that changes in the IV are the cause of changes in the DV. There are three **experimental designs**. In an **independent measures design** there are different participants in each level of the IV, in a **repeated measures design** the same participants are used in all levels of the IV and in a **matched pairs design** the participants are paired up with one member of each pair in each level of the IV. In a repeated measures design **counterbalancing** helps to overcome **order effects** (**fatigue** and **practice effects**) and in an independent measures design **random allocation** helps to overcome the effects of individual differences. In experiments it is important to control variables to raise validity. The most important are **extraneous variables** which could have a confounding effect. If these are left as **uncontrolled variables** they can alter the apparent effect of the IV on the DV. Variables can be described as **participant variables** (due to differences between individuals or between the same individual at different times) or **situational variables** (due to differences in physical setting or the social situation).

In self-reports, different question types can be used, including **open questions** (producing qualitative data) and **closed questions** (producing quantitative data). An interview can be **structured** (fixed), **unstructured** (variable) or **semi-structured**. Observations can be conducted in many different ways, for example **structured** (observing known categories) or **unstructured** (recording any events) and **naturalistic** (observing whatever is happening) or **controlled** (constructing events to observe). The role of the observer may be obvious to the participants (**overt**) or hidden (**covert**) and the observer themselves may be part of the social situations (**participant**) or not (**non-participant**). Correlations look for relationships between two measured variables. They can be **positive** (the two variables increase together) or **negative** (as one variable increases the other decreases) but conclusions cannot be drawn about causal relationships between the variables. All variables, e.g. those in correlations, the IV and DV in experiments and behavioural categories in observations should all be **operationalised**.

Any research begins with an **aim**, which is developed into a testable **hypothesis**. This can be **directional (one-tailed)** or **non-directional (two-tailed)**. This is compared to a **null hypothesis**, which proposes that there is no difference or relationship (or that any pattern in the results has arisen due to chance). To test the hypothesis, a group of participants (the **sample**) is selected from the **population**. This can be done by **opportunity sampling** (choosing people who are available), **random sampling** (selecting participants so that each individual has an equal chance of being chosen) or **volunteer** (self-selecting) **sampling** (inviting participants, e.g. by advertising).

Studies can collect different types of data. **Quantitative data** is numerical and **qualitative data** is descriptive. **Data analysis** of quantitative data includes using various **measures of central tendency** (the **mean**, **median** and **mode**) and **measures of spread** (the **range** and **standard deviation**). Data can be displayed graphically using **bar charts**, **histograms** or **scatter graphs**.

The **normal distribution** is a pattern which can be seen on a frequency histogram which shows that the results have an even (symmetrical) spread around the mean, median and mode.

Research in psychology raises **ethical issues**. Some important issues relate to **informed consent** (knowing about the study and agreeing to do it), **protection of participants** (physically and **psychologically**), the **right to withdraw** (being able to leave a study), **deception** (being misled), **confidentiality** (keeping participants' data anonymous), **privacy** (not invading physical or mental space) and **debriefing** (explaining the study to participants afterwards and returning them to their previous state). There are also ethical guidelines relating to the use of animals, including issues relating to the species used, number of animals, the pain and distress they experience, the way they are housed and rewarded or deprived and their suffering (the need for anaesthesia, analgesia and euthanasia).

Two very important **methodological issues** are **validity** and **reliability**. **Ecological validity** relates to how well the findings from one situation, e.g. a laboratory, represent what would happen in other situations. **Subjectivity** threatens validity because it causes researchers to interpret findings from their personal viewpoint, whereas **objectivity** allows researchers to measure variables in ways that are independent of their own perspective. **Demand characteristics** also threaten validity because they inform participants about the aim of the study which can alter their behaviour. Results of studies should be **generalisable**, that is they should apply to other people, situations and times. **Reliability** refers to the consistency of measures. In an experiment it is important to use **standardisation** of procedures to ensure that all participants are treated in the same way. This raises reliability. When researchers interpreting data are consistent, they have good **inter-rater reliability** (e.g. due to practice of operational definitions). **Inter-observer reliability** is the consistency in the records made by observers who are watching the same events. The reliability of a test, e.g. a questionnaire or a task in an experiment can be evaluated using a procedure to measure **test–retest reliability**, by conducting the test twice and correlating the two sets of data.

41

Exam-style questions

1 A hypothesis in a study says 'Greater emotions will be experienced after an adrenalin injection than after a saline injection'.

   a Is this a directional (one-tailed) hypothesis or a non-directional (two-tailed) hypothesis? Include a reason for your answer. [1 mark]

   b Write a null hypothesis that could be used with the hypothesis given above. [2 marks]

2 Declan is conducting a self-report study about attitudes to people with phobias. He cannot decide whether to use a questionnaire or an interview.

   a Suggest **one** advantage and **one** disadvantage of using a questionnaire for Declan's study. [4 marks]

   b Write **one** open and **one** closed question that Declan could ask. [2 marks]

   c Declan is concerned that his interpretation of the responses to questions might not be consistent. Is this mainly a reliability or a validity issue? Explain your answer. [2 marks]

3 Mary is planning an experiment to find out whether boys or girls in her school doodle more.

   a Describe how Mary could conduct her experiment. [10 marks]

   b Identify **one** possible weakness / limitation with the procedure you have described in your answer to part (a) and suggest how your study might be done differently to overcome the problem. [4 marks]

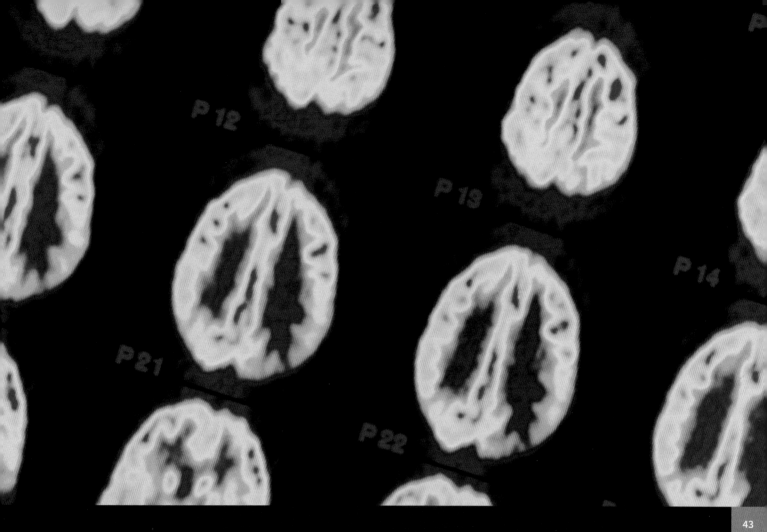

Chapter 2
The biological approach

Introduction

The aim of this chapter is to introduce you to the biological approach to psychology and to explore three studies from this approach. They are:

- **Canli et al. (2000)** which is a brain scanning study looking at the links between the amygdala and memory for emotional experiences.
- **Dement and Kleitman (1957)** which is a study using a range of methods to investigate the relationship between dream content and eye movements.
- **Schachter and Singer (1962)** which is an experiment that explores the of role of two factors, cognition and physiology, in our experience of emotions.

These three studies illustrate the main assumptions of the biological approach, which are that emotions, behaviour and cognition:

- are controlled by biological systems and processes, such as evolution, genes, the nervous system and hormones
- can be investigated by manipulating and measuring biological responses, such as eye movements, brain activity and pulse rate.

In this chapter there are examples of different aspects of biological factors. In each core study you will learn about the background to the research, the way it was conducted, the findings, conclusions and an evaluation of the study. From this you will be able to see how the studies, and the biological approach in general, illustrate a range of aspects from the research methods topic. In addition, you will discover how these ideas can be used to illustrate a range of issues and debates.

A biological being

What have you been thinking, doing and feeling today? Your answer could range from 'nothing at all' to 'I've run a marathon', 'I've sat an exam' or 'I've cried because I couldn't do my homework'. All of those things are ultimately controlled by your biology. Even if you were doing nothing, your brain was active, that is a biological process of electrical and chemical signals along and between nerve cells (neurons) was happening. The movements when you run are controlled by your brain and messages are sent along the neurons inside your arms and legs. The decisions you make answering exam questions are controlled by your brain too. Emotional responses like crying, even though we cannot control them, are governed by the brain, although hormones are important too. A hormone called adrenalin would be released during the excitement of a race and would help you to run faster. Hormones are often involved in emotional responses too, like being very happy or being sad or angry.

Hormones are released in particular situations. For example, adrenalin would be released if you were running away because you were scared. Adrenalin has effects that would help you to run faster, such as providing extra blood to the muscles. Biological responses like this have evolved because they help us to survive – by running faster we can stay safe. In order to be affected by evolution, aspects of a response, or the physiology that controls it, must be genetically controlled. Imagine a situation in which you were sleeping, and dreaming about jumping out of a window. If you actually did this in your sleep, it would be very risky. However, a system has evolved to protect us. When we are dreaming almost all of the muscles we use for movement (except the ones of our eyes) are paralysed.

> **Reflections:** Think of a behaviour or an emotional response that could have been useful to survival in the early **evolution** of humans. Do you think it could be (partly) controlled biologically, by **genes** and hormones or the nervous system?

2.1 Core study 1:
Canli et al. (2000)

Canli, T., Zhao, Z., Brewer, J., Gabrieli, J. D. E., & Cahill, L. (2000). Event-related activation in the human amygdala associates with later memory for individual emotional experience. *Journal of Neuroscience, 20*, 1–5.

Aim

Canli et al. aimed to show that emotive images will be remembered better than those that have little emotional impact on an individual.

The central questions addressed by this study were whether the amygdala is sensitive to varying degrees of emotional intensity to external stimuli and whether the level of intensity enhances memory for the stimuli.

Background

Brain scanning techniques are a huge advance in biological psychology. Psychologists can now study the brains of living people and draw conclusions about the relationship between behaviour and brain structure/activity. There are two basic types of medical scan: functional and structural.

Structural scans take detailed pictures of the structure of the brain whereas functional scans are able to show activity levels in different areas of the brain.

Functional magnetic resonance imaging (fMRI) is a neuroimaging procedure using MRI technology that measures brain activity by detecting changes associated with blood flow. In the simplest fMRI study a participant would alternate between periods of completing a specific task and a control or rest state to measure baseline activity. The fMRI data is then analysed to identify brain areas in which the signal changed between the activity and the rest state and it is inferred that these areas were activated by the task.

KEY TERMS

> **evolution:** the process of natural selection of offspring which have inherited characteristics that make them most likely to survive.
>
> **genes:** inherited instructions that are passed on from parents to children that control our development and influence some aspects of our thinking, behaviour and emotions, such as our personality and intelligence. One way this can happen is by affecting brain function.

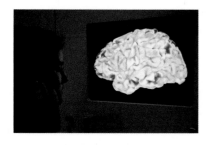

2.1 A computer-generated image using fMRI data showing areas of activity in a human brain

The data from an fMRI scan is used to generate images that can illustrate how the brain is working during different tasks (Figure 2.1). Such a scan allows a living brain to be seen without resorting to surgery. During the scan, patients are placed in a scanner that sends a strong magnetic field through their head. The magnetic field causes the nuclei in hydrogen molecules in the brain to spin in a particular way, and the scanner picks this up. Because hydrogen concentrations vary in different parts of the brain, the scanner is able to create a very detailed picture of the brain.

Over the last few decades, researchers have used fMRI scans to identify areas of the brain that have specific functions (Figure 2.2). Areas that have been shown to have a significant association with emotion and memory are the subcortical areas of the brain, including the amygdala. The amygdala is an almond-shaped set of neurons located deep in the brain's medial temporal lobe and has been shown to play a key role in the processing of emotions such as pleasure, fear and anger. Importantly, the amygdala is also responsible for determining where memories are stored in the brain and which ones are kept.

LaBar and Phelps (1998) suggested that emotional experiences are often better recalled than non-emotional ones and emotional arousal appears to increase the likelihood of memory consolidation during the storage stage of memory (the process of creating a permanent record of the encoded information). Brain imaging studies have shown that amygdala activation correlates with emotional memory in the brain. Previous research by Canli et al. (1999) showed that participants who had a strong amygdala activation in response to a set of emotional stimuli also showed superior memory for those stimuli. However, Canli et al. (2000) suggested that, because an independent measures design was used for these experiments, there could be other explanations for the findings.

The present study used fMRI in a repeated measures, subsequent-memory design to test the predictions that those emotionally intense stimuli that produce greater amygdala activation would be recalled more easily than stimuli that generate less amygdala activation. Participants saw neutral and negative scenes and indicated how they experienced the emotional intensity in each case. A separate fMRI response was recorded in the amygdala for each such emotional experience. Three weeks later, participants' memories for the experiences were assessed to see if those images that generated greater activation of the amygdala were remembered better.

45

> **Reflections:** If you had the use of a brain scanner what behaviour would you want to locate and why?
>
> Is it an advantage for the human brain to have specialised locations for some tasks or is there a benefit to having tasks distributed across the brain?

Method

Research method and design

This was a laboratory experiment as the environment in which the participants were tested was not comparable to an everyday situation. The use of fMRI scanners limits the realism that can be introduced into a study as they are large machines (see Figure 2.3) and participants have to lie very still while the measurements are being taken.

The independent variable was can be seen as the intensity of the emotional arousal to each of the 96 scenes that were presented to each participant. Participants had to choose from four buttons to indicate emotional arousal on a scale from 0 ('not emotionally intense at all') to 3 ('extremely emotionally intense').

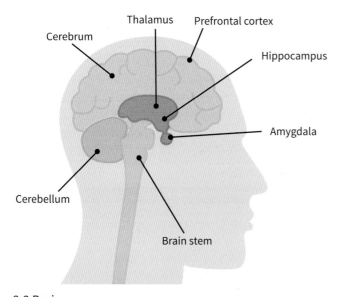

2.2 Brain map

Cerebrum
Thalamus
Prefrontal cortex
Hippocampus
Amygdala
Cerebellum
Brain stem

This experiment is an example of a repeated measures design as participants contributed to each of the four conditions depending on their rating of each scene.

IV Level of perceived emotional arousal	Not emotionally intense at all …		… Extremely emotionally intense	
	0	1	2	3
DVs	fMRI measure of amygdala activation			
	Memory of scene			

There were two key measures of the dependent variable. The first was the level of activation of the amygdala measured by fMRI during the first stage of the experiment when the participants were exposed to each of the 96 scenes. During functional scanning, 11 frames were captured per trial, so therefore for each of the 96 scenes there were 11 fMRI measures of neural activity. The second was the measure of memory when participants had to recognise the images three weeks after the initial experiment.

Sample

Ten right-handed healthy female volunteers were scanned. Females were chosen in this study because it was thought that they are more likely to report intense emotional experiences and show more **physiological** reactions to the stimuli.

Procedure

During scanning, participants viewed a series of 96 scenes that were presented via an overhead projector and mirror to allow them to see it while in the fMRI scanner. All of the participants had given informed consent to be involved in the study and were aware of the nature of the experiment. The individuals who were operating the fMRI scanner were fully trained and competent in the safety arrangements that should be followed during a medical scan.

All of the 96 scenes were from the 'International Affective Picture System' stimuli set. For the scenes used in this study, average ratings for **valence** ranged from 1.17 (highly negative) to 5.44 (neutral).

The order of scenes were randomised across the participants, with each picture presented for a period of 2.88 seconds. There was then an interval of 12.96 seconds, where participants viewed a fixation cross. Participants were instructed to view each picture for the entire time that it was displayed, and after its replacement with a fixation cross they were to indicate their emotional arousal by pressing a button with their right hand. Participants had to choose from four buttons to indicate emotional arousal on a scale from 0 ('not emotionally intense at all') to 3 ('extremely emotionally intense').

To measure activity in the brain, fMRI data were collected by a 1.5 Tesla fMRI scanner (Figure 2.3), which was used to measure blood–oxygen level-dependent contrast. Contrast imaging is a method used in fMRI to observe different areas of the brain which are found to be active at any given time.

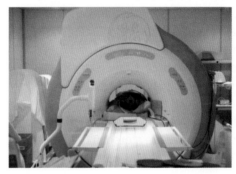

2.3 1.5T General Electric Signa MR imager as used in the research

Three weeks after the first stage, participants were tested in an unexpected recognition test in the laboratory. During this task they viewed all of the 96 previous scenes and 48 new scenes (**foils**). The foils were selected to match the previously presented scenes in their valence and arousal characteristics. Participants were asked whether they had seen each scene before and for images judged as previously seen, participants reported whether they

RESEARCH METHODS

Randomising the order of stimuli helps to overcome order effects, so that seeing one type of stimulus doesn't affect the response to stimuli that follow in a systematic way. This means, for example, that always seeing negative scenes could not consistently affect the perception of neutral scenes. Can you remember the two different types of 'order effects'?

KEY TERMS

physiological: to do with the biological processes in the body, for example hormones.

valence: when discussing emotions this refers to the attractiveness (positive valence) or aversiveness (negative valence) of an event, object or situation.

foil: an unknown or unseen object that is used as a control when testing a participant's memory.

remembered with certainty ('remember') or had a less certain feeling of familiarity ('know').

Research questions

Is the amygdala sensitive to varying degrees of individually experienced emotional intensity?

What degree of emotional intensity affects the role of the amygdala in enhancing memory for emotional stimuli?

Results

Participants' experience of emotional intensity in the present study correlated well with average ratings of emotional valence and arousal. The average **correlation coefficients** between participants' intensity ratings, on the one hand, and normative valence and arousal, on the other hand, were -0.66 and 0.68, respectively. Therefore, participants' ratings of emotional intensity reflected equally well the valence and arousal characteristics of the stimuli.

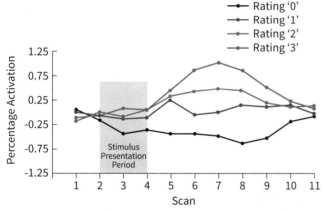

2.4 Graph showing average amygdala activation in response to scenes that were rated in emotional intensity from 0 (least intense) to 3 (most intense)

Amygdala activation was significantly correlated with higher ratings of individually experienced emotional intensity (Figure 2.4). This provides evidence that amygdala activation is related to the subjective sense of emotional intensity and that the participants' perceived arousal is associated with amygdala activation.

KEY TERM

correlation coefficient: a number between –1 and 1 which shows the strength of a relationship between two variables with a coefficient of –1 meaning there is a perfect negative correlation and a coefficient of 1 meaning there is a perfect positive correlation.

The follow-up memory task indicated that memory performance was significantly improved for scenes that were rated as highly emotionally intense (i.e. rated 3) than for scenes rated less emotionally intense. Scenes that were rated mild-to-moderate (ratings 0 to 2) had similar distributions of items that were forgotten, familiar, or remembered, whereas scenes that were rated as emotionally highly salient (rated 3) were recalled better, because fewer items were forgotten and more were familiar and remembered (see Figure 2.5).

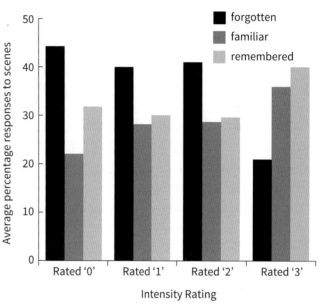

2.5 Average percentage of scenes forgotten or rated as familiar/remembered at the three-week unexpected recognition task

RESEARCH METHODS

This is a special kind of **bar chart**. Imagine it is really three bar charts, one made of each different coloured set of bars. Each bar chart would be drawn on the same axes. By presenting them all together, it is easier to compare the different types of remembering and forgetting. Why is a bar chart being used here rather than a histogram?

For scenes that were rated highly emotional (rated 3), the degree of left (but not right) amygdala activation predicted whether individual stimuli would be forgotten, appear familiar, or be remembered in a later memory test. Therefore, little amygdala activation when viewing a picture rated as highly emotionally intense was associated with the participant's forgetting the stimulus, but intermediate and high amygdala activation was associated with a participant's later report of familiarity or confident recognition.

47

Conclusions

Canli et al. found an association between individual experiences of emotional intensity for stimuli with amygdala activation and subsequent memory for these stimuli, suggesting that the more emotionally intense an image is, the more likely it will be remembered. This conclusion provides evidence to explain why people remember emotionally intense experiences well. The level of arousal a person is under could affect the strength of a memory trace. When exposed to an event that causes this arousal, such as a car crash or witnessing a crime, the memory trace will be more robust.

They also found that the amygdala is sensitive to individuals' experienced emotional intensity of visual stimuli with activity in the left amygdala during encoding being predictive of subsequent memory. Canli et al. do comment that some of their findings are correlational, showing an association between the emotional impact on the participant and the subsequent memory for the item.

Strengths and weaknesses

The main method was a **laboratory experiment** as all of the participants were tested in a standardised environment and given the same items to rate in each condition. The procedure was incredibly standardised to the level of the time that each item was presented for and the duration of the interval between presentations. This means that the research has **internal validity** as the researcher can be more confident that there are fewer confounding variables affecting the variables that they are measuring.

The use of an fMRI scanner to measure one of the dependent variables provided the researchers with vast amounts of **quantitative data** relating to the activation of the amygdala, enabling them to carry out statistical analyses such as correlational analysis about the level of activation and subsequent memory of the scene. Although the task of being scanned in an fMRI scanner is hardly **ecologically valid** it would not be possible for the participants to respond to demand characteristics, which increases the validity of the data collected and allows for very sophisticated analysis.

Using fMRI scanners to measure the biological response on the brain of the different images gives an objective finding for each participant as it does not need the research to interpret any results. However, we need to be careful that we do not infer too much from fMRI results as there are still many unknowns about locations of specific behaviours in the brain. Although the method is widespread, there is insufficient knowledge of the physiological basis of the fMRI signal to interpret the data confidently with respect to neural activity and how this maps onto specific behaviours.

Although most fMRI research uses contrast imaging as a method to determine which parts of the brain are most active, because the signals are relative to the individual rather than measured against a baseline, some question the validity in comparisons across individuals. However, in this research, a repeated measures design was used to minimise the impact of this, as participants' scores were compared against themselves.

The sample in this research consists of right-handed females only and therefore introduces participant variables that could distort the outcomes of the research reducing the validity of the research. Females were chosen as the researchers felt that they would have a higher emotional response and might react differently to the scenes that were presented. Therefore, we must be cautious in generalising the results of this to males and to left-handed individuals, as they may respond differently, for example females were chosen rather than males exactly because they were thought to be more emotionally reactive.

> **SELF-ASSESSMENT QUESTIONS**
>
> 1 Give **two** examples of how Canli et al.'s study lacks ecological validity.
>
> 2 A feature of laboratory experiments is that the researchers have control over the situation and can standardise their procedure. Give **four** examples of controls in this experiment.
>
> 3 a Describe the sample in Canli et al.'s experiment.
>
>   b Evaluate the sample in relation to Canli et al.'s ability to generalise their findings to the general population.

2.2 Core study 2:
Dement and Kleitman (1957)

Dement, W., & Kleitman, N. (1957). The relation of eye movements during sleep to dream activity: An objective method for the study of dreaming. *Journal of Experimental Psychology, 53,* 339–346.

Aim

The aim of this study was to find out more about dreaming. This included three specific research questions:

1. Does dream recall differ between eye movement (**REM**) and quiescent (**nREM**) stages of sleep?

2. Is there a positive correlation between subjective estimates of dream duration and the length of the REM period before waking?

3. Are eye movement patterns related to dream content?

Background

Sleep and dreaming are difficult to study as the participant is not responsive. The sleeper can often give a description of a dream when they awake, but to find out about sleep and dream states, physiological measures are needed too.

Aserinsky and Kleitman (1955) were the first to use physiological measures of sleep to explore the relationship between sleep and dreaming. Like Dement and Kleitman, they used an **electroencephalograph (EEG)** to record brain activity and eye movements and showed that we have several stages during the night, alternating between REM and nREM sleep (see Figure 2.6). They found that participants woken from REM sleep were more likely to report a vivid, visual dream than when woken in other stages. This was the case for both normal and schizophrenic participants.

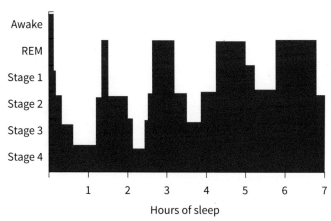

2.6 EEG recording or sleep stages showing four phases of REM sleep with nREM stages (1–4) in between

An EEG produces a chart (an encephalogram) showing how brain waves vary, i.e. how the **frequency** and **amplitude** (height) of electrical activity changes over time (see Figure 2.7). The chart records changes which indicate the sleep stage a person is in. An EEG can also be used to

detect activity in the muscles moving the eyes, so can be used to measure eye movements. This is sometimes called an ElectroOculoGram (EOG).

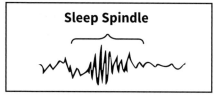

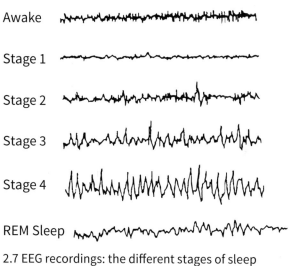

2.7 EEG recordings: the different stages of sleep

Reflections: You have just woken up from a dream. It felt as though it had lasted for a very long time. How long do you think you were actually dreaming for?

2.8 The participant slept in a bed with wires from the EEG electrodes leading into the room where the experimenter sat

Method

Research method and design

This study was conducted in a laboratory but several methods were used. To answer the first question above, about the difference in dream recall between REM and nREM sleep, an experiment with a repeated measures design was used. The independent variable was whether the participant was woken from REM or nREM sleep. The dependent variable was whether they recalled a dream or not. The test of question 2, about the relationship between dream duration and the length of the REM period was a correlation (although the comparison between estimates of 5 and 15 minutes was another repeated measures design experiment). To find out about question 3, the relationship between eye movement patterns and dream content, self-reports were compared to the direction of eye movements observed.

Sample

Seven male and two female adults were used, five of whom were studied in detail. The remaining four were used to confirm the results of the first five.

Procedure

On each day of the study participants ate normally, excluding caffeine-containing drinks (such as coffee) and alcohol. They arrived at the laboratory just before their normal bedtime. The participant went to sleep in a dark, quiet room with electrodes attached beside the eyes and on the scalp (the EEG), which fed into the experimenter's room. The wires were gathered together into a single cord from the participant's head (like a pony-tail) so they could move easily in bed (see Figure 2.8).

Participants were woken (by a doorbell) at various times during the night, asked to describe their dream if they were having one, then returned to sleep. They were not told about their EEG pattern or whether their eyes were moving. The procedure for the three questions differed:

1   Participants were woken either from REM or nREM sleep but were not told which. The choice of REM or nREM waking was decided in different ways for different participants:

    - using a random number table (participants PM and KC)
    - in groups of three REM then three nREM (participant DN)
    - by telling the participant that they would *only* be woken in REM but actually waking them in REM or nREM randomly (participant WD)
    - in no specific order, the experimenter just chose (participant IR).

    Immediately after being woken, the participant stated whether they were having a dream or not and then, if appropriate, described the content of the dream into a recorder. When the participant had finished, the experimenter occasionally entered the room to ask further questions about the dream. There was no other communication between the experimenter and the participant.

2   Participants were woken after either 5 or 15 minutes in REM sleep. The participant guessed which duration they had been dreaming for. Longer REM periods were also allowed. The number of words in the dream narrative was counted.

3   The direction of eye movements was detected using EEG electrodes around the eyes. Participants were woken after a single eye-movement pattern had lasted for more than one minute and asked to report their dream. The eye-movement patterns detected were: 'mainly vertical', 'mainly horizontal', 'both vertical and horizontal' and 'very little or no movement'. Comparison EEG records were taken from awake participants, 20 naive ones and five of the experimental sample, who were asked to watch distant and close-up activity.

The environment was highly controlled, for example the doorbell used to wake participants was sufficiently loud to rouse them immediately from any sleep stage. If the experimenter asked any questions, this was not done until the participant had definitely completed his recording. Also, reports were not counted as 'dreams' if the participant could only recall having dreamt, rather than the content, or had only a vague, fragmented impression of the dream.

Results

Dement and Kleitman reported some general findings, such as that all participants dreamt every night, as well as those relating to their three questions. They found that uninterrupted dream stages:

- lasted 3–50 minutes (with a mean of approximately 20 minutes)
- were typically longer later in the night
- showed intermittent bursts of around 2–100 rapid eye movements.

In addition, they observed that:

- no rapid eye movements were seen during the onset of sleep even though the EEG passed through a stage of brain waves similar to those produced during REM sleep.
- the cycle length (from one REM stage to the next) varied between participants but was consistent within individuals, e.g. between 70 minutes at the shortest and 104 minutes at the longest (with a mean of 92 minutes for all participants).
- When woken from nREM sleep participants returned to nREM but when woken from REM sleep they typically did not dream again until the *next* REM phase (except sometimes in the final REM phase of the night). As a consequence, the pattern of REM and nREM periods was very similar in experimental participants whose sleep was disturbed to those who had an uninterrupted night's sleep.

> **!**
>
> **RESEARCH METHODS**
>
> The **mean** sleep cycle length was calculated for each individual. This would have been worked out by adding together the cycle lengths in minutes for every complete cycle a participant had slept through. This would then have been divided by the number of complete sleep cycles that had been observed for that participant. How variable was the average cycle length?

> **Reflections:** Think about occasions when you have woken up in the middle of the night. Are you more or less likely to remember a dream then than when you wake up in the morning? Why?

In relation to their three questions, Dement and Kleitman's results were as follows.

Does dream recall differ between eye movement (REM) and quiescent (nREM) stages of sleep?

Participants frequently described dreams when woken from REM but rarely did from nREM sleep although there were some individual differences (see Table 2.1). Of awakenings from REM, 79.6% (152/191) of awakenings produced dream recall and 93% (149/160) of awakenings from nREM did not produce dream recall.

This difference was most noticeable at the end of the nREM period. In 17 nREM awakenings soon after the end of a REM stage (within 8 minutes), five dreams were recalled (29% of occasions). However, from 132 awakenings following periods longer than eight minutes after a REM stage, only six dreams were recalled (i.e. less than 5% of occasions). In nREM awakenings, participants tended to describe feelings but not specific dream content. They were least likely to remember a dream if they were woken at the stage of sleep

51

Participant	Rapid eye movements		No rapid eye movements	
	Dream recall	No recall	Dream recall	No recall
DN	17	9	3	21
IR	26	8	2	29
KC	36	4	3	31
WD	37	5	1	34
PM	24	6	2	23
KK	4	1	0	5
SM	2	2	0	2
DM	2	1	0	1
MG	4	3	0	3
Totals	**152**	**39**	**11**	**149**

Table 2.1 Dream recall following awakenings from REM or nREM sleep

in which the EEG has 'spindles' (i.e. stage 2, see Figure 2.7). They tended to be bewildered and report feelings as such as anxiety, pleasantness and detachment.

It is important to note that participant DN was no more accurate even though he could have learned the pattern of awakenings and WD was no less accurate even though he was misled to expect to be dreaming every time. Also, participants did not become any more accurate over time, i.e. they did not improve with practice.

Awakenings from REM sleep did not always produce dream recall, absence of dreaming in REM was more common early in the night. Of 39 REM awakenings when dreams were not reported, 19 occurred in the first 2 hours of sleep, 11 from the second 2 hours, 5 from the third 2 hours and 4 from the last 2 hours. In contrast, awakenings from nREM always produced a low incidence of dream recall.

Is there a positive correlation between subjective estimates of dream duration and the length of the REM period before waking?

The accuracy of estimation of 5 or 15 minutes of REM was very high (88% and 78% respectively). Table 2.2 shows the results of this experimental comparison. REM duration and the number of words in the narrative were significantly positively correlated. The r values for each participant varied from $r = 0.4$ to $r = 0.71$, indicating moderate to strong positive correlations. These were based on between 1 and 35 dreams per participant, with a total of 126 dreams.

One participant often underestimated the dream duration, perhaps because he could only remember the end of the dream. Similarly, narratives from REM periods of recalled after 30–50 minutes of REM were not much longer than those

after 15 minutes even though the participants felt they had been dreaming for a long time. This is probably because they could not remember all the details from very long dreams.

Are eye movement patterns related to dream content?

Eye movement patterns were found to be related to dream content. This part of the study was based on 35 awakenings from nine participants. Periods of only vertical or only horizontal movements were very rare. There were three dreams with mainly vertical eye movements. In one the dreamer was standing at the bottom of a tall cliff operating a hoist (a lifting machine) and looking up at climbers at various levels then down at the machine. In another a man was climbing up a series of ladders looking up and down as he climbed. In the third, the dreamer was throwing basketballs at a net, shooting, looking up at the net, and then looking down to pick up another ball from the floor (Figure 2.9). There was one instance of horizontal movement, in which the dreamer was watching two people throwing tomatoes at each other.

2.9 Dreams of climbing ladders and throwing basketballs produced vertical eye movements

> **Reflections:** Keep a dream diary for a week, writing down the content of any dreams you can remember when you wake up. Think about whether each dream would have had few or many eye movements and whether these would have been vertical or horizontal.

Ten dreams had little or no eye movement and the dreamer reported watching something in the distance or staring at an object. Two of these awakenings also had several large eye movements to the left just a second or two before

Participant	Whether the participants' judgement of 5 or 15 minutes was correct or not			
	5 minutes		15 minutes	
DN	8	2	5	5
IR	11	1	7	3
KC	7	0	12	1
WD	13	1	15	1
MP	6	2	8	3
Total	45	6	47	13

Table 2.2 Results of the comparison of dream duration estimates after 5 or 15 minutes of REM sleep

the awakening. In one, the participant had been driving a car and staring at the road ahead. He approached a road junction and was startled by a speeding car suddenly appearing to his left (as the bell rang). The other dreamer also reported driving a car and staring at the road ahead. Immediately before being woken he saw a man standing on the left of the road and acknowledged him as he drove by.

Twenty-one of the awakenings had mixed eye movements. These participants reported looking at objects or people close to them, for example talking to a group of people, looking for something and fighting with someone. There was no recall of distant or vertical activity.

The eye movement patterns recorded from the awake (control) participants were similar in amplitude and pattern to those occurring in dreams. Similarly, there were virtually no eye movements when watching distant activity and much more when watching close-up activity. Vertical eye movements were rare in awake participants, except during blinking, and when the experimenter threw a ball in the air.

Conclusions

Dreaming is reported from REM but not nREM sleep, participants can judge the length of their dream duration and REM patterns relate to dream content. As a consequence, dreaming is more likely at the end of the night, as the REM stages are longer. These two observations fit with those reported by other researchers. The occasional recall of dreams from nREM is likely to happen because dreams are being recalled from the previous REM phase (as this is more likely closely following REM sleep). The finding that REM sleep occurs in phases during the night helps to explain why participants in other studies who were awoken randomly may not have reported dreaming. Perhaps they were only woken in nREM stages, or were dreaming about distant objects so had few REMs, making accurate detection difficult. Measurement of eye movements and brain waves has shown that dreams progress in 'real time' and that this is a more objective way to study dreaming than using subjective recall of dreams alone, which can also be affected by forgetting.

Strengths and weaknesses

One method used was the **laboratory experiment**. In this part of the study it was therefore possible to control **extraneous variables**. If some participants, or participants in different stages of sleep, had woken more slowly they may have forgotten more of their dream. This was avoided by using a loud doorbell that woke them instantly, from any sleep stage. The participants were not told about their EEG pattern or whether their eyes were moving in order to

avoid possible **demand characteristics**, for example if they expected to remember more detailed dreams in REM sleep they may have made greater effort to do so.

Another method used was a correlation. This demonstrated a positive correlation between REM duration and the number of words in the dream narrative. However, as with any correlation, this could only demonstrate whether there was a link between variables. In order to explore this link in a more controlled way, Dement and Kleitman conducted the additional experiment comparing 5 and 15 minute REM sleep periods.

The definition of a 'dream' was clearly operationalised, as a recollection that included content, rather than just having the impression that they had been dreaming. This helped to raise **validity**, as Dement and Kleitman could be more sure that the details being recorded were of dreams. At the beginning of the study, participants were asked to estimate how long they had been dreaming and although they were roughly (and occasionally exactly) accurate, this task was too difficult, so the method was changed. The task was limited to a choice between 5 and 15 minutes. This also helped to raise **validity** as it reduced **participant variables** such as differences in the ability to recall dreams.

An EEG is an **objective** way to investigate dreaming as it is a biological measure. Differences in narrative length, however, depended not only on the length of the REM phase but also how expressive the participant was, making these reports more **subjective**. Nevertheless, this means that the study collected both **quantitative data**, from the brain waves, eye movement patterns and REM sleep duration, and **qualitative data**, which helped to provide insight into the reason for the eye movements detected. The EEG also provides a very reliable measure because it is unaffected by the experimenter's personal view. The consistent placing of the electrodes ensured that recordings taken from each participant would provide the same information. The reliability of the findings is supported by the similarity of the results to those of previous studies.

As there may be differences in the dreaming of men and women, or between the way they report their dreams, it was useful in terms of **generalisability** that there were both genders in the sample. However, as there were only nine participants in total, the small size of the **sample** limits generalisability.

One aspect of the method that raised an **ethical issue** was the **deception** of participant WD who was misled about the stage of sleep he was being woken in. Participants should not be deceived as it can cause distress and means they cannot give their **informed consent**. However, in some cases the aim cannot be achieved without doing so and in this case it provided a way to test whether expectation of being woken in REM (at least sometimes) would affect a participant's dream reports.

Several aspects of the procedure potentially reduced the ecological validity of the findings. People who were used to drinking coffee or alcohol could have experienced sleep or dreams that were not typical for them as they had been asked to refrain from those drinks. Also, all participants would have found sleeping in a laboratory, connected to machines and under observation, quite different from sleeping in their normal bed. This could also have made their sleeping behaviour less typical.

SELF-ASSESSMENT QUESTIONS

4 Biyu is planning a study on dreams and is worried that if her participants know the aim, they might make dreams up to please her.

   a Explain why this would be a problem.

   b She had decided to solve this problem by telling her participants the study was about insomnia, but her teacher says she cannot do this. Explain why Biyu's teacher has said this.

5 Karl is aiming to find out whether people sleep for longer because they have eaten more. He plans to do a correlation, asking people how much they have eaten during the day and how long they sleep for that night. Karl's teacher says this will not work.

   a Suggest why Karl will not be able to use the information he obtains from his study to come to a conclusion about his aim.

   b Karl decides to do the study anyway. Explain how he could operationalise the variables of sleeping and eating.

Summary

In Dement and Kleitman's study an EEG was used to collect data about sleep stages and eye movements and details of dream content were obtained by **self-report**. This study was conducted in a **laboratory experiment**, allowing for controls such as over what participants were told and how they were woken and objective, quantitative records could be collected as well as **qualitative data**. Three questions were answered: dreams are reported from REM but not nREM sleep, we can accurately judge the length of dreams and REM patterns relate to dream content.

2.3 Core study 3:
Schachter and Singer (1962)

Schachter, S., and Singer, J. E. (1962). Cognitive, social and physiological determinants of emotional state. *Psychological Review, 69, 379–399.*

Aim

The aim of the study was to test the Two-Factor Theory of Emotion. Schachter and Singer (1962) wanted to research if, given a state of physiological arousal for which the individual has no adequate explanation, cognitive factors can lead the individual to describe their feelings with any of a number of emotional labels.

Background

How individuals use either internal or external cues to identify their own emotional state has been of interest to psychologists since the late 1800s. Some of the early research suggested that cognitive factors could influence our emotional state. Cognition can be defined as the mental processes of acquiring and processing knowledge and understanding through experiences, senses and thought. Emotion can be defined as the body's adaptive response to a particular situation.

Following on from this it was suggested that an emotional state may be considered a function of a state of physiological arousal and of a cognition appropriate to this state of arousal. The cognition therefore steers our interpretation of our physiological state so that we can label our emotional responses.

For example, if a criminal tries to mug you by pointing a gun and demanding you give him your wallet, you will experience physiological arousal of the sympathetic **nervous system** (Figure 2.10). Your heart rate and respiration rate will increase, your pupils will dilate and **adrenalin** will be released (this is sometimes referred to as

---

KEY TERMS

nervous system: the brain, spinal cord and all the nerve cells in the body that communicate to control our thinking, behaviour and emotions.

adrenalin: a hormone released from the adrenal glands in response to stress or excitement. It is also known as epinephrine, and is a medication, hormone and neurotransmitter. Common side effects include shakiness, anxiety, sweating; a fast heart rate and high blood pressure may occur. Strong emotions such as fear or anger can cause epinephrine to be released into the bloodstream.

the 'fight or flight' response). You will label this emotional experience as 'fear' because of your knowledge (cognitive interpretation) about criminals with guns and how dangerous they are. Without the knowledge of the danger of guns and criminal behaviour your emotional experience would be different.

What if you were just sitting at home and experienced the same physiological arousal, meaning that you didn't have an explanation for your feelings? Schachter and Singer (1962) suggested that such an individual would look to the situation they were in to gain an explanation.

2.10 Emotional response is a combination of physiological arousal and cognitive understanding of the situation

Schachter and Singer developed what they named the Two-Factor Theory of Emotion (Figure 2.11). They suggest that emotional experience comes from a combination of a physical state of arousal and a cognition that makes best sense of the situation the person is in. For example, the Two-Factor Theory of Emotion argues that when people become aroused they look for cues as to why they feel the way they do from the environment and interpret their arousal in relation to this. Therefore, any emotional experience is a combination of physiological arousal and a cognitive interpretation.

The study by Schachter and Singer investigated emotions, and their Two-Factor Theory argues that we experience emotions as an interaction between physiological and psychological variables. To achieve this, they created a situation where some participants were physiologically aroused through an **epinephrine** injection and put into either a 'happy' or 'angry' situation to investigate if those participants would look to the situation for context cues to explain their arousal.

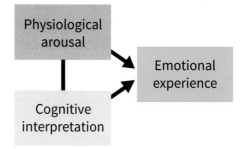

2.11 The Two-Factor Theory of Emotion

Method

Research method and design

This was a laboratory experiment as the environment in which the participants were tested was not comparable to an everyday situation. It was a highly standardised procedure and all participants were exposed to the same environment with a scripted response from the stooge. There were two independent variables in this experiment which resulted in seven different conditions. The first independent variable concerned the knowledge about the injections; whether they were informed, misinformed or ignorant. The second independent variable was the emotional situation that the participant was placed into following the injection; either euphoria or anger. There was also a control group who were not injected with epinephrine but a saline solution. This experiment is an example of an independent groups design as participants only took part in one of the seven groups (see Table 2.3).

There were two key measures of the **dependent variable**. The first was observational data that was recorded by two observers through a one-way mirror during the emotional arousal element of the experiment. The observer had to measure to what extent the participant acted in a euphoric or angry way. During each stage of the stooge's routine the observer kept a record of how the participant reacted and what was said. In the euphoric condition, the categories into which the behaviour was coded were that the participant: joins in the activity, initiates a new activity, watches stooge or ignores stooge. In the anger condition, the observers coded behaviour into six categories depending on the participants' response. These categories were that the participant: agreed with a comment, disagreed with a comment, was neutral to a comment, initiates agreement or disagreement, watches or ignores the stooge. To test the **reliability** of these measures two observers coded their observations independently. The observers completely agreed on the coding of 88% of the behaviour they saw.

The second was a self-report that the participants completed following the emotional arousal element of the research.

55

	Euphoria Informed	Anger Informed
Experimental groups	Misinformed	–
	Ignorant	Ignorant
Control group	Placebo	Placebo

Table 2.3 Conditions within the experiment

RESEARCH METHODS

A **dependent variable** is the factor which is measured in an experiment and which the experimenter expects to be influenced by the independent variable. In this case, there two dependent variables, and they are measured in several different ways. Write out the two dependent variables and list the ways they are measured for each one.

Sample

The 185 participants were all male college students taking classes in introductory psychology at the University of Minnesota, of which many received course credit for taking part in the study. The university health records of all participants were checked prior to the experiment to ensure that no harmful effects would result from the injections.

Reflections: Why might psychologists use psychology students in their experiments? What impact might this have on the validity of any findings?

Procedure

When the participants arrived at the laboratory they were told that the aim of the experiment was to test the effects of vitamin supplements on vision:

'In this experiment we would like to make various tests of your vision. We are particularly interested in how certain vitamin compounds and vitamin supplements affect the visual skills. In particular, we want to find out how the vitamin compound called "Suproxin" affects your vision. What we would like to do, then, if we can get your permission, is to give you a small injection of Suproxin. The injection itself is mild and harmless; however, since some people do object to being injected we don't want to talk you into anything. Would you mind receiving a Suproxin injection?'

RESEARCH METHODS

The participants were misinformed about the aims and procedures of the study, ie they were **deceived**. This means they could not give their informed **consent**. Note that these two uses of 'misinformed' and 'informed' are different from the way these words are used in describing the conditions in this experiment. Can you define the ethical issue of 'deception' and the ethical guideline of 'consent'?

A doctor then entered the room, repeated these instructions, took the participant's pulse and injected the participant with 'Suproxin' (Figure 2.12). The participants were actually injected with either adrenalin or a **placebo** (saline solution). The dosage that the participants were injected with should have caused them to experience the side effects within three to five minutes and these could last up to an hour.

2.12 Epinephrine or a saline solution was injected into participants. Could this have caused arousal regardless of the content?

Those participants who were injected with adrenalin were then put into one of three experimental conditions: informed, ignorant or misinformed. The fourth condition consisted of those participants who had received the placebo injection.

Participants in the *informed* condition were told that they could expect some side effects of the injection and these were that 'your hand will start to shake, your heart will start to pound, and your face may get warm and flushed'. These are the side effects of an injection of adrenalin so the participants would have an explanation for any feelings.

KEY TERMS

reliability: the extent to which a procedure, task or measure is consistent, for example that it would produce the same results we the same people on each occasion.

placebo: a pill or injection given which the patient or participant believes is a drug but which, in reality, has no effect.

In the *misinformed* condition the participants were told that they could expect some side effects of the injection and these were that 'your feet will feel numb, you will have an itching sensation over parts of your body, and you may get a slight headache'. These are not the side effects of an injection of adrenalin so the participants would not have any explanation for the actual side effects they would experience. This condition was introduced as a control condition.

Those participants in the *ignorant* condition were told that they would experience no side effects from the injection. Therefore, these participants would also not have an explanation for the actual side effects that they would experience as a result of the injection of adrenalin.

Immediately after the participant's injection, the doctor left the room and the experimenter returned with a **stooge**. The stooge was introduced as another participant and the experimenter stated that both had had the Suproxin injection which would take 10 minutes to be absorbed into the bloodstream, after which they would both be given the same tests of vision. Participants were then exposed to one of two emotional states at this point: euphoria or anger.

In the euphoria condition when the experimenter departed, he apologetically added that if they needed any rough paper, rubber bands or pencils they should help themselves. The waiting room had been arranged to look in a state of disarray. As soon as the experimenter left the room the stooge introduced himself again, made a few ice-breaker comments and then began his routine which consisted of playing with items (paper, rubber bands, pencils, folders and hula hoops) left in the room (Figure 2.13). The stooge suggested that the participant join in while he used the items. The routine was standardised as far as was possible. The stooge never knew which condition any particular participant was in.

2.13 The stooge in the euphoria condition threw paper to create a fun atmosphere

In the anger condition, after the injection the experimenter introduced a stooge and explained that it was necessary to wait 20 minutes to let the Suproxin enter the bloodstream and that the participants had to complete a questionnaire (Table 2.4) during this time. The stooge was instructed to create a feeling of anger in the room and this was achieved through a variety of comments that he made as the 20 minutes passed:

> '…it's unfair for them to give you shots'
> 'This really irritates me'
> 'The hell with it!'
> 'I'm not wasting any more time'

These increased in intensity and were linked with the questions in the questionnaire. As the participants worked through the questionnaire the questions became more personal, and the stooge became increasingly irate in his behaviour.

7	List the foods you would eat in a typical day.
13	List the childhood diseases you have had and the age at which you had them.
28	How many times a week do you have sexual intercourse?
34	With how many men (other than your father) has your mother had extramarital relationships?

Table 2.4 Example questions asked in the 'anger' condition

KEY TERMS

stooge: a person who appears to be another participant or someone not related to the study, but who is in fact working on behalf of the researcher. They are also sometimes known as '*confederates*' and may be used to mislead real participants within the study.

demand characteristics: features of the experimental situation which give away the aims. They can cause participants to try to change their behaviour, e.g. to fit with their beliefs about what is supposed to happen, which reduces the validity of the study.

How irritated, angry or annoyed would you say you feel at present?

| I don't feel at all irritated or angry (0) | I feel a little irritated and angry (1) | I feel quite irritated and angry (2) | I feel very irritated and angry (3) | I feel extremely irritated and angry (4) |

How good or happy would you say you feel at present?

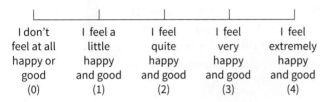

| I don't feel at all happy or good (0) | I feel a little happy and good (1) | I feel quite happy and good (2) | I feel very happy and good (3) | I feel extremely happy and good (4) |

Have you experienced any palpitation (consciousness of your own heart beat)?

| Not at all (0) | A slight amount (1) | A moderate amount (2) | An intense amount (3) |

Did you feel any tremor (involuntary shaking of the hands, arms or legs)?

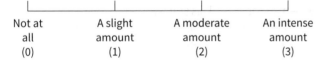

| Not at all (0) | A slight amount (1) | A moderate amount (2) | An intense amount (3) |

2.14 Self-report questions that the participants completed at the end of the experiment

When the participant's session with the stooge was complete, the experimenter returned to the room, took their pulses, and told them there was one final questionnaire that considered their physical responses to the Suproxin (Figure 2.14). This was used as the self-report measure for the dependent variable. When the participants had completed these questionnaires, the experimenter announced that the experiment was over, explained the deception and its necessity in detail, answered any questions and swore the participants to secrecy to protect future runs of the experiment. All participants gave consent to take part in the study and the researchers checked their medical records to ensure that the injections that were given would not cause any harm. To further protect the participant, the injection was administered by a trained doctor who was around for the duration of the experiment to monitor the participants. The researchers did deceive the participants in this research as they were not aware of the true content of the injection, but this was necessary to prevent **demand characteristics** and improve the validity of the results.

Hypotheses

1   If a person experiences a state of arousal for which they have no immediate explanation, they will label this state and describe their feelings in terms of the cognitions available to them at the time.

2   If a person experiences a state of arousal for which they have an appropriate explanation (e.g. 'I feel this way because I have just received an injection of adrenalin'), then they will be unlikely to label their feelings in terms of the alternative cognitions available.

| | | | Physical measure | Self-report measures | |
		N	Change in pulse	Palpitations	Tremors
	Euphoria				
Adrenalin (Epinephrine)	Informed	25	2.9	1.2	1.4
	Ignorant	25	1	1.8	1.8
	Misinformed	25	3.1	1.3	2.0
Control	Placebo	26	−3.3	0.3	0.2
	Anger				
Adrenalin (Epinephrine)	Informed	22	6.5	1.3	1.4
	Ignorant	23	11.8	1.4	1.8
Control	Placebo	23	−4.9	0.6	0.2

Table 2.5 Average scores for the seven conditions

3 If a person is put in a situation, which in the past could have made them feel an emotion, they will react emotionally or experience emotions only if they are in a state of physiological arousal.

Results

All but one of the 185 participants agreed to the injection. Eleven participants were so suspicious about some crucial feature of the experiment that their data was discarded. Five participants had no physiological reaction to the injection of epinephrine and were also excluded from the data analysis. This left 169 participants' data to be analysed (Table 2.5).

The participants who received the injections of adrenalin showed significantly more **sympathetic arousal** (as measured by pulse rate and self-ratings on numbness, tremor, itching, palpitation and headache) compared with the placebo participants. The misinformed condition was only run in the euphoria condition as it was a control condition and inclusion in just one of the categories was adequate to evaluate the possible impacts of receiving information about side effects after the injection. From the data in Table 2.5 it can be immediately seen that on all items those participants in the adrenaline condition show more evidence of physiological response (change in pulse rate) compared to the control groups. Further to this, on the self-report measures, those participants who were in the adrenaline conditions reported higher scores for palpitations and tremors suggesting that they were having a behavioural response to the increased levels of arousal.

In all the adrenalin conditions pulse rate increased significantly when compared with the decreased characteristic of the placebo conditions. On the self-report scales about palpitations and tremors it is clear that the participants in these conditions experienced more of these symptoms in comparison to the placebo conditions. The difference between the adrenalin conditions and the placebo conditions are all significant at the 0.001 level of significance. Therefore, it is clear that those participants in the adrenalin conditions were physiologically aroused during the experiment.

> **KEY TERM**
>
> **sympathetic arousal:** when we are exposed to a stressful situation, the sympathetic nervous system becomes aroused causing the pupils to dilate, an increase in heart rate, digestive activity is inhibited and glucose is released by the liver for extra energy needed to prepare the body to respond to alarm or stress.

From the self-report measures, in the euphoria condition, the misinformed participants were feeling happier than all the others; the second happiest group was the ignorant group. This demonstrates that these participants were more susceptible to the stooge because they had no way of explaining why they felt as they did. The informed group felt the least positive because they were aware why they felt as they did.

In the anger condition, the ignorant group felt the angriest and the second angriest group was the placebo group. The least angry group were those who had been informed. This shows that participants were more susceptible to the stooge because they had no way of explaining why their body felt as it did. Behaviour of the groups was observed through a one-way mirror and matched their self-reports.

Conclusions

Schachter and Singer argue that their findings support their Two-Factor Theory of Emotion, which states that the physiological arousal in different emotions is entirely the same and we label our arousal according to the cognitions we have available. They argued that all three of their hypotheses were supported and concluded that if a person experiences a state of arousal for which they have no immediate explanation, they will label this state and describe their feelings in terms of the cognitions available to them at the time. This study helps us understand how people use different environmental cues to help them interpret their physiological state. It could be useful in treating people who suffer with anxiety and panic attacks as it will allow them to identify environmental triggers that may cause them to become physiologically aroused and fearful.

The Two-Factor Theory of Emotion has been an influential theory of emotions; however subsequent work has shown that the relationship is more complex than this theory predicts. More recent work suggests that attempts to understand an unexplained state of arousal is more extensive than a quick examination of cues in the surrounding environment. When an individual seeks to explain their state of arousal, they do not just use the behaviour of those around, but also call on many other sources of information such as past experience and knowledge about the context of any behaviour.

> **Reflections:** How often do you look to the situation to explain how you feel?
>
> How might information you know influence the way that you feel?

Schachter and Singer's laboratory experiment exerted a large amount of control through their standardised procedure. For example, they were able to randomly allocate different participants to the different conditions, they were able to deceive the participants of the real nature of the experiment and standardise the procedure as much as possible. They even ensured that the stooge did not know which condition the participant was in (**double blind technique**).

KEY TERM

double blind technique: when both the participant and the researcher are unaware of which condition the participant is in to prevent demand characteristics and act as a control to improve the validity of any data collected.

The sample in this research consisted of university students and introduced participant variables that could distort the outcomes of the research reducing the validity of the research. Adrenalin does not affect everyone in the same way, for example five of Schachter and Singer's participants were excluded from analysis because they experienced no physiological symptoms. A further problem with the procedure is that no assessment was made of participants' mood before the injection to gain a baseline from which to measure any change as a result of the stooge. Also, the sample consists of only male participants which further impacts on our ability to generalise the results to all; males could experience emotion differently to females and this has been ignored in this research. People do not usually experience emotions in the way in which Schachter and Singer induced them and are often aware of events before the onset of arousal giving us information to interpret our physical cues.

The use of **questionnaires** as a method to **operationalise** the **dependent variable** allowed Schachter and Singer to further standardise the collection of the data within the experiment. Questionnaires allow researchers to collect **quantitative data** quickly from participants that can be easily analysed and used to compare results across two conditions. Completing a questionnaire may not give the participants the same freedom to express their feelings as a discussion therefore we could argue that there is little ecological validity in this research. However, Schachter and Singer also use other measures such as observation and physical measures to assess both the physical and psychological impact of the arousal.

SELF-ASSESSMENT QUESTIONS

6 Explain why the results support the Two-Factor Theory of Emotion.

7 Explain why the experiment could be seen as unethical.

8 Describe **two** ways in which the researchers measured the emotional response of the participants.

9 Evaluate the measures used by Schachter and Singer to measure the emotional response of the participants.

2.4 Issues, debates and approaches

The application of psychology to everyday life

The use of the EEG allows psychologists to accurately detect dreaming. This could have useful applications for people with sleep and dream disorders, for example people with insomnia or nightmares or people who sleep walk.

Nature versus nurture

The biological approach focuses mainly on the nature side of this debate, which is why it is possible to obtain evidence through procedures like the EEG, which was used in the Dement and Kleitman study to measure brain waves and eye movements. It is useful to be able to collect physiological evidence about brain activity as it provides direct evidence for the underlying biological processes, such as the link between dream content and eye movements.

Dream content relates to our experiences, so is a product of nurture. This, at least partly, explains the differences in dreams between individuals. Nurture influences will vary, thus the content of people's dreams will differ. However, as even a foetus in the uterus experiences REM sleep, the capacity to dream appears to be a product of nature.

Similarly, the biological processes underlying emotions are the product of the brain, and of **hormones**. However, there are clear differences between us in terms of our emotional responses. These can be accounted for by both differences in nature, such as hormone levels, and in terms of our experiences, i.e. nurture.

KEY TERM

hormones: chemicals that are released from glands and travel around the body in the blood to communicate messages between organs.

Using children and animals in psychological research

Although none of the studies in the section used children or animals, it is useful to consider whether they could have been used and what the findings might have shown. For example, there is some debate about whether animals show emotions at all. They certainly show responses such as fear, for example in the presence of a competitor or predator. However, studies exploring such responses are likely to be unethical. The expression of 'feelings' in animals have been explored in more ethical ways, for example by seeing the choices that hens make when presented with situations they do and do not like (Bubier, 1996, quoted in Stamp-Dawkins, 1998).

Reflections: It is possible to use EEGs on the brains and eyes of babies. Could you devise a study to test whether dream content is related to eye movements in babies? If so how, if not, why not?

Non-human animals such as mammals do demonstrate REM sleep, and this has been studied extensively. It is very difficult, however, to determine the content of their dreams. This has been done indirectly, by using brain-cell recording techniques to explore repeated waking behaviours (such as bird song and rats running mazes). It has been found that the patterns of brain activity during sleep closely resemble those of the waking behaviours, indicating what the animals are dreaming about.

Individual and situational explanations

Our tendency to cry at sad films clearly suggests that situational factors matter in our expression of emotions. Although individual factors are present here too – not everyone cries at the same film. Differences such as these were found in both the study by Canli et al. and in Schachter and Singer, for example in the extent to which participants were affected by the mood of the stooge.

Summary

Canli et al.'s study investigated the brain response to emotive images and how they affect memory. Participants had fMRI scans which showed more amygdala activation for emotive than non-emotive images. These images also felt more emotionally arousing to the participants and were better recalled. This laboratory study was well controlled with standardised exposure time and emotional stimuli. Although an fMRI lacks ecological validity and may, in itself, affect emotional responses, participants' scans cannot be affected by demand characteristics. The use of a repeated measures design also ensured that individual differences in emotional responses, brain activity or recall ability could not affect the results. However, the all-right handed, female sample means that the results may not generalise to males or left-handers if they differ in emotional responses.

Dement and Kleitman's study explored the relationship between eye movements during sleep and dream recall. An EEG provided information about participants' sleep stages, such as REM sleep, and about eye movements. Dream recall was measured by self report. The results showed that dreams occurred in REM rather than nREM sleep, that the direction and amount of eye movements during dream sleep is related to dream content, e.g. vertical movements of the eyes and dream events, and that estimates of dream duration are generally accurate. Many variables, such as food and drink that could affect sleep, were controlled and demand characteristics were reduced where possible. However, the laboratory and equipment meant that the situation was unusual for sleeping. Nevertheless, objective, quantitative data was obtained from the EEG, eye movements and timing, allowing for valid and reliable comparisons to be made.

Shachter and Singer tested the two-factor theory of emotion by manipulating physiology with injections of adrenalin and cognition with information (informed, misinformed or not informed) and using an angry or euphoric stooge. The manipulation of cognitions gave the participants different explanations for the physiological effects they were feeling. The results showed that adrenalin did increase physiological arousal (e.g. raising pulse rate) but that this was only interpreted as anger/euphoria when participants had no existing reason for how they felt (if they were misinformed or not informed). This is because they needed a cognitive explanation so took it from the situation (the stooge), so the results support the two-factor theory. The results may not be generalisable, because of individual differences (some participants were not affected by the injection) and because no females were tested. The participants may also have differed prior to the experiment, and this was not measured. Nevertheless, the use of both misinformed and not informed controls, and two different emotional conditions (anger and euphoria), adds validity to the study, as does the range of measures used.

Exam-style questions

1 Describe the variables that were measured in the study by Canli et al. **[6 marks]**

2 Describe **two** conclusions from the study by Canli et al. **[2 marks]**

3 One strength of the biological approach is that it is scientific. Describe **one** way in which the study by Dement and Kleitman is scientific. **[2 marks]**

4 **a** Describe **one** aim from the study by Dement and Kleitman. **[1 mark]**
  b Explain how the results support this aim. **[3 marks]**

5 Explain **two** ways in which the biological approach is different from the learning approach. Use the study by Schachter and Singer as an example of the biological approach. **[4 marks]**

6 There are many ethical problems with the study by Schachter and Singer but also some ethical strengths. Describe **one** ethical **strength** of this study. **[2 marks]**

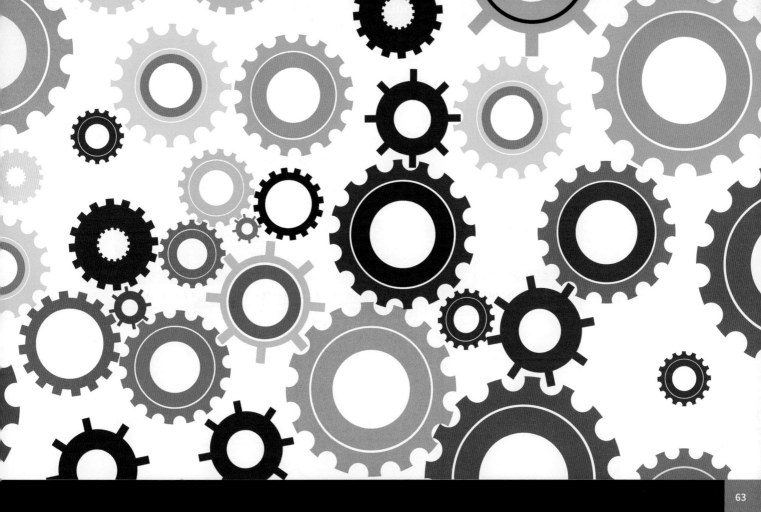

Chapter 3
Cognitive approach

Introduction

The aim of this chapter is to introduce you to the cognitive approach in psychology and to explore three studies from this approach. They are:

- **Andrade (doodling)** which suggests that doodling can improve concentration and the memory of a conversation
- **Baron-Cohen et al. (eyes test)** which investigates how a lack of a 'theory of mind' in adults with Asperger's Syndrome or autism can result in problems recognising emotions
- **Laney et al. (false memory)** which explores how false memories can impact on memories and beliefs in relation to eating asparagus.

These three studies illustrate the main assumptions of the cognitive approach which suggests that:

- behaviour and emotions can be explained in terms of cognitive processes such as attention, language, thinking and memory
- similarities and differences between people can be understood in terms of individual patterns of cognition.

This chapter will examine how different cognitive processes can have an impact on a person's behaviour. In each core study you will learn about the background to the research, the way it was conducted, the results and the conclusions. You will also see how different research methods are used within the cognitive approach and how a range of issues and debates can be applied to the concepts considered in this approach.

Is behaviour all about information processing?

Cognitive psychologists are interested in the processes that work within the mind and how these affect our behaviour. Cognitive psychologists study concepts such as attention, memory, decision making, language development and how cognitive abnormalities can impact on how we behave.

The mind actively processes information that comes in from our different senses. Cognitive processes mediate between stimulus and response. Sometimes this process is compared to a computer and discussed in terms of INPUT > PROCESS > OUTPUT.

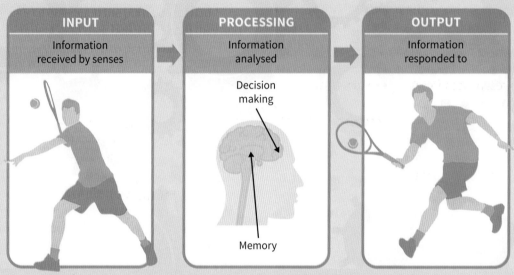

3.1 The process of receiving a stimulus and then responding

For example, when playing a sport our senses process information about other team members, or where the ball is and where we are in relation to it. This is the INPUT element of cognition. All of this sensory information is then processed in the brain with some areas (such as the prefrontal cortex) making decisions about necessary actions, often accessing memories to help inform the process. This is the PROCESS. As a consequence of this process we move, respond and act in an appropriate way. This is the OUTPUT. All of this usually occurs as a seamless subconscious process (Figure 3.1).

Memory is a cognitive process. As a student you spend a lot of time using your memory and hoping that when it really counts you can recall that important piece of information in the exam. Without memory, learning could not take place. Memory is the cognitive ability to encode, store and retrieve information.

When we experience an event, we have to encode (convert) this sensory information into a format that the brain can store. This is the brain's ability to maintain a record of the event without actively using it. Finally, when you need that piece of information, you need to be able to recall, or retrieve, the information (Figure 3.2).

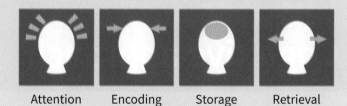

| Attention | Encoding | Storage | Retrieval |

3.2 The memory process

Reflections: How much information have you processed in the last five minutes? What about the last five hours? How much of the information that you have processed have you been aware of and can you recall? You can probably remember a general summary of what you have just read, but could you write it word-for-word?

If you think about what you ate six days ago, can you remember it? You should be able to, since you were there and all your senses were involved: you saw your food, you tasted and smelled it and probably talked about it with those around you. Can you remember it? Probably not.

Now consider this: if you forget something, is it gone forever? What might you need to help you recall what you ate six days ago?

3.1 The cognitive approach

In this chapter we will be looking at how cognitive process like memory can be influenced by doodling and focusing concentration. This suggests that there are ways that we can support our cognitive processes to improve our memories of events. We will look at autism, a problem with cognitive processing that can influence a person's ability to interact with people socially and impair their **social cognition**. Finally we will see how false memories can influence our preferences for different foods.

The cognitive approach often adopts scientific procedures to develop and test hypotheses using experimental techniques. Cognitive theories simplify cognitive processes and allow us to understand mental processes that are not directly observable. However, the cognitive approach tends to ignore biology and genetic influences and provides a mechanistic view of human behaviour (Figure 3.3).

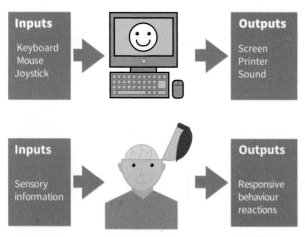

3.3 Cognitive psychologists often compare the way the brain processes information to a computer

Reflections: Can such a scientific approach to understanding mental processes really tell us about how we think, feel and behave? What issues might we encounter trying to measure cognitive processes that we cannot directly see?

KEY TERM

social cognition: the study of how people process social information and how this processing might affect how a person behaves towards or around other people.

3.2 Core study 1:
Andrade (doodling)

Andrade, J. (2010). What does doodling do? *Applied Cognitive Psychology, 24*(1), 100–106.

Aim

Doodling, such as shading in all the Os in 'psychology' on a worksheet, is a common activity. Andrade was interested to know whether this activity assisted information processing, perhaps by enabling people to attend more effectively or by enhancing their memory.

Background

Reflections: The lesson is hard but you're paying **attention**. Your teacher stops talking and asks you what you are writing. You say 'nothing' only to discover a neatly coloured-in shape on the front of your file... You're on the phone and think you're listening properly, but you've doodled an enormous, elaborate leaf pattern during the call. Do you think this doodling is helping you to concentrate or making it more difficult (Figure 3.4)?

KEY TERM

attention: the concentration of mental effort on a particular stimulus. It may be focused or divided.

Teachers often tell students off for doodling. 'I didn't even know I was doing it', you think to yourself in self-defence. Your teacher's complaint is justified: research has shown that we

65

3.4 Doodling – does it help or hinder concentration?

perform less well when our **attention is divided** between tasks. It might make sense to assume that if we are engaged in doodling, we would not be attending as well to any other task, so be worse at them than if we were not doodling. However, in your defence, doodling might be useful. Doodling might aid concentration (Do and Schallert, 2004), for example by reducing **daydreaming** so that you stay **focused**. This idea is based on the **working memory model**. Daydreaming is linked to high arousal when we are bored and it uses important cognitive processing resources (the 'central executive') so inhibits performance on tasks that use this resource – including attention and memory. In Andrade's study, the primary task of listening to a message, was an auditory task whereas doodling is a visuo-spatial task. It is therefore possible that the concurrent task of doodling would interfere less with overall processing than devoting a greater amount of central executive function to daydreaming.

Alternatively, doodling may help to maintain arousal (Wilson and Korn, 2007), for example by giving you something physical to do while you think. It could raise arousal to help to keep you awake if you are sleepy or reduce arousal if you are agitated because you are bored.

Andrade defines doodling the sketching of patterns and figures that are unrelated to the primary task. Such doodling either could take cognitive resources away from the intended (primary) task as if it placed simultaneous demand on cognition by dividing attention, or it could, as

would be the case for the most concurrent cognitive tasks, improve performance by raising arousal and enhancing focused attention on the primary task.

 KEY TERMS

divided attention: the ability to split mental effort between two or more simultaneous tasks (called 'dual tasks'), for example, driving a car and talking to a passenger. Divided attention is easier when the tasks involved are simple, well practised and automatic. You may notice that inexperienced drivers find conversing more difficult, and any driver may stop mid-sentence if the road conditions become difficult. The primary task is the main task, in this case driving, and the additional task is called the concurrent task because it is happening at the same time.

daydreaming: a mildly altered state of consciousness in which we experience a sense of being 'lost in our thoughts', typically positive ones, and a detachment from our environment.

focused attention: the picking out of a particular input from a mass of information, such as an array or a continuous stream, for example, concentrating on your teacher's voice even when there is building work outside and the student next to you is whispering.

working memory model: This model of memory suggests that two different types of current or 'working' memory can be used at the same time, one is vis spatial and the other auditory. These are governed by an overall 'central executive'.

Method
Research method and design

This was a laboratory experiment; the environment was not the normal place in which people would respond to telephone messages and the situation was controlled. The design was independent measures as participants were either in the control group or in the doodling group.

Sample

The participants were 40 members of a participant panel at the Medical Research Council unit for cognitive research. The panel was made up of members of the general population aged 18–55 years and they were paid a small sum for participation. There were 20 participants in each group, mainly females, with two males in the control group and three in the doodling group (one participant in this condition did not doodle and was replaced).

Procedure

All participants listened to a dull (mock) telephone call about a party.

> 'Hi! Are you doing anything on Saturday? I'm having a birthday party and was hoping you could come. It's not actually my birthday, it's my sister **Jane's**. She'll be 21. She's coming up from *London* for the weekend and I thought it would be a nice surprise for her. I've also invited her boyfriend **William** and one of her old school friends, **Claire**, but she doesn't know that yet. Claire's husband Nigel was going to join us but he has just found out that he has to go to a meeting in *Penzance* that day and won't be back in time. I thought we could have a barbecue if the weather is nice, although the way it has been so far this week, that doesn't look likely. I can't believe it has got so cold already. And the evenings are really drawing in aren't they? Anyway, there is plenty of space indoors if it rains. Did I tell you that I have redecorated the kitchen? It is mainly yellow—the wallpaper is yellow and so is the woodwork, although I thought it would be better to leave the ceiling white to make it look lighter. I've still got the old blue fittings—they are pretty battered now but I can't afford to replace them at the moment. Do you remember **Craig**? I used to share a flat with him when we were both working for that bank in *Gloucester*. He has bought a house in *Colchester* now but he promises to take time off from gardening to come to Jane's party. **Suzie** is going to be there too. She's the person I met at the pottery class in *Harlow* last year. Apparently she has got really good at it and may even be having an exhibition of her work soon. Will you be able to bring some food? Maybe crisps or peanuts, something along those lines. **Jenny** from next door is going to bring a quiche and I'll do some garlic bread. I found a good recipe for punch—you warm up some red wine with gin and orange juice plus cloves and cardamom and cinnamon. Add some brown sugar if it's not sweet enough. The boys from the house down the road have promised to bring some of their homebrew. There are three of them sharing that house now—John, Tony and Phil. I think they were all at college together. Phil teaches at a primary school in *Ely* now and the other two commute to *Peterborough* each day. I think they both work in the hospital there—I know Tony was training to be a nurse at one point so maybe he is qualified now. John can't come on Saturday because his parents are coming to stay for the weekend but **Phil** and **Tony** should be there. Tony has to pick their cat Ben up from the vet so he may be a bit late. By the way, did I tell you about our holiday in *Edinburgh*? It was a complete disaster. We were camping and it rained constantly. We spent most of the time in museums, trying to keep dry and then, to make matters worse, Nicky got her handbag stolen. I was quite glad to get back to work after that. Anyway, hope you can make it on Saturday—let me know if you want to stay over. Bye!' (pp 105–106)

During this task they either doodled or did not doodle (the control group). This was the independent variable. They were told beforehand they would be tested on the names of people who were attending the party (and not the ones who were not going to be there). This was the 'monitoring' task. They also had an unexpected test, on the names of places mentioned. This was the 'recall' task. The order of these tests was **counterbalanced**, i.e. half the participants were asked to recall the names of party-goers then the places mentioned. The other half recalled the places first, then the names. These two tasks were the measures of the dependent variable (DV) of recall. To operationalise the DVs, plausible mishearings, such as 'Greg' for 'Craig', were counted as correct. Other names that were on the tape but were not party-goers (e.g. John) were scored as false alarms. Other words relating to people, such as 'sister', were ignored. The final score for monitoring was the number of correct names minus false alarms.

> **Reflections:** Think carefully about the difference between 'mishearings' and 'false alarms'. Why was it important that they were treated differently in the collection and analysis of results?

RESEARCH METHODS

Counterbalancing is often used as a control procedure against order effects in a repeated measures design when participants encounter both levels of the IV. Here it is used to control for potential order effects caused by the two different measures of recall (the DV).

The mock telephone message lasted 2.5 minutes and was recorded in a monotonous voice at an average speed of 227 words per minute. It had eight names of people attending a party, and the names of three people and one cat who could not attend. Eight place names were mentioned, as well as irrelevant details.

The participants were given the standardised instructions: 'I am going to play you a tape. I want you to pretend that the speaker is a friend who has telephoned you to invite you to a party. The tape is rather dull but that's okay because I don't want you to remember any of it. Just write down the names of people who will definitely or probably be coming to the party (excluding yourself). Ignore the names of those who can't come. Do not write anything else.' (pages 101–102).

An A4 sheet was given to the participants in the doodling condition, with alternating rows of squares and circles, ten per row. There was also a wide margin on the left for recording the target information. These participants were also given a pencil and asked to shade in the squares and circles while listening to the tape. They were told 'It doesn't matter how neatly or how quickly you do this – it is just something to help relieve the boredom' (page 102). The control participants were given a sheet of lined paper to write their answers on (which they could also have used for doodling).

Each participant listened to the tape at a comfortable volume and wrote down the names as instructed. The experimenter collected the response sheets, then talked to the participants for one minute, including an apology for misleading them about the memory test. They then completed the surprise test of recalling names of places then people or vice versa.

Results

In the doodling condition, the mean number of shaded shapes on the printed sheet was 36.3, with a range of 3–110 and no participants in the control condition doodled spontaneously.

Task type	Measure	Group	
		Control	Doodling
Names (monitored information)	correct	4.3	5.3
	false alarms	0.4	0.3
	memory score	4.0	5.1
Places (incidental information)	correct	2.1	2.6
	false alarms	0.3	0.3
	memory score	1.8	2.4

Table 3.1 Mean recall for doodling and non-doodling groups

RESEARCH METHODS

Three doodlers and four controls suspected a memory test. This suggests that there were **demand characteristics** that made the aim apparent to the participants. However, none said they actively tried to remember information.

Participants in the control group correctly recalled a mean of 7.1 (SD 1.1) of the eight party-goers' names and five people made a false alarm. Participants in the doodling group correctly recalled a mean of 7.8 (SD 0.4) party-goers' names and one person made one false alarm, see Table 3.1. Overall, the doodling participants recalled a mean of 7.5 names and places, 29% more than the mean of 5.8 for the control group. Recall for both monitored and incidental information was better for doodlers than controls, even when the participants who suspected a test were excluded (to eliminate effects due to **demand characteristics**).

Conclusions

Doodling helps concentration on a primary task as the doodling participants performed better than participants just listening to the primary task with no concurrent task. However, because the doodling group were better on both the monitored and incidental information there are two possible explanations. Either the doodlers noticed more of the target words, an effect on attention, or doodling improved memory directly, for example by encouraging deeper information processing. However, without any measure of daydreaming (which could have blocked attention) it is difficult to distinguish between these two explanations. This could have been done by asking participants about daydreaming retrospectively by self-report. Alternatively, a simultaneous brain scan could have indicated whether doodling reduced activation of the cortex, which is associated with daydreaming.

ISSUES AND DEBATES

Doodling could be a useful strategy when we have to concentrate and don't want to, for example in an important but boring lecture or when you are waiting to hear the faint sound of a friend's car arriving. By stopping our minds from straying we should be better able to focus on the primary task. This would be an **application to everyday life**.

Reflections: Although doodles have some shape and form they are relatively unplanned, so require little processing themselves but may be sufficient to prevent us from daydreaming.

Conduct an interview or a questionnaire to collect self-report data about the types of doodles that people do and the situations in which they doodle.

Strengths and weaknesses

The main method was a laboratory experiment using an **independent measures** design. This means that it was possible to control **extraneous variables**, for example ensuring the participants were listening at a volume comfortable for them and using a recorded telephone message so that there were no differences in stress on the important words between conditions. It was also **standardised** so that the participants were all equally likely to be bored and therefore to daydream. This was achieved by the monotony of the recording, using a dull, quiet room and asking them to do the experiment when they were expecting to go home. This means the research was more **valid** – they could be sure that the differences in results between conditions were due to doodling or not – and more **reliable**, because all participants were similarly bored. The **operationalisation** of doodling was also standardised, using the doodling sheets, otherwise there may have been individual differences in doodling between participants and some more may not have doodled at all. This also increased **validity**. Nevertheless, there is a risk of **participant variables** confounding the results, as the amount of shapes the individuals shaded differed. However, it was an effective strategy as no

participants in the non-doodling condition did doodle (this was discouraged by giving them lined paper) and only one in the doodling condition did not (and they were replaced).

Although the participants were varied in age (18–55 years), so were representative in this respect, they were all members of a recruitment panel and the kinds of people who volunteer for such panels may all be very similar, for example having time to spare or an interest in psychology. This could bias the sample, lowering validity. There was a risk of **demand characteristics** because some of the participants suspected a memory test, but they were roughly equal in each condition and did not actively try to remember, so this is unlikely to have reduced validity. The study collected quantitative data, the number of names and places recalled, which is an objective record of memory. However, it would also have been useful to have asked the participants for self-reports of any daydreaming as this would have helped to explore whether the cause of the difference was attention or memory. It would be important only to ask participants whether they daydreamed, not what they were daydreaming about, as this would be an invasion of their privacy.

This study raised a few ethical issues. The participants were unable to give fully informed consent as they were given an unexpected test on place names. This had the potential to make them distressed if they were unable to remember the names, so could expose them to risk of psychological harm. Although a debrief is not a substitute for good ethical procedures, the experimenters debriefed the participants and apologised for misleading them about the unexpected recall test.

> **RESEARCH METHODS IN PRACTICE**
>
> Individual differences between participants arose. In an **independent measures** design such as this, such differences are a greater problem than they would be in a repeated measures design. This is because they may cause differences in the DV, of memory, that are not caused by the IV but may appear to be so.

3.3 Core study 2:
Baron-Cohen et al. (Eyes test)

Baron-Cohen, S., Wheelwright, J., Hill, J., Raste, Y., & Plumb, I. (2001). The 'Reading the Mind in the Eyes' Test revised version: A study with normal adults, and adults with Asperger Syndrome or High-functioning Autism. *Journal of Child Psychology and Psychiatry,* *42*(2), 241–251.

Aim

The main aim of this research was to test whether a group of adults with Asperger Syndrome (AS) or High-functioning Autism (HFA) would be impaired on the revised version of the 'Reading the Mind in the Eyes' task.

The researchers also wanted to test if there was an association between performance on the revised 'Reading the Mind in the Eyes' task and measures of autistic traits, and to investigate if there were sex differences in those without autism on this task. There were five hypotheses:

- Participants with autism will score significantly lower scores on the revised 'Reading the Mind in the Eyes' task than the control group.
- Participants with autism will score significantly higher on the **Autism Spectrum Quotient Test (AQ)** measure.
- Females in the 'normal' groups (Groups 2 and 3) will score higher on the 'Reading the Mind in the Eyes' task than males in those groups.
- Males in the 'normal' group (Group 3) would score higher on the AQ measure than females.
- Scores on the AQ and the 'Reading the Mind in the Eyes' task would be negatively correlated.

KEY TERM

Autism Spectrum Quotient Test (AQ): a self-report questionnaire with scores ranging from 0 to 50. A higher score suggests that the person completing it has more autistic traits.

Background

Autism is a failure to develop particular cognitive processes linked to social interaction that occurs in approximately 1% of the population. Individuals with autism share difficulties in social functioning, communication and coping with change, often alongside unusually narrow interests. The word autism is used as a general term to refer to a range of disorders from HFA and AS to individuals showing severe forms of autism.

In children, autism is characterised by a triad of impairments:

- difficulties with social interaction
- difficulties with verbal and non-verbal communication
- a lack of imaginative play.

Baron-Cohen suggests that people with autism lack or have an underdeveloped cognitive process called a 'theory of mind'. A theory of mind is a cognitive ability enabling us to realise that others have different feelings, beliefs, knowledge and desires from our own. Individuals with autism find it difficult to understand that other people have their own plans, thoughts or points of view. A theory of mind is often linked to empathy. Empathy is the ability to understand the world as another person does; to appreciate their feelings or emotional state separate from our own.

There are several different tests available to measure a person's theory of mind but most of these are designed for children. Baron-Cohen et al. developed a test called the 'Reading the Mind in the Eyes' task to use with adults to test their ability to attribute emotional labels to others. He suggests that this task tests the first stage of theory of mind: assigning an appropriate mental state to another and that the task of 'Reading the Mind in the Eyes' is a good measure of social cognition.

Two key publications in the field of social cognition are the **Diagnostic and Statistical Manual (DSM)** and the **International Classification of Disorders (ICD)**. Autism was first included as a named category in the DSM 3rd edition (1980) when it was called infantile

KEY TERMS

Diagnostic and Statistical Manual (DSM): published by the American Psychiatric Association, it is used as a classification and diagnostic tool by doctors, psychiatrists and psychologists across the globe.

International Classification of Disorders (ICD): published by the World Health Organization (WHO) and although similar to the DSM, it has a wider scope and covers all health-related conditions, not only mental health and psychological conditions.

autism. In the DSM 5th edition (2014), individuals who are diagnosed with autism need to meet two criteria. These are an impairment of social communication and social interaction skills and evidence of restricted, repetitive patterns of behaviour, interests or activities.

When considering the revisions, it was suggested that there was not enough evidence to show a definite distinction between AS and HFA spectrum disorder. Therefore, it was decided to combine both of these terms into a category called 'autism spectrum disorder'.

Using this 'Reading the Mind in the Eyes' task, in 1997, Baron-Cohen et al. conducted an experiment to investigate whether adults with HFA or AS had problems employing a theory of mind. To test this, Baron-Cohen et al. compared a group of individuals who had HFA or AS with some who did not. The participants were shown photographs of eyes and asked to identify the emotion that was being shown from two options. This was the Reading the Mind in the Eyes Task (see Figure 3.5).

3.5 Fantasising or noticing

Baron-Cohen et al. suggested that this test demands similar cognitive processes as having a theory of mind as it requires the participant to empathise with the person in the photograph to infer their emotional state.

From the results in 1997, Baron-Cohen et al. concluded that those high-functioning adults with autism or AS could identify significantly fewer emotions correctly in the 'Reading the Mind in the Eyes' task than 'normal' participants in the **control group**. However, he suggested that there were several practical issues with the 'Reading the Mind in the Eyes' task.

- It was a forced choice question with only two responses and these were always opposites (e.g. Sympathetic or Unsympathetic).

- The small number of examples in the test (25) led to many in the 'normal' group scoring 24 or 25, causing a **ceiling effect**.
- The 25 sets of eyes illustrated both **basic emotions** and **complex emotions** and the former were too easy.
- The emotion in some of the photos used in the original task could be solved by checking the direction to which the person was gazing (e.g. ignoring).
- There was an imbalance of male and female faces.
- Participants might not have understood the words in the 'Reading the Mind in the Eyes' task.

The following 2001 study attempted to revise the 'Reading the Mind in the Eyes' task as a measure of the theory of mind and aims to check the reliability of the results from the previous 1997 study.

KEY TERMS

control group: often used in experiments, this group does not receive the manipulation of the independent variable and can be used for comparison with the experimental group or groups.

ceiling effect: this occurs when a test is too easy and all participants in a condition score the top score. This is problematic as it does not allow the research to differentiate between participants.

basic emotions: as argued by Ekman (1992), there are six basic emotions that are recognised universally by adults and even very young children developing normally. These emotions, illustrated in Figure 3.6, are happiness, sadness, anger, surprise, fear and disgust.

3.6 Universally recognised emotions

Method
Research method and design
This was a laboratory experiment as the environment in which the participants were tested was not comparable to an everyday situation. Participants in this experiment were asked to identify emotions from photographs, which is not a regularly performed task. It was a highly **standardised procedure** and all participants were exposed to the same photographs, chosen using a **pilot study**.

This is an example of a natural or **quasi-experiment**. In a true experiment, participants can be randomly assigned to any of the experimental conditions. This is not the case in a quasi-experiment, where participants are usually assigned to a condition based on a given characteristic (e.g. whether they have autism).

The independent variable was the type of participant in each condition. There were three control or comparison groups in this study (Groups 2–4) and the experimental group containing participants with AS or HFA (Group 1). This experiment is an example of an independent groups design as participants only took part in one of the four groups (see Table 3.2).

There were two key measures of the dependent variable. The first was a score on the revised 'Reading the Mind in the Eyes Task' (Eyes Task). For those participants in the AS/HFA and the **IQ** matched control condition, there was also the measure of their scores on an AQ test. Baron-Cohen et al. also measured the IQ scores of participants in the AS/HFA condition and the IQ matched comparison group.

Sample

Group	Number	Average
Group 1: Asperger Syndrome / High-functioning Autism (AS/HFA)	15	Age: 29.7 IQ: 115
Group 2: Adult comparison group	122	Age: 46.5
Group 3: Student comparison group	103	Age: 20.8
Group 4: IQ matched group	14	Age: 28 IQ: 116

Table 3.2 The number of participants in separate conditions along with average group characteristics. Groups 2, 3 and 4 are comparison groups

KEY TERM

standardised procedure: a control to reduce confounding variables in laboratory studies where all participants are tested in the same conditions.

KEY TERMS

quasi-experiment: quasi means 'almost', and refers to the fact that these experiments often have lots of control over the procedure, but not over how participants are allocated to conditions within the study.

IQ: a measure of intelligence that produces a score representing a person's mental age. The average range of IQ is between 85 and 115.

Group 1: AS/HFA
The group comprised 15 adult males with AS or HFA with a mean IQ score of 115 and mean age of 29.7 years. The sample was self-selecting through adverts in the Autistic Society magazine and support groups and all had been diagnosed in specialist centres using the DSM or ICD criteria.

Group 2: Adult comparison group
The group comprised 'normal' adults, who did not have a diagnosis of AS/HFA. They were selected from adult community and education classes in Exeter and public library users in Cambridge with a mean age of 46.5 years.

Group 3: Student comparison group
The group comprised 'normal' students, who did not have a diagnosis of AS/HFA, from Cambridge University with a mean age of 20.8 years. Cambridge is a highly selective university so these students are not representative of the general population.

Group 4: IQ Matched group
The group comprised 14 IQ matched participants with those in the AS/HFA group with a mean age of 28 years and mean IQ score of 116. These participants were randomly selected from the general population.

RESEARCH METHODS

A **pilot study** is used to check the validity and reliability of the procedures. It is not a check of whether the study is going to 'work' (although pilot studies might be conducted to find out whether a question is worth investigating). When you have finished reading the procedure for this study, decide why the pilot study was important.

Procedure
Following the changes that Baron-Cohen et al. made to the original Eyes Task, the revised Eyes Task was used in this experiment as a measure of the theory of mind. This consisted of 36 sets of eyes (18 male, 18 female), each with four choices of emotion on the face of the target (e.g. reflective, aghast, irritated, impatient).

For each of the 36 sets of eyes, the target and foil words were developed using groups of eight judges. At least five of the judges had to agree that the target word was the most appropriate for the eyes and no more than two of the judges could select any of the foil words.

Participants in all four groups were tested on the revised Eyes Test and participants in the AS/HFA group were also asked to judge the sex of the target in each photo. Pilot tests had shown that 'normal' adults often achieved 100 per cent on this sex-recognition task so asking them was not part of this experiment.

Participants in all conditions except the 'normal' adult comparison were also asked to complete the AQ test.

Each participant read through a glossary of terms that were to be used throughout the experiment to ensure they knew each word's meaning (Figure 3.7). Throughout the experiment, if a participant did not know the definition of a word, they were asked to refer back to the glossary.

> FLUSTERED
> confused, nervous and upset
> Sarah felt a bit *flustered* when she realised how late she was for the meeting and that she had forgotten an important document.
>
> RELAXED
> taking it easy, calm, carefree
> On holiday, Pam felt happy and *relaxed*.

3.7 Glossary items

Each participant was given a practice item and then presented with the 36 sets of eyes and four possible target words for the emotion shown. Participants were allowed as long as they needed on each set of eyes. Considering the ethics of the research, all participants consented to take part in the study and were aware of the nature of the research. Those participants in the AS/HFA condition had all been diagnosed in specialist centres using established APA criteria. Baron-Cohen et al. also anonymised the data that was collected so that it was not possible to identify any individual from their scores. *(Strengths)*

Results

On the Eyes Test, participants with AS/HFA (Group 1) correctly identified significantly fewer target words than participants in the three comparison groups (Figure 3.8). No participant in any of the conditions checked the glossary for more than two definitions during the experiment. In the Adult comparison (Group 2) and Student comparison (Group 3), sex differences were apparent between males and females on the Eyes Test but this was not significant.

All participants in the AS/HFA condition scored 33 or above out of 36 on the sex recognition task (see Table 3.3).

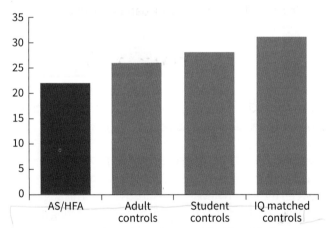

3.8 Average number of words correctly identified on the Eyes Test

Group	Average (mean) scores		
	Number	Eyes test	AQ test*
Group 1: Asperger Syndrome / High-functioning Autism (AS/HFA)	15	21.9	34.4 (N = 14)
Group 2: Adult comparison group	122	26.2	–
Group 3: Student comparison group	103	28.0	18.3 (N = 79)
Group 4: IQ matched group	14	30.9	18.9

* Some participants did not return the AQ tests.
Number in brackets is number of participants.
Table 3.3 Scores gained by the different conditions on the Eyes Test and AQ test

73

On the AQ task, participants with AS/HFA scored significantly higher than the student comparison and IQ matched comparison groups (see Figure 3.9). There was a significant difference between male and female AQ scores in the student comparison group.

> **! RESEARCH METHODS**
>
> The **measure of central tendency** used to calculate the averages used for Figures 3.8 and 3.9 were both **means**. What other measures of central tendency could have been used?

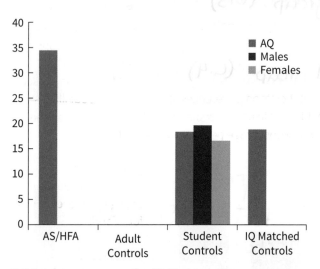

3.9 Average scores on the AQ Test

There was a significant negative correlation between the AQ and Eyes Task scores (–0.53) but no **correlation** between the IQ and Revised Eyes Test scores. This suggests that as a participant's AQ score increases (illustrating higher autistic traits) their ability to correctly identify the correct target word on the Eyes Test decreases.

Conclusions

The results suggest that the participants with AS or HFA have a deficit in a cognitive process that allows a person to identify emotions in other individuals. This lack of a theory of mind, or ability to attribute emotions to another person, is strongly linked to autism spectrum disorders.

There was evidence of a sex difference between males and females in the comparison groups; with males showing more autistic traits and performing worse on the Eyes Test than females. However, some of these differences were not significant so further research would need to be conducted to clarify if there are differences between sexes and their AQ or ability to attribute emotions to others.

It is apparent that the revised Eyes Test used in this study was a more sensitive measure of adult social intelligence than that used in previous studies and will allow future research to discriminate individual differences in a more meaningful way.

Strengths and weaknesses

The main method was a laboratory experiment as all participants completed the task in a standardised way in an artificial setting. This allowed many confounding variables to be controlled for as all participants saw the same set of eyes for exactly the same amount of time. This improves the internal validity of the experiment and allows the research to be repeated to check the reliability of the results. The validity of the Eyes Test has improved on previous versions due to the changes made which have led to normal performance being significantly below the ceiling of the test. As this is a natural/quasi-experiment, it was not possible for Baron-Cohen et al. to randomly allocate participants to the conditions. This introduces a confounding variable, as it could be another factor that is causing the difference between the scores in the different conditions. This research goes some way to attend to this issue by having two different control groups where some were matched on IQ to make the groups as similar as possible.

Although the Eyes Test was vastly improved for this research, there are still several issues that affect the ecological validity of the task. In an everyday situation a person's eyes would not be static and shown for a limited amount of time. Consequently, any attempt to apply the results from this research to an everyday situation will be flawed. Future research might choose to use videos of eyes rather than images to improve the validity of any conclusions.

The experimental sample in this research (AS/HFA participants) is small; therefore when generalising the results from the research we must be aware that the group may not be representative of all individuals who have been diagnosed with AS/HFA.

> **Reflections:** Can we be sure it is really all in the eyes? What else could be important when we are interpreting emotions? To answer this question, think about whether there are any issues with using photographs of eyes rather than a real person in this study. How could this experiment be conducted in a more ecologically valid way? What impact would it have?

75

3.4 Core study 3:
Laney et al. (false memory)

Laney, C., Morris, E., Bernstein, D., Wakefield, B., & Loftus, E. (2008). Asparagus, a love story. Healthier eating could be just a false memory away. *Experimental Psychology, 55*(5), 291–300.

Background

Memory is not always a factual recording of an event and can become distorted by other information both during encoding and after the event. There have been many experiments within memory research that have demonstrated that memories can be distorted by information provided following an event. This has even resulted in people believing that an impossible event has taken place. Braun et al. (2002) found that it is possible to implant these rich false memories by convincing participants that they had met Bugs Bunny (Figure 3.10) at Disneyland (impossible as Bugs Bunny is a Warner Bros creation).

3.10 Could you really meet Bugs Bunny at Disneyland?

Could there be behavioural consequences of false memories? Other studies by Laney et al. (Bernstein et al., 2005) have shown that false memories of sickness following the eating of pickles or eggs resulted in a number of participants changing their willingness to eat the foods when asked about their food preferences. If false beliefs about illness could result in people avoiding foods, could a positive false memory encourage people to eat a food?

3.11 Could a false memory actually change your preference for a food?

This research investigated the impact that implanting positive false beliefs and memories in people

---

RESEARCH METHODS

Questionnaires can contain different types of questions: **open questions** which allow participants to express themselves in their own words and **closed questions** which differ a limited number of fixed choices. Look at the examples of questions below. Are these open questions, closed questions or a mixture?

Food History Inventory (FHI) where respondents rated 24 items on a scale of 1 (definitely did not happen) to 8 (definitely did happen) as to their food experiences before the age of 10 (e.g. 'Loved asparagus the first time you tried it').

Restaurant Questionnaire (RQ) which assessed the respondents' desire to eat each of 32 separate dishes (e.g. sautéed asparagus spears). This questionnaire was designed to look like a menu with five 'courses'. Respondents were asked to imagine they were out for a special dinner and to rate, regardless of price, how likely they would be to order each food on a scale of 1 (definitely no) to 8 (definitely yes).

Food Preferences Questionnaire (FPQ) was a 62 item inventory of items of food (e.g. asparagus) that respondents had to rate on a 1 (definitely don't like to eat, for whatever reason) to 8 (definitely like to eat).

Food Costs Questionnaire (FCQ) was a list of 21 different food items (e.g. a pound of asparagus) with multiple choice answers where respondents had to circle the price they would be willing to pay for each, including a 'would never buy' option. For asparagus, the price options were $1.90, $2.50, $3.20, $3.80, $4.40, $5.00 and $5.70.

Memory or Belief? Questionnaire (MBQ) – respondents were asked to indicate whether they had a memory of an experience with three items from the FHI, including, for the 'love' condition, the critical item of asparagus. The choices were that they had specific memory of the event occurring, a belief that the event had occurred (but lacked specific memory), or were positive that the event had not occurred.

about their liking of eating asparagus as a child would have on their food preferences later. Laney et al. expected to be able to implant memories of loving asparagus the first time it was tried from previous research, but wanted to investigate if these false memories would lead to positive consequences for their participants.

The research consisted of two experiments. The first aimed to see if false feedback about a liking of a food could cause a false memory and change a participant's eating behaviours. As well as checking the reliability of the findings in the first experiment, the second experiment wanted to examine the underlying cognitive mechanisms of the false memory consequence effect.

Experiment 1: Aim
The aim was to investigate whether giving false feedback suggesting that a participant had loved to eat asparagus as a child, would generate a false belief or memory of experiences linked to eating and enjoying asparagus.

Experiment 1: Method
Research method and design
The experiment was a laboratory experiment as the environment the participants were tested in was very artificial and unlike an everyday event, although some small attempts to make one questionnaire look like a menu were taken. Participants were tested in laboratory settings in groups of up to eight people.

The independent variable was whether a participant had the false belief that they had enjoyed asparagus as a child embedded during the second part of the experiment. These participants were compared with a (control group) of participants who received no false belief.

The dependent variable was measured through the use of five questionnaires (see Research Methods box). A questionnaire is a self-report measure where participants respond through writing their answers down.

Sample
This experiment is an example of an independent groups design as participants only took part in one of the two conditions: the 'love' condition or the control group.

All 128 of the participants were undergraduate students at the University of California who received course credit for their time. The sample consisted of 99 females and 29 males who had a mean age of 20.8 years old. The participants were randomly assigned to either the 'love' condition (63) or the control group (65).

Procedure
Participants arrived at the laboratory in groups of up to eight and were told that they were going to take part in a study of 'food preferences and personality'. This deception was necessary to limit **demand characteristics** through awareness of the true aim.

During the first session (week one), all participants were treated identically. Participants first completed the FHI and RQ. The researchers also asked participants to complete three other questionnaires. These were to distract them from the true aim of the study. These other questionnaires included a personality measure, a social desirability scale and an eating habits questionnaire.

Approximately one week later participants were invited back to the laboratory. At this point participants were randomly allocated to the 'love asparagus' condition or the control group. All participants were told that their responses from the first week had been processed by a computer which had generated a profile of their early childhood experiences with food and were given a report that included:

> 'As a young child, you disliked spinach, you enjoyed fried foods, and you felt happy when a classmate brought sweets to school.'

The critical item, 'you loved to eat cooked asparagus', was embedded in the third position of the profile for participants in the 'love' condition. Those in the control group only received the three filler items. Participants were then asked questions about this fake profile to ensure that they had processed the feedback. These questions included:

- Imagine the setting in which this experience might have happened. Where were you? Who was with you?
- On a scale of 1 (not at all) to 9 (very much), to what extent did this experience affect your adult personality?

Following this, participants completed the FHI and the RQ a second time to measure any changes in responses from before the implanting of the false belief. Further to these, participants also completed three further questionnaires: FPQ, FCQ and MBQ.

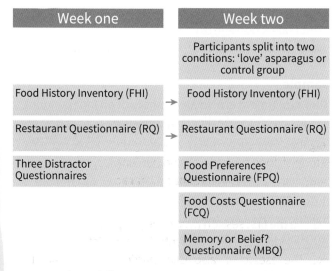

Week one	Week two
	Participants split into two conditions: 'love' asparagus or control group
Food History Inventory (FHI) →	Food History Inventory (FHI)
Restaurant Questionnaire (RQ) →	Restaurant Questionnaire (RQ)
Three Distractor Questionnaires	Food Preferences Questionnaire (FPQ)
	Food Costs Questionnaire (FCQ)
	Memory or Belief? Questionnaire (MBQ)

3.12 Overview of the questionnaires completed by participants at week one and week two

When participants had completed these questionnaires (Figure 3.12) they were fully debriefed by the researchers and told the true nature of the experiment.

Experiment 1: Results

The two key issues the researchers wanted to investigate were whether subjects formed false asparagus-related beliefs and whether these beliefs have consequences.

When asked a second time as part of the FHI if a participant loved asparagus the first time they tried it, participants in the 'love' condition's average (mean) response rose by 2.6 points following the false feedback from the researchers. The responses from those in the control condition only increased by 0.2 points in comparison. This was a statistically significant difference between the conditions.

	Week one	Week two
Love ($n = 46$)	1.5	4.1
Control ($n = 51$)	1.5	1.7

Table 3.4 Mean ratings of the critical item ('Loved asparagus the first time you tried it') on Food History Inventory

Thirty-one participants were excluded from this analysis as they initially believed they loved asparagus the first time, or scored greater than five on the FHI

on the first occasion. This left 97 participants to be included in the analysis.

Memories or beliefs?

For the purpose of this study, memories are the ability to recall specific structured events with some details; the participant 'remembers' an experience. Beliefs are less detailed and not tied to a specific time or place; the participant 'knows' it happened but cannot go into specific detail.

When asked if they had specific memories or a belief that they loved asparagus the first time they tried it, there was a difference between the 'love' condition and the control group. However this was not a statistically significant difference.

	Memory or belief			Not the case
	Memory (M)	Belief (B)	M or B	
Love (46)	22% (10)	35% (16)	57% (26)	43% (20)
Control (51)	12% (6)	27% (14)	39% (20)	61% (31)

Table 3.5 Responses to the question asking if a participant had a specific memory, belief, or it was not the case that they loved asparagus the first time they tried it (MBQ)

This suggests that those participants who were told that they loved asparagus when they first tried it had a greater chance of generating a false memory or belief to substantiate this false memory.

Believers vs nonbelievers

To be classified as a believer, participants had to meet the following three criteria:

- given a low rating on the FHI when initially asked if they loved asparagus (week one)
- increased their rating on the FHI when asked if they loved asparagus on week two
- given positive 'memory' or 'belief' response on the MBQ.

Forty-eight per cent (22) of participants in the 'love' condition met the criteria to be labelled believers and further analysis compared their scores with the other 'non-believers' where the impact of the implanted memory had a lesser effect. The ratings of these 22 believers increased an average of

4.5 points from week one to week two on their FHI item. Nonbelievers increased an average of just 0.9 points. Of the 22 participants classified as believers, 10 claimed to have an asparagus 'memory' and 12 claimed a 'belief' on the MBQ.

To assess the consequence of false beliefs, the believers were compared with those in the control group.

On the RQ, believers reported more desire to eat the critical asparagus item than those in the control group. On the FPQ, in comparison to the control group (mean 3.84), believers (mean 6.14) reported liking asparagus significantly more. Finally, on the FCQ, believers were willing to pay significantly more for asparagus than those in the control group with over a quarter (14) of those in the control group stating that they would never buy asparagus. None of the believers selected the never buy response.

Experiment 1: Conclusions

Participants can be led to develop positively framed false beliefs and these false beliefs can have a consequence on behaviour and food preferences. Participants who had the false belief implanted increased their rating of their love of asparagus and these beliefs had further impacts on how much they would be willing to spend on asparagus, greater intention to eat asparagus in the future, and a greater preference for it.

In the second experiment the researchers wanted to explore why these false beliefs about having loved a healthy food the first time one tried it led to increased liking of that food.

Experiment 2: Aim

The aim of the second experiment was to examine the possible underlying mechanisms of the false memory consequence effect by exploring if, after the false love of asparagus manipulation, the very sight of asparagus was more appealing to participants. A secondary aim was to replicate and extend the results of the first experiment to check the reliability of the findings.

Experiment 2: Method
Research method and design

The independent variable was whether the participant had the false belief, 'you loved asparagus', embedded. These participants were compared with a control group of participants who received no false belief.

The dependent variable was measured through the use of four questionnaires and the participant's feedback to a slideshow of 20 pictures of common foods.

Sample

This experiment is also an example of an independent groups design as participants only took part in one of the two conditions: the 'love' condition or the control group.

All 103 of the participants were undergraduate students at the University of Washington who received course credit for their time. The sample consisted of 64 females and 39 males who had a mean age of 19.9 years.

The participants were randomly assigned to either the 'love' condition (58) or the control group (45).

RESEARCH METHODS

A slideshow was used to present the photographs, which helped to standardise the procedure. This means that differences between conditions were more likely to be due to the IV than to differences in the way the participants were treated. Imagine doing the same test in a classroom using actual photographs that you flip over in a stack in front of the participant. Even if you use a stopwatch to time yourself, you won't be as accurate and the movement of the photographs could distract the participant.

Procedure

Participants arrived at the laboratory and were told that they were going to complete several questionnaires to generate a personal profile of eating experiences based on their responses. There was no deception or cover story for this experiment. All participants first completed the FHI, the RQ and the FPQ. Participants also completed two distractor questionnaires: a personality measure and a social desirability scale.

Similar to the first experiment, approximately one week later participants were invited back to the laboratory. At this point participants were randomly allocated to the 'love' asparagus condition or the control group. All participants were told that their responses from the first week had been processed by a computer which had generated a profile of their expected early childhood experiences with food.

Participants in the 'love' condition were given a profile that contained the critical phrase 'you loved asparagus the first time you ate it' in the third position. After reading the profile, participants then completed an elaboration exercise in which they were required to give details about their memory of eating asparagus, or if they had no memory of it, what might have happened. Those allocated to the control group were told nothing about asparagus and did not complete the elaboration exercise. All participants were then asked: what is the most important childhood, food-related event in your life that your food profile did not report?

3.13 Pictures were rated by participants

A slideshow of 20 colour photographs of common foods were displayed for 30 seconds each to all participants (Figure 3.13). Participants were asked four questions about each slide. On a scale of 1 (not at all) to 8 (very much):

- how appetising they found the food depicted in the photo
- how disgusting they found the food depicted in the photo
- the artistic quality of the photo
- whether the photo was taken by a novice, amateur or expert photographer.

Participants finally completed the RQ, FPQ, and the FHI for a second time, and the same MBQ as in Experiment One (Figure 3.14). When all questionnaires were completed, the participants were fully debriefed.

Week one	Week two
	Participants split into two conditions: 'love' asparagus or control group.
Food History Inventory →	Food History Inventory
Restaurant Questionnaire →	Restaurant Questionnaire
Food Preferences Questionnaire →	Food Preferences Questionnaire
Two Distractor Questionnaires	Common Foods Slideshow
	Memory or Belief Questionnaire

3.14 Overview of the questionnaires completed by participants at week one and week two

Experiment 2: Results

Food History Inventory

As in Experiment 1, the 'love' and control groups rated their liking of asparagus similarly before the manipulation, but differently after they had received their profile distorting their memory. This was a statistically significant difference between the conditions.

	Week one	Week two
Love ($n = 40$)	1.7	4.2
Control ($n = 33$)	1.5	2.5

Table 3.6 Mean ratings of the critical item ('Loved asparagus the first time you tried it') on Food History Inventory

Excluded from this analysis were 30 participants (18 'love' group subjects and 12 controls) who were reasonably sure that they had loved asparagus the first time they tried it before the manipulation (with a rating of five or higher on the FHI).

Memories or beliefs?

Similar to the first experiment, the results from the MBQ suggested that those participants who were told that they loved asparagus had a greater chance of generating a false memory or belief to substantiate this false memory. However this was not a statistically significant difference.

79

	Memory or belief			Not the case
	Memory (M)	Belief (B)	M or B	
Love (40)	28% (11)	28% (11)	57% (22)	45% (18)
Control (32)	6% (2)	38% (12)	39% (14)	56% (18)

Table 3.7 Responses to the question asking if a participant had a specific memory, belief, or it was not the case that they loved asparagus the first time they tried it (MBQ)

Believers vs nonbelievers

Participants were separated into believers or nonbelievers based on the same criteria as in the first experiment. Forty participants in the 'love' condition met the criteria to be labelled believers. The believers were then compared with those participants in the control group.

On the RQ, neither the believers nor the control group reported an increased desire to eat the critical asparagus item when comparing the two weeks. On the FPQ, in comparison to the control group, believers reported a significantly greater desire to eat asparagus. Finally, on the photograph ratings, believers rated the asparagus photo as more appetising than those in the control group (5.10 versus 4.00), and as less disgusting (1.81 versus 3.24).

Experiment 2: Conclusions

Participants can be given positive false food beliefs and these beliefs have consequences on behaviours and attitudes towards foods. Those participants who believed the false feedback were more likely than those in the control group to rate a photograph of asparagus as more appetising and less disgusting.

The photograph measure provides a step towards understanding the cognitive mechanisms associated with false memories as the false memory primed the participant to process the images of asparagus more positively. This positive response is interpreted as familiarity and the participants misattribute it to a childhood experiences (I did love asparagus the first time I tried it) and consequently, an adult preference (I love asparagus).

Across the two experiments it was shown that participants could have false beliefs implanted about whether they had previously had a specific positive experience with asparagus and that this belief had consequences on their attitudes and even memories about that food.

ISSUES AND DEBATES

This study has a clear application to everyday life. If implanting false memories could encourage people to eat more healthily, for example because they began to like fruit and vegetables more, it could contribute to solving problems like obesity. This would be a useful strategy to help people who are already trying to diet but have developed bad eating habits like snacking on crisps and sweets. However, being aware that they were having false memories implanted may prevent the effect from working outside the laboratory.

Strengths and weaknesses

The main method was a laboratory experiment as all of the participants were tested in a **standardised** environment and given the same questionnaires in each condition. The only difference between the experiences of the participants in this experiment was the introduction of the critical 'you loved asparagus' comment on the generated profile for each participant. Each questionnaire was standardised, and further questionnaires were used as distractors to prevent the participants from working out the true aim of the experiment and controlling demand characteristics. This means that the research has more internal validity as we can be more confident that the independent variable is the only variable having an impact on the dependent variable.

The use of questionnaires as a method to operationalise the dependent variable allowed Laney et al. to further standardise the collection of the data within the experiment. Questionnaires allow researchers to collect quantitative data quickly from participants that can be easily analysed and used to compare results across two conditions. However, it is worth noting that we do not know for certain whether these effects will translate to actual eating behaviours. Completing a questionnaire may not involve the same processes as choosing to eat (or not eat) a specific food in a restaurant setting, therefore we could argue that there is little ecological validity in this research.

As this study was conducted in a short space of time and the participants were not followed up, we are not able to ascertain how long the effects of the false memories last. The participants completed the questionnaires within a few minutes of receiving false feedback so there is no way of knowing how long lasting the impact will be. More research of a longitudinal design will be needed to research the durability of any attitude and behavioural consequences of the false memories.

The sample in this research consists of university students and introduces participant variables that could distort the outcomes of the research reducing the validity of the research. Students might react differently to the false information and be more impressionable than an adult or child.

> **Reflections:** Think about a food you have a strong feeling about (either like or dislike) – can you remember why you dislike it? Could this be a false memory? Talk to your parents about it. Could our memories of past events really change your liking or disliking of a food? How could we use the findings from this research to change a person's eating habits?

3.5 Issues, debates and approaches

The application of psychology to everyday life

When we are trying to focus, such as when listening to a lecture, allowing ourselves to doodle might be advantageous. However, any attempt to deliberately 'draw' something specific is likely to be counterproductive as the drawing itself might become the primary task, distracting us from the lecture rather than allowing us to concentrate better.

The eyes provide a lot of information when we are attributing an emotion to an individual. It might be possible to develop a programme to help teach individuals diagnosed with AS/HFA to help them develop skills of interpreting emotions. The Eyes test could also be developed further to help aid initial diagnosis of individuals who could be signposted to appropriate clinical staff to investigate if there is an underlying autistic disorder.

Laney et al. demonstrate that it is possible to impact some people's attitudes towards asparagus by simply giving a small amount of false information. This could be used to help people change their diets and become healthier or help people change their attitudes towards healthier foods such as salad and vegetables.

Individual and situational explanations

As doodling affected recall, this means it has a situational effect information processing. Furthermore, as Andrade deliberately ensured that her participants would be bored so that they were more likely to doodle, this implies that there are situational causes for doodling itself. However, there were very large differences between the doodles of participants initially allocated to the doodling group (from 0 to 110 shaded shapes) and we know that people who doodle do not all doodle in the same way. This means that there are also individual causes behind doodling behaviour.

Those individuals who had a diagnosis of AS/HFA performed significantly worse on the Eyes test than 'normal' individuals, suggesting that the ability to read emotions in the eyes is an individual skill that is developed, rather than being the result of the external environment. The environment was standardised across those participants in both the AS/HFA and 'normal' conditions, providing further support for the individual explanation.

The effect of the false memory embedded by telling one group of participants that they loved asparagus as a child means that the situation could affect an individual's attitude towards the food. As Laney et al. were careful to control that the information presented to the participants was the same, other than the statement about a love of asparagus, this suggests the information from the situation had a consequence on later behaviour. There were individual differences among participants however, with some participants in the control group liking asparagus and others in the 'love' asparagus condition failing to believe that they had experienced this love as a child.

Nature vs nurture

This is a long-running debate, which considers whether we are the way we are because of nature (inherited and genetic) or nurture (experiences and influences after conception). There is no known single cause for autism and there are both generic and environmental arguments. Several different genes appear to be involved in autistic spectrum disorder, with some of these being inherited and others happening spontaneously. Researchers are currently investigating if environmental factors such as viral infections, pollutants or issues during pregnancy could have a role in triggering the disorder.

Children as participants

The research in this area does not focus on children as participants, so it might be useful to consider how similar research could be conducted on younger individuals. Baron-Cohen et al.'s research was conducted on adult male participants using pictures of adult eyes and relatively sophisticated words to describe the emotion displayed. This would not be appropriate for children and alternative methods should be considered to investigate similar aims in children. Baron-Cohen has devised a 'Theory of Mind' test for children called the 'Sally and Anne' test that involves asking children questions following a short scene that is acted out with dolls.

Summary

Andrade's study tested whether doodling could improve concentration on and memory of a conversation. Participants in the doodling condition *remembered* more of the people's names they had been asked to recall and *attended to* the message better, as they recalled more in a surprise test of the place names mentioned. This laboratory experiment was well controlled with a recorded stimulus message and specific shapes to colour in for the doodlers. The data from the words recalled was quantitative and objective. However, it would also have been useful to have had qualitative data about whether the participants daydreamed as this would have helped to distinguish between two possible reasons for the improved memory: deeper processing or better attention.

Baron-Cohen et al.'s study investigated how a lack of a 'theory of mind' in adults on the autistic spectrum relates to problems recognising emotions. The autistic spectrum group's scores on the Eyes test were worse than the control group on the Eyes test even though their IQ was no different. There was also a negative correlation between the revised Eyes test score and Autistic Spectrum Quotient. The test itself was valid because the eyes were shown for a fixed amount of time, although this could also be a weakness as emotions are usually detected on live faces, which move. The findings suggest that the revised Eyes test is better at detecting individual differences in social sensitivity than the previous version, i.e. it is more valid.

Laney et al.'s study explored whether 'false memories' could alter memories and beliefs about eating asparagus. After a suggestion that they loved to eat asparagus as children, participants were more confident that they had loved asparagus the first time they had tried it. This false belief also increased their liking of asparagus, desire to eat it and willingness to pay more for it. This may have been because the false memory made the asparagus look more appealing. Standardisation of the profiles and questionnaires meant that the comparison between the false memory and control groups focused on the 'you loved asparagus' comment, making the study valid. However, the effects may only be short-term as there was no follow up. The findings suggest that adults can be led to believe they had positive food-related experiences as children, which can have healthy consequences.

Exam-style questions

1   Danvir is planning a laboratory experiment about doodling but is worried that the findings may not generalise well to the effects of real-world doodling.

   a Suggest **one** reason why the results may not generalise to real-world doodling. **[2 marks]**

   b Design a natural experiment to test **one** factor that could affect doodling. **[10 marks]**

2   Suggest why it was important to the study by Andrade that the telephone message used was boring. **[2 marks]**

3   In the original Eyes test used by Baron-Cohen et al., there was an imbalance of male and female faces. Explain why this could have been a problem. **[2 marks]**

4   Identify the different types of intelligence measured in the study by Baron-Cohen et al. (Eyes test). **[2 marks]**

5   Explain what the results of the Baron-Cohen et al. study show about different types of intelligence in people on the autistic spectrum. **[4 marks]**

6   Describe **one** aim of the study by Laney et al. (2008). **[2 marks]**

7   Explain why Laney et al. concluded that false beliefs could affect behaviour. **[2 marks]**

Chapter 4
Learning approach

Introduction

The aim of this chapter is to introduce you to the learning approach to psychology and to explore three studies from this approach. They are:

- **Bandura et al. (aggression)** which is based on social learning theory and looks at the effect on children's behaviour of seeing an adult behaving aggressively

- **Saavedra and Silverman (button phobia)** which is a case study of a young boy with a phobia of buttons and the use of classical conditioning to help reduce his fear and disgust

- **Pepperberg (parrot learning)** which explores the comprehension of object categories by a parrot which was trained through social learning and operant conditioning.

These three studies serve to illustrate the main assumptions of the learning approach which are that:

- conditioning helps to explain changes in behaviour
- social learning helps to explain changes in behaviour.

Throughout the chapter you will find out about examples of different types of learning processes and see how these operate with people and with animals. In each core study you will learn about the background to the research, the way it was conducted, the results and the conclusions. From this you will be able to see how the studies, and the learning approach in general, illustrate a range of aspects from the research methods topic. In addition, you will discover how these ideas can be used to illustrate a range of issues and debates.

Live to learn or learn to live?

Think about what you have done today. Apart from basic biological activities, like breathing or blinking, almost everything you have done you will have learned. You are reading this, so you have learned to read, maybe in more than one language. Hopefully you've eaten a meal and maybe travelled to class. How did you learn how to eat or how to get to your classroom?

We can learn through different mechanisms and most of these can also be seen in animals. In some respects, however, our learning is different. Learning means new, permanent changes in behaviour following experience. If you have a pet, or regularly see wild animals, how do you think your learning is similar to and different from theirs? You might have thought of two different kinds of answers. The *way* we learn might differ and *what* we can learn might differ. Both of these are good answers.

When you think about 'learning' the first thing that probably occurs to you is trying to learn your work. In fact this is a memory task. We use 'learning' to refer to the acquisition of new behaviours. Kimble (1961) defined learning as 'a relatively permanent change in behavioural potential which accompanies experience.'

Looking carefully at this statement, we can see that it has three parts:

- learning results in the acquisition of new responses (the relatively permanent change)
- learning may occur without new behaviours necessarily being demonstrated (the behavioural *potential*)
- the environment governs learning (by providing experiences).

In this chapter we will be looking at the changes that occur in learning, how we can measure changes in behavioural potential and how the environment contributes to learning. We will consider repeated exposure to stimuli, rewards and role models, each of which is a feature of the environment.

Looking back over your childhood, think about three different behaviours that you can definitely say you learned, rather than their being purely the product of maturation. Consider how you might have learned them. Did you discover them for yourself or did something or someone in the environment help you? If something or someone was involved, think about what it was that enabled you to learn. Now think about someone quite old. What have they learned recently? Maybe they are developing the ability to use a new piece of technology, or are being told about new games, music or friendships by younger family members. We continue to learn throughout our lifetimes.

Finally, think critically about yourself. Is everything you have learned positive? Have you acquired any bad habits, do you know any words you would not repeat in polite company? The answer to this is likely to be 'yes', even though you probably made no effort to learn these things. This suggests that although some learning involves effort, sometimes we can learn simply by being in a certain environment – and that not all learning is a good thing.

Reflections: Think of something you have learned, such as the meaning of a word. Is it new and permanent? Had you acquired it before actually demonstrating that knowledge? What factor(s) in the environment were responsible for that learning?

4.1 Core study 1:
Bandura et al. (aggression)

Bandura, A., Ross, D., & Ross, S. A. (1961). Transmission of aggression through imitation of aggressive models. *Journal of Abnormal and Social Psychology, 63*(3), 575–582.

Aim

The aim was to investigate whether a child would learn aggression by observing a model and would reproduce this behaviour in the absence of the model, and whether the sex of the role model was important. Specifically, there were four hypotheses:

- Observed aggressive behaviour will be imitated, so children seeing aggressive models will be more aggressive than those seeing a non-aggressive model or no model.
- Observed non-aggressive behaviour will be imitated, so children seeing non-aggressive models will be less aggressive than those seeing no model.
- Children are more likely to copy a same-sex model.
- Boys will be more likely to copy aggression than girls.

nature versus nurture: the importance of the environment, or nurture, can be seen in the role of adults as models for children in the rewards and punishments they give to them.

Background

Children copy adults. This could be because the immediate social setting makes the child imitate what he or she is watching (Figure 4.1). This is just 'facilitation' of behaviour, making it more likely that the child will do what others are doing around them. Alternatively, the observation of a behaviour could lead the child to acquire a new response that he or she could reproduce independently. If this is the case, the new behaviour should generalise to new settings and so would be produced in the absence of an adult model. If this **imitative learning** occurred, it could arise in response to observing either aggressive or non-aggressive behaviour. So whereas watching an aggressive model should lead to more aggressive behaviours being demonstrated, observing a non-aggressive model should lead to more non-aggressive behaviour being produced, i.e. even less aggressive behaviour than normal.

KEY TERM

imitative (social) learning: the learning of a new behaviour which is observed in a role model and imitated later in the absence of that model.

Children are also differentially rewarded for their copying. In general (at least in the mid-twentieth century when this study took place) boys were rewarded for behaviours considered to be sex-appropriate and punished for inappropriate ones, such as cooking or 'playing mother'. Similarly for girls, rewards and punishments would be applied to discourage sex-inappropriate behaviours. This, Bandura et al. suggested, would lead to two kinds of differences. Firstly, boys and girls should be more likely to imitate same-sex models and secondly, they should differ in the readiness with which they imitate aggression, with boys doing so more readily as this is seen as a more masculine-type behaviour.

4.1 A child imitates seen behaviour

Method
Research method and design

This was a laboratory experiment; the environment was not the normal place where the children played and the situation was controlled. The design of the experiment was that of independent measures as different children were used in each of the levels of the independent variables (IVs) (although these children were **matched** for aggression in threes). There were three IVs:

- *model type*: whether the child saw an aggressive model, non-aggressive model or no model
- *model gender*: same gender as child (boys watching a male model and girls watching a female model) or different gender (boys watching a female model and girls watching a male model)
- *learner gender*: whether the child was a boy or a girl.

RESEARCH METHODS

Matched participants design: the participants were divided into threes, all with very similar initial aggression levels. One of each of these individuals was placed into each of the three different conditions of model type (aggressive or non-aggressive model and control).

The dependent variable (DV) was the learning the child displayed. This was measured through a **controlled observation** of the children and measures of aggressive behaviour were recorded.

Sample

Seventy-two children aged three to six years (36 boys and 36 girls) were obtained from Stanford University nursery school.

Procedure

Prior to the experimental part of the study, the children were observed in their nursery school by the experimenter and a teacher who knew them well. They were rated on four five-point scales measuring physical aggression, verbal aggression, aggression to inanimate objects and aggression inhibition (anxiety). They were then assigned to three groups, ensuring that the aggression levels of the children in each group were matched. Of the 51 children, rated by both observers (the rest were rated by only one observer), similar ratings were generally produced. Their ratings were compared as a measure of **'inter-rater reliability'**, which showed a high correlation between the observers, of $r = 0.89$.

> **RESEARCH METHODS**
>
> **Inter-rater reliability** is the extent to which two researchers rate the same activity that they have observed, heard in an interview, etc., in the same way. This is judged using a correlation (an 'r' value) between the two ratings, which will be high (close to 1) if they are reliable.

Twelve boys and 12 girls were allocated to control groups, who saw no model. The remaining children were divided equally by sex between aggressive and non-aggressive model groups and within those, between same and opposite-sex models.

The experimenter and child entered the observation room, where the experimenter showed the child to a table and chair in their 'play area', where they were shown how to make potato prints and sticker pictures – activities previously identified as interesting for children. The opposite corner of the room also contained a table and chair, a Tinkertoy set, a mallet and a five foot (152 cm) Bobo doll – an inflatable clown-like doll which bounced back when hit (Figure 4.2). This is where the model sat, in those conditions where

4.2 Observing and imitating aggressive behaviours with a Bobo doll

there was one. The experimenter remained in the room so that the child would not refuse to be alone or try to leave early but they appeared to be working quietly at their desk.

The three groups were then treated differently. In the non-aggressive condition, the model assembled the Tinkertoys (a wooden building kit) for ten minutes. In the aggressive condition this lasted only one minute, after which the model attacked the Bobo doll. The doll was laid on its side, sat on and punched in the nose, picked up and hit on the head with a mallet, tossed up in the air and kicked. This sequence was performed three times over nine minutes accompanied by aggressive comments such as 'Kick him' and two non-aggressive comments such as 'He sure is a tough fella'. Of children in the model groups, half saw a same-sex model, the others saw a model of the opposite sex. A **control group** did not see any model, and therefore saw no aggression.

The experimental procedure continued with a stage in which all participants were deliberately mildly annoyed. This was done for two reasons:

- because watching aggression may reduce the production of aggression by the observer (even if it has been learned) and it was necessary to see evidence of learning (Figure 4.2)
- to ensure that even the non-aggressive condition and control participants would be likely to express

aggression, so that any reduction in that tendency could be measured.

> **!**
>
> **RESEARCH METHODS**
>
> The non-aggressive model group might appear to be a **control group** because the key factor of 'aggression' is missing. However, the important aspect is the presence of a model – and there is one here. So the real control group is where the IV is absent, i.e. where there is no model at all.

A test of the child's aggression then followed in which the child was observed for 20 minutes using a one-way mirror. For the aggressive model group, this was a test of delayed imitation. This experimental room contained a three foot (92 cm) Bobo doll, a mallet and peg board, two dart guns and a tether ball with a face painted on it which hung from the ceiling. It also contained some non-aggressive toys, including a tea set, crayons and colouring paper, a ball, two dolls, three bears, cars and trucks, and plastic farm animals. These toys were always presented in the same order.

The children's behaviours were observed in five second intervals (240 response units per child). There were three 'response measures' of the children's imitation, with a range of possible activities in each:

*   *Imitation of physical aggression*: striking the Bobo doll with the mallet, sitting on the doll and punching it in the nose, kicking the doll, and tossing it in the air.
*   *Imitative verbal aggression*: repetition of the phrases, 'Sock him', 'Hit him down', 'Kick him', 'Throw him in the air' or 'Pow'.
*   *Imitative non-aggressive verbal responses*: repetition of 'He keeps coming back for more' or 'He sure is a tough fella'.

Reflections: Why might Bandura et al. have chosen to record in five second intervals, rather than one second or one minute intervals?

Partially imitative aggression was scored if the child imitated these behaviours incompletely. The two behaviours here were:

*   *mallet aggression*: striking objects other than the Bobo doll aggressively with the mallet
*   *sits on Bobo doll*: laying the Bobo doll on its side and sitting on it, without attacking it.

Two further categories were:

*   *aggressive gun play*: shooting darts or aiming a gun and firing imaginary shots at objects in the room.
*   *non-imitative physical and verbal aggression*: physically aggressive acts directed toward objects other than the Bobo doll and any hostile remarks except for those in the verbal imitation category (e.g. 'Shoot the Bobo', 'Cut him', 'Stupid ball', 'Horses fighting, biting' 'Knock over people'.

Finally, behaviour units were also counted for *non-aggressive play* and sitting quietly *not playing* at all, and records were kept of the children's remarks about the situation.

One male scored all the children's behaviours and, except for those conditions in which he was the model, he was unaware of which condition the child had been in (although this was typically obvious in the case of the aggressive model children as they performed the very specific behaviours exhibited by the model). To test his reliability, a second scorer independently rated the behaviour of half of the children and the reliability was high, around $r = 0.9$ for different categories of behaviour.

Results

Children exposed to aggressive models imitated their exact behaviours and were significantly more aggressive, both physically and verbally, than those children in the non-aggressive model or control groups. These children also imitated the model's non-aggressive verbal responses. This effect was greater for boys than girls although boys were more likely to imitate physical aggression and girls more likely to imitate verbal aggression (though not significantly so). Boys were also more likely to imitate a same-sex model as, to a lesser extent, were girls. The mean aggression scores can be seen in Table 4.1. Some interesting points are that the mean for imitative physical aggression for male subjects (25.8) is much higher than that for female subjects (7.2). This indicates that the boys imitated the physical aggression of a male model more than the girls. However, with a female model, girls imitated less (5.5) than with the male model.

Children seeing a non-aggressive model were much less likely than either the aggressive model group or controls to exhibit mallet aggression, and this pattern was especially apparent for girls. Although the aggressive model did not appear to affect levels of gun play or punching the Bobo doll, non-imitative physical and verbal aggression other than these activities were higher

following exposure to an aggressive model compared to the other two conditions.

> **Reflections:** Consider the data for the mean aggressive behaviours and the non-imitative verbal responses. Which are qualitative and which are quantitative data?

There were also differences in non-aggressive play. Girls played more with dolls, tea sets and colouring and boys engaged in more exploratory play and gun play. There were no gender differences in play with farm animals, cars or the tether ball. Both boys and girls seeing the non-aggressive model engaged in more non-aggressive play with dolls than either of the other groups, and spent more than twice as much time sitting quietly, not playing.

Response category	Experimental groups				Control groups
	Aggressive		Non-aggressive		
	Female model	Male model	Female model	Male model	
Imitative physical aggression					
Female subjects	5.5	7.2	2.5	0.0	1.2
Male subjects	12.4	25.8	0.2	1.5	2.0
Imitative verbal aggression					
Female subjects	13.7	2.0	0.3	0.0	0.7
Male subjects	4.3	12.7	1.1	0.0	1.7
Mallet aggression					
Female subjects	17.2	18.7	0.5	0.5	13.1
Male subjects	15.5	28.8	18.7	6.7	13.5
Punches Bobo doll					
Female subjects	6.3	16.5	5.8	4.3	11.7
Male subjects	18.9	11.9	15.6	14.8	15.7
Non-imitative aggression					
Female subjects	21.3	8.4	7.2	1.4	6.1
Male subjects	16.2	36.7	26.1	22.3	24.6
Aggressive gun play					
Female subjects	1.8	4.5	2.6	2.5	3.7
Male subjects	7.3	15.9	8.9	16.7	14.3

Table 4.1 Mean aggression scores from Bandura et al.'s study

In the nature versus nurture debate, we can see here that the boys and girls differed. This could be because they are genetically different; a nature explanation. Boys might be biologically predisposed to be aggressive, so more likely to copy aggressive models. Alternatively, boys might be more likely to copy aggressive models because they have been rewarded for aggressive behaviours more than girls have. This would be a nurture argument.

In addition to the observations, records of the remarks about the aggressive models revealed differences, both between reactions to the actions of the male and female models and between boys and girls. Some comments appeared to be based on previous knowledge of **sex-typed behaviour**, such as 'Who is that lady? That's not the way for a lady to behave. Ladies are supposed to act like ladies . . .' and 'You should have seen what that girl did in there. She was just acting like a man. I never saw a girl act like that before. She was punching and fighting but no swearing.' Whereas comments about the female model's behaviour were disapproving, those about the male model were not. This was more likely to be seen as appropriate and approved by both boys and girls, for example in comments such as 'Al's a good socker, he beat up Bobo. I want to sock like Al' and 'That man is a strong fighter, he punched and punched and he could hit Bobo right down to the floor and if Bobo got up he said, 'Punch your nose.' He's a good fighter like Daddy.'

KEY TERM

sex-typed behaviour: actions that are typically performed by one particular gender and are seen in society as more appropriate for that gender. For example, aggression is seen as a masculine-type behaviour and was more commonly imitated by boys.

Conclusions

The results strongly suggest that observation and imitation can account for the learning of specific acts without reinforcement of either the model or observer. All four hypotheses were supported:

- Observed aggressive behaviours are imitated: children who see aggressive models are likely to be more aggressive than those seeing a non-aggressive model or no model.

- Observed non-aggressive behaviours are imitated: children seeing non-aggressive models will be less aggressive than those seeing no model.
- Children are more likely to copy a same-sex model, although this may depend on the extent to which this behaviour is sex-typed.
- Boys are more likely to copy aggression than girls.

Strengths and weaknesses

The main method was a laboratory experiment. This means that it was possible to control **extraneous variables** such as ensuring there was a possibility that the children in any condition would show aggressive behaviour. This was done by showing them nice toys but then taking them to another room. Also, all children in both experimental groups saw a model for the same length of time, and in each condition their behaviours were standardised. This means the research was more **valid** – the researchers could be sure that the differences in results between conditions were due to the differences between the models – and more **reliable**, because each child within a condition experienced exactly the same exposure. **Inter-observer reliability** was also checked for both the initial observations of aggressiveness and for the data recording – and was very high. The pre-testing of the children's aggressiveness was another factor that increased **validity**, because it ensured that differences between conditions were due to the models and not to individual differences between the children who happened to be in each group.

Reflections: The procedure was standardised in many ways. Identify as many of these as you can. Justify why each one of these was necessary – try to think about what might have happened if each participant had not been treated in the same way.

The main measure of the DV was through observation. As the observers were behind a one-way mirror, the children were unaware that they were being watched. This increases validity as they were likely to behave naturally rather than responding to **demand characteristics** as they might have done had they known they were being observed. The observation period was divided into time intervals (of five seconds) and the categories were clearly defined (e.g. imitative and non-imitative behaviours), which also helped to improve both validity and reliability.

Among the weaknesses of the study is that only six children were used in each experimental condition and, although they were matched to reduce the risk of **participant variables** confounding the results, it is still a small sample. Furthermore, it is possible that the children were quite similar, as they all attended the same nursery based at a university, suggesting that they all had academically able parents. This could bias the **sample**, lowering validity.

The study collected both quantitative data, which was an **objective** record of the number of imitative actions in each category and qualitative data, which although more **subjective**, provided some explanation of the reasons behind the tendency of the children to copy some behaviours and not others. It could have been useful to have asked the children for self-reports of their emotions when they were observing the model or reacting towards the Bobo doll. This may have helped to further explain differences such as the influence of sex-typing on imitation. It would also have been useful to have followed the children up to see how long the children's acquired behaviours lasted. If imitation leads to learning, the change in behaviour should be relatively permanent. However, if this were so, it would also raise **ethical issues** with the study as some of the children might have been harmed by becoming more aggressive. Even if this were not the case, the children had been mildly annoyed, which could be psychologically distressing.

Reflections: Think about qualitative and quantitative data as the two ends of a see-saw (Figure 4.3). What are the advantages and disadvantages that weigh the see-saw in each direction?

Can give reasons

Objective

Simple to analyse

Wide range of data can be collected

Can use statistics

Subjective so can be misinterpreted

Fixed categories for data can mean information is missed

Qualitative data

Quantitative data

4.3 The strengths of qualitative data are the opposite of those of quantitative data and vice versa, so they weigh against each other

SELF-ASSESSMENT QUESTIONS

1 The children in Bandura et al.'s study were divided into many different groups according to the various levels of the three different IVs. Draw a table to show how many children were in each of the different conditions.

2 The evidence illustrates several examples of sex-typed behaviours in the children. Identify at least **two** examples.

4.2 Core study 2: Saavedra and Silverman (button phobia)

Saavedra, L. M., & Silverman, W. K. (2002). Case Study: Disgust and a specific phobia of buttons. *Journal of the American Academy of Child and Adolescent Psychiatry, 41*(11), 1376–1379.

Aim

The aim was to examine the role of **classical conditioning** in relation to fear and avoidance of a particular stimulus. In the context of a specific **phobia**, researchers wanted to see if using a type of exposure therapy could reduce the disgust and distress associated with buttons.

KEY TERMS

classical conditioning: learning through association, studied in both humans and animals. It is a learning process in which a new stimulus, which initially has no effect (the neutral stimulus, NS), becomes associated with another stimulus (the unconditioned stimulus, UCS). The UCS already produces a response (the unconditioned response, UCR), which is often an innate (instinctive) reaction. Following pairing of the UCS and NS, sometimes only once by more often repeatedly, the NS will produce a response similar to the existing UCR, so the NS becomes known as the conditioned stimulus (CS) and the newly learned response, the conditioned response (CR). A famous example of this process can be seen in Figure 4.4.

phobia: the irrational, persistent fear of an object or event which poses little real danger but creates anxiety and avoidance in the sufferer.

90

Background

Classical conditioning is a form of learning in which an unconditioned response becomes linked to a previously neutral stimulus to create a learned association. It was investigated by Ivan Pavlov, who observed dogs salivating in a laboratory as part of a totally different experiment. Salivation is an unconditioned (that is, uncontrolled) response to being presented with food (unconditioned stimulus). The dogs came to anticipate the food when they saw researchers in the lab, before feeding times. Pavlov presented the food alongside a range of neutral stimuli, such as bells, which created a learned association. Over the course of several trials, when the dogs heard the bell (conditioned stimulus) they began to salivate (conditioned response), see Figure 4.4.

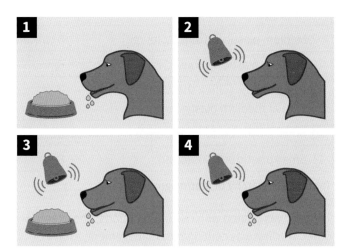

4.4 Pavlov's dog and bell

1   Before conditioning: unconditioned stimulus (food) → unconditioned response (salivation)

2   Before conditioning: neutral stimulus (bell ringing) → no response

3   During conditioning: unconditioned stimulus (food) + neutral stimulus (bell ringing) → unconditioned response (salivation)

4   After conditioning: conditioned stimulus (bell ringing) → conditioned response (salivation).

Some psychologists believe that abnormal behaviour such as phobias can also be both learned (and unlearned) in the same way as any other type of behaviour. There are several subtypes of classical conditioning, including expectancy learning, in which a previously neutral or non-threatening object or event becomes associated with a potentially threatening outcome. The consequence is that the individual *expects* the negative outcome, so experiences fear in the presence of the previously non-threatening situation. Phobias may be caused by evaluative learning, that is, a kind of classical conditioning in which the individual forms an association between a previously neutral stimulus and a negative emotion, but this is a negative *evaluation*, for example disgust, rather than fear. This suggests that disgust, as well as fear, may be an appropriate target emotion for the treatment of phobias, as well as the primary emotion of fear. In the case of phobias, an emotional response such as fear or anxiety becomes associated with a particular neutral stimulus, such as buttons. A strictly behaviourist approach to classical conditioning would suggest that there is little role for thinking and feeling in this learning process. However, the case study we will look at now involves a deeper exploration of the role of cognition and emotion in changing phobic behaviour, known as **evaluative learning**.

> **KEY TERM**
>
> **evaluative learning:** a form of classical conditioning wherein attitudes towards stimuli are considered to be the product of complex thought processes and emotions which lead an individual to perceive or evaluate a previously neutral stimulus negatively. Attitudes acquired through evaluative learning may be harder to change than more superficial associations.

From their study of adults with a blood phobia, Hepburn and Page (1999) suggested that treating patients' disgust, as well as their fear, would helped them to make progress. De Jong et al. (1997) worked with children who had a spider phobia. Although no attempt was made to manipulate feelings of disgust, their feelings of disgust declined alongside their reduction in fear.

> **ISSUES AND DEBATES**
>
> **nature versus nurture** – in classical conditioning, the environment is considered the main influence on behaviour. Individuals are considered to be 'blank slates' when they are born, and are shaped purely by nurture.

Method
Research method and design

This was a clinical **case study** as it involved just **one participant** whose life history and treatment was studied in depth. Data was collected using self-report measures. Both the boy and his mother were interviewed by the researchers about the onset of his phobia and his subsequent behaviour. The results of the treatment were measured using a nine-point scale of disgust known as the 'Feelings Thermometer'.

Sample

The participant was a 9-year-old Hispanic American boy. Along with his mother, he had sought support from the Child Anxiety and Phobia Program at Florida International University, Miami. He met the criteria for having a specific phobia of buttons and had been experiencing symptoms for around four years prior to the start of the study.

Procedure

The boy and his mother both provided informed consent to participate in the study. They were interviewed in order to determine whether any trauma or abuse could explain the boy's phobia. The phobia had begun at age five, when the boy had knocked over a bowl of buttons in front of his class and teacher. He found the incident distressing, and from that time onwards his aversion to buttons steadily increased. When he was interviewed the phobia was interfering significantly with his normal functioning; he could no longer dress himself and had become preoccupied with avoiding touching buttons or clothing that could have touched buttons.

It was necessary for the researchers to understand the boy's specific feelings towards buttons prior to starting treatment. Through discussion with the participant, they created a hierarchy of feared stimuli, with each item on the list provoking increasing fear (see Table 4.2). The most difficult items for the child were small, clear plastic buttons. These were rated at an '8' on the

nine-point Feelings Thermometer. Handling these or touching someone wearing them was the most unpleasant task for the boy.

Stimuli	Distress rating (0–8)
1. Large denim jean buttons	2
2. Small denim jean buttons	3
3. Clip-on denim jean buttons	3
4. Large plastic buttons (coloured)	4
5. Large plastic buttons (clear)	4
6. Hugging Mom when she wears large plastic buttons	5
7. Medium plastic buttons (coloured)	5
8. Medium plastic buttons (clear)	6
9. Hugging Mom when she wears regular medium plastic buttons	7
10. Small plastic buttons (coloured)	8
11. Small plastic buttons (clear)	8

Table 4.2 Hierarchy of fear/disgust

The boy was treated with two interventions, one after the other. The first was contingency management, a form of **positive reinforcement** therapy. This was a behaviour-focused approach which meant the boy was rewarded for showing less fear and for actually handling the buttons. The positive reinforcement was given to the boy by his mother only after he had completed a gradual exposure to buttons. These treatment sessions lasted between 20 and 30 minutes.

Reflections: Imagine a different phobia, one of spiders, mice or peanut butter, for example. Suggest eight different scenarios that could be imagined by a person receiving similar treatment to that described here.

The second form of therapy, and the main focus of the study, was known as 'imagery exposure'. Interviews with the boy had revealed that he found buttons touching his body disgusting, and he also believed that buttons smelled unpleasant. These ideas formed the basis for disgust imagery exercises. Unlike *in vivo* exposure, where the individual actually physically handles or is exposed to fearful stimuli, imagery exposure therapy uses visualisation techniques.

Disgust-related imagery exposures were incorporated with cognitive **self-control** strategies. The boy was asked to imagine buttons falling on him, and to consider how they looked, felt and smelled. He was also asked to talk about how these imagery exposures made him feel. The exposures progressed from images of larger to smaller buttons, in line with the boy's fear hierarchy.

KEY TERM

self-control: a form of cognitive behavioural therapy. It involves using 'self-talk'; the individual is taught to recognise difficult situations, acknowledge troubling thoughts and consider alternative, positive thoughts.

Results
Positive reinforcement therapy

The outcome of this therapy was a successful completion of all the exposure tasks listed in the hierarchy of fear. The boy was also observed approaching the buttons more positively. One example of this was that he started handling larger numbers of buttons during later sessions.

However, his subjective ratings of distress increased significantly between sessions two and three, and continued to rise (see Figure 4.5). By session four, a number of items on the hierarchy such as hugging his mother while wearing buttons had increased in dislike from the original scores. So despite his behaviour towards the fearful stimuli improving, his feelings of disgust, fear and anxiety actually increased as a result of the positive reinforcement therapy. This finding is consistent with evaluative learning; despite apparent behavioural change, evaluative reactions (i.e. disgust) remain unchanged or even increased.

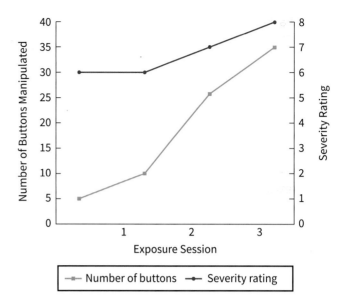

4.5 Ratings of distress: positive reinforcement therapy

Imagery exposure therapy

This appeared to be successful in reducing the boy's rating of distress. One example of this is shown in Figure 4.6, relating to imagery of 'hundreds of buttons falling all over his body'. Prior to imagery therapy, the boy rated this experience the most fearful and disgusting (score of 8 on the Feelings Thermometer). This reduced to 5 midway through the exposure, and just 3 after the exposure was complete.

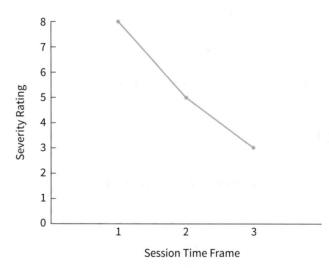

4.6 Ratings of distress: imagery exposure therapy: (1) before, (2) midway and (3) after imagery exposure

93

Following his treatment, six month and 12 month follow-ups were conducted. At these assessment sessions, the boy reported feeling minimal distress about buttons. He also no longer met the diagnostic criteria for a specific phobia of buttons. His feelings towards buttons no longer affected his normal functioning; he was also able to wear small, clear plastic buttons on his school uniform on a daily basis.

Conclusions

The researchers concluded that the treatment was successful. In particular they argue that:

- emotions and cognitions relating to disgust are important when learning new responses to phobic stimuli
- imagery exposure can have a long-term effect on reducing the distress associated with specific phobias as it tackles negative evaluations.

Strengths and weaknesses

This piece of research involved a case study. This means that the sample is small (in this case, one person) and difficult to generalise from. As the participant was diagnosed with a specific phobia of buttons, it makes the case even less likely to be representative of the general population. However, the case study is highly **valid**; the participant was studied over a period of time using several different methods of data collection. The researchers used **standardised** measures such as the Feelings Thermometer before, during and after therapy. Collecting and analysing **quantitative data** means we can be quite sure that the improvement seen in the phobic reactions of the little boy was highly likely to be a result of the treatment he received.

> **Reflections:** This study used only one participant. Can you explain why the results are still useful, despite possibly not being representative of others?

A substantial amount of **qualitative data** was also gathered about the boy. An example of this was the background information obtained by interviewing the boy and his mother about the button incident at his school. This type of data is useful because it can help us to understand the reasons underlying abnormal behaviour.

In many ways this study could be considered to be **subjective**. The participant created his own hierarchy of fear and disgust relating to his button phobia. He also gave personal ratings which were highly individual to his own thoughts and feelings. However, as the aim of this study was to understand the experience of evaluative learning in an individual with specific phobia, these measures were appropriate. A scale created by the researchers for use with all phobic patients would not have been as relevant or informative about personal progress.

Working on a case study involves building rapport with the participant. There is less room for anonymity or objectivity. This means there is a higher risk of **bias** which may compromise the **validity** of the study. There may be researcher bias as the researchers select and report on a particular participant (who may be more likely to have a positive outcome). **Demand characteristics** may be more obvious also. For example, the boy was fully aware he was undergoing therapy with the intention of improving his phobic symptoms. This might have affected the ratings he gave to the different levels of exposure therapy.

When using children as participants, **ethical issues** can be a major concern. In this instance, the boy and his mother gave informed consent to participate in the study. This was important as the therapy involved deliberate exposure to distressing stimuli, whether real or imagined. Overall, the aim of the study was to improve the boy's quality of life and minimise psychological distress, which is less concerning. In addition, the boy's anonymity was preserved, which allowed him to maintain his privacy.

> **SELF-ASSESSMENT QUESTIONS**
>
> 3   Briefly explain why the study by Saavedra and Silverman was carried out.
> 4   Describe the conclusions from this study.

4.3 Core study 3: Pepperberg (parrot learning)

Pepperberg, I. M. (1987). Acquisition of the same/different concept by an African Grey parrot (*Psittacus erithacus*): Learning with respect to categories of color, shape, and material. *Animal Learning & Behavior, 15*(4), 423–432.

Aim

The aim of this study was to see whether a parrot could use vocal labels to demonstrate a symbolic understanding of the concepts 'same' and 'different'.

Background

Humans are not the only animals capable of making meaningful communication. There has long been interest in non-human primates, such as chimpanzees and gorillas, and their abilities to talk to one another. Researchers have even been able to teach them to express their ideas and needs through pointing at symbols or using sign language (see Figure 4.7). Some of these studies have produced surprising results; namely that non-human primates have the cognitive capacity to express abstract ideas and, in some cases, form meaningful sentences.

4.7 Teaching sign language to a primate

Although some language skills appear to be confined to primates, one specific cognitive capacity is thought to be present in other species. The conceptual categorisation of items as the same or different is thought to be present in other animals. Identifying items as the same or different requires a particular set of cognitive abilities. Firstly, the animal must recognise the category that is being shared (for example, that both items are green in colour). From this single attribute, they must also realise that this sameness can be applied to other items that they have not yet encountered. This requires a skill known as symbolic representation. This means the concept of sameness or difference learned from one experience can be applied to an entirely new and different situation.

The focus of much language training has been on non-human primates because their advanced cognition makes them useful participants in such research. However, there is evidence to suggest that the capacity to recognise same/different items is present in many bird species. This may be the case as it serves an adaptive function; it benefits a bird's survival.

Method

Research method and design

This was an animal case study involving one subject who was trained and tested over a couple of years.

Sample

This study focused on one African Grey parrot (Figure 4.8) called Alex. Alex had been involved in prior research on communication and cognition for around ten years. During the day, the parrot had free access to all areas of the laboratory and at night he was confined to a wire cage. He was fed a diet suitable for his species and given toys to play with.

4.8 African Grey parrot

Procedure

Prior to training, Alex already had a considerable vocabulary as a result of his previous experience as a research subject. For example, he could already name the colours red, green, yellow, blue and grey, several shapes (e.g. triangle, square) and different kinds of material (wood, cork, hide, paper and some metals). He also had experience of replying to verbal prompts. When asked 'what colour?' he could often correctly name the colour of an item presented to him. He could even combine responses to describe items, e.g. to name 'green wood'.

The purpose of training was to teach Alex to respond to questions with a categorical label, rather than simply describing an item's appearance, or stating whether it matched or did not match a paired item. This is a more complex task which required abstract thinking. He engaged in training sessions two to four times a week, each session lasting between five minutes and one hour. Alex also engaged in training for other studies during this period.

4.9 Different shapes were used in the trials

The training method used in this study is known as the model/rival or M/R approach. It is based on the concept of modelling demonstrated in the first study in this chapter by Bandura et al. (1961). One human acts as the trainer of the second human by presenting the second with objects (Figure 4.9), then asking questions about the objects and offering reward or praise to desirable responses. Thus, the second or learner human acts as a model to the parrot who is watching the interaction. The parrot can be considered a 'rival' for the trainer's attention; if they offer the right vocalisation when the question is asked, they receive the reward or praise rather than the model human. The roles of trainer/model are then reversed.

At the beginning of training, a system of **continuous reinforcement** was used. This was intended to create the closest possible association between the object or category and label to be learned. During training on same/different, the trainer would ask the model 'what's the same?' or 'what's different'? The model would either respond with the correct category label and be rewarded by being given the object, or would give an incorrect response and be scolded and have the object taken away.

KEY TERM

continuous reinforcement: when a learner receives a reward each time they perform a desirable behaviour. It is one of several possible schedules of reinforcement.

RESEARCH METHODS

It was important in terms of **validity** that Alex's responses could be understood. This is why testing was delayed. If testing had been started earlier, and any sounds Alex made that were a bit like 'matter' were counted as correct, this may have resulted in an over-estimate of his ability.

Task

At the start of the study, Alex could already say the labels 'colour' and 'shape'. However, it took some time to master the vocalisation for matter (he pronounced 'mah-mah') so the testing phase was delayed for the purposes of accuracy. Alex was tested by secondary trainers who had not worked with him on learning same/different. The materials were paired from a selection given to a student who had nothing to do with the study, in order to create an unbiased set of stimuli. They also randomly ordered the set of questions used in each trial. Although researchers were only interested in data from the same/different questions, other questions were included to prevent boredom effects such as:

- What colour?
- How many?
- What shape?

In each trial, Alex was presented with two objects that could differ in one of three categories: shape, colour or material. For example, the group might include a blue wooden triangle and a blue wooden square. In some trials, Alex was asked by the trainer: 'what's the same?' and 'what's different?' The correct response would be for Alex to name the categories that were the same (in this example colour and material), and those which were different (shape). The

task would either involve pairs of familiar items (familiar trial) or one or both items which he had not yet encountered in training (novel trial).

Reflections: Why do you think Alex was asked to make judgements on items that had three dimensions (shape, colour and material) rather than just two?

The principal trainer was present in each trial, but sat facing away from Alex and was unable to see the objects being presented. After each of Alex's responses, the trainer repeated the vocalisation aloud. If Alex's response had been correct, he was rewarded with praise and given the items. Getting the answer right first time counted towards the 'first-trial' response rate. If it was an incorrect or indistinct vocalisation, Alex was told 'No!' and had the object removed while the trainer turned their head away from the parrot (known as a 'time-out'). This correction procedure was repeated until the correct response was given, and the number of errors was recorded.

Reflections: Alex's primary trainer was present in each trial. However, they didn't look at the parrot and were asked to repeat his responses. Can you explain why they were given this role?

Results

In tests involving familiar objects, Alex correctly responded to 99/129 trials (76.6%). This was for first trials answered correctly and those that involved correction procedures. For first trials only, Alex answered correctly in 69/99 instances (69.7%). However, this finding gives a conservative picture of the success of the training. One reason for this is that the response was only counted as correct if it was the first vocalisation Alex gave in response to the question; but rather than giving the 'wrong' answer on the remaining trials, Alex might not respond with an answer at all, but instead make a request for another object or actions unrelated to the trial.

RESEARCH METHODS

In recording Alex's responses, an **operational definition** was used. The response was only counted as correct if it was the first vocalisation Alex gave. Operationalisation of variables helps to improve reliability because it means that the experimenters are likely to be more consistent in the way that they collect data.

The tests also involved novel objects which measured the extent to which Alex could generalise his understanding and communication around the concepts of 'same' and 'different' to entirely new situations. Here Alex actually performed slightly better on the task, scoring 96/113 on all trials (85%), and 79/96 (82.3%) on first-trial performance only. While we might expect Alex to have found it more difficult to judge items which he had never encountered before, he was actually more accurate at doing so. One reason the researchers suggest for this difference is that Alex received the items involved in each trial as his reward. As such, he might have been motivated to do better on novel trials because he was curious to investigate newer reward items.

Conclusions

The researchers concluded from the case study of Alex that after training:

- parrots have the potential to demonstrate comprehension of the symbolic concepts 'same' and 'different'
- they may also learn to respond to verbal questions to vocalise categorical labels.

Strengths and weaknesses

This study involved one male African Grey parrot, making it a case study. Like the previous piece of research on phobias, this method makes it difficult to generalise from. As the parrot was a trained laboratory animal, it would be hard to say that it is representative of the general population. The researchers mention that Alex suffered from boredom at times, hence they varied his training and testing schedules in order to **control** for repetitive behaviours that were unrelated to the leaning process. This species is intelligent and prone to self-injurious behaviour in captivity as a result of boredom; a major challenge for those conducting research with them.

Reflections: How do you think the lab-based environment differs from the parrot's natural environment (Figure 4.10)? What effect might this have on their behaviour?

There were attempts to maintain the **validity** of the research; for example, the question order and materials were selected by a student with no connection to the project. Similarly, the trainer conducting the trials had not trained Alex on the same/different task. Both of these controls meant that researcher bias was limited.

4.10 African Grey parrots in the wild

It also meant Alex did not respond to any **demand characteristics** from interacting with his usual trainer. The research involved collecting **quantitative data** in the form of correct responses to the same/different questions. This allows us to make an objective analysis of whether or not Alex was able to understand the abstract concepts. Usefully, it also enabled comparison of two different sorts of tests, one involving familiar objects and one involving novel objects, so researchers could establish whether the rules of same/different had been generalised beyond training materials.

When using animals as participants, different sorts of **ethical issues** must be considered. In this instance, Alex is reported to be well treated and does not appear to have been physically harmed as a result of the research. There is no suggestion he was underfed or understimulated in order to encourage his participation in training. For example, Alex's conditions are described in a way that suggested he had adequate space to explore the laboratory for a considerable part of the day, and was given toys and interactions to prevent boredom. However, the researchers acknowledge that the species of parrot involved in the study is fairly intelligent, and being kept in an artificial environment for such an extended period of time while participating in non-naturalistic behaviours could be considered unethical.

SELF-ASSESSMENT QUESTIONS

5 Outline the aim of the study by Pepperberg.
6 Discuss **two** strengths and **two** weaknesses of this study.

4.4 Issues, debates and approaches

The application of psychology to everyday life

There are clear implications from Bandura et al.'s work. Children all over the world are exposed to aggression, both real, such as domestic violence in the home or violence on the news, or fictional, such as in cartoons, films and computer games. This study shows how such models can influence the behaviour of children, especially of boys. One consequence of the recognition of such potential effects is that many countries have restrictions on viewing, such as TV times before which programmes with inappropriate content for children cannot be shown (this is called the 9 p.m. 'watershed' in the UK) and certifications for films and games which indicate the age of child it is deemed suitable for viewing.

Similarly, the study by Saavedra and Silverman shows how therapy based on the principles of classical conditioning can be used to treat specific phobias. A phobia is a distressing mental health condition which can negatively affect people's quality of life. Methods such as disgust imagery exposure are used in clinical practice to challenge the fearful associations with phobic stimuli. This piece of research demonstrates the potential long-term improvement that can result from exposure therapies.

The research by Pepperberg into parrot cognition and communication raises interesting questions. It shows how non-primate animals can also be taught to communicate using modelling and reinforcement. Using these learning techniques has enabled us to see that other animals are able to reason about abstract categories, and generalise such concepts to novel situations.

Nature versus nurture

In the study by Bandura, situational influence of models on the acquisition of aggressive behaviours (and the suppression of them by the non-aggressive model) are examples of nurture. However, the differences between the responses of boys and girls to the same models could be explained by either nature or nurture. Boys were more likely to imitate aggressive behaviour than girls, possibly because boys have more of the hormone testosterone which is a nature factor. Alternatively (or additionally), boys may be more likely to imitate aggression because they have already acquired stereotypes about what is acceptable behaviour for males or have been rewarded for masculine-type behaviours. These would be examples of nurture.

The theory underlying the acquisition and treatment of phobias in the study by Silverman and Saavedra is classical conditioning. Classical conditioning relies solely on a nurture-based explanation of learning. Phobias are not considered innate or genetically inherited. Instead they are considered to be products of negative experiences with previously neutral stimuli. Treatment is based on the same principles; that subsequent neutral or positive experiences with the phobic stimuli (along with cognitive therapy) can reduce fearful responses.

Once again, both the theories of operant conditioning and social learning demonstrated in Pepperberg rely on a nurture-based approach to learning. As human training shaped the parrot's behaviour through rewards, it was able to demonstrate an important aspect of its cognition. However, there are clearly differences in the parrot's abilities and those of humans and other primates which cannot be attributed to factors in the environment, but rather in-born traits and abilities unique to different species.

Individual and situational explanations

This debate is relevant to the study by Bandura. Imitation clearly suggests that situational factors matter in that the model is an aspect of the situation, as are differences between male and female models. However, individual factors could also explain some differences in imitation. Individual factors in operant conditioning can explain why, even when girls and boys are exposed to the same models, their acquisition of behaviours differs because boys and girls may be differently rewarded for sex-typed behaviours. For example, a daughter may be praised for *not* fighting but a son praised for 'sticking up for himself'.

Individual and situational explanations can also be considered in the context of the study by Pepperberg. Alex the parrot's abilities in the familiar and novel testing did show significant differences; namely a higher rate of success on object pairs which were unfamiliar to Alex in some way. This suggests that situational factors (the familiarity of objects) can affect an animal's ability to offer a correct response.

The use of children in psychological research

The children used in Bandura et al.'s study did not appear to have been given the opportunity to consent to the study, or to withdraw. Since children are particularly vulnerable, and this study had the potential to cause distress, if this were the case these would be issues for ethical concern. Although the headteacher at the nursery school is thanked in the study, so she was clearly aware of the procedure, there is no indication of whether the parents' consent was obtained. When children are used in studies, ethical guidelines typically suggest that parents' or guardians' consent should be obtained in addition to the child's own.

On a practical level, the use of children rather than adults in Bandura's study was ideal. Children have been exposed to much less violence than adults and there are likely to be fewer extraneous factors affecting their aggression levels (such as a bad day at work). In general, children are more naive than adults, so the participants would have been less likely to suspect that they were being shown aggressive models in order to investigate the effects of these on their own behaviour. These considerations all lead to the greater potential for representative effects of the procedure on children than if the same study were conducted with adult participants.

In the study by Silverman and Saavedra, the child participant (aged nine) was asked for consent. In accordance with ethical guidelines, his mother also consented to his participation. This study was potentially highly distressing, as it involved both real and imagined exposure to frightening stimuli. Furthermore, the boy could be considered vulnerable as his specific phobia is a recognised mental health condition. However, the intention of the researchers was to treat his phobia and improve his quality of life, which may justify the temporary distress caused during treatment.

The use of animals in psychological research

Although the Bandura study was conducted on humans, similar research could, and has, been done with animals. Clearly there are some reasons why this would be better – it removes the potential risk of causing short-term distress or long-term harm to children. In addition, although it is assumed that the children remained naive to the purpose of the activity, it is still possible that they believed that they were 'supposed' to copy the adult's behaviour. This would not be a risk if animals were used, and the possibility that some animals had been exposed to more aggression prior to the study could be controlled.

Conversely, there would be disadvantages. Although there are biological sex differences in the behaviours of animals, they do not acquire sex-typed behaviours that are a consequence of cultural factors in the way that children do. Because this has been shown to be important, an animal study would not be able to test such social influences.

The research by Pepperberg was a case study of the training and testing of a single male African Grey parrot. Use of this participant was necessary as the researchers were particularly interested in the cognitive abilities of non-primates. Practically there were some advantages to working with this animal; it was relatively easy and cheap to care for. It had already been involved in training for other studies and was known to respond well to training in vocabulary exercises. Furthermore, there is no evidence that Alex was harmed as a result of the learning techniques of modelling and positive reinforcement. The study was conducted over a number of years and involved training on at least a weekly basis, which would have been difficult to achieve with a human participant. The parrot was also motivated by receiving the reward of the object in each trial; again motivating a human participant to continue with on-going trials might have been harder.

4.11 Is it right to keep animals in captivity for the purposes of research?

On the other hand, there are some practical limitations to working with animals in studies of this kind. The researchers had to devise a method for testing the cognitive abilities of the animal without having direct access to that animal's understanding. The parrot was unable to explain its reasoning in great depth. Fortunately the design of the task meant the investigation went beyond a simple match or no-match test, and the parrot was also able to demonstrate its learning in novel situations. There are also ethical concerns around keeping an animal in captivity away from its natural environment (Figure 4.11), and engaging it in artificial tasks such as imitating human speech.

Summary

Bandura et al.'s study used adults being aggressive to a Bobo doll to show that children's behaviour can be affected by that of a model. Exact aggressive behaviours were imitated although non-aggressive modelling was also effective. Children were more likely to copy a same-sex model and boys engaged in more aggressive imitation than girls. This was a well-controlled laboratory experiment measuring the dependent variable through objective observations which were reliable. Qualitative data suggested that the children recognised sex-typing and were surprised by behaviour that did not fit the pattern. The findings suggest practical applications for protecting children, e.g. through film certification.

The study by **Saavedra and Silverman** aimed to investigate the role of evaluative learning in treating a specific phobia of buttons. They used a case study of a young boy to explore the origin of his phobia, and treated him using both reinforcement and imagery exposure therapies. He responded best to the imagery exposure technique which relates closely to the thoughts and feelings associated with learned responses. This was a unique piece of research which gained both qualitative and quantitative data about the participant's progress through therapy. It has practical applications for the treatment of specific phobias, e.g. through imagery exposure relating to disgust.

Pepperberg's study used a single male African Grey parrot to show that birds of this species are capable of learning through modelling and reinforcement. Through a lengthy process of training and testing, researchers were able to establish that the animal could comprehend and apply the cognitive constructs of 'same' and 'different' to both familiar and unfamiliar objects. This was a lab-based study which had limited generalisability and lacked ecological validity. Using objective, quantitative measures of correct responses however did show that abstract categorical constructs may not be limited to humans and other non-human primates.

Exam-style questions

1   In their conclusion, Bandura et al. suggest that social imitation can speed up the learning of new behaviours as they can be acquired without the need for reinforcement, that is, without operant conditioning. Suggest why acquiring new behaviours through social imitation would be quicker than through operant conditioning. **[2 marks]**

2   If Bandura et al.'s study were performed today, the researchers would be required to obtain informed consent from both the children and their parents or guardians. Explain why this would be necessary. **[3 marks]**

3   There are several explanations for how learning occurs, including classical conditioning, operant conditioning and social (observational) learning. In the study by Saavedra and Silverman on button phobia, one technique for therapy used operant conditioning.

   a   Explain what is meant by operant conditioning. **[3 marks]**

   b   Describe how operant conditioning was used to help reduce the boy's phobia in the study. **[2 marks]**

4   One debate in psychology is the nature versus nurture debate. This is illustrated in the study by Pepperberg (parrot language).

   a   Explain what is meant by 'nature' and 'nurture'. **[2 marks]**

   b   One cognitive capacity present in many animals is the ability to understand that things can be 'the same' or different'. This categorisation requires the symbolic representation of 'sameness'. This ability is found in many species. Explain why this suggests it is controlled by '**nature**'. **[2 marks]**

   c   Describe **one** way that '**nurture**' is illustrated in Pepperberg's study. **[4 marks]**

Chapter 5
Social approach

Introduction

The aim of this chapter is to introduce you to the social approach to psychology and to explore three studies from this approach. They are:

- **Milgram (obedience)** which is based on the conflict between individual conscience and obedience to authority and considers how far a person would obey instructions which involved hurting another person
- **Piliavin et al. (subway Samaritans)** which looks at how bystanders behave in real-life situations and factors that affect their desire to help, including diffusion of responsibility
- **Yamamoto et al. (chimpanzee helping)** which considers pro-social behaviour and instrumental helping in chimpanzees, and looks at whether chimpanzees have the ability to help others based on specific needs.

These three studies serve to illustrate the main assumptions of the social approach which are that:

- behaviour, cognitions and emotions can be influenced by other individuals
- behaviour, cognitions and emotions can be influenced by groups or social contexts.

Throughout the chapter you will find out about how the presence of others can influence the thinking and behaviour of humans and animals. In each core study you will learn about relevant background to the research, how the study was carried out, the findings and the conclusions. You will also see how research methods in psychology are used in different ways within the social approach. You will explore how a range of issues and debates can be applied to the concepts considered in this approach.

Just fitting in?

Imagine you are walking to a friend's house. You notice an older person about to cross the road into busy traffic. Perhaps you might stop and ask if they need help. Perhaps you would like to help but do not feel confident approaching them, or maybe you do not feel it is your place to help. You might even have felt bad about just walking away from the situation. Have you ever wondered why and how we make these decisions about interacting with others?

Many factors are involved when we consider how we behave in social situations. Social psychologists argue that all of our thoughts, feelings and behaviour take place in the real or imagined presence of others. Do you agree? Consider whether you are the same 'self' in private, with friends and family, at school, work or in public. The social approach to psychology is concerned with many group processes in our daily lives, including prejudice, conformity, **obedience** and helping.

Some social behaviours might seem so normal and everyday that you might wonder why psychologists are concerned with them. We are surrounded by authority figures, including parents, teachers and politicians, who make and enforce rules for us to follow. We do much of this without even noticing; following signs which remind us to 'Keep off the grass' or 'Keep out' is an act of obedience.

Throughout history, and indeed, still today we are surrounded by examples of obedience to authority which has crossed from the everyday to the extreme. This is known as '**destructive obedience**'. What exactly then are our motivations for doing something that others tell us to do, even when it goes against our personal beliefs? Can you think of some historical examples of destructive obedience?

> **Reflections:** In one of the most shocking and infamous acts of civilian violence during the Vietnam War, a group of American soldiers carried out a mass murder in the small village of My Lai in March 1968. Read more about the cause of this massacre. What explanations might there be for this kind of destructive obedience?

KEY TERMS

obedience: following a direct order from a person or people in authority.

destructive obedience: obedience that has potential to cause psychological or physical harm or injury to another.

5.1 Core study 1:
Milgram (obedience)

Milgram, S. (1963). Behavioural study of obedience.
Journal of Abnormal and Social Psychology, 67, 371–378.

Aim

The aim of the study was to investigate how obedient individuals would be to orders received from a person in authority. Specifically, Milgram wanted to know whether people would be obedient even when it would result in physical harm to another person. To test this, he arranged his laboratory-based procedure to involve administering electric shocks to a victim under the orders of a researcher.

Background

The concept of obedience, in particular destructive obedience, had a particular relevance to Milgram. In Europe around the time of the Second World War, 11 million innocent people were systematically murdered on command by the Nazis during Adolf Hitler's regime (Figure 5.1). The Holocaust took the lives of those from a range of minority groups, including six million Jews. For such a large-scale atrocity to be possible required the obedience of many, indeed a majority of ordinary citizens as well as Nazi officers and guards. Some of those later tried as war criminals in the Nuremberg Trials argued in their defence that they were 'just following orders'.

5.1 Why did so many people obey the orders to commit mass murder in Nazi concentration camps?

One theory used to explain the tragic events of the Holocaust is that German citizens possessed some defective personal traits which made such extreme levels of obedience possible. This is a **dispositional** argument which seems to suggest that Germans are somehow different from others. Stanley Milgram, who was himself born into a Jewish family, sought to challenge this hypothesis. He suggested a **situational** explanation for obedience; that many people who found themselves in a similar situation would harm or even kill other human beings under the orders of an authority figure.

Prior to his study, Milgram told psychology students and some of his own colleagues about the procedure he would use involving destructive obedience, and asked them how many participants would apply the maximum voltage shocks. Those asked believed that less than 3% of participants would deliver the maximum voltage shock, with many stating they felt that no one would deliver such strong punishment.

ISSUES AND DEBATES

The **dispositional/situational** debate considers whether the person's individual characteristics or the conditions of their environment are more influential on levels of obedience.

Method

Research method and design

This study is perhaps best described as a **controlled observation**. It took place in a laboratory setting where all the variables and measurements were controlled, while the behaviour of participants was observed and recorded. Milgram originally described his study as a laboratory experiment. In this particular study each participant underwent the same procedure and there was no control condition. However, he later replicated the procedure in other studies using different variations to allow comparisons to be made.

In this study, participants' levels of obedience were measured through observation. This was operationalised as the maximum voltage given in response to the orders. Observers also noted the participants' body language and any verbal comments or protests made throughout the procedure.

RESEARCH METHODS

A **controlled observation** is where the researcher watches and records the behaviour of participants in an artificial environment, in contrast to a naturalistic observation which takes place in the individual's normal environment.

Reflections: Milgram collected both quantitative and qualitative data in this study. Can you identify these from the description given here? Consider why both types of data might be useful in understanding destructive obedience.

Sample

A newspaper advertisement was used to recruit 40 men between the ages of 20 and 50 years old. This meant it was a **volunteer sample**, composed of those who lived in the New Haven area of the United States. The men came from a range of different backgrounds and occupations, and represented unskilled workers, **white collar workers** as well as professionals.

KEY TERMS

white collar workers: refers to individuals who work in professional occupations, as compared to 'blue collar' workers which refers to those who perform manual work.

confederate: someone who is playing a role in a piece of research and has been instructed as to how to behave by the researcher.

RESEARCH METHODS

A **volunteer sample** is also known as a 'self-selected' sample. Participants are recruited through advertisements which can be a quick and easy recruitment tool. However, they may not attract a particularly representative sample.

Procedure

After responding to the newspaper advertisement, each participant was promised $4.50 for taking part. This was not conditional on their completing the study, but simply for being willing to participate. The study took place at Yale University, in a modern laboratory. The location was

103

chosen in order to make the procedure seem legitimate, an important situational factor in obedience.

The participants arrived individually to the lab, and were then introduced to another man whom they believed to be another participant. This man was in fact a **stooge** or **confederate**; he was a likeable, middle-aged man who worked for Milgram and had been trained in the procedure which followed. Both men were told that they would be allocated the roles of 'teacher' or 'learner' in what was to be an experiment about the effects of punishment on learning. They drew pieces of paper from a hat to determine the roles, but it was fixed so that the real participant was always allocated the role of teacher.

> **Reflections:** Why might Milgram have gone to the trouble of giving slips of paper to the stooge and real participants to 'allocate' the roles of teacher and learner?

Next the participant was taken to another room, where the stooge was strapped to a chair and had electrodes attached to him by the experimenter. The participant was presented with the shock generator (see Figure 5.2), which consisted of rows of switches labelled with voltage readings ranging from 15 V to 450 V. The shock voltage was also labelled in ascending order with words such as 'moderate shock', to 'danger: severe shock' and for the final two switches 'XXX' (Figure 5.3).

5.2 Milgram's participants were shown the shock generator before the procedure began

5.3 The simulated shock generator used in the study

The participant was told that although the shocks were painful, they were not dangerous. They were also then given an example shock of 45 V as a demonstration. After this, they were seated behind a wall so that they could hear but not see the stooge who was attached to the machine. Although the stooge

'learner' at no point in the procedure received any kind of shock, the elaborate machine was set up to convince the participants that they were really able to injure the learner. The experimenter remained with the participant; the same experimenter was used in each trial. He was a 31-year-old teacher who wore a grey technician's coat and had a stern manner throughout.

The participants were instructed in the 'memory' task, which involved reading pairs of words aloud to the learner, and subsequently testing the learner on their recognition of the words. Whenever the learner made a mistake, the participants were told by the experimenter to give him a shock by pressing a switch on the generator. They were ordered to increase the level of shock each time by 15 V for each error the learner made. Since the learner was a stooge, they could follow a pre-set plan of mistakes, deliberately giving the wrong answers at particular times.

Until 300 V were reached, the learner had remained silent when receiving the punishment. However, once the punishment level had reached 300 V, the learner began to pound on the wall in protest to the participant. After this time, the learner made no further noises and stopped responding to the memory task altogether. If and when the participants asked the experimenter what they should do, the experimenter insisted that they continue with reading the words aloud and punish the learner, treating no response as an incorrect answer. When participants protested at this, the experimenter continued to give them verbal prods in the sequence: Please go on / Please continue / The experiment requires that you continue / It is absolutely essential that you continue / You have no other choice, you *must* go on. These verbal prods or orders had a set wording, and were given in a standard order to any participants who protested at the task.

> **Reflections:** What do you think the real participants might have been thinking when the learner stopped pounding the wall and did not give any more answers to the task?

The procedure was considered to be complete when the participant refused to give any more shocks, or when they had given the maximum 450 V available. One-way mirrors were used to record the physical behaviours of the participants, and observers noted any comments that were made. After the procedure was complete, each participant was interviewed and had the deception explained to them fully. As part of the interview, participants were asked to estimate how painful they thought the final 450 V shock was, on a scale of 0–14 ('not at all painful' to 'extremely painful'). They were given the chance to meet the learner again, in order to reassure them that they were not injured and to restore the participant's well-being.

Results

Most participants were convinced that all aspects of the situation were real; that they were delivering electric shocks to another person which were extremely painful. The **mean** estimate of the pain of the 450 V shock was 13.42 out of a maximum 14 (as reported in the debriefing interview), meaning that participants were fully aware that they were causing serious pain.

> **RESEARCH METHODS**
>
> The **mean** is a measure of average calculated by dividing the sum of all participants' scores by the number of participants. In this study, 368 V is the mean average shock administered by participants. The mode is a different measure of average: it represents the most frequently occurring score amongst a group of participants. Using the data in Table 5.1, calculate the mode of the participant's shock scores. What conclusion can you draw from this?

Despite the findings being clear that participants believed the situation was real, participants showed extremely high levels of destructive obedience. The mean voltage given by participants was 368 V. All participants gave at least 300 V, and 65% gave the maximum 450 V shock (see Table 5.1). This is a startling contrast with the 0-3% obedience rate estimated by Milgram's students and colleagues prior to the study.

However, the qualitative data collected in this study revealed that participants showed signs of tension when undertaking the procedure. Observers reported signs of nervousness in participants, which increased as they gave more powerful electric shocks. The participants were also frequently observed to be sweating, shaking and groaning, with 14 out of the 40 men showing signs of nervous laughter or smiling. One participant could not complete the experiment because he went into a violent seizure, presumably as a result of the high level of stress he was experiencing.

> **ISSUES AND DEBATES**
>
> **The application of psychology to everyday life**: this study shows us how likely it is that we follow the orders of an authority figure, even when we are not comfortable doing so. Think about how this might affect people in the military, or working in hospitals where they have to carry out orders which may conflict with their own consciences or personal beliefs.

Comments made by the participants who protested at the orders given included 'I don't think I can go on with this…I don't think this is very humane', and 'I'm gonna chicken out…I can't do that to a man, I'll hurt his heart'. Nonetheless, the verbal prods given by the experimenter were generally successful in persuading the participants to continue. After the procedures ended, the participants showed visible signs of relief, wiped their faces, sighed and shook their heads. A small minority of participants, however, did not show elevated levels of stress and appeared calm during the procedure.

Voltage label	Voltage range (v)	Number of participants for whom this was maximum voltage
Slight shock	15–60	0
Moderate shock	75–120	0
Strong shock	135–180	0
Very strong shock	195–240	0
Intense shock	255–300	5
Extreme intensity shock	315–360	8
Danger: severe shock	375–420	1
XXX	435–450	26

Table 5.1 Distribution of participants' maximum shocks

Conclusions

Milgram's study supports the idea of a situational explanation for obedience. He identifies a number of factors which contributed to the high level of obedience recorded in his study. One of these factors is the perceived legitimacy of the study; the professional academic environment of the study and use of uniform by the experimenter. Other important factors which may encourage obedience include the feeling of financial obligation the participants had towards the experiment, and their belief that both they and the learner had freely volunteered to participate.

Milgram went on to draw two main conclusions from this study:

- Individuals are much more obedient to authority than we might reasonably expect. This seems to be true for the majority of people.
- Despite high levels of obedience, people find the experience of carrying out destructive acts under the orders of authority figures triggers feelings of stress. This is due to a conflict between two important social phenomena: the need to obey those in authority and the need to avoid harming other people.

Strengths and weaknesses

The method used in this study was a controlled observation. This means that it was possible to control extraneous variables in the environment, such as the age and appearance of the actor playing the stooge. This meant that the level of shock administered by each participant was not based on whether the participant felt more or less sympathetic towards different stooges (e.g. they might have been less willing to deliver shocks to an older individual). Also, the procedure was standardised throughout; the verbal prods used by the experimenter were the same each time. The level of control and standardisation of the procedure means the research was more **reliable**, because each participant went through exactly the same experience. The clever design of the electric shock generator and the example shock given to participants improved the **validity** of the design, because it ensured that participants were convinced that the study was real and that their actions actually mattered.

Reflections: Why is validity so important in this study? Why was it so essential participants believed that they were delivering real shocks? Consider the evidence in Milgram's results which support the idea that the study was believable.

The participants in this study were all males, and came from the same local area. This could mean that the **sample** was low in **generalisability**; it would not be possible to predict what differences there might be in obedience levels between men and women, for example. However, Milgram carefully selected participants to ensure a range of ages and backgrounds. This means that the sample has greater **validity**. It showed that even those with professional backgrounds who are more likely to be in positions of power are susceptible to obeying the commands of an authority figure.

The main measure of obedience was through the voltage of shocks delivered. This is a quantitative measurement, which offered an **objective** record of obedience for each participant. It made it easy to compare the results of the participants and draw conclusions about the overall amount of destructive obedience seen in this study. However, this measure alone did not fully explain the experience of the participants. Qualitative measures such as the notes of observers were used to capture the physical and verbal behaviour of those administering the shocks. Although this data is more **subjective**, it provided a richer understanding of the tension between wanting to obey orders and wanting to obey one's own conscience. Furthermore, interviews with the participants after the procedure also helped explain some of the behaviour of the participants.

This study had major **ethical issues**. Although participants had consented to take part in the research, they did not give their informed consent as they were told the study was about memory and punishment. Participants were repeatedly deceived throughout the study, as well. For example, they were led to believe they had chosen the role of teacher by chance when in fact it was a set-up. Furthermore, participants were arguably denied their right to withdraw. Although they were told they could keep the payment for participation no matter when they left, many felt as though they had to keep going with the shocks out of obligation to the research and as a result of the verbal prods.

ISSUES AND DEBATES

Ethical issues are particularly important to Milgram's research, which caused outrage at the time of its publication. In some ways this research can be considered harmful to the reputation of psychology. It tells us uncomfortable truths about the power of situational factors over ordinary individuals. It might also lead to distrust by the general public who may not want to take part in future research studies.

Participants were not protected from psychological harm; many underwent visible and extreme distress, yet in only one trial was the procedure stopped. All participants were debriefed and told the true aim of the study, as well as being reassured that they had not done any real harm. However, there is the potential for lasting negative consequences to the participants, who may have felt deeply disturbed by their own behaviour.

SELF-ASSESSMENT QUESTIONS

1 The study by Milgram collected both quantitative and qualitative data. Give **one** quantitative and **one** qualitative finding.

2 Milgram's findings support the situational explanation for obedience. Identify **two** features of the situation which may have contributed to the high levels of obedience seen in this study.

5.2 Core study 2:
Piliavin et al. (subway Samaritans)

Piliavin, I. M., Rodin, J., & Piliavin, J. (1969). Good Samaritanism: An underground phenomenon? *Journal of Personality and Social Psychology, 13*(4), 289–299.

Aim
Following on from previous laboratory-based studies, the researchers aimed to study **bystander** behaviour in a natural setting. They also wanted to investigate the effect of four situational variables on helping behaviour or '**Good Samaritanism**':

- the type of victim
- the race of the victim
- the behaviour of a 'model'
- the size of the group of bystanders.

🔑 **KEY TERMS**

bystander: a person who is present at, but may not be directly involved in, a particular situation. 'Bystander apathy' or the 'bystander effect' refers to the actions of bystanders who don't help others in the event of an emergency.

Good Samaritan: this term originates from the New Testament in the Bible. It refers to a story of a Samaritan (person originating from ancient Samaria) who stops to offer help to an injured stranger.

Background
A key trigger for research into bystander behaviour was the murder of a young woman called Kitty Genovese (Figure 5.4) in New York City in 1964. After returning from her work during the early hours of the morning, Miss Genovese was followed and assaulted by an assailant near her home. One witness had called down to warn off her attacker as Miss Genovese screamed that she was being stabbed. Her attacker was scared off but returned to continue the assault. It was alleged in news reports of the time that around 38 individuals living nearby were either eye or ear witnesses to the crime, but failed to prevent her murder. While it is impossible to say what each person saw or interpreted, the event triggered the interest of social psychologists who tried to understand the behaviour of the bystanders.

5.4 Newspaper article about Kitty Genovese

Reflections: With so many witnesses to the murder of Kitty Genovese, stop and ask yourself why people might have been reluctant to get involved. Did they just not care, or could there be other explanations? Try to think of as many explanations as you can.

One explanation for the lack of bystander helping was outlined by Darley and Latané (1968). They found that bystanders who believed that there were other people witnessing an emergency, such as over-hearing someone having an epileptic seizure, were significantly less likely to help than those who believed they were alone in hearing the event. The explanation for this is known as the **diffusion of responsibility** hypothesis. Alternatively, if we witness those around us assisting or 'modelling' helping behaviour, we may be more likely to imitate and engage in helping.

There is also evidence to suggest that we are more likely to help some people than others. For example, we may be more willing to assist those whom we perceive as more similar to ourselves. Some studies have shown that bystander helping occurs more when victims are not seen as responsible for their circumstances (Schopler and Matthews, 1965). This may be because they evoke less sympathy from those around them.

KEY TERM

diffusion of responsibility: a person is less likely to take action in an emergency where there are others there also able to help. In a large group, the perceived sense of individual responsibility towards those in need is 'diffused' or reduced to the extent that people feel little obligation to intervene. An explanation for the bystander effect.

Method

Research method and design

This study was a **field experiment**. This means it took place in a realistic environment; in this case, the New York City subway. It can be described as using an independent groups design, as the trials were repeated on different days and involved different participants in each condition.

Reflections: The study intended to use different participants for each of the trials. Why might this not have been guaranteed? Consider the impact this might have had on the results of the study.

There were four independent variables (IVs) which corresponded to the factors outlined in the aims of the study. They were operationalised as:

- the type of victim: the levels were 'drunk' or 'ill' victim
- the race of the victim: the levels were black or white victim

- the behaviour of a 'model': the levels were a model who was either close to or distant from the victim helped, either early or late in the event
- the size of the group of bystanders: this level was the naturally occurring number of passengers present in the subway carriage.

The dependent variable (DV) was the level of bystander helping. In quantitative terms, this was operationalised as the time taken for the first passenger to help, as well as the total number of passengers who helped. The race, gender and location in the carriage of each helper were also recorded. Qualitative data was recorded in the form of verbal remarks made by passengers during each incident.

RESEARCH METHODS

A **field experiment** is a type of study that takes place in everyday locations, rather than the controlled environment of a lab. It still has an experimental design, meaning that independent variables are manipulated by the researcher, while the dependent variables are measured.

Sample

This study took place on the New York subway. Participants were passengers travelling on an underground service between Harlem and the Bronx weekdays between 11 a.m. and 3 p.m. We might regard this 'unsolicited' sample as an opportunity sample as they were not deliberately selected for participation. The total estimated number of participants was 4450 people, of whom around 45% were black and 55% were white. The mean number of passengers per carriage was 43, and the mean number of people in the critical area (where the incident took place) was 8.5.

Procedure

Four teams of student researchers carried out the study, following a standard procedure. On each trial, two male and two female students boarded the train using different doors. The female confederates sat in the area adjacent to the immediate 'critical' area where the incident took place (see Figure 5.5). They observed the passengers and recorded data during each trial. The male confederates took the roles of the victim and the model. The victim stood at the pole in the centre of the critical area, and the model remained standing throughout the trial.

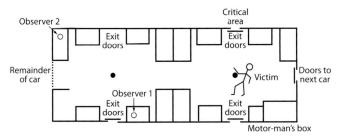

5.5 Layout of adjacent and critical areas of the subway carriage

Each trial used the same route, because it included a 7.5 minute gap between two stations. At approximately 70 seconds into the journey, the 'victim' staggered forward and collapsed. He remained lying on the floor looking upwards. If he received no help, the model would help him to his feet at the next stop.

RESEARCH METHODS

Even though this is a field experiment, there was considerable **standardisation** between trials and **controls** that ensured there were few differences between different conditions. For example, the 'victim' was always identically dressed and behaved in the same way for all trials.

The victim was played by different males during the study, but all were made to look similar. They were aged 26 to 35 years; three were white and one was black. They were dressed in identical, casual clothing (jacket, old trousers, no tie). On 38 out of 103 trials the victim smelled of alcohol and carried a bottle of alcohol wrapped in a brown bag. On the remaining 65 trials they appeared sober and carried a black cane. In all other ways they behaved identically.

Reflections: There were an uneven number of 'drunk' and 'cane' trials. The student confederates reported that they did not like playing the drunk victim. Why might this be?

The models were all white males aged 24 to 29 years of age, who were also dressed informally. When helping, the model raised the victim to the sitting position and stayed with him until the train reached the next stop.

Trials were split into the following conditions:

- Critical/early: model stood in critical area and waited 70 seconds to help victim
- Critical/late: model stood in critical area and waited 150 seconds to help victim

- Adjacent/early: model stood in adjacent area and waited 70 seconds to help victim
- Adjacent/late: model stood in adjacent area and waited 150 seconds to help victim
- No model condition: the model did not help the victim until after the trial was over and the train had reached the next stop.

Results

Overall, the frequency of helping recorded in this study was much higher than had previously been reported in laboratory studies. The majority of the helpers were male. Nearly 80% of victims received spontaneous help (i.e. helped before model intervened or in a no-model condition), and in around 60% of cases more than one person helped.

There were key differences in levels of helping between different conditions of the study, as seen in Table 5.2. In terms of the type of victim, participants were more likely to help the victim with the cane than the drunk victim (the cane victim received help in 62/65 trials; the drunk victim received help in 19/38 trials). In the cane trials, spontaneous helping also occurred earlier than in the drunk trials. For example, in all but three of the cane trials that were also model trials, helping occurred before the model could give assistance.

Trial	White victim		Black victim	
	Cane	**Drunk**	**Cane**	**Drunk**
No model	100%	100%	100%	73%
Model trial	100%	77%	–*	67%

*No model trials for the black 'victim' were run for the cane condition

Table 5.2 Percentage of trials in which help was given

In terms of race, both black and white cane victims were equally likely to receive help. However, there was some minor evidence of same-race helping in the drunk condition, with participants being more willing to offer help to those of their own race. In the drunk condition, black victims were found to receive less help overall. Although these results were non-significant, they would have supported research suggesting people are more likely to help those similar to themselves, as they feel more empathy towards them.

The effect of modelling was difficult to analyse, because most of the helping that occurred was spontaneous. However, it appeared that early model intervention at 70 seconds was slightly more likely to result in helping behaviour than waiting until 150 seconds had passed.

Reflections: Piliavin et al. found that people are more likely to help when they had watched a model help quite quickly after the victim collapsed. What explanation might there be for this?

Surprisingly, unlike previous studies, this research found no evidence to support the diffusion of responsibility hypothesis. In fact, there was some evidence to suggest that when more passengers were present, rates of helping were also slightly higher. Looking at the graph in Figure 5.6 we can see that the hypothetical speed to respond for seven-person groups, as predicted by the diffusion of responsibility theory, is slower than for three-person groups. This is because in seven-person groups the responsibility should be diffused or shared between more individuals. In fact, natural seven-person groups were faster to respond than predicted, and faster to respond than the three-person groups. This directly opposes the prediction of diffusion of responsibility.

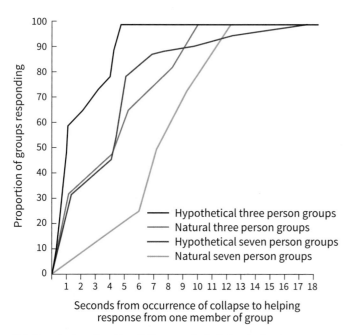

Key
- Hypothetical three person groups
- Natural three person groups
- Hypothetical seven person groups
- Natural seven person groups

Seconds from occurrence of collapse to helping response from one member of group

5.6 Graph showing the difference in helping behaviour between the groups

Additional observations showed that the majority of helpers were male. Observers noted that in around 20% of trials, passengers actually moved away from the critical area where the incident was taking place. There were a higher number of comments made during trials without helping. There were also more comments made during trials with a drunk victim.

Piliavin et al. proposed an alternative explanation for their findings, known as the **'cost–benefit model'** (Figure 5.7). They suggest that witnessing an emergency raises an individual's level of arousal. They may either become more likely to feel disgust and aversion, or even sympathy and courage. This heightened arousal level prompts individuals to act, in order to reduce difficult feelings.

> **KEY TERM**
>
> **cost–benefit model:** involves a decision-making process in which a person weighs up both the advantages and disadvantages of helping. If it seems beneficial to help, then the person is more likely to do so; if the risks are too great, they may refrain.

5.7 Weighing up the pros and cons of helping

Reflections: Using the cost–benefit model proposed by Piliavin et al., consider the costs and benefits of helping and not helping in both the cane and drunk conditions. Does this support the findings of the study?

Potential responses include helping directly (as seen in most trials in this study) or indirectly (asking others to help). Individuals may alternatively leave the area where the incident is taking place (as seen in some trials) or determine the victim should not be helped. This final response is evidenced in comments by passengers who expressed disgust or dismissal at the drunk victim's collapse.

Conclusions

This study found that in a natural setting, many people would offer spontaneous help to a stranger, even in a group situation. This study found no evidence of diffusion of responsibility, but did identify several factors which may determine decisions to help:

- the type of victim (someone using a cane will be helped more than a drunk person)
- the gender of the helper (men are more likely to help than women)

- people may be more likely to help members of their own race, especially if the victim is drunk
- the longer an emergency continues, the less likely it is that anyone will help, and the more likely it is they will find another way of coping with arousal.

Strengths and weaknesses

The method used in this study was a field experiment which used independent measures. This meant that it had good **ecological validity**; the participants were ordinary train passengers who were unaware they were taking part in the experiment. They would have behaved naturally as they believed the emergency situation to be real. However, one limitation of this method is that there is less control over extraneous variables, such as the weather conditions or train delays, which could affect the participants' behaviour and lower the **validity** and **reliability** of the study.

There are other methodological issues with the study. For example, the experimenters cannot be sure that participants only took part in the experiment once; as they used the same route each time there is a chance participants may have been exposed to more than one condition of the experiment. Suspecting that the emergency was a set-up might have made the participants more or less likely to offer help, creating **demand characteristics**.

Reflections: Field experiments are often affected by a lack of control of extraneous variables. Can you identify ways in which the researchers improved validity through standardising their procedure?

The participants in this study were all subway passengers from New York City, which means that the **sample** is unrepresentative. It would not be possible to predict levels of bystander helping in other countries from this study. However, the design of the study meant that around 4500 individuals participated in the study, which included a mix of ethnicities and genders. This large sample therefore is likely to be quite representative and has greater **validity**.

The main recorded measure of bystander helping was the number of helpers and how long they took to help. This quantitative measurement ensured an **objective** record, made more **reliable** by the presence of two observers. The observers also recorded qualitative data including the remarks and movements made by the passengers during each trial. This allowed the researchers to understand the thoughts and behaviours associated with helping in more depth.

This study raised serious **ethical issues**. Firstly, participants did not give their consent to take part in the research, nor were they debriefed after the study had finished. Participants were deceived during the study, as they believed the victim had genuinely collapsed and needed help. They might have suffered psychological distress as a result of the study, guilt at not helping or concern about the well-being of the victim.

111

5.3 Core study 3: Yamamoto et al. (chimpanzee helping)

Yamamoto, S., Humle, T., & Tanaka, M. (2012). Chimpanzees' flexible targeted helping based on an understanding of conspecifics' goals. *Proceedings of the National Academy of Sciences, 109*(9), 3588–3592.

Aim

The aim of the study was to learn more about helping behaviour in chimpanzees. Specifically, the researchers wanted to find out:

- whether chimpanzees can understand the needs of **conspecifics**
- whether chimpanzees can respond to those needs with targeted helping.

KEY TERM

conspecific: member of the same species. Therefore, in this study, 'conspecifics' refers to other chimpanzees.

Background

In order to maintain cooperative societies, humans engage extensively in helping behaviours (Figure 5.8). Other animals engage in helping, but more often at the request of their conspecifics. In other words, they may not help spontaneously or voluntarily but rather at the direct request of others. The ability to offer targeted help to members of our own species relies on an understanding of their goals, which is linked to 'theory of mind' (ToM) ability.

5.8 Altruistic helping in human society

As you may remember from Section 3.2, ToM refers to our capacity to understand the intentions and needs of others. Some people believe that ToM is unique to humans, and can explain why they are the only species to demonstrate **altruistic** helping. However, some recent studies have shown that some primates have the capacity for helping and food sharing, without direct benefit to themselves (Figure 5.9)

KEY TERM

altruistic: acting helpfully towards others without obvious benefit to oneself. An example of this might be chasing after a stranger in order to return their wallet, which involves no guarantee of reward.

5.9 Direct requests for help elicit more responses in chimpanzees

One explanation for conspecific animal helping is known as targeted or instrumental helping. It is a cognitive explanation for social behaviour; where the type of care or help given is based on a cognitive understanding of the need or situation of others. There is some evidence to suggest that chimpanzees can engage in targeted helping following direct requests (e.g. an outstretched arm requesting food), but little is known about whether they have any ability to interpret the needs of conspecifics.

Reflections: Can you think of some everyday examples of targeted helping? Try to think of three different situations. Consider how we might guess that someone needs our help, even if they don't directly ask for it.

Method
Research method and design

This study was a laboratory experiment. It took place in an artificial environment where the chimpanzees were seated at adjacent experimental booths (see Figure 5.10).

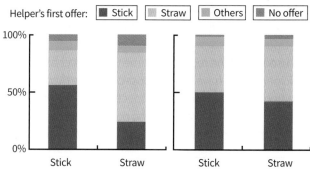

5.10 Illustrations of the 'can see' and 'cannot see' conditions

The independent variable (IV) was the ability of the chimpanzee to give targeted helping to another chimpanzee. There were two conditions in the task. In the first, the potential helper chimpanzee was able to see the other's tool-use situation, in the second they could not see. The study used a repeated measures design, which means that all the chimpanzees took part in both conditions of the experiment.

Reflections: This study used a repeated measures design. Why do you think this design was chosen for this experiment, in preference to an independent measures design?

The dependent variable was the targeted helping behaviour. This was operationalised as the items offered by the participants to conspecifics. The item offered was either the correct tool (stick or straw, depending on situation) or an incorrect non-tool item (e.g. a piece of string). The behaviour of the participants was recorded on video camera and was used to produce quantitative data; the number of correctly targeted offers per condition. The video also captured the behaviour of the chimpanzees, such as how they moved, responses to gestures, as well as where they were looking while they sat in the experimental booths.

Sample

Five chimpanzee participants who were socially housed within the Primate Research Institute at Kyoto University took part in this study. Each had previously been a part of a number of other perceptual and cognitive studies, including some investigating helping behaviour in a similar setting to the present study. In each trial, the chimpanzee participants were paired in mother and child pairs. This was because each pair had already demonstrated frequent tool-giving interactions in previous experiments. Also, they were familiar with the tool-use tasks used in this study.

Reflections: Experiments with primates often rely on the use of charts composed of symbols. In this study, the chimpanzees communicated directly with one another. This meant that their natural communicative abilities could be observed in situations of flexible and spontaneous helping. What do you see as the challenges of directly observing chimpanzee communication?

Procedure

The experimenters designed the experimental task in order to examine the ability and flexibility of chimpanzees to help a conspecific, depending on their need. A chimpanzee had to select a tool that would help the other chimpanzee to solve a problem. One task required a stick and the other required a straw. Solving the task allowed the second chimpanzee in the pair to obtain a reward: a juice drink.

Seven objects (including a stick and a straw) were placed in a booth occupied by a potential helper (see Figure 5.11). This could not be reached by the potential recipient but could be requested by the chimpanzee poking his or her arm through a hole to gesture. This allowed the experimenters to examine whether the potential helper chimpanzee was able to understand what the other needed. Before any trials started, the chimpanzees went

through a familiarisation phase each day where they could examine and manipulate all the objects without the need to use them as tools or offer them to others.

5.11 Tray of items presented to participants

When the experimental trials began, each chimpanzee experienced the conditions in the same order. Firstly they were placed in the 'can see' booth in which the panel between the two chimpanzees was transparent. Next they completed the task in the 'cannot see' booth, in which the panel was opaque. Finally the 'can see' condition was repeated in order to confirm that any difference in object choice between the first two conditions was due to intentional, targeted helping and not an **order effect**.

RESEARCH METHODS

An **order effect** is when the order of conditions in an experiment has an effect on participants' behaviour. This can be a confounding variable; meaning that the validity of the results can be lowered because participants are tired, bored or have worked out what they are supposed to be doing in the study. How else could the experimenters in this study avoid creating an order effect?

Forty-eight trials were carried out in each condition; this consisted of a random order of 24 stick-use and 24 straw-use situations. Trials began when the tray of objects was presented. The trial ended when the recipient received the object and succeeded in obtaining the juice reward or after five minutes had elapsed without an object being passed. 'Offers' were counted when the chimpanzee held out the object to the recipient, whether the recipient took the object or not. Only the first offer of help was counted; subsequent offers of different items were not included in the data. Between two and four trials were conducted per day.

Results

The experimenters found that chimpanzees are capable of flexible targeted helping based on an understanding of

113

the other's goals. In the 'can see' condition, objects were offered in 91% of trials, and this mostly occurred following requests from the paired chimpanzee (i.e. holding out hand through the hole in the panel). This can be compared to the pre-test familiarisation trials, where 'offering' occurred in only around 5% of trials.

Apart from one individual, all chimpanzees first offered tools (stick or straw) on significantly more occasions than non-tool objects. This bias suggests that the chimpanzees were able to discriminate between potential tools and non-tools. In addition, the chimpanzees selected the correct tool (stick or straw) to offer their partner over a significant number of trials. This suggests the chimpanzees used targeted helping through understanding of the task confronting their partner.

In the 'cannot see' condition, at least one object was offered in 96% of trials. Again, offering occurred mostly at the request of the paired conspecific. Like the first condition, all but one chimpanzee first offered a potential tool significantly more often than non-tools. This chimpanzee, 'Pan', mainly offered the brush item at first. When this item was removed from her tray, she made appropriate tool offers similar to the other chimpanzees.

An important difference was observed between 'can' and 'cannot see' conditions: in the 'can see' condition, there was a significant difference in which tool (stick or straw) was offered, depending on the task requirement (Figure 5.12). In the 'cannot see' condition there was no significant difference in which tool was offered in all but one of the chimpanzees. The one chimpanzee named Ayumu who did select the correct tool more often was able to stand and peer through a hole in the wall. He did so in order to view his partner chimpanzee (his mother) and observe the task that she was facing.

The results suggest that the chimpanzees were only able to understand their partner's goals when able to see the task themselves. The partner chimpanzees performed request actions with similar method and frequency in both conditions; this behaviour did not communicate information regarding specific needs (such as the appropriate tool required).

The third trial, a repeat of the 'can see' condition, was undertaken with three chimpanzees who had previously shown a significant difference in tool selection in the 'can see' condition and a non-significant difference in the 'cannot see' condition. Object offer was observed in 98% of trials; offer upon request accounted for around 80%. There was a significant difference in offer of stick or straw,

depending on the partner chimpanzee's situation. This confirms flexible targeted helping with an understanding of the tool needed to complete the task, when the chimpanzees could see the task for themselves.

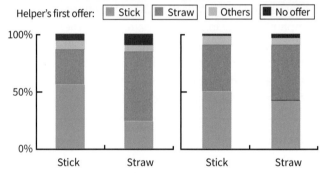

5.12 Results of the helping conditions

Conclusions

Chimpanzees can understand the needs of conspecifics in order to help them in successfully solving tasks.

- They will offer help to conspecifics who require it in the majority of cases, but usually as a response to a direct request rather than as a spontaneous act.
- Chimpanzees rely on visual confirmation of conspecifics' needs in order to offer targeted helping.

Strengths and weaknesses

The method used in this study was a laboratory experiment. There were high levels of control in the study and a standardised procedure. For example, the presentation of the objects on the tray was the same for each trial, and the chimpanzees sat at the same booths to undergo each trial. These measures increased the **reliability** of the study. Furthermore, the experiment used a repeated measures design. This design meant that the chimpanzees participated in both or all the conditions of the study; reducing any risk of individual differences and increasing **validity**.

The study had low **ecological validity** because it was conducted in an artificial environment. The chimpanzees were given tasks and tools that they would not normally use in their natural environment. However, as the chimpanzees had previously taken part in laboratory studies and were therefore familiar with the task and materials used in this research, they probably showed normal behaviour. In this way it could be argued that the study was **valid**.

On the other hand, concluding that offering the correct tool is an intentional cognitive decision that involves theory of mind may not be an accurate assumption. It could be argued that the findings of this study could be a result of an automatic association created by previous experience. For example, Pan repeatedly offered the brush to her partner in early trials. This might suggested that her previous experiences with similar tasks created **bias** in her responses to this study.

The participants in this study were five chimpanzees, and came from the same research institute. This means it was a very small **sample** that is arguably low in **generalisability**. It would be difficult to say this sample of captive chimpanzees is representative of wild chimpanzee populations, although there is nothing to suggest that any of the animals was unique or unusual.

> **RESEARCH METHODS**
>
> You might think that only humans respond to **demand characteristics** but there is a range of evidence that suggests some animals do too. By looking over the top of the opaque panel, and peeking through the hole, chimpanzees in this study made it clear that they understood the nature of the task. This suggests they had an awareness of the demands of the task.

Targeted helping was observed using video recording and quantified in a standard way as no offer, offer of tool or offer of other item. Both the way in which the data was recorded and the type of data recorded provide an **objective** record of helping for each participant. Other qualitative data was gathered during the experiment such as the behaviour of one chimpanzee who looked over the opaque panel in the 'cannot see' condition. This data is important in helping us understand why the chimpanzee then showed an increase in correctly targeted helping.

> **Reflections:** No physical harm was caused to the chimpanzees during this study. What other types of harm should psychologists consider when conducting research with animals? Do you think any of these issues apply to the study by Yamamoto et al.?

This study involves animals and has some specific **ethical issues**. Although issues of consent and right to withdraw do not apply to research of this kind, there are important considerations for the animals' well-being. The researchers state that the study was approved by the Animal Care Committee of the Primate Research Institute at Kyoto University. Chimpanzees were tested and cared for in accordance with the guide produced by this committee. While specific details are not given in this study, guidance of this type typically recommends that treatment of animal participants is humane. This might involve ensuring that the basic needs of animals are met, such as adequate access to food and shelter (Figure 5.13). This study focuses on helping tasks, and does not involve punishment or physical harm to the chimpanzees.

5.13 Chimpanzees in captivity

> **SELF-ASSESSMENT QUESTIONS**
>
> 5 The research by Yamamoto et al. used experimental booths in their set-up. Give **two** details describing the set-up of the booths.
>
> 6 This study used a repeated measures design. Identify both conditions of the IV which all participants completed.

5.4 Issues, debates and approaches

Application of psychology to everyday life

Milgram's study has important implications for understanding obedience in the real world. Previously it was believed that acts of extreme, destructive obedience such as the Holocaust had a dispositional explanation (i.e. that Germans were somehow very different from other people). However, Milgram's later research (1974) and other work inspired by his findings has shown that situational variables such as the legitimacy of authority can elicit destructive obedience in nearly anyone. A result of this is a raised awareness of the power of authority in the workplace. For example, some hospitals have introduced whistle-blowing policies to encourage reporting of mistakes by doctors or other senior staff in order to protect the safety and well-being of patients.

Piliavin et al.'s study has interesting practical applications as well. It tells us about specific situational factors which may make bystanders more likely to help. For example, it may be useful to know that people may be more willing to help if they are of the same sex or race as the victim, or in a situation that they cannot easily just walk past. It shows us that a person in need may be more likely to get help from a stranger if they do not risk embarrassing, intimidating or disgusting them.

The study by Yamamoto et al. demonstrates that chimpanzees, like humans, have the capacity and inclination to help conspecifics. It can also help us to understand more about how chimpanzee societies work in the wild.

Individual and situational explanations

Milgram's research was particularly significant in highlighting the importance of situational factors in influencing how obedient we are to authority figures. Findings from his study showed that the majority of people will be destructively obedient if they feel that the authority figure is legitimate or the cause is worthy, for example.

However, some individuals are more resistant to authority than others – not all participants inflicted the full voltage on the learner as directed. This suggests that there is a role for individual factors, which may affect overall levels of obedience as well.

> **Reflections:** Piliavin et al. also considered situational factors. Can you explain how each of the trial conditions (victim type, race, model, size of group) influenced helping behaviour?

Yamamoto et al.'s study is interesting in that it shows the influence of individual and situational factors on the helping behaviour of chimpanzees. Most chimpanzees demonstrated similar patterns of behaviour in a social situation because they offered tools to conspecifics in need. However, one chimpanzee showed a clear preference for a specific non-tool, possibly as a result of their own prior learning. Another chimpanzee initiated problem-solving in the 'cannot see' condition by peering over the opaque panel to observe his partner. Both of these cases demonstrate the influence of individual personalities on common social behaviours.

Use of animals in psychological research

The study of flexible, targeted helping by Yamamoto et al. is useful in that it can allow us to make some comparisons between chimpanzees and humans. For example, a more recent study has shown that such chimpanzee helping approximates the level of helping shown by 18-month-old toddlers (Svetlova et al., 2010). They have capacity for understanding the needs of others, as well as a willingness to help. In contrast, by around 30 months, humans have developed capacity for spontaneous helping. However, the cognitive processes involved in theory of mind in humans and primates are not yet well understood. Furthermore, the culture of chimpanzee societies is quite different from humans (e.g. family structures, group sizes and hierarchies), which makes direct comparison difficult.

Summary

Milgram's study investigated the extent to which ordinary people obey the orders of an authority figure when they involve physically harming an innocent person. All participants were willing to give high levels of electric shocks at the command of a researcher, with a significant majority of people willing to give the maximum shock level possible. This was a well-controlled naturalistic observation collecting measure of the dependent variable through objective measurements which were reliable. Qualitative data suggested that most participants showed signs of stress during the destructive obedience. The findings suggest that situational factors may be better at explaining obedience to authority than dispositional ones.

Piliavin et al.'s study considered different factors which affect bystander behaviour. It looked at how specific circumstances might make subway passengers more or less likely to help a man who had collapsed on a train. This was a field experiment involving a large number of participants. Quantitative measurements showed that victims who were ill were more likely to receive help than those who appeared drunk, and that the number of bystanders does not affect the amount of bystander helping. The findings suggest that diffusion of responsibility is not typical of bystander helping in natural environments.

Yamamoto et al.'s study looked at flexible targeted helping in chimpanzees. As a laboratory experiment it was well controlled and was able to show that chimpanzees can offer carefully targeted help to conspecifics. Chimpanzees were able to offer tools to their partners in most cases, and usually only when assistance was directly requested. Careful observation of the participants' behaviour provided reliable measures of helping, although the experiment only used a small sample. The findings show that humans may not be unique in possessing some capacity for theory of mind as they suggest chimpanzees can understand the goals and needs of others.

Exam-style questions

1 Although Milgram's study (obedience) is often used as an example of poor ethics, there were many ways in which he made good ethical decisions.
   a Describe **two** guidelines which Milgram could be said to have tried to follow. **[2 marks]**
   b Explain how **each** of these two ethical guidelines was followed by Milgram. **[4 marks]**

2 Piliavin et al. (subway Samaritans) concluded that their results did not support the 'diffusion of responsibility' hypothesis. Explain this conclusion using evidence from the study. **[6 marks]**

3 State **two** aims from the study by Yamamoto et al. (chimpanzee helping) and explain whether each one was supported by the study. **[6 marks]**

117

Issues and debates at A Level

From your AS Level you will have gained an understanding of some of the important debates and issues in psychology, including the application of psychology to everyday life, individual and situational explanations, nature versus nurture, and the use of children and animals in psychological research. You will need to learn to apply these ideas to the new topics you explore at A Level. As the A Level course is based on applied topics, you will find that the 'applications to everyday life' are very obvious, so you can consider the extent to which these applications are useful and how valid and reliable you feel the research is that supports them.

In addition to the AS issues and debates, there are five additional issues and debates at A Level. These are:

- cultural bias
- reductionism
- determinism
- psychometrics
- longitudinal research.

Cultural bias in research is important as much evidence is collected on narrow samples; exclusively or predominantly from one ethnic group. The findings of such research may not apply to other cultures. This would mean that any decisions based on the evidence would be potentially flawed. You will need to consider whether this applies to the research you are reading about and, if so, whether it is important in this instance.

Reductionism relates to the extent to which a psychological phenomenon, such as a feature of our emotions, thinking or behaviour, is explained by a theory or concept in terms of its most basic elements. In practice this means 'reducing' explanations to biological factors such as the actions of

neurotransmitters (the chemicals that send messages between nerve cells) or genes. However, in a wider sense, reductionism may refer to considering only some of many elements that are important in explaining a phenomenon, such as looking only at cognitive factors (to do with the way we think) and excluding biological or social ones.

Determinism refers to the extent to which a psychological phenomenon, such as a feature of our emotions, thinking or behaviour is governed by processes that are beyond our control. A 'deterministic' view suggests that we have little free will to choose how we feel, think or behave and we are the product of biological, social or other environmental influences.

Two aspects of research methods are also issues at A Level. **Psychometrics** refers to the measurement of psychological phenomena, such as intelligence, personality or pain. Debates surround the appropriateness and effectiveness of such measures.

Finally, much research in psychology looks at participants over a short time span – the period they spend in the laboratory to complete a study for example. **Longitudinal research**, in contrast, follows participants over a period of time so we can see developmental changes or other kinds of progress. The relative strengths and weaknesses of this approach can be considered in relation to short timespan studies. For example, experiments are typically done in a few hours, so consider each individual for only a brief moment. That time may or may not happen to be typical of that individual and can only capture their behaviour at that instant. A longitudinal study, or case study in contrast, may explore an individual for many days, or over a much longer period. Such studies can therefore see both fluctuations in behaviour and progressions over time.

Chapter 6
Psychology and abnormality

Introduction

This chapter introduces you to five key topics within abnormality:

- **schizophrenic and psychotic disorders**, including the characteristics of the disorder, and a closer look at symptom assessment and treatments

- **bipolar and related disorders**, including definitions and types of such as unipolar depression and bipolar depression, with a range of explanations and treatments

- **impulse control disorders and non-substance addictive disorders**, including measures of addiction and ways of managing these disorders, such as positive reinforcement techniques

- **anxiety disorders**, including types of phobias and treatment options like cognitive-behavioural therapy

- **obsessive compulsive and related disorders**, including common obsessions and compulsions such as hoarding, along with comparison of different explanations and treatments.

You will find out about the nature of a range of mental health disorders and how they are classified and diagnosed. You will discover competing explanations for the origin of these disorders from different approaches to psychology, as well as considering several treatment options for each. Relevant issues and debates will be explored throughout each of the topics, and you will be reminded throughout about how psychological research methods are used in the study of abnormality.

Understanding abnormality

Abnormal psychology looks at how we define normal and abnormal behaviour in society. Consider for a moment what normality means to you. Would you find it abnormal to kiss or hug a person when you greet them? Would it seem more normal if they were a close friend or family member? What is normal and acceptable in one situation or culture can be offensive and appear abnormal in others. When does behaviour that is socially unconventional become 'abnormal', or even a sign of mental disorder?

Mental disorders are not just something that happens to other people. The majority of people will at some point in their lives be affected by these issues either directly, or have a friend or family member who receives a mental health diagnosis. Psychology can help us to understand the different sorts of disorders that exist, as well as possible causes and options for treatment. In this way, psychology can encourage individuals to seek help for their illness, whilst challenging myths and stigma around particular disorders.

For the most part, psychologists and psychiatrists rely on a system of classification for mental disorders, much like we have systems for categorising physical disorders of the body. This is determined by considering the abnormal symptoms an individual might be experiencing. Having a recognised system for diagnosis and standardised measurement tools arguably improves the validity and

reliability of diagnosis. We will also consider controversies and challenges in this section.

There is huge debate over what causes mental disorders. Each approach in psychology can offer competing and, in some cases, complementary explanations. Biological or biomedical explanations focus on physical causes of disorders, such as chemical imbalances in the brain or genetic links. By contrast, the cognitive approach looks at factors relating to mental processes, such as dysfunctional thought patterns, whereas behaviourists believe abnormal behaviour is a result of learning. Once appropriate mental health diagnoses are reached, there are a range of treatment options. Current psychological research can offer insight as to how successful competing approaches to managing disorders can be, helping to improve the lives of millions of people worldwide.

> **Reflections:** Determining the best treatment may take into consideration any identifiable cause of the disorder as well as the patient's own wishes. Consider someone who has experienced a very traumatic event and suffers from a mental health disorder as a result. How much say should patients, their families and their healthcare providers have in deciding how to manage their illness?

6.1 Schizophrenic and psychotic disorders

Psychotic disorders involve a major break from reality in which the individual perceives their world in a way that is very different from how others perceive it. Schizophrenia is a particularly severe type of psychotic disorder that affects all aspects of a person's thinking, emotions and actions.

Characteristics of schizophrenia spectrum and psychotic disorders

These disorders share some common symptoms. The schizophrenia spectrum refers to several different but similar disorders which vary in their **duration** and **severity**.

KEY TERMS

duration: length of time the individual experiences the symptoms or illness.

severity: the intensity with which the individual experiences the symptoms or illness.

Definitions, types, examples and case studies

The current **Diagnostic and Statistical Manual** of Mental Disorders (DSM-5, American Psychiatric Association, 2013) defines schizophrenic spectrum and psychotic disorders as sharing one or more of the following (the first four are sometimes called 'positive symptoms'):

- Delusions – beliefs individuals hold which are not based on reality. For example, falsely believing that other people are trying to harm or kill you.

- Hallucinations – sensory experiences that may involve seeing and hearing things that do not exist, e.g. 'hearing voices'.
- Disorganised thoughts – thoughts may be mixed up and racing; the person's speech might be jumbled and impossible to understand.
- Catatonic behaviour – the person may not react to things in the environment and remain rigid and unmoving in awkward poses, or engage in constant, repetitive movements.
- Negative symptoms – a loss of normal functioning, such as loss of speech, or lack of typical facial expressions.

The main types of schizophrenia spectrum and psychotic disorders are listed in Table 6.1. Schizotypal personality disorder, for example, is characterised by great difficulty in developing emotionally meaningful relationships with others and showing extreme 'coldness' and flat **affect**. Another example of these types of disorder is substance or medication-induced psychotic disorder. Heavy, prolonged use of alcohol over many years can lead to this disorder, as can withdrawal from certain types of illegal substances.

 KEY TERM

affect: a person's feelings or emotions. A 'flat' affect can refer to a lack of visible response such as a frown or smile.

Schizotypal (personality) disorder
Delusional disorder
Brief psychotic disorder/schizophreniform disorder
Schizophrenia
Schizoaffective disorder
Substance/medication-induced psychotic disorder
Psychotic disorder due to another medical condition
Catatonia associated with another mental disorder or condition
Unspecified schizophrenia spectrum and other psychotic disorder

Table 6.1 DSM-5 Schizophrenia spectrum and other psychotic disorders (adapted from Black and Grant, 2014, page 62)

Perhaps the most well-known disorder in this category is schizophrenia. Those with schizophrenia show at least one of the following symptoms: delusions, hallucinations and/

or disorganised speech, and may also include catatonic behaviour or negative symptoms. These signs must have been present for at least six months and cannot be attributed to use of illegal substances or medication. The individual must also show a reduction in normal functioning (for example, difficulty maintaining personal relationships, caring for themselves or going to work or school).

Case study:
Conrad (male aged 23)

Conrad had his first psychotic episode whilst on holiday when he was 22 and was later diagnosed with schizo-affective disorder. At first he was reluctant to seek treatment as he was unsure that he would recover, and subsequently spent the eight months following his diagnosis in a psychiatric hospital. Through trial and error Conrad has found the right drug treatment, though maintaining a healthy weight remains a challenge.

Schizophrenia and delusional disorder

Delusional disorder is a disorder characterised by persistent delusions, but people suffering from it otherwise have quite normal behaviour, unlike those with classic schizophrenia. It also excludes those suffering other psychotic symptoms (hallucinations, disorganised speech, catatonia or negative symptoms). Examples of some of the types of delusional disorder are given in Table 6.2.

Type	Description
Erotomanic	Belief that another person is in love with them
Grandiose	Convinced they have a great unrecognised skill or status
Jealous	Belief that partner is being unfaithful
Persecutory	Belief that the person is being conspired against or pursued by others who intend to harm them

Table 6.2 Types of delusional disorder

Reflections: Using the table above, can you write your own examples of delusional thoughts for each type of delusional disorder?

Some delusions may also be 'bizarre'. This means that they are clearly impossible or beyond the realm of

121

ordinary occurrence. For example, delusional disorder with bizarre content might involve believing that one's internal organs had been removed and replaced with those of another, without leaving any wounds or scars. Non-bizarre delusions might include the belief that one's partner is cheating on them, or that their boss wants to fire them. The main difference is that non-bizarre delusions could be true or possible (but unlikely) whereas bizarre delusions may be logically impossible or difficult to understand.

In order to receive a **diagnosis** of delusional disorder, the individual must have been experiencing symptoms for one month or longer. The DMS-5 states that symptoms should be unrelated to physiological effects of substance use, and are not better explained by another psychological or medical disorder.

> **KEY TERM**
>
> **diagnosis:** the process of understanding which mental disorder can best explain an individual's symptoms. Like diagnosing physical problems, it involves looking for particular signs that meet the criteria for known illnesses.

Symptom assessment using virtual reality (Freeman, 2008)

Difficulties with diagnosing schizophrenia and related disorders can relate to interpretation of the individual's experiences in the social world. Social interaction may involve misinterpretation of other people's behaviour and can lead to distrust, paranoia and withdrawal. In one study, Freeman (2008) explores the potential for the use of virtual reality to eliminate such challenges when checking symptoms and developing treatment for schizophrenia. Virtual reality (VR) involves using the technology for presenting different social environments to the user, and has been applied successfully in the treatment and management of other disorders, such as social phobias.

Typically, symptom assessment has relied on an interviewer and patient sitting in a clinical room and discussing behaviour over the previous week or month. One problem with this approach is that it relies on the individual answering truthfully. Also, discussing existing personal circumstances cannot rule out that beliefs of persecution are unfounded. Using VR, the assessment can be novel and standardised while assessing actual behaviour. It also can ensure that paranoid thoughts and behaviour are genuine, as the social situation is totally artificial.

The technique used for VR in Freeman's research involved a specifically designed library or underground train scene where the user takes a walk or ride in the presences of other neutral avatars (see Figure 6.1) wearing VR headgear (Figure 6.2). This was trialled on a **non-clinical population** of around 200 students. Prior to the virtual reality test, a large number of validated measurement tools were used to profile each individual's levels of paranoid thinking, emotional distress and other social and cognitive traits, such as the 16 item Green et al. Paranoid Thoughts Scale (GPTS) Part B. Measures of persecutory thinking were also taken after being in the virtual environment, along with visual analogue rating scales, and an assessment of their degree of immersion in the virtual environment.

The researcher found that those who scored highly on questionnaire assessment of paranoia experienced high levels of '**persecutory ideation**' during the VR trial. This meant that they were more likely to make comments such as '*Lady sitting down next to me laughed at me when I walked past*', rather than positive or neutral comments such as '*Getting on with my own business*'. In related laboratory studies, Freeman reports that individuals who experience auditory hallucinations in the real world also experienced them in the VR environment.

> **KEY TERMS**
>
> **non-clinical population:** a term used in the study of health which refers to a group who are not specifically targeted in contrast to a clinical population which is a group of particular interest, such as those with a medical or mental health disorder.
>
> **persecutory ideation:** the process of forming an idea that one is at risk of being ill-treated or harmed by others.

6.1 The tube train virtual environment

6.2 Virtual reality headgear

Reflections: Freeman suggests that VR technology could also be used to develop treatments for schizophrenia. Can you outline a design for a simple experiment to test the effect of a particular drug on reducing persecutory ideation using a VR environment?

Evaluation

The study by Freeman (2008) used a fairly large **sample**; however, it did not represent a clinical population. The specially designed VR programme adopts a **standardised** approach to assessment which increases the **reliability** of measurement. However, it compromises the **ecological validity** of the assessment, as it involves a simulated environment quite different from what one would typically experience. It also continues to rely on **self-report** in that users of VR are asked to make comments about their experiences, which may lead to **response bias**.

ISSUES AND DEBATES

The VR **trials** outlined by Freeman (2008) have good **relevance to everyday life**, meaning that they can be used to assess patient symptoms, as well as potentially identify causal factors and treatment strategies. However, the method has not been used extensively in clinical populations at the time of Freeman's writing, meaning it is yet to be determined whether it can replace conventional clinical interviews and questionnaires in diagnosing schizophrenia.

Freeman's suggestions should also make us consider the issue of **cultural bias**. The diagnosis of schizophrenia and other psychotic disorders is particularly open to criticism because it relies on culturally based expectations of what constitutes normal social behaviour. This is important, because some cultures

ISSUES AND DEBATES (continued)

are more tolerant than others in what is considered normal with regard to hearing voices. There are also social norms around interacting in public, levels of eye contact and personal space which vary among cultures. Use of VR in diagnosing symptoms would need to take such factors into consideration to avoid creating biased interpretations of individuals' behaviour and comments.

RESEARCH METHODS
The findings of Freeman's VR trials suggested that it may be a useful technique for diagnosing schizophrenia and related disorders. What ethical considerations might there be **trialling** VR with patients presenting with possible schizophrenic symptoms?

Explanations of schizophrenia and delusional disorder

Psychologists offer competing explanations for these disorders. Here you will discover possible biological causes (genetics and biochemical) as well as a cognitive explanation.

Genetic (Gottesman & Shields, 1972)

Gottesman and Shields (1972) carried out **twin study** research into the genetic inheritance of schizophrenia. One biological explanation for mental disorders such as schizophrenia is that genes or particular combinations of genes are passed on to offspring which may cause the disorder to develop.

General symptoms of disorders like schizophrenia include features such as psychosis. On a more basic level, the experience of psychosis consists of a series of abnormalities of function; such as sensory dysfunction and working memory impairment. These specific difficulties have known genetic origins and are otherwise known as 'endophenotypes'. Thus, schizophrenic symptoms are believed to have identifiable genetic markers which may be inherited.

Twin studies are thus highly useful in the study of genetic influence, because they allow researchers to establish the relative influences of nature and nurture. For example, identical or monozygotic (MZ) twins share their entire DNA, whereas non-identical or dizygotic (DZ) twins only share around 50% of their DNA. If the occurrence of the disorder is no higher in MZ twins than DZ twins, researchers may conclude that there is little genetic **concordance**.

> **KEY TERMS**
>
> **twin study:** a type of study which compares sets of twins to analyse similarities and differences. This may include concordance for intelligence or mental disorders. Both monozygotic (MZ) and dizygotic (DZ) twins are studied, as well as twins who have been raised together or separately (i.e. adoption studies). Results may be compared with other family members such as parents or siblings to isolate the effects of nature and nurture.
>
> **concordance:** the presence of a particular observable trait or disorder in both individuals within a set of twins.

The researchers in this study drew their sample from 467 twins who were registered at the Maudsley Hospital in London between 1948 and 1964. Identifying 57 pairs of twins, they conducted a series of tests on 24 sets of MZ twins and 33 DZ twins. Twins were identified as MZ or DZ using blood group and fingerprint analysis. The researchers interviewed both the patients and their twins, some of whom also had a diagnosis of schizophrenia. Participants also undertook cognitive tests such as object sorting. In order to ensure the validity of diagnosis, case summaries of each participant were independently evaluated by judges external to the research.

Gottesman and Shields found that approximately 50% of MZ twins had a shared schizophrenic status, but that concordance was much lower in DZ twins (around 9%). In MZ twins, the co-twin was more likely to be schizophrenic if the illness of their twin was severe. For example, if one twin had been hospitalised within the last six months or had catatonic symptoms, this was classified as severe. There was then a high likelihood their co-twin also showed some schizophrenic symptoms, whereas in mild cases co-twin concordance was far lower (see Table 6.3).

Reflections: Gottesman and Shields (1972) suggested that environmental pressures also play an important role in triggering the onset of schizophrenia and related disorders. How does this contribute to our understanding of the nature vs nurture debate in psychology?

Biochemical (dopamine hypothesis) (Lindström et al., 1999)

The dopamine hypothesis essentially states that the brains of those with schizophrenia produce more dopamine than those without the disorder. Dopamine is a neurotransmitter, meaning it is a chemical substance which enables communication between two neurons. In order to allow the nerve impulse to pass between two cells, it moves across a small junction known as a 'synapse' (see Figure 6.3).

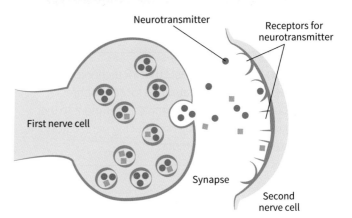

6.3 Diagram of neuron cells showing neurotransmitters

The dopamine hypothesis identifies a link between excessive amounts of dopamine or dopamine receptors and positive symptoms of schizophrenia and related disorders. Neurons that use the transmitter dopamine are thought either to fire too often, or to send too much information. Additionally, it is thought that an excess of dopamine in particular brain regions can be related to certain symptoms. For example, such an increase in the Broca's region (responsible for formation of language) can impair logical speech, a classic symptom of schizophrenia.

Evidence to support this theory comes from drug trials involving those with schizophrenia and those without the disorder. Drugs that increase the level of dopamine in the brain include amphetamines and cocaine. Large increases in dopamine production are correlated with an increase in the reporting of hallucinations and delusions.

Criteria for severity	Concordance for schizophrenia in co-twins with 'mild diagnosis'	Concordance for schizophrenia in co-twins with 'severe diagnosis'
Not working or in hospital within past six months	17%	75%
In hospital for more than two years	38%	77%
Classified as catatonic by independent judge	33%	91%

Table 6.3 Relationship between severity and concordance in MZ twins

In those with schizophrenia, the effect of ingesting these drugs is to worsen positive symptoms. Patients with Parkinson's disease are often treated with a synthetic form of dopamine called L-dopa. If their dosage is too high, it also creates symptoms in these individuals identical to those in people with schizophrenia, such as hallucinations (Lindström et al., 1999).

Post-mortem studies and brain scans can also help us to understand the neurochemistry involved. Autopsies have found that the brains of deceased individuals with schizophrenia have a larger number of dopamine receptors than those without the disorder. Wise et al. (1974) found that brain fluid from deceased patients had abnormally low levels of the enzyme which breaks down dopamine, suggesting it may have been present in excessive quantities.

Positron emission tomography (PET) scan analysis of dopamine usage indicates a greater number of receptors in the striatum, limbic system and cortex of the brain in those with schizophrenia than in those without (Figure 6.4). Excessive dopamine activity in these areas may be linked to positive symptoms, while some research (Nestler, 1997) suggests that decreased dopamine activity in the prefrontal cortex of schizophrenia patients may correlate with negative symptoms such as flattened affect.

> **KEY TERM**
>
> **Positron emission tomography (PET) scanning:** a technique which uses gamma cameras to detect radioactive tracers such as glucose which is injected into the blood. The tracer accumulates in areas of high activity during the scan, allowing them to become visible for analysis.

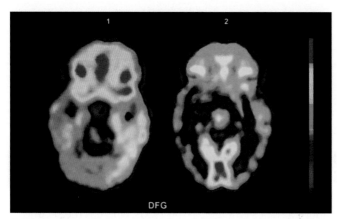

6.4 PET scans of non-schizophrenic (1) and schizophrenic (2) individuals

Cognitive (Frith, 1992)

The cognitive approach to **abnormality** recognises that biological factors contribute in some way to the positive symptoms of schizophrenia. For example, Frith (1992) accepts the role of biochemical processes, brain structure and genetic influence on the disorder. However, since no one genetic, structural or biochemical cause has been identified, he sought to frame the signs and symptoms of schizophrenia in a cognitive manner. This essentially means schizophrenia and related disorders are viewed as involving faulty mental processes, rather than relying solely on physiological explanations.

> **KEY TERM**
>
> **abnormality:** can be defined in psychology in many ways. It can mean behaviours that are rarely seen in most people, such as experiencing hallucinations. It can also be used more subjectively to refer to behaviours that are not considered normal in a particular society, or that harm the individual or those around them.

Frith describes schizophrenia as an 'abnormality of self-monitoring'. This occurs when patients fail to recognise that their perceived hallucinations are in fact just inner speech (the kind of self-talk people normally experience). It leads them to attribute what they are hearing to someone else, e.g. a voice speaking to them from an external source. He tested this idea with schizophrenic patients by asking them to decide whether items that had been read out loud were done so by themselves, an experimenter or a computer. Schizophrenic patients with incoherent speech as a symptom performed worst at the task, which may be linked to memory and attention difficulties crucial for self-monitoring.

Frith suggests that another major positive symptom, delusional thinking, may also arise from a misinterpretation of perception. Those experiencing delusions may be applying logical reasoning to their hallucinations, for example. So thoughts that are actually self-generated instead appear to be coming from an external source, and become incorporated in the individual's set of beliefs. These failures in monitoring can lead to delusions of alien control, auditory hallucinations and thought insertion. Conversely, inability to monitor the intentions of others can lead to delusions of paranoia and incoherence.

Frith explains that those experiencing negative symptoms such as a lack of action have difficulty generating spontaneous actions. This means that they are better at reacting to external stimuli in order to produce a response. This may arise in part due to impaired theory of mind, which creates problems in recognising the intentions of others (see Section 3.2). A flattening of affect, lack of speech and social withdrawal all result from difficulties in monitoring their own mental states and the states of others.

Reflections: In Section 3.2 you considered the work of Baron-Cohen et al. in exploring theory of mind in those with autistic spectrum disorder. Here, Frith suggests theory of mind impairment could be used to explain delusional thinking in those with schizophrenia. Can you give a real-life example of how a paranoid delusion might result from such impairment?

Evaluation

The study by Gottesman and Shields (1972) used a large **sample** of MZ and DZ twins. Although the results are likely to be **representative** of twins with schizophrenia because of the sample size, the findings may not be generalisable to non-twin individuals. Also, the sample was drawn from only one hospital. However, assessments were made in part by independent judges, reducing **researcher bias**. They also collected data using **qualitative** methods such as interviews, which can gain **in-depth** data about participants, though may be more **subjective**.

ISSUES AND DEBATES

The **nature versus nurture** debate is particularly relevant to understanding explanations of schizophrenia and related disorders. The **longitudinal** twin study technique employed by Gottesman and Shields (1972) attempts to establish a causal link between genetics (nature) and mental disorder. However, it is difficult to isolate nature from nurture. It is likely that MZ twins are not only more genetically similar than DZ twins, but are more likely to be treated more similarly by others. This is because they are always the same gender (unlike DZs), and may look much more alike. DZ twins, although they are the same age and live in the same environment, may experience life more like ordinary non-twin siblings. This means that not all differences between MZ and DZ twins can be simply attributed to genetics.

ISSUES AND DEBATES (continued)

Biological and cognitive explanations are often considered **reductionist**. Gottesman and Shields attribute the origin of schizophrenia to particular genes or gene combinations; the most simple biological explanation possible. However, they do acknowledge that environmental factors are important to the onset of the disorder. The dopamine hypothesis also indicates a specific biological origin, namely disruption to the normal uptake of a particular neurotransmitter.

The cognitive theory put forward by Frith is more holistic as it takes into account mental processing as well as biological causes, but could still be said to ignore social and environmental causes for the disorder. Essentially, the three explanations offered in this section therefore all point to **individual explanations** not **situational** ones. Psychologists from the social or psychodynamic traditions would look towards situational factors that contribute to the disorder, such as traumatic events or difficulty with forming early relationships.

RESEARCH METHODS

The research of Gottesman and Shields (1972) involves a **longitudinal design**, meaning the same participants were studied over an extended period of time. Why is this important for studying the concordance rate of twins with schizophrenia?

Treatment and management of schizophrenia and delusional disorders

Schizophrenia and related disorders can be especially complex to treat because of their impact on all aspects of functioning. Individuals may require treatment for acute episodes as well as help to manage independent living.

Biochemical

Although there are many different medications used to treat schizophrenia and related disorders, they can be broadly divided into two types: antipsychotics and atypical antipsychotics. These are also known as first and second generation antipsychotics, respectively. First generation antipsychotics emerged in the 1950s, whereas the second generation of these drugs came into usage during the 1990s. Both types reduce the severity of psychotic symptoms in those suffering from schizophrenia and related disorders.

Chloropromazine and other similar antipsychotics work by blocking dopamine and serotonin receptors in the cortical and limbic areas of the brain. They also affect different neurotransmitters such as serotonin and norepinephrine, depending on the individual antipsychotic. After one week, patients may appear less hostile and agitated, and after two or three weeks many report diminished positive symptoms.

> **Reflections:** With which theoretical explanation for schizophrenia does this treatment best fit?

The use of antipsychotic drugs has been thoroughly researched using randomised control trials (RCT). These trials are often **double-blind placebo controlled**, and consistently show that around 50% of those taking antipsychotic medication show significant improvement in their condition after four to six weeks. Around 30–40% show partial improvement; however a substantial minority of those remaining patients show little to no improvement in their functioning. This is what is known as 'treatment-resistant' schizophrenia.

Relapse rates using antipsychotics can be quite high. One reason for this is that patients are usually directed to keep taking medication after acute psychotic episodes, even in periods of remission (albeit at lower doses). However, the medication can cause unpleasant side effects such as weight gain, drowsiness, extrapyramidal symptoms (EPS) and tardive dyskenesia (TD). The latter two are conditions which affect motor control, and can result in involuntary spasms and abnormal movements of the face and body. When an individual experiences a reduction in symptoms combined with unpleasant side effects, **non-adherence to medication** may be the result (see Section 8.2).

KEY TERM

non-adherence to medication: this occurs when a patient goes against a physician's instructions for drug dosage, for instance by stopping taking their medication.

Atypical antipsychotics are less likely to produce unwanted side effects such as EPS and TD, yet are usually at least as effective as first generation antipsychotics. Atypical antipsychotics may also carry increased risk of side effects such as weight gain and obesity, which can lead to heart disease and diabetes.

Electro-convulsive therapy

Electro-convulsive therapy (ECT) is another biological treatment which has been applied to help alleviate symptoms of schizophrenia and related disorders. For hundreds of years, inducing seizures by other methods had been used to treat psychiatric problems. By the 1930s it was mistakenly believed that schizophrenia was very rare in those who suffered from epilepsy, which inspired the first trials of ECT on schizophrenic patients. Physicians Ugo Cerletti and Lucio Bini had discovered the potential for electricity to be used to induce seizures and unconsciousness by observing the effect electric shocks had on cattle. They modified this technique to be applied to humans; however, without the use of anti-anxiety drugs or anaesthetic, patients were often traumatised and suffered broken bones.

Modern ECT involves passing electricity through the brain with the intention of inducing a seizure; the seizure is the 'treatment' rather than the electricity (Figure 6.5). Patients usually undergo a course of ECT treatments ranging from six to 12 sessions, although some may need fewer. It is typically given twice a week during the treatment period, or less commonly at longer intervals in order to prevent relapse of symptoms. Instead of applying ECT bilaterally (across both brain hemispheres), it is now applied unilaterally to the non-dominant hemisphere to reduce memory loss. Despite improvements to the technique, there are still significant risks involved to the individual. The procedure affects the central nervous system and cardiovascular system, which can be dangerous for those with pre-existing medical conditions. Memory loss is still a common side effect of ECT, but this is usually temporary. More serious but extremely rare side effects can include lasting neurological damage or even death.

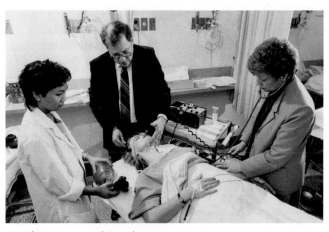

6.5 Electro-convulsive therapy

There is still no generally accepted explanation for the effect ECT has on the treatment of mental disorders. One theory is that it affects post-synaptic responses to central nervous system transmitters. ECT is rarely used in the treatment of schizophrenia because of a lack of evidence to suggest it is more effective than other forms of therapy, such as antipsychotics. Evidence suggests that ECT can be effective during acute episodes of psychosis where fast, short-term improvement of severe symptoms is needed. There is also some evidence indicating it may be most effective for individuals experiencing catatonic symptoms (NICE, 2015).

Token economy (Paul & Lentz, 1977)

The behavioural approach to schizophrenia considers that symptoms of the disorder occur as a learned response. This approach is not concerned so much with the individual's internal experience (e.g. auditory hallucinations) as with the effect this has on their behaviour (e.g. acting as though they are hearing voices). Behavioural therapies therefore focus on helping patients 'unlearn' individual symptoms in order to get better.

Paul and Lentz (1977) investigated the effectiveness of one **operant conditioning** strategy to reinforce appropriate behaviour with schizophrenic patients. The participants in this study were 84 individuals with **chronic** admissions to psychiatric institutions who were split into different groups. Over around four and a half years, Paul and Lentz used an independent measures design to compare the outcomes of three different forms of treatment; **milieu therapy**, traditional existing hospital management of schizophrenia and a token economy system in a hospital ward. A token economy is a system that is based on the main principle of operant conditioning; that desirable behaviours can be reinforced through use of reward. Patients in this condition were given a 'token' as a reward for appropriate behaviours such as self-care, attending therapy and engaging socially (Figure 6.6). Although the tokens had no value in themselves, they could be exchanged for luxury items, such as clothing, TV use, sweets and cigarettes.

 KEY TERMS

chronic: something that occurs for a long time or is on-going. It can be used to refer to a mental or physical disorder, or to a course of treatment.

milieu therapy: a type of treatment which involves the use of a therapeutic community. Patients live collectively in a clinic or treatment centre and are encouraged to look after both themselves and each other, to promote social engagement and relationship building.

6.6 Tokens such as these are used to exchange for rewards

The behaviour of the patient groups was monitored through time-sampled observations, standardised questionnaire scales and individual interviews. Some overall reduction in both positive and negative symptoms was observed. The system was most effective at reducing catatonic behaviour and social withdrawal but less successful in reducing hallucinations and delusional thinking. Perhaps most significantly, 97% of the token economy group were subsequently able to live independently in the community for between 1.5 and five years, compared to 71% in the milieu group and 45% in the hospital group. The researchers concluded that operant conditioning can be an effective method of managing the symptoms of schizophrenia and ensuring good potential for long-term discharge of patients.

> **Reflections:** Can you explain how the use of tokens reinforces desirable behaviour in a token economy?

Cognitive behavioural therapy (Sensky et al., 2000)

Cognitive behavioural therapy (CBT) is an approach to the treatment of mental health disorders which incorporates principles of both the cognitive and behaviourist approaches to psychology. It departs from the behaviourists' strict focus on observable behaviour in order to recognise the influence of invisible cognitive processes on learning. CBT is a talking therapy designed to help people change through recognising thoughts which underlie their behaviours. It has been identified as a promising treatment for reducing the distress, disability and hospitalisation that occurs in individuals with schizophrenia who do not respond well to antipsychotic medication.

Sensky et al. (2000) carried out a **randomised control trial** to compare the effectiveness of CBT with a control group who engaged in 'befriending'. Befriending sessions included informal one-to-one discussions about hobbies, sports or current affairs. Ninety patients aged 16–60 years with a diagnosis of treatment-resistant schizophrenia from five clinical services received a mean average of 19 sessions of CBT or befriending over the treatment period. They were randomly allocated to either treatment condition, making this an independent groups design.

Each intervention was delivered by two experienced nurses. The CBT treatment followed distinct stages, including engaging with the patient and discussing the emergence of their disorder, before tackling specific symptoms. For example, those with auditory hallucinations engaged in a joint critical analysis with the nurse to challenge beliefs about the nature and origin of the voices. Patients kept voice diaries to record what they were hearing in order to generate coping strategies.

Participants were assessed by blind raters before the start of their treatment, at treatment completion (up to nine months) and at a nine month follow-up. They used a number of standardised, validated assessment scales such as the Comprehensive Psychiatric Rating Scale (CPRS) and Scale for the Assessment of Negative Symptoms (SANS). Results showed that both groups showed a significant overall reduction in both positive and negative symptoms of schizophrenia. At the follow-up stage, the CBT group continued to improve in reduction of positive symptoms, whereas those in the befriending group did not (see Table 6.4).

Outcome measure	CBT (n = 46)	Befriending (n = 44)
CPRS total	29	17
SANS total	23	23

Table 6.4 Patients with 50% or greater reduction of symptoms at nine month follow-up

Reflections: Calculate the percentage of participants in each group from the raw data given above. What do the two measures show about the differences between the CBT experimental group and the befriending control?

Evaluation

The study by Paul and Lentz (1977) using token economies involved intensive staff training to ensure rewards were administered **reliably**. Staff were monitored and issued with a manual to ensure procedures were **standardised**. Such rigorous enforcement in other hospitals and indeed the outside world might not be possible, which lowers the **ecological validity** of the study. There are also **ethical issues** with denying privileges to patients who do not behave appropriately and may become de-motivated and distressed by the therapy.

Sensky et al. (2000) used an RCT design, which increased **validity**. Assessors were blind to the treatment group they were assessing, which removes any **bias** they might have felt for or against the treatment. Also, since participants were from several different clinics across the UK, the sample was probably fairly **representative**. A further strength was that the nurses in both conditions were carefully trained and monitored which ensured they used a **standardised** approach to the CBT.

ISSUES AND DEBATES

The treatment of schizophrenia and related disorders has important **application to real life**. Biochemical treatment in the form of antipsychotics is usually the primary treatment for the disorder, and has been shown to be effective in reducing the positive symptoms of schizophrenia in the majority of people. This reduces hospitalisation and can improve quality of life. ECT, however, is far less effective and is likely only to be used in urgent, acute cases or those with primarily catatonic symptoms. The lasting impact of token economies on those with schizophrenia was evidenced in the study by Paul and Lentz (1977); however, implementing the system requires specific conditions and rigorous training and enforcement by clinical staff. Other treatments include CBT; as Sensky et al. (2000) have shown, the effectiveness of this treatment is fairly significant, and may offer hope to individuals who have not responded well to antipsychotic medication.

RESEARCH METHODS

The study of Sensky et al. (2000) was a **randomised control trial** (RCT) using independent groups. Can you evaluate this design in terms of strengths and weaknesses?

SELF-ASSESSMENT QUESTIONS

1 What is the advantage of using virtual reality as a form of symptom assessment (Freeman, 2008) instead of a face-to-face interview?

2 Why do you think clinicians might limit the number of PET scans they give to a patient, or avoid using this technique with certain groups?

3 In the study by Sensky et al. (2000) using CBT for schizophrenia, the participants were evaluated by blind raters. Explain why this was important.

6.2 Bipolar and related disorders

Bipolar and related disorders are some of the oldest recognised psychiatric disorders, and are more common in the general population than schizophrenic disorders. They are also associated with lower life expectancy and suicide.

Characteristics of bipolar and related disorders

These disorders can be separated into two types: unipolar (depression) and bipolar (mania), the definitions and characteristics of which we will consider in this section.

Definitions and characteristics of abnormal affect

All disorders in this category involve an abnormality of affect; they are also classified as 'mood disorders' in DSM-5. This is to distinguish them from brief feelings of sadness or joy. Emotions are amplified beyond the normal ups and downs we all experience, in either extremely negative or positive directions which can persist for long periods of time. Individuals might experience strong feelings of despair and emptiness; in other instances they may also feel anger or euphoria. So while it may be easier for us to relate to these difficult emotions than to imagine what a psychotic episode feels like for example, these disorders are still distinct from everyday experience. Disorders involving abnormal affect significantly impair the individual's ability to function normally.

Types: depression (unipolar) and mania (bipolar)

Unipolar depression is one type of affective disorder. The central characteristics of this type of disorder are the sadness and hopelessness experienced by the individual for most of the day, on most days. The disorder ranges from mild to moderate or severe. Those with the disorder often find they no longer enjoy activities they used to find pleasurable. Their mood may or may not be noticeable to those around them. They may appear angry, withdrawn or tearful. Individuals with unipolar depression may also experience change in appetite (including weight loss or gain) and sleep disturbances (insomnia or excessive sleeping). Along with these changes come feelings of fatigue and exhaustion and reduced concentration which make normal functioning difficult. In some cases, individuals may also experience psychomotor agitation; physical movements such as pacing or handwringing.

Another major disorder in this category is bipolar depression. This disorder has also been known as 'manic' depression in reference to manic symptoms which make it distinct from unipolar depression. Instead of remaining at one 'pole' (i.e. the lows associated with depression), the moods of someone with bipolar involve a marked swing between depressive symptoms and manic symptoms. Some important symptoms of bipolar disorder are detailed in Table 6.5.

Bipolar disorder can present differently in individuals. The manic or depressive phases can last for varying periods of time, and may even be mixed, i.e. experienced in quick succession or even simultaneously. Sometimes an individual may not recognise the signs that they are unwell; the feelings of happiness and purpose that can accompany a manic state may not lead them to believe anything is wrong (Figure 6.7). These dramatic changes in mood and behaviour may be more noticeable to those around them.

Manic symptoms	Depressive symptoms
Changes in mood	**Changes in mood**
• Long period of feeling euphoric or 'high'	• Long period of feeling sadness and despair
• Rage; irritability	• Loss of interest in enjoyable activities
Changes in behaviour	**Changes in behaviour**
• Becoming easily distracted, having racing thoughts	• Struggling to concentrate or remember easily
• Sudden interest in new activities or projects	• Withdrawing from activities or friends
• Over-confidence in one's abilities	• Fatigue or lethargy
• Speaking quickly	• Finding it difficult to make decisions
• Sleeping less or appearing not to need sleep	• Change to appetite or sleeping patterns
• Engaging in risky behaviours (e.g. gambling, sexual promiscuity)	• Considering or attempting suicide

Table 6.5 Symptoms of bipolar disorder

6.7 Throwing oneself into projects with little need for sleep can be a symptom of bipolar disorder

Measures: Beck Depression Inventory

One way depression is commonly measured by healthcare professionals is through psychometric testing. A good example of this is the Beck Depression Inventory (BDI). This 21-item self-report measure assesses attitudes and symptoms of depression, and is the most widely used tool for detecting depression. Each item in the inventory consists of at least four statements, of which the person taking the test must choose the one that best fits how they have been feeling during a recent period of time. This may be the past week or two weeks, depending on the version of the test that is being used. An example item is given here (Beck, 1979, page 398), with the corresponding score listed in brackets:

I get as much satisfaction out of things as I used to (0)

I don't enjoy things the way I used to (1)

I don't get real satisfaction out of anything anymore (2)

I am dissatisfied and bored with everything (3)

Other items relate to the known symptoms of depression; feelings of guilt and hopelessness and physiological symptoms such as fatigue and weight loss. The total score across the test is used to determine the severity of the disorder, with a score of 10 being the minimum for diagnosing mild depression, 19–29 moderate depression, and a score or 30 or more indicating severe depression.

Since its initial introduction, this influential tool has been updated twice. The current version BDI-II was issued in 1996 and, whilst retaining the same structure as the original, has been revised to include both increase and loss of appetite and fatigue as symptoms.

Evaluation

The BDI is a robust instrument; numerous studies have demonstrated that it has high levels of **reliability** and **validity**. This means it is fairly accurate and consistent in measuring the severity of an individual's level of depression. It is a **quantitative** measurement, as it provides a numerical score for each person. This gives it a level of **objectivity** which could not be achieved through an unstructured interview. Although it cannot capture the detail and richness that a less structured approach would offer, it is a tool which allows clinicians treating those with depression to measure improvement or deterioration of their condition over time or with treatments. However, as a self-report there is a risk that **validity** may be reduced as the person taking the test may either exaggerate or play down their symptoms.

> **ISSUES AND DEBATES**
>
> The BDI is an important diagnostic tool which has **application to everyday life**. It can be used in clinical settings to aid in the diagnosis and treatment of depression. The inclusion of items around suicide and death can also aid healthcare professionals in identifying those individuals who may be most at risk to themselves. It has also been adapted for use with children below the age of 13 who may suffer from depression.

> **Reflections:** Consider whether you think the BDI is a useful tool. Can it help us to understand what it is really like to experience depression? Why or why not?

Explanations of depression

Biological: genetic and neurochemical (Oruc et al. 1997)

First degree relatives such as parents and siblings share 50% of their DNA. Just like physical illnesses, some mental disorders are thought to have a genetic basis, meaning they can be transmitted from one generation to the next. Current evidence for bipolar depression suggests that there is at least some genetic explanation for why some individuals are more at risk of developing such disorders.

One study examining the genetic basis for these disorders is Oruc et al. (1997). A sample of participants aged between 31 and 70 years of age with a diagnosis of bipolar disorder (42 participants: 25 female and 17 male) were drawn from two psychiatric hospitals in Croatia. A control group of 40 participants with no personal or family history of mental health disorders matched for sex and age were also included in the study.

Sixteen of the bipolar group also had at least one first degree relative who had been diagnosed with a major affective disorder such as bipolar. This information was collected from participants and their family members, with diagnosis confirmed through medical records. DNA testing was carried out with participants to test for **polymorphisms** in serotonin receptor 2c (*5-HTR2c*) and the serotonin transporter (*5-HTT*) genes. These genes were chosen since alterations in them can lead to disturbances in specific biochemical pathways with known links to depressive disorders.

Results of the testing showed that there were no significant associations in the sample. However, serotonin as a neurotransmitter is understood to be **sexually dimorphic**. So, when participants were analysed separately by gender, trends for association with both polymorphisms in female participants were observed. This analysis suggested that polymorphisms in these genes could be responsible for an increased risk of developing bipolar disorder in females only.

KEY TERMS

polymorphism: a variation in a gene or genes. Rather than the term 'mutation' which suggests a unique change, polymorphism refers to the different expressions that may be present in a normal population, even if that expression occurs infrequently.

sexually dimorphic: any differences between males and females of any species which are not just differences in organs or genitalia. These differences are caused by inheriting either male or female patterns of genetic material.

Reflections: The research by Oruc et al. (1997) shows a genetic predisposition towards bipolar and related disorders. What alternative explanations might there be to explain why two family members develop the same disorder?

Cognitive (Beck, 1979)

Cognitive theorists such as Beck (1979) believe that the negative views of someone with depression form a reality for that person, even if they seem far-fetched to others. The reason for the individual's low mood and physiological symptoms is an underlying process of incorrect information processing.

Another term for this irrational thinking is 'cognitive distortion'. According to Beck, cognitive distortion is an automatic process which develops as a result of earlier life experiences, through developing **schemas**. Adverse events activate the potential underlying assumptions, creating a negative bias towards new events. The result of cognitive distortion is the emotional, cognitive and behavioural symptoms typical of depression.

KEY TERM

schemas: units of knowledge about the world. As we grow and learn, information from our senses is arranged meaningfully in our minds; it helps us to categorise new experiences and details. Our individual systems of schema underlie virtually all cognition, such as reasoning, memory and perception.

Cognitive processes involved in depression can be understood to form a triad (see Figure 6.8). The first component of this model relates to the individual's view of themselves. Unpleasant experiences are attributed internally; the individual thinks that they are worthless and not capable of being happy. Secondly, the individual perceives the world as presenting them with insurmountable obstacles to happiness and well-being. They misinterpret external forces as being against them. The third component is a negative view of the future; when considering undertaking a specific task in future, the person anticipates failure or rejection.

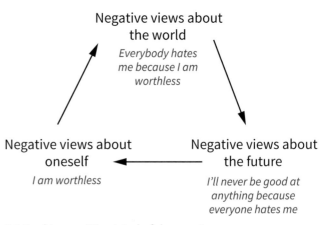

6.8 Beck's cognitive triad of depression

Learned helplessness and attribution style (Seligman et al. 1988)

Learned helplessness is behaviour that occurs as a result of a person having to endure an unpleasant situation, when they perceive the unpleasantness to be inescapable.

In theory the individual learns that they are unable to control the situation and prevent suffering, so they eventually cease to resist it. The theory was developed in the 1960s by Martin Seligman and his colleagues, who believed that the phenomenon of learned helplessness might help explain depression. Their view was that depression was a direct result of a real or perceived lack of control over the outcome of one's situation.

This theory is the basis of '**attributional** style' or 'explanatory style'. As life experiences teach us to develop trust or distrust in our environments, so we develop particular patterns of thinking towards the world and ourselves. A person who has had a difficult upbringing, or experienced parental loss, for example, might be more likely to perceive a lack of control over the negative events in their lives (learned helplessness), and subsequently be more inclined towards a negative attributional style. This means they will consistently view things that happen in the future as internal, stable and global. If something bad happens they might think it is their fault (internal), or that it will stay this bad forever (stable) and that it means more things are likely to go wrong now (global).

Seligman et al. (1988) investigated how well attributional style could predict depressive symptoms. Thirty-nine patients with unipolar depression and 12 patients with bipolar disorder participated in the study during a depressive episode. All the participants came from the same outpatient clinic, included a mix of genders and had a mean age of 36 years. They were compared with a non-clinical control group of ten participants. At the start of the study, participants completed a short form of the BDI to assess severity of symptoms. They then completed an Attributional Style Questionnaire consisting of 12 hypothetical good and bad events. The participants had to make causal attributions for each one and then rate each cause on a seven-point scale for internality, stability and globality.

Both the bipolar and unipolar participants were found to have more pessimistic, negative attributional styles than the non-patient control group. The more severe the depression score on the BDI, the worse the pessimism on the Attributional Style Questionnaire. For those with unipolar depression undergoing cognitive therapy, an improvement in attributional style correlated with an improvement in BDI scores. This suggests that the way we make attributions is an important mechanism underlying the experience of depression.

KEY TERM

attribution: the cognitive process by which individuals explain the causes of behaviour and events. Our attributions may be faulty or biased; tending to always look to specific causes for behaviour on the basis of our previous life experience.

Reflections: Imagine your favourite football team has just lost a match. To what would you attribute this disappointing outcome? Consider the many explanations; what might someone with a negative attributional style consider to be the reason behind this failure?

Evaluation

Seligmann et al. (1988) used **standardised** questionnaires to assess participants. The **Attributional Style Questionnaire** and BDI are considered to be **valid** and **reliable** measurement tools. However, the link between BDI and positivity of attribution was correlational, meaning it is impossible to determine **cause and effect** in this research. It could be, for example, that as one's symptoms of depression improves, this causes attributional style to also become more positive. It is not clear that the link between the two is actually causal.

The study by Oruc et al. (1997) is limited in terms of its **sample size**, meaning it is difficult to generalise from the results. Typically, genetic studies require fairly large samples for accurate and valid analysis to take place. Establishing the importance of the serotonin-related genes in increasing risk of depressive illness in females would require a larger sample. Furthermore, some participants in the study were still within range for detecting onset for the bipolar disorder. This means the findings might have changed if the researchers had used an older population and so age is an **extraneous variable**. However, the study collected DNA samples which were analysed in a laboratory setting with automated equipment, which increases the **validity** of the measurement and removes **researcher bias**.

RESEARCH METHODS
Seligmann et al. (1988) collected quantitative data using the **Attributional Style Questionnaire**. What are the strengths and weaknesses of collecting this type of data in this piece of research?

133

The biological explanation for depression reflects the influence of nature in the **nature vs nurture** debate. As particular genes and neurochemicals are implicated in developing these illnesses, biology is seen as the primary cause. One example of this is the study by Oruc et al., which showed a possible genetic cause for bipolar in the female population. However, there are other complementary explanations which might explain why depression is 'triggered', such as adverse life events. This view reflects the nurture side of the debate, and is seen in the explanation of learned helplessness.

Learned helplessness and a negative attributional style develop as a result of an individual's interaction with their environment, thus offering an **individual** explanation. The cognitive account also assumes that the depression results from an individual's dysfunctional thinking, rather than explaining the symptoms as a result of **situational** variables such as a difficult childhood.

The genetic explanation for depression can also be considered **reductionist**; as it focuses on a very narrow set of genes (such as those relating to serotonin) that may be responsible for the disorder. Despite this, it cannot account for all instances of depression, or why not all first-degree relatives develop the same disorder. Yet, as we cannot change our DNA, this explanation is somewhat **deterministic** as it demonstrates that individuals with a family history of depression or bipolar are at much higher risk of developing a similar disorder. However, in this case, the findings of Oruc et al. suggest only a small genetic susceptibility for females; this indicates there must be other causes of the disorder, which may or may not be genetic in origin.

A further issue for this section might be the use of psychometric testing. The Beck Depression Inventory for example is popular because it is easy to administer and score. This makes it a useful tool for clinicians. However, as a self-report measure it is subject to bias; individuals may downplay symptoms to appear more socially desirable which reduces its validity.

Treatment and management of depression
Biochemical: MAOIs and SSRIs

There are numerous biochemical treatments for depression. As a group they are commonly known as antidepressant drugs. Each works in slightly different ways, though they have a similar effect on particular neurotransmitter levels in the brain.

Monoamine oxidase inhibitors (MAOIs) were one of the first groups of antidepressants to come into widespread use. They **inhibit** the work of an enzyme known as monoamine oxidase. This enzyme is responsible for breaking down and removing the neurotransmitters norepinephrine, serotonin and dopamine. Thus, MAOIs prevent these neurotransmitters from being broken down, and allow them to remain at higher levels in the brain. The effectiveness of MAOIs has been evidenced from as early as the 1950s. However, they have numerous side effects such as headaches, drowsiness/ insomnia, nausea, diarrhoea and constipation. This type of antidepressant can also cause patients issues with withdrawal, and may interact with other medications. For this reason, current MAOI use tends to be a course of action reserved only for atypical depression, when other antidepressants or treatments have been unsuccessful.

 KEY TERM

inhibit: to hinder or prevent. In neuropsychology, inhibition occurs when a chemical or chemical process is reduced or stopped.

More recently developed antidepressants include the group known as selective serotonin reuptake inhibitors (SSRIs). These include well-known brands such as Prozac. SSRIs act on the neurotransmitter serotonin to stop it being reabsorbed and broken down once it has crossed a synapse in the brain. SSRIs are now the most commonly prescribed antidepressant drug in most countries. They tend to have fewer and less severe side effects than MAOIs, though different individuals may respond better to particular drugs.

Both MAOIs and SSRIs are agreed to be more effective treatment for depression than placebos, as evidenced by a multitude of large clinical studies. However, there is growing evidence to suggest that the impact of these drugs on individuals is far more noticeable in patients with moderate to severe symptoms, and less so in patients diagnosed with mild depression (Fournier et al., 2010).

Electro-convulsive therapy

ECT is another biological treatment for depression. You may wish to remind yourself of how it is administered and the potential side effects of treatment as outlined in Section 6.1. Again, using ECT to manage symptoms of depression tends to be a last resort, if the patient has not responded well to biochemical or other forms of therapy such as CBT. In a study which included over 1000 patients with either unipolar depression or bipolar disorder, Dierckx et al. (2012) found that ECT had similar levels of effectiveness, both resulting in around a 50% remission rate.

However, unlike antidepressants, ECT is administered in short sessions, so the benefits of treatment can be quite short term, in contrast to a 'maintenance' effect created by on-going drug therapy. This means that relapse rates are just as high as in individuals who cease antidepressant use; it is likely that an individual will experience a reoccurrence of symptoms which necessitate further treatment (Jelovac et al., 2013).

Cognitive restructuring (Beck, 1979)

Cognitive restructuring aims to gain 'entry into the patient's cognitive organisation' (Beck 1979, page 142). It is essentially a talking therapy, based on one-to-one interactions between the patient with depression and their therapist. It involves techniques such as questioning and identifying illogical thinking to determine and change the patient's ways of thinking.

Cognitive restructuring as a form of therapy begins with explaining the theory of depression to the patient (see previous section on Beck's cognitive theory of depression). Explaining how the cognitive triad works is intended to help the patient understand that their way of thinking about themselves and the world contributes to his or her depression. A further stage is to train the patient to observe and record their thoughts; this is critical for helping them to recognise irrational or inaccurate beliefs and statements.

Once the individual is able to recognise their own cognitions, the therapist helps them to understand the link between their thoughts, affect and behaviour, and how each affects the others. The patient is often directed to try to 'catch' automatic, dysfunctional thoughts and record them. This is practised outside therapy sessions, to help them identify such thoughts as they occur in a real-life context. Such thoughts can be discussed and challenged in therapy, to explore with the patient whether they really are an accurate reflection of reality.

The purpose of this 'reality testing' for patients is to investigate and begin to notice negative distortions in thinking for themselves. The therapist can then use techniques such as 'reattributing' where they discuss whether the cause of problems or failures the patient has experienced are internal or external. As a result of this, the patient can reframe their thinking about an upsetting situation and perhaps realise that they were not responsible. Ideally, the therapy completes when the patient is able to employ cognitive restructuring for themselves, and is able to see a reduction in their depressive symptoms.

Cognitive therapy is now a well-established way to manage depression, particularly in cases where drug treatment is unsuitable. Wiles et al. (2013) showed that it can reduce symptoms of depression in people who fail to respond to antidepressants. A group of 469 individuals with depression were randomly allocated either continued usual care (including on-going antidepressants) or care with cognitive behavioural therapy. Those who received the therapy were three times more likely to respond to treatment and experience a reduction in symptoms.

> **Reflections:** What type of experimental design was used in the study by Wiles et al. (2013)? Outline its strengths and weaknesses.

Rational Emotive Behavioural Therapy (REBT) (Ellis, 1962)

Rational Emotive Behavioural Therapy (REBT) is a psychological approach to treatment based on the principles of Stoicism. Stoicism is a philosophy, one of the principles of which is that in the majority of cases, the individual is not directly affected by outside things but rather by their own perception of external things. Albert Ellis (1962) placed this belief at the core of his theory on how depression should be recognised and treated. A person becomes depressed as a result of internal constructions; because of their perceptions and attitudes towards things that happen to them in their lives.

In REBT, the therapist helps individuals to understand the process known as the ABC model (see Table 6.6). The most important element of the model is 'B', one's beliefs about the event. This is because, while we all experience adversity and setbacks to some degree, Ellis argues that it is how we think about those experiences that have greatest impact on our emotional well-being and behavioural outcomes. People who consistently develop negative, fixed or irrational beliefs are at greater risk of depression.

Components	Example	Description
A Activating event	Unsuccessful at a job interview	Activating event or adversity in one's life (not directly the cause of emotional upset or negative thinking)
B Beliefs about event	I'll never get anywhere I'm just not good enough	Beliefs about the activating event which lead to emotional and behavioural problems
C Consequences: emotional and behavioural responses	Feeling sad, tearful or angry Withdrawal from friends and family Refusal to apply for other work	

Table 6.6 The ABC model of psychological change

The goal of therapy therefore is to help individuals create and maintain constructive, rational patterns of thinking about their lives. This means identifying and changing thoughts which lead to guilt, self-defeat and self-pity, or negative behaviour such as avoidance, withdrawal and addiction. The main way this is achieved is through a process known as 'disputing'. The REBT therapist forcefully questions irrational beliefs using a variety of different methods in order to reformulate dysfunctional beliefs.

Thus the therapist enables the individual to recognise that whatever setbacks befall them, they can choose how they think and feel about it. Individuals must begin to see that the consequences (C) they experience are only partly a result of an activating event (A). They then must accept that holding on to negative and self-defeating beliefs (B) is a destructive tendency, but one that can be changed by disputing them and replacing them with healthier thoughts. Ellis argues that the tendency to hold on to irrational and unhealthy beliefs is ingrained in people over time, and thus REBT has a great focus on the present, with little concern for exploring past experiences as would psychoanalysis.

Lyons and Woods (1991) conducted a meta-analysis of 70 REBT outcome studies. A total of 236 comparisons of REBT to baseline, control groups or other psychotherapies are examined. They found that individuals receiving REBT demonstrated significant improvement over baseline measures and control groups. Recent research comparing the effectiveness of REBT to antidepressants suggests that both methods of treatment are equally effective in relieving symptoms of depression (Iftene et al., 2015).

Evaluation

Studies in this section investigating the effectiveness of antidepressants such as MAOIs and SSRIs consist of generally well-controlled experimental research using large **samples** which is highly **replicable**. Similarly, research considering the use of cognitive therapy and REBT such as Wiles et al. (2013), Lyons and Woods (1991) and Iftene et al. (2015) also include the use of control groups. This allows the experimenters to draw **valid** conclusions about cause and effect. For example, Lyons and Woods assessed results between those receiving REBT and the control group who did not receive the therapy.

ISSUES AND DEBATES

Individual vs situational explanations are highly relevant to this topic. All the forms of treatment outlined in this section focus on the individual's requirements. For example, the individual is considered to have problematic levels of neurotransmitters which require correction through antidepressant usage, or irrational thinking which needs to be challenged. Little consideration is given to changing situational factors which may contribute to depression, such as trying to alleviate social isolation.

In terms of the **nature versus nurture** argument, the biochemical treatments such as MAOIs, SSRIs and ECT consider biological factors (nature) as most important in reducing symptoms of depression. By contrast, cognitive therapy and REBT regard dysfunctional patterns of behaviour and thinking as learned from our experiences with the world. For example, Ellis argued that adverse or activating events in one's life can trigger irrational beliefs, meaning depression can be treated only when we consider how we react to situational variables.

There are serious ethical considerations around the use of antidepressants and ECT, because they involve the potential for physical and psychological harm. MAOIs and SSRIs can have mild, temporary side effects such as causing headaches, or more severe ones such as increase in suicidal thoughts. Likewise, the risks of ECT include memory loss, and so healthcare professionals and patients must balance the risks and benefits of each treatment.

SELF-ASSESSMENT QUESTIONS

4 Identify whether each of the following are symptoms of mania or depression:
- Long periods of euphoria
- Loss of interest in normal activities
- Sudden interest in new activities
- Fatigue or exhaustion
- Changes to usual sleep patterns

5 In the study by Seligmann (1988), participants with depression were more likely to have more negative attributional styles than those without. Why is this described as a correlational not causal relationship?

6.3 Impulse control disorders and non-substance addictive disorder

For the majority of the time, most of us are able to resist inappropriate impulses. Impulse control and non-substance addictive disorders, however, involve difficulties in such self-regulation of our thoughts and behaviour.

Characteristics of impulse control and non-substance addictive disorders

Here we will consider some features of these disorders and look at a common framework for defining addictions. Individuals are diagnosed when their symptoms cannot be better explained by other psychotic or developmental disorders.

Definitions (Griffiths, 2005)

According to Griffiths (2005), there is now a growing acceptance that a number of behaviours can be defined as 'addictions', not just those that involve taking drugs. These commonly include gambling (Figure 6.9), sex, exercise, videogame playing and internet use. Although these behaviours are quite different from one another, they share

a number of common components which form a definition of addictive behaviours. He identifies these as: salience, mood modification, tolerance, withdrawal, conflict and relapse. Here we will consider the meaning of each in turn and how they can be applied to certain behaviours.

Salience is when a particular activity takes over as the most important activity in a person's life. It may dominate their thinking, feeling and behaviour. They may be preoccupied with thoughts about and cravings for the activity, which may mean their behaviour can become problematic. For example, a person who is addicted to gambling may always be thinking about the next time they can place a bet, and may jeopardise relationships or finances to satisfy this need.

6.9 The act of gambling can dominate addicts' thoughts

The experience of having this need met can create 'mood modification' where the person with the addiction experiences a 'buzz', 'high' or even feelings of peace and escape. Over time, tolerance may develop. This refers to the process whereby increasing amounts of the particular activity are required to sufficiently modify mood. Conversely, the person with the addiction will experience 'withdrawal'; unpleasant feelings or physical effects that occur when the behaviour is reduced or stopped.

Reflections: Can you give an example of how tolerance might affect a gambler's behaviour? Consider how this might create conflict in their lives.

Conflict can occur either between the addict and those around them or within the addict themselves. They may compromise personal relationships, their work or education and other social activities. Addicts often want to cut down or stop the behaviour but find they are unable to do so, which causes internal conflict. Even when reduction of addiction occurs (e.g. if a gambler stops gambling), they are at risk of relapse (i.e. returning to gambling) even after many years of controlling their addiction.

Types

Kleptomania is an impulse control disorder. It involves an on-going inability to resist stealing objects not needed for personal use or because of their monetary value (Figure 6.10). Individuals with kleptomania may feel tension before the act of theft, then pleasure or gratification afterwards. Far more women than men present with the disorder, though this may be because women are more likely to seek treatment. It occurs in between 0.3% and 0.6% of the population, and often is diagnosed with other disorders such as anxiety or substance misuse. It is characterised by intrusive thoughts and urges to steal, which can significantly affect the person's ability to concentrate. The individual may feel guilt and shame, and the inability to control the behaviour can lead to arrest, prosecution and subsequent embarrassment and loss of employment.

6.10 Kleptomaniacs may steal from shops, or even from friends and relatives

Pyromania, as described by Burton et al. (2012), is also an impulse control disorder. It is characterised by the impulse to start fires. The diagnosis for this disorder requires that individuals have deliberately and intentionally set fires on more than one occasion. Like kleptomania, individuals with pyromania feel tense or emotionally charged before the act, and relief and pleasure when setting a fire or participating in their aftermath. Those with pyromania are fascinated with fire and its situational context, such as accelerants (substances that accelerate fires or explosions such as gasoline). People with pyromania cannot resist the impulse to start fire, set off false fire

alarms or watch explosions or fires burning. It may even lead them to seek employment or voluntary work as fire-fighters. Some individuals with pyromania are indifferent to the destructive consequences of fire on people and property, though many report feeling severe distress after starting fires.

Gambling disorder, on the other hand, is a non-substance addictive disorder. In fact, it is the only one of its kind listed in DSM-5. Other behaviours such as internet addiction or shopping addictions are not yet well enough understood to be given their own classification. Like the disorders outlined above, gambling disorder involves a difficulty in controlling impulses. However, gambling disorder has been shown to stimulate the brain's reward centre in a way that is similar to substance abuse. Gambling disorder involves persistent and problematic gambling behaviour such as difficulty withdrawing from gambling, lying to conceal involvement with gambling, and loss of significant relationships as a result of the behaviour. Gambling disorder may, understandably, have a devastating impact on the individual, their family and others in society.

Measures (Kleptomania Symptom Assessment Scale)

Diagnosis of these disorders can be made with a clinician using an appropriate self-report measure. One such measure for the diagnosis of kleptomania is the Kleptomania Symptom Assessment Scale (K-SAS; Figure 6.11). This is an 11-item self-rated scale which measures impulses, thoughts, feelings and behaviours related to stealing. The individual taking the assessment is asked to consider this in relation to the past seven days. Each item is rated on a point-based scale, typically 0-4 or 0-5 (0= no symptoms, 4 or 5= severe, frequent or enduring symptoms), with the highest scores reflecting the greatest severity and duration of symptoms.

1) If you had urges to steal during the past WEEK, on average, how strong were your urges?
Please circle the most appropriate number:

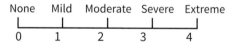

6.11 Sample item from the K-SAS

Reflections: The K-SAS is an example of a self-report measure. Consider the advantages and disadvantages of using this tool to diagnose kleptomania.

Evaluation

The **K-SAS** has scored well for **retest reliability**. It has also been compared with other validated tools such as the Global Assessment of Functioning Scale and found to have good **concurrent** validity. However, it relies on self-report, which means there could be **response bias**, as individuals may feel ashamed of their behaviour and may under-report symptoms. Nonetheless, it provides **quantitative** data which makes it easy to compare the outcomes of interventions, as we shall see in the next section.

RESEARCH METHODS

The **K-SAS** is a recognised assessment tool for measuring the severity of symptoms of kleptomania. Describe one way in which it could be checked for reliability.

ISSUES AND DEBATES

Measuring how severe the symptoms of impulse disorders are is **relevant to everyday life**. When individuals are working with psychiatrists or psychologists to change behaviours, tools such as the K-SAS can be useful in helping to monitor reduction in their symptoms. It allows the person with the disorder to gain insight into their thoughts and feelings, helping them to understand their behaviour. It is also useful for psychologists researching ways to reduce symptoms of the disorders, as we will explore later in this chapter.

Causes of impulse control and addictive disorders

Biochemical: dopamine

We considered the function of the neurotransmitter dopamine in relation to schizophrenia earlier in this chapter. It has also been linked to impulse control and addictive disorders. Dopamine is sometimes referred to as a 'happy' chemical. This is because its release is triggered by rewarding stimuli, such as engaging in enjoyable behaviours. So when someone with kleptomania steals something, their reward centres are stimulated and release dopamine. When these behaviours become compulsive, however, levels of dopamine in the striatum are reduced. This area of the brain is responsible for reward and behavioural control, and so deficiency in dopamine can lead to the perpetuation of compulsions and addictions. The kleptomaniac will then increasingly engage in stealing behaviours. This mechanism is otherwise known as 'reward deficiency syndrome' (Comings & Blum, 2000) and may also explain other forms of addiction.

Reflections: Dopamine has been shown to be an important neurotransmitter implicated in these disorders. Consider the principle of cause and effect: could we say for certain reduced dopamine causes compulsive symptoms? Why or why not?

Kleptomania is a possible side effect of using synthetic dopamine for treatment of disorders such as Parkinson's. There is also some evidence that symptoms of gambling disorder and compulsive shopping emerge alongside the use of these drugs, which further suggests a relationship between dopamine and impulse control disorders. We will look more closely at how dopamine uptake can be managed using medication in order to treat this group of disorder.

Behavioural: positive reinforcement

An alternative explanation for these disorders also relates to the idea of rewards. Rather than a biological focus, the behavioural approach considers the action of the person involved in the compulsive behaviour, whether it is setting fires, shoplifting or gambling. One behavioural theory that can account for these patterns of behaviour is 'positive reinforcement'.

Positive reinforcement is one aspect of operant conditioning. This occurs when someone's learned behaviour is a result of previous trials of that behaviour. Take, for example, a person who goes for a night out at a casino with friends and enjoys the experience of playing poker. Playing the game makes them feel good, and winning may make them feel even better. The enjoyment of winning acts as a **positive reinforcer** (a reward that increases the likelihood of their repeating the behaviour).

You might wonder why gamblers don't stop playing once they start losing. This can be explained by the 'schedules of reinforcement' they receive while gambling. Instead of constant positive reinforcement, most betting games involve a lot of losing! Some fruit machines, for example, may pay out only one in every 500 plays. In other words, gambling on a fruit machine involves partial positive reinforcement; you do not receive a reward each time. This reduces the chance that the player will ever feel fully satisfied with their reward, and means they are much more

139

likely to keep playing in order to recoup losses, believing that the pay-out could happen if they play just one more time, and so on. Research into schedules of reinforcement suggests that the type of partial reinforcement used in fruit machines, for example, changes people's behaviour very quickly, is fairly addictive.

Cognitive: Feeling-State Theory (Miller, 2010)

A third explanation for impulse control and addictive disorders is Feeling-State Theory. It relies on underlying thoughts about particular behaviours to explain obsessions. Miller (2010) uses this cognitive approach to explain how intense, positive feelings can become linked with specific behaviours such as gambling. Miller proposes that impulse control disorders are caused because these links form a 'state-dependent memory' which he refers to as a feeling-state (see Figure 6.12).

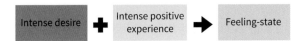

6.12 Creation of a feeling-state

The feeling-state is all the sensations, emotions and thoughts a person experiences in relation to a particular event. It can also include physiological arousal (e.g. increased heart rate, release of adrenaline). It is this feeling-state composed of the positive emotions and memory of the behaviour which leads to impulse-control problems. If a person's feeling-state about starting a fire is 'I am a powerful human being', combined with the positive emotions, physiological arousal and memory of setting the fire, then this could create a compulsion for fire-setting behaviour.

These feeling-states persist over time and different circumstances, so even early positive feeling-states can affect later behaviour. It is also important to note that normal behaviours that occur in moderation only become problematic because of fixated, intense feeling-states. Miller states that an underlying negative thought or experience is most likely to create the feeling-states that lead to impulse control disorders. For example, the pyromaniac who has the feeling-state 'I am powerful' when setting a fire may have underlying negative beliefs about themselves; such as that they are weak or unimportant. This makes the feeling-state achieved during the act of fire-setting highly intense and desirable. However, further negative beliefs occur when the behaviour becomes out of control, typically because behaviours such as gambling, stealing and setting fires have highly negative consequences for the individual and those

around them. Table 6.7 summarises the three sets of beliefs associated with these disorders.

Belief type	Example of belief
Negative belief about oneself or the world	'I'm a loser'
Positive belief created during event (e.g. gambling)	'I'm a winner'
Negative belief created from out-of-control behaviour	'I mess up everything'

Table 6.7 Beliefs and impulse control disorder

ISSUES AND DEBATES

The theory of feeling-states (Miller, 2010) has **application to everyday life**. It shows how gaining awareness of how our beliefs can relate to treating addictive behaviours. This insight is invaluable when engaging in therapies discussed in the next section. Likewise, understating the role of dopamine in these disorders has led to the development of biochemical treatments for symptoms of impulse control disorders.

The **individual versus situational debate** is relevant to these explanations, as the neurochemical account of impulse control explains addiction as relating to individual impairment of brain function. The cognitive explanation for impulse control disorders reflects a more balanced view; naturally some experiences will be stimulating, rewarding or upsetting, but as individuals we each develop our own feeling-states in relation to these, which lead to overall patterns of behaviour.

Within the **nature versus nurture debate**, the behaviourist account of positive reinforcement (Skinner, 1938) is entirely based on nurture factors and how they influence behaviour. In other words, the rewards we gain from interacting with our environment (e.g. through compulsive stealing) reinforce and shape our subsequent behaviour. By contrast, the biological account is based on natural influences; the effect of dopamine uptake on symptoms of addiction and impairment of impulse control.

Treatment and management of impulse control and non-substance addictive disorders

As we have seen, these disorders involve habitual, compulsive behaviours that the individual finds rewarding but may also be highly detrimental. Here we will consider several ways of managing these disorders.

Biochemical (Grant et al., 2008)

Existing research suggests that a group of drugs known as **opiates** may be successful in treating gambling disorder. Grant et al. (2008) wanted to systematically examine how individuals responded to this biochemical form of treatment. They invited 284 participants (a roughly equal split of genders) to participate in a double-blind experiment in which participants took either a 16 week course of the opiate nalmefene or 18 week course of naltrexone, or a **placebo**.

Gambling severity was assessed with the Yale Brown Obsessive Compulsive Scale (Y-BOCS). We will explore this method of measurement later in the chapter; in this study it was specially modified for gambling disorder. Grant et al. wanted to see if taking the opiates would lead to a reduction in gambling behaviour, operationalised as a 35% or greater reduction in their scores on the Y-BOCS for at least one month after the study had taken place. They also considered the participants' depression, anxiety and psychosocial functioning as a response to treatment.

The opiate groups produced a significant reduction in symptoms. There were also significant individual differences, with specific factors contributing to a greater reduction in Y-BOCS scores. Those participants with a family history of alcoholism and those who received the highest dose of the opiates showed the greatest reduction in gambling disorder symptoms. This suggests that opiates may be even more effective in some gambling addicts than in others.

KEY TERM

opiates: a group of powerful drugs which have historically been used as painkillers. Many opiates are considered high risk for drug abuse (heroin is one type of opiate).

Cognitive-behavioural

As we have learned, cognitive and behavioural therapies may rely on changing distortions in the thoughts and feelings of clients, in order to enact behavioural change. Below are three types of therapy that have been used to treat impulse control disorders.

Covert sensitisation (Glover, 2011)

This procedure is conditioning, in which an unpleasant stimulus such as nausea or an anxiety-producing image is paired with an undesirable behaviour in order to change that behaviour. It therefore draws on classical conditioning, and is less concerned with underlying reasons regarding the origin of behaviour. Glover (2011) describes one case study using covert sensitisation to treat an instance of kleptomania. A 56-year-old woman with a 14 year history of daily shoplifting who was seeking help for her behaviour took part in this therapy. Her behaviour started after her husband was convicted of embezzlement. Finding it difficult to forgive him, the woman had then become isolated from their close friends, reluctantly taken a low-status job and become depressed. Compulsive thoughts of shoplifting each morning entered her head which were repulsive but nonetheless impossible to resist. Her shoplifting was without purposeful gain. For example, she once stole baby shoes, despite not having anyone to give them to.

After seeking treatment, Glover reports that the imagery of nausea and vomiting was used in order to create an unpleasant association with stealing. The woman underwent four sessions at two-weekly intervals. For the first two sessions, **muscle relaxation** was used in order to enhance her ability to immerse herself in the visualisation. Increasing nausea visualisation was used over each session; she imagined vomiting as she lifted the item to steal and attracting attention and disgust of those around her. She practised these visualisations outside the formal sessions as 'homework'. During the last session she imagined the sickness going away as she replaced the item and walked away without shoplifting. The participant learned to associate the unpleasant sensations of vomiting with the undesirable stealing behaviour. At a 19 month check-up she had decreased desire and avoidance of the stealing, with a single relapse. Additionally she reported improvements in her self-esteem and social life.

KEY TERM

muscle relaxation: used in therapies to relieve tension from within the body and mind. It can be induced using medication, visualisation exercises or repetition of calming phrases. Progressive muscle relaxation is achieved through systematically tensing and relaxing the muscles of the body in turn, for example from head to toe.

Imaginal desensitisation (Blaszczynski & Nower, 2003)

This therapy relies on the use of images to help individuals who have specific types of impulse control disorders, such as gambling disorder, trichotillomania (compulsive hair-pulling), kleptomania and compulsive shopping. Blaszczynski and Nower (2003) describe this form of therapy and explore some evidence of its effectiveness.

Firstly, the therapist teaches a progressive muscle relaxation procedure. Clients must then visualise themselves being exposed to a situation that triggers the drive to carry out their impulsive behaviour. So, for example a gambler might be instructed to imagine they are coming back from a long, stressful day at work. They are then asked to think about acting on the impulse to gamble, then to mentally leave the situation. This should all be done in a state of continued relaxation, without having acted upon the impulse to gamble. The sessions are often audio-recorded to assist with practising the technique outside therapy sessions.

Imaginal desensitisation has been found to be effective in several studies. It has been shown to reduce the strength of a compulsive drive by reducing levels of psychological and physiological arousal associated with these disorders. In those with gambling disorders, for example, imaginal desensitisation was found to significantly decrease arousal and anxiety levels associated with gambling impulses, even at a five year follow-up. Clients who have undertaken the therapy generally also report that they feel better able to control their impulses.

Impulse control therapy (Miller, 2010)

The goal of this therapy is not to eliminate the behaviour itself, but to establish normal, healthy behaviour. So, a compulsive shopper can still shop but without triggering the problematic behaviours of overspending, hoarding, etc. Essentially this involves changing distorted thoughts a person has about their behaviour, and is directly linked to the feeling-state explanation of impulse control disorders.

Firstly, the aspect of the behaviour which produces the most intense feelings will be identified with the patient. The intense positive feeling associated with the act will also be identified, along with any physical sensations created by the behaviour. These are measured on a standardised scale known as the 'Positive Feelings Scale' to allow for later comparisons. The client then is asked to combine the image of performing the compulsive behaviour, the positive feelings and the physical sensations (recreating the feeling-state in their mind). During this time, they are directed to perform **eye movement desensitisation and reprocessing (EDMR) exercises** (Figure 6.13). The client is also directed to undertake reflections on the therapy between sessions, then return to re-evaluate their feeling-state in relation to the problematic behaviour using the feeling scale. Subsequent sessions of visualisation and eye movements are repeated until the person's drive towards compulsive behaviour is reduced and change has been achieved (usually around three to five sessions).

6.13 Eye movement desensitisation and reprocessing exercises

KEY TERM

eye movement desensitisation and reprocessing (EDMR) exercises: the individual recalls problem behaviour or memories while the therapist directs their eye movement in one of several patterns, using their hands or other stimuli.

Miller outlines supporting evidence for this therapy in the form of a case study of a compulsive gambler. Prior to therapy, John had lost his first marriage, had experienced depression as a result of gambling and had got into debt. With his impulse control therapist, John was able to identify the feeling-state of a particular gambling memory, which involved 'winning', and a powerful feeling connected to his compulsive behaviour. After visualising this feeling-state along with EMDR, John began noting a reduction in the urge to gamble and less excitable feelings towards gambling. His behaviour and feelings continued to change over a further four sessions. At a follow-up interview three months post-therapy, John reported he enjoyed twice-weekly poker nights and could leave the table after a set period whether he was winning or losing. He also reported that he was doing well in his job and relationship.

Evaluation

Grant et al. (2008) used a **double-blind trial**, so neither the experimenter nor participant knew which drug or placebo they were receiving. This eliminated the possibility

RESEARCH METHODS
Grant et al. (2008) used a **double-blind trial**. Explain what the term 'double-blind' means and why it might help increase the validity of a piece of research such as this.

of **participant** or **researcher bias** and increased the **validity** of the results. The data collected in this study was **quantitative**; using this **objective** measurement made it easy to compare improvement of symptoms through the **standardised** Y-BOCS. However, as with all experiments involving placebos, there are **ethical issues** around deceiving participants into believing they are receiving real drug treatment.

The study by Glover (2011) shows how covert sensitisation can be used effectively to reduce symptoms of kleptomania, over several months. However, this research is a case study, meaning it cannot be **generalised** to a larger number of people. Also, as the study is about an individual with kleptomania, we cannot be sure the improvements would be as good for other impulse control disorders. The same criticism could be made of the research by Miller (2010), who outlines the case study of John.

In both cases, the follow-up interviews with participants occurred within a year post-treatment; a longer-term review could check for relapses in behaviour. Furthermore, it is the therapist who is assessing the participants, meaning they may be **biased** in reporting improvements as a result. However, the main strength of both these studies is that they allow for the collection of in-depth **qualitative** data, which helps us understand the experience of the person undergoing treatment.

> **Reflections:** Can you see any ethical issues with cognitive-behavioural treatments such as covert sensitisation? What measures should be put in place to make sure participants are protected from harm?

ISSUES AND DEBATES

The treatments you have explored in this section can be **applied to real life**. The study by Grant et al. (2008) shows the effectiveness of opiates in treating individuals with a gambling disorder, and also gives us an idea of which individual circumstances might make this treatment most effective. Likewise, the cognitive-behavioural treatments we have explored can be used in conjunction with drug therapy or to improve the symptoms of those with treatment-resistant impulse control disorders.

One criticism all the treatments in this section share is that they offer fairly **reductionist** management

ISSUES AND DEBATES (continued)

of an individual's disorder. The use of opiates has been shown to effectively manage the symptoms of impulse control disorders. However, this ignores the circumstances in a person's life which may have triggered the problem behaviour in the first place. Similarly, the cognitive and behavioural approaches to treatment such as covert sensitisation place little value on understanding the person's social and emotional situation, meaning they rely on **individualistic** approaches to treatment.

> **Reflections:** What do you see as the risks of ignoring issues in a person's life which may trigger impulse control disorder symptoms? What situational factors might lead to a relapse?

6.4 Anxiety disorders

These are some of the most frequently occurring mental health disorders worldwide. Those with the disorder are more likely to have other mental or physical health problems.

Characteristics of anxiety disorders

Anxiety refers to fear that is disproportionate to a given situation. Different conditions may be triggered by particular stimuli, but all produce excessively fearful reactions in the individual.

Characteristics, examples and case studies

Anxiety disorders are characterised by a pattern of frequent, persistent worry and apprehension about a perceived threat in the environment. The key aspect of this is that the actual threat posed is minor or non-existent, yet the individual perceives it as highly threatening. Individuals may or may not realise that their anxiety is disproportionate, but they will almost certainly find it difficult to manage and control their worry. Panic attacks are a common feature of some anxiety disorders (see Figures 6.14 and 6.15), and can last minutes or even hours. They can be very frightening experiences for the individual as well as those around them.

143

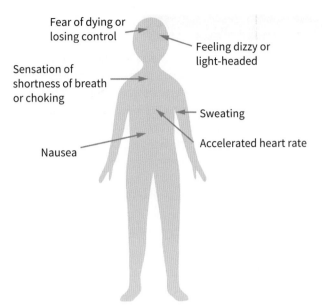

Fear of dying or losing control

Feeling dizzy or light-headed

Sensation of shortness of breath or choking

Sweating

Accelerated heart rate

Nausea

6.14 Panic attack signs

6.15 Panic attacks can last a few minutes or several hours

The high level of anxiety experienced by the individual can manifest itself in a number of different ways. These may include restlessness, muscle tension and constantly feeling 'on edge'. The individual may find it difficult to concentrate because they are preoccupied with their worry; they may also feel tired and irritable. This can be partly explained by sleep disturbance, as the individual has difficulty falling asleep or staying asleep. Anxiety may be generalised, i.e. occur in response to many different stimuli, such as in the case of Generalised Anxiety Disorder. On the other hand they can be very specific, as when experienced in relation to a unique stimulus. We will consider some of these **phobias** in the next section.

Case study:
Kimya (female aged 39)

Kimya has been afraid of birds for as long as she can remember. She has no idea what caused her extreme anxious reactions towards them. Kimya cannot bear to even look at photographs of birds; she finds the sound of birds flapping their wings particularly upsetting. The thought of looking at or having to touch feathers makes her feel sick. Kimya avoids places where she might be

exposed to birds such as town centres, beaches or woodlands, which limits her social life.

Types and examples

Agoraphobia is commonly known as the fear of public places. It is characterised by a fear of two or more of the following:

- standing in line or being in a crowd
- being in open spaces
- using public transport
- being outside the home by oneself.
- being in enclosed spaces

The situations above cause fear and anxiety to the individual, meaning that they will actively avoid agoraphobic situations, or experience real distress while enduring them. Due to the nature of the phobic stimulus, the fear and avoidance can cause significant impairment to the individual's social and working life. They may be unable to visit friends, commute to work or do their own shopping, for example.

Other specific phobias include blood, animal and button phobia. Blood phobia (**haemophobia**) is the irrational fear of blood, and can also extend to needles, injections or other invasive medical procedures. Individuals with blood phobia may actively avoid receiving injections, or situations and occupations which involve exposure to blood, such as visiting a hospital. Haemophobes are known to experience an increase in heart rate when they see blood. Combined with a drop in blood pressure, this physiological response can often lead to fainting.

Animal phobias commonly include dog, insect, bird and spider phobias. Individuals would again avoid contact with these animals, and experience distress or even a panic attack if faced with them. There are numerous other specific phobias, some of which may seem quite unusual. 'Koumpounophobia' is the fear of buttons: individuals cannot bear to touch buttons, or even look at them. The case of a boy with koumpounophobia was discussed in Section 4.2.

Measures (BIPI, GAD-7)

The Blood-Injury Phobia Inventory (BIPI) is a way of measuring this specific phobia. It comprises 18 situations involving blood and injections (see Table 6.8 for an example). The self-report measure lists possible situations and asks the individual to evaluate different reactions that might occur to them in each. These include cognitive, physiological and behavioural responses. They are then asked to rate on a scale of 0–3 the frequency of each symptom (0 = never, 1 = sometimes, 2 = almost always, 3 = always).

Example situation	Example cognitive response (rated 0–3)
When I see blood on my arm or finger after pricking myself with a needle	I don't think I will be able to bear the situation
	I think I am going to faint
	I think that something bad is going to happen to me

Table 6.8 The Blood-Injury Phobia Inventory (BIPI) (adapted from: Mas et al., 2010, page 70)

By contrast, the Generalised Anxiety Disorder 7 (GAD-7) questionnaire is a screening test often used to enable further referral to a **psychiatrist** or counsellor. It has seven items which measure the severity of anxiety. These include 'Feeling nervous, anxious or on edge', 'Being so restless that it is hard to sit still' and 'Feeling afraid as if something awful might happen'. Participants also score between 0 and 3 for each item; however, in this test the scores refer to the frequency of occurrence of symptoms (0 = not at all, 1 = several days, 2 = more than half the days and 3 = nearly every day). This tool is typically used by general practitioners and in primary care settings rather than by specialists. As such, it can be described as a screening tool, useful for recommending further referral rather than providing the level of detail needed for a formal diagnosis.

Evaluation

In this section we have considered two assessment tools for measuring symptoms of anxiety and related disorders: the BIPI and the GAD-7. Both the GAD-7 and the BIPI have been shown to have good **concurrent validity** with other measures, and thus are valid and reliable instruments for assessing anxiety and blood phobia respectively (Mas et al., 2010; Spitzer et al., 2006). However, both measures rely on the accuracy of the individual's self-reporting of symptoms. If a person is having a particularly 'bad' day (perhaps they have accidentally cut their finger that morning), then their BIPI score might be distorted by this.

KEY TERM

psychiatrist: a doctor with specialised medical training to deal with the diagnosis and treatment of disorders. (Most psychologists are not doctors.)

concurrent validity: a way to judge validity by comparing measures of the same phenomenon in different ways at the same time to show that they produce similar results in the same circumstances.

Both measurement tools described here can be considered to be **psychometric** assessments. This means they analyse one dimension of a person's thinking, behaviour and emotions, e.g. towards blood in the case of the BIPI. This type of assessment can be controversial; it relies on a single quantitative measurement of what is actually a complex and all-consuming lived experience for individual sufferers. Some psychologists might feel that these assessments alone do not tell us enough about what it is like to have a specific phobia, and how symptoms may change over time and with treatment.

Cultural bias is also an issue that can affect the diagnosis of phobias. There are cross-cultural differences in the diagnosis of social phobia, for example (Figure 6.16). In North America, agoraphobia is a well-known, recognised disorder, but in South East Asian countries it is rarely diagnosed. These differences may have to do with the emphasis different cultures place on either independence and self-sufficiency or social interdependence and collectivism (Hofmann et al., 2010). In cultures where individuals derive their sense of well-being and reassurance from those around them rather than in competition or contrast with others, diagnostic rates of social phobia seem to remain low.

145

6.16 Diagnosis of social phobia varies cross-culturally

Explanations of phobias

Behavioural (classical conditioning, Watson & Rayner, 1920)

One behavioural explanation for phobias is based on classical conditioning. An individual may develop a phobia of a harmless stimulus if it is paired with a frightening experience. For example, a person might develop agoraphobia following an assault or mugging in public.

Watson and Rayner (1920) used the principles of classical conditioning to create a phobia in a young boy. A normal, healthy 11-month-old infant known as 'Little Albert' was the participant in their case study (Figure 6.17). Prior to the conditioning, he was shown a range of different stimuli. These included a white rat, a rabbit, a dog, a monkey, masks with and without hair, cotton wool, burning newspapers, etc. He reacted normally and neutrally throughout with no outward signs of fear. The white rat was chosen as the neutral stimulus (NS). They also placed a metal bar above and behind Albert's head and struck it loudly with a hammer. This was the unconditioned stimulus (US) as it produced an unconditioned response of fear (UCR) in the boy.

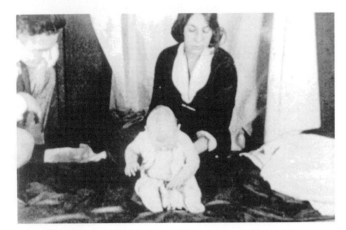

6.17 Little Albert in Watson and Rayner's study

The next phase was the conditioning (see Table 6.9). When Albert was shown the rat he began to reach for it, but just as his hand touched the animal the researchers made a loud noise by striking a hammer against a metal bar just behind his head. Understandably this made the infant very distressed. Watson and Rayner repeatedly paired the loud noise with presentation of the white rat over several trials one week after the initial trial. Eventually Albert only had to see the rat and he began to demonstrate a fearful response (crying, trying to move away from it). The white rat had become a conditioned stimulus (CS), producing a conditioned response of fear (CR). The researchers wanted to see if Albert's fear of the rat was generalised to other similar-looking animals or items. When presented with a rabbit he also had a similarly distressed reaction. These results suggested that fear could indeed be learned through classical conditioning.

Psychoanalytic (Freud, 1909)

Freud suggested that anxiety and fear can result from the impulses of the **id**, usually when it is being denied or repressed. Phobias are one way this internal conflict can manifest in human behaviour. According to Freud's theory of psychosexual stages, such sources of conflict are common at different times in our development. The phobic object comes to symbolise the conflict typical of the stage.

Freud (1909) offered an account of a boy who was suffering from a phobia of horses and a range of other symptoms in order to illustrate the **Oedipus complex**. Hans was a five-year-old Austrian boy whose father had referred the case to Freud and provided most of the case detail; Hans met Freud no more than twice during the period of the study.

When he was three, Hans had developed an intense interest in his penis. He frequently played with himself which angered his mother, who threatened to cut it off. This upset the boy and he developed a fear of castration. Around this time, Hans' younger sister was born and his mother was separated from him in hospital. He also witnessed an upsetting incident where a horse fell down and died in the street.

Quite soon after this time, Hans' horse phobia emerged. He was particularly worried that he would be bitten by a white horse (Figure 6.18). Hans' father felt this concern was related

Before conditioning	unconditioned stimulus (UCS)	→	unconditioned response (UCR)
	Loud noise of metal bar		Fearful crying and avoidance
During conditioning	neutral stimulus + unconditioned stimulus	→	unconditioned response (UCR)
	(NS) + (UCS)		Fearful crying and avoidance
	White rat + loud noise		
After conditioning	conditioned stimulus (CS)	→	conditioned response (CR)
	White rat or similar animal/ item		Fearful crying and avoidance

Table 6.9 Stages of Little Albert's classical conditioning

to horses' large penises. Conflict began to emerge at this time between Hans and his father, who had begun denying him the chance to get into his parents' bed in the mornings to sit with his mother. Hans' phobia lessened as he reached age five. His father reported Hans had experienced two notable fantasies at this time. One was that he had several children of his own with his mother, and imagined that his father was in fact his grandfather. He also fantasised that a plumber had come and removed his penis and replaced it with a new, larger one.

6.18 Hans developed a phobia of horses

Freud felt that the object of fear, the horse, represented Hans' father. Hans was particularly afraid of white horses with black nosebands, which symbolised his moustached father. The anxiety Hans experienced was related to his castration fear from his mother's threat and the banishment of Hans from his parents' bed. Further evidence of the Oedipus complex came from the two fantasises which represented the dynamic of the three-way relationship between Hans and his parents.

Reflections: Freud suggested Hans' phobia of horses was caused by his Oedipus complex. Can you suggest an alternative explanation?

Biomedical/genetic (Öst, 1992)

This explanation suggests that we are born prepared to fear certain objects. In other words, there are particular stimuli in the environment which may pose a threat to survival that we are more genetically set up to avoid. This is transmitted in our DNA through the generations to help our survival.

One study which considers the genetic explanation for phobias is Öst (1992). Participants in this study included 81 blood phobic and 59 injection phobic patients. These were also compared with a sample of other participants who had been diagnosed with different specific phobias (animal, dental and claustrophobia). Participants underwent a screening interview with a clinician, and also completed a self-report questionnaire on the history and nature of their phobia. This included discussing the impact the phobia had on their normal lives, as well as giving ratings to particular situations which might trigger a fearful response.

Participants also underwent a behavioural test. The blood phobics were shown a 30 minute silent colour video of surgery being performed. They were told not to close their eyes but to try to watch for as long as they felt they could. The experimenter tracked gaze direction and if participants looked away or stopped the video using a remote, the test would be terminated. The injection phobic test was 'live' and involved 20 steps, from cleaning a fingertip to performing a fingertip prick. Each step was described to the subjects, who had to say whether or not it was OK to perform. If they said 'no' the test ended.

The measures included a score relating to the percentage of maximal performance (e.g. how long they watched the video), the experimenter's rating of the patient's fainting behaviour (0 = no fainting and 4 = fainting), and a self-rating of anxiety (0 = not at all anxious and 10 = extremely anxious). Participants also completed a questionnaire on their thoughts during the test, and had their blood pressure and heart rate monitored. This is because the fainting associated with these phobias has been found to be related to changes in blood pressure and heart rate.

The family histories of participants revealed that around 50% of blood phobics and 27% of injection phobics had one or more parents with the same fear (Figure 6.19). Around 21% of the blood phobics also reported having at least one sibling who shared the disorder. Another key finding of this study is that a high proportion of the participants with blood phobia and injection phobia had a history of fainting when exposed to their respective phobic stimuli (70% blood phobics and 56% of injection phobics). These results are much higher than those participants with other specific phobias or anxiety. The mean number of fainting instances was 10.8 in the blood phobic group and 7.7 in the injection phobic group. Öst concluded that there seemed to be a strong genetic link for these phobias, which are more likely than other phobias to produce a strong physiological response (fainting).

6.19 Blood phobia may have a genetic basis

Cognitive (Di Nardo et al., 1988)

Cognitive psychologists view the origin of phobias as involving the individual's thought processes. Those with phobias are biased in their reasoning about what is harmful. This means that they are more likely to perceive ambiguous stimuli (like heights or spiders) as more threatening than would most other people. They may also have negative self-beliefs, such as that they would not cope with being exposed to the phobic stimulus.

Di Nardo et al. (1988) conducted a study which examined the origin of cynophobia, the fear of dogs. Prior to this study, much research on specific animal phobias had focused on fear of snakes, and findings about the origin of such phobias were very mixed. Using a participant group of 14 dog-fearful and 21 non-fearful female college students, Di Nardo et al. conducted individual structured interviews in order to obtain information on the aetiology or origin of the phobia. They wanted to investigate whether particular unpleasant events known as conditioning events involving dogs were more common in cynophobes or non-cynophobes. They also wanted to compare fearful and non-fearful participants' expectations of physical harm and fear upon encountering a dog.

From a sample of female psychology students aged 18–21, 37 women took part in this study. They were chosen from a larger student population as they either rated themselves highly fearful of dogs and reported anxiety on encountering a dog in a live behavioural test (fearful participants), or rated themselves as not fearful and felt little anxiety in the test (non-fearful participants).

In the interviews, the participants were asked to discuss frightening and painful encounters with dogs, their expectation of fear or harm coming to them in such an encounter and their estimate of the likelihood associated with this expectation. The results showed that conditioning events, i.e. upsetting or painful encounters with dogs were reported by 56% of fearful participants. However, similar results were found in the non-fearful group, with 66% reporting similar conditioning events. The majority of such events in both groups involved bites or scratches. However, all of the fearful participants expected to experience fear or come to harm during an encounter with a dog compared with a small minority of the non-fearful group. Thus, the anticipation of harm occurring was far greater in the fearful group than in non-fearful participants.

So, while non-fearful participants had a different expectation of what would happen when encountering a dog, painful experiences with dogs were common among both groups. Di Nardo et al. therefore concluded that factors other than conditioning events must affect whether or not these painful experiences will develop into dog phobia, such as the individual's own interpretation and rationalisation of events.

Evaluation

Both the studies by Watson and Rayner (1920) and Freud (1909) were **case studies**. This means we cannot reasonably generalise about the acquisition of phobias from Little Albert's or Hans' experiences alone. However, Watson and Rayner conducted a number of trials using different stimuli to check whether Albert was a particularly fearful boy and **control** for any changes that occurred during the study. As Albert appeared healthy and confident, it may well be that phobias could be acquired by other children in the same way. Freud's study lacked **objectivity** as he was a friend of Hans' father, who also provided him with the case study detail. This research lacks **validity** as it may be subject to bias in an attempt to fit Freud's existing theories about the subconscious and psychosexual stages.

In comparison, the research by Öst et al. and Di Nardo et al. could be considered more objective, because they both used **standardised** behavioural tests and interviews with larger groups of participants. Their findings could be **generalised** more easily and had better levels of **control**. However, both studies were **cross-sectional** and did not consider the different participant's experiences in depth.

The studies in this section are directly **applicable to real life**. In understanding how phobias are acquired, the right method of treatment can be selected. To give one example, in the study by Di Nardo et al., conditioning events may well play a role in developing a phobia of dogs; however, they do not seem to be the only explanation. As we will consider in the next section, therapies for treating phobias which rely on cognitive techniques have a good success rate, which supports this explanation of phobia acquisition.

ISSUES AND DEBATES

The **nature versus nurture** debate can help us consider the merits of different theories about what causes phobias. Biological explanations such as Öst et al. rely solely on genetic factors to account for the prevalence of fear, such as in blood phobia. In direct contrast, the behaviourist account relies entirely on conditioning events which are a product of our environment. So, although Little Albert was born a happy, confident boy, he was conditioned by his experience to fear rats; purely a result of his nurturing.

Both studies by Watson and Rayner and Freud use **children as participants**. Interestingly both pieces of research were conducted in the early part of the twentieth century, where ethical issues were not of as such significant concern as they are today. Little Albert underwent a traumatic experience in being classically conditioned to fear rats; he was visibly upset and this was taken as a successful measure of the training. Although Freud was not directly involved with Hans, there are also questions around the boy's consent in this study.

The debate over **determinism** and free will can also be considered in light of two of the studies in this section. The behaviourist explanation of phobias is deterministic and states that a conditioning event (such as the training administered by Watson and Rayner) will produce a conditioned response of fear in individuals. However, the research by Di Nardo et al. counters this assertion, through evidence that conditioning events are common to both fearful and non-fearful individuals, and that there must be more complex explanations for our behaviour.

Both the behaviourist and biological explanations of phobia acquisition can be considered **reductionist**. Watson's explanation for Little Albert's rat phobia relies entirely on his classically conditioned experience. Öst et al. look only at a specific biological explanation for blood phobia: the genetic link. By contrast, the cognitive theory used by Di Nardo et al. considers that conditioning events may have a role in causing phobic responses, yet emphasises this cannot be the only explanation because non-fearful individuals also have bad experiences with the animals. A more **holistic** explanation would consider the range of experiences, thinking and environment of the individual. This is more evident in Freud's case study of Hans, who takes into account Hans' fears, dreams, conversations and fantasies over a number of years to trace the origin and resolution of his horse phobia. Use of **longitudinal** research in this way can build an in-depth picture of a participant's experience which can help us understand causal factors in specific phenomenon, such as the development of phobias.

Treatment and management of anxiety disorders

Systematic desensitisation (Wolpe, 1958)

Systematic desensitisation is a way of reducing undesirable responses to particular situations. This makes it a particularly appropriate way of managing phobic reactions. Its principles are based within behavioural psychology; namely it holds the assumption that nearly all behaviour is a conditioned response to stimuli in the environment. If a phobia can be learned as in the case of Little Albert (Watson and Rayner, 1920), then it can also be unlearned. Systematically desensitising a patient requires that a once frightening stimulus should eventually become neutral and provoke no real anxiety.

> **Reflections:** Systematic desensitisation is based on the theory of classical conditioning. Can you explain using the correct psychological terms the process by which a phobic response is unlearned?

Wolpe (1958) introduced the idea of 'reciprocal inhibition', which is the impossibility of feeling two strong and opposing emotions simultaneously. The key to unlearning phobic reactions through systematic desensitisation is to put the fearful feelings associated with a phobic stimulus directly in conflict with feelings of deep relaxation and calm. A therapist practising systematic desensitisation follows particular stages which are outlined below:

- Teach patient relaxation techniques. These can be progressive muscle relaxation exercises, visualisation, or even anti-anxiety drugs.
- The patient and therapist work together to create an anxiety hierarchy (see Table 6.10 for an example). This is a list of anxiety-provoking situations relating to the specific phobia that increase in severity. The list is unique to the individual who works through *in vitro* or *in vivo* exposure to each stage in turn.
- At each stage of the anxiety hierarchy, the patient is assisted to remain in a calm, relaxed state using their chosen technique. The patient does not move on to the next stage in the hierarchy until they report feeling no anxiety in relation to their current stage.

149

RESEARCH METHODS

The research by Di Nardo et al. (1988) involved a sample consisting of female psychology students. What are the advantages and disadvantages of such a sample?

KEY TERM

in vitro: instances where exposure to the phobic stimulus is imagined, such as through a visualisation exercise.

in vivo: instances when the individual is directly exposed to the stimulus in real life.

Stage	Situation relating to phobic stimulus (spider phobia)
1	Looking at a drawing of a spider (Figure 6.20)
2	Looking at a detailed photograph of a spider
3	Watching a spider making a web on a video
4	Being in the same room as a caged spider
5	Standing in front of the spider's cage
6	Standing next to another person who is holding a spider
7	Touching the spider whilst someone else holds it
8	Holding the spider in their own hand

Table 6.10 Sample anxiety hierarchy

6.20 A picture of a spider might feature on an anxiety hierarchy

As the two emotions of fear and calm are incompatible, the fearful response to the stimuli is gradually unlearned and will no longer produce anxiety in the patient. There is good research evidence to support the effectiveness of systematic desensitisation in treating phobias such as agoraphobia (Agras, 1967) and fear of snakes (Kimura et al., 1972). However, since the 1970s and 1980s, this form of therapy has declined in popularity and other treatments which involve more direct forms of exposure are now more commonly used.

Applied tension (Öst et al., 1989)

The introduction of behavioural therapy for anxiety disorders such as systematic desensitisation paved the way for further forms of treatment, including applied tension. This form of treatment involves applying tension to the muscles, in an effort to increase blood pressure throughout certain areas. As you may remember, blood phobia in particular is associated with drops in blood pressure and fainting. By training individuals with blood phobia to increase muscle tension, the aim is to reduce instances of fainting and other unpleasant responses.

In a study by Öst et al. (1989), 30 patients from the same hospital with phobia of blood, wounds and injuries were individually treated using applied tension, applied relaxation

or a combination of these two methods. Participants were all otherwise healthy individuals between the ages of 18 and 60, including 19 women and 11 men. The aim was to establish which if any of these was the most effective treatment, and also to see whether applied tension could produce quicker improvements for phobic patients.

Using an independent groups design, those undergoing applied tension had five sessions, while those in the applied relaxation and combined groups had nine and ten sessions respectively. Each session lasted between 45 and 60 minutes. Prior to commencing treatment, participants were assessed by self-report, as well as behavioural and physiological measures to establish tendencies towards anxiety and fainting. These included being observed while watching videos involving surgical operations, and having their heart rate and blood pressure measured.

The applied tension technique used by Öst et al. involved the patient learning to tense their arm, chest and leg muscles until they experienced a feeling of warmth rising to their face. Once the participants had mastered the technique, they then practised it during exposure to several different situations involving blood (e.g. watching blood donation, looking at slides of pictures involving wounds). The applied relaxation technique used involved progressive muscle relaxation during exposure to the same stimuli.

After completing their treatment and six months after treatment, all participants were given the same set of measures to establish whether they had experienced any changes. There were similar improvements across all groups, with around 73% of participants across all groups showing a noticeable improvement in their behavioural and physiological responses to blood. Since applied tension had been at least as effective as the other treatments in around half the time, the experimenters suggested it may be the most appropriate treatment choice for blood phobia.

Cognitive behavioural therapy (Öst & Westling, 1995)

So far we have considered two forms of treatment for phobias which are based on behavioural models. By contrast, cognitive behavioural techniques (CBT) such as that employed by Öst and Westling (1995) also take into consideration the need to change the individual's thoughts and beliefs about the source of their anxiety.

In their study, Öst and Westling (1995) aimed to compare the effectiveness of CBT with applied relaxation (AR) in the treatment of individuals with **panic disorder**. Thirty-eight patients were treated individually across 12 weekly sessions. The sample was recruited through a mixture of newspaper advertisement and psychiatrist referrals. They were assessed before, after and in a one year follow-up. In order to draw a comparison, they were rated using a self-report scale as well as through self-observation of panic attacks. This included keeping a diary in which they recorded instances of panic attacks and rated their severity.

> **KEY TERM**
>
> **panic disorder:** a recognised mental health disorder characterised by spontaneous and unexpected panic attacks. The attacks may range in frequency from several per day to only a few per year.

Both groups worked with experienced therapists. The first step of therapy for the cognitive group involved identifying the misinterpretation of bodily sensations, i.e. thinking that when their heart beats more rapidly, they believe that they are having a heart attack. In the second step, participants were encouraged to generate alternative, non-catastrophic interpretations of their bodily sensations. Finally, through discussion the therapist challenged the patient's evidence for their beliefs, using behavioural experiments to induce the misinterpreted sensations. In the applied relaxation group, progressive muscle relaxation techniques were taught to the participants who were then asked to practise these both in panic- and non panic-inducing situations.

Results of these measures showed that there was no significant difference between the group that underwent applied relaxation and those who completed the CBT course (Figure 6.21). There were no relapses in either group at follow-up, which suggests that both methods were successful in short- to medium-term alleviation of panic attack symptoms.

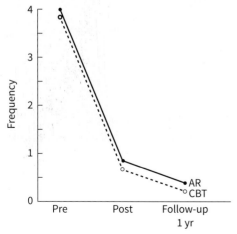

6.21 Graph to show frequency of panic attacks per week (source: Öst and Westling, 1995, page 156)

Evaluation

The study by Öst et al. (1989) used a **sample** of participants from the same hospital, which limits its **generalisability**. However, it did include both males and females, meaning the results can be applied to both sexes. Using an independent groups design meant that although differences between the three conditions could be compared, there is a chance that **participant variables** could have affected the outcome. Although the participants consented to participate, they were exposed to videos of surgical procedures which were especially upsetting given their phobias. This is an important **ethical issue** with the study.

In comparison, Öst and Westling (1995) asked participants to keep records of naturally occurring panic attacks (rather than inducing fear so directly), which could be seen as more ethical. This was a well-controlled study; for example therapists gave standardised training to participants in applied tension or muscle relaxation. This increases the validity of the research, as it is less likely **extraneous variables** affected the outcome. In this research, participants were followed up after one year to evaluate the effectiveness; this may show a longer-term effect than the six month follow-up used by Öst et al. (1989) in the applied tension research.

151

> **ISSUES AND DEBATES**
>
> These forms of treatment are useful in their **application to real life**. For example, Öst et al. (1989) demonstrated that, compared with applied relaxation, applied tension was a quicker and equally effective technique. Offering this treatment to those with blood phobias could reduce waiting times for therapy and give the potential to treat more individuals in need.
>
> The use of systematic desensitisation to treat phobias and anxiety disorders relates to the **nature versus nurture** debate. Based on the behaviourist principles of classical conditioning, it assumes that individuals are born a 'blank slate' with few if any specific behaviour tendencies. However, the evidence is not clear in all cases of phobias that they develop from traumatic events that have created negative associations. Some phobias are common because they are believed to have served an evolutionary purpose (e.g. fear of heights or water might have been useful for survival). Thus, systematic sensitisation and other behavioural therapies may be most suited to those phobias that have clearly been learned, rather than those with a possible evolutionary basis.

RESEARCH METHODS

The study by Öst et al. (1989) used quantitative measures to collect data. Identify one example of this type of data in this piece of research and explain why it is useful.

6.5 Obsessive compulsive and related disorders

You may be familiar with these disorders, which we commonly associate with highly repetitive behaviours such as hand-washing. Underlying such visible behaviour are obsessive thoughts which create deep anxiety for the individual.

Characteristics of obsessive compulsive and related disorders

Here we will consider the different types of obsessions and common obsessive thoughts and compulsions, looking at two disorders in particular.

Types of common obsessions, common compulsions, hoarding and body dysmorphic disorder

These disorders are unified by the presence of obsessive thinking. This means the person with the disorder will experience intrusive, recurrent thoughts and urges that are unwanted. They also involve compulsive behaviour; the person is driven toward repetitive rituals which significantly impair their normal functioning. Disorders of this type are relatively common, affecting between 1% and 5% of the population, with obsessive compulsive disorder (OCD) being one of the leading causes of disability worldwide (Black and Grant, 2014).

Criteria for diagnosis of OCD in the DSM-5 include the presence of obsessions and/or compulsions. Often individuals will attempt to suppress unwanted obsessive thoughts by performing behaviours to stop them. Such behaviours are intended to reduce anxiety and may give temporary relief. However, these behaviours are clearly excessive and not realistically a way to relieve the source of worry. For example, a person who has the obsessive worry that they might accidentally hit someone with their car might be compelled to engage in continuous counting (something which would not actually help prevent an accident). These thoughts and behaviours can be extremely time-consuming, e.g. taking more than one hour a day and have a negative effect on the individual's ability to work and

socialise. Some common obsessions and compulsions are outlined in Table 6.11.

Hoarding is an obsessive compulsive disorder in which individuals experience great difficulty getting rid of possessions. For many hoarders, this means they collect so many possessions their homes may be unsafe, due to access or hygiene issues (Figure 6.22). The homes of hoarders may be difficult to clean, leading to infestations, for example. Frequently hoarded items include clothes and newspapers; those with hoarding disorder find it difficult to part with these items, regardless of their actual value. Individuals experience distress associated with discarding possessions, which can then impact their ability to live with their families, have visitors and so on.

Obsessions	Compulsions
Fear of deliberately harming oneself	Frequent and excessive hand-washing
Fear of illness or infection	Putting things in order (e.g. all labels on food in cupboard facing same way)
Fear about harming or killing other people	Checking things repeatedly (e.g. checking oven 20 times to ensure it is 'off' before leaving home)
Fear of accidentally injuring oneself or others	
Strong desire for order and symmetry	Repeating words to oneself or repetitive counting

Table 6.11 Examples of common obsessions and compulsions

6.22 Hoarding disorder can result in crowded, cluttered living spaces

Body dysmorphic disorder (BDD) involves obsessive thoughts regarding perceived faults in one's physical appearance. These faults are likely to be slight or not at all obvious to others. These obsessions are often focused on imagined flaws or defects on the skin around the face and head. The anxiety caused by these intrusive thoughts leads to compulsive, repetitive behaviours such as frequent mirror-checking or excessive grooming (hair-washing, shaving, tooth-brushing) and constantly comparing one's appearance with others. These behaviours are intensely time-consuming with individuals with BDD spending several hours a day performing rituals to hide their defect, for example.

Examples and case studies ('Charles', Rapoport, 1989)

One example of an individual living with an obsessive compulsive disorder comes from Rapoport (1989). Charles was a 14-year-old boy with OCD who spent three hours or more each day showering, plus at least another two hours getting dressed. He had elaborate, repetitive routines for holding soap in one hand, putting it under water, switching hands and so on. His mother contacted Rapoport (1989) after this behaviour had been going on for around two years. Prior to this time, Charles had been a good student with a particular interest in the sciences. He had had to leave school because his washing rituals were making it impossible for him to attend on time. He had also been in and out of hospital for his condition, and had already received standard treatments of medication, behavioural therapy and psychotherapy.

Charles was, however, still utterly obsessed with the thought that he had something sticky on his skin that had to be washed off. In an attempt to help her son overcome this worrying thought, his mother had helped him clean his room and kept things he touched clean with rubbing alcohol. He had only one friend because his rituals left him little time to leave the house. He underwent a drug trial for clomipramine (a type of antidepressant), which gave effective relief of his symptoms; he was able to pour honey, for instance. Yet after a year, he had developed a tolerance for his medication. Charles relapsed and returned to ritualistic washing and dressing.

Measures: Maudsley Obsessive-Compulsive Inventory (MOCI), Yale-Brown Obsessive Compulsive Scale (Y-BOCS)

There are several tests used to assess obsessive compulsive disorders. We will consider two in this section.

The Maudsley Obsessive-Compulsive Inventory (MOCI) is a short assessment tool that contains 30 items that are scored either 'true' or 'false'. It assesses symptoms relating to checking, washing, slowness and doubting. It takes

around five minutes to complete and produces scores that range between 0 and 30. Example items (Hodgson and Rachman, 1977, p 391) include:

- I frequently have to check things (gas or water taps, doors, etc.) several times. (Checking)
- I am not unduly concerned about germs and diseases. (Washing)
- I do not take a long time to dress in the morning. (Slowness)
- Even when I do something very carefully I often feel that it is not quite right. (Doubting)

The MOCI was designed as a quick assessment tool for clinicians and researchers, rather than a formal diagnostic tool.

The Yale-Brown Obsessive Compulsive Scale (Y-BOCS) developed by Goodman et al. (1989) is a widely used test designed to measure the nature and severity of an individual's symptoms. The Y-BOCS involves a **semi-structured interview** that takes around 30 minutes to conduct. It also involves a checklist of different obsessions and compulsions (see Table 6.12), with a ten-item severity scale. The severity scale allows individuals to rate the time they spend on obsessions, how hard they are to resist and how much distress they cause. Sometimes the checklist is administered on its own, as a way of helping plan treatment, or assessing how treatment is progressing. Scores range from 0 (no symptoms) to 40 (severe symptoms); those above 16 are considered in the clinical range for OCD.

Obsessions	Aggressive, Contamination, Sexual, Hoarding, Religious, Symmetry, Body-focused, Other
Compulsions	Cleaning, Washing, Checking, Repeating, Counting, Ordering/arranging, Hoarding, Other

Table 6.12 Y-BOCS obsessions and compulsions categories

Reflections: Compare the two assessment tools outlined in this section. What are the advantages or disadvantages of each?

Evaluation

The **reliability** and **validity** of assessment tools such as the MOCI and Y-BOCS have been evaluated in a number of studies. They have good levels of **concurrent validity**; meaning that individuals will score similarly on different tests for obsessive compulsive disorder (Esfahani et al., 2012). They also both offer good **test–retest reliability**, meaning that individuals who repeat the measures at different times are likely to get the same results. This is important for researchers wanting to use the tools in trialling psychological interventions.

Both tests use a self-report measure, however, which means that they rely on the individual to give accurate and honest answers to each item. This can be quite a **subjective** process for several reasons. For example, those who are resistant to treatment or fear being thought of badly might downplay the severity of their symptoms. It can therefore be difficult for researchers or clinicians to obtain a true picture of the nature of someone's condition.

> **ISSUES AND DEBATES**
>
> Using the assessment tools discussed in this section might be considered **reductionist**. The symptoms of obsessive compulsive disorders can be very specific and unique to individuals, which makes designing generic tests difficult. Often they may end up being very lengthy, in order to identify a person's main obsessions. They may also end up being too 'one-dimensional', looking at the impact of situations as being 'not at all distressing' up to 'severely distressing'. However, some argue that this fails to capture the complex impact obsessive thoughts and compulsive behaviours have. 'Distress' might also include different feelings and experiences such as depression, anxiety and functional impairment (Abramowitz et al., 2010).
>
> The case study (Rapoport, 1989) is useful in helping us understand the experience of OCD in everyday life. The experience of Charles and his mother demonstrates the impact of compulsive behaviours on normal functioning, such as the extremely lengthy washing rituals which prevented the young man from attending mainstream schooling. It can also highlight the unique obsessive thoughts (e.g. Charles' 'stickiness') that are symptomatic of these disorders.

Explanations of obsessive compulsive and related disorders

In the next section we will examine the explanations offered by different psychological approaches and consider their strengths and weaknesses.

Biomedical (genetic, biochemical, neurological)

There are several biomedical explanations for obsessive compulsive and related disorders, all of which use physiological processes to explain symptoms.

- *Genetic:* Recent research suggests that OCD may have a genetic basis. Mattheisen et al. (2015) conducted a large-scale study involving 1406 patients with OCD and other members of the general population to analyse and identify genes that may be linked to OCD symptoms. The gene PTPRD was implicated, along with a gene called SLITRK3, both of which interact to regulate particular synapses in the brain. Other studies have found evidence to suggest a role for the gene DRD4, which is related to the uptake of dopamine (Taj et al., 2013). We explored the role of this neurotransmitter in Section 6.3.

- *Biochemical:* Oxytocin is commonly referred to as the 'love hormone'. This is because it is involved in enhancing trust and attachment. However, it has also been shown to increase distrust and fear of certain stimuli, particularly those which might pose a threat to survival. By analysing cerebral spinal fluid and patient accounts of behaviour, Leckman et al. (1994) found that some forms of OCD were related to oxytocin dysfunction. This could mean that OCD-type behaviours may be at the extreme end of a normal range of behaviours moderated by the hormone.

- *Neurological*: Abnormalities of brain structure and function offer a third possible biomedical explanation for OCD. The area of the brain known as the basal ganglia has been implicated by studies of brain-damaged patients as related to the obsessive thinking symptomatic of OCD. The basal ganglia and two associated regions (orbitofrontal cortex and the anterior cingulate gyrus) usually work together to send and check warning messages about threatening stimuli. In individuals with impaired function in these areas, this checking 'loop' does not work as it should; meaning the basal ganglia continues to receive worrying messages that 'something is wrong'.

Cognitive and behavioural

As you have discovered, OCD is composed of two aspects; cognitive obsessions and behavioural compulsions. The cognitive explanation considers that obsessive thinking is based on faulty reasoning (Rachman, 1977). For example, the belief that hands are covered in harmful germs that could kill (Figure 6.23) is due to errors in thinking.

These mistakes in cognition can also worsen under stressful conditions. Compulsive behaviours are the outcome of such erroneous thinking, attempts to alleviate the unwanted thoughts and the anxiety they create. Compulsive behaviour can be explained through the principles of operant conditioning. Engaging in behaviour such as hand-washing may alleviate the obsession over germs, albeit temporarily. The hand-washing has become a **negative reinforcer** because it has relieved something unpleasant (the worrying obsessive thoughts). It is also a positive reinforcer, because the person is 'rewarded' by knowing that they have clean hands. The influence of negative and positive reinforcement can shape obsessive-compulsive behaviours, meaning they are *learned* behaviours.

6.23 Compulsive hand-washing may result from dysfunctional thinking

Psychodynamic

This approach looks to unconscious beliefs and desires to explain the occurrence of OCD. Psychodynamic theorists claim that symptoms of these disorders appear as a result of an internal conflict between the id and the ego. Freud suggested that such conflict arises in the anal stage of psychosexual development, around the time most children begin toilet training (Figure 6.24). This process may involve tension between children and their parents, who may wish to control how and when the child defecates or urinates, against the child's wishes. In order to regain control the child may soil themselves, which causes upset and arguments. Alternatively, the child may fear harsh responses from their parents and retain faeces or urine in order to regain control.

6.24 Can traumatic toilet training really cause OCD?

Both these behaviours (anally expulsive and anally retentive) can lead to later behavioural disturbances, as the individual has become 'fixated' in this stage. Essentially, the obsessive thoughts which come from the id disturb the rational part of the self, the ego, to the extent that it may lead to compulsive cleaning and tidying rituals later in life, in order to deal with the earlier childhood trauma.

Evaluation

The biomedical explanations each have their respective strengths and weaknesses. The scientific analysis used in identifying genes relating to OCD is **objective** and usually conducted under well-controlled laboratory conditions. This also makes it highly **replicable.** However, it does not offer a complete picture in that it cannot explain why some individuals may carry genes that are implicated in OCD, yet never develop symptoms.

Biochemical explanations such as the oxytocin hypothesis are also supported by laboratory-based studies. However, it is difficult to establish a **cause and effect** relationship between the hormone and OCD symptoms. The third biomedical account considers brain structure and function. Evidence suggesting a role for the basal ganglia in OCD is supported by case studies of brain-damaged individuals. This method may lack **generalisability**, however, as these individuals may not be representative of a wider population. More research is needed into examining the structure and function of this and related areas of the brain.

Cognitive and behavioural accounts fit well with the experience of OCD symptoms reported by individuals with the disorder. However, much research in this area relies on **self-report**, including measures such as the Y-BOCS or MOCI. This introduces **bias** as individuals may deliberately or inadvertently mislead researchers.

The psychodynamic explanation, by contrast, is not supported by empirical research. This is because you cannot accurately measure or **control** the variables involved. It means it would be difficult to demonstrate a **cause and effect** relationship between harsh parenting during toilet training and a child's later compulsive washing, for example.

ISSUES AND DEBATES

Biomedical explanations for OCD are **applicable to everyday life** as they can indicate potential areas for research on treating and management of the disorder. For example, understanding the role of the basal ganglia, orbitofrontal cortex and the anterior cingulate gyrus has led to innovations in neurosurgery which may offer symptom relief. Similarly, cognitive-behavioural and psychodynamic accounts have also led to treatment options for OCD, including psychoanalysis and CBT (which we will consider below).

However, biomedical, cognitive and behavioural explanations focus on the **individual**, their hormonal abnormalities or faulty thought processes (Rachman, 1977). This ignores the role of **situational** factors and can also be considered **reductionist**. The psychodynamic explanation, however, places more emphasis on early social relationships and considers the effect these can have on an individual's development.

Likewise, the biomedical accounts all rely on physiological factors (genes, hormones, brain function) which relate to the nature side of the **nature versus nurture** debate. By contrast, the behavioural explanation of compulsions suggests that they are learned behaviours, making individuals with OCD a product of their environment. Although these accounts sit either side of the nature vs nurture debate, they can also be considered to be **deterministic**; we have no free will to influence our genetic make-up or the automatic learning processes that may lead to developing OCD.

Treatment and management of obsessive compulsive and related disorders
Biomedical (SSRIs)

We considered the use of SSRIs in treating depression earlier in Section 6.2. They have also been used to treat OCD and related disorders. These medications are selective in the sense that they work on the neurotransmitter serotonin alone. In a meta-analysis, Soomro et al. (2008) reviewed the results of 17 studies which compared the effectiveness of SSRIs with placebos. In all studies, totalling 3097 participants, SSRIs as a group were more effective at reducing OCD symptoms 6–13 weeks after treatment using the Y-BOCS. The effect of taking SSRIs to treat OCD is that they reduce the severity of obsessive compulsive symptoms as they seem to lessen the anxiety associated with the disorder. They have been shown to work in individuals with and without depression, though generally a higher dosage of medication is given as it has been shown to be more effective (Pampaloni et al., 2009).

Psychological therapies: cognitive (Lovell et al., 2006) and exposure and response prevention (Lehmkuhl et al., 2008)

The alternative to biomedical treatment is psychological therapy. Here we will consider two such examples that have been applied to the management of OCD.

Lovell et al. (2006) used a randomised control trial to compare the effectiveness of CBT delivered by telephone (Figure 6.25) with the same therapy offered face-to-face in those with OCD. This was a randomised control trial. Seventy-two participants from two different outpatient hospital departments each underwent ten weekly sessions of therapy either delivered by telephone or face-to-face. Changes in participants' well-being were measured using the Y-BOCS, Beck Depression Inventory and a client satisfaction questionnaire. At six months post-treatment, the change in Y-BOCS scores prior to therapy and after therapy showed significant improvement in symptoms for both groups. Participants were also found to be highly satisfied with both telephone and face-to face CBT. This suggests that the patients with OCD may benefit equally from telephone or face-to-face CBT.

6.25 Cognitive therapy via telephone

Exposure and response prevention (ERP) is a form of CBT. Lehmkuhl et al. (2008) researched the application of this form of treatment in a case study with a 12-year-old boy referred to as Jason who had both OCD and **autism (or autistic spectrum disorder, ASD)**. Approximately 2% of children with ASD are also diagnosed with OCD. It can be difficult to distinguish ASD rituals and behaviour from

 KEY TERM

autism (or autistic spectrum disorder, ASD): developmental disorders characterised by difficulty in social, communicative and imaginative areas. They are also associated with repetitive physical behaviours.

compulsive behaviour seen in OCD; however cleaning, checking and counting tend to be common in those with OCD. Jason had been diagnosed with high-functioning autism (normal IQ score), and also experienced contamination fear, excessive hand-washing, counting and checking. He would spend several hours each day engaged in compulsive behaviour and reported significant anxiety when prevented from completing his rituals.

ERP consists of (1) gathering information about existing symptoms, (2) therapist-initiated ERP and (3) generalisation and relapse training. Jason attended ten 50 minute CBT sessions over 16 weeks. Some of the ERP techniques were modified to meet Jason's specific ASD needs; he was not asked to do visualisation exercises as he would find it impossible to imagine pretend situations. Jason first identified feelings of distress and with the help of the therapist, learned coping statements for when he felt anxious (e.g. 'I know that nothing bad will happen…').

The next step involved exposing Jason to stimuli which he felt were contaminated and produced feelings of anxiety or disgust. These include common objects such as door handles and elevator buttons. The exposure involved Jason being asked to touch these items, and repeatedly to do so until he became **habituated** and his anxiety levels dropped. Exposures became increasingly difficult, so that Jason was engaging in behaviours that held increasing anxiety for him. In between sessions he practised this exposure through specific tasks in his normal environment, handing out papers in a classroom or using 'contaminated' items at home.

After completing his therapy, Jason's score on the Y-BOCS had dropped from a severely high pre-therapy score of 18 to just 3, well within the normal range. At a three month follow-up his score remained low, and both he and his parents reported a significant improvement in both his OCD symptoms and his participation in school and social activities.

Evaluation

The research by Lovell et al. (2006) used an **independent measures** experimental design in which participants were randomly allocated to one of two conditions, thus removing the possibility of **researcher bias**. The face-to-face CBT group acted as the **control group** for the experiment, meaning researchers could compare the effectiveness of

telephone therapy effectively. The duration of the therapy was kept the same in both conditions, and outcomes were measured using the same validated scales. This meant the study had high levels of **validity** and **reliability**.

> **Reflections:** Why do you think Lovell et al. (2006) did not include a third group of OCD patients who received no therapy during the experiment?

Lehmkuhl et al. (2008) used a case study to investigate the effectiveness of ERP as a treatment for OCD. This method offers limited generalisability, particularly so in this case because the participant also had ASD, meaning he was not **representative** of the general population of OCD sufferers. As a 12-year-old, Jason was a child with additional needs, which also raises **ethical issues** around briefing, consent and the risk of psychological harm. However it does give us an in-depth understanding of the experience of going through ERP and captures both **quantitative** and **qualitative data** through interview and Y-BOCS scores.

ISSUES AND DEBATES

SSRIs have a fairly high success rate in reducing symptoms of OCD. They are generally considered safe, though their use is sometimes restricted in cases of children or young people with OCD, as the risks of harmful side effects may be higher. Similarly, the case study of Jason (Lehmkuhl et al., 2008) also raises issues around the ethics and practicalities of **conducting research with children**. His parents would have had to give consent on Jason's behalf, and some of the procedures of his ERP therapy were altered to accommodate his age and ASD needs. Nonetheless, cognitive-behavioural therapies and SSRIs are the most frequently used treatments for OCD, meaning research in this area is **applicable to real life**.

In terms of **individual vs situational explanations**, the use of SSRIs to manage OCD treats only one aspect: the individual's serotonin uptake. This treatment does not alter their environment or take into consideration what might have caused the OCD symptoms to emerge in the first place. Thus it is also a **reductionist** approach to treating mental health disorders. Cognitive-behavioural therapies such as those used by Lovell et al. (2006) and Lehmkuhl et al. (2008) consider the environment in which the person's compulsive behaviour takes place. For example, Jason's therapy addressed triggers in his home and school environment in order to help pre-empt relapse post-treatment.

KEY TERM

habituated: when a person becomes accustomed to something. When someone is frequently exposed to a certain stimulus then over time they become used to it.

Summary

Throughout this chapter, we have explored five major categories of mental health disorders. For each we have considered the specific characteristics of disorders, a range of explanations, as well as treatment and management options. The studies and theories we have looked at involve a variety of psychological approaches, such as biological, cognitive and behavioural perspectives. In considering the research into psychology and abnormality, we have also encountered a range of issues and debates.

In the section on schizophrenic and psychotic disorders, the focus was on defining and diagnosing schizophrenia. Specifically we explored the possibility of using virtual reality to assess symptoms in the paper by **Freeman (2008)**. We compared biological explanations of the disorder, such as large-scale genetic studies (**Gottesman and Shields, 1972**) and the dopamine hypothesis with cognitive accounts, such as that by **Frith (1992)**. This allowed us to consider the effectiveness and ethics of a range of treatments, including the use of anti-psychotic medication, ECT, token economies (**Paul and Lentz, 1977**) and CBT (**Sensky, 2000**). Amongst other issues, cultural bias and nature-nurture were relevant to assessing biological predisposition and cultural attitudes towards these disorders.

Similarly, in the topic on bipolar and related disorders, we outlined what is meant by 'abnormal affect', distinguished bipolar from unipolar depression and learned about the Beck Depression Inventory. Beck's work had further relevance in comparing his cognitive explanation for depression with **Oruc's (1997)** biological research, as well as **Seligman's (1988)** theory of learned helplessness. A range of treatments were considered in detail, including biological approaches such as drug therapy and ECT. These were contrasted with cognitive and behavioural models proposed by **Beck (1979)** and **Ellis (1962)**. The effectiveness of research in this area means it can be applied to real-life. We looked also at the use of psychometrics as a key issue in this area.

Different types of impulse control disorders were described in the next sub-topic, such as pyromania (**Burton et al., 2012**). We looked at the explanatory value of dopamine, positive reinforcement and the feeling-state theory (**Miller 2010**) in relation to these disorders. Likewise, one biochemical treatment study by **Grant et al. (2008)** was compared to a range of cognitive-behavioural treatments (**Blaszczynski and Nower, 2002; Glover, 2008** and **Miller, 2010**). This raised the debate over determinism and free will; the extent to which individuals could control and change their impulsive behaviours.

The topic on anxiety disorders primarily focused on what is meant by the terms 'anxiety' and 'phobia'; and how different disorders can be defined and measured (e.g. the BIPI and GAD-7). We looked at a range of explanations for these disorders, covering a wide spectrum of approaches (behavioural, psychoanalytic, biological and cognitive). We examined treatment techniques such as systematic desensitisation (**Wolpe, 1958**), applied tension and CBT (**Öst et al., 1989; Öst and Westling, 1995**). Issues relevant to this section included the use of psychometrics, as well as the use of children in psychological research, as seen in the research case studies.

In the final section, obsessive compulsive disorders were specified in terms of types, case studies (Charles by **Rapoport (1989)**) and measures (MOCI and Y-BOCS). Key explanations for OCD included biomedical, cognitive and behavioural, as well as psychodynamic approaches. Lastly, we looked again at the use of SSRIs to manage OCD symptoms, in contrast with psychological therapies such as cognitive (**Lovell et al., 2007**) and exposure and response prevention (**Lehmkuhl et al., 2008**). Once again, the use of children in psychological research was a salient issue, as well as there being implications for the debate over reductionism in terms of biomedical explanation and treatment.

Exam-style questions

1   **a** Explain what is meant by the term 'agoraphobia'. **[2 marks]**

  b Describe one measure of obsessive-compulsive and related disorders. **[4 marks]**

  c Discuss one strength and one weakness of the behavioural explanation of phobias (Watson, 1920). **[6 marks]**

Chapter 7
Psychology of consumer behaviour

Introduction

This chapter introduces you to five key topics within:

- **The physical environment:** This section considers the effect of various factors of the retail or leisure environment, including architecture and layout. This section also examines the effect of music on consumers and the influence of lighting, colour and smell.

- **The psychological environment:** This section considers the way that consumers make sense of their environment, the impact of menu design and the importance of personal space.

- **Consumer decision-making:** This section considers the way that individuals make decisions as well as choice

blindness and false memory and their applications to consumer behaviour.

- **The product:** This section considers a variety of factors relevant to the product. These include packaging, positioning and placement, sales techniques and purchasing decisions and behaviours.

- **Advertising:** This section considers advertising techniques, communication models and issues relating to children's brand recognition, the importance of the consumer personality and what makes an effective slogan.

What is consumer psychology? This is a relatively new area of applied psychology which looks at why and how individuals and groups engage in consumer behaviours (Boyd-Jannson, 2010). This chapter will consider some of the key areas of consumer psychology.

You may be able to think of some applications already based on the psychology you learned in your AS course. Social psychology may be relevant when considering issues such as attitudes and attempts to change attitudes, the effects of other people on our consumer behaviours and so on. The learning approach is also important in considering how advertisers might use knowledge about classical and operant conditioning to develop successful advertising techniques. Aspects of the cognitive approach such as memory and decision making are also crucial in understanding how individuals make sense of advertisments and other marketing techniques.

Finally, although there is little biological research in this chapter, some recent research has made use of fMRI technology to see if it is possible to predict the decisions that we might make before we respond to questions. Much of the research that we will be covering in this chapter uses research methods that will be familiar to you from other parts of your course. The same evaluation issues will also be relevant to this research although you should bear in mind that the research conducted in this area, as in all areas of applied psychology, tends to be conducted in the real world rather than the laboratory.

> **Reflections:** Before reading any further, think about all the psychology that you have learned so far. Make a note of all the things you can think of that might be relevant to the study of consumer behaviour.

7.1 The physical environment

Retail/leisure environment design

Retail store architecture

Shoppers may respond to the atmosphere of a retail environment in one of two ways: approach or avoidance. Approach behaviours would be positive responses such as the desire to stay in the environment longer and to explore it further. Avoidance behaviours would be the opposite; not wanting to stay in the environment any longer and feeling no desire to explore these further. Turley and Milliman (2000) identified and reviewed 60 studies which all found a statistically significant relationship between some aspect of atmospherics and shopping behaviour. Their article argues that it is possible to create atmospheres which influence consumers to spend money.

They grouped atmospheric variables into five categories:

- External variables: signs, displays, size of building, style, location and so on
- General interior variables: colour schemes, flooring, lighting, music, scents and aisle width
- Layout and design variables: allocation of space, placement of merchandise, placement of cash registers, waiting space and changing rooms
- Point of purchase and decoration variables: wall decorations, certificates and point of purchase displays
- Human variables: employee characteristics, uniforms, crowding, customer characteristics and privacy.

> **!**
>
> **RESEARCH METHODS**
> Think about the last time you went shopping. Try to identify at least two features (variables) about a shop that made you want to spend time in the shop and at least two features about a shop that made you want to leave.

Research into external variables has identified the importance of store exterior and window displays, as well as parking and location. Interestingly this group of variables has not been extensively studied and one conclusion drawn by Turley and Milliman is that far more research needs to be done in this area, especially as these exterior variables are usually the first set of cues seen by a consumer.

Far more research has been conducted into the effect of general interior variables. Research has shown that general perceptions of the interior can affect approach/avoidance behaviours. Music has been extensively studied and has been shown to affect sales, arousal levels, perceptions of and actual time spent in the environment, and flow through the store. Music influences our behaviour even when we are not consciously aware of the music. A more recent focus of research has been odour (smell or aroma) and colour. Both of these have been shown to influence purchases, time spent in the store and pleasant feelings and can be used to attract a customer to a specific display. Lighting has also been shown to influence store image.

Research into variables in the layout and design category is also under-explored. There is some research which suggests that layout can be used to influence purchases and also research which highlights the importance of the relationship between consumer knowledge of store layout and unplanned purchasing. Unplanned purchases are higher when consumers are unfamiliar with the store layout which may explain why large supermarkets rearrange items frequently!

Studies into point of purchase and decoration variables reveal that product displays can be used to manipulate sales, as can in-store signage (such as special offer information). However, results from research into the use of shelf space (where an item is located, how much space is allocated to the item) is inconclusive and there are obviously many other variables impacting on this relationship.

Finally, the newly added category was that of human variables. Turley and Milliman divided these into two: the influence of other shoppers and the influence of retail employees on customer shopping behaviour. One of the key areas here is crowding. Perceived crowding tends to have a negative influence on shopping satisfaction, with customers doing less browsing and comparison shopping, fewer purchases and lower ratings of enjoyment and excitement. The other category relates to the appearance of the retail staff. Professionally dressed staff have a positive effect on satisfaction and the number of staff available in a store can also have a positive effect on ratings of service quality.

Reflections: Design a store selling one of the following products: designer clothing, budget clothing, electronics, confectionary. Identify at least one characteristic from each of the five categories discussed here.

Turley and Milliman established that the retail environment can be shaped in many ways to elicit a variety of behaviours from shoppers. Purchasing behaviour is obviously the most important dependent variable in most studies although time spent in the store and ratings of enjoyment are also common. We will be meeting many of these variables throughout this chapter. Turley and Milliman identified some areas that they felt would benefit from further research. These included exterior building shape and style, landscaping and signage from the exterior variables category and research into different odours and the relationship between different groups of people and their responses to different odours and the effect of different floor coverings from the interior variables category.

Reflections: Design an experimental study to investigate the effect of different floor coverings (carpet, wood, tiles etc.) in a retail environment on either sales or customer perceptions. State a clear hypothesis for your study and explain how you would manipulate the independent variable and how you would measure the dependent variable.

Turley and Milliman also suggested that research could be usefully conducted into a number of areas, as shown in Table 7.1. They concluded their review by identifying the need for the development of theory in the area of consumer psychology. This is an important issue to consider as new areas of research need to build up a considerable amount of research evidence before this can contribute to theoretical explanations.

Layout and design	How are customers asked to wait to be served? Is there a long queue where customers are called to the next available checkout or multiple queues? Do these impact on customers' perceptions of waiting time or on approach/avoidance behaviour?
Waiting room design and furnishings (for example in a doctor's surgery or in a hairdressing salon)	How does this affect customer attitudes? Within the area of point of purchase and decoration variables, how do artworks and certificates demonstrating staff qualifications and competencies, and television sets for customers to watch while they are waiting to be served have an effect?
Employee uniforms	The impact of staff wearing uniforms is far more significant than has previously been recognised but more research is needed.

Table 7.1 Areas of research

Leisure environments

The study by Finlay et al. (2006) compared two different casino designs. The first was the 'playground model' proposed by Kranes (1995) who suggested that a casino should be a simple and easy to understand space with familiar, pleasing and natural elements. This model proposed that casinos should include environmental elements such as sunlight, green space and moving water to induce feelings of security, intimacy, pleasure, freedom and vitality. In contrast, Friedman (2000) proposed that the machines should be the dominant feature of the décor. Any other design elements should be limited to highlighting the machines. This means that ceilings should be low and no signs should draw the gamblers' attention away from the machines. The casino should be divided into small areas with short pathways that 'twist and turn'. This layout was predicted in this study to reduce legibility and coherence (i.e. decrease feelings of relaxation). A sample of the Friedman macro design is displayed in Figure 7.1.

7.1 Friedman macro design

This study used a quasi-experimental design as the researchers simply identified three casinos constructed on each design (Finlay et al., 2006). Measures of emotional reactions to the casinos were collected from people who had gambled in all six casinos. The participants were 48 individuals (26 males) recruited from casinos in Las Vegas, Nevada in May 2002. The mean age was 28 years, and all participants had attained at least a high school degree. Groups of two or three participants were paired with one of the researchers. That group went on to visit four casinos in succession. This recruitment process was replicated for each of four researchers so that across the researchers, each of 16 casinos reviewed by Kranes and Friedman was rated by at least three individuals.

The results showed that the Kranes-type casinos yielded significantly higher ratings than did Friedman-type casinos on pleasure and restoration (relief from environmental stress). The authors conclude that future research should focus on design variations that can be built into a Friedman-type setting to enhance restoration.

> **Reflections:** This study has discussed the design of casinos. To what extent could you apply the findings of this study to the design of very different retail environments such as a beauty salon or a car salesroom?

Store interior layout

We have already considered the way in which several aspects of a retail store may be crucial to its success. Vrechopolous et al. (2004) argued that the design and, in particular, the layout of a virtual store is equally as crucial to virtual retail store success. In this study, the authors manipulate the virtual layout of an online grocery store by creating three different layouts: a free-form layout, a grid layout and a racetrack layout (Figure 7.2).

7.2 Store layouts: (a) free-form; (b) grid; (c) racetrack

Reflections: Study the images of the different layouts given in Figure 7.2. Do any of the shops that you visit on a regular basis have these layouts?

Some 120 participants were recruited from both Greece and the UK to take part in a laboratory experiment where they were given a planned shopping task with money to spend and completed this task in one of the three virtual store layouts. Each participant was given a budget of £20 (or 12 000 Greek drachmas) and whatever was 'purchased' during the experiment was subsequently purchased by the researchers and physically delivered to the participants.

The online store offered mainly European brands (the researchers mention Coke, Heineken, Pringles, Tide and Johnny Walker in their report) but also included some own-brand products. To make the online experience as similar to a visit to a grocery store as possible, participants were given a blank shopping list and information about what was available in the store in order to plan their purchases.

The results showed that the free-form layout was more useful in terms of finding items on a shopping list. It was also reported to be the most entertaining to use. The grid layout was reported to be significantly easier to use than the other two layouts (with the racetrack layout the hardest to use). Finally, the layout significantly affected the length of time that customers spent shopping, with the racetrack and free-form layouts engaging shoppers for longer, as would be predicted by conventional retail theory.

The results suggest that conventional retailing store layout theory is not readily applicable to online grocery retail and that customers visiting a virtual grocery store prefer a hierarchical/tree structure. Such a structure is only provided by a grid layout which was perceived as the easiest to use. Shopping behaviour was also facilitated by being able to reach any place in the store directly (that is from the home page or from any other 'place' in the store). This was only provided by the free-form layout which was perceived as the most useful for conducting planned purchases.

Evaluation

All three of the articles considered here demonstrate the relationship between the individual and the situation (retail environment). Turley and Milliman identify a large number of variables that can be manipulated to affect shopping behaviour and shopper attitudes and these have obvious practical applications for retail organisations. Obviously it is not always going to be possible to manipulate every aspect of a retail environment but knowledge of these factors can only be useful. For example, if sales of a particular item are low, this might be addressed by the addition of an appropriate artificial odour or style of music – a relatively inexpensive strategy to attempt. However, all three articles also highlight the importance of individual factors as well.

Turley and Milliman's article is a review; that is they did not conduct any of this research themselves but have brought together the findings of many pieces of research to see if any general conclusions can be drawn. This is an important stage in the development of a body of research. Finlay's study comparing two different styles of casino design can be described as a **quasi-experiment**. There is an **independent variable** (type of design) but this was not manipulated by the experimenter. This means that there may be many **extraneous variables** that have not been taken into account although clearly research that is conducted in 'real' rather than artificial laboratory environments will have high levels of **ecological validity**. Much of the research reported in the review by Turley and Milliman is likely to have used the same approach. High ecological validity but some lack of control will be a theme that we return to throughout this chapter as most of the research is conducted in real retail environments rather than the controlled environment of the laboratory.

Both this study and the study by Vrechopolous et al. have many useful applications. Finlay's work suggests useful modifications that could be made to casinos based on the least preferred design although it is interesting to consider whether the findings of this study would generalise to environments other than casinos. The study by Vrechopolous et al. suggests that online retail stores need to take care when applying principles and guidelines drawn from traditional retail environments, although increasing the number of hyperlinks to make it easier for customers to find the products that they are looking for would seem to be justified by the research. This study differs from the previous one as it was conducted as a laboratory study although the ecological validity was increased by the use of a real shopping task and the **generalisability** is also increased by the fact that the samples were drawn from two countries.

Sound and consumer behaviour
Music in restaurants

The aim of the study by North et al. (2003) was to investigate the effect of musical style on the amount of money customers spent in a restaurant.

This was a **field experiment** which was conducted in a restaurant in the UK. The independent variable was the type of music played and the dependent variable was the amount of money spent. There were three conditions of the independent variable: classical music, pop music and no music. On one evening only classical music was played, on the following evening pop music and then the control condition of no music. This was done for 18 evenings. The research employed an independent subjects design such that each participant was exposed to only one of the music conditions. All other aspects of the restaurant, such as lighting, decoration, temperature and menu, were held constant throughout the research.

In total 393 restaurant customers participated in the research. This was the number of people that ate in the restaurant during the 18 evenings that the study was conducted (February/March 2002), excluding a small number of customers who ate at the restaurant on more than one occasion (to ensure that there were no confounding effects from this). There were approximately equal numbers of males and females and no participants were aware that they were taking part in psychological research.

Of the participants, 142 were exposed to the pop music condition, 120 to the classical music condition, and 131 to the no music condition. Overall, a total of 141 parties of diners were investigated: 49 parties in the pop music condition, 44 parties in the classical music condition, and 48 parties in the no music condition.

Two 76-minute CDs were prepared for each music condition, making a total of two hours and 32 minutes of music to ensure that no single piece of music was repeated for any customer. The music was played at a constant background volume on the restaurant's usual CD system. An **independent samples t-test** indicated no difference between the pace of the music in the two conditions.

Reflections: Why do you think it is important to make sure that the music did not differ in pace?

The research was carried out in a restaurant situated in a small affluent town located in the UK. The restaurant served high-quality food at prices which the researchers described as 'well above' the market average. The study was carried out over a period of three weeks for the entire duration of the restaurant's evening opening hours (Monday to Saturday, inclusive from 7 p.m. to approximately 11.30 p.m.). There were no significant public or school holidays within

the three weeks. An experimenter collected data while working as a waitress in the restaurant.

Reflections: What is the research technique called when a researcher becomes part of the environment in order to research this? What are the strengths and weaknesses of this?

The **dependent variable** was the mean amount of money spent per person. This was calculated separately for starters, main course, desserts, coffee, bar drinks, wine and then for overall drink bill, overall food bill and total spend. The researchers also recorded the total amount of time that each person spent in the restaurant.

Reflections: This study conducted quantitative data only. Suggest what qualitative data could also have been collected.

The results showed that on the evenings when classical music was played, the average spend was higher than in both the other two conditions (pop music and no music). Customers were also more likely to have starters and coffee in the classical music condition. **Statistical analysis** revealed that there was an overall significant difference between the conditions with classical music leading to higher spending than both no music and pop music. Statistical analysis indicated that there were significant differences between the conditions on mean spend per head on starters, coffee, total spend on food and overall spend.

The authors conclude that these findings were consistent with the limited previous research, which had suggested that the playing of background classical music led to both (a) people reporting that they were prepared to spend more and (b) higher actual spending. The results indicate that restaurant managers can use classical music to increase customer spending, and the results are discussed in terms of three possible explanations. The first is that classical music is **synergistic** with other aspects of the restaurant

KEY TERMS

statistical analysis: involves the use of statistical tests which measure the likelihood of differences or relationships in data being due to chance.

synergistic: leading to the interaction of more than one condition which creates a combined effect greater than the sum of either of their effects separately.

(stylish décor, etc.) and that this synergy promotes spending. However this does not explain the results found here as the same effect of classical music was found in the study by North and Hargreaves (1998) conducted in a student cafeteria. This study also showed that classical music increased spending and the music was most definitely not synergistic with the surroundings.

The second explanation is that classical music was the preferred music of the customers and that this increased liking somehow produced higher spending. This is also unlikely to be the reason in the North and Hargreaves study, and without self-report data on musical preferences, this explanation cannot be usefully applied here.

The third explanation is the one preferred by the researchers. They suggest that classical music promotes an upmarket atmosphere which 'primes contextually appropriate, congruent behaviour' (page 717) such as increased spending. This explanation would not only explain the results of this study but also of previously conducted studies such as North and Hargreaves.

> **Reflections:** Suggest how this third explanation could be investigated further. How might a researcher measure whether classical music produces an upmarket atmosphere? Be as creative as you like!

Music in open air markets

Many experiments have shown that music, particularly classical music, increases spending. These studies have been conducted in a range of retail environments but according to the authors of our next study, the effect of music on spending has never been tested in outdoor environments. This study was conducted at one stall (selling trinkets and toys for €10 or less) at an open air market in France and aimed to test the hypotheses that popular music would increase both length of stay at the stall as well as the amount that was spent.

The article by Gueguen et al. (2007) describes a **field experiment** as it was conducted in a real environment but maintained control over the **independent variable** which was whether music was being played or not being played. The music chosen was described as 'joyful' and it was selected through a pre-test which established its appropriateness for association with the selling of trinkets and toys.

Some 154 men and 86 women were selected from visitors to a stall at an open air market in France on two sunny Saturdays. The three female stall holders acted as confederates of the experimenter and if the subject was in the music condition, the confederate would start the music (playing on a portable system) as soon as the subject approached the stall. Only one confederate knew who had been selected as the subject and she did not interact with the subject in any way. One confederate would time the length of stay at the stall and the amount that had been spent was recorded once the customer had left.

Data was examined for differences between male and female customers and as none were found, the data for both males and females was combined. The results showed that when music was played, customers stayed significantly longer at the stall than when no music was played. Customers in the music condition stayed at the stall for an average of 5.27 minutes whereas customers in the no music condition stayed for an average of 3.72 minutes. This was **significant** at $p<0.001$.

> **RESEARCH METHODS**
> Explain what is meant by 'This was **significant** at $p<0.001$'.

There was a difference between sales in the two conditions. In the music condition, 18% of people bought something compared with 10% in the no music condition. However this was only significant at $p < 0.07$ which in many studies would not be regarded as a large enough difference to be considered significant. Finally, although customers in the music condition spent an average of €6.3 compared to an average spend of €5.67 in the no music condition, this difference was not statistically significant.

The authors offered several possible explanations for their findings. Firstly the finding that people stayed longer at the stall when music was being played may be explained by the finding that music may influence our perception of time. Secondly, although the differences in amount spent were not significant the authors claimed that music can be used to increase sales. There are other studies which support these arguments, such as that by Areni and Kim (1993) who showed that classical music led to customers in an upmarket wine shop buying more expensive bottles of wine than when other music was played. However, there are also limitations to this study such as the fact that music at an outdoor stall is considered something of an oddity by the researchers and it may be this rather than the music itself that was keeping customers at the stall.

Background noise and food perception

Woods et al. (2011) used a **laboratory experiment** to investigate the effect of auditory background noise on the perception on gustatory food properties (or taste), including reported saltiness, sweetness, food crunchiness and food liking.

The independent variable was the background noise. There were three conditions of background noise (no sound, quiet background white noise and loud background white noise). The dependent variables were the ratings that the participants had to give. In experiment 1 participants had to rate the food they ate in terms of sweetness, saltiness and liking. In experiment 2 participants had to rate the food they ate in terms of overall flavour, crunchiness and liking.

In the first experiment, 48 students (39 female and nine male) between 19 and 39 years of age (mean = 29 years) from Manchester University participated. They volunteered to take part in this experiment in return for either course credits or payment. Participants were told that the study involved judging foods on several different characteristics. At the time of the study, five smoked and five reported mild cold symptoms. None of the participants reported any food allergies. All participants gave informed consent.

Commercially available foods were used as stimuli. Both savoury and sweet stimuli were selected for the soft and crunchy food categories. Water crackers were included as a dummy stimulus to promote full scale-usage (crackers are neither salty nor sweet). The food was broken into mouth-sized pieces (approximately 1 cm cubed or 2 cm squared in size).

The participant sat at a table upon which there was a panel to hide the food from view (Figure 7.3). The participant wore headphones which were open backed to minimise the distortion of chewing sounds. White noise was delivered through these at either at 45–55 dB (quiet) or 75–85 dB (loud). There was also a no white noise condition to give a baseline measure.

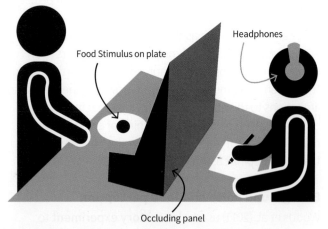

7.3 Experimental set up, showing how food was hidden from the participant

Participants were told at the start of each trial to close their eyes and rest their hands on the table in front of them. The experimenter placed a paper plate containing a food stimulus on the table touching the participant's fingers to indicate to the participant to pick up the stimulus and eat it. After swallowing, the participant opened their eyes and then rated the stimulus on saltiness, sweetness and liking. Participants were asked to take a sip of water between each trial. There were 25 trials per participant, which took approximately 30 minutes. Afterwards, all participants were fully debriefed as to the nature of the experiment.

The second experiment had two aims:

- To test whether sound conveyed food cues are affected by background noise and how this compares to the ratings of gustatory food cues.
- To assess whether the liking (or disliking) of the background noise affects the liking of food consumed in the presence of the noise.

The participants were 34 students (19 female and 15 male) from Manchester. Participants' ages ranged from 20 to 49 years (mean = 28 years). None reported any food allergies.

As with the first study, all foods used were commercially available and fell into three categories: sweet, salty or as dummy stimuli. Participants rated flavour, crunchiness and liking. They also rated how much they liked the background noise over the whole study. The remainder of the design and procedure was identical to experiment 1.

Remember that in experiment 1 participants had to rate the food they ate in terms of sweetness, saltiness and liking. In experiment 2 participants had to rate the food they ate in terms of overall flavour, crunchiness and liking.

The results are fascinating. Reported sweetness and saltiness were significantly lower in the loud condition compared with the quiet sound condition (experiment 1), but crunchiness was reported to be more intense in the loud condition (experiment 2). This suggests that food properties unrelated to sound (sweetness, saltiness) and those conveyed via auditory channels (crunchiness) are affected differently by background noise. A relationship between ratings of the liking of background noise and ratings of the liking of the food was also found (experiment 2).

The authors concluded that background sound which is unrelated to food diminishes gustatory food properties saltiness, sweetness while enhancing food crunchiness.

Reflections: Can you think of any another environmental variable that might affect taste? Design an experiment to measure its effect.

Evaluation

It is important to consider the application of these studies to everyday life. They certainly seem to suggest that music will have a positive effect on customer spending in very different environments. However, it may not be quite that simple. Would classical music lead to increased spending in a different type of restaurant, a pizza chain for example, or would some other music be more likely to have this effect here?

We also need to consider the effects of cultural differences. Would these effects be the same in different cultures where the use of music or the level of background noise may be very different or have very different cultural meanings? This is not to suggest that the studies themselves suffer from any form of bias but that their application to different cultures needs to be carefully considered.

Finally, the issue of individual versus situational explanations is also important. Although the three studies considered in this section provide strong support for the importance of situational factors in determining our behaviour, it is likely that individual characteristics such as personality type are also important and should be considered in further research.

The studies by North and by Gueguen were **field experiments**: they manipulated an independent variable and measured its effect on a dependent variable in a 'real' environment (a restaurant and an outdoor market stall) rather than in the artificial environment of a laboratory. This gives the research high levels of **ecological validity** but relatively low levels of control. In contrast the study by Woods et al. was a **laboratory experiment** which would lead to higher levels of control but relatively lower levels of ecological validity. The participants in the field experiments were not aware that they were participating in a study so their behaviour should have been natural. In the laboratory, you will obviously know that you are taking part in an experiment and this is likely to produce demand characteristics. Woods et al. claimed that the levels of control in their study were superior to those used in other previous studies and that participants wore headphones across all conditions to remove this as a potential confounding variable.

Lighting, colour and smell

Models of effects of ambience: pleasure–arousal and cognition–emotion

What effect does smell really have? In some cultures, the sales of scented candles, room fragrancers and other products are growing rapidly, while in others aromatherapy products have been popular for many years. But what effect do they really have on us? There are claims that lavender relaxes and peppermint invigorates, ginger creates a romantic atmosphere and rose can help to combat depression. Although retailers may be more interested in whether a product sells than whether there is scientific evidence to support its use, there is a growing body of research in this area.

One useful model to consider here is the pleasure–arousal model first proposed by Mehrabian and Russell (1974) who proposed that mood is a mediating factor between environmental cues and behaviour. We can react to our environment with either approach or avoidance behaviours (stay and explore further or leave). Clearly anything that produces approach behaviours in consumers is worth exploring further. Positive responses to music, smell or any other variables will increase the length of time a consumer spends in a shop and may in turn increase the amount of money that they spend.

Alternatively, we could look at the relationship between cognition and emotion. There are two ways to look at this. The first is the emotion–cognition model proposed by Zajonc and Markus (1984).This proposes that an emotion can take place without antecedent cognitive processes and that emotions can be generated by biological, sensory or cognitive events. So cognition may produce emotion but it is not a necessary cause of emotion. The second model is the cognition–emotion model proposed by Lazarus (1966). This suggests that cognitions are a necessary but not sufficient precursor to emotions. What is required is a personal appraisal of the situation. In the study by Chebat and Michon (2003) later in this section, these two models are tested. In the first model olfactory cues (smell) stimulate positive emotions which influence customer perception of the environment and the product. In the second, scent mediates the perception of the shopping environment and product quality, thereby enhancing the customer mood.

Lighting and colour in retail stores

Kutlu et al. (2013) aimed to investigate how customer perception of a high-quality brand is influenced by colour and light. Previous research has suggested that bright/fluorescent light and the use of popular music produces a 'discount' image, whereas having a combination of soft/incandescent lights and classical music produces images of higher quality. They predict that a well-illuminated and well-designed store will increase the likelihood of passers-by stopping, looking in the window and entering the shop.

> **Reflections:** Imagine you had an unlimited budget to set up an expensive jewellery store. How would you use lighting to help the atmosphere that you need?

Kutlu et al. began by predicting that there is a relationship between store image and product type which will determine the type of lighting that will be most effective. They refered to this as the 'Square method' (see Figure 7.4) although this is not a recognised research method.

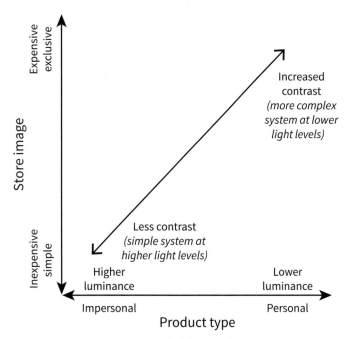

7.4 Square method for retail lighting design

The researchers visited four stores of the same high-quality brand (Nautilus) in Istanbul and collected data in two ways:

- data on the lighting levels in various parts of the store (the display units, the 'circulation' areas, the till, the windows and the changing rooms)
- data on customer perceptions of the store, which they collected using a questionnaire.

They recruited 121 participants with an age range of 15–60, of whom 15% were male and 85% were female. They were asked to complete a questionnaire. The questionnaire asked them to answer eight questions which were designed to evaluate the store image.

The results suggested that the lighting levels were above average for the windows, display units and circulation areas but not for the cash desk or the changing rooms. The questionnaire results showed that around 75% of the sample thought that the lighting colour scheme of a store had an effect on the brand image; 83.3% of them felt that the image was stylish, 12.7% thought it was luxurious and 4% thought it was simple. In addition, 31.7% of the respondents felt that the lighting colour scheme of the store was relaxing, 24% believed it was pleasing, 20.6% thought it was lively and 23% that it was boring.

They concluded that the perceived image and identity of a store/brand are strongly influenced by light and colour. In this particular store, the high levels of illumination along with the light coloured, highly reflective colour scheme contribute to the exclusive brand image.

> **Reflections:** Kutlu et al. suggested that sound and temperature are both features of the environment that could be manipulated to create different atmospheres. Choose either sound or temperature and suggest how you would manipulate this in your exclusive jewellery store.

Effects of odour on shopper arousal and emotions

Chebat and Michon (2003) conducted a field experiment in a shopping mall in Canada. The experiment was conducted in two consecutive weeks known to be identical in terms of sales volume and shopper traffic. The mall director cancelled all special promotions by the retailers during the two weeks of the experiment.

> **Reflections:** Why do you think that the shopping mall director cancelled all other special promotions during the two weeks of the experiment?

In the first week, the shopping mall's 'ambient olfactory atmosphere' (page 533) was not modified in any way. During the second week a light, pleasing scent was vaporised in the mall's main corridor. Ten diffusers released a citrus scent for three seconds every six minutes, maintaining a constant intensity. Pilot studies ensured that the odour intensity reached perceptual thresholds without starting to bother people.

Graduate students (who were asked not to wear any perfume) handed out the questionnaires. Those sampled were unaware of the true aim of the study and were simply asked to complete a questionnaire on the shopping trip.

Some 145 participants completed the questionnaire during the scent phase of the experiment. The experimenters had collected the same data from 447 people during the control week and explained that this larger number was to ensure that they had data for other experiments.

Questionnaires asked about perceptions of product quality, and about their perceptions of the shopping mall in general. Participants were also asked how much they had spent, excluding groceries, in this visit to the mall.

Findings

The researchers concluded that scent contributes to a favourable perception of a shopping environment and indirectly to an increased perception of product quality (thus supporting the cognition–emotion model discussed earlier). The use of an ambient scent is a relatively inexpensive technique for a retailer to consider. Although a product-related scent may be effective in increasing the sales of a particular product it may also reduce the sales of other products. The ambient scent needs to support all products in the store.

> **Reflections:** Suggest appropriate scents for a furniture store, grocery store and a high-end fashion store.

Evaluation

The studies conducted by Kutlu et al. and by Chebat and Michon were conducted in real retail environments; Kutlu et al. in Instanbul and Chebat and Michon in Canada. Kutlu et al. did not manipulate any variables but simply measured the lighting levels in the store and measured customers' perception of this. In contrast, Chebat and Michon manipulated the presence of a pleasing citrus odour and

compared both customer perceptions and spending with a 'no odour' condition. Despite the differences in method, there are similar strengths and weaknesses here. Both studies would have struggled to control other variables that may be influencing consumers, although it is possible to generalise the findings from both studies to other environments and these studies have clear applications to everyday life. Both clearly showed the impact that environmental cues such as colour, light and scent (situation) may have on the individual and their cognitions and behaviours. This supports the importance of situational rather than individual factors in determining behaviour although we should always be aware that individual characteristics are going to be important as well. As with other topics in this section, the exact effects of factors such as light, colour and scent are likely to vary significantly from one culture to another.

There are few ethical issues to consider here as neither study could be considered to cause any type of psychological distress to the participants who would have consented to being questioned. Although it could be argued that Chebat and Michon's participants were not aware that they were taking part in an experiment, we are subject to this kind of experimenter manipulation every time we walk into a store.

7.2 The psychological environment

Environmental influences on consumers
Cognitive maps of retail locations

The aim of the study by Mackay and Olshavsky (1975) was to explore the use of **cognitive maps** (Figure 7.5) in understanding consumer behaviour

 KEY TERM

cognitive map: an internal representation of an external geographical reality sometimes described as a mental map of one's physical environment. Asking someone to draw a map of their environment is one way of exploring what the important features of the environment are for them.

The researchers recruited 78 supermarket shoppers from eight busy supermarkets in Bloomington, Indiana, USA, during both day and evening. They made sure that the subject was the principal grocery shopper for his or her household, that the store was their main store for grocery shopping, that they had access to a car for grocery shopping and that they were familiar with (had heard of) the other seven grocery stores.

If they met all four of these criteria they were invited to participate in a laboratory study for which they

> **SELF-ASSESSMENT QUESTIONS**
>
> 1. Outline the results of the study conducted into leisure environments by Finlay et al.
> 2. Explain how the dependent variable was measured in the study by North et al. into music in restaurants.
> 3. Outline one strength and one weakness of the use of a field experiment in the study by Gueguen et al. into music in open air markets.
> 4. In the study by Chebat and Michon (effects of odour on shopper arousal and emotions) the graduate students collecting the data from shoppers were instructed to not wear perfume. Explain why this instruction would be given.

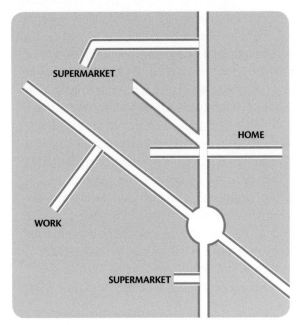

7.5 A cognitive map

would be paid $5. Approximately ten participants were recruited from each of the eight stores. Once in the laboratory, the participants were interviewed about their shopping patterns and knowledge of the location of the eight supermarkets. They were asked to rate the eight supermarkets in order of preference and then to assign points to the different supermarkets on the basis of:

- prices charged for identical goods
- distance from the subject's usual place of departure (usually home or work if people shopped after work)
- size of the store
- overall quality of the merchandise offered.

Subjects were then asked to draw a map of their departure point and the location of the eight supermarkets in Bloomington. No guidance was given on this task meaning that participants were able to give as much or as little detail as they felt necessary. Another map was also constructed using **multi-dimensional scaling**.

 KEY TERM

multi-dimensional scaling: a statistical technique that can take a range of responses (such as preferences and perceptions) from respondents and present them visually.

The researchers concluded that cognitive maps correlated better with preferences and with actual behaviour than did actual maps. Cognitive maps generated by multi-dimensional scaling are better

related to shopping preferences and frequencies than hand drawn maps. The authors conclude that cognitive maps are a useful technique for understanding shopping behaviour.

Crowding in retail environments

Reflections: Look at Figure 7.6. Imagine you are out shopping. How do you feel when the shops are overcrowded? If you thought the shops would be overcrowded would you still go shopping?

7.6 Overcrowded shops are often not much fun!

Machleit et al. (2000) claimed that an increase in perceived **crowding** in a retail store can decrease customer satisfaction with the store and their research considered a number of factors which might affect this relationship. These include emotional reactions experienced while shopping, prior expectations of crowding, tolerance for crowding and type of store. Machleit et al. argued that retail crowding will produce stress and weakened coping abilities, which in turn will produce an increase in negative emotions (most notably anger caused by frustration) and a corresponding decrease in positive emotions. This would also suggest the opposite; that the experience of a non-crowded retail environment will produce an increase in positive emotions (most notably interest and joy) and a decrease in negative emotions.

 KEY TERM

crowding: the subjective experience of density.

These arguments led to the hypotheses that

- Perceived retail crowding will be positively **correlated** with negative and neutral emotions and negatively correlated with positive emotions.
- Higher levels of perceived retail crowding will result in lower levels of shopper satisfaction.
- Shopper satisfaction will be higher when perceived crowding falls short of or meets crowding expectations, and lower when perceived crowding exceeds expectations.

170

In other words, when an individual perceives shops or malls to be crowded, they will be stressed and less satisfied with their shopping experiences. This relationship is affected by expectations: if we expect an environment to be crowded and it is less crowded than we expected, then satisfaction will be higher.

They also proposed that individuals vary in their ability to tolerate crowds. They suggested that individuals with a high tolerance for crowding will not be affected by crowding levels, but for individuals with a low tolerance for crowding, crowding will negatively affect satisfaction. This is an interesting suggestion. In addition to the first three predictions, they are now suggesting that individual differences will also be important and that the predicted relationships will be stronger for those with a low tolerance for crowding.

Finally, they predicted that the type of store will also be important. For discount-type stores, high levels of crowding will not affect shopping satisfaction. For other store types there will be a negative correlation between crowding and satisfaction. This is interesting as it suggests that in a discount-type store, we are far less likely to be bothered by crowding. Perhaps we expected the crowds or perhaps the bargains simply outweigh the negative effects of crowding.

To investigate these questions, the researchers conducted three studies.

In Study 1, 722 students from both undergraduate and postgraduate marketing courses were given a survey and asked to complete this after their next shopping trip. They were to name the store or shopping mall where they had been shopping (even if they hadn't bought anything) and then to answer the questions. The survey asked about their purchases, the purpose of the trip, their past experiences in the same store/shopping mall and then asked about their perceptions of crowding, satisfaction and outcome of the trip. Finally they were asked traditional emotion measurement questions, crowding tolerance questions and basic demographic questions.

Examples of perceived crowding questions included

- *The store seemed very crowded to me*
- *There were lots of shoppers in the store*
- *I enjoyed shopping at the store.*

The results of Study 1 supported the hypothesis that an increase in perceived crowding was associated with a decrease in positive emotions. However, perceived crowding did not significantly affect arousal. If the shopper felt the store was crowded, then the arousal (excitement) experienced by shopping was decreased.

Study 2 was a replication of Study 1 with a more diverse adult sample, recruited from a number of parenting groups and schools and asked to participate as part of a fundraising activity. The results from this study confirmed the results of Study 1 although results did not show the same effect of expectation as in Study 1 and this is likely to be explained in terms of a smaller sample and a very small proportion falling into the 'more shoppers than expected' group.

Study 3 was a laboratory experiment. A professional photographer made short films in the university bookstore which varied the numbers of shoppers in the store (**human density**) and the placements of 3 foot (86 cm) high bookshelves (spatial density).

KEY TERM

human density: the number of people in a given space.

RESEARCH METHODS

The authors claim that this final study addresses the problem of self-selection in the previous two studies. Explain why this might have been a problem and how Study 3 has overcome this.

A total of 231 participants were given a short passage to read which described the bookstore as either a discount store or an upmarket bookstore and stated that the participant was searching for an important book for their job hunt. They then watched one of four 55 second videos (which had different levels of spatial density and different numbers of people visible) and imagined themselves shopping for this book in this store. They then had to respond to a series of questions as in the previous studies.

Reflections: This study manipulates density rather than perceived crowding. Explain the difference between density and crowding.

This study found that that a decrease in shopping satisfaction can be mediated by expectations of crowding and by personal tolerance for crowding which confirms the findings of the previous two studies. This laboratory experiment also demonstrated that the relationship between perceived crowding and shopping satisfaction varied by store type. The earlier studies suggested that in discount stores, crowding would not be related to satisfaction. Interestingly in Study 3, crowding was related to satisfaction and the authors suggested that they may have identified a ceiling effect such that there is a point at which the environment gets so crowded that satisfaction levels are inevitably affected.

Shopper movement patterns

This study examined patterns of shopper movement and behaviour in a supermarket. Gil et al. (2009) interviewed and tracked movements of over 480 shoppers to produce shopper profiles. They referred to their study as a **space syntax** study. This is a non-experimental study as the researchers did not manipulate any variables.

> **KEY TERM**
>
> **space syntax:** a science-based, human-focused approach that investigates relationships between spatial layout and a range of social, economic and environmental phenomena.

The researchers were particularly interested in whether store layout has an impact on shopper behaviours, specifically movement patterns, shopping duration and interaction with products. They attempted to identify distinctive movement patterns and to determine whether these patterns can be associated with certain shopper groups.

Shoppers were initially approached to take part in a survey, and basic information (such as age, gender and size of group) was recorded. They were given a coloured tag which allowed them to be identified on the store CCTV system so that their movements around the store could be followed. This also allowed them to be identified on leaving the store so that a more detailed interview could be conducted.

> **Reflections:** The authors claim that any effect on the shopper behaviour would be minute as the initial approach was extremely brief and the observation was unobtrusive. Do you agree with this claim?

The interview covered a range of topics, asking the shopper about the purpose of their trip, their use of a shopping list, satisfaction with their shopping and the amount of money spent as well as asking about more general shopping habits such as the frequency of shopping trips.

The video recordings were processed to extract data on the store areas visited, the time spent in each area and the type of product interactions. The researchers concluded that shopper behaviour is strongly affected by the location of

products within the store (which is to be expected). Also as expected, some areas are more popular than others, with milk, fruit and vegetables and bread being the busiest and non-food and baby products being the least busy. A more interesting result is that it is possible to identify four distinct patterns of movement around the store. The authors refer to these as 'short trip', 'round trip', 'central trip' and 'wave trip' and these are shown in Figure 7.7. No significant differences in the types of people making each type of trip were identified.

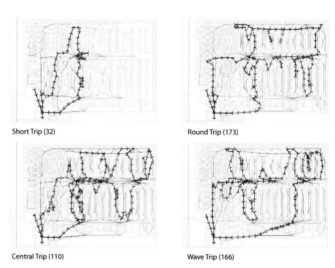

Short Trip (32) Round Trip (173)

Central Trip (110) Wave Trip (166)

7.7 The four spatial movement patterns identified by Gil et al.

Five types of spatial behaviour patterns were also identified and termed the specialist, the native, the tourist, the explorer and the raider, and the authors conclude that this information about shopper behaviour could be further investigated in other stores with other layouts.

Evaluation

These three studies can all be seen to be part of the cognitive approach to psychology as they investigate the way that we perceive and make sense of the consumer environment. The three studies use a range of techniques to explore consumer behaviour. The study by Mackay and Olshavsky was conducted in a laboratory, which means that it would have been much easier to control **extraneous variables** such as noise levels and distraction. In contrast the study by Machleit et al. was conducted in both laboratory and field conditions. Clearly the first two studies, conducted in real shopping environments, will have greater **ecological validity** than the third study, which was conducted using filmed consumer environments watched in a laboratory. However, it is important to remember that this would give the researcher a great deal more control over the environment. The final study by Gil et al. was also conducted in a real consumer environment. Research conducted in the real world gains in terms of ecological validity but loses in terms of control and this pattern is reversed for laboratory-based research. When considering applied research such as consumer psychology, the ecological validity and the ability to apply the results directly to consumer environments are obviously crucial. This means that it is likely that consumer psychologists would consider field research (even with its obvious disadvantages) to be the most useful technique. However, when researchers can demonstrate the same effect in both field and laboratory environments, as Machleit et al. have done, this obviously strengthens the conclusions and the applications that follow.

How can the studies looked at in this section be applied? The study by Mackay and Olshavsky simply concludes that cognitive maps are 'a useful technique for understanding consumer behaviour' rather than making specific suggestions in terms of manipulating behaviour. This is important as this area of research is relatively new and it is important for the techniques to be developed which will help researchers explore the field further. In a sense, the study by Gil et al. can also be understood in this way. Gil et al. have identified shopper types and further research will no doubt not only explore these types in greater detail but begin to apply the understanding of these types to the design of store layouts. Perhaps smaller convenience-type stores are better suited to 'short trip' shoppers and can be designed to suit this type of behaviour. This may mean designing a layout that allows a 'short trip' to be completed even faster, so that customers find everything they need and pay quickly, or it may involve trying to slow them down slightly and exposing them to products that they otherwise might not see. There is a reason that large supermarkets do not have the bread, milk and fruit and vegetables close together (or even near the entrance of the store) as they want you to walk around and see other products.

The study by Machleit et al. has more specific applications; perhaps most obviously to the 'luxury' end of the market and very clearly demonstrates the importance of situational factors in understanding consumer behaviour. Consumers will have more positive emotional responses to feelings of space (as opposed to feelings of being crowded) and it is reasonable to expect will visit stores more often, spend more time in the store and thus hopefully spend more money. Although the research discussed here has not demonstrated the link between space and spending, there is evidence enough here for a shop to focus on creating a feeling of a space rather than filling the space with as much merchandise as possible.

Finally, as with all the studies in the chapter, it is important to consider their findings in a cross-cultural context. Two of these studies were conducted in the USA and the third in the UK. We should therefore be cautious about applying the results globally. We would need to consider the size, number and location of supermarkets and shopping centres, population density, cultural norms and expectations as well as economic factors before assuming that research conducted in these countries could be applied effectively in different cultures.

Menu design psychology
Eye movement patterns, framing and common menu mistakes

Pavesic's article (2005) did not report on a piece of empirical research but was an account of some psychological principles that can be applied to the design of menus. Pavesic began by pointing out that the menu is the most important marketing tool that a restaurant has and that it is important to understand how it can be used to increase sales and improve customer loyalty.

Common mistakes are failing to spend enough time considering the design of the menu and using font sizes, types and paper colours that are difficult to read (especially in low light). Poor use of space, crowding the information together or failing to vary the presentation can make menus less attractive to the customer. Making the prices too obvious can lead to customers discounting some items simply on price. Finally, failing to design the menu to fit with the décor, style or personality of the restaurant is another common mistake, which is particularly important if menus are displayed away from the restaurant.

The concept of 'menu psychology' was introduced by Seaberg in 1971. He pointed out the importance of highlighting certain items so that they grab the customer's attention and increase the likelihood that they will select certain items rather than others. We will be returning to this idea in the next study. Pavesic reported that the average time spent reading a menu is 109 seconds. This is an important piece of information for someone designing a menu. Some large restaurant chains now have extensive menus that take a very long time to read. This increases the time each table spends deciding and ordering and will inevitably reduce the turnover in the restaurant. It would be better to have shorter, attractive menus (Figure 7.8) and reduce not only ordering times, but also the range of stock needed and the potential wastage.

7.8 A typical non-linear menu

Customers' attention can be drawn to certain items if the restaurant wants to sell more of these and so these should be the items that have the greatest profit margins and are the easiest to prepare. Making a menu item stand out and increasing orders also means that the item can be prepared in larger quantities. This can be done with boxes, images and the use of different fonts and different colours.

The paper then goes on to apply cognitive psychology, particularly the **primacy–recency** effect, to menu design. This refers to the position of items on the menu and within subsections of the menu. We will be examining this in more detail in the next study.

> ### KEY TERM
>
> **primacy–recency effect:** an effect identified in memory research which finds that the items at the beginning of a list and the items at the end of a list are more likely to be recalled than the items from the middle of the list.

Primacy, recency and menu item position

Dayan and Bar-Hillel (2011) reported two studies which manipulated the position of items on a menu in order to increase or decrease the frequency of choice. For example they predicted that placing healthier options at the beginning or end of the menu and less healthy options in between should produce an increased choice of healthy options.

The first study was an experiment. A total of 240 Hebrew University students were randomly allocated to four conditions. These were four different menu designs, differing only in terms of order of item presentation within each category. The menus all offered four appetisers (A), ten entrées (main courses, E), six soft drinks (S) and eight desserts (D).

The names of the items and their descriptions were copied from an Israeli pizza chain. No prices were displayed. The four menus (in Hebrew) presented the items in different orders within each category:

- baseline – arbitrarily ordered
- mirror – complete reverse of the baseline
- inside out baseline – reversed the baseline order within the top and bottom half of each category separately, therefore turning middle items into top/bottom items and vice versa
- inside out mirror – as inside out baseline but reversing the mirror version.

Each participant was given one version of the menu and asked to choose one item from each of the categories. They were told that one participant would be chosen at random to receive a real meal at the pizza restaurant.

The results showed that participants were significantly more likely to select items at the extremes (that is the beginning or end of the list) than they were to select items placed in the middle. This was true even for relatively unpopular items. Overall the advantage of being listed at the beginning and end was 56% which was significant to $p < 0.001$. Interestingly no primacy–recency effect was found. 50.5% of the choices were from items in the top half of their category and 49.5% from the bottom.

The authors accepted that although the results of Study 1 were convincing, they represented a hypothetical choice rather than one made in a real restaurant. In order to address this criticism, the authors conducted a second study in a small coffee shop in the centre of Tel Aviv. The coffee shop had 60 items on the menu in three categories: coffee, soft drinks and desserts.

This field experiment took place over 30 days in one summer period. The baseline menu (the coffee shop's standard menu) was alternated with the inside out version which changed the position of items in the three categories by exchanging items from the two ends of the category with items from the middle. Staff recorded orders made during this time and data was excluded from any customers who ordered without reference to a menu. It is not possible to say exactly how many customers were involved, only that 459 orders were recorded from the baseline menu and 492 from the inside out menu.

175

> **Reflections:** Identify the strengths and weaknesses of using staff to record the data. What alternative methods could have been used?

The mean advantage in this study was 55% and the results confirmed the findings from Study 1. In this study there was an even larger gain when an item was moved from the exact middle to the extreme end (55%) than when moved from the near middle to the near end (51%). The results also seemed to suggest an advantage (59%) from being in the top half of the category although this study did not use a mirror conditions.

The results of this research confirmed the recommendation made by menu design consultants to place items at the beginning or end of the category if you want them to be ordered more often. Although it is most likely that this would be used to manipulate purchases of the highest profit items or of items that have been overstocked, the authors also suggest that there may be practical implications from this study in terms of manipulating people's choices towards healthier options.

Sensory perception and food name

Wansink et al. (2005) reported on a six week experiment in a cafeteria in an American university. Six products were selected which were popular enough to be offered twice a week and which represented a wide variety of foods. Food labels were changed from the regular to the descriptive and included geographic labels, nostalgia labels and sensory labels:

- Red Beans with rice became *Traditional Cajun Red Beans with Rice*
- Seafood Filet became *Succulent Italian Seafood Filet*
- Grilled Chicken became *Tender Grilled Chicken*
- Chicken Parmesan became *Homestyle Chicken Parmesan*
- Chocolate Pudding became *Satin Chocolate Pudding*
- Zucchini Cookies became *Grandma's Zucchini Cookies*

On two days of each of six test weeks, two items were presented with their regular labels and two were presented with their descriptive labels (the other two were not offered). These were rotated until all items had been offered in all conditions and were then repeated to minimise any unexpected variables that might have affected either preferences or participation such as weather, religious holidays or sporting events. During the six week period, each item was available six times.

Every person selecting one of the six target menu items was asked to complete a one page questionnaire by the person at the cash register. Nearly all (98%) of the questionnaires were returned.

> **Reflections:** 98% return rate is a huge return rate. Suggest why the return rate was so high in this study.

Diners were asked questions related to sensory perceptions on nine-point Likert scales with the end points labelled 'strongly agree' and 'strongly disagree'. The statements were:

- *This item was appealing to the eye*
- *This item tasted good*
- *After finishing this item, I felt comfortably full and satisfied.*

Diners were also asked to estimate how many calories the menu item contained. On the back of the questionnaire, people were able to comment further, and 537 comments were received (2.4 per person).

There were 140 participants of whom 87% were university staff, 9% graduate students and 5% visitors. Ages ranged from 23 to 74, with the average being 43.2. No differences were found in terms of age, gender or education in terms of who bought which menu items, in terms of how healthy they considered themselves to be or whether they claimed to be watching their weight. The fact that there were no significant differences between the two groups gave the researchers confidence that any differences they found in the results would be due to the labelling of the food and not to any differences in sample.

The key results were that the descriptive labels led to the food being described as more appealing and also as more calorific. The descriptive labels encouraged diners to give a greater number of favourable comments about the product compared with those who saw only the regular label. While all people were relatively positive about the products, those given the descriptive labels were more so. The use of these descriptive names increased post-consumption sensory ratings and calorie estimations compared to the regularly labelled food.

The authors concluded that the way that food is labelled is an important criterion for decision making and make several suggestions for extending their research. These included looking at how descriptive labels would interact with poor quality or average quality food and whether labelling might encourage people to eat more of the food. They raised the interesting question that if a person perceives the food as more calorific they may in fact eat less.

Evaluation

This selection of studies can also be understood to be largely cognitive. Once again we can consider the relative strengths and weaknesses of laboratory-based research and field-based research. Although the study by Wansink et al. conducted a **field experiment** examining the effects of food labelling, the research on menu position by Dayan and Bar-Hillel repeats the pattern seen in the study by Machleit et al. in the previous section and has conducted both a **laboratory experiment** and two field experiments. Once again, the findings are confirmed in each replication, which not only strengthens the applications to real life but also suggests that research conducted in the laboratory can produce results which are very similar to results produced in real consumer environments. These two studies have attempted to manipulate behaviour (in contrast to the studies discussed in the previous section which attempted only to understand and categorise behaviour) and so the issue of ethics may be worth considering. This can be done in two ways. First we need to consider the **ethical issues** raised by the research that was conducted. Participants in Dayan and Bar-Hillel's first study were aware that they were taking part in a piece of research and would have been able to give their consent. Were they deceived? They weren't told that the research was looking at the effect of menu position as this would obviously have produced demand characteristics but it is hard to imagine that anyone would have felt upset with this level of deception. In a similar way, although the participants in the second study in the coffee shop were not aware they were taking part in research and neither (until afterwards) were the participants in the study by Wansink et al., it is unlikely that this would have caused problems for anyone. Interestingly Wansink et al. needed to let their participants know that they had been part of a research study because the data they wanted meant that they had to ask questions. Dayan and Bar-Hillel did not need to ask their participants anything at all as their menu choices were the data. Interestingly, this level of manipulation is typical in all consumer environments and business owners will be constantly 'experimenting' with design, layout, labelling and many other variables in order to see how changes affect consumer behaviour. This is the

second way in which ethics might be considered. Research such as this (and others still to come) is applied directly in the consumer environments you visit.

> **Reflections:** If a researcher demonstrates that there is a 'best position' for an item to be listed on a menu and a business uses this information to manipulate customers to buy the most expensive item on the menu, is this unethical?

You can also consider the use of **qualitative** and **quantitative data** in this section. The study by Dayan and Bar-Hillel collected only quantitative data – how many of each item/item position were ordered. Quantitative data is easily analysed and allows for very clear comparisons to be drawn. It could be argued that this is sufficient in this study and there was no need to collect qualitative data. However in the study by Wansink et al., researchers collected both quantitative and qualitative data. The quantitative data was collected from the rating scales and the estimates of calorie content and the qualitative data was collected from the additional comments that people made.

The applications of this research are fairly easy to see and once again relate to the importance of situational factors in understanding consumer behaviour. Where you place an item on a menu and the words you use to describe this item have both been shown to have statistically significant effects on how often these items are selected. To put this into practice in a café or restaurant would be very straightforward and relatively cheap.

Finally, in this section we have only two pieces of research. One was conducted in a university restaurant in the USA and the other in Israel. This gives a broader representation of cultures than the studies in the first part of this section, although we should still be cautious in assuming that these findings would be replicated worldwide.

Personal space
Theories of personal space: overload, arousal and behaviour constraint

Personal space is a concept that was first identified by Katz in 1937 and was defined by Somner (1969) as 'an area with invisible boundaries, surrounding a person's body, into which intruders may not come' (cited in Cave, 1998, page 67). Some descriptions use the concept of a bubble surrounding us which can expand or contract according to the situation (Figure 7.9).

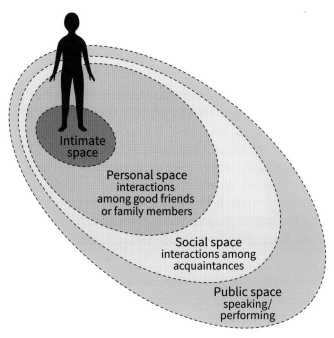

Intimate space

Personal space
interactions
among good friends
or family members

Social space
interactions among
acquaintances

Public space
speaking/
performing

7.9 Zones of personal space

Reflections: Think about all the different places you have been in the last week. Some of them may have been very busy environments such as trains or buses where people get very close to you. How does this make you feel? Have you been to see a doctor, a dentist or a hairdresser or barber? How close do they get to you and how does this make you feel? Have you cuddled anyone this week? How did this make you feel?

Maintaining our personal space allows us to avoid becoming stressed or even threatened by people coming too close. One well-known study that investigated the effects of invasion of personal space was conducted by Felipe and Somner (1966) in a university library where a confederate would sit either very close to or at varying distances from a target person. The closer they sat, the faster the target person would remove themselves from that situation. The researchers also reported the same defensive behaviours such as turning away from the invader or building 'barriers' out of books.

Responses to the invasion of our personal space can be explained with reference to three concepts: overload, arousal and behaviour constraint. The concept of overload suggests that we maintain our personal space in order to reduce (and to maintain control over) the amount of information that needs to be dealt with. If people are too close, we have no choice but to process information relating to their features, their smell, their body heat and possibly even their touch. This produces an overload of information to process as well

as a lack of control over the information that we process producing feelings of stress.

A slightly different way to explain this is to use the concept of arousal. When our personal space is invaded, we may feel a heightened sense of arousal. Of course, our response to this arousal depends on the interpretation we put on the invasion of personal space. At a football match or a concert, or if someone hugs you, the arousal produced by the invasion of your personal space is likely to be interpreted positively. A stranger sitting too close to you on a bus or someone walking right behind you would be interpreted very differently.

The invasion of personal space can also be understood in terms of behaviour constraint, such as having the freedom to choose how to behave taken away from us. Research shows that crowds behave very differently from individuals, aggression is often increased and helping behaviours are decreased. It is possible that the stress experienced by lack of personal space may be responsible for these changes in behaviour.

Reflections: One of the best known (and probably the most unethical) was conducted by Middlemist et al. (1976) in a men's public toilet. Find out what Middlemist et al. did and what they found. How many ethical issues do you think their study raises?

Space at restaurant tables

The study by Robson et al. (2011) examines the importance of personal space in user's perceptions of comfort in a restaurant. The authors conducted a web-based survey of more than 1000 American participants who were asked to respond to a scenario where they visited a restaurant where the tables were spaced at 6, 12 or 24 inches (approximately 15, 30 or 60 cm) apart.

The first part of the survey asked people for information about themselves, including their gender, age, ethnicity, place of residence (urban, suburban or rural), restaurant use frequency and whether they had any work experience in the restaurant industry. The second part of the survey measured emotional, intentional and anticipated behavioural reactions to one of three images of tables for two placed at a distance of 6, 12 or 24 inches away from each other. Questions invoked one of three dining scenarios: business, friend or romantic.

Respondents were randomly assigned to one of nine possible scenarios (e.g. 24 inch spacing and friend) and asked to respond to a series of 32 statements that measured their emotional and behavioural responses to the specific distances.

For all the pleasure, stress, control and comfort variables and for all but one of the privacy variables there was a statistically significant difference between the 6 inch spacing and the other two conditions. Close table spacing made people feel less private, more crowded, less likely to have a positive meal experience and more dissatisfied with the table to which they were assigned. They also reported being more concerned with disturbing others or being overheard. Stress scores were also significantly higher in the tightly spaced table condition. Respondents strongly objected to the tightly spaced tables, particularly in a 'romantic' context.

The authors conclude that context is a key factor in consumer preference for table spacing. Gender is also important, with women reporting that they would be much less comfortable in tightly spaced environments than men. Although these are clear findings, the implications for restaurant owners are more complex. Tightly spaced tables mean that people eat and leave more quickly without spending any less, meaning that more customers can be served and more profit made. However they may be less likely to return if they felt uncomfortable which may be more important for businesses that rely on repeat custom.

Defending your place in a queue

Reflections: Look at Figure 7.10 and imagine you are standing in a long queue when someone pushes in in front of you. How this would make you feel and more importantly, what would you do? Do you think Milgram et al.'s study raises any ethical concerns?

7.10 How would you feel in this situation?

This is what was investigated by Milgram et al. (1986) in a series of experiments conducted in real-life environments, including train stations, betting shops and other New York City locations. Queues had an average of six members.

A confederate calmly approached a point between the third and fourth person in line and said in a neutral tone 'excuse me; I would like to get in here'. The confederate would then simply join the queue without waiting for a response. If someone asked them to leave the queue explicitly then he or she would. Otherwise the confederate stayed in the line for one minute before leaving. Five students served as intruders and an observer was stationed nearby to record physical, verbal and non-verbal reactions to the intrusion.

The researchers also varied the number of intruders – sometimes one and sometimes two. They also used buffers – these were confederates who passively occupied a position between the point of intrusion and the next naive queuer. This allowed the researchers to see if the responsibility for objecting would be displaced from the person immediately at the point of intrusion to others. In some conditions two buffers were used standing immediately behind each other. In these cases, the buffers would join the end of the queue and the 'intruders' would wait until they reached the appropriate position in the queue. Therefore there are two independent variables: number of intruders (one or two) and number of buffers (zero, one or two) resulting in six experimental conditions. In total, confederates intruded themselves into 129 naturally occurring waiting lines and the reactions of the queuers were observed.

Results showed that queuers following the intruder were far more likely to object than those who were ahead of the intruder. Two intruders provoked far more reaction than one and buffers (passive confederates standing in line) dampened the queue's response to the intruder. Physical action against the intruder happened in 10% of queues. This included any physical contact between a queuer and the intruder. This contact including tugging the sleeve, tapping the shoulder and even, in a few cases, physically pushing the intruder out of line. This type of response normally originated from the person standing immediately behind the intruder. Verbal objections were the most common, occurring in 21.7% of queues. These ranged from polite to hostile but all demanded that the intruder get out of the queue or go to the back of the line.

Generalised expressions of disapproval were also coded in this category – these included more tentative comments such as 'excuse me, this is a queue'. Non-verbal objections included dirty looks, hostile glares and gestures to the intruder to get into line. They occurred in 14.7% of queues.

Milgram et al. conclude that the queue can be considered to be a social system with a shared set of beliefs governing the behaviour of the participants. They conclude that this means that individuals 'no longer act in terms of purely personal wishes but instead, by reference to a common social representation' (page 688). The force of this representation may differ widely from one social situation to another or indeed from one culture to another.

Evaluation

These studies all take a social approach to understanding the consumer. These three pieces of research are looking at the environmental or **situational variables** which influence how we feel and how we behave. To begin with we examined the theory of personal space. This allowed you to understand the effect of the situational factor of **crowding** and particularly the effects produced by an invasion of personal space. This was then demonstrated in the study by Robson et al. which showed that tables placed very close together made people feel less comfortable, and more dissatisfied. However although this was an experimental study (compared a number of different conditions) participants' responses were to an imagined scenario rather than a real-life experience of the different environments, giving this study lowered **ecological validity**. This was an **independent measures** study (participants were allocated to one condition only), meaning that individual differences could have played a significant part here. Finally the study by Milgram et al. was conducted in the real world, making this a **field experiment**. This gives the study a much greater level of ecological validity than the other studies in this section. However, it also raises ethical issues of consent, deception and potential distress although, as Milgram notes, every effort was made to reduce the possible distress caused by the intruders. The intruder left the queue as soon as they were challenged although, obviously, it would have been fascinating to know what would have happened if they had stayed! Although Milgram et al.'s conclusions take a situational perspective on queues, they also acknowledge the importance of individual differences, in particular age and gender effects, as well as the effects of different types of queues, especially those for items that are in short supply.

How can these results be applied to everyday life? Robson et al. suggest that their findings may be useful in deciding how many tables to fit into a space in a café or restaurant. Too many tables and people may feel uncomfortable. However, this may mean that they finish their meal faster and leave, meaning that the business actually makes more money as they serve more customers. However, if they felt too

uncomfortable they may never return, so businesses that rely on repeat custom may need to ensure a little more space than a business that is not so dependent on repeat custom, for example one that is near a popular tourist destination.

The findings from this study might also be applied in a broader context to the use of space in a variety of consumer locations such as shops or banks. Would increased arousal, overload and behaviour constraint make someone more or less likely to make a large purchase or agree a large financial transaction?

Cultural differences also need careful consideration here. If there are cultural differences in personal space and in social norms relating to behaviours such as queuing, then the results of these studies are unlikely to be replicated in other cultures. Both Robson et al.'s and Milgram et al.'s studies were conducted in the USA and there is no guarantee that these findings would be the same if conducted in other countries. In fact, it is likely that they would not be the same. This is an important point in applied research like this.

SELF-ASSESSMENT QUESTIONS

5   Explain the effect of perceived crowding on the shopping experience from the study by Machleit et al.

6   Identify the two methods used by Dayan and Bar-Hillel in their study of menu item position.

7   Outline two effects of the descriptive labels used to describe the food in the study by Wansink et al.

8   Outline one ethical issue raised by the study into queueing behaviour conducted by Milgram et al.

7.3 Consumer decision making

Utility theory, satisficing and Prospect theory

Utility theory was proposed by Neumann and Morgenstern (1944). It suggests, simply, that consumers make rational decisions based on the likely outcomes of their actions. However, it is unlikely that consumers are as rational as this model predicts or even that they are aware of the process of decision making within a retail environment.

> **Reflections:** Think about some of the decisions that you have had to make recently. Would you describe your decision making as logical, rational and consistent?'

Simon (1956) proposed an alternative model called satisficing in which he describes consumers as getting '*approximately where they wanted to go*' and then stopping the decision-making process. For example if you were looking for a new car, Utility theory would predict that you would evaluate every available car against all the pertinent variables (cost, size, mileage, make, etc.) and then select the one that scored highest on all of these variables. From a satisficing point of view, you might look at a few cars and stop the process when you find one that is 'good enough'.

Although this model may explain behaviour more accurately than Utility theory, it still does not offer a good predictor of consumer behaviour that can be effectively used in a retail environment. Prospect theory was developed by two psychologists, Kahneman and Tversky, in the 1970s. Their theory added two new concepts to the explanation of consumer decision making; these were value (rather than utility in the earlier utility model) and endowment, which is when an item is more precious when owned than when owned by someone else. This suggests that people value gains and losses in different ways and are more likely to base their decisions on perceived likelihood of gains rather than perceived likelihood of losses. For example, we buy a lottery ticket because we might win, not because we are highly likely to lose. Most investment opportunities will be presented to potential investors in terms of the likely gains.

Strategies: compensatory, non-compensatory and partially compensatory

The next development in the area of consumer decision making was the identification of a number of possible consumer decision making strategies which could be exploited by those working in consumer fields. These strategies can be described as compensatory, non-compensatory and partially compensatory (Green and Wind, 1973). In compensatory strategies, a consumer may allow the value of one attribute to compensate for another. To return to our car buying example, you might decide that a very low mileage compensates for the fact that this was not your first choice of make or your preferred colour. Alternatively you may choose the car based on the colour, allowing this to compensate for the high mileage.

Richarme (2005) suggests that the attributes that we use for our decision making may have equal weight or different weights. The first is termed the Equal Weight Strategy and the second is termed Weighted Additive Strategy. For example someone might value the low mileage on a car much more highly than the make or the colour.

In non-compensatory strategies each attribute is evaluated individually, rather than allowing one variable to compensate for another. This would mean that however high a car scores

on variables such as make, mileage and price, it would be immediately eliminated if it was not the correct colour.

Simon suggests that there are there non-compensatory strategies and these include:

Satisficing: the first product to meet the basic requirements is chosen and no further consideration takes place. For example if an essential piece of household equipment fails, such as a kettle, someone might simply purchase the first kettle they see.

Elimination by aspects: this strategy sets a 'cut off' value for the most important attribute and then allows everything that meets that attribute to remain under consideration. The remaining items are then assessed against the next attribute and so on.

Lexigraphic: in this strategy the most important attribute is evaluated and if one item is considered superior in terms of this attribute, this immediately stops the decision making process and the item is chosen. If no one item emerges as superior on the most important attribute then the consideratin moves to the next attribute and so on.

Finally, consumers may use one of two partially compensatory strategies. The first is termed Majority of Conforming Dimensions. An individual using this strategy would evaluate two products against all relevant attributes and retain the one that does best. This one is then compared to the next product and so on until there is only one product left. The second partially compensatory strategy is called Frequency of Good and Bad Features, and here all the products are compared to the appropriate cut-off values and the product that has the most positive features exceeding the cut-off values will be chosen.

> **Reflections:** Apply the ideas of compensatory and non-compensatory strategies to choosing a new mobile phone.

Marketing theories: consideration and involvement

We also need to examine two major areas of marketing theory which also help to provide additional explanations of consumer decision making strategies (Richarme, 2005). These are called 'Consideration' and 'Involvement'. Consideration involves forming an initial subset of items to consider. We may be able to name a great many makes of cars, but when we start considering purchasing a car, it is likely that the shortlist will be a much smaller sub-set of this. The more complex the decision the more steps or stages there are likely to be in the decision making process. We might begin with all the cars we can name but we will reduce these to all the cars we can afford, all the cars for sale nearby and so on. Effectively we are ensuring that we focus our cognitive effort on the cars that belong to the final subset that might be considered. Involvement examines the amount of cognitive effort applied to the decision-making process and proposes that this is directly related to the importance of the decision. This makes sense as obviously we would put more effort into the choice of a new car than the choice of a sandwich! However, price does not necessarily determine the level of involvement we might have in the decision, which might also be determined by the 'perceived impact on the quality of life of the consumer' (Richarme, 2005, p.3).

Richarme (2005) summarises some of the key ways in which psychology has been applied directly to an understanding of the decision making processes used by consumers. Having a theoretical basis like this is useful both for researchers exploring the effects of different variables on this process as well as retailers attempting to understand and manipulate the decision making process.

Evaluation

All the concepts considered in this section have useful applications for retailers. An understanding of the way in which consumers make decisions can be applied to the shopping experience. This is frequently applied in the design of shopping websites, allowing customers to directly compare products. This was investigated by Jedelski et al. (2002), who suggested that websites that were designed to allow easier comparisons would lead to better (more compensatory) decisions.

They began by briefing their participants on the differences between compensatory and non-compensatory decision making strategies and then gave them access to two different websites to purchase specific items from. Website 1 allowed the customer to choose the attributes that were important to them and then to compare items by displaying them side by side. Website 1 also allowed customers to sort the products against lots of different criteria. Website 2 gave the customer exactly the same information but in a way that made making comparisons much more difficult. The results showed that compensatory strategies were used more often when using Website 1 than when using Website 2. This strongly suggests that an understanding of decision making strategies can be used to improve the shopping experience.

Another issue for consideration here is one of individual differences. Utility theory makes the assumption that consumers are all rational decision makers. Later models challenged this assumption but it may also be useful to consider the extent to which individuals differ in terms of their preferred decision making strategies or indeed, whether the decision-making strategy they use is more likely to be determined by the situation (the type of product, store or website) or by individual characteristics. There may be differences in the strategies used for purchasing different items, with rational, compensatory strategies being more in evidence for necessary household purchases but not for luxury items such as shoes and handbags.

There may also be cultural differences in terms of the consumer experience as a whole which also need to be taken into consideration here. We will be returning to this later in this chapter when we consider the topic of advertising. If an advertiser understands the decision making strategies that consumers tend to use, then they can tailor their advertising strategy to make the decision to purchase seem like the only sensible decision.

Choice heuristics

Availability, representativeness

We are constantly making decisions and have developed cognitive processing strategies or shortcuts to help us make decisions more easily. These are called **heuristics**.

KEY TERM

heuristics: mental shortcuts that help us make decisions and judgements quickly without having to spend a lot of time researching and analysing information.

Most of the time, heuristics are helpful but they can sometimes lead to errors in judgement. Two of these heuristics are the availability heuristic and the representative heuristic.

Availability heuristics are mental shortcuts based on how easy it is to bring something to mind. They are often useful ways of thinking about situations and can be beneficial, for example by making us more cautious in dangerous situations as we can easily bring examples of negative outcomes to mind. However this is often based on inaccurate information or faulty thinking.

For example, Hoyer et al. (2009) suggest that if you had purchased a DVD player that kept breaking down, your 'available' perception of that brand is likely to be a negative one, meaning that you would be unlikely to purchase a DVD player or any other product made by that company. Communication from others might also create an availability heuristic. If your friend had problems with a particular make, then this information is likely to influence your thinking even though this may be an isolated instance.

This is because we ignore base rate information – how often something really occurs – in favour of information that is readily available or easily memorable. A study reported by Hoyer et al. demonstrated this bias using the example of refrigerator breakdowns. Participants who were given 'stories' to read from unhappy consumers made significantly higher estimates of the likelihood of the appliance breaking down than participants who were given statistics referring to the actual breakdown rates.

Representative heuristics are mental shortcuts that allow us to make judgments by making comparisons with the best known (most representative) example of a category. If we are looking for a mobile phone, we are likely to compare a newly released model to the current market leader. If it appears similar, then we are likely to assume that this is also a quality product. Manufacturers take advantage of the fact that we use this heuristic, by making products (or their packaging) look like an established product so that the consumer assumes they will be similar.

Reflections: Imagine you have to do the weekly food shopping for your family. How will you decide what to buy? Identify all the heuristics that you might use.

Anchoring and purchase quantity decisions

Wansink et al. (1998) examined the issue of what factors might influence how many units of a product a consumer chooses to buy. Prior research on consumer behaviour looked in great detail at many aspects of the consumer decision making process, such as which brand and how frequently something was purchased. In this paper the authors looked specifically at the decisions relating to quantity.

They suggested how **point of purchase promotions** could increase sales. The paper reported on two field experiments and two laboratory experiments which showed that anchor-point promotions – presented as multiple unit prices, purchase quantity limits and suggestive selling – can increase purchase quantity.

A potential quantity anchor is a promotion which presents the price for multiple units. For example a product may have a sign saying 'On Sale – 6 cans for $3' versus 'On Sale – 50c'. The authors suggest that this kind of promotion works in retail environments to increase sales by making consumers see a larger than normal purchase as attractive.

The authors conducted a one week field experiment comparing multiple with single unit promotional pricing in 86 stores, which were assigned randomly to either the single or multiple unit promotion conditions. A baseline score was calculated as the average weekly sale during the previous six months (with no promotions) and the dependent variable was calculated as a percentage change in sales compared with this baseline. The same size shelf label was used in every store and this displayed the original price as well as either the single unit promotion price (75 cents) or the multiple unit price (2 for $1.50). Thirteen items were included in the experiment which included cookies, candy, frozen meals, cereals, tinned soup and tinned tuna.

The results showed that multiple-unit promotional prices resulted in a 32% increase in sales over the single-unit control. For 12 of 13 products, sales were higher with multiple-unit pricing, and for 9 products the difference was statistically significant. A meta-analysis of all 13 tests indicates that the multiple-unit pricing effect is highly reliable ($p < .0001$).

However, the authors are rightly cautious of the conclusions that can be drawn from this study. They acknowledge that consumer confusion may have been an important factor and that consumers shopping in the multiple promotion condition shops might have believed that they had to purchase multiple items in order to get the promotional price. This first study did not include any self-report data so it is impossible to know if this was the cause, although they suggest that it was unlikely to explain all of the increased sales. They also note that as they are dealing only with store level data (that is total sales for that store) they have no way of knowing whether the increased sales were a similar number of customers purchasing more items or an increased number of customers.

Study 2 looked at the effect of purchase quantity limit anchors such as 'Limit 4 per customer'. There is limited research evidence in this area and what evidence there is tends to have examined the use of low purchase limits, for example restricting customers to one item appears to make the deal look very good, and low purchase limits such as two or four also seem to increase sales. In this study Wansink et al. wanted to look at the effect of a relatively high purchase decision: 12 items per customer.

This was also a field experiment conducted over three consecutive evenings in three supermarkets in Iowa, USA. Each supermarket created an aisle end display of Campbell's soups for 79c each. The regular price was 89c, which implied a modest 12% discount. Each supermarket presented one limit notice each evening so that each store offered each limit condition on one evening. These limits were 'No limit per person'. 'Limit of 4 per person' and 'Limit of 12 per person'. Shoppers were observed unobtrusively. For each of the 914 shoppers observed, data was collected on whether they purchased the soup and how many cans they purchased. Data for eight shoppers was excluded from the final analysis as they purchased more than the limit allowed by the sign.

The results showed that shoppers who bought soup from the displays with no limit purchased an average of 3.3 cans of soup, whereas buyers with limits of 4 and 12 purchased an average of 3.5 and 7.0 cans, respectively. The buyers in the limit 12 condition purchased significantly more cans than consumers in either the no-limit condition ($p < .01$) or the limit 4 condition ($< .01$). The limit 12 signage increased sales per buyer by 112%.

The third study is slightly different as it examined the effect of anchor-based suggestive usage slogans such as 'Snickers bars – buy them for your freezer' and also examined the effect of these anchors when accompanied with or without a price discount.

Some 120 undergraduates from a large university participated in a shopping scenario study. Each participant was offered six well-known products at one of three price levels: an actual convenience store price (no discount), a 20% discount, and a 40% discount. All subjects were given suggestive selling claims that included either no product quantity anchor ('Snickers bars – buy them for your freezer') or an explicit product quantity anchor ('Snickers bars – buy 18 for your freezer'). Participants were given no indication whether the price was a discount and were asked to provide purchase quantity intentions for all products.

The results suggested that both the suggestive anchor and the discount level increased purchase quantity intentions. However, the authors claimed that supermarket shoppers might be able to resist point-of-purchase (external) anchors by using self-generated (internal) anchors. They examined this in their fourth and final study, which provided evidence that anchoring is the psychological mechanism driving the results of the previous experiments.

Course credits were given to 139 undergraduate students from a large university who participated in the study. Each participant was told that he or she was involved in a shopping study for a local grocery store and was given a shopping scenario involving 25 30% discounts on single servings of well-known products (e.g. Coca-Cola, Oreo cookies, Snickers candy bars, Sunkist oranges, Wrigley's five-pack gum). There were four purchase quantity limits: a no-limit control, limit 14, limit 28 and limit 56. After studying the details of the promotional deal (i.e. product description, regular and discounted prices, and quantity limits if any), subjects were immediately asked to answer the question 'How many units of this product [e.g. packs of gum] do you usually buy at a time?' After writing down a number, each student indicated his or her intended purchase quantity for the item. After seeing the deal, subjects were asked, 'On each of the lines below, please write down a different situation in which you might imagine yourself [consuming this product (e.g. chewing some gum)].' After listing different examples, they were asked, 'How many [units of this product (e.g. packs of gum)] do you think you might [use (e.g. chew)] in the next month?' Finally, subjects provided their intended purchase quantities.

In the no-limit control condition, the default anchor led to purchase intentions close to those produced when no internal anchor was elicited (4.2 versus 5.0). The expansion anchor, in contrast, increased intended purchase quantities considerably, an increase of 150%. The results support the anchoring model by showing that both low (past purchase quantities) and high (future usage quantities) internal anchors can overpower the effects of external anchors.

Pre-cognitive decisions

It is predicted that purchases are driven by a combination of consumer preference and price. The study by Knutson et al. (2007) on the neural predictors of purchases uses fMRI scanning technology to investigate brain activity during purchasing decisions.

Subjects were scanned while engaging in a novel task. The researchers called this a SHOP task (Save Holdings or Purchase). The task consisted of a series of images. First the subject saw the product for four seconds and then the product with a price for four seconds and was then shown a third screen which asked them to choose whether to purchase this product at this price. This choice screen was also shown for four seconds. They then had to fixate on a crosshair for two seconds before the next trial began.

The researchers predicted that during the product consideration task, preference would be shown by activation of neural circuits associated with anticipated gain. Secondly, they predicted that during the price presentation phase, excessive prices would be associated with the activation of neural circuits associated with anticipated loss. Finally, they predicted that activation prior to the purchase decision would predict, above and beyond self-report variables, whether individuals would subsequently choose to purchase a product.

Participants were 26 healthy right-handed adults; 12 were female and 14 were male and their age ranged from 18 and 26. All were screened for use of psychotropic drugs and ibuprofen, substance abuse in the last month and any history of psychiatric disorders prior to collecting informed consent. A further six participants were excluded as they purchased fewer than four items (less than 10%) and this did not produce sufficient data to model and a further eight participants were excluded due to excessive head motion during the sessions.

Participants were paid $20 for their participation. To ensure engagement in the task they were told that one trial would be selected at random to count 'for real'. If an item had been purchased in this trial they would pay the price (out of their $20) that they had seen in the scanner and would be shipped the product. Products ranged in retail price from $8 to $80 but were discounted by 75%.

Subjects purchased a mean of 23.58 items out of 80 products shown. There was no significant difference in the number of products purchased by men and women and so further analysis was done in respect of this.

Purchasing was consistent over several presentations of the same product. Reaction time did not differ between products that were purchased and products that were not purchased. However, for purchased products, reaction time correlated negatively with preference. In other words, there was more time spent in considering whether to purchase an item that they only showed a weak preference for and less time considering whether to purchase an item that they showed a strong preference for. The opposite was found for unpurchased products, in that subjects spent longer deciding before buying a product for which they had a relatively weak preference as well as prior to not buying something that they had a relatively strong preference for. This suggests that the reaction time indicates some form of response conflict (*I want it but it is too expensive*).

The findings were consistent with previous neuroimaging studies which showed that there are distinct circuits which anticipate gain and loss. Product preference activated the **nucleus accumbens (NAcc)** and excessive prices activated the **insula** and deactivated the **mesial prefrontal cortex** prior to a purchase decision. Activity from these regions was able to predict immediately subsequent purchases above and beyond self-report variables.

The findings suggest that the activation of distinct brain regions related to anticipation of gain and loss can be used to predict purchasing decisions. They were controlled for increased motor preparation as the buttons for 'purchase' or 'not purchase' were not the same each time.

Evaluation

The content of this section can be applied to everyday life. The understanding of **heuristics** has much to offer the retailer. If a brand sells well, we can maintain these sales by ensuring that the customer can simply and easily identify 'the one I always buy'. However, for new products or for products that are not selling well, we may need to understand this way customers use heuristics in order for us to try to break into this processing and make them consider something different or by using packaging that makes the new product look like something familiar and trusted. This could be achieved with the use of promotional materials, special offers and eye-catching displays. All of these will be considered elsewhere in this chapter. There are two studies to consider in this chapter. The study by Wansink et al. is a **field study** conducted in a number of supermarkets and although there will always be problems in controlling all the possible variables that may influence customer spending, there is clear evidence here that point of purchase promotions increase sales. This study gives us a deeper understanding of how these situational variables work and could be usefully applied in a variety of retail environments and in different cultures. In contrast, the study by Knutson is a **laboratory-based study** and will have been highly controlled. Although there are limitations of the fMRI technique, the possible implications of this study are huge. If we can identify customer intentions without using self-report then we remove all of the conscious cognitive processing which might 'interfere' with the response. If computers can be controlled by thought it is scary to imagine that retailers may one day be able to make sales based on the fact that an advertisement activated a certain brain region.

It is likely that the findings of the research described in this section would apply equally to all cultures, even though the studies are not conducted cross-culturally.

Intuitive thinking and its imperfections
Thinking fast-thinking slow/system 1 and system 2

Kahneman's (2011) book '*Thinking, Fast and Slow*' presents his theory of thinking and has been summarised and reviewed by Schleifer (2012). System 1 thinking corresponds to 'thinking fast' and System 2 to 'thinking slow'. System 1 is described as intuitive, automatic, unconscious and effortless, uses associations and resemblances and is non-statistical, gullible and heuristic. System 2 is very different, it is conscious, slow, controlled, deliberate, effortful, statistical, suspicious and costly to use.

Kahneman and Tversky (1979) have done a great deal of research into the consequences of System 1 thinking, which they claim is the way most people think, most of the time. This does not mean that we are incapable of System 2 thought but that we use this rarely and this may be why predictions of decision making are so difficult to get right.

One of their best known experiments asked Americans to respond to this statement: '*Steve is very shy and withdrawn, invariably helpful but with very little interest in people or in the world of reality. A meek and tidy soul, he has a need for order and structure, and a passion for detail.*' Is Steve more likely to be a librarian or a farmer?

Not surprisingly, most Americans respond that Steve is more likely to be a librarian than a farmer. Steve sounds more like a librarian than a farmer. We do not consider the fact that there are at least five times as many farmers in the USA as there are librarians and that male librarians are even rarer than female librarians. From this statistical (System 2) approach it is surely much more likely that Steve is a farmer. However, this is System 2 thinking and we use this rarely.

In another example participants are asked to estimate the total number of murders in Detroit in a year while others are asked to estimate the total number of murders in Michigan in a year. Typically, the first group on average estimates a higher number of murders than the second. Again, System 1 thinking is in evidence. Detroit evokes a violent city, associated with many murders. Michigan evokes idyllic apple-growing farmland. Without System 2 thinking, the fact that Detroit is *in* Michigan does not come to mind for the second group of participants.

Reflections: To get a feel for System 1 thinking, respond to these questions:

- Add 2 and 2
- Complete the phrase 'Bread and...' .

These are typical, rapid, intuitive, automatic responses, which will usually, but not always produce the right answers. The first question should produce the same answer from everyone but the typical response to the second question may differ by culture.

Kahneman (2011) also discusses the role of heuristics (rule of thumb thinking) and biases in our thinking. One of the examples given in the article illustrates the way that irrelevant material can influence our answers.

Kahneman calls this the anchoring heuristic. Imagine a wheel of fortune marked from 0 to 100. It has been rigged by the experimenters to stop at either number 10 or number 65. When it stops, students are asked to write down the number at which it stops and they are then asked two questions:

- Is the percentage of African nations in the United Nations larger or smaller than the number you just wrote down?
- What is your best guess of the percentage of African nations in the United Nations?

Remember that the number the student has just written down has absolutely nothing to do with the questions that have been asked. Despite this, students who saw the wheel stop at 10 gave an average guess for the second question of 25%. Those who saw the wheel stop at 65 gave an average guess of 45%. There are many studies like this which show how the first question (and the irrelevant material) anchors the answer to the second question. Kahneman describes this as an extreme example of System 1 thinking – planting a number in someone's head makes it relevant to decisions.

Another category of heuristic is the representativeness heuristic. The following task described by Kahneman illustrates this. Participants are asked to read the following description:

Linda is 31 years old, single, outspoken and very bright. She majored in philosophy. As a student, she was deeply concerned with issues of discrimination and social justice, and also participated in anti-nuclear demonstrations.

Participants are then asked to rank in order the likelihood that Linda is:

1 an elementary school teacher

2 active in the feminist movement

3 a bank teller

4 an insurance salesperson

5 a bank teller who is also active in the feminist movement.

Time after time, respondents choose scenario 5 over scenario 3, completely ignoring the fact that scenario 5 is a special case of scenario 3 and thus considerably less likely to be correct. Not only do a great number of people get this wrong, but they also object strongly when the correct answer is explained to them. Kahneman would explain this as the use of heuristics; the description given of Linda creates associations in the person's mind and when asked to match that picture to each of the above scenarios they see that scenario 5 is more similar to the picture in their head than scenario 3. System 1 thinking can 'tell a story' which fits 5 better than 3. Fitting the mental picture to 3 is harder as the stereotypical bank teller is not a college radical. Of course, it is possible to walk people through a System 2 approach to this problem and explain to them that there are more bank tellers than feminist bank tellers then you can get them to reach the correct answer. But the conclusion drawn by Kahneman is that people do not do this automatically.

Choice blindness

Hall et al. (2010) conducted a study into **choice blindness** for the taste of jam and the smell of tea. Shoppers (180 in total, 118 female) at a supermarket in Sweden were recruited as they passed a tasting venue that had been set up in store. Participants were asked to sample different varieties of jam and tea and to decide which one out of a pair they preferred. Immediately after making their choice, the participant was asked to sample the chosen item again and to verbally explain why they chose the way they did. The experimenters then switched the contents of the sample containers (without the participant's knowledge) so that the rejected item was now the preferred item.

The stimulus material was three pairs of jam and three pairs of tea, selected from a pre-test in which independent participants rated the similarity of eight pairs of jam and seven pairs of tea. Experimenters selected one pair from the middle of the distribution and the two most dissimilar pairs.

For jam the chosen pairs were Blackcurrant vs Blueberry, Ginger vs Lime and Cinnamon Apple vs Grapefruit. For tea the chosen pairs were Apple Pie vs Honey , Caramel & Cream vs Cinnamon and Pernod (Anise/Liquorice) vs Mango.

In order to manipulate the choice, two small containers were glued together bottom-to-bottom, creating a single jar with two independent sections with separate screw-

KEY TERM

choice blindness: ways in which people are blind to their own choices and preferences. People often do not notice when they are presented with something which was not what they asked for. They will also suggest reasons to defend these choices.

on lids. A paper wrapping was then applied over the mid-section to complete the illusion of a single unbroken container (colour coded in red and blue to make it easier to distinguish among the alternatives). In each trial two of these containers were used, filled with either two different sorts of jam or tea (i.e. each jar was a mirror of the other one, except for the coloured label, and which compartment was facing upwards at the beginning of the experiment).

The experiment took place at a local supermarket. Participants were asked to take part in a quality control test of the jam and the tea. Participants were simply asked to state which one of each pair they preferred. In addition, half of the participants were told that they would receive the chosen package of tea or the chosen jar of jam as a gift at the completion of the test.

Two experimenters were present during the test. Experimenter 1 asked questions, took notes, and managed the recording device, while Experimenter 2 conducted the preference test. Each participant completed a total of two trials, one for jam and one for tea. For each participant, either the tea or the jam condition was manipulated. The order of presentation, the type of manipulation, and which pair of jam or tea that was included was randomised for each participant. In a manipulated trial, the participants were presented with the two prepared jars. After tasting the jam or smelling the tea, they were asked to rate how much they liked this on a 10-point scale. Participants were told that they could revise their first rating after the second sample and that they would also be asked which one they preferred. While Experimenter 1 interacted with the participants, Experimenter 2 screwed the lid back on the container that was used, and surreptitiously turned it upside down. After the participants had rated the first option, they were offered the second sample, and once again rated how much they liked it. As with the first sample, Experimenter 2 covertly flipped the jar upside down while returning it to the table. Immediately after the participants completed their second rating, they were then asked which alternative they preferred, and asked to sample it a second time.

After the tastings, participants were asked whether they felt that anything was odd or unusual with the way that the tasting session had been conducted. This was to allow participants to spontaneously indicate that some form of change or mismatch had taken place.

After this, participants were debriefed and again given the opportunity to indicate whether they had noticed or suspected the manipulation. The experimenters classified any detections into three categories:

Concurrent detection	the participants voiced any concerns immediately after tasting or smelling the manipulated jam or tea. In these cases, the experiment continued as normal but the results were not used in the final analysis.
Retrospective detection	the participant claimed to have noticed the manipulation but reported this at the end (either before or after the debriefing).
Sensory-change detection	the participants did not report detecting the manipulation, but described the taste or smell as somehow different the second time round.

In total, 33.3% of the manipulated jam trials, and 32.2% of the manipulated tea trials were detected. (This included 14.4% of the jam trials and 13.8% of the tea trials detected concurrently, 6.2% of the jam and 6.9% of the tea trials were detected retrospectively, and 12.4% of the jam and 11.5% of the tea trials were registered as a sensory-change.) Manipulations were detected more frequently in the least similar pairs compared with the most similar pairs (but not compared with other pairs) and rated discrepancy of preference within a pair was higher for detected manipulated jam trials compared to the undetected trials; however this was not true for detected tea trials. Contrary to the prediction, the participants that received the gift incentive had a lower detection rate (19.6%) than participants not receiving a gift (46.3%) in the tea condition but no difference was found for the jam condition.

No more than one-third of the switches were detected, even when remarkably different tastes were used such as Cinnamon Apple and bitter Grapefruit, or very different smells such as Mango and Pernod; the switch was detected in less than half the trials. This demonstrates considerable choice blindness. The authors recognise that this was a decision with few if any consequences and that it is likely that consumers may be more likely to recognise a manipulation in a higher-stakes decision and that there is a great deal more research to do in this area. In this situation, there were few if any consequences to the decision; the consumers were not even purchasing the item, although it is interesting to note that the participants offered a gift of their preferred jam before taking part were in fact less likely to notice the manipulation than other participants. This

indicates that choice blindness can remain robust even in the face of real world consequences.

Advertising and false memory

Recent research in consumer psychology has demonstrated that **reconstructive memory** can have a powerful **retroactive** effect on how people remember past events. In the following study by Braun-LaTour et al. (2004), the researchers aim to test whether this can be applied to advertising. Can post-experience advertising influence our recollection?

> **KEY TERMS**
>
> **reconstructive memory:** a theory of memory recall which suggests that the act of remembering is influenced by various other factors such as cultural beliefs, expectations and stereotyping.
>
> **retroactive:** retroactive interference is where new information interferes with the memory of old information. For example learning your new phone number interferes with the memory for the previous one.

Experiment 1 was conducted to investigate whether true and false autobiographical advertising would be processed and remembered in the same way. The researchers exposed the participants to false information about Disney (a character that was not a Disney character) and they expected that this would change what the participants remembered about their experience at Disneyland. They also expected that those who recognised the falseness would be less likely to create false memories than those who did not notice the discrepancy.

Participants were 66 undergraduate students in an US university; 32 females and 34 males with an average age of 21 were randomly allocated to one of two conditions. This was an independent measures design. The advertisements were autobiographical in nature with a vignette of a typical Disney experience.

The true advertisement includes a picture of Mickey Mouse (a Disney character) and makes reference to shaking hands with this character, whereas the false advertisement replaces this with a picture and a reference to shaking hands with Bugs Bunny, who is a Warner Brothers character and would not be part of a Disney attraction.

Adverts were given out in a classroom setting. Participants were asked to read and evaluate the advert and then rate their own attitude, affect and likelihood of visiting

Disneyland in the future. They were then asked about their own past experiences visiting Disneyland and whether they had seen certain characters at the park. They were debriefed and informed about false memory research.

Although a small number of participants identified that Bugs Bunny should not be on an advertisement for Disneyland, there were no significant differences between the way that the true and false adverts were processed or in terms of the attitudes they had towards Disney. Neither was there a difference in the recollections of participants who received the true or false adverts. However, those receiving the false Bugs Bunny information were significantly more likely to recall Bugs Bunny memories (22% vs 7%). It is important to note that even some in the 'true' condition were likely to confuse Bugs Bunny with a Disney memory.

Interestingly, the researchers report that none of the participants guessed the true purpose of the study and most thought that it was to see if an advert could get people to remember their past. Only a very small number of participants believed that the advert changed what they remembered. The false advert did seem to affect memory.

RESEARCH METHODS

Note that the inclusion of the false material is essential here – if someone recalled (falsely) that they had shaken hands with Mickey Mouse after being exposed to advertising containing this story, we would be unable to determine whether this did take place or not. However we know that no one can be accurately recalling shaking hands with Bugs Bunny at a Disney theme park. Suggest another piece of false information that could be used in this study.

Experiment 2 was similar but contained three false conditions:

1   False information was provided as a picture.

2   False information was provided in words.

3   False information was provided as both words and pictures.

Some 100 students in a different US university participated in this study and were randomly assigned to one of the three conditions. The procedures and measures were identical to Experiment 1. The pictures had a stronger effect than the words. Both conditions containing a picture of Bugs Bunny produced the greatest number of false memories.

Reflections: Interestingly the verbal only condition also produced the largest numbers of 'Bugs detectors' (participants recognising that this was false information) who in turn showed less favourable responses to the ads, less involvement with the ads and a more negative attitude towards Disney.

Suggest why detecting the false information would affect the way that participants responded to the adverts.

There are two ways to interpret the findings of Experiment 2. One possibility is that the participants in the 'verbal only' condition processed the information more deeply than in the other conditions – this might be why they were more likely to detect Bugs and thus less likely to create a false memory. The alternative is that they did not process it deeply enough – that apart from those who detected Bugs others overlooked it as it was not as prominent or attention grabbing as the picture.

Experiment 3 added a memory test to the end of the experiment to try and distinguish between these explanations. The researchers predict that if information is more deeply processed then the memory of it will last for longer and participants will be more likely to remember the information. If the second explanation is the more accurate one then we would predict that less information would be recalled.

The same advertisements as in Experiment 2 were used and 110 participants were randomly allocated to one of three conditions. Participants were placed in groups of around 30 in a computer lab. They were given the advertising information and were asked to provide feedback on it for several minutes. They were then given ten minutes to write about their own first childhood experience at a Disney resort. They then completed the computer task. This was in two parts: recognition of items from their own childhood visit to Disney and then an **Implicit Association Test (IAT)**. In the recognition task the main focus of interest was whether the participants would identify Bugs Bunny as part of their childhood experience and how confident they would be that they did or did not meet him. The main interest in the IAT test was the whether the participants would categorise Bugs as belonging to the Disney or 'Other' theme park category.

 KEY TERM

Implicit Association Test (IAT): this is a test to see what associations people make. In this study the IAT presented the participants with a series of words to classify into two groups: Disney and Other by pressing computer keys.

Finally, participants were given a written advertising memory task in which they were asked to recall everything they could remember from the Disney ad they saw earlier and were asked specific questions, including; 'What character did the child shake hands with?', 'What pictures appeared in the ad?' and 'What appeared in the ad's headline?'

Results confirmed findings from Experiment 2 in that more 'Bugs detectors' were found in the verbal only condition and that more false memories were created in the pictorial conditions.

Participants remembered significantly more items in the pictorial condition. They remembered an average of 6.2 items in the 'both' condition, 5.1 items in the pictorial only condition and 4.7 in the verbal only condition. 88% of participants in the both condition recalled Bugs Bunny, 76 % in the pictorial only condition and 47% in the verbal only condition.

Evaluation

It is clearly useful to be able to see how our thinking can be faulty. Not only is this useful in mainstream psychology but it is also useful in terms of how it may be applied in the consumer environment. The descriptions of 'thinking; fast and slow' and of choice blindness are important examples of this. The study by Hall et al. into **choice blindness** was a field experiment conducted in a supermarket in Sweden. It involved a relatively large sample of participants who did not realise that they were taking part in anything more than a usual 'taste test'. The study involved a very clever manipulation of the jars and revealed that the majority of people do not notice when the products are swapped. This has interesting implications for retailers. If a consumer makes a commitment to a specific product, then as long as they believe that they have received that product they should be happy. This might suggest that packaging is extremely important. Perhaps if a 'value' or 'budget' brand were to be placed in the packaging of the preferred more expensive brand then customers will still claim that they like it more. Our earlier examination of heuristics would suggest that we might! The study by Braun-LaTour et al. into false memory also involved creative manipulation of variables and shows clearly that information received after an event can alter our memory for that event. Psychologists were aware of this effect from the context of eyewitness testimony where it has been shown by many studies that post-event information in the form of leading questions can influence memory (e.g. Loftus and Palmer, 1974) but its application to advertising is relatively new. The two studies in this section show clearly the influence of situational variables on our

behaviour whilst the discussion of the way we think brings in a focus on individual cognitive processes..

SELF-ASSESSMENT QUESTIONS

9   Explain what 'satisficing' means.
10 Briefly explain the task that the participants in Knutson's study of pre-cognitive decisions had to complete.
11 Explain what is meant by 'choice blindness'.
12 Briefly explain how Braun-LaTour et al. knew that a participant reporting a memory of meeting Bugs Bunny at a Disney attraction was a false memory.

7.4 The product
Packaging, positioning and placement
Gift wrapping

This section will examine expectations surrounding the wrapping of a gift. Previous research (Howard, 1992) suggests that the use of wrapping signals that the object is actually a gift. There is no ambiguity. This means that both the giver and the receiver know exactly the roles that they are supposed to play. Poruvleb et al. (2009) note that there is only limited research into the expectations of what a gift should look like. They claim that gifts can be presented in one of three ways: unwrapped (or 'naked'), wrapped in a non-traditional manner where it may be difficult to determine that the gift is actually a gift (they give the example of brown paper but perhaps also just giving someone something in the bag it came in from the shop) or wrapped in a traditional manner. Howard conducted a study in which he examined how the appearance of a gift influenced mood. He found that people were happier when presented with a traditionally wrapped gift than with either a non-traditionally wrapped or a naked gift.

Reflections: If someone hands you a wrapped gift, how does this make you feel?

Naked gifts can be acceptable – there are going to be clear cultural differences here. For example if you took a bottle of wine or box of chocolates to someone's house as a gift you would probably not wrap them, although if they were birthday presents you probably would.

In the study by Poruvleb et al. three data collecting techniques were used: (a) observations conducted at a Christmas gift wrapping stall; (b) 20 in-depth interviews where respondents were asked to reflect on gift wrapping (including questions such as 'Do you prefer to receive gifts that are wrapped or unwrapped?', 'In what instance do you wrap gifts?', 'In what instance do you not wrap gifts?'); and (c) six workshops where, in pairs, participants were asked to wrap two gifts, one for someone they were close to and one for an acquaintance and to have a conversation about gift wrapping while doing so.

Results from both the workshops and the interviews revealed that most participants (25–35-year-olds from Victoria, Australia) preferred to receive a gift that was wrapped and that there were clear expectations of what a gift should look like.

The researchers used qualitative data to support their findings that gifts should be wrapped. For example one of their participants said '*I prefer wrapped. I like the reveal … I like a gift under any circumstances, but it does mean somebody's taken a little bit of extra time and put extra thought into it'*. Another suggested that they would be embarrassed to give a gift that was not wrapped while another identified that even though there may be environmental issues to do with wasting paper, they still prefer receiving a wrapped gift. Participants also identified that gift wrapping was traditional and that people probably do it without thinking too much about why they are doing it – it is just 'what you do'.

There was also a preference for a gift to look like a gift (Figure 7.11). An analysis of the gifts created in the projective workshops showed that all 24 of them looked like gifts, with traditional wrappings; paper, decorative bags with ribbons, bows and other embellishments. The authors claim that this indicates social expectations of what a gift should typically look like. Participants in the gift wrapping task reported 'playing it safe' with wrapping the gift for an acquaintance although when wrapping a gift for a close friend or family member they were able to relate this directly to the person, choosing colours and patterns that

they knew they would like. In conclusion, they claimed that gifts should be wrapped because wrapped gifts make it easier for the exchange to occur because they 'enable the giver and receiver to fall into their roles without any confusion as to the purpose of the exchange'.

7.11 Wrapping a gift makes it clear that it is a gift

The researchers claimed that this study has contributed to the field of consumer behaviour by helping us to better understand the role that gift wrapping plays in the giving and receiving of gifts and also provides a starting point for further research into the symbolic meaning of wrapping gifts. The findings also have useful implications for retailers, perhaps particularly at the luxury end of the market, where gift-wrapping could be a significant differentiator.

Product colour and associative learning

Grossman and Wisenblit (1999) have summarised what is known about consumers' colour choices. Advertisers have been aware of the importance of colour for many years. Car companies now update car colours regularly and will plan these changes up to four years in advance. Traditionally domestic appliances were always white but producing them in a variety of colours has increased sales significantly (Figure 7.12).

7.12 Domestic appliances – no longer just white!

Reflections: Suggest why producing fridges in different colours increases sales.

The ideas of **classical conditioning** have been used to understand colour preferences. You will have studied classical conditioning at AS Level but briefly this is associative learning. We form associations between different aspects of our environment. For example a favourable experience with a colour will lead to a preference for this colour, or we may learn to associate certain colours with certain products. This approach has even been used to alter colour preferences. Grossman and Wisenblit report a study by Gorn (1982) in which different coloured pens were paired with either pleasant or unpleasant music. When participants were asked to choose a pen to take home at the end of the study, they chose the colour that had been associated with the pleasant music.

Associative learning can also be used to explain the physiological reactions that we have to colour. Some suggest that these associations will have been formed early in human history when people first associated blue with night – and therefore passivity – and yellow with sunlight – and therefore arousal. Even now, we assume that cool colours are calming (blue, green) and warm colours (red and orange) are arousing. This has been applied in several environments, for example pink is used to calm inmates in institutions and dentists often paint their surgeries blue to calm patients. However, different cultures have different associations with colour as well as different colour preferences and any product application would need to take note of these differences.

Reflections: A prison in Georgia, USA, trialled the use of bright pink uniforms for prisoners. Suggest why this idea might have been proposed and whether you think it would be successful. Design a study to test the effect of this or the use of different colour uniforms in a different context.

Different colour associations exist for different products and this is of obvious importance for manufacturers and retailers. It is not enough to know what someone's favourite colour is as this will not necessarily predict purchases in all product categories. For example, someone might love the colours green and orange when buying clothes but we shouldn't assume that they would therefore buy a carpet, a car or a dining room table in those colours! Several studies including those by Holmes and Buchanan (1984) support the finding that people's colour preference differ depending on the product. Cars are preferred in blue, grey, red, white and black whereas beige is often preferred for carpeting, soft furnishing and paint.

These findings suggest that colours have meanings for consumers and several researchers have attempted to decode these meanings and to use these meanings to understand consumer choices. Grossman and Wisenblit give the example of a vitamin supplement that was packaged in a black container with white lettering. Interviews with potential purchasers showed that they were mistaking this for poison as black is commonly used in the packaging of dangerous products. A change of packaging to beige and brown changed customer perception. However, black created a successful association when used to package a men's cologne where the colour was used to signify strength and masculinity.

Grossman and Wisenblit also suggest that colour can be used to signify the attributes of a product and give the example of Cheer laundry detergent. Researchers tested the use of blue, yellow and red flecks in the white detergent, concluding that blue signified cleanliness to the consumer. Once again, culture is important here. One fascinating example is that grey is associated with expensive products in the USA but with cheaper products in China and Japan.

Finally, colour may actually be more important in relatively low involvement decision making, which is often conducted in an automatic manner. This means that simple product attributes such as colour might be surprisingly influential in a decision over which candy bar to buy for example. This does not necessarily mean that they will choose their favourite colour, rather that a complex set of associations will lead to their choice.

All of this suggests that the choice of colour, for the product and for the packaging, is crucial.

Reflections: Choose a colour for the packaging of the following products and explain your choice.
- An expensive set of art materials
- Face paints for children
- A high quality food hamper
- A jewellery store carrier bag

Attention and shelf position

Atalay et al. (2012) used eye tracking technology to identify the customer tendency to choose the option in the centre of the array. An 'offline' study also confirmed that the centrally located item is chosen more often, even when this is not the centre of the visual field.

They conducted several studies. Study 1A involved 67 undergraduate students in France. They participated for additional course credits. The average age was 20.4 and the sample was 54% females. Each participant was seated in front of an eye tracker. The eye tracker screen is 17 inches (43 cm) wide and the screen is refreshed 50 times per second. As participants look at the screen, a discreet infra-red camera records their eye gaze and is able to track the exact location of eye fixations on the screen.

Participants reviewed two product categories: vitamin supplements and meal replacement bars. Two separate **planograms** were displayed. These were displayed in a 3 × 3 matrix design. There were three brands and each brand appeared three times. The brand names used were fictitious – Priorin, Alpecin and Labrada for vitamins and Bega, Niran and Salus for meal replacement bars.

KEY TERM

planogram: a diagram that shows how and where specific retail products should be placed on retail shelves or displays in order to increase customer purchases. *Planogramming* is a skill used in merchandising and retail space planning.

Participants were asked to carefully review each product on the screen as if these were on the shelf in a shop and to hit the enter key when they had finished reviewing the product and were ready to make a choice. Once they hit the enter key, the stimulus disappeared from the screen to ensure that any further visual processing was stopped and participants indicated their choice. Participants indicated their choice by ticking the box that matched the position of the product on a 3 × 3 matrix that mirrored the planogram.

Results of Study 1A demonstrated that brands in the centre received more frequent eye fixations and overall were looked at for longer. Further analysis revealed that products placed in the centre were chosen more often and this choice was unrelated to other inferences made about the product and solely to increased visual attention.

Study 1B extended this research by considering whether the effect of horizontal central location on choice and the central gaze effect are explained by horizontal centrality (in the centre of the display) or simply by centrality on the computer screen. Participants were 64 undergraduate students in Paris. This study was a replication of Study 1A with the addition of displaying planograms that were shifted away from the centre of the computer screen (to either the left or the right). These planograms were reduced in size and were shifted to the left or right by 50% such that the centrally located item in the planogram was not the centrally located item on the screen.

Results showed that the brand in the horizontal centre of the array received more frequent eye fixations as well as longer duration of fixations. The preference for the central item was a robust finding. Therefore the results from Study 1B converged with the results from Study 1A. The tendency to choose the central item was robust and maintained even when the planogram was shifted off the centre of the computer screen. The results showed that the centrally located item in a horizontal array gets more visual attention and that the central gaze cascade effect that emerges in the last few moments of the gaze duration is involved in the choice making process.

Study 2 was conducted to see if the results could be replicated in a more realistic context. Categories of items on shop shelves are not always in the centre of the shelf space or indeed the centre of a consumer's visual field. It is important therefore to determine whether the product placed in the centre of an array of products within a category, but to the left or right side of the shelf would still be chosen more often. Conducting this study in a 'real' environment with physical products also addressed the issue of the previous studies being conducted on screen.

A total of 84 students at Concordia University took part in this experiment. The products used in this study were fictitious brands of energy drink named Cebion, Niran and Viba. Each brand had one feature attribute: high intensity, extended endurance or muscle recovery but these attributes were rotated around the brands to eliminate any possible effects of these attributes.

Items were displayed in categories of three items so that each product could appear in a left, centre or right position within the category. The category could then be positioned towards the left or the right hand side of the shelf. Filler products from other categories were included on the shelf.

Participants were tested one at a time and were positioned in the middle of the display such that the category they were asked to choose from was to their left or their right (but never exactly in the centre of their visual field). They were not allowed to reposition themselves (which would have put the category in the centre of their visual field) and were simply asked to review the items and to choose one of the energy drinks.

Results showed that the centrally located brand within a product category is more often chosen even when it is not in the centre of the visual field. This again shows just how robust the central gaze effect is and that it is not a product of screen-based presentation.

Interestingly, although the brand in the centre was chosen more often and received more visual attention, it was not evaluated any more positively than the other items. This suggests that more research is required into this effect.

Finally, in line with other researchers claims that consumers have 'lay beliefs' about how items are displayed in supermarkets, one additional measure was taken in Study 1A although the researchers only report this in their discussion. They asked participants to rate the following statement on a scale from 1 to 9.

> 'On the supermarket shelf, I believe that most popular products are always placed in the middle'.

The mean response was 5.8, considerably above the centre of this scale, although there were no significant correlations between individual participants' ratings and the central gaze effect suggesting that this belief cannot be an explanation for any of this effect.

Evaluation

The study by Poruvleb et al. investigated an under-researched area of consumer psychology; the importance of gift wrapping. This reveals some interesting conclusions about the way that wrapping a gift helps the social interaction process as it is much clearer to the recipient that this is a gift. This might have useful applications for retailers and the designers of packaging. Many products are packaged so that they look like gifts when they are purchased – perhaps the idea behind this is that the buyer makes a positive association between the appearance of the product and the feelings of receiving a gift making them more likely to purchase. In a similar way, many high-end beauty products often come with 'gifts' which are wrapped as if you are being given a present by the store. The research methods used in this study are also interesting as we have not come across this kind of group methodology before and these are relatively common in consumer research. These are often referred to as focus groups and bring

together groups of people to discuss and feedback on new products before they are released. However, important differences between cultures in terms of both gift giving and gift wrapping need to considered. The study by Atalay et al. also used an interesting approach; eye-tracking technology is relatively new and has been used to explore a range of consumer situations. This study has high levels of control; the use of fictitious products means that no other criteria (such as differences in packaging, colour, price, familiarity) can be used to base a choice on. Where names were different (but still fictitious) this has been controlled. Therefore any differences in choice can only be attributed to the location. The researchers claim that this is not the case in much previous research and that their research is considerably less confounded than other research in this area. This study suggests that **situational variables** (positioning) are hugely influential in determining consumer behaviour and have obvious implications for the positioning of products within a store. It is particularly interesting that the 'first in display' is not at an advantage especially when you consider the findings of the menu position study discussed earlier in this chapter.

Selling the product

Sales techniques: customer/competitor/product focused

There are several strategies that can be used to sell a product, although as we shall see, they tend to overlap. The first is the customer-focused sales technique. From this perspective, the seller would look carefully at potential customers and identify what they want. They would then tailor their sales techniques to match these needs. This is sometimes called 'solution-selling' and advertisements based on solution-selling will highlight exactly how the product suits the customer. In order for a customer-focused sales technique to be effective the seller will need as much information as possible about the customers and their needs and they will need to think long term rather than just short term. This is not only because loyal customers will spread the word and advertise your business for you but also because satisfied customers will come back. If a car dealer listens carefully to what a customer says they need and finds a car that perfectly suits their needs, there is every chance that this customer will come back to the same dealer next time they are buying a car. Admittedly, people tend not to buy cars very often but the same principle would apply in many other areas. If you were a business and you needed to find a firm to produce all your printed materials for you, you would return regularly to the one that provided the service best suited to your needs rather than the one that tried to manipulate you into buying one of their already existing packages.

The second strategy is the competitor-focused sales technique. From this perspective the seller would focus on how they compare to their competitors. This is common in supermarkets in the UK for example, where advertisements regularly draw direct comparisons between prices in different supermarkets. Competitor-focused sales techniques are also crucial if your product is relatively similar in price to your competitors. In this case the retailer will need to 'sell' other advantages of buying from them and this might include factors such as customer service, after-sales care or guarantees.

> **Reflections:** Imagine that you wanted to buy an electronic product such as a television or a laptop. You do some research and you identify five different retailers selling the product you want for the same low price. What other information might you look at before deciding which retailer to buy from?

The final strategy is the product-focused sales technique. This largely ignores the needs of individual customers and focuses primarily on producing or selling a quality product. The assumption here is that if you have the best product then the customers will come to you and that also the creation of a new, high-quality product might in fact create the customer need where this did not exist before. Apple is a perfect example of an organisation which focuses on the product.

However, in practice, it is difficult to separate out these three strategies. A customer-focused sales pitch may well include elements of competitor comparison as well as product quality. Perhaps, as with many areas of consumer psychology, it is about matching the most appropriate strategy to the product.

> **Reflections:** Which sales technique (customer-focused, competitor-focused or product-focused) would you use for each of the following products?
>
> - Coffee
> - Washing powder
> - A wristwatch computer
> - A hover-board
> - TV subscription services
> - Car rental

Interpersonal influence techniques; disrupt-then-reframe

The 'disrupt-then-reframe' (DTR) technique is intended to confuse consumers with a disruptive message and then reduce this confusion (or ambiguity) by reframing the message. For example, Davis and Knowles (1999) asked participants if they would like to purchase Christmas cards sold by a charity. In some of the conditions the experimenters used the DTR technique – by saying 'The price is 300 pennies ... I mean 3 dollars'. The use of this technique doubled sales. Fennis, Das and Pruyn (2004) also showed that using the disrupt-then-reframe technique reduced the amount of counterarguments and disagreements from customers.

The study by Kardes et al. (2007) involved two field experiments and one laboratory experiment to test the following hypotheses:

- *The DTR technique should increase compliance with a monetary request presented in a commercial context.*
- *The DTR technique should be more effective as the customer's* **need for cognitive closure (NFCC)** *increases.*

The DTR effect should be mediated by perceived ambiguity. In other words, the DTR effect will be stronger when there are higher levels of ambiguity.

Study 1 was a field experiment conducted in a European supermarket. The researchers set up a sales stand presenting a special offer on candy. Five confederates acting as sales personnel would introduce themselves to any customer who stopped near the stand. The confederate would tell the customer that 'as Christmas is approaching, these boxes of Christmas candy are on special offer today'. In the DTR condition, the confederate would then say, '*The price is now 100 eurocents* (2 second pause), *that's 1 euro. It's a bargain*'.

> **Reflections:** Identify the disruption and the reframe in this sentence, '*The price is now 100 eurocents* (2 second pause), *that's 1 euro. It's a bargain*'.

KEY TERM

need for cognitive closure (NFCC): (sometimes just referred to as need for closure) a dislike of ambiguity and uncertainty and a preference for definitive answers to questions.

In the control condition (reframe only) the confederate would simply say *'The price is 1 euro. It's a bargain!'* The confederate then observed the customer response. Adding one or more boxes of candy to their shopping cart was recorded as complying with the sales request.

A total of 147 customers listened to the whole presentation and 54% subsequently bought candy. However, 65% of those in the DTR group bought candy compared with 44% of those in the control group.

Experiment 2 was also a field experiment. A male confederate claimed to be from a fictitious student interest group and approached students on the campus of a Dutch university, asking them to join the group for a small cost (3 euros). Half the students were exposed to a DTR message and the other half were not. After the request had been made the participant was also asked to complete a 20-item scale measuring need for cognitive closure. In both groups the students were informed that membership of the group would be 3 euros. In the DTR groups they were told that *'You can now become a member for half a year for 300 eurocents. (2 second pause.) That's 3 euros. That's a really small investment.'* In the control group (reframe only), they were told that *'You can now become a member for half a year for 3 euros. That's a really small investment'.*

Overall 22% of the students approached agreed to become a member, with 30% of those in the DTR group agreeing to join compared with only 13% of the control group. Compliance also increased as NFCC increased: 43% of high NFCC individuals complied in the DTR condition compared with only 17% in the control condition. Although there was a slight difference for low NFCC individuals (16% versus 9%) this difference was not significant.

As predicted the DTR effect was stronger for those individuals who were high in NFCC. The final experiment examined this further. Here, 137 undergraduate students in an American university participated for course credit. They were randomly assigned to one of three conditions: DTR, reframe only or disrupt only. The study was a laboratory study conducted on computers. Participants were told that the study was about 'campus issues' and that the researchers were interested in the differences between various forms of communication; written, oral and video and that they had been randomly assigned to the video condition.

In the DTR condition the video showed a male actor (a theatre studies student who was blind to the aims of the study) stating that research is essential to the quality of education at university and that money is necessary for research. For these reasons, he continued, the Student Advocacy Council is arguing for *'an increase intuition of 7500 pennies. (2 second pause.) That's $75, it's a really small investment'.* In the reframe only condition, the participants heard the actor argue for *'an increase in tuition of $75; it's a really small investment'* and in the disrupt only condition they heard *'an increase in tuition of 7500 pennies'.*

All participants then completed the NFCC scale. Participants were then asked to complete a series of other scales measuring perceived ambiguity, attitudes and behavioural compliance.

Perceived ambiguity was measured using three scales which were rated from 1 (strongly disagree) to 6 (strongly agree):

- *Right now I would describe myself as indecisive.*
- *I am struggling with the decision about tuition fees.*
- *I feel uncertain about what to do.*

Attitudes were measured on six scales ranging from 1 to 9 with the following anchors: very negative–very positive, very bad–very good, very unfavourable–very favourable, very unpleasant–very pleasant, very harmful–very beneficial and very foolish–very wise. Behavioural compliance was measured by informing students that sometime in the future, they would be looking for students to volunteer to phone other students to tell them about the benefits of this increase. Participants were asked to say how much time they would be prepared to devote to making these calls on a scale of 1–9 where 1 was no time and 9 was 36–40 minutes. They were also asked to indicate their willingness to vote for the tuition fees on a scale from 1 (definitely against) to 9 (definitely in favour).

The analysis of this data is complex but the key findings are that when NFCC was low, the DTR manipulation had no effect on perceived ambiguity but when it was high, the disruption manipulation was successful in increasing ambiguity and the reframing was successful in decreasing ambiguity. When NFCC was high, more favourable attitudes towards the tuition increases were formed in the DTR condition than in the reframe only condition, which in turn produced more favourable outcomes than the disrupt only condition. When NFCC was low, the DTR technique was no more effective than the reframe only technique but was more effective than the disrupt only technique. Overall the findings suggest that the DTR technique was more effective as NFCC increased. This was also found when analysing the behavioural measures.

The researchers conclude that the effectiveness of the DTR technique increases as the need for cognitive closure increases and that disruption motivates consumers to accept a reframed message that aids closure through the reduction of ambiguity.

Ways to close a sale

Most techniques for closing a sale involve psychological principles drawn from social psychology and persuasion techniques. Cialdini (1984) suggests that there are six ways of getting people to say yes. These are as follows:

Reciprocity: This is the idea that if someone gives us something, that we have to give them something in return. So free samples in a supermarket or the promise of a free gift with our purchase (common with cosmetics and beauty products) is more likely to make us agree to buy something.

Commitment and Consistency: If you can persuade someone to make a small commitment, then you will increase the likelihood that they will make a larger commitment. For example, if an online retailer can get someone to sign up to their newsletter (which costs nothing) they increase the chances of that person buying something in the future. If signing up to something implies a commitment (to lose weight, to exercise more, to de-clutter or learn a new skill) then making associated purchases is consistent with this initial commitment. Social psychology tells us that people are more concerned with appearing consistent than appearing rational. Other techniques which can increase commitment include offering a free 'try at home' service (commonly used by online opticians so that you can try frames at home) or by offering free returns. Free returns might make a customer think they could order several items and then decide which ones to send back, whereas in reality, they are likely to keep all of them.

Liking: It may sound obvious to say that someone is more likely to buy something that they like, but liking is wider than the individual product. If we like the salesperson, or the friendliness of a store, then we are more likely to purchase from that store. If a product has been endorsed by a celebrity and we like that celebrity, then we are more likely to purchase the product. As an example, look at how many brands of celebrity perfume there are. Store design is also important, whether a physical store or an online one. If we like the brand image created by the store then we want to be associated with that image and we will purchase the products. Another way to create liking is to use social media such as Facebook to show you that your friend likes a product or has just bought a product. Hotel booking sites will tell you that '5 rooms have been booked in this hotel in the last hour' and online auction sites such as eBay will tell you how many views an item has had. All this creates liking for the product through associations and this can help to achieve a sale.

Authority: We know that authority is powerful. The experimenter in the lab coat was thought to be responsible for the high levels of obedience in the infamous Milgram experiment and authority is equally effective in persuading us to buy. Product advertising which includes 'scientific' or 'expert' evidence will convince us to buy.

Social proof: We like to have our decisions 'supported' by others. Knowing that lots of other people have bought a particular item, or booked into the same hotel can act as 'proof' that we are making the right decisions. Fashion websites that give us the option of selecting 'best sellers' are taking advantage of this social psychological need. Looking at the reviews left by other people in sites such as Amazon is also very influential and many manufacturers will offer free products to customers in return for a review. The principle of reciprocity (above) is likely to mean that we will write a positive review in these circumstances.

Scarcity: If we think that we might miss out on something, we are likely to make a purchase, even on something we didn't know we wanted. Shops will often have 'last few days' signs to encourage us to buy now and online retailers make increasing use of limited time period sales such as the American 'Black Friday' which is spreading to other countries.

> **Reflections:** Suggest some good closing techniques for selling the following items:
>
> - Tickets to a concert
> - A limited edition handbag
> - A television

Evaluation

The materials on different sales techniques and on ways to close a sale are based on both research and experience in the consumer environment. The applications of this material can provide the retailer with useful guidance on successful techniques which can be applied and evaluated. Clearly different techniques are more suited to different situations and to different products, as well as to different consumers and it can never be as simple as saying that one technique is the most successful.

Customer focused strategies suggest the importance of individual variables whereas the use of competitor focused strategies suggest the importance of situational factors. Clearly both interact to provide the optimal selling experience. The study by Kardes et al. is a fascinating example of the effectiveness of the 'disrupt-then-reframe' technique and the inclusion of two field experiments and one laboratory experiment in their article strengthens their findings even further.

This too reveals the importance of both situational and individual variables. The effect of the situational variable of the 'disrupt-then-reframe' technique was stronger in those individuals who had a greater need for cognitive closure (NFCC), suggesting the interaction of both situational and individual influences. This study also used rating scales to measure behavioural compliance and attitudes. Although the use of rating scales is useful in gathering large amounts of easily compared data quickly and easily, there are weaknesses too. Different individuals may interpret the values on the scale in different ways and there is no way of knowing whether a measure of compliance like this would actually translate into actual behaviour.

Buying the product

Purchase decisions: theory of planned behaviour (Ajzen, 1991)

One critical factor in the theory of planned behaviour is intention; the individual's intention to perform a given behaviour, for example to make a specific purchase. The stronger the intention, the more likely the behaviour. If someone desperately needs a car, they have a strong intention and it might be reasonable to assume that it is highly likely that this intention will result in the behaviour of buying a car. However, other factors may affect this. Someone may have a genuine need for a car, hence a strong intention, but no money to buy a car. This shows the importance of the perceived behavioural control. Buying a car is not within my control if I have no money. However, what is within my control is all the possible ways in which I might raise money, and the strength of the original intention is likely to determine how hard I work to achieve the funds to enable me to turn my intention to purchase into a purchase. Looked at like this, perceived behavioural control may overlap with other similar concepts such as locus of control and achievement motivation.

Azjen's theory of planned behaviour is a model that attempts to predict behaviour and can be applied to

a variety of situations (Figure 7.13). The theory states that attitudes towards behaviour, subjective norms and perceived behavioural control together shape an individual's behavioural intentions and behaviours. Therefore exploring people's attitudes and intentions in relation to products and services can help us to predict their likely purchase behaviours. This could simply be used to make sure that we target the people most likely to be interested in our product or it could be used to see how attempts to change attitudes ultimately change behaviours.

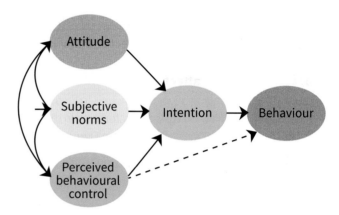

7.13 Azjen's theory of planned behaviour

Black box (stimulus–response) model

A well-developed and tested model of buyer behaviour is known as the stimulus–response model, which is summarised in Figure 7.14. This is a behaviourist model, in that it simply looks at the stimuli (what goes in) and the response (what comes out) and places all the intervening factors (cognitive, emotional, etc.) into the 'black box'. The stimuli come from the environment and include factors such as the 4Ps of marketing (product, price, place and promotion) as well as other environmental stimuli such as cultural, social, personal and psychological factors. The first set of stimuli are under the control of the retailer who can, for example set the price of the product, but the other factors are not. However an understanding of these factors and how they influence buyer behaviour is crucial and will allow the retailer to design their product or marketing strategy with specific buyer groups in mind. The reaction to these stimuli takes place in the black box and two key factors are crucial here: the characteristics of the buyer and the decision making process of the buyer. The outcome of what takes place within the black box are the buyer responses: their buying choices and behaviours.

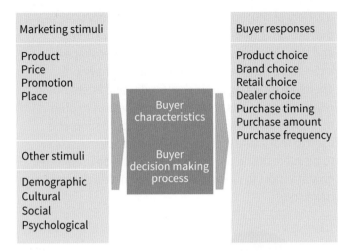

7.14 Stimulus–response model of buyer behaviour

Characteristics that affect customer behaviour

One way of understanding buyer behaviour is to focus on the factors that determine the 'buyer characteristics' in the 'black box'. These can be summarised as shown in Figure 7.15.

Engel, Blackwell and Kollat (1968) proposed a model of the consumer decision process which contains five steps:

- problem (or recognition of need)
- information search
- evaluation of alternatives to meet this need
- purchase decisions
- post-purchase behaviour.

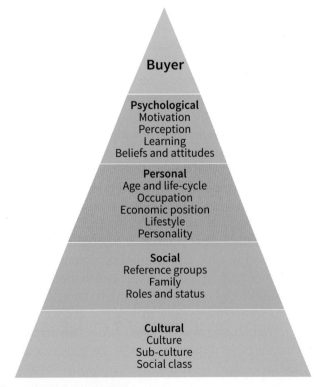

7.15 Buyer characteristics

The first step is recognising that there is no need. The authors suggest that if there is no need, then there is no purchase. There are different sorts of needs – internal stimuli such as hunger or thirst can produce certain needs whereas the 'need' for those shoes you saw last Saturday or that cake in the bakery window is a need caused by external stimuli.

> **Reflections:** Could Maslow's hierarchy of needs help us understand this step?

The second stage is about finding information about how to meet that need. This may involve information that the consumer already has based on previous experience or they may need to research this further. Thirdly, the information is evaluated and the consumer is able to choose the one that is most suited to his or her needs. This would be followed by the purchase, although previous experiences, associations and a host of other factors could still determine which store the product is purchased from. Finally, the authors suggest a post-purchase behaviour stage. This is where the consumer will evaluate the purchase that they have made. If this is positive this will produce customer loyalty and repeat purchases. This may also mean that the next time the consumer needs a similar item, they will use a mental shortcut (heuristic) and simply purchase 'the one I bought last time'. If the post-purchase behaviour is negative, then the whole set of stages will start again next time there is a perceived need.

Evaluation

The three models in this section attempt to understand buying behaviours. All three have useful applications for retailers and especially for advertising (which will be discussed in the following section). As all the models focus on general categories of behaviour such as 'intention' or 'evaluation of needs' there is no reason to suppose that these models would not fit the purchasing process in all cultures and in a wide variety of contexts. For example, the theory of planned behaviour offers us a way of understanding why intentions might not always translate into purchases as well as helping the retailer to identify techniques to try and increase the likelihood that intentions will result in purchases. Perhaps targeted online advertising, where the adverts that you see are determined by your previous internet searches, are a way of tapping into the buyer intentions and buyer decision making processes and providing a solution to the 'need'. In this way these models incorporate both situational and individual characteristics and make it clear that purchases are the result of the complex interaction between the two which can be successfully manipulated by the retailer.

7.5 Types of advertising and advertising techniques

Advertising media television, etc.; persuasive techniques

Types of advertising

There has been a dramatic increase in advertising in most cultures. We are constantly exposed to advertising on television, radio and social media as well as by paper-based and electronic direct mailings. Adverts are on billboards on the side of the road or on the sides of buildings, on buses and trains and in newspapers and magazines.

Reflections: How many adverts do you think you see in a day? Have a guess at the total and then spend a day recording every advert that you see. If you multiple this number by 365 it will give you an estimate of how many adverts you are exposed to in a year!

It is an interesting finding that most people think that adverts affect other people but not themselves (Wilson and Brekke, 1994, cited in Boyd-Jannson, 2010) but clearly advertising must be effective or companies would not spend so much money on it. In this section, we will be looking at a range of persuasive techniques and marketing models.

Attracting, and keeping, the attention of the audience is crucial. Before any other aspect of the advert can work, we need to make sure that people notice it! We are more likely to notice (and therefore attend to) adverts containing something that makes it 'stand out' (these are sometimes referred to as vivid stimuli). Adverts by Benetton are renowned for containing particularly vivid stimuli and you may be able to think of others.

7.16 Benetton adverts always have visual impact

However, you need to be careful when using vivid stimuli that people don't just remember the vivid stimuli and not the product that it is advertising. In other words the vivid stimuli can detract from the message. Other stimuli that can attract attention include changes in volume or brightness levels when television adverts begin.

The point of advertising is to persuade and we will be looking at this in more detail throughout this section of the chapter.

Marketing mix models: The 4 Ps (McCarthy, 1960), The 4 Cs (Lauterborn, 1990)

There are several marketing mix models and this section will look briefly at two of these: the 4 Ps model proposed by McCarthy and the 4 Cs model proposed by Lauterborn.

The 4 Ps of marketing are *Product* (this could be a physical product or a service), *Place, Price* and *Promotion*. We will look briefly at each of these concepts.

Product refers to the product or service being marketed. Someone wanting to market a product or service will need to consider a range of issues relating to the product. There are several listed below but you may be able to think of more.

- What is the customer looking for from the product?
- What features do they need? Does this product have all these features and does it have any that are unnecessary?
- What is the product name?
- How can it be branded (design, logo, slogan, etc.)?
- How is it different from other similar products?
- How much does it cost to produce and how much can it be sold for?

Place refers to where buyers will find the product or service. This might include considering where someone might look for the product (in a shop, in a mail order catalogue or online for example), what type of shop they might look in and how the product can be distributed appropriately. For example, one very common 'place' to look for a high variety of items in most countries in the world would be the online retailer Amazon. Managing to 'place' a product in the Amazon store would be a real bonus for a small organisation.

Price is self-explanatory but the seller needs to consider the value of the product or service to the buyer and whether there are established price points for these products. Is the price the crucial factor which determines whether the customer will buy the product or are other factors more important? It may be that a price cut will not gain any more customers. In fact sometimes when prices are very low people are suspicious of the quality and will not purchase it and there are examples of large stores shifting stock that was not moving, not by reducing the price, but by increasing it!

> **RESEARCH METHODS**
>
> Why might an increase in price increase sales? Design an experiment to test the effect of price on purchase intentions.

The final 'P' is *promotion*. How is information about the product going to get to the intended customers? Would an advert on television be the most effective or would some other form of advertising be more appropriate? It would also be important to consider when to advertise. This could refer to the timing of television adverts, even down to which programmes they follow but also when in the year. Not surprisingly, in Europe and America at least, toy adverts on television increase dramatically as Christmas approaches.

Of course, all four of these 'P's overlap and some authors stress that it is not important in which order they are listed. They all need to be taken into account to produce an effective marketing strategy.

7.17 The 4 Cs model

The second marketing mix model is the 4 Cs model. In the 1990s Lauterborn proposed this model, stating that the 4 Ps were 'dead' and that the 4 Cs model was more focused on the consumer. The 4 'C's are as follows:

Customer want or need: This replaces the 'product' in the earlier model. This shifts the focus to what the customer perceives themselves wanting or needing and makes it clear that customer needs and wants should be thoroughly researched. After all, there is no point in producing products that no-one wants to buy.

Cost to satisfy: This replaces 'price' in the earlier model. Lauterborn explains that the price of the product is only part of what he calls the total 'cost to satisfy' a consumer want or need. This total cost might include cost of time (perhaps someone will pay more for something that is closer to home or can be delivered faster). Cost may also reflect psychological aspects such as the guilt associated with not buying something that your children are asking for. We may be prepared to pay more for a fairtrade product again suggesting that 'cost to satisfy' is a more useful concept that simply the price.

Convenience to buy: The internet has changed shopping. Place is no longer an important consideration. We can shop 24 hours a day, buy direct from the manufacturer and use a range of price comparison sites. Convenience is the focus of the new model, taking into consideration the ease of finding the product, finding information about the product, buying the product and receiving delivery of the product. The retailers that provide the most convenient shopping experience will gain the most sales.

Communication: Lauterborn argues that 'promotion' is manipulative and one-way. Communication, on the other hand is co-operative and involves a two way dialogue.

Product placement in films (Auty & Lewis, 2004)

Product placement is where a branded product is given a prominent position within a scene in a television or film. This might be the characters drinking a branded soft drink or eating a branded chocolate bar or smoking a recognisable brand of cigarettes. Although thought to be highly influential, there are remarkably few studies which examine the effectiveness of product placement. The study by Auty and Lewis (2004) investigates the effect of product placement on children's subsequent choices and they also consider the effect of age (in terms of cognitive processing ability) on this.

Two age groups of children were used: 6–7-year-olds were selected as **limited processors** and 11–12-year-olds as

cued processors. Roedder (1981) characterises children as being either strategic, cued or limited processors. **Strategic processors** (12 plus) are able to use a variety of cognitive strategies for storing and retrieving information such as verbal labelling, rehearsal and the use of retrieval cues. Cued processors (7–11) can use similar strategies but only with explicit prompts or cues and do not produce them spontaneously. Children under seven are regarded as limited processors and often have difficulty using storage and retrieval cues even when prompted to do so.

The researchers wanted to see if the children's choice of a soft drink was related to the brand that had been displayed in the film clip they had just watched. They also wanted to investigate whether the children choosing this brand recalled the brand that had been displayed in the film clip, which would indicate some form of cognitive processing taking place.

Participants were 105 children from state schools in the UK. They were randomly allocated to either the experimental group or the control group.

KEY TERMS

strategic processors: individuals (generally over 12 years of age) who can use a variety of cognitive strategies for storing and retrieving information.

limited processors: individuals (generally children under 7) who are unable to use storage and retrieval cues even when prompted to do so.

cued processors: individuals (generally children aged between 7 and 11) who are able to use storage and retrieval cues with explicit prompts or cues and do not produce them spontaneously.

Reflections: The researchers reported that parents gave permission, not only for their children to take part in the study, but also for the researchers to offer the child a soft drink as part of the study. Why was it important to ask for this permission?

Children in the experimental group were shown a short clip from the film *Home Alone*. The clip showed the family around the table eating pizza and drinking milk and Pepsi. Pepsi is also mentioned by name in the dialogue. The control group were shown a similar length clip from the same film, in which Kevin, the main character in the film, is shown eating macaroni cheese and drinking milk.

After watching the film clip (in groups) children were questioned individually. Before asking any questions the researcher asked the child if they would like to help themselves to a drink from the table where two small cans of Pepsi and two small cans of Coca-Cola were set up. The researcher looked away while the child made his or her choice. This is called an implicit preference test.

In the experimental group, the children's choice of drink was recorded while the child was being asked to describe as much as they could remember about the film. If they did not mention the Pepsi specifically they were given a series of prompts: 'What were they doing?', 'What were they eating and drinking?', 'Was it a fizzy drink?', 'What was it called?', and so on. The number of prompts needed to elicit the name of the cola brand was recorded together with the brand name that the child identified. They were asked if they had seen the film before and if so how many times.

The control group followed a similar procedure and were also asked about what was drunk in the clip and this was to see if prior viewing of the film brought about mistaken identification of Pepsi as the drink being consumed.

Results showed that the product placement had an effect. Children in the experimental group were more likely to choose Pepsi (a ratio of 62:38) compared with the control group (a ratio of 42:58). The market share in the UK is 75:25 in favour of Coke.

There was no statistically significant difference between the age groups in terms of their ability to recall Pepsi, although the younger age group required more prompts to get there (mean number of prompts was 4.43 for the younger group and 2.06 for the older group). However the more times the children had seen the film was negatively correlated with the number of prompts that were required. In other words, the more times they had seen the film, the fewer prompts were needed.

Evaluation

There are clearly many different advertising techniques and many different strategies which are useful. It is almost impossible to isolate variables in controlled studies to see which ones are the most effective. The marketing mix models are useful for advertisers as they identify the key factors that the advertiser should consider when designing their advertising strategy.

201

The shift from the 4 'P's of marketing to the 4 'C's of marketing reflect a shift away from the 'one-way' marketing of previous years to more of a two-way dialogue with the customer or consumer. The internet has obviously enabled marketers to significantly change the way that they interact with their customers and, as we saw in our discussion of these models, has also produced other significant changes, with a range of situational variables such as place being far less important than they used to be.

The study by Auty and Lewis demonstrates that product placement can work. There are other studies that do this although this one is one of the few to do this with children, and it is important to consider the issues that arise when working with children. These may be practical issues or **ethical issues**. It is difficult to see any ethical issues with the study by Auty and Lewis. They obtained permission from parents, not only for the children to take part in the study but also for them to be offered a soft drink and the film they chose was one appropriate to the age group. There would have been practical issues: children may have struggled to try to understand what the researchers were looking for and may have been subject to demand characteristics.

We would also need to ask whether the results from a study like this would have been the same had it been conducted with adults. Are children more or less likely to be influenced by product placement? As this study only looked at children, we are unable to answer this question. As this study only looked at children in one culture, we are also unable to draw conclusions about the universality of this finding. Perhaps children in some cultures are far more (or far less) influences by product placement and by advertising techniques in general.

Communication and advertising models
Changing attitudes and models of communication (source, message, etc.)

Advertisements are attempts to communicate with potential consumers and to change their attitudes towards a product in the hope that they will buy it. Factors which affect the ability of a communication to persuade can be divided into three main categories; the source, the message and the audience.

The source is where the message (or advert) is coming from. The credibility and trustworthiness of the source are crucial aspects and will determine whether the audience will have a positive reaction to the message. Experts are generally thought to be more credible than others, so an advert for toothpaste presented by a dentist may be seen as having credibility. Trustworthiness is linked to how much we like someone – the more we like them, the more we trust them. This is why advertisers often use famous, well-liked celebrities such as David Beckham to advertise their products. However if the same celebrity is used to endorse too many products, then they lose their trustworthiness. Men are generally perceived as more persuasive than women but similarity is also important. We tend to be more easily persuaded by someone that we perceive as similar to ourselves. Boyd-Jannson (2010) even cites evidence that the more similar the source's name is to the recipient of the message, the more we like the source and the more likely we are to comply with the request. Attractiveness can also be a powerful effect although the more the attractiveness is linked to the product the more this effect will be seen.

The way the message is presented can also determine its effectiveness. It is often better to present a two-sided argument (where comparisons are made to competitors for example) than a one-sided argument but only when the product being advertised is unfamiliar to consumers. Boyd-Jannson explains that this leads consumers to think that you are being truthful. One-sided arguments have been shown to work better when consumers are familiar with the products advertised. If messages are too obviously trying to persuade, this can backfire. Repetition of message and of the image also makes the message more likely to be believed and will also aid recall when shopping.

> **Reflections:** If you ask a group of people to name the first brand of the following products that they can think of – coffee, tea, toothpaste, computers, chocolate – the chances are that they will name the brands that spend the most on advertising. Why not try it and see if most people give you the same brand names?

Finally, it is also important to consider aspects of the audience (sometimes called the receiver). It might be important to consider their existing attitudes or opinions in relation to the product or message as it is easier to convince someone who already has a similar set of attitudes than someone who holds very different ones. It is also worth considering self-esteem. It is harder to persuade someone with either very high or very low self-esteem than it is to persuade someone with moderate self-esteem. Women are also easier to persuade than men.

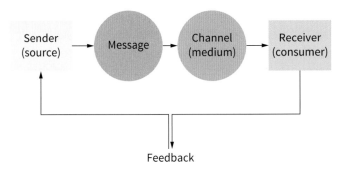

7.18 Communicating with potential customers

Reflections: Using the information given here about sources, message and audience, design an advertising campaign to advertise one of the following products:

- A new mobile phone
- A treatment for baldness
- A budget price car.

The AIDA model

The AIDA model was developed to describe what might happen when a consumer engages with an advertisement. The letters stand for

A – attention (or awareness)

I – interest

D – desire

A – action

In other words, an advertisement should attract the attention of the customer, hold their interest, produce or increase their desire or need for the product and influence their future actions. This model is typically presented in visual form as a funnel, as shown in Figure 7.19. However this model is considered dated and has been revised. Some more recent models have simply added new phases such as satisfaction (creating AIDAS) or satisfaction and confidence (AIDCAS), while the AISDALS Love model adds Search, Like/Dislike, Share and Love/Hate to the model.

Other modifications reduce the number of items in the model. The CAB model simply identifies Cognition, Affect and Behaviour such that Cognition refers to our awareness of the product or what we know about it, Affect refers to our feelings about the product and Behaviour refers to the actions that we are likely to take.

Other models have also been developed which focus more directly on the decision-making process. One of these is

The AIDA Model

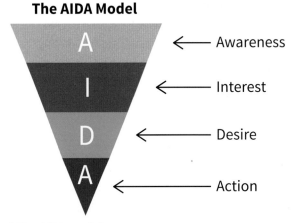

7.19 The AIDA model

the TIREA scale which identifies T – Thought, I – Interest (Desire), R – Risk (Evaluation), E – Engagement, A – Action. Thought alone does not necessarily mean attention as we can be aware of something (an advert on the television for example) without being interested in it or motivated to learn more. The interest stage starts when we want or need something. If we are significantly interested then we may move on to the next step, Risk or Evaluation, where we weigh up our options, such as comparing different products or deciding whether we can afford something. The authors of this model describe the next stage, Engagement, as the emotional response that occurs when interest and desire exceed risks and the final stage, Action, is when we respond in some way, such as purchasing the product.

A similar model, the REAN model, is more specifically focused on the customer life cycle. The letter R refers to Reach – the set of activities needed to promote your brand, product or service; E refers to Engage – the activities needed to engage those who are interested; A refers to Activate – the activities that you need the potential customers to take; and N to Nurture – the activities needed to nurture the customer relationship you just managed to create.

Finally an even more complete model was proposed by Betancur (2014): the NAITDASE model. This begins with the identification of a Need (an opportunity or a problem that can be solved). After the Attention and Interest, there needs to be Trust (i.e. confidence). Without this, customers cannot move forward towards the Desire and Action of purchase. However, in this model the process does not end with the purchase, and the final two stages are Satisfaction and Evaluation. This will lead to customers making repeat purchases and recommending the product or organisation to others.

Hierarchy of effects model

The Hierarchy of effects model was created in 1961 by Lavidge and Steiner. This is a model of marketing communication which proposes six steps from viewing an advert to purchasing the product. The advertiser needs to create an advert which increases the likelihood of the target audience moving through all six steps and purchasing the product (Table 7.2).

Six steps and behaviour

Lavidge and Steiner suggested that the six steps can be split into three stages of consumer behaviour: cognitive, affective and conative (behaviour). The job of the advertiser is to promote the three behaviours:

- cognitive (thinking) so that the consumer becomes product aware and gathers product knowledge. This is Steps 1 and 2 in Table 7.2.
- affective (feeling) so that the consumer likes the product brand and has conviction in it. Steps 3 and 4.
- conative (behaviour) so that the consumer buys the product brand. Steps 5 and 6.

Conclusion

This model is known as a 'hierarchy' because the number of consumers moving from one stage to the next reduces, as you move through the model. A lot of consumers may see the product advert but not everyone will make a purchase. It takes a lot of work to take a consumer from awareness to the final stage of purchase, so advertisers need to focus on all the stages to try and make sure that as many people as possible reach the final stage and make purchases.

Evaluation

There is no empirical research in this section which has focused solely on communication and advertising models. Models are useful ways of looking at complex behaviours as they attempt to simplify them, often through the use of diagrams illustrating stages and processes. Models of communication and advertising processes are useful for advertisers both in the planning stage to ensure that everything has been considered and in any evaluation process. For example it might be possible to conduct experimental research into the Hierarchy of effects model to see how many people move from one stage to another and where the greatest losses are.

These models tend to be produced in the West and although it is highly likely that the same processes will be relevant everywhere in the world, it is worth considering whether Western thought processes and elements of Western culture

Step 1	Awareness	The customer usually becomes aware of the product through advertising. However, it is important to design advertising that will create awareness as customers see many adverts every day and will retain information about a very small number of them.
Step 2	Knowledge	Customers need to obtain some knowledge about the product, depending on the type of product. Not much information is needed before buying a chocolate bar for the first time, but think about buying a mobile phone, a computer, a car or a house! The internet allows customers to get the information they need very easily, but equally they can get information about competitor brands and organisations. The advertiser's job is to ensure that their information is easily available and more attractive and accessible to the consumer than that of their competitor.
Step 3	Liking	What can the advertiser do to make sure that the consumer likes this product more than the competition?
Step 4	Preference	Builds on Steps 2 and 3. At this stage, consumers may like several products and could end up buying any one of them. What unique selling points can the advertiser highlight?
Step 5	Conviction	Strengthening the customer's desire to purchase the product. Offering free samples of food or beauty products or allowing a potential customer to test drive a car may increase conviction.
Step 6	Purchase	This must be easy to complete or the customer may go elsewhere. If the checkout queues are very long, or the checkout page for an online store is not working properly it is likely that the sale will be lost.

Table 7.2 The hierarchy of effects model

may be biasing these models in favour of understanding communication and advertising in this part of the world.

Advertising applications
Brand recognition in children (Fischer et al., 1991)

There have been studies examining brand recognition in consumers but the participants in these studies are usually adults. Fischer et al. (1991) have conducted one of the only studies into brand recognition by children. Fischer et al. comment that 'children are consumers in training' (page 3147) and that consumer behaviours are 'taught to our children along with toilet training, toddling and talking' (page 3147).

They acknowledged that the usual survey methods that are used to investigate brand recognition will be difficult to use with children so they developed a game technique to measure the recognition level for brand logos.

They collected 22 brand logos from a range of products (Figure 7.20). These included ten 'children's brands':

- The Disney Channel
- McDonalds
- Burger King
- Domino's Pizza
- Coca-Cola
- Pepsi
- Nike
- Walt Disney
- Kellogg's
- Cheerios.

A further seven brands were seen as 'adult brands' and these included car brands and electronics firms as well as television news channels aimed at adults:

- Chevrolet
- Ford
- Apple
- CBS
- NBC
- Kodak
- IBM.

Finally, they included five cigarette brands:

- Old Joe
- Marlboro
- Marlboro Man
- Camel and Pyramids
- Camel.

7.20 The logo of the Disney Channel

Each logo was printed on a card and no information was included that might give clues to the product. For example the picture of Old Joe the Camel did not include the packet of cigarettes and the camel was not shown smoking. Recognition was measured by asking the children to match the 22 logo cards to one of 12 product categories pictures on a game board (for example, cigarettes, television, cereal).

Participants came from ten pre-schools in the USA. Parents gave consent and were also asked to complete a short questionnaire asking about how much television the child watched, the frequency with which they requested specific brands and whether anyone in the home smoked. 229 children were tested in all and they ranged in age from three to six years.

Children were tested individually in a quiet part of the classroom. They were told that they were playing a matching game. Each of the 12 product categories on the board was named (these were generic pictures) and the child was then given the first test card to match. When they had placed this on the board, they were simply told 'that's good' regardless of whether this was placed correctly or not and no feedback was given. The card was then removed from the board and the child was given the next test card. Card order was randomised for each child.

> **Reflections:** Why would it be important to randomise the order of the cards? What problems might there be if all children were given the 22 cards in the same order?

The results showed that, not surprisingly, the children showed good recognition rates for the children's brand logos. This ranged from 91% for The Disney Channel to 25% for Cheerios. A random guess would produce a recognition rate of 8.3%, that is a one in 12 chance of getting the right category.

Old Joe the Camel had the highest recognition rate with over half of the children correctly matching the image with a picture of a cigarette. The other cigarette brands were recognised between 18% and 32% of the time. Other adult products were recognised between 16% and 54% of the time with car brand logos being recognised the most.

Recognition increased with age. For example, 30% of three-year-olds recognised Old Joe the Camel and 91% of six-year-olds did. Three-, four- and five-year-old children recognised The Disney Channel logo significantly more frequently than Old Joe the Camel, but the six-year-olds were able to identify these two images equally well. There was no effect from race or gender. Children from homes where parents smoked were more likely to recognise cigarette logos.

The researchers concluded that children demonstrated high recognition rates for products targeted at both children and adults. While it may not be surprising that American children recognise the golden arches of McDonalds, or the logo for the Disney Channel, or even car logos as these manufacturers advertise frequently on television, it is more surprising (and worrying) that they are able to recognise cigarette brands with such accuracy, especially as cigarettes are no longer advertised on television. The researchers claim that this shows the power of 'environmental advertising'; billboards and sponsorship displays as well as T-shirts and other items.

Advertising and consumer personality

Another way to investigate the effectiveness of advertising is to consider the ways in which different personality types respond to different types of advertising. Snyder and DeBono (1985) investigate how high and low self-monitoring individuals respond to two different advertising strategies; appeals to product image and appeals to product quality.

They begin by outlining the soft sell and the hard sell approach. Hard sell advertising uses a direct approach that tells the consumer how they can directly benefit from purchasing or using the product. This approach assumes that customer decisions are rational and reasoned. This would be an appeal to product quality.

> **Reflections:** What evidence have we met so far in this chapter that would challenge the assumption that consumers make rational and reasoned decisions?

Soft sell advertising is indirect and subtle. It does not emphasise direct benefits of the product but will attempt to create positive associations with the product, such as

humour, comfort or style. This approach assumes that decisions to purchase are largely emotive rather than rational. This would be an appeal to product image.

Do different types of people respond differently to these different types of advertising? The authors suggested that the trait of self-monitoring may be the crucial one here. Self-monitoring is the extent to which we monitor and adapt our behaviour to fit the situation we are in. High self-monitors are constantly aware of the situation and are effectively asking 'Who is the best person to be in this situation?'. Low self-monitors are less concerned about the situational factors and more focused on 'how best to be me in this situation'.

Study 1 used three sets of fictitious magazine advertisements for whisky, cigarettes and coffee. Each set of adverts contained two adverts which were identical in all aspects except for the written message or slogan associated with the picture. One advert had a slogan appealing to the image associated with the use of the product and the other advert had a slogan about the product's quality (see Table 7.3).

Participants were 50 male and female undergraduates from an American university who took part in this study for course credits. On the basis of a median split of their self-monitoring scale scores, they were divided into a group of high self-monitors and a group of low self-monitors.

Participants were tested alone and were shown all the advertisements. They were told that their role was to help to evaluate the relative merits of the advertisements. After seeing each set of two adverts, the participant filled out a 12-item questionnaire which asked them to make comparisons between the two adverts. Examples of the questions included:

- *Overall, which ad do you think is better?*
- *Which one appeals to you more?*
- *Which ad do you think would be more successful?*

The researchers predicted that the high self-monitors would react more favourably to the image-oriented adverts and that low self-monitors would react more favourably to the quality-oriented adverts. This was supported by the data from all three sets of adverts. The researchers concluded that high and low self-monitors have different evaluative reactions to appeals to quality and appeals to image but they wanted to take this research further and investigate whether the way a product was advertised would affect how much they might be willing to pay for the product.

In Study 2 the researchers predicted that high self-monitors would be prepared to pay more for products that were advertised with appeals to their image rather than appeals to their quality. They also predicted that the opposite would be true for low self-monitors; they will be prepared to pay more for products that were advertised with appeals to their quality rather than appeals to their image.

Forty male and female participants from the same American university participated for course credits. They were divided into high and low self-monitors by means of a median split.

This study used the same sets of adverts that were used in the first study but this time the participants were either shown the image oriented advertisements or the quality oriented advertisements and then asked 'How much would you willing to pay for this item?'. They were given price ranges to select, for example for the Canadian Club Whisky the range was $5 to $15.

As predicted the results showed that high self-monitors were prepared to pay more for products if they were advertised with an image orientation than if they were advertised with a quality orientation. The reverse was true for low self-monitors; they were prepared to pay more for products that were advertised with a quality orientation than if they were advertised with an image orientation.

Finally the researchers investigated whether these differences would also influence actual decisions to consume products. Study 3 offered consumers the opportunity to try a new shampoo. Forty male and female undergraduates from the same American university participated for course credit. As in the previous two studies, a median split divided the sample into high and low self-monitors.

The experimenter posed as a market researcher and contacted the participant by telephone. He offered them the chance to participate in a test marketing study.

He said '*Hi, my name is XXXXX and I work for a marketing research firm here in the Twin Cities. Presently, we are surveying college students, to see if, in the future, they would be interested in trying out a new shampoo that our client plans to market. However, before you tell me if you would be interested in trying this shampoo, let me tell you a little more about it.*'

This was followed by one of the following scripts.

- Image message: *The results of recent laboratory tests have indicated that while compared to other shampoos, this brand usually rates about average in how it cleans your hair; it consistently rates above average in how good it makes your hair look.*
- Quality message: *The results of recent laboratory tests have indicated that while compared to other shampoos, this brand usually rates about average in how good it makes your hair look, it consistently rates above average in how clean it gets your hair.*

Finally, the experimenter asked the participant to answer two questions; the first asked them how willing they would be to use this shampoo (definitely not, probably not, unsure, probably yes or definitely yes) and secondly they were asked to indicate what percentage (between 0 and 100) best describes their willingness to try this shampoo.

As expected, high self-monitors were more willing to try the shampoo if they thought it would leave their hair looking good and low self-monitors were more likely to try the shampoo if they thought it would leave their hair very clean.

Product	Advert	Image slogan	Quality slogan
Canadian Club Whisky	A bottle of Canadian Club whisky resting on a set of house blueprints	You're not just moving on, you're moving up	When it comes to great taste, everyone draws the same conclusion
Barclay cigarettes	Handsome man, about to light a cigarette, looking in a mirror at his female companion. Her hand is resting on his shoulder	Barclay … you can see the difference	Barclay … you can taste the difference
Irish Mocha Mint (coffee)	A man and a woman relaxing in a candle-lit room, smiling at each other as they drink the coffee	Make a chilly night become a cosy night with Irish Mocha Mint	Irish Mocha Mint: a delicious blend of three great flavours – coffee, chocolate and mint

Table 7.3 Details of the advertisements and messages

The authors conclude that they have been successful in identifying two types of advertising strategy (image and quality) and two types of individuals (high and low in self-monitoring) who will react in very different ways to these two strategies. This may suggest that the reason that both the image oriented soft sell approach and the claim oriented (quality) hard sell approach have both been successful is that they appeal to different groups of consumers. Adverts that combine elements of both may succeed in appealing to both sets of consumers.

Effective slogans (Kohli et al., 2007)

The use of slogans is common in current marketing.

Reflections: Which marketing slogans are you familiar with?

- Nike – Just do it!
- IBM – Solutions for a smart planet
- Sony – Make Believe
- Playstation – Live in your world. Play in ours.
- McDonalds – I'm loving it
- Red Cross – The greatest tragedy is indifference

Can you think of any more? You could test the effectiveness of these slogans by making a list of about ten slogans and seeing if people can identify the brand that the slogan is associated with (or the other way around).

Kohli et al. (2007) have reviewed many other articles and industry publications, which attempt to put together a series of guidelines for creating effective slogans. They begin by identifying the three key elements of brand identity; the brand name, the logo and the slogan. Taken as a whole, this is how the brand communicates itself.

However each of three elements can be considered separately. The brand name is the anchor for the brand image and cannot easily be changed. The logo is a visual cue which allows us to process information faster – we recognise the golden 'M' of McDonalds or the red and white script on a Coca-Cola can without having to read the whole name. Logos are sometimes updated but rarely changed significantly. Slogans play an important role in brand identity; they can communicate more than a name or a logo and will help to 'communicate what the brand is about' (Kohli et al., 2007, page 416). Slogans can be more easily changed and updated. Pepsi, for example have changed their slogan numerous times in 100 years, from 'Cures everything, Relieves exhaustion' in 1902 to 'Generation Next' in 1998 and to 'The Joy of Pepsi' in 2015.

In the UK, several confectionary brands have changed their names. Opal Fruits became Starburst and Marathon became Snickers. However they kept the same packaging design and colours so they were still easily recognisable on the shelf. It is important that people recognise brands and the two key elements of brand knowledge are brand awareness and brand image. Brand awareness is determined by brand recall and brand recognition. Recall is what can be remembered without any cues and recognition is being able to identify the brand from a list, which is an easier task. Slogans can enhance brand awareness and in turn, brand knowledge.

Slogans have two main aims – to enhance brand awareness and to positively affect the brand image. The effects that slogans have on brand awareness have been investigated through 'priming' effects. This refers to the fact that ideas that you have been exposed to recently will tend to come to mind first – so if a slogan talks about a particular attribute of a product, for example the taste, and if this slogan is heard repeatedly then when you are asked to rate the product on a range of attributes, you are likely to rate taste more highly than if you hadn't heard the slogans. This was confirmed in a study by Boush (1993). Slogans are often presented as jingles as this is thought to do a better job of enhancing memory and recall. Yalch (1981) investigated this by presenting participants with a list of commonly used advertising slogans (some jingle slogans and some non-jingle slogans) and asking them to say which brands were associated with which slogans. This was a recall test rather than a recognition test so participants were not given any cues, such as a list of brands to choose from. Yalch found that brands with jingle slogans were more easily recalled than brands without jingles. However there were no differences between the two when the task was a recognition task rather than a recall task. However jingles should be used with care as there is also some evidence that music can interfere with other cognitive processing. They may be better suited to small companies with limited budgets who are primarily looking to advertise on radio.

If slogans are too complex, they may be harder to recall and to recognise. However this seems to be quite a complex relationship as more complex slogans may have to be processed more deeply. In a similar way, Lagerwerf (2002) found that complexity in the form of ambiguity (especially where this involves a pun) can increase brand awareness. This is only effective when the ambiguity is recognised and can be resolved. If it is not recognised as ambiguous or the meanings are unclear then this may even have a negative effect.

It is crucial to link the slogan to the brand. This may sound obvious but there is evidence that there is actually quite a high level of inaccurate recall for slogans especially in product categories with many brands. Finally, there is the problem of bogus recall, where people report that they have seen a slogan used in advertisements even though it has been created solely for the purposes of the experiment. In some studies the recall rates were so low that the researchers questioned their own methodology.

The authors conclude that their review has not identified any specific guidelines for the creation of effective slogans, but they attempt to produce a list of suggestions. These include taking a long-term view of the product, positioning the brand clearly, making sure that the slogan links to the brand effectively, and using the slogan from the outset of the advertising campaign. They also argue for the use of jingles, repetition and creativity.

Evaluation

The studies by Fischer et al. and by Snyder and DeBono used experimental methods to investigate aspects of advertising, whereas the final article by Kohli is a review article. Both the experimental studies have designed simple, yet effective techniques for the collection of data. Fischer's study is only one of two in this chapter that has used children, which may be surprising giving the consumer power that children, particularly in western cultures, appear to have. As with any research using children, we need to consider ethical issues as well as practical issues. The study by Fischer et al. does not appear to raise any strong ethical issues as children are only being exposed to images that they are exposed to in every day life. Fischer's matching game is an ingenious

way to determine the associations that children have with different brand images. The results could be seen as disturbing especially in relation to the recognition levels for cigarette brands as familiarity may be a significant factor in determining whether someone smokes later in their life and has supported the change to package cigarettes in plain packets. We do not really need to consider whether the results of the study also apply to adults as the aim of the study was to measure the strength of brand recognition in children. However, it is interesting to consider whether the same results would be found with equivalent brands in other cultures.

Snyder and DeBono also created a simple, effective technique for comparing the 'image versus quality' messages of adverts and also looking at this in relation to the level of self-monitoring of the individual. This demonstrates that **situational factors** (the advert) interact with individual factors (personality) and help us to understand why two very different approaches to advertising may both be effective. An application of their findings would be to consider whether the potential market for the product is likely to contain more high self-monitors or more low self-monitors and tailoring the advertisement appropriately.

SELF-ASSESSMENT QUESTIONS

16   What are the 4 'P's in McCarthy's 4 Ps marketing model?

17   Outline the aim of the study into product placement in films by Auty and Lewis.

18   Describe the game that was designed by Fischer et al. to test brand recognition in children.

19   Explain the difference between a 'hard sell' and a 'soft sell'.

Summary

This chapter has covered five major areas of consumer psychology. These have been wide ranging and reflect the rapid development of research in this area.

We began by considering the importance of the physical environment. This included an examination of retail store architecture (**Turley and Milliman, 2000**) and the design of leisure environments (**Finlay et al., 2006**). We also considered a range of evidence relating to the importance of music and sound in consumer environments including an examination of the powerful effect of classical music on spending in restaurants (**North et al., 2003**). Finally in this section we considered the importance of lighting, colour and smell in influencing the whole consumer experience. One of the key issues discussed here was the fact that much of this research was conducted in real consumer environments (using the field experiment method or the natural experiment method) giving the research strengths such as high levels of ecological validity but meaning that it is always important to consider the role of confounding variables and the fact that consumer environments are all so different, making generalisation from one to another more difficult.

We then moved on to examine the psychological environment. This section began by looking at cognitive maps (**Mackay and Olshavky, 1975**), crowding (**Machleit et al., 2000**) and shopper movement patterns (**Gil et al., 2009**). We then looked at the importance of menu design (**Pavesic, 2005**), menu position (**Dayan and Bar-Hillel, 2011**) and the effect that the name given to a dish can have on the perception of that food (**Wansink et al., 2005**). Finally in this section we considered the importance of personal space, particularly in restaurants (**Robson et al., 2011**) and in queues (**Milgram et al., 1986**). There was a range of experimental methodology used in the research covered in this section allowing us to compare the strengths and weaknesses of research conducted in the real world with that conducted in laboratory environments.

The next section examined a range of theoretical approaches to consumer decision making. We considered a number of models of decision making as well as research looking at decision making in supermarkets (**Wansink et al., 1998**), choice blindness (**Hall et al., 2010**) and advertising and false memory (**Braun-LaTour et al., 2004**). We considered the usefulness of applications of these models as well as the strengths and limitations of the research.

The product is obviously a crucial focus in consumer research and the next section examined packaging, position and placement, selling the product and buying the product. We examined studies that considered the importance of gift wrapping (**Porublev et al., 2009**), the importance of colour (**Grossman and Wisenblit, 1999**) and the importance of shelf position (**Atalay et al., 2012**). We also examined the 'disrupt-then-reframe' technique of selling and a number of ways to close a sale. Once again we considered the usefulness and application of the research findings as well as the strengths and weaknesses of each study.

Finally, we looked at advertising. We examined a range of advertising techniques and models as well as a study examining the role of product placement in films (**Auty and Lewis, 2004**). We also examined the importance of slogans (**Kohli et al., 2007**), brand recognition in children (**Fischer et al., 1991**) and the complex relationship between advertising and consumer personality (**Snyder and DeBono, 1985**). Along with an evaluation of the usefulness and applications of this research, we were also able to consider the issue of children in research and were able to consider the strengths and weaknesses of a number of innovative research procedures designed to be suitable to use with children.

Exam-style questions

1   Auty and Lewis conducted an experiment to see if product placement could influence children's choices. Their sample was 105 children from UK schools randomly allocated into either the experimental group or the control group. Both groups were shown a short clip from the movie *Home Alone*. The clip shown to the experimental group showed images of Pepsi and the clip in the control group did not. After watching the clip, the children were asked if they would like a drink and were given the choice of Pepsi or Coca-Cola.

   a Identify the independent variable and the dependent variable in this study. **[2 marks]**
   b Describe **one** alternative way in which the dependent variable in this study could have been measured. **[4 marks]**
   c Identify **one** strength and **one** weakness of the way this study was conducted. Give reasons for your answer. **[4 marks]**
   d Discuss the advantages and disadvantages of using children in psychology experiments. **[5 marks]**

Chapter 8
Psychology and health

Introduction

This chapter introduces you to five key topics within health psychology:

- The patient–practitioner relationship, including studies and concepts relating to practitioner and patient interpersonal skills, patient and practitioner diagnosis and style and misusing health services
- Adherence to medical advice, including studies, theories and concepts relating to types of non-adherence and reasons why patients don't adhere, measuring non-adherence and improving adherence
- Pain, including studies, theories and concepts relating to types and theories of pain, measuring pain and managing and controlling pain
- Stress, including studies, theories and concepts relating to sources of stress, measures of stress and management of stress

- Health promotion, including strategies for promoting health, health promotion in schools, worksites and communities and individual factors in changing health beliefs.

Throughout the chapter you will find out about examples of theories that attempt to explain psychological phenomena within the application of health. Studies exploring these ideas are presented, as well as ways to measure psychological variables relating to health, such as following advice or the experience of pain, and treatments and strategies which aim to overcome problems such as failing to follow advice, pain, stress and improving health. Within these contexts we will remind you of the role played by research methods in psychology and encourage you to consider way these topics illustrate the issues and debates.

Healthy thoughts and thinking about health

Health psychology considers both how psychological factors affect health and how psychology helps us to understand health care. In both cases, a knowledge of psychology can improve a patient's welfare, either by improving their health directly (or reducing their risk of ill health) or through improvements to the quality, accessibility or effectiveness of the care offered by health professionals.

For patients to gain from the knowledge of their practitioner, they must be able to communicate effectively with them and follow their advice. In these respects, psychology helps us to understand some of the issues faced by patients and practitioners in their interactions. If a patient is unable to express their concerns to their doctor, or does not follow the instructions they are given, they are unlikely to benefit fully from the health care available. Psychology helps to identify such problems and find ways to overcome them.

Physical pain is, in theory, just that – physical. However, as you may be aware, the same pain can feel better or worse depending on context. If you stub your toe at home it is really painful and makes you stop, yet you can injure yourself much more seriously on the sports field and keep playing. Our knowledge of the psychology of pain helps to explain how pain arises, and accounts for differences such as this. Stress, too, can have both an external cause (such as your teacher demanding work), and be influenced by internal factors. For example, you might be more resilient if you get a bad mark on some days than others, or you might find the stress of forthcoming exams makes you work

harder. Recognition of such influences helps psychologists to piece together an understanding of stress.

Both medical and psychological care for ill health is improving but much can be gained from avoiding ill health and maintaining good health. This is the province of health promotion: 'prevention is better than cure'. Psychological interventions can help to reduce the risk of health problems arising in healthy people, through ways to raise health awareness and increase the likelihood that people will do what they know is good for them. This is an important difference. Think about the people you know: some probably have 'healthy' behaviours – such as exercising or eating plenty of fruit and vegetables – and others engage in unhealthy ones – such as eating fatty or salty foods, or smoking. Both groups probably have similar access to information about what is healthy, but differ in the extent to which they follow that advice. Psychology can help us to understand why and to influence not just people's awareness but also their behaviour.

> **Reflections:** Imagine Jeff, who has a busy job but cannot keep up with his credit card payments. He is stressed, and getting severe headaches that make it hard to sleep, so he is even less able to cope. He wants to go to the doctor to get help but the doctor always looks so formal and serious; he wonders if this is too trivial a matter. When he finally does go to see his doctor, he is given a choice between therapy and some tablets. When he gets them home he can't remember how to take the tablets. Our knowledge of psychology might be able to help in several ways. Think about what benefits our understanding might bring.

8.1 The patient–practitioner relationship

In order for patients to gain the most they can from seeing a health-care practitioner, they must go to see them, be able to communicate with them and have confidence in them. In this section we will explore some of the factors that influence the trust between a patient and their practitioner and the effectiveness of their interactions.

Practitioner and patient interpersonal skills

The first step for a patient needing health care is typically to make an appointment to see a general practitioner. This may be someone they have never seen before or a familiar

doctor. The confidence this individual inspires in the patient through their verbal and non-verbal communication – their **interpersonal skills** – could affect several important variables, for example how happy they feel and therefore how much they are likely to tell the doctor and whether they have confidence in the doctor's ability to help them. McKinstry and Wang's study shows that the doctor's clothing is one factor that may influence this trust.

KEY TERM

interpersonal skills: 'inter' and 'personal' mean 'between people'; the abilities we have (or don't have) that allow us to communicate effectively with others.

Non-verbal communications (McKinstry & Wang, 1991)

McKinstry and Wang (1991) investigated doctors' clothing as a form of non-verbal communication. A total of 475 patients, seeing 30 different doctors from five general medical centres in one area of Scotland, were interviewed about their opinions based on eight photographs. The images were of a male doctor or a female doctor, each dressed differently but in a similar pose (see Figure 8.1). They were asked:

- which doctor they would feel happiest seeing for the first time (scoring 0–5)
- whether they would have more confidence in the ability of one of these doctors (based on their appearance)
- whether they would be unhappy about consulting any of them
- which doctor looked most like their own doctor.

Finally, they were asked a series of general, closed questions about doctors' dress (see Table 8.1). The interviewer sampled patients at different times of day on five occasions at each surgery, seeing on average just over 70% of available patients.

The results showed that patients significantly preferred male doctors wearing a formal suit and tie. They also preferred female doctors in a white lab coat, although not significantly more so than females in a smart skirt and blouse. The preferences for traditionally dressed doctors were most apparent in older patients, and those in higher social classes. Although 28% of patients reported that they would be unhappy seeing one of the doctors shown, usually the informally dressed one, some patients said they disliked their doctor wearing a white lab coat. Nevertheless, 64%

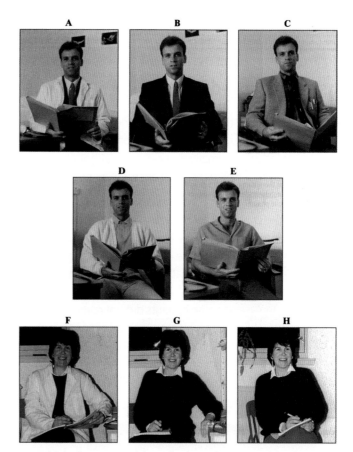

8.1 Which doctor would you be happiest consulting?

said that the way their doctor dressed was quite or very important. Overall, female doctors received higher ratings than male doctors, but with regard to gender differences between patients, only one was found, that female patients

213

Acceptability score	Number of patients (out of 475 for each clothing type)							
	Male doctor wearing:					Female doctor wearing:		
	white coat over formal suit	formal suit, white shirt and tie	tweed jacket, informal shirt and tie	cardigan, sports shirt and slacks	jeans, open-necked short sleeved shirt	white coat over skirt and jumper	skirt, blouse and woollen jumper	pink trousers, jumper and gold earrings
5	183	238	141	76	60	263	222	104
4	122	116	120	77	44	118	194	86
1	39	19	4	31	154	7	2	20
0	9	8	6	48	83	6	2	34

Table 8.1 Partial results table for the distribution of scores for different styles of doctors' clothing

ranked the male doctor in a tweed jacket higher than male patients did. However, there was variation between patients from different medical centres, with some showing much stronger preferences for a male doctor in a suit and against a male doctor in jeans and others being less extreme.

When asked about their confidence in the doctor's ability, 41% expressed a preference for one photograph, predominantly the formally dressed ones (although nine had most confidence in the male doctor in jeans and 13 in the female doctor in trousers).

Based on the way the doctors were dressed in the photographs, 41% of patients said that they would have more confidence in one of the doctors, suggesting that the way a practitioner dresses matters to their performance. The data about similarity to the patient's own doctor was difficult to analyse as some patients did not respond or gave two answers. However, many more patients in one practice said their doctor looked most like the smartly dressed one, while in another few did. This difference was reflected in their choices, with those having a formally dressed doctor preferring one dressed like that.

Percentage of patients who:		
believe that doctors should usually wear a	white coat	15
	suit	44
	tie	67
would object to male doctor	wearing jeans	59
	wearing an earring	55
	having long hair	46
believe female doctors should usually wear	white coat	34
	skirt (rather than trousers)	57
would object to female doctor wearing	jeans	63
	lots of jewellery	60

Table 8.2 Patients' responses to closed questions about specific items of doctors' dress

The data in Table 8.2 was also analysed by social class and gender and revealed few differences, although higher social classes objected more to male doctors wearing an earring and to female doctors wearing lots of jewellery, and more male than female patients thought that women doctors should wear white coats.

In general, the findings show that patients prefer formally dressed doctors although this is somewhat affected by age, social class and the particular medical practice used.

Patients also preferred doctors dressed in the manner of their current doctor, although it may be that doctors dress according to their perception of their patients' preferences.

McKinstry and Wang observe that it would have been useful to have included a photograph of a female doctor in a formal suit, and that had this been included the preference for the female in the white coat might not have been so apparent. Conversely, the pressure for women to conform to a formal stereotype may be greater, for example more patients objected to the idea of a female than a male doctor in jeans. On this basis, McKinstry and Wang were reluctant to advise that female doctors wear white coats. Nevertheless, the study did appear to successfully avoid the risk of patients giving the answer they thought was wanted rather than the one they felt to be correct, i.e. demand characteristics were reduced. This is illustrated by the findings that many patients who said they felt the way the doctor dressed was not important, still gave discriminatory scores in assessing the photographs.

> **Reflections:** Would the way a doctor dresses affect the way that you perceived them? How about other professions? Should there be a doctors' uniform that all doctors wear instead?

Verbal communications (McKinlay, 1975; Ley, 1988)

Here are some examples of the medical vocabulary used in interviews with patients:

ANTIBIOTIC: If a doctor told a patient that she's going to put her on antibiotics, what's she going to do?

BREECH: If a doctor told a patient that she's going to have a breech, what do you think is going to happen?

NAVEL: If a doctor, while examining a patient, mentions the word 'navel', what is he talking about?

PURGATIVE: If a nurse tells a patient that she is going to give her a purgative, what is she going to give her?

RHESUS: Doctors sometimes, while examining a woman who is expecting, say she's 'rhesus positive'. What are they talking about?

The focus of much research into barriers to communication between patients and their doctors has been on patient failings, such as being unable to hear, unwilling to receive unpleasant information, anxiety caused by differences in status, social class or ethnicity and the inability to comprehend common medical terms. Few studies have considered responsibility for failings in communication

214

by the doctor, and those which have typically had methodological flaws, such as not using independent raters for the patients and doctors. The research discussed below attempted to overcome these problems.

McKinlay (1975) conducted a pilot study into the words which the doctors used in a Scottish maternity hospital. They were either classed as commonly used among patients (all would use), incomprehensible to patients (none would use) or were in between these two extremes. Of the 57 words tested, only 13 fell into a middle bracket, i.e. that some but not all doctors would use. These 13 words became the focus of the study as they represented a 'grey area' of verbal comprehension. In an interview to test patients' understanding, they were read each word, heard it used in the context of a sentence and were then asked to say what it meant. This interview began with a reassuring introduction saying 'This is not a test. We are trying to find out if doctors use words that patients can't understand, so it's really a test of them.' The patients' responses were recorded verbatim on a standard form identified only by the participant's number and then scored independently by two doctors (one male and one female). These scorers were working 'blind'; they were unaware of individual participant or the other doctor's score.

One year after the collection of the original word-list data, the group of doctors working on the ward were asked to indicate for each word whether the level of understanding they would expect for a typical patient at the hospital (a lower working class woman) to have for each word, using this scale:

A   not understand at all and say so

B   get the meaning quite wrong

C   have an incomplete or vague understanding

D   understand pretty well.

The two scorers were generally reliable, giving the same or similar ratings. Very few differences arose in the A/B category (assigned to A), more in B/C (the two were combined) and C/D (assigned to D). Where differences arose, the male scorer credited the women with less understanding than the female scorer.

In scores obtained the patients were compared in relation to the women's service use. Those who underused the maternity services were less likely to have an adequate understanding of the words in comparison to regular users, whose comprehension was worse only for 'navel' and 'rhesus'. There appeared to be few differences based on whether the women had already had a child although among the 'users', women who already had at least one child were slightly more likely to comprehend words than those attending the hospital in their first pregnancy. The results also show how the women often had a far better understanding than the doctors anticipated. Only for one word, 'purgative', was the women's comprehension lower in both groups than anticipated. Where low levels of comprehension were demonstrated, the women did have some knowledge, for example suggesting that 'rhesus' was about 'your blood group', which was not deemed to be an adequate understanding by the scorers.

Ley (1988) reported on the frequency with which patients forget the verbal advice given to them by their doctor. This forgetting is linked to factors such as the amount, order, perceived importance and nature of the information given, as well as the patient's age, anxiety level and medical knowledge. To improve their relationship, Ley suggested that a practitioner should use simple language, state the key information first, giving concrete-specific advice which is categorised (e.g. into diagnosis, treatment, self-help and

---

ISSUES AND DEBATES

There is a risk that the doctors' beliefs will have a **deterministic** effect on patients' behaviour. By underestimating comprehension, the doctors bring about a situation in which patients cannot demonstrate their understanding, thus perpetuating the doctors' false beliefs about their ability knowledge.

The findings of McKinlay appear to have **relevance to everyday life**, suggesting doctors should provide more information to patients because they understand more than is typically assumed, but care should be taken not to use words the doctors know to be incomprehensible to patients. However, the narrow sample of lower working class participants at one hospital means that the findings

may not generalise to other, potentially better informed, populations who may ask more questions or elicit different beliefs from doctors. McKinstry and Wang's findings also offer advice for doctors, although with some caution in relation to women.

McKinlay's findings also illustrate **individual versus situational explanations**, as although there are clearly individual differences in knowledge, the situation created by the doctors' expectations is a limiting factor to improving the patients' access to information. Situational explanations also prevail in the conclusions from McKinstry and Wang, as patients' confidence in their doctor is partly determined by what they are wearing.

prognosis) and repeat the key points e.g. by summarising the essentials at the end of the consultation.

Evaluation

In McKinstry and Wang, in addition to a wide representative sample from different doctors and medical centres, demand characteristics were successfully reduced. This is illustrated by patients saying that the way the doctor dressed was not important, but still giving discriminatory scores in assessing the photographs. However, if a photograph of a female doctor in a formal suit had been used, the preference for a white coat might not have been so apparent. There may also be pressure for women to conform to a formal stereotype, for example more patients objected to a female than a male doctor in jeans. Advising female doctors to wear white coats might therefore be wrong.

In McKinlay, the scorers were working blind and the interview with patients was both clear, e.g. with words in context to ensure data collection was valid and standardised, to ensure it was reliable. The use of qualitative data as well as quantitative data helps to explain patients' perceptions. The interview with patients began with 'This is not a test. We are trying to find out if doctors use words that patients can't understand, so it's really a test of them.'. This ethical step followed the guideline to 'avoid psychological harm' by reassuring patients.

The proposals from Ley, 1988 have direct, practical applications to improving practice, so are useful. This is especially the case as the recommendations are easy for doctors to implement.

SELF-ASSESSMENT QUESTIONS

1 A new doctor's surgery is using McKinstry and Wang's findings to decide on a dress code for female doctors. Suggest one reason for wearing white lab coats and one reason against.

RESEARCH METHODS

In the study by McKinlay, why was it important to know the doctor's actual use of the 13 words used in the interviews?

Although most of the findings presented in the study are quantitative, the data originally collected from patients were qualitative, and the patient quote is also an example of qualitative data. What are the advantages of collecting qualitative data in this study?

Patient and practitioner diagnosis and style

Many studies have been conducted that investigate the style of practitioner diagnosis. Some studies, like Byrne and Long, have investigated the style of communication of the doctor and how this is interpreted in satisfaction ratings. Savage and Armstrong also looked at the relationship between the patient and the doctor in regard to the approach that the doctor takes when diagnosing illness. Others have focused on why some doctors might want to be cautious when diagnosing patients to reduce errors.

Practitioner style: doctor- and patient-centred (Byrne & Long, 1976; Savage & Armstrong, 1990)

Byrne and Long (1976) carried out a study of interactions between patients and practitioners. They tape recorded and analysed about 2500 medical consultations in several countries. They found that each practitioner tended to use a consistent style for all patients being treated. Most of the styles were classified as **doctor-centred** or patient-centred.

They commented that few doctors at that time could reflect on the dynamics and process of the consultation when asked questions such as: 'What are you doing?' or 'How are you doing it?' From the tape recordings Byrne and Long recognised six phases that doctors went through in the process of consultation:

1 Establishes a relationship with the patient

2 Attempts to discover, or actually discovers, the reason for the patient's attendance

3 Conducts a verbal or physical examination or both

4 The doctor, the doctor and the patient, or the patient (in that order of probability) consider the condition

5 The doctor, and occasionally the patient, details further treatment or further investigation

6 Ends the consultation.

Most of the 2500 consultations went through this process, but Byrne and Long were able to classify different approaches to dealing with the patients during their consultations. They identified seven different styles that they placed on a continuum from being extremely doctor-centred to extremely **patient-centred** (Table 8.3). Doctors who were classified as doctor-centred tended to ask questions that required only brief answers – generally 'yes' or 'no' and focused mainly on the first problem the patient mentioned. These doctors tended to ignore attempts by a patient to discuss other problems he or she might have had.

'Prescribing' style	Incidence in sample (N = 1965)	Example	Additional information	Typical behaviours*
Style 1: The doctor *makes* a decision about the patient and his treatment and then *instructs* the patient to seek some service	624	*'I want you to take these tablets and come back in two weeks, Bye-bye'*	Notice there is no mention of a diagnosis	Directing Direct termination
Style 2: The doctor *makes* a decision and *announces* it	680	*'This is an infection of the lung. I want you to go upstairs and have an X-ray now. When you have had that come back here and I will detail the treatment'*		Giving information Directing Terminating
Style 3: The doctor *sells* his decision to the patient	57 on its own 70 as a back-up strategy = 127	*'Now then, I would like you to take this to the chemist… don't worry it is no more serious than last time… right then, off you go. Cheerio!'*	Diagnosis, treatment and reassurance	Giving information Directing Reassuring Seeking patient ideas (but not using them) Direct termination
Style 4: The doctor *presents* a *tentative* decision subject to change	279	*'I think you need a long rest. Now then, how do you think you can cope with that?'* Afterwards there is a discussion on length and time of rest agreed	Diagnosis, treatment and mutual understanding Danger of 'I will if you will' game (page 108)	Giving information or opinion Directing Advising Answering patient questions Reassuring Seeking patient ideas Indicating understanding Using patient ideas
Style 5: The doctor *presents* the problems, and *makes* decisions	159	Similar to the previous style but the doctor directs the patient to come up with suggestions which he takes up		Giving information or opinion Advising Clarifying Reflecting Exploring Seeking patient ideas Using patient ideas Offering collaboration Termination (indirect)

→

'Prescribing' style	Incidence in sample (N = 1965)	Example	Additional information	Typical behaviours*
Style 6: The doctor *defines* the limits and *requests* the patient to make a decision	35 primary strategy 39 secondary strategy after failing with styles 1 and 2 = 74	'... this condition is no more than a simple appendicitis. It can be quickly treated by surgery, although at this stage that is not the best possible answer. I can also treat you at home with some drugs. This treatment will take a short time if you rest. If you have to keep working then the treatment will take rather longer, and may not be so effective. The choice is yours.' '... Well you know medical opinion can be a terribly fickle thing. Years ago we would have had it out by now ... Given what you have, I don't think I would advise an operation ...'		Giving information Answering patient questions Seeking patient ideas Using patient ideas Summarising to open up Pre-directional probing (i.e. 'If I said X how would you react?')
Style 7: The doctor *permits* the patient to make his own decision	22	'... what I want you to think about is what we should do next ...'	Doctors have very different opinions about this style as a treatment for hypochondriacs [negative attitude] or when they face an emotional problem and do not know what to do about it [more positive attitude]	Reflecting Encouraging Seeking patient ideas Using patient ideas

*As defined in Byrne and Long (1976)

Table 8.3 'Prescribing' styles (Byrne and Long 1976 page 106)

In contrast those doctors classified as patient-centred took a less controlling role. They tended to ask open-ended questions, such as 'Can you describe the situation when the pain occurs?', which allowed the patient to relate more information and introduce new facts that may be pertinent. They also tended to avoid medical jargon and allowed the patient to participate in some of the decision making.

They concluded that many doctors were a 'product and prisoner of own medical education' which did not enable doctors to deal with the psychological or social issues related to patients' problems.

Savage and Armstrong (1990) wanted to compare the effect of **directing** and **sharing** styles of consultation by a general practitioner on patients' satisfaction with the consultation (Table 8.4). They used a more scientific approach with randomised allocation to conditions to test how satisfied patients felt following these different approaches.

Some studies have reported the benefits of general practitioners adopting a sharing style during consultations. These studies have argued that by making patients part of the process of making decisions the doctor becomes clearer about the nature of the patient's problem and the

Part of consultation	Style of consultation	
	Directing	**Sharing**
Judgment on the consultation	*'This is a serious problem'* or *'I don't think this is a serious problem'*	*'Why do you think this has happened'* *'Why do you think this has happened now?'*
Diagnosis	*'You are suffering from …'*	*'What do you think is wrong?'*
Treatment	*'It is essential that you take this medicine'*	*'What have you tried to do to help so far?'* *'What were you hoping that I would be able to do?'* *'Would you like a prescription?'* *'I think this medicine would be helpful; would you be prepared to take it?'*
Prognosis	*'You will be better in … days'*	*'What do these symptoms or problems mean to you?'*
Follow-up and closure	*'Come and see me in … days'* *'I don't need to see you again for this problem'*	*'Are there any other problems?'* *'When would you like to come and see me again?'*

Table 8.4 Examples of directing and sharing styles of consultation by general practitioner during five parts of consultation

patient is more committed to any advice given. However, others argue that the doctor's primary function is to make the patient feel better through a top-down, authoritarian approach to medical consultations.

A random sample of 359 patients between the ages of 16 and 75 presenting with any symptoms were eligible to take part in the study; 200 results were used (see Table 8.5). Each patient was asked for their consent to have their consultation recorded. Patient satisfaction was measured by two questionnaires that asked about the quality of the communication in the consolation and any thoughts afterwards; one immediately and one a week later.

Overall a high level of satisfaction was found in both conditions, but it was higher for the directed group who reported more 'satisfaction with explanation of doctor' and with 'own understanding of the problem'. They were also more likely to report that they had been 'greatly helped'.

Savage and Armstrong's results suggest that the directing style had a better effect in terms of patient satisfaction as measured by their perception of the doctor's understanding of the problem, the quality of the doctor's explanation, and the subjective improvement one week later. This provides more evidence that authoritarianism and certainty are elements of the doctor's style that satisfy the patients most and again show the importance of style on satisfaction within the doctor–patient relationship.

219

Assessment	Initially		One week later	
	Directing style	**Sharing style**	**Directing style**	**Sharing style**
I was able to discuss my problem well	79/96 (73)	75/102 (74)	55/90 (61)	50/95 (53)
I received an excellent explanation	44/97 (45)	24/101 (24)	30/90 (33)	16/96 (17)
I perceived the general practitioner to have complete understanding	60/97 (62)	38/103 (37)	35/90 (39)	17/96 (18)
I felt greatly helped	52/97 (54)	45/100 (45)	44/89 (49)	27/97 (28)
I felt much better	32/96 (33)	32/100 (32)	29/89 (33)	25/97 (26)

Table 8.5 Assessment of a doctor's style of consultation by 200 patients who completed questionnaires initially and one week later. Figures are numbers (percentages) of patients.

Evaluation

In Byrne and Long's research the study used tape recordings, focusing on verbal communication. Therefore, the study did not recognise the many forms of non-verbal communication, which are important factors in successful interpersonal skills. The study only attempted to classify interactions into two styles: doctor-centred and patient-centred. This is very simplistic because many interactions would surely fall between the two styles. There was a large number of recordings that were coded during this experiment which suggest that a **representative sample** allowed **generalisations** to be made to different contexts within the medical profession. Each of the consultations that were recorded had to be coded by the researchers which allowed a large amount of qualitative data to be analysed, however, coding of consultations could be subjective and lead to problems with the reliability of classifications.

Savage and Armstrong's (1990) research used an **independent measures design** as participants were only in one of the two conditions. This could introduce confounding variables because of the individual participant preferences. Some participants may have preferred a computer based questionnaire whereas others may prefer face-to-face consultation and this preference was not

collected. The data only refers to individuals who were attending a Genito-urinary (GU) clinic where there is a higher rate of personal information that is required during a consultation therefore similar findings might not be found in a general practitioner's office where there are a wider range of illnesses.

Practitioner diagnosis: Type I and Type II errors

Doctors undergo years of training and study to be able to interpret any symptoms that a patient may exhibit and diagnose the correct illness. It is important for the doctor to gain as much information as they can about the illness, symptoms and medical history of the patient, and even their immediate family, to help them make a correct diagnosis. Sometimes a doctor will get it wrong though. These errors can be classified into two categories.

8.2 Doctors can make both Type I (false positive) or Type II (false negative) errors

There are two types of error that doctors and researchers are concerned with: Type I and Type II (Figure 8.2). A Type I error occurs when the results of a test show that a difference exists but in reality there is no difference. Therefore, a Type I error, or false positive, is declaring an illness when one does not exist. A Type II error, or false negative, is declaring that a person is well when he or she is ill (Table 8.6).

	Doctor diagnoses illness	Doctor does not diagnose illness
Patient is ill	Correct	Type II error (false negative) Calling a sick patient healthy
Patient is not ill	Type I error (false positive) Calling a healthy patient sick	Correct

Table 8.6 Type 1 and Type II errors

Type I and Type II errors can happen at any point throughout a patient's illness from initial **screenings**, consultations and treatment stages. Throughout a patient's illness there may be several opportunities for errors to be made by doctors, nurses and those analysing samples or scans.

Screening involves relatively cheap tests that are given to large populations, many of whom will not manifest any clinical indication of disease (e.g. smears/mammograms). Testing involves far more expensive, often invasive, procedures that are given only to those who manifest or are expected to manifest some clinical problem or disease, and are most often applied to confirm a suspected diagnosis.

> **Reflections:** Is it better for a doctor to make a Type I or a Type II error? What are the consequences for each type of error?

Disclosure of information (Robinson and West, 1992)

An important element of the patient–practitioner relationship is the information that is disclosed by the patient. If the patient does not disclose all of their symptoms, is not honest, or exaggerates their symptoms it will increase the likelihood of Type I and Type II errors in diagnosis. Robinson and West (1992) wanted to investigate the difference between, and effectiveness of, a computer-based medical questionnaire against a paper-based questionnaire, in eliciting medical histories from patients.

In this study they wanted to find out whether computerisation leads to greater disclosure from respondents when information is being sought on a highly personal topic. It consisted of a comparison of

the data collected by a computer interview with a paper questionnaire in a genito-urinary (GU) clinic. Both of these were also compared with the physician's records of the same patients.

> **Reflections:** Would you be more honest if you were answering questions on a computer than face-to-face with a doctor? Why?

The participants were 33 male and 36 female patients of a GU clinic in northern England. Their ages ranged from 15 to 49 with a mean of 27 years. Owing to the withdrawal of some participants and some having issues with their computers, there were 37 participants in the computer group and 32 in the paper questionnaire group.

> **RESEARCH METHODS**
> Why was it important that participants were allowed to withdraw?

On arrival at the clinic patients were randomly allocated to either the 'computer' condition or the 'paper questionnaire' condition. Patients were then asked to complete their case histories either through a computer questionnaire or on a paper questionnaire and returned to the waiting room. Following this, each patient had a medical consultation with a doctor which included a physical examination.

The data collected from the questionnaires was compared with the patients' medical notes from the doctor's interview. Three key items were compared:

- The number of the symptoms the patient reported
- The number of reported previous attendances at a GU clinic
- The number of sexual partners the patient had had in the last 12 weeks.

Both the computer interview and the paper questionnaire yielded significantly more symptoms than were recorded by the doctor from their consultation (Table 8.7). Although the mean number of sexual partners reported to the computer was greater than to the paper questionnaire or in the physician's notes, the differences were not statistically significant.

		Computer		Physician	
		Mean	SD	Mean	SD
Computer group (N = 37)	Number of symptoms	3.0	2.3	1.1	0.7
	Number of previous attendances	1.2	2.3	0.6	1.1
	Number of sexual partners	2.4	5.7	1.3	1.7
Questionnaire group (N = 32)	Number of symptoms	1.9	1.9	0.9	0.6
	Number of previous attendances	0.8	1.3	0.8	1.6
	Number of symptoms	1.1	0.5	1.1	0.3

Table 8.7 Information disclosed to the paper questionnaire, computer and recoded by the doctor (page 81)

The results support the view that the computer interview will elicit more information from patients than the paper questionnaire with regard to personal symptoms. Both the computer interview and the questionnaire also elicited significantly more symptoms than were recorded in the doctor's consultation. This suggests that patients are unwilling to disclose all of their symptoms to doctors within a consultation and that other measures, such as computer questionnaires, should be employed to elicit this information to support doctor's diagnosis.

Misusing health services

Sometimes it is the patient who gets things wrong, misinterprets their symptoms or delays in getting medical treatment or advice. In this sub-topic we will look at the factors that influence patients delaying their treatment with the study by Safer et al. researching the different types of delays. We will also look at two disorders: hypochondriasis, or a fear or illness, and Munchausen syndrome where individuals make themselves ill to get attention from medical professionals.

Delay in seeking treatment (Safer et al., 1979)

Safer et al. (1979) wanted to investigate what factors influence delays in seeking medical treatment for the first time for a particular symptom. The study was conducted in the waiting rooms of four clinics in a large inner-city hospital. Interviewers approached patients who were waiting to see a doctor or nurse and asked them if they were going to tell the doctor about a new symptom. If the patient was presenting a new symptom they were asked to take part in the study. Ninety-three patients (38 males and 55 females) with an

average age of 44 years were interviewed about their health behaviours leading up to their current illness and their reaction to their symptoms (Figure 8.3).

When making reference to delays, Safer et al. categorised delays in four ways. Total delay was the number of days elapsing from the time a patient first noticed his symptoms to the time he was interviewed in the clinic. This was sub-divided into three further stages. He believed that there were different factors that would affect one's likelihood of seeking help at the different stages of delay (Table 8.8).

- *Appraisal delay*: the first stage of delay, defined as the number of days that elapsed from the day the patient first noticed their symptom up to the day they concluded they were ill. The patient was questioned about both of these events during the interview.
- *Illness delay*: the second stage of delay defined as the number of days from the end of appraisal delay, when the patient concluded they were ill, up to the day when they decided to seek professional help.
- *Utilisation delay*: the final stage of delay – defined as the number of days from the end of illness delay, the point at which the patient decided to seek professional help, to the time of the interview, when the patient was actually seen in the clinic.

The independent variable was operationalised by asking the patient about their symptoms and their reactions to those symptoms. The patient was also asked about the length of delay at various stages of the illness episode which was the dependent variable. The interview lasted approximately 45 minutes.

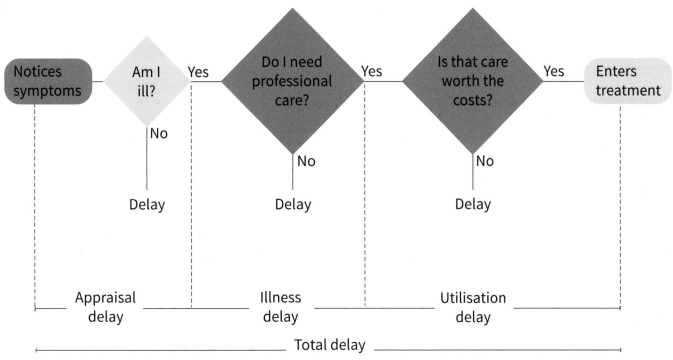

8.3 Decisions to seek or delay care in three stages of an illness episode

Appraisal delay	Illness delay	Utilisation delay
• Frequency, severity and location of symptoms • Perceived importance of symptoms • Lack of awareness of the nature of the symptoms • Trying a 'home remedy' • Lack of monitoring • Family pressure	• Awareness that you cannot treat the illness yourself • Perception of the consequences of the illness as severe • Beliefs about the benefits of any treatment • Fear about illness	• Obstacles to receiving care (money/time) • Lack of familiarity with medical services • Demographic factors (age, sex, education, marital status and ethnicity)

Table 8.8 Proposed factors influencing the types of delays in Safer et al. (1979)

- *Appraisal delay* (average length = 4.2 days): two variables correlated significantly with the delay: severe pain which reduced appraisal delay (2.5 days) and researching the symptoms which increased appraisal delay (4.9 days).
- *Illness delay* (average length = 3.1 days): two variables correlated significantly with the delay: increase in the number of symptoms reduced illness delay (2.5 days) whereas those who had negative images about the outcome of their disorder had an increased illness delay (11.3 days).
- *Utilisation delay* (average length = 2.5 days): three variables correlated significantly with the delay: concerns about the cost of treatment increased the delay (9.7 days), presence of pain decreased the delay (1.6 days) and the belief that they could be cured reduced the delay (1.8 days).

Safer et al. concluded that a variety of factors, perceptual, situational and appraisal strategies, affect delay in seeking medical treatment. As they expected, strong sensory signals, such as increased pain and bleeding, led to shorter delays, whereas those who procrastinated by researching their symptoms had an increase in the total delay. This goes against common belief that those who delay seeking treatment do so because they deny their symptoms; delays appear to come from a failure to appraise the situation adequately.

223

> **Reflections:** What would delay you in seeking medical treatment?

Misuse: hypochondriasis (Barlow & Durand, 2011)

Hypochondriasis is a persistent fear of having a serious medical illness. People with this disorder often interpret normal sensations, minor symptoms and bodily functions as a sign of an illness with a negative outcome. For example, a person may fear that perspiring, the normal sounds of digestion or a bruise may be a sign of a serious disease. Some symptoms of hypochondriasis are:

- clinical distress or functional impairment
- misinterpretation of body symptoms
- persistent fear despite medical reassurance
- absence of delusions or psychosis
- preoccupation with having a serious illness.

Hypochondriasis is often accompanied by other psychological disorders. Bipolar disorder, clinical depression, obsessive-compulsive disorder (OCD), phobias and somatisation disorder are the most common accompanying conditions in people with hypochondriasis, as well as a generalised anxiety disorder diagnosis at some point in their life. It is a chronic (long-lasting) condition that can begin at any time of life, although it is most common between ages 20 and 40.

Although hypochondriasis is currently classified as a somatoform disorder, the underlying cognitive processes may be more consistent with an anxiety disorder. This observation has important implications for treatment and subsequent revisions of the diagnostic classification of hypochondriasis. The Integrative model of causes of hypochondriasis (Figure 8.4) suggests that those individuals suffering with hypochondriasis will initially react to an external trigger. From this they will perceive the threat to their health which causes apprehension and physiological responses to this apprehension. This can then be misrepresented as sensations indicating illness, which further compounds the individual's belief that their health is under threat.

Munchausen syndrome (Aleem & Ajarim, 1995)

Munchausen syndrome is one of the most intriguing of factitious disorders and is named after a German aristocrat, Baron Munchausen, who became famous for telling wild, unbelievable tales about his exploits. Factitious disorders are characterised by physical or psychological symptoms that are intentionally produced or faked in order to assume the sick role. People with the condition intentionally produce or pretend to have physical or psychological symptoms of illness. Their main intention is to assume the 'sick role' to have people care for them and be the centre of attention. Any financial benefit for them in pretending to be sick – for example, claiming government benefits – is not the reason for their behaviour.

People with Munchausen syndrome may spend years going from one doctor to another, or even move from hospital to hospital, pretending to have an illness. People with Munchausen's syndrome may pretend to have psychological symptoms (hearing voices), physical symptoms (pains and aches) or actually try to make

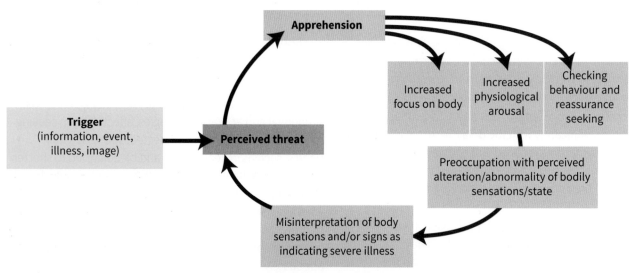

8.4 Integrative model of causes of hypochondriasis (based on Warwick and Salkovskis, 1990)

themselves ill by deliberately infecting themselves. There are four main ways in which these individuals will behave:

- lying about symptoms
- tampering with test results
- self-infliction (cutting or burning themselves)
- aggravating pre-existing symptoms.

The cause of Munchausen syndrome is not known, but researchers are looking at the role of biological and psychological factors in its development. Some suggest that a history of abuse or neglect as a child, or a history of frequent illnesses that required hospitalisation might be factors in the development of the syndrome. Researchers are also studying a possible link to personality disorders, which are common in people with Munchausen syndrome.

Aleem and Ajarim (1995) report the case of a 22-year-old female who attended their hospital in Saudi Arabia (see below) and state that most doctors will encounter at least one patient with a factitious disorder during their career, of which Munchausen syndrome is the most extreme type. The details below are from a real case that the researchers were involved with and illustrates the extent that individuals who suffer with Munchausen syndrome will go to in order to get the medical attention that they desire.

A 22-year-old female (university student) was referred to the hospital with a painful swelling over the right breast and a history of similar recurrent swellings over the abdominal wall during the past few months which needed repeated surgical drainage in other hospitals. From the age of 17 she had been seen by hospitals regularly for issues relating to her menstrual cycle during which she developed symptoms suggestive of deep vein thrombosis which did not respond to increases in medication.

The patient's father was a teacher and described by her as a supportive and friendly man. Her mother had breast cancer. She had six sisters and no brothers; she was the third in line. The patient was intelligent but seemed to have only modest knowledge of the medical field.

Soon after the swelling, she again presented with complaints of swellings in the groin area associated with weakness of the lower limbs. Following physical examination and investigations (ultrasound and CT scans) a diagnosis of suspected haematoma (a solid swelling of clotted blood within the tissue) was given. Physical examination during the current admission revealed an intelligent young female, afebrile, with normal pulse and blood pressure.

She was treated with antibiotics but later, surgical drainage had to be completed as features of an abscess fully developed. After about four days of hospitalisation, the patient developed a similar abscess in the opposite breast and this had to be drained surgically as well. Cultures were taken from the abscesses and they were found to contain several different bacteria.

At this stage, suspicion was raised regarding the possible factitious nature of her problem because of an inability to explain the cause of her abscesses and the growth of multiple bacteria around them. A psychiatric consultation was made after counselling the patient without giving her a hint about suspected factitious disorder.

Finally, one day when the patient was not in bed, the nurses found a syringe full of faecal material along with needles. When the patient came back, one of the other patients told her about this. She became very angry and hostile and left the hospital against medical advice and did not return to the hospital again. A diagnosis of factitious illness (Munchausen syndrome) was confirmed.

ISSUES AND DEBATES

Research like Safer et al.'s into reasons for delay in seeking treatment has a real **application to everyday life**. If we can understand why a patient would fail to seek treatment, we can put interventions into place to reduce these as a preventative measure. In addition to this, understanding hypochondriasis could further support the development of treatment programmes that could reduce the number of times a patient presents themselves to a medical centre, reducing costs, and allowing doctors and nurses to concentrate on those who genuinely need medical attention.

There are **individual and situational explanations** for mental disorders like hypochondriasis and Munchausen syndrome. Some suggest a history of abuse or neglect as a child, or a history of frequent illnesses, whereas others are also studying a possible link to personality disorders. This further links with the **nature versus nurture** debate where we need to consider if there is a biological cause that could trigger an individual to act in a way that misuses the health systems, or if it is a consequence of upbringing, attachments and relationships throughout one's life.

Much of the research into hypochondriasis and Munchausen's syndrome has been conducted on western patients which could lead to a **cultural bias** in understanding the disorders and possible treatment programmes that are developed to support these individuals. Further research should be conducted across a wider range of individuals to investigate the symptoms that individuals exhibit in similar situations.

Evaluation

Safer et al. used a variety of self-report measures to investigate why patients had arranged a doctor's appointment, the length of time they had been suffering with a particular symptom and reasons for delaying accessing treatment. With any self-report measure there are issues of validity and respondents answering in a socially desirable way. Many participants might have been concerned about how they were perceived so changed their answers about the duration of the symptoms and reasons for accessing help. The sample that Safer et al. used was relatively large and represented both males and females so it is possible to argue that there is **population validity** which would allow the researcher to generalise the findings to a wider range of patients.

SELF-ASSESSMENT QUESTIONS

3 A doctor is talking to the sister of one of his patients. The man's sister is worried because he always seems to be ill. He sees the doctor often, with diarrhoea, different allergies producing strange red rashes and wounds that don't seem to get better. He knows everyone at the surgery well and seems to find any diagnosis comforting. His sister says she has seen him rubbing dirt into his wounds. Identify the features of this situation that suggest he might have Munchausen syndrome.

8.2 Adherence to medical advice

One of the issues to consider with **adherence** to medical requests is the type of behaviour we are asking someone to do. The types of requests fall into a number of categories:

- requests for short-term compliance with simple treatments, e.g. take these tablets twice a day for three weeks
- requests for positive additions to lifestyle, e.g. eat more fruit and vegetables
- requests to stop certain behaviours, e.g. stop drinking alcohol
- requests for long-term treatment programmes, e.g. diabetic diet or renal dialysis diet.

KEY TERM

adherence: sticking. 'Adherence to medical advice' means following advice given by a medical practitioner.

Chronic diseases can be well managed only if the patient adheres to their prescribed treatment. It is important to be able to measure how well people are adhering to medical requests so that medication can be improved and appropriate decisions made in the delivery of care.

Types of non-adherence and reasons why patients do not adhere

Many different psychological reasons have been given for why patients do not always adhere to medical advice. Explanations for why patients do and do not adhere to medical advice fall into two categories: some studies look for the explanation within the patients and some studies look for the explanation by looking at the doctor's behaviour.

Types of non-adherence and problems caused by non-adherence

Non-adherence with medication is a complex and multidimensional health-care problem. The causes may be related to the patient, treatment and the type of health care provider. As a consequence, substantial numbers of patients do not benefit from correct diagnosis and treatment, resulting in increased **morbidity** and **mortality** as well as an increase in both direct and indirect costs. Patients might not adhere during any stage of their treatment (Table 8.9).

> **KEY TERMS**
>
> **morbidity:** the incidence of a disease across a population and/or geographic location during a predefined timeframe.
> **mortality:** the rate of death in a population.

Before treatment	Poor description of the treatment programme leading to lack of awareness
During treatment	Take more or less of a drug than has been prescribed
	Take the drug at a different time from that instructed
	May not complete their prescription
	Only attend some clinics or medical follow-up appointments
	Not complete all instructed activities (exercise/physiotherapy)
End of treatment	May end their course of treatment early or fail to attend follow-up sessions
	May revert straight back to behaviours that were changed through the treatment

Table 8.9 Possible ways that a patient might not adhere to medical requests

Adherence can be defined as the extent to which a patient's behaviour and following of treatment programmes coincides with the advice and guidance provided by doctors and other health care professionals. The reasons for non-adherence could be intentional (*I am not taking any of these drugs*) or non-intentional (*I forgot to take my medication*).

The reason for the non-adherence could be due to issues with the patient, the treatment programme or the doctor's instructions (Table 8.10). In the context of disease, medication non-adherence can be termed an epidemic. It is suggested that some older-adult hospital admissions may be due to non-adherence with medication regimens and these could have been avoided if medical instructions were followed.

Patient	Patient decides that they do not need the treatment
	Patient does not understand the treatment
	Patient decides the costs of the treatment (time or money) are more than the expected benefits
	Social support and demographic factors
Treatment programme	Treatment programme is expensive, time consuming or difficult to administer
	Access to the treatment programme is not made easy (clinic at the other side of the city)
Health care provider	Doctor does not stress the importance of the treatment
	Doctor does not give adequate details about how to administer the drug

Table 8.10 Influences on why a patient might not adhere to medical requests

> **SELF-ASSESSMENT QUESTIONS**
>
> 4 Is each of the following reasons for non-adherence due to the patient, programme or provider?
>   a The gym is too busy to get onto the exercise bikes to do the required exercises.
>   b How to take the medication was not explained clearly.
>   c Running out of the drug and not putting in a repeat prescription.
>   d Forgetting how often to take pills.

Failure to adhere to medical requests could lead to increased need for medical intervention, more frequent visits to the doctors, additional medical tests and treatments, emergency admissions or even death. At best, non-adherence will cause a delay in improvement from the illness, and at worst could increase the chances of the illness developing into a more dangerous illness.

Of all age groups, older persons with chronic diseases and conditions benefit the most from taking medication, and risk the most from failing to take them properly. Among older adults the consequences of medication non-adherence may be more serious, less easily detected and less easily resolved than in younger age groups.

Why patients don't adhere: rational non-adherence (Bulpitt, 1994)

Rational choice theory is a framework for understanding and modelling why an individual will behave in a particular way. In everyday life we all make rational decisions based on the information that is available to us at the time. When such decisions are made, we weigh the costs and the benefits: what is the cost now and in the future and what will the benefits be? If the costs are higher than the benefit, an individual will not change their behaviour to adhere to a medical request. This suggests that one reason for non-adherence is actually a result of a well-considered and reasoned thought process that leads the patient to believe that non-adherence is a better choice of behaviour than adherence.

KEY TERM

rational: based on or in accordance with reason or logic.

Bulpitt (1994) considers that one of the reasons for non-adherence is a rational 'cost–benefit' analysis of the situation that patients make and puts forward the risks and benefits of drug treatment for hypertension (abnormally high blood pressure) in the elderly.

In Bulpitt's 1994 paper, he reviews several pieces of research that suggest that individuals conduct 'cost–benefit' analyses when deciding on the course of action that they are going to take. Within the research Bulpitt considers costs and benefits of drug treatment for elderly individuals with hypertension separately and looks at research that has been conducted within these areas.

When considering risks Bulpitt found that both the EWPHE trial and the SHEP studies found there were many health risks to drug treatment in the elderly such as gout, chest pains and change in bowel habits. When considering the benefits in the MRC trial for elderly participants he found that coronary events were reduced by 44% with a mixture of drugs that were prescribed.

He concluded that the benefits from treating combined systolic and diastolic hypertension in elderly patients far outweigh the disadvantages. When considering the benefits of antihypertensive treatment, it is important to consider benefits other than stroke reduction. He also makes reference to the difficulty in measuring 'cost–benefit' interactions in individuals.

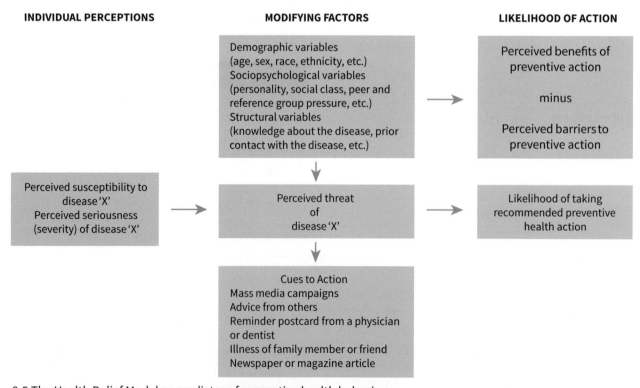

8.5 The Health Belief Model as predictor of preventive health behaviour

The Health Belief Model (Becker, 1974)

The Health Belief Model aims to predict when a person will engage in preventative health behaviours such as stopping smoking, taking up exercise, attending check-ups and yearly screening tests. According to the Health Belief Model, the likelihood that individuals will follow medical advice depends directly on two assessments that they make: evaluating the threat and a cost–benefits analysis (see Figure 8.5).

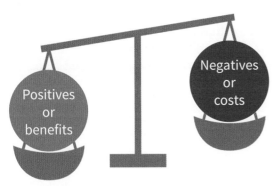

8.6 Weighing up positives and negatives

When evaluating the threat, there are several factors that can influence a person's perceived threat of illness, including: perceived seriousness, perceived susceptibility and cues to action. Other factors also likely to affect this assessment are demographic variables (such as income and level of education), age and sex of the individual.

For example, if a person is obese they might be in danger of developing a heart condition. They might understand that this is a serious condition, but they might believe that because they are still quite young they are unlikely to develop this problem just yet. Therefore, they might judge the threat as minor. Even if we judge the threat to be serious, we are only likely to act if we have a reason to act. This cue might be an advertising campaign, or it might be the diagnosis of a friend with heart disease.

The cost–benefit assessment looks at whether the perceived benefits exceed the perceived impediments. The barriers might be financial (prescription charges are about to rise again), situational (difficult to get to the health clinic) or social (don't want to face ageing). The benefits might be improved health, relief from anxiety and reducing health risks.

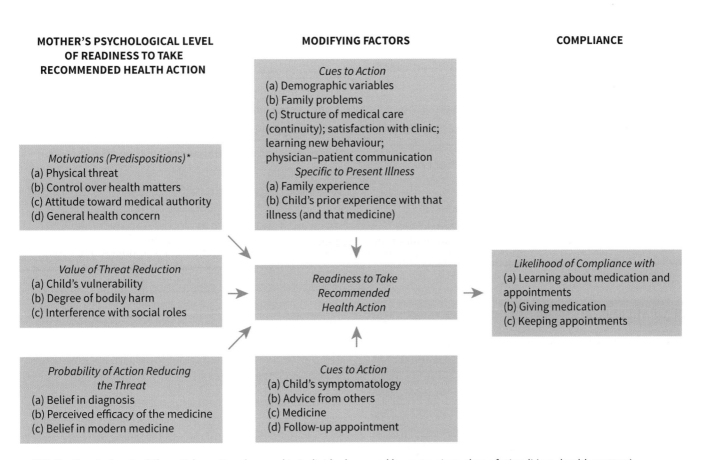

MOTHER'S PSYCHOLOGICAL LEVEL OF READINESS TO TAKE RECOMMENDED HEALTH ACTION

MODIFYING FACTORS

COMPLIANCE

Cues to Action
(a) Demographic variables
(b) Family problems
(c) Structure of medical care (continuity); satisfaction with clinic; learning new behaviour; physician–patient communication
Specific to Present Illness
(a) Family experience
(b) Child's prior experience with that illness (and that medicine)

Motivations (Predispositions) *
(a) Physical threat
(b) Control over health matters
(c) Attitude toward medical authority
(d) General health concern

Value of Threat Reduction
(a) Child's vulnerability
(b) Degree of bodily harm
(c) Interference with social roles

Readiness to Take Recommended Health Action

Likelihood of Compliance with
(a) Learning about medication and appointments
(b) Giving medication
(c) Keeping appointments

Probability of Action Reducing the Threat
(a) Belief in diagnosis
(b) Perceived efficacy of the medicine
(c) Belief in modern medicine

Cues to Action
(a) Child's symptomatology
(b) Advice from others
(c) Medicine
(d) Follow-up appointment

*'Motivations' refers to differential emotional arousal in individuals caused by some given class of stimuli (e.g., health matters).

8.7 Reformulated Health Belief Model as predictor of compliance in paediatric situations

In 1974 Becker developed the Compliance Model, building heavily on the Health Belief Model, to explain why a patient might comply or adhere with medical requests. The model could be used to predict factors that would influence the likelihood of a patient adhering to any medical requests. The perceptions of the child's (patient's) mother are examined within this model as it was believed that it was usually the mother who decided whether or not the child was sick and what care would be accessed at that point.

The Compliance Model (Figure 8.7) introduces the concept of health motivation. It considers both negative aspects of health that could motivate action (physical threat) as well as positive aspects such as a general awareness of health concerns. The second concept introduced in this model is that of incentive value of adherence. These are factors about the illness that contribute to the decision to adhere, such as the child's vulnerability and the degree of harm. The third factor is the mother's perception that the doctor's instructions will result in a reduction of the threat (a belief in the diagnosis and the treatment prescribed).

As this is a model of compliance, the patient has already seen the doctor and is presenting symptoms; therefore, the cues to action are present. However, readiness to take the recommended action is still susceptible to the influence of positive and negative modifying (such as demographic and previous experience). This may prevent adherence to medical requests.

Becker suggests that these five variables (motivations, value of threat reduction, reducing threat, cues to action and modifying factors) combine to predict the likeliness of a mother taking the recommended health action prescribed by a doctor.

This model was supported by a study conducted in 1971 where a random sample of 125 cases was drawn from a population of children being treated in the Comprehensive Child Care Clinic at a large teaching hospital. The children

ISSUES AND DEBATES

The reasons for patients not adhering to medical requests could have both **individual and situational explanations**. Situational explanations would stress the importance of environmental and demographic factors such as levels of education, income, cues to action and family networks. These could influence how likely a patient is to adhere to the requests of their doctors. Individual explanations would put more emphasis on

ISSUES AND DEBATES (continued)

personality factors of the individual and the risks that they perceive they are under from the illness compared to the perceived costs of following the medical advice. The Health Belief Model attempts to blend these two factors and give a framework to help us predict when a patient is more likely to adhere to medical requests. This therefore has **applications to everyday life** and could be used to help train doctors to stress the gains that a patient would see by following the medical advice and reducing the perceived costs.

There could be **cultural biases** in the models used to explain why patients might not follow medical advice that ignore the importance of healthy behaviours, the amount of trust in doctors and the belief in alternative medicines. Wider ranging research would need to be conducted to improve the understanding of adherence from a range of countries with different levels of health provisions. For example, some countries have free health services that all residents are able to access whereas others rely on free clinics to support those who cannot afford the health insurance that would give them access to the superior health care. This could be a significant factor in the importance of the advice given by the doctors.

were aged from six weeks to ten years and all were placed on a course of liquid oral antibiotic and a follow-up visit. An hour-long interview was conducted with each patient immediately after their doctor's appointment.

Adherence was **operationalised** by asking the name of the medication, the number of times a day it should be given, and the date of the follow-up appointment, together with subsequent behaviours such as administering the medication and keeping the follow-up appointment.

The results showed that mothers who adhered to various aspects of the prescribed treatment were more interested in their child's health in general, and were more concerned about the present illness. They perceived that illness was a substantial threat to their child, but had confidence in the ability of physicians and medication to reduce this threat. The mothers who worried about the child's health engaged in behaviour they felt would prevent future illness.

The model appears to be useful in the explanation and prediction of compliance behaviour. Variables are found in each major category of the model which are related to compliance both at a general level and at a level dealing with the specific illness studied.

Evaluation

Both Rational Choice Theory and the Health Belief Model have supporting empirical evidence that provides credibility to their underlying ideas about adherence to medical requests. However, the research often relies on self-report measures to gain an insight into the reasons for adherence. These are open to respondents answering in a **socially desirable** way as they could be concerned about the implications of reporting that they did not follow the advice of the doctors.

SELF-ASSESSMENT QUESTIONS

5 Using your knowledge of models of adherence to medical requests, suggest three questions a doctor could ask a patient to assess their likelihood of adhering to medical requests.

Measuring non-adherence

There are various ways to measure how well patients adhere to medical requests. These can be divided into those that use physical measures, such as pill counting, recording repeat prescriptions and biochemical tests, and those that use self-report measures. However, like all methods in psychology, they only produce estimates of behaviour and they all contain some degree of error.

There are a number of physical measures of adherence. For example, using blood or urine tests, researchers can determine whether the medication has been used recently and in some cases how much has been used. Adherence can also be measured by outcome. That is, if the patient gets better we can assume that they have taken their medication. A further physical measure is to do a pill or bottle count and compare it with the number that should be left in the bottle.

Subjective: self-reports (Riekart & Droter, 1999)

Self-report measures involve asking the patient or the doctor if the patient is following their treatment programme (such as taking their antibiotics, reducing their alcohol intake). The validity of self-reports are limited because of the challenges associated with gaining information from patients without response biases.

Subjective measures can affect the validity of any data collected as it is open to any response bias from the participant. The response bias could be in the form of answers in a **socially desirable** way, lying about adhering to a medical request, or simply not responding to a self-report measure. Studies that rely on these subjective self-report measures need to consider the impact that they have on their data and conclusions.

KEY TERM

socially desirable: responding to a question in a way that you feel is expected by the researcher or socially accepted.

Reflections: Would you lie about adhering to a medical request? If you were told to complete a course of medication and you had not, would you answer honestly when the doctor enquired about it? Why might patients lie about adhering to medical requests?

Riekart and Droter (1999) wanted to examine the implications of non-participation in studies using self-report measures to investigate adherence to medical treatment for adolescents with diabetes (see Research Methods box). It was felt that those patients who chose not to be involved with research might actually show less adherence than those who did agree to take part, therefore suggesting a bias in all research of adherence. The participants in the study were adolescents between the ages of 11 and 18 who were living with at least one parent. The adolescents were excluded from the study if they had been diagnosed with diabetes within the last year, had an additional chronic illness or had evidence of a learning difficulty.

The respondents were asked to complete a series of questionnaires and interviews. The adolescent completed an adherence interview immediately after their appointment at the clinic while the parent(s) completed a demographic questionnaire. Both the adolescent and the parent(s) were given a further questionnaire to be completed at home with a self-addressed return envelope. If the questionnaires were not returned within ten days of the interview, the family was called once to remind them.

RESEARCH METHODS

Self-report measures used in Riekart and Droter (1999):
- Adherence and IDDM Questionnaire-R: a semi-structured interview to assess the adolescent's adherence to treatment such as dietary behaviours, insulin adjustment and glucose testing.
- Demographics Questionnaire: a questionnaire including questions on age, gender, ethnicity, disease duration and family demographics.

Eighty families, out of 94 approached, consented to participate in the study, took part in the adherence interview and completed the demographic questionnaire. Fifty-two of these families had at least one family member return the follow-up self-report questionnaires. Medical records were reviewed for each of these participants to gain information about the number of blood sugar tests taken per day as a measure of their adherence to medical requests. The families were categorised into three groups: participants (52), non-returners (28) and non-consenters (14).

The results showed significant differences in adherence levels between study participants and those who did not return their self-reports. The families that returned their questionnaires had adolescents who had higher adherence interview scores and tested their blood sugar more frequently than adolescents in families who did not return their questionnaires.

The implications of this research are that those participants who did not return their self-report differed on several adherence variables when looking at medical records. This suggests that when self-report measures are used, there is an association with lack of adherence and failure to respond to questionnaires. This needs to be considered when interpreting the results of any study that utilises self-report measures to collect data on adherence, as such data might be distorted if the responses of only those that completed the self-report are considered.

RESEARCH METHODS
Would the bias in data caused by differences in adherence between patients who do and do not participate in research tend to make adherence rates appear better or worse than they really are?

Objective: pill counting (Chung & Naya, 2000)

Pill counts are often used to measure adherence, but there is little data on how they affect adherence. During clinical visits, health professionals are trained to count the number of tablets left in a pill bottle (Figure 8.8) and to advise the patient about adherence if the patient missed dosages based on the expected number of pills compared with those remaining. The health professional will record the result of the pill count on the medical record of the patient.

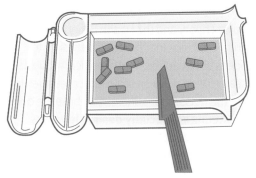

8.8 Is physically counting pills a reliable method of measuring adherence?

Adherence with prescribed asthma medication is commonly estimated from tablet counts for oral medications and canister weights for inhaled medications. Developments in technology mean that electronic medication monitoring devices have been developed to measure adherence as well as drug use patterns. In patients with asthma, non-adherence is thought to play a major role in the unacceptably high morbidity and mortality associated with the disease. Chung and Naya (2000) were the first to electronically assess adherence with an oral asthma medication.

Fifty-seven patients, of whom 32 were male and 25 female, between 18 and 55 years of age, with a history of asthma took part in this research. An initial screening period of two to three weeks was followed by a 12-week treatment period during which patients were instructed to take their medication twice a day. The purpose of the screening period was to find out if patients were suitable candidates for the asthma therapy.

At the start of the treatment period, each patient received 56 tablets (enough for three weeks) with one week's supply to spare. Tablets were dispensed in screw-top bottles fitted with a TrackCap medication event monitoring system (MEMS®) device. The system comprises two parts: a standard plastic container and a lid containing a computer chip that registers the time at which the bottle is opened and closed. Patients were scheduled to return to the clinic every three weeks for four more visits where tablet counts were taken to compare with the TrackCap monitoring. Each participant was told: 'Take one tablet in the morning and one tablet in the evening approximately 12 hours apart. Do not take the tablets at mealtimes.'

As calculated from TrackCap events, median adherence was 89% and the distribution of percentages of days with full adherence can be seen in Figure 8.9. On days when patients took exactly two tablets, the mean time between doses was

12 hours 34 minutes with tablets taken eight to 16 hours apart on 86% of treatment days. On the basis of tablet counts, median adherence was 92%, which was slightly higher than compliance calculated from TrackCap events.

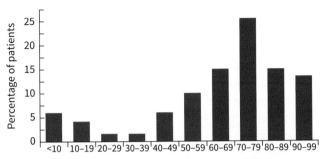

8.9 TrackCap MEMS® 6 is an electronic monitoring system designed to compile the dosing histories of patients prescribed oral medications

Chung and Naya concluded that the study showed that it is possible to assess adherence with an oral medication using a medication event monitoring system like TrackCap. They reflect that direct methods, such as biomedical tests, are ultimately inconvenient, and indirect methods such as pill counting, with inference of drug use, are problematic in determining the extent of full adherence and accounting for patient behaviours as they can be inconsistent. The fact that adherence calculated from the returned-tablet counts was greater than that calculated from TrackCap events may be attributed to accidental loss of medication, removal of multiple tablets at bottle openings, or deliberate disposal of tablets to disguise under usage.

Biochemical tests (Roth, 1978)

In his 1987 review of measuring adherence to medical requests, Roth considers the relative merits of a variety of methods that can be used by researchers and doctors to investigate the levels of patient adherence. From the review, Roth suggests that patient self-reports are usually correct when they say that they are taking little or no medicine, but commonly overestimated when they say that they are taking their medicine regularly and that doctors usually overestimate their patients' intake of medicine. Reliability in keeping appointments is not a good indication of adherence with other aspects of a medical treatment. Further, he states that pill counts provide an indication of medicine intake, but it cannot be presumed that all pills were taken and medication monitors can only indicate when as well as whether medication was removed from a container.

Levels of a medication or its metabolites in blood or urine usually provide a reasonably good indication of amount of medicine taken and clinical responses or side effects can be indications that medicine was taken. Urine and blood levels are the best available measures of medicine intake. Biochemical tests that measure drugs and their metabolites can be used to monitor plasma concentrations of a number of drugs used on the cardiovascular system.

By taking blood or urine samples from patients it is possible to see if some of the drug has been taken. The precise concentrations are useful in demonstrating whether there is a clinically effective dosage to treat particular disorders and if the dosage needs to be altered.

Biochemical testing can be used as a way to monitor adherence to medical treatment programmes and empirical evidence has shown that adherence for prescribed medications is higher with frequent urine monitoring. These measures of adherence are reliable and objective measures, but they can only be used to measure adherence to medications, not physical treatments such as changes in diet, exercise or physiotherapy.

Repeat prescriptions (Sherman et al., 2000)

One way that a patient could exhibit non-adherence behaviour is by failing to have their prescription fulfilled at a pharmacy. A prescription is given to a patient by a doctor and instructs a pharmacy as to what drugs the pharmacy is to provide to the patient and the amount to be taken each day. When a patient needs a long-term treatment, they are able to get a repeat prescription from their doctors without having to make another appointment. If the patient fails to have their prescription fulfilled this is a clear measure of non-adherence to medical advice and is an objective measure.

Sherman et al. (2000) wanted to determine if a prescription refill history obtained by calling the patients' pharmacies identified poor adherence with asthma medications more frequently than the doctor's assessment from clinical appointments. The sample consisted of 116 children with asthma who were interviewed with their parents or carers on a visit to the clinic. Among the questions asked were measures of estimated adherence on a checklist and a question asking where they obtained their drugs.

Patient adherence was operationalised by calculating the number of doses refilled divided by the number of doses prescribed over a period of up to 365 days (range,

233

63–365 days). The patient's doctor was also asked to make a judgement about their adherence by estimating if their patients were taking the required doses of their inhaler based on case history and their best clinical judgement.

Information provided by pharmacies was 92% accurate and the mean adherence was 72%, 61% and 38% for the three different inhalers that were prescribed to the patients within the study. Doctors were only able to identify 21 (49%) of 43 patients who refilled less than 50% of their prescribed doses of long-term symptom controllers and only three (27%) of 11 patients who used their inhalers excessively. This suggests that checking prescription refills is an accurate and practical method of identifying patients who are not adhering to medical requests and that doctors are not reliably able to tell if a patient is taking their inhaler through consultations alone.

> **Reflections:** If you were designing a study to measure non-adherence, what measure of adherence would you use? Why? Could a mixed methods study be a way of improving reliability of adherence measures?

234

ISSUES AND DEBATES

Being aware of the effectiveness of different measures of non-adherence has **applications to everyday life** by signposting the most **reliable** methods for investigating if a patient has been adhering to the medical advice they have been given. Within the area we have seen that **self-reports** can be questioned on how valid a measure they are because patients can easily lie about their interactions with any treatment programmes that are prescribed by a doctor. Physical measures (pill counting and repeat prescriptions) and biochemical tests are more trustworthy as they provide **objective** measures of the levels of drug in the blood, or the number of pills that are remaining after a period of time.

When **using children as participants**, as Riekart and Droter did, it is important to consider the ethical implications, particularly consent and protection. Children might be more likely to be susceptible to **demand characteristics** or answering in a socially desirable way. Depending on the age of the children, they might not be capable to giving informed consent, and in this case, it's important to gain the consent of their parents or carers.

Evaluation

Self-report measures are a quick way to identify if a patient has adhered to the advice of their doctors. It is useful as it can be used to query the patient about any treatment programme, not just a drug based prescription. For example, it is possible to ask about health behaviours such as diet, exercise and alternative therapies, that could not be measured in physical or biochemical ways. In comparison, biochemical measures of adherence are a subjective way to identify if a patient has been adhering to medical advice, but could involve invasive medical treatments to take the blood, saliva or urine. Further to this, these specimens then need to be sent for analysis which can be costly and time consuming.

It can be argued that pill counting is a reliable method of measuring the number of pills or amount of a medicine that has been consumed by a patient. Using a method like this, it is easy to compare the level of use to the prescribed dosage. Just because pills are not in the container does not mean that the participant has consumed the drug; it is possible that they disposed of the drug to deceive the doctors. Tools such as the TrackCap allow researchers to identify the frequency and patterns of drug usage that is far more detailed than simply counting the number of pills at regular intervals during a treatment programme. Similarly, using repeat prescriptions as a measure only informs the researcher that the drugs have been collected from a pharmacy, not that the patient is engaging with the treatment programme.

SELF-ASSESSMENT QUESTIONS

6   Why would it be better to use two measures of adherence to measure if a patient has completed a course of treatment rather than one?

Improving adherence

Ley (1988) reviewed a selection of studies of GP and hospital patients and found that 28% of patients in the UK had low satisfaction ratings of the treatment they received. Dissatisfaction in hospital patients was even higher with 41% giving low satisfaction ratings of their treatment and interaction with their doctors. Further to this, Ley suggested that patients were 'information seekers' and wanted to know as much about their disorder and any subsequent treatment rather than being 'information blunters' who wanted to be kept from the truth about their status.

Ley suggested that this dissatisfaction came from a lack of emotional support and understanding on the doctors' part, lack of information when prescribing drugs or failure to provide adequate explanations about their disorders. To improve adherence, Ley suggested that doctors should consider their attitudes and style of communication to improve the information that they give patients. It appears that the more information that patients receive and the more they feel they have been listened to as part of their consultations the greater the impact on their subsequent adherence.

Although the problem of poor adherence has been researched, the rates of non-adherence have not changed much in the past three decades. Health care providers play an important role in assisting patients to make healthy behavioural changes. Atreja et al. (2005) conducted a review of the current literature to help providers become more familiar with proven interventions that can improve patient adherence. They created the mnemonic SIMPLE that brings together all the elements a successful adherence improvement intervention should have (Table 8.11).

For interventions that are complex and require lifestyle modifications, it is worthwhile addressing patients' beliefs, intentions and self-efficacy, because knowledge alone is not sufficient to improve adherence. Patients must be motivated to adhere to medical requests.

Improving practitioner style
Behavioural techniques

There has been much research looking at the impact that various prompts, feedback, monetary incentives and other **reinforcers** have on increasing adherence to medical requests. Here are two studies that show the effectiveness of such behavioural techniques to change health behaviours. These techniques are often based on the behaviourist approach. Behaviourists offer a number of suggestions to improve adherence, such as changing habits using classical conditioning or aversion therapy, using positive reinforcements (operant conditioning) to encourage positive behaviours and using role models (social learning theory) show the importance of adherence to medical requests.

Money as an incentive (Yokley & Glenwick, 1984)

The purpose of the study by Yokley and Glenwick (1984) was to evaluate the relative impact of four conditions for motivating parents to take their children to be immunised. The conditions were: (a) a mailed general prompt, (b) a mailed specific prompt, (c) a mailed specific prompt plus expanded clinic hours (i.e. increased clinic access, convenience condition) and (d) a mailed specific prompt plus a monetary incentive (i.e. a lottery). It was

235

Strategies	Specific interventions
Simplifying regimen characteristics	Adjusting timing, frequency, amount and dosage
	Matching to patients' activities of daily living
	Using adherence aids, such as medication boxes and alarms
Imparting knowledge	Discussion with physician, nurse or pharmacist
	Distribution of written information or pamphlets
	Accessing health-education information on the web
Modifying patient beliefs	Assessing perceived susceptibility, severity, benefits and barriers
	Rewarding, tailoring and contingency contracting
Patient and family communication	Active listening and providing clear, direct messages
	Including patients in decisions
	Sending reminders via mail, email or telephone
	Convenience of care, scheduled appointment
	Home visits, family support, counselling
Leaving the bias	Tailoring the education to patients' level of understanding
Evaluating adherence	Self-reports (most commonly used)
	Pill counting, measuring serum or urine drug levels

Table 8.11 Commonly used interventions in successful adherence-enhancing strategies (from Atreja et al.)

expected that the monetary incentive and specific prompt combination would have the greatest impact on attendance as it provided a reward for taking the child to the clinic.

The study was conducted on the entire population of a medium-sized mid-west city (population of approximately 300 000). The **target population** consisted of children five years or younger who needed one or more inoculations for diphtheria, tetanus, pertussis, polio, measles, mumps or rubella.

KEY TERMS

reinforcers: something that encourages the replication of a desired behaviour. This could be external (money), internal (a positive feeling) or vicarious (by observing other people).

target population: a target population is the group of people that a researcher is interested in investigating. The sample is then taken from this group of people.

Prompts were constructed for each study child by researchers based on information from medical records. The four conditions differed in the type of message that was presented to them on their postcard.

General prompt (*n* = 195) received the message:

> Dear Parent: Unless your doctor decided differently, your child needs X doses of X vaccines at X ages. If your child is behind in any of them (the inoculations mentioned), I urge you to make an appointment and get your child caught up.

Specific prompt (*n* = 190) received a more personalised message containing details of the exact immunisations that the child needed:

> To the Parents of (child's name), our records show that it is time for (name) to receive the following shot(s): ... (specific list provided)... Shots may be obtained FREE of charge at the: ... [specific clinic location, dates, and times].

Increased access group (*n* = 185) received the specific prompt as well as a second page that opened with the statement:

> Attention: for your convenience, two special 'off hours' clinics are being held at the [clinic name] clinic [clinic address].

Then there was an announcement of the additional clinic hours (Wednesday from 5 p.m. to 10 p.m. and Saturday from 9 a.m. to 5 p.m.) with child-care facilities that included food and entertainment. The message ended with the statement:

> Just sign all of your children in at the clinic and you may go out for the evening or day while we take care of them FREE of charge. Hope to see you there!

Monetary incentive group (*n* = 183) received the specific prompt plus a second page that opened with the statement:

> Attention: in an effort to get parents to have their children immunized against childhood diseases, the Akron Health Department with support from B. F. Goodrich is giving away $175 in cash prizes to parents who turn in the ticket attached to this page.

Instructions for lottery eligibility were made further contingent on the child's clinic attendance for immunisation by instructing parents to bring their child into the clinic for inoculation, tear off their ticket, and deposit it in the lottery box. Parents were informed that three monetary prizes ($100, $50 and $25) would be drawn in a lottery held subsequent to the intervention period.

The message ended with the statement:

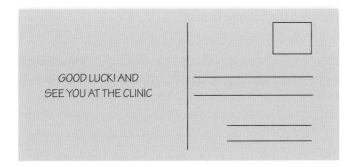

GOOD LUCK! AND
SEE YOU AT THE CLINIC

and a lottery ticket was attached to the bottom of the page.

The impact of the different prompts was measured over the following 12 weeks to assess how many of each group would attend the clinics for the immunisation injections. The results show (Figure 8.10) that the monetary incentive group had the biggest impact on attendance, followed by the increased access group, specific prompt group and general prompt group, respectively.

The data suggests that relatively powerful and immediate adherence can be produced by monetary incentives in conjunction with patient-specific prompts. However, the specific prompts alone appear to be the most cost-effective of the interventions as they were almost as effective as the monetary condition but have significantly reduced costs.

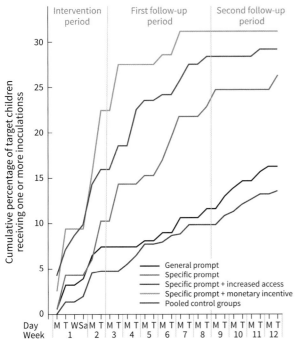

8.10 Cumulative percentage of target children receiving one or more inoculations across time periods

The Funhaler (Watt et al., 2003)

Especially with young children, making medical treatment programmes fun and engaging can have positive consequences on the levels of adherence and engagement with the medication. A novel asthma spacer device, the Funhaler (Figure 8.11), incorporates incentive toys to a child's inhaler. If the correct breathing technique is used, the child is rewarded by a fun whistle sound and a spinning toy within the inhaler.

8.11 The Funhaler

In their 2003 study Watt et al. stated that poor adherence to prescribed frequency and technique remains a major problem for paediatric asthmatics on inhaled medication and aimed to demonstrate that the Funhaler does not interfere with drug delivery and can improve a child's adherence to using their inhaler. The device incorporates a number of features to distract the attention of children from the drug delivery itself and to provide a means of self-reinforcing through the use of effective breathing techniques.

Watt et al. also stated that a study of the effect of the Funhaler on measures of paediatric adherence in the home setting found it was associated with improved parental and child compliance. For example, when surveyed at random, 38% more parents were found to have medicated their children the previous day when using the Funhaler, compared with their existing small volume spacer device, and 60% more children took the recommended four or more cycles per aerosol delivery when using the Funhaler compared with the standard spacer. This provides support that behavioural techniques can be developed to reinforce positive health behaviours and improve adherence with children.

237

ISSUES AND DEBATES

The concepts and theories discussed in this area all have **practical applications** to doctors and the medical profession in general as they signpost behavioural interventions that can be used to improve adherence to medical requests. The evidence strongly suggests that patients are more likely to adhere to a medical request if there is some form of incentive such as a monetary reward (Yokley and Glenwick) or making the process of taking the drug more enjoyable (Watt et al.).

The Yokley and Glenwich study could be considered to take a **longitudinal research** approach to studying adherence to medical requests as the research looked at the development of several levels of intervention to engage parents in a childhood inoculation programme. This type of research allows the researcher to see the impact of an intervention over a period of time and reflect on the impact that this is having on behaviour.

Much research on adherence is focused on adult adherence, or adherence directed by adults on the behalf of their children. **The use of children** as participants allows researchers to look directly at how and why children adhere to medical requests and what interventions can be put into place to improve their engagement with drug taking. The research by Watt et al. illustrates how psychological reinforcers in the form of turning the process of administering an inhaler into a fun experience, can improve a child's use of their inhaler.

Evaluation

Yokley and Glenwick's research was conducted on a large sample of people within a city suggesting a large amount of population validity. The parents who were sent the invitations to take their children to get their inoculations were not aware that they were taking part in a piece of research, which could raise ethical considerations in relation to **deception** and **informed consent**. As the researchers were asking parents of children to come in for inoculations the research is very true to life, or ecological valididity and can therefore be generalised back to many different populations.

8.3 Pain

Most people do not want pain but without it we would have serious issues. Pain seems to have three useful functions:

- It can occur before a serious injury develops; for example, the pain experienced when picking up something hot will immediately cause a person to drop it.
- It can aid learning and help people avoid harmful situations in the future.
- When it occurs in damaged joints and muscles, pain sets a limit on activity and this helps the person both to recover and to avoid further damage.

The current medical definition of pain states pain is 'an unpleasant sensory and emotional experience associated with actual or potential tissue damage, or described in terms of tissue damage, or both'. This definition is the culmination of centuries of ideas and work that have explored the concept of pain.

There are many theories (or explanations) of pain. These theories can be roughly divided into two types – physiological explanations and psychological explanations. An example of a physiological explanation is specific theory. The Gate Theory of pain is an example of an explanation of pain which combines both physiological and psychological approaches.

The way in which we experience pain is very complex. All sorts of factors influence our experience, including our thoughts and feelings. Several theoretical frameworks have been proposed to explain the physiological basis of pain, although none yet completely accounts for all aspects of pain perception.

Types and theories of pain

Until about 100 years ago pain was most frequently considered a direct consequence of physical injury, and its intensity was generally thought to be proportional to the degree of tissue damage. However, most investigators now agree that pain is both a physical and psychological phenomenon. How we actually experience pain is not merely the result of the intensity of physical injury but is a result of a number of psychological factors such as anxiety, depression, suggestion, prior conditioning, attention and cultural learning. Pain is subjective and how we experience it will differ from individual to individual.

Definitions of pain
Acute and chronic organic pain

One of the distinctions that psychologists make about types of pain is between acute pain and chronic pain. Acute pain is an intense pain that lasts until healing has begun (the pain of appendicitis or of a broken limb). Chronic pain is much more persistent, and can be constant or intermittent. Pain is said to be chronic if it has lasted for three months or more.

Acute pain begins suddenly and is usually sharp in quality. It serves as a warning of disease or a threat to the body. Acute pain might be caused by many events or circumstances, including, but not limited to:

- surgery
- broken bones
- dental work
- burns or cuts
- labour and childbirth.

Acute pain might be temporary and not too severe, or it might be severe and last for weeks. Usually, acute pain does not last longer than three months, and it disappears when the underlying cause of pain has been addressed or has healed. Untreated acute pain, however, might lead to chronic pain.

Chronic pain persists despite the fact that the injury has healed. Pain signals remain active in the nervous system perhaps for years. Physical effects include tense muscles, limited mobility, a lack of energy and changes in appetite. Emotional effects include anxiety, anger, fear of re-injury and depression. Such a fear might impact on a person's ability to return to normal work or leisure activities. Common chronic pain complaints include:

- cancer pain
- headache
- low back pain
- arthritis pain
- psychogenic pain (pain not due to past disease or injury or any visible sign of damage inside)
- neurogenic pain (pain resulting from damage to nerves).

Chronic pain might have originated with an initial trauma, injury or infection, or there might be an ongoing cause of pain. However, some people suffer chronic pain in the absence of any past injury or evidence of body damage.

Reflections: Think of as many words as you can to describe different types of pain that you have experienced. Consider what life would be like without pain. What difficulties would a person face if they did not experience pain?

Theories of pain
Specificity Theory (Descartes)
René Descartes was one of the first western philosophers to describe a detailed somatosensory pathway in humans. Descartes described pain as a perception that exists in the brain and makes the distinction between the neural phenomenon of sensory transduction (today known as **nociception**) and the perceptual experience of pain.

One of the earliest theories of pain was Specificity Theory. Specificity Theory argued that the body has a separate sensory system for perceiving pain – just as it does for hearing and vision – and this system contains its own special receptors for detecting pain stimuli and its own area of the brain for processing pain signals. When a **noxious** event stimulates a pain receptor, a signal travels to the pain centre in the brain where it is perceived as pain. This theory suggests that pain is purely a sensory experience. The more noxious an event, the more pain experienced.

KEY TERMS

nociception: the encoding and processing of harmful stimuli in the nervous system, and, therefore, the ability of a body to sense potential harm.

noxious: harmful, poisonous, or very unpleasant.

Gate Control Theory (Melzack, 1965)
Gate Control Theory takes a step further than Specificity Theory and suggests that pain perception is a combination of sensory experience and psychological gates that can increase or decrease the perception of pain. For example, you will probably be aware that there are times when, even though you have pain, you are only just aware of it. This can happen when you are really engrossed in doing something interesting or in a situation that demands all your attention.

A good example of this is the stories you might have heard about people who are able to carry on physically moving despite terrible injuries. On the other hand, it is well reported that pain can feel more severe the more time you devote to thinking about it.

Melzack (1965) suggested that the Gate Control Theory of pain is a helpful way of making sense of our pain experience to account for the clinically recognised importance of the mind and brain in pain perception. The Gate Control Theory of pain attempts to combine a physiological and psychological approach to pain. The theory argues that the nerve impulses which produce pain pass through a series of 'gates' on their way to the brain, and that these gates are influenced by messages descending from the brain and by other information that we are receiving (Table 8.12).

239

Conditions that open the gate	Conditions that close the gate
Physical conditions	*Physical conditions*
Extent of the injury	Medication
Inappropriate activity level	Counter-stimulation, e.g. massage
Emotional conditions	*Emotional conditions*
Anxiety or worry	Positive emotions
Tension	Relaxation
Depression	Rest
Mental conditions	*Mental conditions*
Focusing on pain	Intense concentration or distraction
Boredom	Involvement and interest in life activities

Table 8.12 Some of the conditions that can open or close the pain gate

Psychogenic pain (phantom limb pain)

Psychogenic pain is physical pain that is caused, increased or prolonged by mental, emotional or behavioural factors. The pain has a psychological origin or cause rather than a physical one. Headache, back pain and stomach pain are some of the most common types of psychogenic pain.

Phantom limb pain refers to ongoing painful sensations that seem to be coming from the part of the limb that is no longer there. The limb is gone, but the pain is real. The onset of this pain most often occurs soon after surgery. After amputation of a limb, an amputee continues to have an awareness of the limb and experiences sensations from it. These phantom limb sensations are also present in children born without a limb, suggesting that perception of our limbs is 'hard-wired' into our brain and that sensations from the limbs become mapped onto our brains. Therefore, if the limb is removed, there are still areas of the brain specialised to interpret sensations from nerve cells around the site of the removed limb which can be perceived as phantom limb pain.

Melzack (1992) reviewed the evidence on phantom limbs and noted that they have the following remarkable features:

- Phantom limbs have a vivid sensory quality and precise location in space – at first people sometimes try to walk on a phantom leg because it feels so real.

- Phantoms have a wide range of sensations including pressure, warmth, cold, dampness, itchiness and different kinds of pain (around 70% of amputees suffer pain in the phantom).

- In most cases, a phantom arm will hang down at the side when the person sits or stands, but moves in coordination with other limbs when the person is walking.

- Sometimes a limb gets stuck in an unusual position – for example, one person had a phantom arm bent behind them, and could not sleep on their back because the limb got in their way.

- Patients perceive phantoms as an integral part of the body – even when a phantom foot is felt to be dangling in the air several inches below the stump and unconnected to the leg, it is still experienced as part of the body and moves accordingly.

- Phantoms are also experienced by some people with spinal injuries and some paraplegics complain that their legs make continuous cycling movements, producing painful fatigue, even though their actual legs are immobile on the bed.

- Wearing an artificial arm or leg enhances the phantom, and it often fills the extension like a hand fits a glove.

The syndrome occurs in at least 90% of amputees; in two-thirds of those it manifests as an insatiable itch in the missing limb, and many feel extreme discomfort or even chronic pain. In most cases, painkillers and surgical treatment have no effect. Melzack gave an explanation for these findings, suggesting that the brain contains a neuromatrix or network of neurons. This neuromatrix responds to information from the senses and also generates a characteristic pattern of impulses that indicate that the body is whole and is also your own. You could think of this as a mental hologram but Melzack called it the neurosignature. If a limb is removed, the sensations cease from that region but the hologram is still created in the neuromatrix.

New approaches, based on a better understanding of the brain's role in pain, may be opening the way to new treatments such as the mirror box (see Figure 8.12). A mirror box is a box with two mirrors in the centre (one facing each way), invented by V. S. Ramachandran to help relieve phantom limb pain. The patient places the good limb in one side of the mirror box, and the stump in the other. The patient then looks at the mirror on the side with the good limb. Because the subject is seeing the reflected image of the good hand moving, it appears as if the phantom limb is also moving. Through the use of this artificial visual

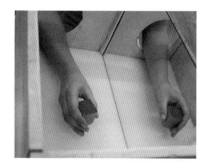

feedback it becomes possible for the patient to 'move' the phantom limb, and to unclench it from potentially painful positions.

8.12 The mirror box for amputees

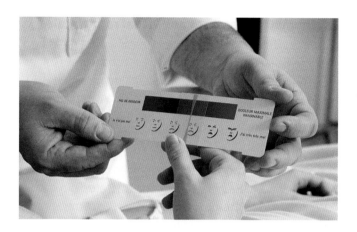

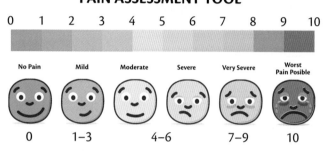

Measuring pain

Pain is a subjective experience and it is therefore impossible to feel or observe other people's pain directly, so it has to be measured indirectly, by communicating with the sufferer. The measurement of pain is important for research and as a diagnostic tool for medical treatment. There are three main ways in which we can measure pain: to use a physiological method such as an EEG (electroencephalogram) which records brain activity, to observe pain behaviour and lastly to ask the patient, using self-report measures (Figure 8.13).

Measures of a patient's pain must be reliable and accurately reflect the intensity of pain being experienced. The practice of assessing pain as 'the fifth vital sign' has become widespread, despite a lack of published evidence demonstrating the accuracy and effectiveness of screening strategies.

Self-report measures (clinical interview)

Self-report of pain intensity is the preferred approach to pain assessment. There are several tools available to reliably assess pain; however, there is no accepted criterion standard. Chronic pain is a complex phenomenon, involving not just the intensity of the pain, but location, type and duration of the pain. It is most common to focus on pain intensity, but good pain assessment should consider as many criteria as possible to get an overview of how the patient is experiencing the pain and not just ask patients 'how much does it hurt?'.

Pain intensity, pain quality, pain location and duration of pain all need to be considered when discussing a patient's experience of pain. *Pain intensity* can be measured through several different means such as psychometric measures like the McGill Pain Questionnaire, observation or by measuring the impact of the pain (counting the number of painkillers a person is taking).

Pain quality is usually measured by self-report measures which consider the level of unpleasantness on two measures (deep and surface pain) and several descriptions such as

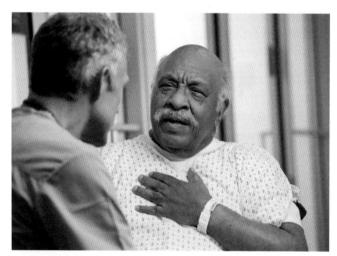

8.13 Self-report measures

sharp, cutting, throbbing and tingling. The second part of the McGill Pain Questionnaire used this method of measurement.

Pain location is usually measured by asking patients to identify the area of the body where they are experiencing pain. This can sometimes be in a limb that has been removed (such as those suffering with phantom limb pain). For those who have difficulty verbalising the location of pain, such as young children or those with impaired language, an outline of a body may be used on which the patient can draw where they are experiencing the pain. An example of this can be seen in the Paediatric Pain Questionnaire.

241

Psychometric measures and visual rating scales

A visual analogue scale (VAS) is a tool that is used to measure a characteristic, attitude or feeling across a continuum of values. The VAS usually takes the form of a line 100mm in length with descriptors at either end showing alternative ends of the spectrum. The patient marks on the line the level of pain that they are currently suffering and a VAS score can be calculated by measuring the distance from the starting point to the mark. This allows scores over time to be compared and recorded. It is particularly useful for measuring things that are difficult to quantify by allowing respondents to give a relative measure of their current state. This is more similar to the perception of pain as it does not take measured 'steps' from one stage to another like other psychometric measures suggest (e.g. providing groups of words in increasing severity).

Because pain is a subjective, internal experience, the measurement of pain is usually carried out using patient self-reports. The McGill Pain Questionnaire, developed by Melzack (1975), was the first proper self-report pain-measuring instrument and is still the most widely used today.

To compile the adjectives for the self-report measure, Melzack used a sample of doctors and university graduates to classify adjectives into groups describing different aspects of pain. The three groups or dimensions of pain were:

- *Sensory*: what the pain feels like physically – for example 'burning', 'throbbing'
- *Affective*: what the pain feels like emotionally – whether it is frightening, worrying and so on
- *Evaluative*: what the subjective overall intensity of the pain experience is – for example 'unbearable', 'distressing'.

A similar sample then had to rate each word for intensity.

Patients are asked to tick the word in each class that best describes their pain. Based on this, a Pain Rating Index (PRI) is calculated. In addition, patients are asked to indicate the location of the pain on a body chart (Figure 8.14).

Behavioural and observational methods

Behaviourists believe that we should not investigate subjective feelings, cognitions or emotions but should consider only observable behaviour. Behaviourists have noticed that people tend to behave in certain ways when they are in pain, such as complaints, gestures and postures, and from this finding have designed pain behavioural scales. One such scale, the UAB Pain Behavioural Scale (Figure 8.15), consists of target behaviours (body language, mobility, posture and so on). The observer has to judge how frequently each behaviour occurs.

Part 1. Where is your pain?
Please mark, on the drawing below, the areas where you feel pain. Put E if external, or I if internal, near the areas which you mark. Put EI if both external and internal.

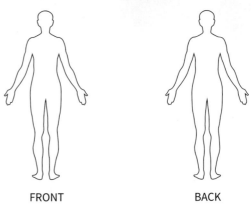

FRONT   BACK

Part 2. What does your pain feel like?
Some of the words below describe your *present* pain. Circle *ONLY* those words that best describe it. Leave out any category that is not suitable. Use only a single word in each appropriate category – the one that applies best.

1	2	3	4
Flickering	Jumping	Pricking	Sharp
Quivering	Flashing	Boring	Cutting
Pulsing	Shooting	Drilling	Lacerating
Throbbing		Stabbing	
Beating		Lancinating	
Pounding			

5	6	7	8
Pinching	Tugging	Hot	Tingling
Pressing	Pulling	Burning	Itchy
Gnawing	Wrenching	Scalding	Smarting
Cramping		Searing	Stinging
Crushing			

9	10	11	12
Dull	Tender	Tiring	Sickening
Sore	Taut	Exhausting	Suffocating
Hurting	Rasping		
Aching	Splitting		
Heavy			

13	14	15	16
Fearful	Punishing	Wretched	Annoying
Frightful	Gruelling	Blinding	Troublesome
Terrifying	Cruel		Miserbale
	Vicious		Intense
	Killing		Unbearable

17	18	19	20
Spreading	Tight	Cool	Nagging
Radiating	Numb	Cold	Nauseating
Penetrating	Drawing	Freezing	Agonising
Piercing	Squeezing		Dreadful
	Tearing		Torturing

Table 8.14 Rating pain

UAB Pain Behaviour Scale

Name: ....

Rater: ....

		M	T	W	T	F	S	S	M	T	W	T	F	S	S	M	T	W	T	F	S	S
1 Vocal complaints: verbal	None	1	1	1	1	1	1	1	1	1	1	1	1	1	1	1	1	1	1	1	1	1
	Occasional	½	½	½	½	½	½	½	½	½	½	½	½	½	½	½	½	½	½	½	½	½
	Frequent	0	0	0	0	0	0	0	0	0	0	0	0	0	0	0	0	0	0	0	0	0
2 Vocal complaints: non-verbal *(moans, groans, gasps, etc.)*	None	1	1	1	1	1	1	1	1	1	1	1	1	1	1	1	1	1	1	1	1	1
	Occasional	½	½	½	½	½	½	½	½	½	½	½	½	½	½	½	½	½	½	½	½	½
	Frequent	0	0	0	0	0	0	0	0	0	0	0	0	0	0	0	0	0	0	0	0	0
3 Down-time *(time spent lying down per day because of pain: 8 am–8 pm)*	None	1	1	1	1	1	1	1	1	1	1	1	1	1	1	1	1	1	1	1	1	1
	0–60 min	½	½	½	½	½	½	½	½	½	½	½	½	½	½	½	½	½	½	½	½	½
	>60 min	0	0	0	0	0	0	0	0	0	0	0	0	0	0	0	0	0	0	0	0	0
4 Facial grimaces	None	1	1	1	1	1	1	1	1	1	1	1	1	1	1	1	1	1	1	1	1	1
	Mild and/or infrequent	½	½	½	½	½	½	½	½	½	½	½	½	½	½	½	½	½	½	½	½	½
	Severe and/or infrequent	0	0	0	0	0	0	0	0	0	0	0	0	0	0	0	0	0	0	0	0	0
5 Standing posture	None	1	1	1	1	1	1	1	1	1	1	1	1	1	1	1	1	1	1	1	1	1
	Mildly impaired	½	½	½	½	½	½	½	½	½	½	½	½	½	½	½	½	½	½	½	½	½
	Distorted	0	0	0	0	0	0	0	0	0	0	0	0	0	0	0	0	0	0	0	0	0
6 Mobility	No visible impairment	1	1	1	1	1	1	1	1	1	1	1	1	1	1	1	1	1	1	1	1	1
	Mild limp and/or laboured walking	½	½	½	½	½	½	½	½	½	½	½	½	½	½	½	½	½	½	½	½	½
	Marked limp and/or laboured walking	0	0	0	0	0	0	0	0	0	0	0	0	0	0	0	0	0	0	0	0	0
7 Body Language *(clutching, rubbing site of pain)*	None	1	1	1	1	1	1	1	1	1	1	1	1	1	1	1	1	1	1	1	1	1
	Occasional	½	½	½	½	½	½	½	½	½	½	½	½	½	½	½	½	½	½	½	½	½
	Frequent	0	0	0	0	0	0	0	0	0	0	0	0	0	0	0	0	0	0	0	0	0
8 Use of visible supportive equipment *(braces, crutches, cane, leaning on furniture, TENS, etc). Do not score if equipment prescribed.*	None	1	1	1	1	1	1	1	1	1	1	1	1	1	1	1	1	1	1	1	1	1
	Occasional	½	½	½	½	½	½	½	½	½	½	½	½	½	½	½	½	½	½	½	½	½
	Dependent: constant use	0	0	0	0	0	0	0	0	0	0	0	0	0	0	0	0	0	0	0	0	0
9 Stationary movement	Sits or stands still	1	1	1	1	1	1	1	1	1	1	1	1	1	1	1	1	1	1	1	1	1
	Occasional shifts of position	½	½	½	½	½	½	½	½	½	½	½	½	½	½	½	½	½	½	½	½	½
	Constant movement, position shifts	0	0	0	0	0	0	0	0	0	0	0	0	0	0	0	0	0	0	0	0	0
10 Medication	None	1	1	1	1	1	1	1	1	1	1	1	1	1	1	1	1	1	1	1	1	1
	Non-narcotic analgesic and/or psychogenic medications as prescribed	½	½	½	½	½	½	½	½	½	½	½	½	½	½	½	½	½	½	½	½	½
	Demands for increased dosage or frequency, and/or narcotics, and/or medication abuse	0	0	0	0	0	0	0	0	0	0	0	0	0	0	0	0	0	0	0	0	0
TOTAL																						

Table 8.15 The UAB Pain Behaviour Scale

RESEARCH METHODS

Why would it be important to have operational definitions for the behaviours and the frequencies on the UAB?

The UAB Pain Behaviour Scale can be used to track the severity of chronic pain over time. This can help determine the level of pain control and identify temporal associations that can influence management. There are ten types of question and each item is scored on a three-point scale (0, 0.5, 1). The higher the score, the more marked the pain-associated behaviour and the greater the level of impairment. Therefore, a patient can get a score of between 0 and 10.

1. vocal complaints – verbal
2. vocal complaints – non-verbal (groans, moans gasps, etc.)
3. down time (time spent lying down because of pain per day from 8 a.m. to 8 p.m.)
4. facial grimaces
5. standing posture
6. mobility
7. body language (clutching/rubbing site)
8. use of visible support equipment (braces, crutches, cane, leaning on furniture, transcutaneous electrical nerve stimulation (TENS), etc.)
9. stationary movement (ability to stay still)
10. medication use.

Pain measures for children
Paediatric Pain Questionnaire (Varni & Thompson, 1987)

We already know that measuring pain in adults is very difficult due to validity and reliability issues. Various pain assessment tools are available for children who are old enough to communicate. Pain scales have been developed using numbers, colours and facial expressions. In pre-verbal children, several pain scales have been validated. The CHEOPS (Children's Hospital of Eastern Ontario Pain Scale) is a well-validated tool for the assessment of pain in children. It was initially developed for post-surgical patients, but has been used broadly since.

Varni and Thompson's Paediatric Pain Questionnaire (PPQ) is a multidimensional questionnaire for assessing childhood pain, with separate forms for the patient (child),

the parent and the doctor. It was created after the McGill Pain Questionnaire and assesses the perceptions of the patient's pain experience in a child-friendly format. Specifically, this instrument measures pain intensity, location and the sensory, evaluative and **affective** qualities of the pain.

KEY TERM

affective: relating to mental disorders in which disturbance of mood is the primary symptom.

The PPQ allows a comprehensive assessment of pain in children with chronic pain. The different forms use different formats, such as using colours for younger children and descriptive terms for adolescents.

Children are first asked to circle words that best describe the pain that they are suffering and then must choose the three that describe the pain they are in at the time of completing the questionnaire.

Circle the words that best describe your pain, or the way you feel when you are in pain:

cutting	pounding	tingling	tiring	deep
squeezing	throbbing	horrible	stabbing	burning
pulling	sickening	biting	screaming	scraping
aching	uncomfortable	cold	miserable	stretching
pricking	hot	scared	lonely	jumping
pinching	unbearable	sad	itching	grabbing
stinging	sharp	sore	flashing	pins and needles

The child is then asked to rate how they feel at the time on a continuum as well as rating the worst pain they had this week on the same scale.

Not hurting
No discomfort ———————— Very uncomfortable
No pain
Hurting a whole lot
Severe pain

8.16 Asking children about how they perceive pain

244

Finally, they are asked to pick four colouring pens and colour in the picture of themselves, with one colour meaning no pain, another for mild pain, a third for moderate pain and the final colour for severe pain (see Figure 8.17).

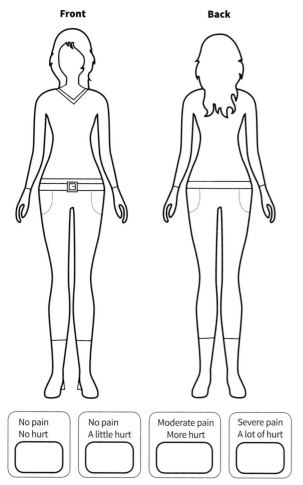

Front   **Back**

| No pain
No hurt | No pain
A little hurt | Moderate pain
More hurt | Severe pain
A lot of hurt |

8.17 Asking children about how they perceive pain

Wong-Baker Scale

The Wong-Baker FACES Rating Scale (Figure 8.18) was developed for young patients to communicate how much pain they are feeling. The scale shows a series of faces ranging from a happy face at 0, 'No hurt', to a crying face at 10, 'Hurts worst'. The patient must choose the face that best describes how they are feeling. The rating scale is recommended for children aged three and older.

Wong-Baker FACES® Pain Rating Scale

| 0
No
hurt | 2
Hurts
little bit | 4
Hurts little
more | 6
Hurts even
more | 8
Hurts
whole lot | 10
Hurts
worst |

8.18 Wong-Baker FACES Rating Scale

The child is told that each face is for a person who feels happy because he has no pain (hurt) or sad because he has some or a lot of pain.

Face 0   is very happy because he doesn't hurt at all.

Face 2   hurts just a little bit.

Face 4   hurts a little more.

Face 6   hurts even more.

Face 8   hurts a whole lot more.

Face 10 hurts as much as you can imagine, although you do not have to be crying to feel this bad.

The child is asked to choose the face that best describes how they are feeling.

This scale has been validated outside the emergency department, mostly for chronic pain. Garra et al. (2010) were able to demonstrate a significant difference in the visual analogue scale for each of the Wong-Baker FACES Scale ordinal categories. The visual analogue scale was found to have an excellent correlation in older children with acute pain and had a uniformly increasing relationship with the Wong-Baker FACES Scale.

245

> **Reflections:** Is using faces a good way to ask children how much pain they are in? Can you think of any other ways that a doctor could use to gauge how much pain a child was suffering?

ISSUES AND DEBATES

Although specificity theory contains features that have received research support, the theory cannot adequately explain pain perception as it is **reductionist** and only focuses on biological explanations of behaviour. One of the problems with specificity theory is that the pain area of the brain it proposes does not exist. Perhaps the most serious problem with specificity theory (and other mechanistic theories of pain) is that it does not attempt to explain how the experience of pain is affected by psychological factors. Specificity theory uses a physiological approach and does not recognise the psychological factors which influence how we perceive pain.

All of the theories of pain have **useful applications to everyday life** as they help health practitioners understand why individuals perceive pain and as a result should be able to develop intervention strategies and

ISSUES AND DEBATES (continued)

treatment programmes to help with this. For example, theories, like the Gate Control Theory of pain, that suggest that the brain can have a top-down influence on pain perception, have led to practitioners developing techniques such as imagery and meditation to help people control their pain perceptions. The improved understanding of pain through research into phantom limb pain has also allowed researchers to develop treatments (such as the mirror box) for those individuals who have had amputations and experience phantom pain following this.

SELF-ASSESSMENT QUESTIONS

8   What do intensity, duration and location refer to when discussing pain perception?

Managing and controlling pain

Psychologists have investigated the many different ways in which people can manage and control pain. A major distinction can be made between medical techniques used to manage pain, such as taking drugs or surgical treatment, and psychological ways of managing stress such as cognitive training to cope with pain. We will also discuss some alternative methods for controlling pain such as acupuncture and stimulation therapy. The Gate Control Theory of pain would suggest that we use a combination of psychological and physical treatments.

Medical techniques

Surgical treatments are used when medication doesn't relieve pain. Such treatments can consist of cutting nerve pathways or making lesions in special centres in the brain. Surgical treatment is usually only recommended for people with terminal illnesses. There are also several physical therapies that are used to ease and manage pain. These include manual therapies such as massage, mechanical therapies such as ultrasound and traction and heat treatments such as microwave diathermy, cold treatments such as ice packs, and electrotherapy such as electrical nerve stimulation.

Reflections: If you were in pain, what would you turn to first to reduce it? Drugs? Would you ever consider a different method of pain relief?

Biochemical methods may be used to relieve pain. An analgesic or painkiller is any member of the group of drugs used to achieve analgesia (relief from pain). Analgesic drugs act in various ways on the central nervous system. The type of medicine that you need to treat your pain depends on what type of pain you have. The aim of taking medication is to improve your quality of life. All painkillers have potential side effects, so you need to weigh up the advantages of taking them against the disadvantages.

For pain associated with inflammation, such as back pain or headaches, paracetamol and anti-inflammatory painkillers work best. Pain caused by sensitive or damaged nerves is usually treated with tablets that are also used for epilepsy and depression. These tablets change the way the central nervous system works.

The most popular chemical treatment for pain is aspirin. Aspirin and other similar drugs such as ibuprofen have three therapeutic actions: first, against pain; secondly, against inflammation; and thirdly, against fever. They appear to work on the damaged tissue that is causing the pain and inflammation, and they have no known effect on the nervous system. These drugs are heavily used today and the only physical drawback is the number of side effects such as gastric irritation and bleeding and also (with large doses) deafness.

Other drugs include paracetamol and opiates. Opiates inhibit pain messages from travelling to the brain; in other words, they close the gate, preventing the pain signals getting to the brain. Morphine and morphine-like drugs (for example, oxycodone, fentanyl and buprenorphine) are the strongest painkillers there are. Some come as a patch, but they all work in similar ways and should only be used for severe pain. They will only be prescribed after consultation with a GP or a pain specialist and the dose and response will be closely monitored.

Psychological techniques: cognitive strategies

Over the past few years there has been a growing acceptance of the value of psychological interventions in the treatment of pain. Included in these interventions are relaxation, biofeedback, hypnosis, cognitive coping skills, operant techniques, mental imaging, self-efficacy and counselling.

Attention diversion, non-pain imagery and cognitive redefinition

Cognitive redefinition is where an individual attempts to alter their thinking to replace thought of apprehension about the pain with other more positive thoughts. This cognitive approach is related to distraction therapies and involves the patient replacing thoughts such as "*this is really going to hurt*" with "*this is not the worst pain in the world*". It is a top-down approach that suggests that the brain can have a significant impact on the way that pain is perceived. Further to this, it can involve therapists attempting to 'redefine' the perception of pain as some other feeling by encouraging a patient to consider the pain sensation as a different sensation such as warmth.

Attention management is often included in cognitive behavioural treatments (CBT). Patients vary in their response to attention diversion strategies and there are individual differences in what diversion techniques are effective as a method of pain relief. The core concept of attention diversion is to divert attention from the pain by refocusing or directing attention to something other than the pain. According to the Gate Control Theory this will help close the gates and reduce the perception of pain.

Deliberately using imagery, attention diversion and mindfulness to cope with pain can take many forms as there are many ways to divert attention away from pain. People who suffer chronic pain have reported that engaging in an activity that is enjoyable is the most effective attention diversion. Interesting activities and mental distracters can become effective methods of attention diversion and pain relief. It is rare to offer a single form of coping strategy like attention management in isolation from other aspects of a cognitive behavioural approach to pain management.

Morley, Shapiro and Biggs (2004) developed a training programme in which they taught patients how to use attention diversion strategies such as:

- use of imagery and mindfulness: creating vivid and pleasant images to concentrate on
- basic attention management: brief relaxation, internal and external attention focus
- pain coping strategies: coping self-statements, signal breathing

- discussion on dealing with pain and relationship to pain and its chronic nature, discussion of all sessions and the use of skills
- attention diversion and mindfulness: focus on the details of experience, mindfulness breathing exercises, integrating mindfulness in everyday activities, external, mental and somatic focus of attention
- intense pain and flare-ups: identifying responses to pain and vicious cycles in thoughts, images and behaviour, defusing catastrophising and breaking vicious cycles
- pain transformation images: creating images to transform pain.

In the first time period until the three month follow-up, pain intensity reduced significantly and this pain reduction was maintained at the six month follow-up, but to a lesser degree. Participants reported they used brief relaxation, use of imagery and distraction towards external objects most regularly, and reported benefits such as developing skills to deal with pain (*n* = 9), altered attitudes to pain (*n* = 10), improved sleep patterns (*n* = 8) and stress reduction (*n* = 4).

Alternative techniques

Acupuncture is a treatment derived from ancient Chinese medicine in which fine needles are inserted at certain sites in the body for therapeutic or preventative purposes (Figure 8.19). It is often seen as a form of complementary or alternative medicine. Western medical acupuncture is the use of acupuncture after a proper medical diagnosis. It is based on scientific evidence that shows the treatment can stimulate nerves under the skin and in muscle tissue.

247

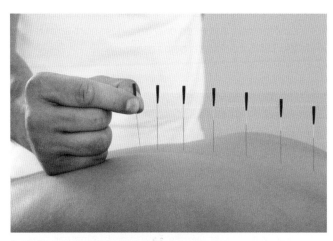

8.19 A patient undergoing acupuncture

This results in the body producing pain-relieving substances, such as endorphins. It is likely these substances are responsible for any beneficial effects seen with this form of acupuncture. Traditional acupuncture is based on the belief that an energy, or 'life force', flows through the body in channels called meridians. This life force is known as *Qi* (pronounced 'chee'). Acupuncturists believe that when *Qi* can not flow freely through the body, sickness can result. They also believe acupuncture can restore the flow of *Qi*, and so restore health.

Transcutaneous electrical nerve stimulation (TENS) is a method of pain relief involving the use of a mild electrical current. A TENS machine is a small, battery-operated device that has leads connected to sticky pads called electrodes (Figure 8.20). When the machine is switched on, small electric impulses are passed through the pads to areas of the body where you are experiencing muscle pain. These impulses can reduce the pain signals passing along nerves in the body and can help an individual relax. As well as the tingling sensation that you might get when

using the machine, it is suggested that the electric impulses can also stimulate endorphins which are the body's natural opiates (painkillers).

8.20 A TENS machine

Health care professionals have reported that it seems to help some people, although how well it works depends on the individual and the condition being treated. The main use of TENS is to help reduce the perception of deep muscle pain, or pain in muscles due to anxiety and stress. TENS is not a cure for pain and often only provides short-term relief while the TENS machine is being used.

ISSUES AND DEBATES

When developing methods to control and manage pain, it is important to recognise that both biological and psychological factors combine when we perceive pain. Consequently, any method used to manage pain effectively should not be **reductionist**, like the biomedical approach, and attempt to explain and treat the pain in a simplistic and narrow way, but instead take

ISSUES AND DEBATES (continued)

a more holistic approach to treat the entire individual, both physiologically and psychologically. The alternative techniques discussed often tend to focus heavily on psychological influences when treating pain, whereas the cognitive methods of imagery also fail to recognise the biological factors in how we experience pain.

The most **useful application** that comes from our understanding of pain is that the most effective pain relief will probably come from combining the different biological and psychological techniques. Further to this, it is important to note the improved quality of life that someone can experience when they are not in pain, especially those who suffer from chronic pain, and anything that can improve the quality of life for an individual is of significant importance to psychology. Especially with techniques such as imagery or cognitive behavioural therapy, it is a relatively simple way of managing pain that can be learned by most people regardless of level of their age, sex or cultural background.

SELF-ASSESSMENT QUESTIONS

9   Why might imagery or a cognitive therapy be the most effective pain relief for all types of pain?

8.4 Stress

Stress is caused by two things: levels of anxiety and your body's reactions to your thought processes. The instinctive stress response to unexpected events is known as 'fight or flight'. Stress happens when we feel that we are not in control of events in our lives and comes in many forms, both positive and negative, and can have many triggers and physiological responses.

Many of life's demands can cause stress, particularly work, relationships and money problems. When you feel stressed, the stress itself can get in the way of sorting out these demands, and can affect everything you do.

Stress is an inevitable part of life, but it is not a purely negative phenomenon. It can also result from intense joy or pleasure as well as fear or anxiety. Researchers have coined the term *eustress*, or beneficial stress, to reflect the fact that positive experiences such as a promotion, marriage, having children and many others are also stressful.

Reflections: What events in your life have caused you stress and anxiety? Is it the small things mounting up or big life events that cause you the most worry?

Sources of stress

There are many different ways of investigating the causes or sources of stress. One way is to investigate environmental changes which cause stress. Such changes are called *stressors*. Modern life is full of frustrations, deadlines and demands. For many people, stress is so commonplace that it has become a way of life. As discussed above, stress isn't always bad. Stress within your comfort zone can help you perform under pressure, motivate you to do your best, even keep you safe when danger looms. But when stress becomes overwhelming, it can damage your health, mood, relationships and quality of life.

Top 5:
Sources of Stress

What causes our stress? In an annual survey by the American Psychological Association, here are the top sources of stress, and the percentage of respondents who identified each as a "very significant" source of stress.

❶ Money		**76%**
❷ Work		**70%**
❸ The economy		**66%**
❹ Family responsibilities		**59%**
❺ Relationships		**55%**

Source: APA Stress in America survey, 2010 (most recent stats available)

8.21 Sources of stress, as found by the American Psychological Association in 2010

Physiology of stress and effects on health

The physiological model is primarily concerned with what happens within the person, usually as a response to stressors. Central to our understanding of the physiological basis of stress is the concept of arousal. Arousal refers to a general physiological state in which the **sympathetic division of the autonomic nervous system** is activated (Figure 8.22). The function of the sympathetic division is to rouse the body to action, and it does so by activating a number of physiological mechanisms which produce or maintain alertness and energy.

KEY TERM

sympathetic division of the autonomic nervous system: the autonomic nervous system controls the internal organs of the body and plays an essential role in keeping the body's internal environment stable. It also plays a major part in our emotional experience to external situations. The sympathetic division is our emergency system. It prepares the body to produce energy and to protect it from the effects of stress and injury: this is sometimes referred to as the 'fight or flight' response.

The GAS Model (Selye, 1936)

Immediate responses to stressful or anxiety-provoking events generate a high level of arousal. The human stress response involves many components, as Selye's work portrayed. He observed that long-term adaptation to stress followed a three-stage pattern, which he named the General Adaptation Syndrome (GAS) (Figure 8.23). GAS is a term describing the body's short- and long-term reactions and adaptations to stress in order to restore **homeostasis**.

KEY TERM

homeostasis: the control of internal conditions, be it temperature, specific blood conditions or other variables within living organisms.

Selye suggested that there are three stages that lead to illness, linking stress and illness. He believed that stress

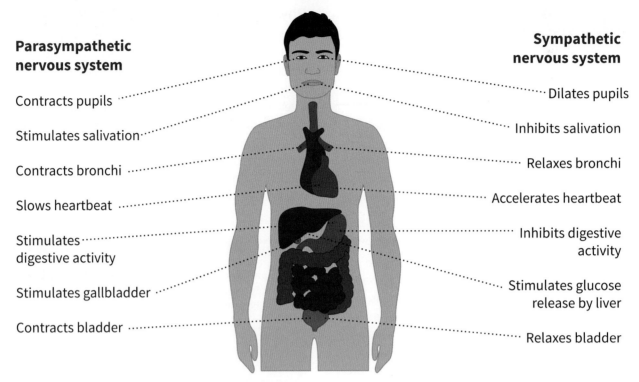

Parasympathetic nervous system

Contracts pupils

Stimulates salivation

Contracts bronchi

Slows heartbeat

Stimulates digestive activity

Stimulates gallbladder

Contracts bladder

Sympathetic nervous system

Dilates pupils

Inhibits salivation

Relaxes bronchi

Accelerates heartbeat

Inhibits digestive activity

Stimulates glucose release by liver

Relaxes bladder

8.22 Comparison of the parasympathetic and sympathetic nervous system

250

results in the depletion of physiological resources, lowering resistance to infection. The three stages of Selye's GAS are: alarm, resistance and exhaustion.

- *Alarm*: like the 'fight or flight' response, the stressor upsets the homeostasis of the body. The function of this stage is to prepare the body's resources. We might respond to narrowly missing a serious car accident in the same way. Our bodies immediately release hormones, including cortisol and adrenaline, to provide instant energy.
- *Resistance*: the body adapts to the stressor and physiological arousal declines but is still above normal. This is the body fighting back by adjusting to the stress.
- *Exhaustion*: this occurs when long-term stress is not removed. Eventually the body's energy reserves become depleted and the ability to resist declines. If stress continues then disease, damage and death can follow.

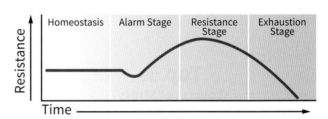

8.23 Selye's General Adaptation Syndrome

Selye suggested that early symptoms of almost any disease or trauma are virtually the same, that is, the body responds identically to any stressor. In modern life, however, we rarely respond to perceived threat with actual action. Moreover, perceived threats do not have to be present in a physical form and so they are difficult to quantify or avoid. They might also be continuous. This means that the threat may be continuous and nebulous. For example, the concern that financial problems might result in homelessness does not represent a direct physical threat, but it may result in an acute and ongoing perceived threat.

Causes of stress
Work (Chandola et al., 2008)

Workplace stress is the result of a conflict between the demands that a job might place on its employees and the extent of the control an employee has to meet the demands. It can be a damaging physical and emotional response. In general, the combination of high demands in a job and a low amount of control over the situation can lead to stress. Stress in the workplace might come from one single event or many sources. It can impact on both employees and employers alike. In 2001, the Higher Education Funding Council of England conducted a three year study of occupational stress. The main causes of stress identified were: long hours, job security, particularly in relation to terms of employment, work relationships, access to resources and communications.

Stress at work is associated with an increased risk of **coronary heart disease (CHD)** but the reasons underlying this association remain unclear. Chandola et al. (2008) wanted to determine the biological and behavioural factors linking work stress with CHD.

KEY TERM

coronary heart disease (CHD): Coronary heart disease (CHD) occurs where a waxy substance called plaque builds up inside the coronary arteries. These arteries supply oxygen-rich blood to your heart muscle. Hardened plaque narrows the coronary arteries and reduces the flow of oxygen-rich blood to the heart.

Chandola et al. analysed data collected from the Whitehall II study to investigate the following three questions:

- Is the accumulation of work stress associated with higher chances of developing CHD?
- Is this association stronger among the working-age population?
- Does work stress affect CHD directly through **neuroendocrine mechanisms** (Figure 8.24) or indirectly through behavioural risk factors?

KEY TERM

neuroendocrine mechanisms: the system by which the hypothalamus maintains homeostasis, regulating reproduction, metabolism, eating and drinking behaviour, energy utilisation and blood pressure.

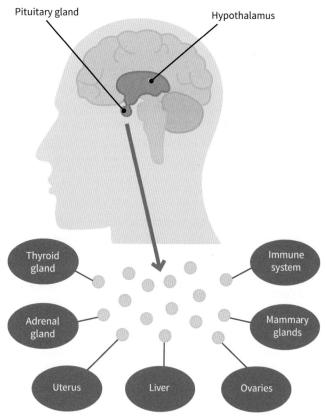

8.24 Neuroendocrine mechanisms

The Whitehall II study was established to explore the relationship between socio-economic status, stress and cardiovascular disease. A sample of 10 308 participants aged 35–55, of whom 3413 were women and 6895 men, was recruited from the British Civil Service in 1985. Since this first wave of data collection in 1985, self-report questionnaires and clinical data have been collected from the cohort every two to five years with data collection intended to continue until 2030.

Evidence from the Whitehall II study suggests that workers who report work stress more often in their working careers have increased risks of heart disease, obesity and cardiovascular risk. A job strain questionnaire was used at two points in the study to provide a measure of cumulative work stress. Job strain was defined as a high job demand with low personal control over the job and decision making. People who have job strain and who are socially isolated at work (without supportive co-workers) were said to have work stress.

Chandola et al. recorded the number of non-fatal heart attacks as well as deaths due to heart disease that occurred during the study. They also collected information on biological risk factors for heart disease such as cholesterol, blood pressure, blood sugar levels, waist circumference, cortisol levels and heart rate variability; and behavioural risk factors such as alcohol, smoking, diet and exercise.

The results suggest that cumulative work stress is a high risk factor for developing CHD, especially among the younger, working-age population. Around 32% of the effect of work stress on CHD can be explained by the effect of work stress on health behaviours such as low physical activity and poor diet. Chronic work stress was associated with CHD and this association was stronger among participants under 50.

There were similar associations between work stress and low physical activity, poor diet and lower heart rate variability. Work stress was associated with a higher morning rise in cortisol. Around 32% of the effect of work stress on CHD was attributable to its effect on health behaviours and the metabolic syndrome.

Life events (Holmes & Rahe, 1967)

People use the word 'stress' to describe a wide variety of situations: from your mobile phone ringing while you are busy on another task, to the feelings associated with intense work overload, or the death of a loved one. Perhaps the most useful and widely accepted definition of stress is: *a condition or feeling experienced when a person perceives that demands exceed the personal and social resources they are able to make use of.* In other words, we feel stressed when we feel that things are out of control.

Life events are defined as experiences that disrupt an individual's usual activities, causing a substantial change and readjustment. Examples of life events include marriage, divorce, illness or injury, and changing or losing a job. Lots of research into stress has focused on life events and these have been considered as an important type of stressor.

When investigating the causes and sources of stress, Holmes and Rahe (1967) looked at what makes a situation stressful. This is often called the stressful life event approach or the engineering model. They suggested that living through life events that were stressful could cause serious damage to an individual's health. One of their major findings was that stress generated by such events seemed to build up. Whether a particularly stressful period produced illness later on depended on just how much stress had been accumulated and people who had experienced a very high number of stressful life events in a certain period were very much more likely to experience a prolonged illness in the following year than people who had not.

Using medical case histories and interviews, Holmes and Rahe studied a large number of people who were suffering, or had suffered, from extreme stress. From this data, they developed a social readjustment scale, which ranked life events according to how much stress they appeared to give people. Not every life event was the same: for example, going through a divorce or suffering bereavement was very much more stressful than changing one's eating or sleeping habits. Using a sample of 394 patients, Holmes and Rahe were able to rank 43 life events on their scale, from those that cause the most stress (death of a spouse) to those that cause the least stress (minor violations in law and Christmas) as shown in Table 8.13.

Rank	Life event	Mean value
1	Death of spouse	100
2	Divorce	73
3	Marital separation	65
4	Jail term	63
5	Death of close family member	63
6	Personal injury or illness	53
7	Marriage	50
8	Fired at work	47
9	Marital reconciliation	45
10	Retirement	45
11	Change in health of family member	44
12	Pregnancy	40
13	Sex difficulties	39
14	Gain of new family member	39
15	Business readjustment	39
16	Change in financial state	38
17	Death of close friend	37
18	Change to different line of work	36
19	Change in number of arguments with spouse	35
20	Mortgage over $10 000	31

Rank	Life event	Mean value
21	Foreclosure of mortgage or loan	30
22	Change in responsibility at work	29
23	Son or daughter leaving home	29
24	Trouble with in-laws	29
25	Outstanding personal achievement	28
26	Wife begin or stop work	26
27	Begin or end school	26
28	Change in living conditions	25
29	Revision of personal habits	24
30	Trouble with boss	23
31	Change in work hours or conditions	20
32	Change in residence	20
33	Change in schools	20
34	Change in recreation	19
35	Change in church activities	19
36	Change in social activities	18
37	Mortgage or loan less than $10 000	17
38	Change in sleeping habits	16
39	Change in number of family get-togethers	15
40	Change in eating habits	15
41	Vacation	13
42	Christmas	12
43	Minor violations of the law	11

Table 8.13 Social readjustment rating scale

Personality (Friedman & Rosenman, 1974)

Friedman and Rosenman (1974) believed that the causes of stress come from the individual and that a person's personality will determine whether they are susceptible to stress or not. This approach to personality, known as Type A and Type B personality, was originally developed as an attempt to explain why it was that some people seemed to be particularly prone to CHD, while peers who also work hard, were not.

Type A characteristics	Type B characteristics
Highly competitive	Non-competitive
Works fast	Works more slowly
Strong desire to succeed	Lacking in desire to succeed
Likes control	Does not enjoy control
Prone to suffer stress	Less prone to stress

Table 8.14 Type A and Type B characteristics compared

Friedman and Rosenman (1974) observed that the people who seemed to be particularly susceptible to CHD also tended to have certain personality similarities (Table 8.14). These they argued formed the Type A pattern, which consists of three major facets.

The first is a competitive achievement orientation, in that these people are critical of themselves and set goals without feeling any sense of happiness when they accomplish them. The second personality characteristic is time urgency. Type A individuals are very conscious of time, arranging a huge number of commitments, attempting to complete more than one thing at once and expressing impatience with delays. The third facet of Type A personality is a high level of anger and/or hostility, which may or may not show outwardly. In contrast, type B individuals are less competitive, show less time urgency and experience less hostility.

RESEARCH METHODS

This study used a very large sample. Why is a large sample so important?

In a **longitudinal study**, 3000 healthy men between ages 39 and 59 were assessed to determine their personality type, and then followed up throughout the following nine years. The men were split into two roughly equal groups,

KEY TERM

longitudinal study: a study that is conducted over a long period of time. They are usually conducted to follow the development of participants' behaviour, illnesses or response to interventions like treatment programmes.

depending on whether they were assessed as Type A or Type B. Over the course of the study, 70% of the 257 men who died were from the Type A group. People who are of Type A are more susceptible to stress because of their behaviour traits, and are consequently more likely to suffer stress-related illness such as CHD.

> ### ISSUES AND DEBATES
>
> It is important to be able to identify what are the biggest sources of stress as this then allows individuals to identify triggers in their life that may be impacting on their health and implement appropriate interventions. This has **applications to everyday life** as correctly identifying stress triggers and the sources of stress in one's life could help with diagnosing stress early and preventing illnesses like coronary heart disease and other illnesses relating to stress.

There are **cultural differences** between different areas in what might be a source of stress. These different cultural expectations and beliefs, and how they are internalised by individuals within that culture, could have a significant impact on what they perceive as a trigger to stress. We must be aware of this and not be ethnocentric when discussing sources of stress; what you consider a source of stress might be something of little significance to another culture. Similarly, something that would not cause you stress could be the source of significant anxiety and stress to another individual.

When considering sources of stress, the **nature versus nurture** debate would suggest that we need to consider if an individual's response to triggers and the impact this has on stress is due to the environment or a biological predisposition. How we respond to stressful or anxiety provoking events and our body's physiological response to these triggers could be a result of genes that we have inherited from our parents or actually learned from our parents. Selye provides evidence to suggest that our response to stress, and likelihood of suffering negative consequences following an anxiety provoking situation is a combination of our physiology and how we choose to respond to this.

The use of **longitudinal research** allows researchers to see how different sources of stress impact individuals over a period of time and how the stress response develops. The research by Chandola et al. gives an insight into how a large population of over 10 000 people respond to different life events, and the impact this had on their chances of developing coronary heart disease. This is far more useful than a **snapshot study** that only shows how a sample of people are reacting at one point in time.

Stress is a complicated concept, and it is unlikely that any one explanation will be able to account for everyone's experience of stress following a life trigger. It is important that we consider how **reductionist** any explanation is when trying to explain what sources of stress are. There are a variety of factors that could influence our stress response, from a depletion in physiological reserves (Selye) to life triggers like work, or even the type of personality that we have and the impact this has on the way that we approach stressful situations. It is likely to be a combination of these factors that will best explain how an individual experiences and deals with stressful situations.

Measures of stress

Stress is not an illness itself, but it can cause serious illness if it is not addressed. It is important to recognise the symptoms of stress early since this will help a patient work out ways of coping, and so save them from adopting unhealthy coping methods, such as drinking or smoking.

There are two main ways to measure stress: physiological and psychological. Physiological measures look at physical characteristics, such as blood flow and levels of chemicals and hormones in the body. Psychological measures tend to rely on self-report measures to gain feedback from the person experiencing stress.

Physiological measures: recording devices and sample tests (Wang et al., 2005; Evans & Wener, 2007)

One way to investigate the impact of stress on the brain is to use brain imaging techniques. Functional magnetic resonance imaging (fMRI) is a neuroimaging procedure using MRI technology that measures brain activity by detecting changes associated with blood flow. In the simplest fMRI study, a participant alternates between periods of completing a specific task and a control or rest state to measure baseline activity. The fMRI data is then analysed to identify brain areas in which the signal changed between the activity and the rest state. It can be inferred that these areas were activated by the stressful task.

254

Despite the prevalence of stress in everyday life and its impact on happiness, health, and cognition, little is known about the neural experience of stress in the brain. Wang et al. (2005) used an fMRI scanner and a technique called **arterial spin-labelling perfusion MRI** to measure cerebral blood flow.

> **KEY TERM**
>
> **arterial spin-labelling perfusion MRI:** arterial blood is labelled or tagged and, after a delay, moves into the imaging plane or volume, during which time there is decay of the label. Snapshot images are acquired in labelled and control conditions and subtracted, producing an image that illustrates cerebral blood flow to areas of the brain.

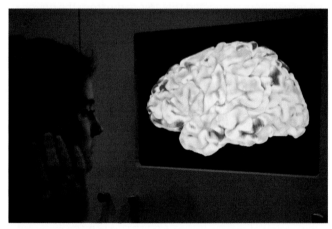

8.25 An fMRI scan

The data from fMRI scans are then used to generate images that can illustrate how the brain is working during different tasks (Figure 8.25). They allow us to view active brains without a neurosurgeon having to cut into the head of the patient. Patients are positioned in a large scanner that sends a strong magnetic field through their head. The magnetic field causes the nuclei in hydrogen molecules in the brain to spin in a particular way, and this is picked up by the scanner. Because hydrogen concentrations vary in different parts of the brain, it is possible for the scanner to produce a detailed picture of the brain based on the amount of hydrogen molecules it identifies in different areas.

In Wang et al.'s research 32 participants were split into a stress condition (25) and the control experiment (7). Participants were instructed to perform a mental arithmetic task, responding verbally while in the fMRI

scanner. Throughout, participants were prompted for faster performance and were required to restart the task if an error occurred. This high-stress condition was preceded by a low-stress condition, during which subjects counted aloud backward from 1000 (to control for activation of verbal and auditory centres). Self-report of stress and anxiety levels (on a scale of 1 to 9) and saliva samples were collected straight after each task (Table 8.15).

Stress	Effort	Difficulty	Frustration
Low-stress task	4.4	3.4	3.4
High-stress task	7.0	6.6	6.1

Table 8.15 Self-report of effort, difficulty and frustration during low- and high-stress tasks (scale 1–9)

Regression analyses were carried out to search for the specific brain regions associated with individual participants' experience of stress. The hypothesis was that the cerebral blood flow change induced by the high-stress task compared with the low-stress task should be correlated with the change in perceived stress between these two conditions.

The results provide neuroimaging evidence that psychological stress induces negative emotion and that the ventral right prefrontal cortex plays a key role in the central stress response. It further suggests that it is possible to use a physiological scan to measure the influence of stress on blood flow in the brain.

Cortisol is released in response to fear or stress by the adrenal glands as part of the 'fight or flight' mechanism. Salivary cortisol is frequently used as a biomarker of psychological stress and is a technique that has been preferred by researchers as it is non-invasive. In addition, as opposed to blood sampling, saliva collection does not require the collaboration of skilled personnel, allowing for an uncomplicated and trouble-free sample collection. One issue to identify, though, is that stress mechanisms, which trigger a physiological reaction, can only indirectly be assessed by salivary cortisol measures.

Evans and Wener (2007) conducted research looking at how easily and how frequently personal space may be intruded upon and how this may be one of the key underlying processes that underlie stressful experiences when travelling. A total of 139 adult commuters (54% male) who had been commuting to work by passenger train between New Jersey into Manhattan, New York City, were recruited to the study. Each participant was provided a free monthly rail pass for their participation. Participants had been on the same commuting route for an average of 82 months, with a 12 month minimum and their average duration of the commute to work was 83 minutes.

Two measures of crowding were taken for each participant's journey: car (carriage) density and seat density. Car density was calculated by dividing the total number of passengers within the train car by the total number of seats. Seat density was a more proximal measure of crowding local to where the participant was sitting and was calculated by dividing the number of people sitting on the same row as them by the total number of seats on the row (five).

Salivary cortisol was collected from each participant through a chewable swab. The results showed that the density of the train car was inconsequential for levels of stress whereas the seating density near to the passenger significantly affected both self-reported stress and levels of cortisol in the participant's saliva. Evans and Wener concluded that the ease and how frequently personal space is intruded upon may be one of the key processes that underlie the experience of crowding.

This study showed that it is possible to measure the impact of stressful experiences, such as a morning commute to work, on an individual by using a physical measure such as taking a sample of saliva and measuring the levels of cortisol at different points.

Psychological measures: self-report questionnaires (Holmes & Rahe, 1967; Rahe et al., 1970; Friedman & Rosenman, 1974)

As mentioned above, Holmes and Rahe (1967) investigated the causes and sources of stress and focused on life events as stressors. Through this they developed the Social Readjustment Rating Scale. The scale consisted of 43 different life events which each had a stress score. Respondents would add up the stress scores of all of the events that they had experienced within the last 12 to 24 months to get their total score.

An interesting observation suggested a relationship between the Social Readjustment Scale and subsequent health. A score of 300 or higher puts a person at risk of illness, 150–299 shows a moderate risk of illness, and a score of less than 150 predicts only a slight risk of illness. The researchers suggested that this came from the physical drain on the body produced by the continual arousal and the general adaptation to long-term or repeated stress.

Rahe et al. (1970) tested the reliability of the scale again in 1970. He asked 2500 US military members (sailors) to rank stressful events in their lives against the scale. He tracked the sailors for six months, noting their visits to the dispensary, to see if there was a correlation between their visits to the doctor and the stressful events they had reported. The study once again proved the reliability of the scale, with the exact same positive correlation between reported stress and illness as found in the original examination of medical record: 0.118 (Table 8.16).

1	Marriage
2	Troubles with the boss
3	Detention in jail or other institution
4	Death of spouse
5	Major change in sleeping habits (a lot more or a lot less sleep, or change in part of day when asleep)
6	Death of a close family member
7	Major change in eating habits (a lot more or a lot less food intake, or very different meal hours or surroundings)
8	Foreclosure on a mortgage or loan
9	Revision of personal habits (dress, manners, association, etc.)
10	Death of a close friend
11	Minor violations of the law (e.g. traffic tickets, jay walking, disturbing the peace)
12	Outstanding personal achievement

13	Pregnancy
14	Major change in the health or behaviour of a family member
15	Sexual difficulties
16	In-law troubles
17	Major change in number of family get-togethers (e.g. a lot more or a lot less than usual)
18	Major change in financial state (e.g. a lot worse off or a lot better off than usual)
19	Gaining a new family member (through birth, adoption, oldster moving in, etc.)
20	Change in residence
21	Son or daughter leaving home (e.g. marriage, attending college)
22	Marital separation from mate
23	Major change in church activities (e.g. a lot more or a lot less than usual)
24	Marital reconciliation with mate
25	Being fired from work
26	Divorce
27	Changing to a different line of work
28	Major change in the number of arguments with spouse (e.g. either a lot more or a lot less than usual regarding childrearing, personal habits, etc.)
29	Major change in responsibilities at work (e.g. promotion, demotion, lateral transfer)
30	Wife beginning or ceasing work outside the home
31	Major change in working hours or conditions
32	Major change in usual type and/or amount of recreation
33	Taking on a mortgage greater than $10000 (e.g. purchasing a home, business)
34	Taking on a mortgage or loan less than $10000 (e.g. purchasing a car, TV, freezer)
35	Major personal injury or illness
36	Major business readjustment (e.g. merger, reorganisation, bankruptcy)
37	Major change in social activities (e.g. clubs, dancing, movies, visiting)
38	Major change in living conditions (e.g. building a new home, remodelling, deterioration of home or neighbourhood)
39	Retirement from work
40	Vacation
41	Christmas
42	Changing to a new school
43	Beginning or ceasing formal schooling

Table 8.16 Social readjustment rating questionnaire

As discussed above, it is possible to categorise individuals as either Type A or Type B personality types (Friedman and Rosenman, 1974). Classifying behaviour into these categories is usually done by interview or by questionnaire (i.e. a psychometric test). Examples of questions are:

'Has your partner or friend ever told you that you eat too fast?'

- Type As are likely to say, 'Yes, often'.
- Type Bs are likely to say, 'Yes, once or twice' or 'no'.

'How would your partner, or best friend, rate your general level of activity?'

- Type As are likely to say, 'Too active, need to slow down'.
- Type Bs are likely to say, 'Too slow, need to be more active'.

'Do you ever set deadlines or quotas for yourself at work or at home?'

- Type As are likely to say, 'Yes once a week or more often'.
- Type Bs are likely to say, 'Only occasionally'.

'When you are in the middle of a job and someone (not your boss) interrupts you, how do you feel inside?'

- Type As are likely to say, 'I feel irritated because most interruptions are unnecessary'.
- Type Bs are likely to say, 'I feel OK because I work better after an occasional break'.

The idea that people can be categorised is desirable to doctors as it allows practitioners to predict behaviour based on the results of a personality test. Such a simplistic approach can be criticised for trying to explain human personality in such basic terms and it should be recognised that there are more than two types of personality.

The major problem with Type A and Type B theory is actually determining which factors are influencing stress and CHD. Some research has concentrated on hostility, arguing that the Type A behaviour pattern is characterised by underlying hostility which is a major factor leading to CHD. Research by Friedman and Rosenman has demonstrated that it is the negative experience of stress that those with Type A personalities are exposed to that is the major factor leading to CHD. Therefore, it would seem

that a much more sophisticated model is needed to predict CHD than this simple Type A–Type B approach.

ISSUES AND DEBATES

Some of the methods used to measure stress are types of **psychometric tests**, that allow the practitioner to better understand the feelings and perceptions of the individual who is experiencing the anxiety. Psychometric tests can be developed to help medical professionals explore not only how much anxiety and stress is being experienced, but also possible personality and environmental criteria that could increase the experience of the stress. On the other hand, physiological measures, such as measuring cortisol in saliva or using brain imaging techniques are far more objective and not subject to the same biases increasing the reliability of any data collected.

All of the measures of stress provide **useful applications to everyday life**, both in a medical setting and at home. If we can measure stress and identify when an individual is experiencing stress, it is possible that a medical professional could get involved early and prevent any more dangerous illnesses.

Evaluation

Those stress measures that are reliant on self-report mechanisms can be susceptible to social desirability where patients answer in a way that they feel they should answer, rather than giving the truth. Similarly, there are issues of subject bias as stress perception is a unique experience, and there are massive individual differences in stress thresholds. Two people could experience the same trigger but react in very different ways to this anxiety.

Physiological measures are a more **objective** measure of stress. This could be achieved by looking at brain activity, or levels of hormones produced by the body, however, these are time consuming and expensive. Further to this, using physiological measures like fMRI (Wang et al.) require a technician to interpret the results of the scan; there is still a lot that researchers do not know about areas of the brain and how activity links to the experience of emotion, so any inferences about stress and anxiety from these results should be treated with care.

SELF-ASSESSMENT QUESTIONS

10 If you were trying to conduct a study where you needed to measure the amount of stress a participant was under, what problems would you face in collecting reliable data?

Management of stress

Reflections: How do you manage your stress and anxiety? When you feel anxious about a situation, like a college exam, how do you deal with the situation?

Medical techniques

Drugs can be used as a quick and relatively easy way of dealing with stress, especially in the short term. Stress is often accompanied by anxiety and depression and so drugs used to treat these disorders are often prescribed when a person is experiencing many symptoms of stress.

The antidepressants most widely prescribed for anxiety are selective serotonin reuptake inhibiters (SSRIs) such as Prozac. These work by regulating serotonin levels in the brain to elevate mood and have been used to treat panic disorder, obsessive-compulsive disorder (OCD), and generalised anxiety disorders (GAD).

Anti-anxiety drugs decrease arousal and relax the body by reducing tension in the muscles. Since the stress response involves high arousal, tranquillisers may in some cases reduce stress. Benzodiazepines are drugs that can be used to treat anxiety (which often results from stress) and work by releasing inhibitory neurotransmitters, meaning that the brain is less aroused so the person is calmer and less anxious.

The effectiveness of benzodiazepines was researched by Kahn et al. (1986) who gave a group of patients the drug, while another was given a placebo (a substance that has no therapeutic effect, used as a control in testing new drugs). They followed 250 patients for eight weeks and found that benzodiazepines reduced stress significantly more than the placebo.

Psychological techniques: biofeedback and imagery
Biofeedback (Budzynski et al., 1969)

Biofeedback is a technique in which an electromechanical device monitors the status of a person's physiological processes, such as heart rate or muscle tension, and immediately reports that information back to the individual. This information enables the person to gain voluntary control over these processes through operant conditioning. If, for instance, the person is trying to reduce neck muscle tension and the device reports that the tension has just decreased, this information reinforces whatever efforts the individual made to accomplish this decrease.

Principles of biofeedback

The patient has electromyography (EMG) electrodes attached to the skin surface over a particular muscle.

Subjects hear a tone with a pitch proportional to the electromyographic activity in a given muscle group (Figure 8.26).

As the patient gets better at this they have to maintain a higher level relaxation in the muscle to hear a low tone.

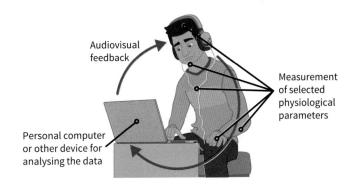

Audiovisual feedback

Measurement of selected physiological parameters

Personal computer or other device for analysing the data

8.26 The principles of biofeedback

Biofeedback has been used in stress management by helping people learn to relax specific muscles. It has also been employed to treat stress-related health problems, for example, in reducing chronic muscle-contradiction headaches. Biofeedback is based on the principle of operant conditioning and receiving reinforcement for behaviour that reduces the stress response.

Most often, biofeedback helps people control their stress response, by realising when a stress response is happening and employing relaxation techniques like deep breathing, visualisations and meditation to calm their physiological arousal.

Budzynski et al. (1969) wanted to assess the effect of biofeedback in reducing tension headaches. Tension headaches are associated with sustained contraction of the scalp and neck muscles, therefore relaxing the frontalis muscle (from the top of skull to the forehead) will have a positive impact on reducing the suffering of a patient (Figure 8.27).

8.27 The frontalis muscle (top of skull to forehead)

Each participant had electrodes attached to their head one inch (25 cm) above the eye across the forehead. There were three conditions in the experiment and each of the 15 participants was randomly allocated to one of these conditions. The experimental group were told that the pitch of the tone would vary with the level of muscle tension in the forehead. They were told to relax as deeply as possible and to keep the tone low pitched. The other two conditions were **control groups**. The constant low tone irrelevant feedback condition was told to relax deeply, especially the forehead muscle; they were also told that the constant tone should help them relax. The final group was told to relax as deeply as possible and to do this in silence.

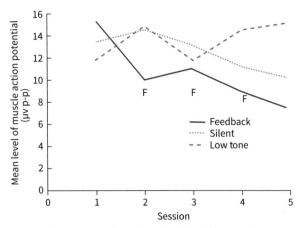

8.28 Patients can be trained to voluntarily lower their muscle through the use of biofeedback

The results were collected over five sessions and the mean level of muscle tension was measured to operationalise the dependent variable. It was evident that those participants in the feedback condition saw a significant reduction in their muscle tension over the course of the five sessions, and this reduction was greater than the two control groups.

The study showed that patients can be trained to voluntarily lower their muscle through the use of biofeedback, see Figure 8.29. This study suggests that operant conditioning techniques and 'shaping' of behaviours could be applied to a wide variety of physiological events in the body. The practical implication of these results would seem apparent. Biofeedback can have beneficial effects of profound muscle relaxation in alleviating a number of anxiety and stress-related disorders.

Imagery (Bridge, 1988)

Visualisation and imagery (sometimes referred to as guided imagery) techniques offer yet another avenue for stress reduction. These techniques involve the systematic practice of creating a detailed mental image of an attractive and peaceful setting or environment. There is no single correct way to use visual imagery for stress relief. However, something similar to the following steps is often recommended:

- Find a private calm space and make yourself comfortable.
- Take a few slow and deep breaths to centre your attention and calm yourself.
- Close your eyes.
- Imagine yourself in a beautiful location, where everything is as you would ideally have it. Some people visualise a beach, a mountain or a forest, or being in a favourite room sitting on a favourite chair.
- Imagine yourself becoming calm and relaxed. Alternatively, imagine yourself smiling, feeling happy and having a good time.
- Focus on the different sensory attributes present in your scene so as to make it more vivid in your mind. For instance, if you are imagining the beach, spend some time vividly imagining the warmth of the sun on your skin, the smell of the ocean, seaweed and salt spray, and the sound of the waves, wind and seagulls. The more you can invoke your senses, the more vivid the entire image will become.
- Remain within your scene, touring its various sensory aspects for five to ten minutes or until you feel relaxed.

- While relaxed, assure yourself that you can return to this place whenever you want or need to relax.
- Open your eyes again and then re-join your world.

Guided imagery has many uses. You can use it to promote relaxation, which can lower blood pressure and reduce other problems related to stress. You can also use it to help reach goals (such as losing weight or quitting smoking), manage pain and promote healing.

A study on the impact of imagery is reported by Bridge (1988) who detailed an experiment looking at the effect of relaxation and imagery on the stress levels of women who were undergoing treatment for cancer. Studies of patients with cancer showed that the systematic use of positive thought and imagery when patients were in a relaxed frame of mind helped prolong their lives.

Bridge wanted to see whether stress could be alleviated in patients being treated with radiotherapy for early breast cancer using a controlled randomised trial lasting six weeks. All of the 139 women were outpatients having a six week course of radiotherapy at the Middlesex Hospital, London, and were under the age of 70.

The patients completed the Leeds General Scales Measure, which gives the severity of depressive and anxiety symptoms in patients who have not received a primary diagnosis of affective illness, both before and after the six week trial. They also completed a mood scale: the profile of mood states uses 65 items to yield scores on subscales for tension, depression, vigour, fatigue, anger and confusion. The women were fully aware of the experiment and were randomly allocated to one of three conditions: relaxation, relaxation plus imagery or a control condition (Table 8.17).

There were no significant differences on the Leeds General Scales but the total mood disturbance score on the profile of mood states differed significantly in the predicted way. This indicated that relaxation positively affected mood state and that this positive effect was further enhanced when relaxation was combined with imagery.

Relaxation plus imagery was more effective than relaxation alone as the simplicity of the imagery, suggesting a peaceful, pleasant scene of the patient's choice, meant that it was within everyone's grasp. Bridge reported that often the image made the patient smile, at a time when smiles were perhaps few and far between. Therefore, this provides support for the use of imagery techniques in reducing stress in women undergoing cancer treatment.

Preventing stress (Meichenbaum, 1985)

Stress inoculation training (SIT) consists of three overlapping phases (Table 8.18). A key part of the training is the idea that stressors are creative opportunities and puzzles to be solved rather than obstacles. SIT is a form of **cognitive behavioural therapy** in that it attempts to get the patient to recognise the cognitions (thoughts) that trigger a stressful experience and then skill them with intervention strategies to help relieve the stressful experience.

KEY TERMS

cognitive therapy: a key influence on behaviour is how a person thinks about a situation, so cognitive therapy aims to change maladaptive or unwanted thoughts and feelings.

behavioural therapy: a key influence on behaviour is the previous learning process, so behavioural therapy aims to produce a new set of more desirable behaviours.

cognitive behavioural therapy (CBT): a combination of cognitive therapy and behavioural therapy.

Relaxation (*n* = 47)	Relaxation plus imagery (*n* = 44)	Controls (*n* = 48)
These patients were taught a relaxation technique which by a process of direct concentration focuses sensory awareness on a series of individual muscle groups. They were also taught breathing techniques that induce a calmer state and reduce tension.		Women in the control group were encouraged simply to talk about themselves and their interests.
These patients were given a tape recording of the instructions and told that they should practise these techniques at home for 15 minutes each day.		
	Also taught to imagine a peaceful scene of her own choice as a means of enhancing the relaxation.	

Table 8.17 Participant allocation

Conceptualisation	Education phase emphasising development of a warm, collaborative relationship through which a careful assessment and problem reconceptualisation are completed. During this stage, the patient is taught about the concept of stressors and how these affect their body.	'I realise that I'm most stressed in social situations and I always react by thinking "I can't handle this, I'm going to make a fool of myself".'
Skills acquisition and rehearsal	New skills and coping strategies are acquired and rehearsed. These techniques will be chosen with the patient and specifically tailored to their cognitive strengths but could involve a variety of emotion regulation skills, relaxation and problem solving strategies. The development of these skills, and the subsequent growth in confidence about their effectiveness, will empower the patient as they begin to realise that they are able to control their stress response.	'Relax, I'm in control. I just need to focus on the job. I must take slow, deep breaths and make sure my muscles are relaxed.'
Application and follow through	Focuses upon activities that transfer coping skills to real life and prevent relapse.	'I'll try to chat to colleagues during the lunch break. I'll then move on to starting an evening class and talking to new people there. If it all goes wrong, I'll talk it through with my therapist.'

Table 8.18 The three overlapping phases of SIT

The goal of SIT is to equip the patient with a variety of coping strategies that they can implement when they identify that they are having negative, or stressful cognitions (Table 8.19). Meichenbaum (1985) believed that people could inoculate themselves against stress, in the same manner as being inoculated from disease.

Cool relaxed thoughts	Just stay cool. Getting all anxious and upset won't help.
	It's just not worth it. Who is going to know or care in a month anyway?
	Just relax. That's it, take those three deep breaths…
	OK, if I need to, I will just switch on that calm relaxation image and calm myself down
Cognitive restructuring of maladaptive thoughts	Is this an all-or-none situation? Things aren't usually black and white.
	Don't jump to conclusions. Check out the possibilities.
	Don't take it so personally. What's my share of the responsibility pie anyway? Even if I am responsible for this problem, it doesn't mean I'm a bad person.
	Put it into context. If you look at it the right way, it's pretty funny.
	One new snowflake doesn't make a blizzard. Just stay with what's going on.
	It's not going well, but that doesn't mean that I'm worthless or it's hopeless, just that it didn't work out for me this time.
	I don't 'have to' do it 'perfectly' or 'right'. I am just going to do *my* best. That's all I can ask of myself or anyone else.
	Don't worry. Worrying doesn't help.

Table 8.19 Examples of types of self-statements rehearsed in stress inoculation training

SIT proposes that stress occurs whenever the perceived demands of a situation exceed the perceived resources that are available to the individual. The word 'perception' is important here as it reflects the concept that stress is an individual view of the situation and this can be modified through interventions and coping strategies.

Evaluation

In Bridge, the sample was focused on women who were undergoing therapy for cancer. This biased sample means that any conclusions that are gained from the research cannot necessarily be generalised to men as well. This limits the usefulness of the findings somewhat, but it is important to note that the significant improvement when using imagery could lead to further research to test the reliability of the findings with a male sample. The use of random allocation as a **control** is a strength of the research, however, as the patients were aware that they were in a study on the impact of pain management; this could have created demand characteristics. The use of a single-blind technique, where the patient is not aware of the condition that they are in, or the aim of the research could have been used to avoid this.

Budzynski's research was focused on a small sample of 15 participants which reduces the population validity of the research. A group of 15 people cannot represent the wide range of individuals within a population, so we have to be careful in how we interpret the results and not over-generalise the findings. There were many controls in the experiment, and each participant had to follow a standardised procedure throughout the trials. This standardised procedure allows the researchers to be confident about the reliability of the results, however, the researcher needs to be cautious about how long lasting any changes in behaviour would be as this is only a snapshot of behaviour over five weeks.

ISSUES AND DEBATES

When developing methods to manage stress, it is important to recognise that both biological and psychological factors combine in how our bodies react to anxiety. Any method developed should attempt to combine as many techniques as possible, and not focus on one narrow approach. The most **useful application** that comes from our understanding of stress management and prevention is that the most effective stress relief will probably come from combining the different biological and psychological techniques.

SELF-ASSESSMENT QUESTIONS

11 How could you measure the effectiveness of a stress management technique?

8.5 Health promotion

Although the term health education is quite new, there have been attempts made for centuries to persuade people to change their behaviour to ensure good mental and physical health. How best to encourage them to do so is a fundamental issue that hasn't yet been resolved. There has been an increasing move among health professionals towards primary care: promoting behaviour that facilitates the avoidance of disease, ill health or injury.

Treating an illness once it has developed is the familiar and established medical model of 'secondary care'. Health psychologists are increasingly recognising that such a reactive stance is inadequate if we are one day to achieve a healthy society and that a more proactive primary care approach of **health promotion** is needed.

Strategies for promoting health

This is a report of a study conducted by Cowpe (1989). At the time this research was conducted, chip-pan fires were a major cause of domestic fires in the UK. Approximately one-third of all domestic fires were caused by chip-pans. In 1981, there were 21 deaths and 1372 injuries caused by 15 000 chip-pan fires in the UK. Not only this but chip-pan fires were a major cost to the taxpayer in terms of providing emergency rescue crews and police and the associated costs to the National Health Service.

The aim of this study was to test the effectiveness of an advertising campaign warning people about chip-pan fires. This can be understood as a quasi-experiment. The advertisement was shown on television in ten UK regional television areas. The findings revealed a net decline in each area over the 12 month period from between 7% and 25%. The largest reduction was actually during the time that the campaign was running. Questionnaires showed a significant increase in awareness.

The conclusion was that the advertising proved effective as shown by the reduction in chip-pan fires. However, as time passes the effectiveness of the campaign passes away as well. Viewers are also less likely to be influenced by the campaign if overexposed.

263

Health professionals and health psychologists have investigated many different methods of promoting health. Some psychologists have suggested that health can best be promoted by using health education campaigns and others have suggested that it is done best by direct intervention.

There are several competing theories on what makes an effective strategy for promoting a health behaviour. Janis and Feshbach (1953) consider fear arousal the most effective way of changing behaviour, but recognise that it is possible to scare people too much so that they do not take the message on board. The Yale Model of Communication goes further by considering the different elements of a health promotion and how each of these needs to be considered separately to be effective.

Fear arousal (Janis & Feshbach, 1953)

Fear arousal is a key feature of many health promotion campaigns. It works by letting people know bad things will happen to them unless they change their ways. One of the most studied variables affecting health promotion is the degree of fear inspired by a message. An early study by Janis and Feshbach (1953) compared high-fear, medium-fear and low-fear presentations of information about dental hygiene, each presented to a group of 50 high-school students (mean age 15 years). There was also a **control group** who received a presentation on human eye function. The aim was to test if level of fear would have a behavioural consequence in relation to the participants' brushing of teeth.

The greatest immediate impact was on the students in the high-fear group, of whom 76% said they were worried about tooth decay (an increase of 42% after watching the film). In contrast, of students seeing the low-fear presentation, only 46% reported feeling worried about tooth decay (an increase of only 24%).

After a week, **questionnaires** were administered asking how tooth-brushing behaviour had changed. They found 28% of the high-fear group reported that they had changed their habits, but 50% of the low-fear group reported better habits. Clearly the low-fear group learned from their presentation, even if they found it boring. Students in the high-fear group had a quick emotional reaction but less behaviour change. Something worth noting about this study is that the low-fear group received specific, practical instructions. Those instructions may have been lost amid the 71 fear-arousing images in the high-fear presentation.

Janis and Feshbach found on one hand that the message arousing strong fear elicited the most favourable appraisals of the communication by the audience and proved equally as effective as the other versions in teaching factual information. Different results were obtained, on the other hand, concerning acceptance of the message's recommendation. The minimal fear appeal was far more effective than the other two messages in encouraging students to adopt the recommended practices of oral hygiene, whereas the message that aroused strong fear was the least effective. The same finding was demonstrated when students subsequently were asked to react to a statement which contradicted the message's emphasis on the use of the proper type of toothbrush. Minimal fear elicited the most resistance to the counter-propaganda and strong fear, the least resistance.

Yale Model of Communication

The Yale Model of Communication (Figure 8.29) states that there are several factors that will affect how likely a person is to change their behaviour in response to a cue in the environment. It takes into account the fact that a person's behaviour is unlikely to change unless their

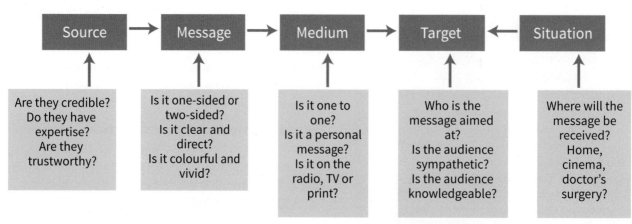

8.29 Yale Model of Communication

thoughts or attitude towards the behaviour change first. The model focuses on three aspects of communication: the communicator (who says it), the communication (what is said) and the audience (to whom it is said).

- The *communicator*: it is crucial that the source of any message has credibility. This can be achieved through use of academic advice, appropriately qualified people, relevant personal experience and those who are trustworthy. For example, many group therapies for drug users are led by an ex-drug user which gives them credibility when empathising with their situations. Also, many advertising campaigns will be sponsored by government agencies to further add to the weight and credibility of any message contained within.
- The *communication*: the Health Belief Model suggests that perceived threat is a prerequisite for positive health behaviours. The Yerkes–Dodson Law of Arousal (Figure 8.30) states that each individual has their own optimal level of arousal and it is important for an effective message to be strong enough to increase attention, but not too unpleasant as to produce high levels of anxiety.

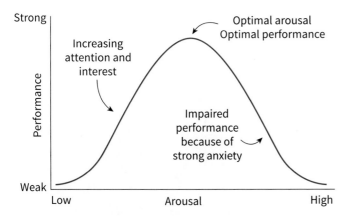

8.30 The Yerkes–Dodson Law of Arousal states that each individual has an optimal level of arousal. Over-arousal will reduce the effectiveness of any programme

- The *audience*: when considering how the message is to be conveyed it is important to consider the demographic of the audience and the type of issue that is being promoted. With complicated issues it is better to spell out the conclusions whereas when there is a simple message or it is addressing well-informed people, let them make their own conclusions. Also, where possible, the audience should be involved in some way by posing questions or using point of view filming.

Health Belief Model

According to the Health Belief Model people are likely to practise healthy behaviour if they believe that by not doing so they are susceptible to serious health problems. In other words, they are motivated by fear to protect their health.

Leventhal (1967) demonstrated this with an experiment on cigarette smokers. Those who were exposed to a high-fear appeal, involving watching a film of an operation to remove a diseased lung, changed their attitudes and intentions regarding smoking more than those shown a moderate-fear appeal.

Providing information (Lewin, 1992)

Giving patients information to help them make informed decisions could be a good way of promoting many health behaviours. A home-based exercise programme has been found to be as useful as a hospital-based one in improving cardiovascular fitness after a heart attack.

To find out whether a comprehensive home-based programme would reduce psychological distress, Lewin (1992) randomly allocated 176 patients who had suffered a heart attack to a self-help rehabilitation programme based on a heart manual or to receive standard care plus a placebo package of information and informal counselling.

Psychological adjustment, as assessed by the Hospital Anxiety and Depression Scale, was better in the rehabilitation group at one year. They also had significantly less contact with their general practitioners during the following year and significantly fewer were readmitted to hospital in the first six months.

The improvement was greatest among patients who were clinically anxious or depressed at discharge from hospital. The cost-effectiveness of the home-based programme has yet to be compared with that of a hospital-based programme, but the findings of this study indicate that it might be worth offering such a package to all patients who have had a heart attack.

ISSUES AND DEBATES

When considering strategies for promoting health behaviours it is important to look at both **individual and situational explanations** for their behaviour. Some individuals may be more likely to follow a health promotion strategy if there are situational gains for them, whereas others may be more affected by campaigns that are directed towards them personally (by age, behaviour or sex for example). The interaction between these needs to be considered so that theories do not become too deterministic and promote the ideas that a person's health behaviour can be changed through the use of one simple strategy. It is not the case that if you do give a cue to action to an individual they will follow it.

The fear arousal model and the Yale Model of Communication have **useful applications to everyday life** as they signpost strategies that can be employed by marketing campaigns and those within the medical profession to change patient's health behaviours. Prevention of illness is a more effective way of dealing with illness and if campaigns can be devised that encourage people to live healthier lives then this helps not only the individual but the strains that are being put on health services around the world.

Health promotion in schools, worksites and communities

Schools - Tapper et al. (2003)

Often, healthy eating campaigns rely on educating individuals as to the negative consequences of continuing to eat unhealthy foods. Researchers at the Bangor Food Research Unit have approached the problem of encouraging healthy eating from a different angle. Instead of attempting to change knowledge about healthy eating, or attitudes towards particular foods, they tackled food consumption itself. Through their research they developed three different strategies to use with young children to change their eating behaviours: taste exposure, modelling and rewards (Table 8.20).

Based on the these strategies, Tapper et al. (2003) recently completed the development and evaluation of a whole-school Food Dudes programme (Figure 8.31) for use across the primary age range (4–11 years). The programme is designed to be implemented entirely by school staff and contains the following elements:

- a Food Dudes video containing six short adventure episodes
- a set of Food Dudes rewards
- a set of letters from the Food Dudes that provide praise and encouragement and remind children of the reward contingencies
- a Food Dudes home pack to encourage children to eat fruit and vegetables in the home context as well as at school
- a staff manual and staff briefing video to help teachers implement the programme correctly
- a set of education support materials to help teachers meet curriculum targets using the Food Dudes theme.

The main intervention phase of the programme lasts for a period of 16 days during which children watch the Food Dudes video episodes and listen to their teacher read out the Food Dudes letters. Children also receive rewards when they eat the fruit and vegetables that are presented to them. They receive a Food Dudes sticker for tasting a food, or a sticker and a small prize for eating a whole portion. The intervention phase is followed by a maintenance

8.31 The characters from the Food Dudes programme

Taste exposure	Modelling	Rewards
Increasing the exposure to a new food group over a period of weeks.	Research shows that certain factors make modelling (imitation and observational learning) more effective.	Positive reinforcement for eating the new food.
The more you taste a novel food the more you learn to like it.	A child is more likely to imitate another person if that person is liked by the child (Bandura, 1977).	Rewards should imply the importance of the healthy eating behaviour rather than become a compensation for eating something unpleasant.

Table 8.20 Strategies developed by Tapper et al.

phase during which there are no videos and the letters and rewards become more intermittent.

Both teachers and parents evaluated the programme positively. The children had engaged with the programme, were enthusiastic about curriculum work using the Food Dudes theme, had better attendance and previously lower achieving children were more confident. After four months, the children were still eating significantly more fruit and vegetables than they had been before the programme began.

Worksites (Fox et al., 1987)

Token economy programmes use the principles of operant conditioning to modify behaviour; specifically, reinforcement. Such programmes are used in prisons to encourage pro-social behaviour and involve giving tokens to offenders if a desired behaviour is performed. The tokens may then be swapped for certain rewards in the hope that desired behaviour is repeated.

Fox et al. (1987) reported on a token economy system that used stamps as tokens that was instituted at two dangerous open-pit mines. Employees earned stamps for working without lost-time injuries, for being in work groups in which all other workers had no lost-time injuries, for not being involved in equipment-damaging accidents, for making adopted safety suggestions, and for unusual behaviour which prevented an injury or accident. The workers lost stamps if they or other workers in their group were injured, caused equipment damage, or failed to report accidents or injuries. The stamps could be exchanged for a selection of thousands of items at shops on the site.

Following the implementation of the token economy, large reductions in the number of days lost from work because of injuries were recorded. The reductions in costs far exceeded the costs of operating the token economy and the improvements were maintained over several years.

The tokens given to workers for periods without lost time injuries or equipment damaging accidents apparently benefitted all parties immediately involved. Both the number of days lost from work and the number of lost-time injuries declined at both mines following the introduction of the token economies.

Communities: Five City project (Farquhar et al., 1985)

The Stanford Five City Multifactor Risk Reduction Project (FCP) completed by Farquhar et al. (1985) is a long-term field study of the feasibility and effectiveness of community-wide health education directed at lowering cardiovascular

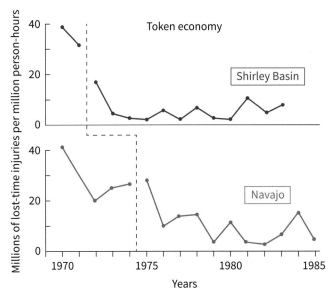

8.32 The yearly number of work-related injuries, per million person hours worked, requiring one or more days lost from work

disease (CVD) risk, morbidity and mortality. The FCP as originally planned included six years of education (mid-1980 to mid-1986), four independent (cross-sectional) population surveys, four surveys of a cohort, and continuous surveillance for cardiovascular disease events.

The population surveys provide the major source of data relating to CVD risk and risk factor reduction in the FCP. These surveys are designed to obtain information on health attitudes, knowledge and behaviour, and selected measures of CHD risk. They are conducted on randomly selected samples of young and older adults, ages 12–74, from four communities: Monterey, Salinas, Modesto and San Luis Obispo.

The two treatment cities were Salinas (1980 population 80 500) and Monterey (population 44 900), and the two control cities were Modesto (population 132 400) and San Luis Obispo (population 34 300). Santa Maria was the third control city where only morbidity and mortality events were monitored. People aged 12–74 who resided in randomly selected households in the four surveyed cities, were eligible to participate with each survey comprising approximately 1800–2500 participants.

The major goals of the population surveys included the following:

- to develop or adopt appropriate measurement instruments and procedures for the survey
- to hire, train and supervise a staff to operate the centres

267

- to establish survey centres in each of the four communities
- to identify and recruit randomly selected samples from each community with an objective of achieving a response rate of at least 66%
- to conduct the surveys in a manner that provides accurate and reliable data, and to maintain an effective relationship with the general public and medical/health care professionals in the community.

As well as the surveys, physiological measures of some of the participants were taken. These included:

- body height and weight
- blood pressure by two methods (mercury manometer and a semi-automated machine)
- resting heart rate
- non-fasting blood sample analysed for plasma thiocyanate (as a measure of smoking rate)
- expired air carbon monoxide
- urinary sodium potassium and creatinine (as an index of prior sodium chloride intake)
- a low-level bicycle exercise test (as a measure of fitness).

The short-term impact of the project saw knowledge of CVD risk factors steadily increase in both the treatment and control groups, but improvement in the treatment group was significantly greater. There was a significant decline in cholesterol over time. A significant net decrease in blood pressure occurred. Net decreases in the resting heart rate favoured intervention participants. In the 24 hour diet recall, dietary saturated fat intake declined significantly in women, but not in men.

The long-term impact found that both CHD and all-cause mortality risk scores were maintained or continued to improve in intervention cities while levelling out or rebounding in control cities.

During a follow-up in 2014, results suggest that frequent, regular, systematic contact with media professionals and provision of materials influence newspaper coverage of health-related topics, which has important implications for shaping public opinion and policy change.

Future efforts should combine general mass media education with programme development for special populations and environmental changes that focus on increasing the availability of lower-fat fast foods. Those at the highest risk for CVD reported the lowest use of preventive interventions. These findings indicate the need

for systematic research and application of behavioural science theory in developing interventions that are age-appropriate, gender-specific and culturally relevant, as well as research examining links between low socioeconomic status and risk of disease.

ISSUES AND DEBATES

The use of **longitudinal research** within this area provides lots of in-depth awareness of how health promotion campaigns can impact on large communities. Research such as Fox et al. identified the positive effects that token economy systems can have in improving safety in the workplace and how this can be sustained over a long period of time. This is also the case when looking at the research conducted by Farquhar with the Five City Project which was able to look at the long term impact of mass media campaigns, the impact of which is still being measured in 2014.

The research in this are provide useful **applications to everyday life** in the way it provides evidence to support the implementation of health campaigns in a variety of different areas, and that these interventions can be very successful at changing health behaviours. Knowing that health promotion campaigns can be effective at motivating people to change behaviours supports more research into why these are effective.

The **use of children as participants** is raised through the work by Tapper et al. who researched the impact of a healthy eating campaigns within primary schools. Researching the impact of these campaigns is important, as developing healthy eating habits as a child will support the development of positive adult health behaviours too. When using children as participants it is important that their parents are involved in the research and are aware of the interventions that are being put into place.

Individual factors in changing health beliefs
Unrealistic optimism (Weinstein, 1980)

Weinstein (1980) investigated unrealistic optimism about future life events. He classified unrealistic optimism as an error in judgement where people tend to believe that they are invulnerable and expect others to be victims of misfortune and illness, not themselves. There are several factors that cause a person to be optimistically biased: their desired end state, their cognitive mechanisms, the information they have about themselves versus others, and overall mood.

The research attempted to test six hypotheses:

- People believe that negative events are less likely to happen to them than to others, and they believe that positive events are more likely to happen to them than to others.
- Among negative events, the more undesirable the event, the stronger the tendency to believe that one's own chances are less than average; among positive events, the more desirable the event, the stronger the tendency to believe that one's own chances are greater than average.
- The greater the perceived probability of an event, the stronger the tendency for people to believe that their own chances are greater than average.
- Previous personal experience with an event increases the likelihood that people will believe their own chances are greater than average.
- The greater the perceived controllability of a negative event, the greater the tendency for people to believe that their own chances are less than average; the greater the perceived controllability of a positive event, the greater the tendency for people to believe that their own chances are greater than average.
- When a stereotype exists of a particular type of person to whom a negative event is likely to happen, people will tend to believe that their own chances are less than average.

In the first study, 258 college students estimated how much their own chances of experiencing 42 events (given in Table 8.21) differed from the chances of their peers. The 42 events were randomly split between two rating forms; positive and negative events were intermixed. Instructions on the forms stated 'Compared to other students – same sex as you – what do you think are the chances that the following events will happen to you?'

Beneath the description of each event participants had a 15-point scale on which they had to choose their relative probability of this happening to them. The lowest choice possible was 100% less than average, since this indicated a probability of zero. At the other extreme, no probability could exceed 100%, but this upper limit could be many times the average probability.

Overall, the participants rated their own chances to be above average for positive events and below average for negative events. The present data provide evidence of unrealistic optimism for both positive and negative life events.

Positive life events	Negative life events
Like post graduation job	Having a drinking problem
Owning your own home	Attempting suicide
Starting salary > $10 000	Divorced a few years after married
Travelling to Europe	Heart attack before age 40
Starting salary > $15 000	
Good job offer before graduation	Contracting venereal disease
Graduating in top third of class	Being fired from a job
Home doubles in value in five years	Getting lung cancer
Your work recognised with award	Being sterile
	Dropping out of college
Living past 80	Having a heart attack
Your achievements in newspaper	Not finding a job for six months
No night in hospital for five years	Decayed tooth extracted
	Having gum problems
Having a mentally gifted child	Having to take unattractive job
State-wide recognition in your profession	Car turns out to be a lemon
Weight constant for ten years	Deciding you chose wrong career
In ten years, earning > $40 000 a year	Tripping and breaking bone
Not ill all winter	Being sued by someone
Marrying someone wealthy	Having your car stolen
	Victim of mugging
	Developing cancer
	In bed ill two or more days
	Victim of burglary
	Injured in auto accident

Table 8.21 The 18 positive and 24 negative life events used in Weinstein (1980)

Although all six hypotheses were supported, different factors appeared to govern responses to positive and negative events. For negative events, optimism and perceived controllability had an impact on participants' judgements. When an event was judged to be controllable, a stereotype existed in participants' minds of the kind of person to whom the event generally occurred. We can assume this person was seen to be at risk because he or she did not take any action to control the risk. Participants seemed to compare themselves with a stereotypical victim, leading them to decide that their own risks were less than average. For events perceived to be uncontrollable, there was no stereotype of the victim, and subjects did not show any systematic bias.

Transtheoretical Model (Prochaska et al., 1997)

The Transtheoretical Model suggests that, as individuals start on the trajectory of a health behaviour, they move through six stages of change: pre-contemplation, contemplation, preparation, action, maintenance and termination (Figure 8.33). At each stage different intervention strategies are most effective to support an individual to move from one state to the next and finally to maintenance.

- *Pre-contemplation*: people do not intend to take action in the foreseeable future (defined as within the next six months)
- *Contemplation*: In this stage, people are intending to start the healthy behaviour in the foreseeable future (defined as within the next six months). Even with this recognition, people may still feel ambivalent toward changing their behaviour.
- *Preparation* (determination): In this stage, people are ready to take action within the next 30 days. People start to take small steps toward the behaviour change, and they believe changing their behaviour can lead to a healthier life.
- *Action*: In this stage, people have recently changed their behaviour (defined as within the last six months) and intend to keep moving forward with that behaviour change. People may exhibit this by modifying their problem behaviour or acquiring new healthy behaviours.
- *Maintenance*: In this stage, people have sustained their behaviour change for a while (defined as more than six months) and intend to maintain the behaviour change going forward. People in this stage work to prevent relapse to earlier stages.
- *Termination*: In this stage, people have no desire to return to their unhealthy behaviours and are sure they will not relapse. Since this is rarely reached, and people tend to stay in the maintenance stage, this stage is often not considered in health promotion programmes.

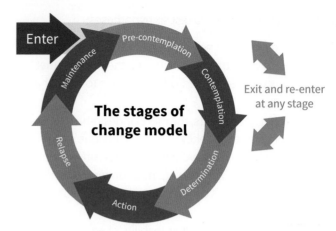

8.33 The Transtheoretical Model

Processes of change are the actual activities that a person can complete to move through the different intervention stages. You can consider these the methods of moving from one stage to another. There are ten processes that have received the most empirical support (Table 8.22). These can be used during any of the stages to move from one to the next.

To help individuals progress through the stages, health professionals need to understand the processes of change. One of the fundamental principles for progress is that different processes of change need to be applied at different stages of change.

Prochaska et al. (1992) believe that the future of health promotion programmes lies with stage-matched, proactive and interactive interventions. Much greater impacts can be generated by proactive programmes because of much higher participation rates, even if efficacy rates are lower.

Health change in adolescents (Lau, 1990)

Lau (1990) conducted a longitudinal study to explore how sources of stability and change in young adults might affect their health beliefs for behaviours such as drinking, diet, exercise and wearing seatbelts. The data for this study were collected as part of a larger piece of research of students who were enrolled at Carnegie Mellon University for classes ending in 1983. Of 1106 students who were sent questionnaires, 947 of these provided data which included responses from both the student and the student's parents. These 947 parent-child pairs are the participants within the study. The data collected via questionnaires from these students over a period of three years were collated to investigate six research questions:

1   Is there a link between the health beliefs of parents and students when they initially leave home for college?

270

2 How do parents exert their influence on their children?

3 How much do young adults' health beliefs change during the first years of college life?

4 How strong is the association between the health beliefs of the young adults and their peers at this time?

5 How do peers exert their influence over these young adults?

6 How strong is parental influence compared to peer influence?

The results found that there was a substantial change in the performance of health behaviours during the first three years of college and that peers have an increasing influence on these. In total, parents' influence on health beliefs is much more significant than that of peers. Lau suggested that direct modelling of behaviour is the most powerful influence on an individual's health beliefs. This provides support for the pattern of behaviour that saw increasing parental influence over the child in the early years of development while they are at home. This influence subsides as the child leaves for college as the peers that they spend their time with have a greater influence over their behaviour. Therefore, this suggests that proximity to individuals is a presiding factor over a person's health beliefs. Even though parental influence plays a large part in the early years, once a child leaves home, they are affected more by those that are around them.

ISSUES AND DEBATES

Understanding the individual factors in changing health behaviours has **useful applications to everyday life** in that they can be used to identify who is more likely to change their behaviours following a health promotion campaign. This could help direct campaigns to specific groups of individuals or identify factors, such as unrealistic optimism, that can then be exploited to make heath promotion campaigns more effective.

There are **cultural biases** in the individual factors that may influence a person to change their health behaviours. Different cultures could see health behaviours as more central to their beliefs and expectations. Also, within cultures, social comparison is often a powerful factor when considering health behaviours; individuals will often compare themselves to others in their community to make a judgement about their behaviour and if it is 'normal'. If within a culture, obesity is more common, it is likely that the individual will see their own weight issues as less important.

	Process	Intervention strategies
Consciousness raising	Involves increased awareness about the causes, consequences, and cures for a particular problem behaviour	Feedback, education, confrontation
Dramatic relief	Initially produces increased emotional experiences followed by reduced affect if appropriate action can be taken	Role playing, grieving, personal testimonies and media campaigns
Self re-evaluation	Combines both cognitive and affective assessments of one's self-image with and without a particular unhealthy habit	Healthy role models and use of positive imagery
Environmental re-evaluation	Both affective and cognitive assessments of how the presence or absence of a personal habit affects one's social environment are explored	Empathy training, documentaries, and family interventions
Self-liberation	The belief that one can change and the commitment and recommitment to act on that belief	New Year's resolutions, public testimonies, and multiple rather than single choices
Social liberation	This requires an increase in social opportunities to demonstrate new, positive behaviours	Advocacy, empowerment procedures and appropriate policies can produce increased opportunities

	Process	Intervention strategies
Counter-conditioning	Requires the learning of healthier behaviours that can become substitutes for problem behaviours	Relaxation techniques, and nicotine replacement and fat-free foods can be safer substitutes
Stimulus control	This removes cues for unhealthy habits and adds prompts for healthier alternatives	Planning parking lots with a two minute walk to the office and putting art displays in stairwells are examples of re-engineering that can encourage more exercise
Contingency management	Provides consequences for taking steps in a particular direction	Overt and covert reinforcements, positive self-statements and group recognition are procedures for increasing positive behaviours
Helping relationships	Develop relationships with caring, trust, openness and acceptance as well as support for the healthy behaviour change	Rapport building, a therapeutic alliance, counsellor calls and buddy systems can be sources of social support

Table 8.22 The ten processes of change

Summary

From this chapter you will have gained an understanding of how psychology helps us to understand aspects of health care, and to improve it, as well as providing an understanding of how aspects of health such as pain and stress can impact on an individual. In terms of non-verbal communication, a doctor's clothing can make a patient more or less confident, with more formal clothing typically inspiring trust. In verbal communication there are potential problems too. Although doctors tend to underestimate patients' understanding of medical terminology, they nevertheless continue to use medical terms. Studies of the patient–practitioner relationship have shown that, although less often used by doctors, a patient-centred consultation style is beneficial, so psychology can both provide tools for measuring doctor effectiveness and suggest ways to improve practices.

We considered how and why patients might not adhere to medical requests even though they have been to see a doctor to gain their guidance. Rational choice and consideration of a cost–benefit analysis of following the advice seemed to have a big impact on engagement with medical treatment. Measuring adherence is problematic, with no single measure able to reliably and non-invasively report on patient adherence over a long period of time. Self-report measures can easily give feedback about adherence, but are susceptible to response biases, whereas physical measures can give an account of the number of pills that have been removed from a container as a proxy for adherence. It seems that to improve adherence to medical requests, behavioural techniques can be effective with adults, by using monetary incentives, and children, by making the process of adhering to the medical requests fun.

The personal experience of pain was considered by looking at different theories of understanding how we perceive pain; from the biological theories suggesting pain is merely proportionally linked to the extent of the injury to more psychological theories, suggesting we are able to affect the perception of pain by opening and closing 'gates'. Measuring the experience of pain raises issues about relative self-reports and objectivity. Self-reports can be used with both children and adults and are a quick and easy method of data collection, but are open to individual biases. We considered methods of managing pain from the use of drugs to medically influence our experience of pain, to the use of imagery and acupuncture.

Within the stress sub-topic, we considered another individual experience that has an impact on many millions of people worldwide. Initially, we considered a variety of causes of stress such as work, life events and personality, and how our body reacts to stress with the GAS model. As with the other areas, the measurement of stress was considered by considering both physiological and psychological measures and how these could be used together to give an overview of a person's level of stress experience through the use of psychometric tests. Both drug therapies and alternative treatments for stress such as biofeedback and imagery were considered, as well as more proactive ways of preventing stress.

Finally, we looked at how we can use psychology to promote health behaviours using strategies such as fear arousal and providing enough information for the general population to make informed decisions. Three health promotion campaigns were looked at as case studies in schools, on a mining worksite and within the general communities. Consideration was then given to the individual factors that change health behaviours and how we can change health behaviours in adolescents.

Exam-style questions

1   A marketing firm has approached you to develop a health promotion campaign to encourage parents to get their children to have a yearly vaccination at their local clinic. They have asked you to consider different approaches that could be taken to promote this programme and the psychological research that would support the approach you would like to take.

   a Identify **two** named strategies for promoting health. [2 marks]

   b For one of the strategies named in (a), give **one** strength and **one** weakness of using that strategy to design a health promotion campaign. [4 marks]

   c Describe **one** individual factor that could affect whether a person will change their health beliefs. [4 marks]

   d Discuss the strengths and weaknesses of using health promotion campaigns to change an individual's health behaviours. [5 marks]

2   a Design an experiment to test the effectiveness of a physical measure of adherence compared to a self-report measure of adherence to medical requests. [10 marks]

   b Explain the psychological and methodological evidence on which your experiment is based. [8 marks]

Chapter 9
Psychology and organisations

Introduction

This chapter introduces you to five key topics within organisational psychology:

- **Motivation to work:** including theories of motivation, motivational techniques and the importance of perceived equity
- **Leadership and management:** including ways of measuring leadership, leadership styles and whether leadership can be learned
- **Group behaviour in organisations:** including group behaviours and team roles, the way that groups think and make decisions, and conflict and the management of conflict

- **Organisational work conditions:** including the famous Hawthorne effect, bullying at work, the effect of different office environments, the effect of shift work on health and accidents, the use of token economy in improving safety
- **Satisfaction at work:** the measurement of workplace satisfaction and the quality of working life, employee sabotage, the effects of job involvement and organisational commitment on turnover and absenteeism, workplace commitment.

What is organisational psychology?

Formerly referred to as occupational psychology (with a focus specifically on jobs or occupations), organisational psychology brings together theories and research from across psychology and applies this to the study of organisations. This chapter will consider the world of work, and how individuals and groups within an organisation function and influence each other and have an impact on the organisation itself.

You may be able to think of some applications already based on the psychology you learned in your AS course. Social psychology may be relevant when considering issues such as leadership and followership, motivation, quality of working life, employee sabotage and group processes. The learning approach is vital in considering whether personality characteristics such as leadership can be explained from a nurture or a nature perspective. This approach is also key when considering the role of reward and reinforcement not only in producing workplace satisfaction but also in training programmes such as those designed to make sure that safety procedures are followed. Aspects of the cognitive approach such as memory and attention, and also theoretical models of decision making and other cognitive processes are also crucial in understanding how individuals make sense of their roles within organisations. Finally, although there is little biological research in this chapter, the study of motivation considers the ways in which work can satisfy our varying physiological needs. Much of the current research into working conditions looks at the effects of different work conditions such as office layouts or shift work patterns on our physical and psychological health. We will also be considering psychometric approaches within this chapter and these are attempts to measure personality and cognitive functioning in order to ensure that people and their organisational roles are well suited.

> **Reflections:** There are lots of ways in which organisational psychologists may be able to benefit an organisation. Imagine you have been asked to help the management team of a large manufacturing organisation. There is a very high turnover of staff and those staff who remain are taking many days off as sick leave and reporting high levels of stress. Suggest some of the steps you could take to begin to address the problem.

275

9.1 Motivation to work

Need theories

Maslow's hierarchy of needs

Maslow's original hierarchy of needs (Maslow, 1943) is one of the best known theories of motivation and proposes that basic human needs need to be satisfied before we can begin to satisfy higher needs. Maslow claimed that all needs of humans could be arranged in a hierarchy. A person moves through the hierarchy by fulfilling each level, so that the basic physiological needs need to be met before moving up. Some people may never move through the entire hierarchy. Maslow's original hierarchy lists five levels of needs as shown in Figure 9.1.

> **Reflections:** Is it possible for people in all parts of the world to reach self-actualisation? Try to identify areas of the world where this may and may not be possible. It may be important to consider the effects of recent conflicts on this issue.

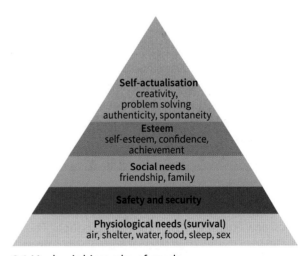

9.1 Maslow's hierarchy of needs

Maslow continued to develop his theory through the 1960s and the 1970s.

The updated model now has eight stages which are described below:

1   Biological and physiological needs: This stage is as it was described in the original model and focuses on our basic survival needs.

2   Safety needs. This stage covers a range of safety and security needs including those provided by a stable society with appropriate legal and justice systems. If a country is in the middle of a civil war, or people are living as refugees, they are unable to meet their safety and security needs.

3   Love and belongingness needs: This was called 'social needs' in the earlier model and focused primarily on friendship and family. In this later model, this focus has been widened slightly to include all the groups that we belong to: work, family, friends as well as romantic relationships.

4   Esteem needs: This level is the same as in the original model and refers to achievements; skills, status, independence, and so on. These esteem needs could be met very differently in different people. Some may feel a great sense of esteem through their family roles, through their well-paid jobs, through voluntary work that helps others or through the creation of something that achieves critical acclaim.

276

Reflections: The internet did not exist when Maslow proposed his theory. To what extent might social media such as Facebook allow us to meet our 'love and belongingness' (social) needs?

Maslow inserted two new stages into his theory at this point.

5   Cognitive needs: This relates to our need for information, knowledge and meaning. Once again it is worth considering how the internet may have changed not only our ability to access information but also our need for it.

6   Aesthetic needs: Maslow described this as our need and appreciation of beauty.

7   Self-actualisation: These new stages are followed by the original final stage; that of self-actualisation. This is described in the way that Maslow originally described this; self-actualisation is reaching our personal potential and becoming fulfilled.

8   Transcendence needs: Maslow also made one final amendment to his model and added a level above the level of self-actualisation. This was called 'transcendence needs' and refers to our ability to help others to also achieve self-actualisation.

Reflections: Can you think of anyone who might be considered to be at the transcendent level?

Alderfer's ERG Theory

Alderfer's ERG Theory (1972) is a revision of Maslow's theory and simplifies Maslow's eight categories into just three. These are the E, R and G of the title and refer to:

- **E**xistence needs: the basic survival needs described in the first two levels of Maslow's hierarchy; the physiological and the safety needs.
- **R**elatedness needs: the social and self-esteem needs. This is equivalent to the social needs identified by Maslow. Alderfer proposes that self-esteem needs can be divided into two: external and internal and our need for relatedness satisfies the external element of our self-esteem needs. If other people like us and want to spend time with us, we must be likeable people.
- **G**rowth needs: the needs related to self-development and advancement. This refers to the internal element of our self-esteem needs and allows us to meet needs related to the self-esteem and self-actualisation needs in Maslow's theory.

Alderfer's Theory is not a hierarchical approach and people can be motivated by needs from more than one level at the same time. We do not progress from satisfying needs at one level to satisfying needs at the next level. Ideally paid work will provide for all three of these needs and this is where the individual experiences the greatest motivation. For example, your job should provide at least for all your existence needs but you will be more motivated if your job also provides for some of your relatedness and growth needs as well. Alderfer's theory also suggests that the relative importance of these needs may change throughout our lives. Relatedness needs may be the most important in adolescence and early adulthood, followed by growth needs as we establish a career and then relatedness needs again when we start a family.

Reflections: What is your ideal job? Would it provide for all three of the needs?

McClelland's Theory of Achievement Motivation

McClelland's Theory of Achievement Motivation dates back to 1965 but the concept of achievement motivation is still commonly referred to today. This theory proposes that there are different needs that motivate people and that these differences are measurable. There are three types of needs identified in this theory:

- Need for *achievement*: the need to get things done, to achieve things, to be a success. People who have a high need for achievement (N-Ach) will be driven to succeed and are highly motivated by challenges and appraisals.
- Need for *affiliation*: the need to be liked by others, to be accepted as part of a group, to put effort into developing and maintaining social relationships. People who have a high need for affiliation will tend to prefer working with others to working alone and will be motivated by cooperative tasks.
- Need for *power*: the need to have influence and control over others. People with a high need for power will be motivated by the chance to gain status or prestige or to be looked up to by others.

Reflections: Can you think of people you know that fit these categories? Which one of these do you think best describes you? Think about the study by Milgram that you covered at AS Level (Section 5.1). Could any of these three types explain the behaviour of the participants in this study?

This theory is commonly applied in organisational settings as these are measurable qualities of a person; one person may have a higher need for power than another. It is likely that someone who will make a good manager will have a need for power but not a need for affiliation. We will be looking at leadership later in this chapter.

Need for achievement (or N-Ach) can be measured with the use of the Thematic Apperception Test or TAT. These are a series of ambiguous images which the individual is asked to interpret. For example they might be given the picture in Figure 9.2 and asked to consider what is happening, what has just happened, what is going to happen next and what the people in the picture are thinking.

Reflections: What story do you think this picture in Figure 9.2 is telling? If someone else gives a very different interpretation, do you agree that this tells us something about them?

9.2 What story is this picture telling you?

Evaluation

ISSUES AND DEBATES

277

It is important to begin any evaluation of theories of motivation by recognising that it has been difficult to support the notion that needs are organised in a hierarchical manner. This could be used to argue that Alderfer's approach may be more accurate. Another criticism of Maslow's work is that it has been difficult to test the notion of self-actualisation and Maslow's own work was based on a small number of people that he thought could be described as 'self-actualised'. However, theories of motivation can be usefully applied to the workplace in many ways: as well as working to earn enough money to satisfy our physiological and safety needs (at least) organisations must ensure that they meet these needs while we are at work. Workers should have breaks so that they can eat, drink and go to the toilet regularly. Organisations must ensure their workers' safety – this might simply mean ensuring that the building is safe but may also involve a complex set of safety procedures and the need for appropriate clothing and equipment. Some organisations also attempt to provide for workers' social needs through the provision of social clubs or events. They might also provide education and training, rewards and bonus schemes to meet self-esteem needs. Similarly McClelland's theory can be applied in the workplace to help understand personal characteristics and to ensure that people are given roles that suit their particular need for achievement.

Reflections: Consider how a workers' social club might improve workers' lives. Make reference to theory in your answer.

RESEARCH METHODS

The work covered in this section is primarily theoretical and you are not required to know details of any research carried out by these theorists. However, research on McClelland's Theory of Achievement Motivation comes under the heading of a **projective test**. Although these tests are widely used (most frequently in a clinical context), they are subjective and low in both **reliability** and **validity**.

KEY TERM

projective test: a personality test that uses ambiguous stimuli such an ink blots or the Thematic Apperception Test images discussed here. The response given to the stimuli is thought to reveal hidden emotions and conflicts which the individual projects onto the image.

RESEARCH METHODS

McClelland used projective tests to measure the need for achievement. Give one strength and one weakness of projective tests.

Cognitive theories

Goal Setting Theory

Goal setting theory opposes McClelland's idea that internal motives were largely unconscious and measurable only by projective tests. Locke and Latham based their work on the claims made by Ryan (1970) who argued that 'it seems a simple fact that human behaviour is affected by conscious purposes, plans, intentions, tasks and the like' (page 18).

Locke (1981) suggested that goal setting was a key motivator in getting people to work hard and improve their performance. In their co-authored text 'Goal setting: a motivational technique that works', Locke and Latham (1984) suggest that setting specific goals produces higher levels of performance than setting vague goals. For example stating as a goal 'I want to earn more money' is too vague and is less likely to affect the way a person behaves whereas someone who states 'I want to earn $50 more each week' will be more likely to achieve this. Specific goals are harder to achieve and present a greater challenge and goal-setting theory claims that this will make the individual try harder.

This may sound counter-intuitive but their book provides evidence from many studies which support this claim.

Goal setting theory provides guidance on how to set goals and these are based on five key principles which are referred to as 4C F standing for Clarity, Challenge, Complexity, Commitment and Feedback.

- *Clarity*: goals should be clear, specific, unambiguous and measurable.
- *Challenge*: goals should be relevant and linked to rewards.
- *Complexity*: Goals must be achievable within a specific time period.
- *Commitment*: Goals must be understood and accepted in order to be effective.
- *Feedback*: Goal setting must involve feedback on task progress and achievement.

The importance of feedback in this model is crucial. If the only assessment was whether the goal had been reached or not, it is possible that many weaknesses in performance may be missed. There may be easier, quicker or even more effective ways of achieving the same goal. Feedback needs to be positive and constructive and focus on the strategies used. This process should also allow for reflection by the individual rather than simply feedback from a superior.

The SMART method of goal setting developed from these five principles and is discussed in the Reflections box below. A final method of goal setting is 'Backward Goal Setting' in which the individual is encouraged to work backwards from the end goal in order to determine the most appropriate way of reaching this goal.

Reflections: SMART targets are targets or goals which are Specific, Measurable, Attainable, Relevant and have a Timescale. For example, a SMART target in business would look like this:

Specific: I want to set up a business selling jewellery I have made myself.

Measurable: I will aim to sell five items on eBay to begin with.

Attainable: I will start with an eBay store and then research other options.

Relevant: I will be turning my hobby into a money-making enterprise.

Timescale: I will aim to list five items on eBay within one week and 20 items within two weeks.

SMART targets are used in many schools. Try and write some SMART targets for your A Level Psychology course and decide whether you think this is a useful strategy.

Expectancy Theory

Expectancy Theory (Vroom, 1964) proposes that workers are rational beings whose decision making is guided by logical thought processes in which potential costs and rewards play a significant role. Vroom recognised that a worker's performance would be influenced by a wide range of factors, including knowledge, skills and experience as well as individual characteristics such as personality and different ambitions and goals. Despite this, he claims that all workers can be motivated if there is a clear relationship between effort and performance, if the favourable performance is rewarded, if the reward satisfies a need and finally, if the desire to satisfy the need is strong enough to make the effort worthwhile. Vroom proposes an equation which states that

$$\text{Motivation} = \text{expectancy} \times \text{instrumentality} \times \text{valence}$$

Expectancy is the perception of how much effort relates to performance as well as a worker's confidence in what they are capable of doing. Expectancy can be modified by the provision of additional resources or by training and supervision. Instrumentality is the perception of how much effort will be rewarded and whether workers actually believe that they will be given the reward that has been offered. Instrumentality will be positively affected if the management makes sure that rewards are always given as promised. Valence is the perception of the strength or the size of the reward as well as the extent to which this reward is needed or wanted. It is likely that a small reward will produce low motivation regardless of the values of expectancy and instrumentality, and similarly if the value of any one of the three is low, then overall motivation is likely to be low.

Equity Theory

Finally, Equity Theory was proposed by Adams (1963). This is an application of social psychology, where Social Exchange Theory predicts that people will weigh up what an action will cost them in terms of the benefits it will produce.

Reflections: Think about the study by Piliavin et al. (in your AS course, Section 5.2). Could equity theory be used to explain helping behaviour?

Equity Theory was an application of this idea to the workplace. It proposes simply that workers expect things to be fair. They expect pay, status and recognition to equate to the amount of effort that they put in. The significant factor in Equity Theory is comparison with others. If we perceive others as being treated better than us, then the perceived inequality will lead to decreased motivation.

This theory suggests that workers bring certain things to the job, such as skills, qualifications, energy, enthusiasm and effort. These are referred to as INPUT (I) and may be perceived (I_p) or actual (I_a). Workers expect certain things from their job, including pay, recognition, involvement and many other benefits, all referred to as outcomes (O) and again these may be perceived (O_p) or actual (O_a).

The key proposal of this theory is that workers compare themselves with other workers in similar posts to check the fairness or the equity of their own position. If they believe that the situation they are in is one of inequity (unfairness), this can result in low motivation. Inequity can be of two types: underpayment or overpayment. This is strongly related to the concept of organisational commitment which will be considered later in this chapter (Section 9.5).

Underpayment equity might be felt if you find out that someone else in the same post as you is being paid considerably more, despite being less experienced and less qualified. In order to bring the situation back to one of equity you have several options: you could try to increase the outcomes from your job, perhaps by asking for a salary increase or you could try to decrease your input – after all if you are not being paid as much as someone else, why would you work as hard as they do? These are the most obvious outcomes from identifying a state of inequity although there are other cognitive strategies that also could be used. You could decide that you had made an inappropriate comparison and find someone else to compare yourself to which will make you feel better about the situation, or find some other way to distort the way that the inputs and outcomes are perceived. A final option might be to leave and find another job.

What if you experienced an overpayment equity? What if you felt that you were being rewarded more than you deserved or at least, more than the people you were comparing yourself to? You might decide to work harder as your input doesn't match the outcomes. It is unlikely that you would look for options that decreased the outcomes such as asking for a pay cut or asking for more work. You could use the cognitive strategies described above, decide that you need to compare yourself to different people or find some other way to distort either the input or the outcomes to reach a state of equity.

Reflections: If you have a part-time job as well as being a student, how would you feel if a newly appointed member of staff, doing the same job as you, was being paid more? What reasons might there be for this? What if they were being paid less? What if you found out that someone who had been working there longer than you, doing the same job, was being paid less?

Evaluation

ISSUES AND DEBATES

In this section we have been examining motivation from the cognitive approach. All three of the theories outlined here focus on the way that the individual perceives the situation that they are in, rather than the situation itself. As with the previous section, all three theories can be usefully and effectively applied to the workplace. If goals are specific, measurable and achievable they will be more effective. Roberts (1994) points out that a manager cannot simply say 'do your best' and expect this to be effective. It is therefore crucial that we understand exactly what types of goals and what type of feedback will be most effective. Expectancy Theory can also be applied in similar ways such as involving workers in the goal setting process and ensuring that rewards are appropriate and will be valued by workers.

Finally, Equity Theory demonstrates the importance of understanding the way that the individual makes sense of their role in comparison to others. A field study conducted by Martin and Peterson in 1987 and reported by Hayward (1996) provides some support for Equity Theory. It showed that when new workers in a retail environment were taken on at a lower pay scale than existing workers, they perceived underpayment inequity as they were being paid less than other workers for doing the same job. However the existing workers did not perceive overpayment inequity as they were not comparing themselves to the new workers and maintained the comparisons they were making prior to the introduction of the new scheme.

RESEARCH METHODS

As with the previous section, much of this work is theoretical although clearly these ideas have been tested in real-life situations. Whilst this will give the research high **ecological validity**, it is likely to be difficult to **generalise** to other different organisations due to the huge number of variables involved. In other words, it will never be possible to conduct highly controlled research when dealing with real organisations and their employees and so conclusions need to be considered carefully.

Motivators at work
Intrinsic and extrinsic motivation

'People do work for money – but they work even harder for meaning in their lives. Companies that ignore this fact are essentially bribing their employees and will pay the price in a lack of loyalty and commitment.' (Pfeffer, 1998)

Reflections: Do you have a job? Why do you have one? Write down all the reasons you can think of before reading any further. Now think about the job that you would like to have when you have finished your education. Write down all the reasons why you would like to have this job.

Motivation can be internal or external. Internal (or intrinsic) motivators come from within and include factors such as enjoyment or a sense of satisfaction or achievement as motivators. This means that motivation comes from the actual performance of the task rather than from the potential consequences of completing the tasks. These potential rewards would be called external motivators. External (or extrinsic) motivators create a sense of motivation because of an external reward such as money, promotion and bonuses. Clearly different organisations might offer different types of motivators. Someone who works in finance may experience high levels of external motivators such as the amount they earn and the potential for additional bonuses, whereas someone who chooses to work in some aspect of health and social care is unlikely to experience the same level of financial reward but may be rewarded and motivated by different things, such as a sense of helping others and making a difference.

Reflections: Now look at the list you made earlier regarding a job you would like to have in the future. How many of the reasons you wrote down would be internal motivators and how many would be external motivators? Was there a difference between the job you have now and the job that you would like to have in the future?

Reward systems

Reward systems vary from organisation to organisation and can include pay, bonuses, profit sharing and performance-related pay. Pay may be linked to performance such that the harder someone works, or the faster they complete tasks, the more money they can earn. Bonuses are sometimes offered in addition to a salary and can be significant sums of money in some sectors, particularly in Finance. Profit sharing by an organisation means that a percentage of the company profit is shared among all the workers. This gives workers a stronger sense of belonging to the organisation and can lead to increased motivation. These systems might not be available in all organisations as not all organisations are set up to make a profit. Most health and education organisations for example do not have profit as their primary aim.

It is hard to tell if monetary rewards are successful in improving productivity and evidence exists on both side of this debate. A paper by de Waal and Jansen (2011) summarises a number of research findings in this area. They cite studies demonstrating that over half the growth in productivity in Chinese State industries could be attributed to the use of bonuses (Yao, 1997) and studies demonstrating the positive effects of performance-related pay (Belfield & Marsden, 2005). Hollowell (2005) claimed that those organisations paying their senior executives on high performance-related pay scales maintained strong stock markets presences.

However, de Waal and Jansen also include contradictory evidence. They cite studies which demonstrate that in organisations with very high inequalities (the difference between the highest paid and the lowest paid member of the organisation) there is also very high turnover of staff. This is also true in baseball where the teams with the highest pay inequalities lose more games (Bloom, 1999). This would suggest that any gains in productivity shown by the high performers are outweighed by the costs to the low performers. Finally research conducted in a number of organisations in the UK (Fattorusso et al., 2007) and Holland (Duffhues and Kabir, 2008) found no relationship between the size of bonus payments and performance.

Non-monetary rewards

Non-monetary rewards include praise, respect, recognition, empowerment and a sense of belonging.

Rewards and recognition are different. In an organisational context rewards are promised from the start. For most employees there will be a clear understanding of how much they will be paid, for example. This may affect your extrinsic motivation – you go to work in order to earn a salary. Recognition is not promised from the start and is when a worker is recognised for their contributions or achievements. An example may make this clearer. Giving someone a medal for bravery is recognition for their behaviour. It is not a reward as it was not promised from the start and as Hansen et al. (2002) explain; 'we would never think of promising a cash reward for every act of courage under fire. In fact, the thought of remuneration for such deeds actually cheapens them. On the other hand, try to get a teenager to clean his room without some clear contract of "what is in it for him"'.

However, not everyone is motivated by money and not all organisations are designed to make a profit. There are several effective motivators which are not monetary. Many of these you will understand as forms of positive reinforcement.

Reflections: Which studies at AS Level involved the concept of reinforcement?

Praise, respect and recognition come from other people and can be extremely motivating. Think about how you feel when you are praised for an achievement in the classroom. This is not quite an external reward like money – this is reward that makes you feel good about yourself. Achievement of a difficult task or even simply the completion of a task can lead to a feeling of empowerment. Empowerment makes you feel as though you can achieve anything!

Recognition can take many forms. At its simplest, recognition may be the employer thanking an employee for a job well done. This might be made more formal by the employee receiving a formal letter of thanks from their manager or even from someone more senior. More public forms of recognition might be in the form of award ceremonies or 'employee of the month' schemes. Achieving a difficult task, or meeting a challenging goal, can produce a sense of empowerment which is also motivating and creates a sense of belonging, within a team or the whole organisation.

Rose (1998) estimates that around 75% of organisations in the UK had some form of non-monetary recognition scheme and also noted that these were even more commonly found in organisations that rely heavily on customer contact.

There are many advantages to an organisation of having a non-monetary recognition scheme. Such a scheme can highlight desired behaviours and through recognition, create role models for other to imitate. The recognition may be given immediately, strengthening the association between the behaviour and the consequence, and these schemes are often very low-cost. Evidence suggests that staff turnover can also be positively affected. Building positive affective relationships between managers and workers and making sure that workers know that they are appreciated and that their efforts are valued makes people more likely to stay and increases their satisfaction ratings (Brown and Armstrong, 1999). Reed (a large UK based recruitment company) found that recognition was rated as the most important factor in achieving job satisfaction, whereas salary was rated sixth. The issues of staff turnover, absenteeism and job satisfaction will be explored later in this chapter.

Reflections: How would you feel if you were nominated as employee of the month?

Evaluation

> ### ISSUES AND DEBATES
>
> This section has considered motivation in a more practical sense. Rather than the theories that we met in the previous sections, here we have considered what factors may act as motivators in work. This is obviously useful information in several ways. It may be useful for you to consider what motivates you and this may help you in deciding the type of job that you want to aim for in the future. It may also be useful for managers of teams and organisations when considering what motivates their workers. For example, a monetary award is not always possible and recognising that non-monetary rewards such as praise and recognition can be equally effective (in some organisations at least) may ensure

> ### ISSUES AND DEBATES (continued)
>
> that managers recognise the value of these rewards to ensure the motivation of their workers. This section can be considered to take a behaviourist approach to the topic of motivation as it considers the effect of certain outcomes (reinforcements) on behaviour rather than focusing on the cognitive aspects. However, we can also consider individual differences here; what motivates one person may not motivate another – and also the **individual–situational debate** as the situation may well interact with the individual in determining the most effective motivators. Someone working in a highly creative environment is likely to be motivated by praise and recognition for their creativity whereas non-monetary rewards may not be as effective in the competitive business world.

> ### RESEARCH METHODS
>
> The material covered in this section has not included any empirical research although it is easy to see that all of these ideas could be tested experimentally. We could design a whole range of studies, in **laboratory** or **field situations** to test the effectiveness of different rewards.

Reflections: Design a laboratory-based study to test whether praise or money would be a more effective motivator for the completion of a boring, repetitive task. What strengths and weaknesses does your study have?

> ### SELF-ASSESSMENT QUESTIONS
>
> 1 Describe what Maslow meant by 'self-actualisation'.
> 2 McClelland used projective tests to measure the need for achievement. Give one strength and one weakness of projective tests.
> 3 Equity theory proposes that workers expect things to be fair. Suggest how somebody might respond if they discovered that someone doing the same job as them was being paid more.
> 4 Describe the difference between internal and external motivation.

9.2 Leadership and management

Traditional and modern theories of leadership

Universalist and behavioural theories

> **Reflections:** Research the meanings of leadership and management. Are they the same or different?

Universalist theories of leadership look at the personal qualities or characteristics which are shared by great leaders. One of the best known of these theories is the 'Great Man Theory' first proposed by Woods in 1913 and now more commonly referred to as the 'Great Person Theory'. This theory argues that great leaders are born and not made – in other words this can be understood as part of the nature–nurture debate and this will be considered in the evaluation section.

Another way to look at this is to consider the notion of a charismatic or transformational leader – someone with the charisma and the interpersonal skills to inspire and lead others. Such people tend to have excellent public speaking skills and high levels of confidence. They are sometimes described as 'visionaries' and are often unconventional in their approach.

> **Reflections:** Can you think of anyone who might be described as a transformational leader? Ask a few people of different ages and see what they say. Research anyone whose name you do not recognise.

Behavioural theories of leadership look at the specific behaviours shown by leaders as opposed to the personal qualities of leaders. Researchers at Ohio State University (R.M. Stogdill and A.E. Coons) have collated data from numerous studies of leaders and their workers and have identified over 100 different behaviours shown by leaders. Through further analysis these behaviours were shown to fall into two distinct categories:

- *Initiating structure*: this includes allocating tasks to people, creating groups and defining their goals, setting deadlines and ensuring that they are met and making sure that workers are working to a set standard.
- *Consideration*: this is the category of behaviours which are shown by leaders who express a genuine concern for the feelings of workers. These leaders will establish a rapport with workers and show trust and respect.

They will listen to workers more often than the other category of leader and will try to improve performance by boosting self-confidence.

A similar set of studies were conducted at the University of Michigan and this also produced two main types of behaviours shown by leaders which were:

- *Task-oriented behaviours*. Not surprisingly this refers to behaviours which focus specifically on the task to be completed. Leaders focus on the structure (as in the 'initiating structure' leadership behaviour category described above) and will set targets and standards, supervise and monitor workers and progress.
- *Relationship-oriented behaviours*. These have a focus on the well-being of the workforce. Leaders would spend time examining and understanding the interpersonal relationships between workers and those between workers and managers and this has clear overlaps with the 'consideration' leadership behaviour described above.

Adaptive leadership

As organisations grow ever larger and more complex, it is possible to argue that traditional forms of leadership may be failing. If these traditional methods are not working, then there is a need to change or a need for adaptation. Working practices and organisational norms and values that made an organisation successful in the past may now be irrelevant and the organisation must confront the need for change. This is where Heifetz et al.'s (1997, 2009) concept of adaptive leadership comes in. They define leadership as the 'art of mobilising people (in organisations and communities) to tackle tough issues, adapt and thrive' (2009). They argue that leadership itself has to change; that rather than leading by providing solutions, the leader of an organisation facing adaptive challenges must be able to shift the responsibilty for change to the entire workforce. This may be distressing for some people as employees may have to take on new roles, learn new skills, align with new values or even accept that there is no longer a place for them within the organisation. Employees are used to management solving problems for them and this will also have to change. This may mean that adaptive leaders can no longer protect their workers from the problems facing the organisation so that they understand the need to change. The role of the adaptive leader is no longer to maintain and support the organisational norms and values but to allow disorientation, conflict and challenge to create a new organisation that can survive. The differences between traditional leadership and adaptive leadership are summarised in Table 9.1.

Traditional leadership	Adaptive leadership
is about authority and the issuing of directions to others	is about helping others to find their inner authority
is about maintaining organisational norms and traditions (*we have always done it like this*)	is about challenging these norms and traditions and exploring new ways of working
makes use of the skills and competencies available	pushes boundaries and attempts to extend skills and competencies
is about tried and tested solutions or directions based on prior experiences	is about new solutions or new directions which have not been tested and have unknown outcomes
is useful in times of certainty	is most useful in times of uncertainty

Table 9.1 Leadership styles compared

There are six key principles of adaptive leadership and these are as follows:

1   'Get on the balcony'. An adaptive leader needs to see the whole picture and to view the organisation and the way it works as if they were observing from above.

2   Identify the adaptive change. An adaptive leader needs to not only identify the need for change but be able to determine the nature and extent of the change required, be that to organisational structure, values, working practices or working relationships.

3   Regulate distress. Adaptive change will both stress and distress those who are experiencing it. This cannot be avoided but it can be managed. The pressure needs to be enough to motivate people to change but not so much that it overwhelms them. The adaptive leader needs to be able to tolerate the uncertainty and frustration and to communicate confidence.

4   Maintain disciplined attention. An adaptive leader must be open to contrasting points of view. Rather than avoiding or covering up issues that are difficult or disturbing, they must confront the issues directly.

5   Give the work back to the people. An adaptive leader must recognise that everyone in the organisation has special access to information that comes only from their experiences in their particular role. Adaptive leaders must step back from the traditional role of telling people what to do and, by allowing them to use their special knowledge, recognise that they are best placed to identify the solutions to the problems.

6   Protect voices of leadership from below. Heifetz et al. argue that 'giving a voice to all people is the foundation of an organisation that is willing to experiment and learn'. In many organisations, those who speak up are silenced. An adaptive leader needs to listen to these voices to learn of impending challenges. Ignoring them can be be fatal for the organisation.

As an example of leadership styles, Heifetz and Linsky, in their book *Leadership on the Line (2002)*, refer to Henry Fonda's character in the film *12 Angry Men* as an example of the adaptive leader in action. Henry Fonda plays the only jury member who initially votes 'not guilty' in a murder trial. Through the film, his behaviour encourages the other jurors to explore their own prejudices and biases and to look at the evidence from different perspectives. Heifetz and Linksy claim that this is a powerful display of adaptive leadership.

The three levels of leadership

The idea of three levels of leadership was introduced by James Scouller in a book published in 2011, which explains how leadership presence can be developed and is sometimes referred to as the 3P model of leadership after the three key elements:

- public leadership
- private leadership
- personal leadership.

The model is usually presented in diagram form as three circles and four outwardly-directed arrows, with personal leadership in the centre (Figure 9.3).

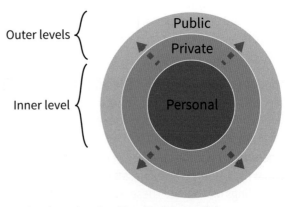

9.3 The three levels of leadership model

Public and private leadership are described as the 'outer' or 'behavioural' levels of the model. Public leadership concerns the behaviours required to influence groups of people and private leadership concerns the behaviours involved in influencing individuals.

> **Reflections:** How do you think these might be different? What skills might you need to influence an individual? What skills might you need to influence a group?

The third level, shown in the centre of the diagram, is described as the 'inner' level and relates to the leadership qualities shown by the individual. This will include their skills and beliefs but also their emotions, subconscious behaviours and their 'presence'. Scouller argued that leaders need to 'grow their leadership presence, know-how and skill' through developing their technical know-how and skill, cultivating the right attitude towards other people and working on psychological self-mastery. This final aspect is the most crucial aspect of developing a leadership presence.

> *'At its heart is the leader's self-awareness, his progress toward self-mastery and technical competence, and his sense of connection with those around him. It's the inner core, the source, of a leader's outer leadership effectiveness.'*
> (Scouller, 2011)

Scouller argues that personal leadership is the most powerful of the three levels. He likened its effect to dropping a pebble in a pond and seeing the ripples spreading out from the centre (Figure 9.4) – hence the four arrows pointing outward in Figure 9.3.

9.4 Personal leadership spreads like ripples

Evaluation

ISSUES AND DEBATES

Theories of leadership raise a number of crucial evaluation issues. To begin with, we will consider the **nature versus nurture debate**. Are leaders born or made? The Great Person Theory described above would certainly be on the nature side of this debate while the other theories may leave room for some development of leadership skills. Scouller in particular, whose theory brought together many of the older theories, including trait theories, behaviour theories and theories of leadership style, would argue that leadership presence can be developed but the arguments proposed by Heifetz et al. also suggest that leadership needs to able to adapt and change and that leadership skills can be learned.

The 3 Ps model and the Theory of Adaptive Leadership also allow us to consider the **individual–situational debate** as it clearly shows that different skills will be required for different situations, for example in trying to persuade an individual rather than trying to persuade a group. Heifetz et al. argue strongly for the need for adaptive leadership particularly where the more traditional styles of leadership have failed or when the situation is one of great uncertainty. As with the earlier theories of leadership we can also consider whether some individuals may be better able to provide adaptive leadership as well as considering the extent to which personal leadership skills may be developed. Finally, it is important to consider the issue of usefulness or application to everyday life. The theories that have been discussed here have been applied in organisations all over the world and make a significant contribution to the success or otherwise of a wide variety of organisations.

RESEARCH METHODS

The work conducted by Ohio State University and by the University of Michigan brings together huge amounts of data collected from a wide range of organisations and individuals. This gives their findings a great deal of support, and conclusions drawn from these findings can be generalised easily. Heifetz et al. and Scouller present largely theoretical models of leadership although this is a good point to introduce the issue of psychometric testing. In any study where leadership is being measured, some form of psychometric test will be used. These have a number of strengths and weaknesses which will be discussed in the next evaluation section.

Leadership style
Leadership effectiveness

There have been several attempts to explain different styles of leadership and this is what will be examined next. The first is the Theory of Leadership Effectiveness proposed by Fiedler (1967) which examines the interaction between the style of leadership and the situation. This identifies an important point that different leadership styles will be effective in different situations. This is not only because of the goals of the organisation – a different leader would be required to run a school, a prison, a charity and a financial institution – but also because different organisations will give their leaders differing amounts of power and control and so different types of leader will fit better into different types of organisations.

Reflections: Choose three of the following organisations: a school, a prison, a bank, a hospital, a newspaper and a small convenience store. Identify what you think would be the most appropriate way to lead each of your chosen organisations.

In order to measure leadership effectiveness, Fiedler developed the LPC or least preferred co-worker scale (see Table 9.2). This 16-item questionnaire asks leaders about the person with whom they work least well. Fiedler assumed that everyone's LPC is probably equally unpleasant and so the LPC is not about the least preferred co-worker but rather is about the person taking the test. The analysis of the answers determines whether the individual has a low LPC score and is task oriented (such that they would give harsh ratings to their least preferred co-worker) or a high LPC score and is relationship-oriented (such that they would give positive ratings to even their LPC).

Pleasant	8	7	6	5	4	3	2	1	Unpleasant
Friendly	8	7	6	5	4	3	2	1	Unfriendly
Rejecting	8	7	6	5	4	3	2	1	Accepting
Tense	8	7	6	5	4	3	2	1	Relaxed
Cold	8	7	6	5	4	3	2	1	Warm
Supporting	8	7	6	5	4	3	2	1	Hostile
Boring	8	7	6	5	4	3	2	1	Interesting
Quarrelsome	8	7	6	5	4	3	2	1	Harmonious
Gloomy	8	7	6	5	4	3	2	1	Cheerful
Open	8	7	6	5	4	3	2	1	Closed
Backbiting	8	7	6	5	4	3	2	1	Loyal

Untrustworthy	8	7	6	5	4	3	2	1	Trustworthy
Considerate	8	7	6	5	4	3	2	1	Inconsiderate
Nasty	8	7	6	5	4	3	2	1	Nice
Agreeable	8	7	6	5	4	3	2	1	Disagreeable
Insincere	8	7	6	5	4	3	2	1	Sincere
Kind	8	7	6	5	4	3	2	1	Unkind

Table 9.2 Least preferred co-worker (LPC) scale

The Situational Theory of Leadership

The Situational Theory of Leadership was suggested by Hersey and Blanchard (1988) and proposed that there is no single effective leadership style (Figure 9.5). Although leaders may have their preferred style, it is not appropriate for a leader to use the same style all the time. A truly effective leader must be able to adapt their leadership style to suit the situation.

9.5 Situational leadership model

The two key concepts in this model are the *leadership style of the leader* and the *individual's or group's **maturity** level*. An effective leadership style must be relevant to the task and the most successful leaders are those who can adapt their leadership style to the maturity level of the group they are leading.

KEY TERM

maturity: in this context is the capacity to set high but attainable goals, willingness and ability to take responsibility for the task, and relevant education and/or experience of an individual or a group for the task.

Reflections: Look at the list you made in response to the previous reflection. Do you think that the maturity level of the group you were leading was something you considered?

Leadership style can be described in terms of task behaviour and relationship behaviour. This produces four types of leader behaviour:

- *Style 1 (S1) telling.* This is behaviour that is largely directive, the leader will define the role for the members of the group and will explain (or tell) the group members how, why, when and where to do the task.
- *Style 2 (S2) selling.* This behaviour type is still directive but will involve more two-way communication and will also involve the use of relationship skills that will allow the group members to 'buy into' or feel a part of the process.
- *Style 3 (S3) participating.* The leader provides less direction and this style is characterised by shared decision making. A high use is made of relationship skills.
- *Style 4 (S4) delegating.* The leader is still involved with the decision making process but the responsibility has been delegated to the group. The leader is likely to take a monitoring rather than a directive role.

Reflections: Imagine you are a teacher of A Level Psychology students and you have set your class a group activity to research some aspect of organisational psychology. Which style of leader behaviour would you choose to use and why?

The right leadership style will depend on the person or group being led. This is where the second important concept, the maturity level of the individual or group comes in. The Hersey–Blanchard Situational Leadership Theory identifies four levels of maturity:

- M1 – the individual or group lacks the specific skills required for the job in hand and is unable and unwilling to do or to take responsibility for the task.
- M2 – they are unable to take on responsibility for the task being done; however, they are willing to work at the task. They are enthusiastic but need more training and support.
- M3 – they are experienced and able to do the task but lack the confidence or the willingness to take on responsibility.
- M4 – they are experienced at the task, and comfortable with their own ability to do it well. They are able and willing to not only do the task, but to take responsibility for the task.

Maturity levels are also task-specific rather than person-specific. A person might be generally skilled, confident and motivated in their job, but would still have maturity level M1 when asked to perform a task requiring skills they do not possess.

Reflections: Make a list of some tasks that you feel you could complete at maturity level 4. Now make a list of some tasks where you think you might be at maturity level 1. What sort of leader would you like to have for each of these tasks?

287

Style of leader behaviour

Research conducted since the 1960s has tended to focus on the superiority of the democratic style of leadership. However, Muczyk and Reimann (1987) argue that democratic leadership may not always be the most effective and that it may not work at all in some situations. They argue that 'leadership is a two-way street, so a democratic style will be effective only if followers are both willing and able to participate actively in the decision making process. If they are not, the leader cannot be democratic without also being "directive" and following up very closely to see that directives are being carried out properly' (page 301).

They argue that the importance of direction to successful leadership has neither been fully recognised nor properly investigated and this, they claim, is due to the common failure to distinguish between participation and direction. They further argue that some researchers appear to understand direction as being the exact opposite of participation and that this has had the effect of making directive leadership appear anti-democratic.

Their article is an argument for direction as a separate dimension of leadership and one that is not necessarily inconsistent with participation. Combining direction with participation produces four styles of leadership and may help us understand the question of which style of leadership is best in which situation.

One of the key problems in previous research is that researchers have tended to see decision making and the execution of this decision to be the same thing. This is a crucial point as clearly the process of making a decision is quite separate from the process of ensuring that this decision is carried through. Deciding that something should happen is not the same as ensuring that it does happen.

> **Reflections:** Is deciding that something should happen all that an effective leader should have to do?

Although participation may well be the more effective style in decision making, direction (or directive leadership) may be crucial to ensure correct implementation of this decision. Research has tended to focus on the superiority of the participative (or democratic) style of leadership during the decision making process. It is important to realise that a leader may be participative during the decision making phase and directive during the later stages, meaning that they follow progress carefully to ensure that the decision is fully achieved.

This means that there are two leadership factors which need to be considered:

- *Participation*: low participation would be an autocratic leader and high participation would be a democratic or participative leader.
- *Direction*: low direction would be permissive with little or only general supervision and high would be directive, close supervision, constant follow-up.

An autocratic leader would assume that their role is to make decisions and that these decisions will be carried out by others who are subordinate to them and have no role in the decision making process. A democratic leader on the other hand will ensure that subordinates are involved in the decision making process even though they may retain the right to make the final decision.

The directive behaviour refers to how the leader deals with what happens after the decision has been made. A non-directive leader (permissive) will leave their subordinates free to decide how to reach the goal and will offer little if any direction. A directive leader on the other hand will specify how tasks are to be completed and will follow up progress throughout the implementation stage.

Classifying leaders as high or low on these two variables produces four types of leader behaviour, as given in Table 9.3.

		Degree of participation in decision making	
		Low	**High**
Amount of leader direction	**High**	*Directive autocrat:* Makes unilateral decisions Supervises workers closely Useful when there is a need for quick decisions and supervision of new staff or poor managers.	*Directive democrat:* Invites full participation in decisions monitors closely Useful when there is a need for complex decisions involving many experts, needing an overall direction
	Low	*Permissive autocrat:* Makes decisions themselves Allows staff to choose how to implement these decisions Useful where tasks are relatively simple or where staff are highly skilled and need little supervision	*Permissive democrat:* Seen as 'ideal' leader in (primarily American) literature Invites high degree of participation in decisions Allows for autonomy of implementation Good for highly skilled, trusted employees

Table 9.3 Four types of leader behaviour

Evaluation

The most obvious evaluation issue to begin with is the **individual–situational debate**. Fiedler examines the relationship between the individual (leader) and the situation directly and makes the point that different leadership styles will be effective in different situations. Hersey and Blanchard take this further and state that the leader must be able to fit their leadership style to the situation and that the mark of an effective leader is the extent to which they are able to do this. This has obvious applications to organisations, and organisations that recognise the importance of the 'fit' between the leader and the group or who can appoint leaders with the skills required to adapt their behaviour will be the most successful organisations.

Remaining with the theme of usefulness and applications, the contribution made to this area by Muczyk and Reimann has been significant. Highlighting the difference between making a decision and ensuring that that decision is implemented (followed through to its completion) is extremely valuable and will allow organisations to recognise that as with leadership in general, there are many styles and these styles suit different situations and groups. Ensuring that the right leader is in charge will ensure the successful completion of the task.

RESEARCH METHODS

As with previous sections, we have considered several theoretical models but again it would be possible to test these models in real-life situations. We have also considered the LPC scale and so we need to discuss the strengths and weaknesses of this. Some critics argue that ratings of LPC tells us little about an individual's leadership style. Other criticisms of this scale are ones that could be made about any psychometric test; individuals are prone to social desirability bias. It is difficult to construct a culturally fair (unbiased) test and tests may reveal more about the assumptions of the test-maker than anything else. However tests like the LPC scale are relatively easy to administer and to mark, produce quantitative data that can be easily analysed and are relatively objective ways of measuring personality characteristics.

KEY TERM

social desirability bias: trying to present oneself in the best light by determining what a test is asking.

Leaders and followers

Leader–member exchange model

A number of different models have been proposed to help explain the manager–worker relationship. One of these is the leader–member exchange model proposed by Danserau et al. (1995). Originally Danserau et al. had proposed the Vertical Dyad Linkage Theory (1975) which suggested that leaders can treat their followers in two different ways: they may treat some of them as trusted followers and others in more formal ways. This theory has now become known as the leader-member exchange model (1994). A further model, the individualised leadership model, was developed in 1995 and suggests that each follower should be understood as independent and each leader viewed as unique.

Vertical Dyad Linkage Theory claims that the relationship between a manager and his or her followers is developed through three stages. The first of these is the role-taking stage. This is where individuals become team members and meet their leader. Leaders need to make expectations clear and team members need to make their skills and abilities evident to the leader so that he or she can determine how each person may contribute to the team. In the second stage, the role-making stage, members of the team become integrated into the team and begin work. This allows them the opportunity to further prove their skills as well as their ability to work with others. The leader may then determine who becomes part of the in-group and who belongs in the out-group. The final stage is described as the role routinisation stage and this is where in-group members and the leader engage in 'mutual and high quality leader and subordinate exchanges' which further develops their relationships. This can also lead to improvements within the group. A study by Erdogan et al. (2015) showed that this is due to the out-group members attempting to communicate well with the in-group members as they are closely connected to the leader. This may allow them to achieve a move from the out-group to the in-group. Danserau's individualised leadership model extends the theory described above by focusing on the one-to-one relationship between a superior and a specific subordinate, involving (1) the supervisor's investments in and returns from the subordinate, and (2) the subordinate's investments in and returns from the superior.

Followership

Followership refers to a role held by certain individuals in an organisation, team or group. Specifically, it is the way in which an individual actively follows a leader. It is important to recognise that the role of leader can only be understood by also examining the reciprocal role of follower: Kelley (1988) claims that the study of 'followership' will lead to a better understanding of leadership. The success or failure of a group may not be solely down to the ability of a leader but may also be dependent on how well the followers can follow.

Kelley described four main qualities of effective followers:

- *Self-management*: this refers to the ability to think critically, to be in control of one's actions and to work independently. It is important that followers manage themselves well as leaders are able to delegate tasks to these individuals.
- *Commitment*: this refers to an individual being committed to the goal, vision or cause of a group, team or organisation. This is an important quality of followers as it helps keep one's (and other member's) morale and energy levels high.
- *Competence*: it is essential that individuals possess the skills and aptitudes necessary to complete the goal or task or the group, team or organisation. Individuals high in this quality often hold skills higher than their average co-worker (or team member). Further, these individuals continue their pursuit of knowledge by upgrading their skills through classes and seminars.
- *Courage*: effective followers hold true to their beliefs and maintain and uphold ethical standards, even in the face of dishonest or corrupt superiors (leaders). These individuals are loyal, honest and, importantly, candid with their superiors.

Kelley also identified two characteristics (dimensions) which help to identify the difference between followers and non-followers. The first of these is critical thinking and the second is whether the individual is active or passive. This gives us five types of followers, described as follows:

- The *sheep*: passive, lack commitment and require external motivation and constant supervision from the leader.
- The *yes-people*: these individuals are committed to the leader and the goal (or task) of the organisation (or group/team). These conformist individuals do not question the decisions or actions of the leader. Further,

yes-people will defend their leader when faced with opposition from others.
- The *pragmatics*: these individuals are not trail-blazers; they will not stand behind controversial or unique ideas until the majority of the group has expressed their support. These individuals often remain in the background of the group.
- The *alienated*: these individuals are negative and often attempt to stall or bring the group down by constantly questioning the decisions and actions of the leader. These individuals often view themselves as the rightful leader of the organisation and are critical of the leader and fellow group members.
- The *star followers*: these exemplary individuals are positive, active and independent thinkers. Star followers will not blindly accept the decisions or actions of a leader until they have evaluated them completely. Furthermore, these types of followers can succeed without the presence of a leader.

Measuring leadership

Kouzes and Posner (1987) argue that leadership is a 'measurable, learnable and teachable set of behaviours'. They developed the Leadership Practices Inventory (LPI) to measure the extent to which an individual engages in each of the five practices of exemplary leadership which they established through their research with successful leaders. These include modelling desired behaviours, inspiring others, challenging the status quo, enabling others and encouraging and rewarding others. The LPI consists of six behavioural statements for each of these practices and examples of these statements are given below.

1 Model the Way.
   - 'sets a personal example of what he/she expects of others'
   - 'is clear about his/her personal philosophy of leadership'.

2 Inspire a shared vision.
   - 'describes a compelling image of what our future could be like'
   - 'appeals to others to share an exciting dream of the future'.

3 Challenge the process.
   - 'experiments and takes risks even when there is a chance of failure'
   - 'challenges people to try out new and innovative ways to do their work'.

4 Enable others to act.
- 'Treats others with dignity and respect'
- 'Supports the decisions that people make on their own'.

5 Encourage the heart.
- 'Praises people for a job well done'.
- 'Makes it a point to let people know about his/her confidence in their abilities'.

The LPI consists of the individual's self-ratings of the frequency with which they demonstrate these behaviours as well as a number of observer ratings. These are combined on the final profile. Kouzes and Posner strongly believe that leadership is learned rather than something one is born with. This means that the profile that is produced after completion of the LPI does not simply provide a picture of the behaviours that someone exhibits but can be used to identify areas for personal development. They claim that there are many different ways in which different types of people (for example introverts versus extroverts) can be developed into successful leaders.

Reflections: Kouzes and Posner's views would be on the 'nurture' side of the nature-nurture debate as they believe that leadership is something that is learned rather than something that one is born with. What do you think?

Evaluation

> **ISSUES AND DEBATES**
>
> We will begin this evaluation by considering the **nature versus nurture debate**. Kouzes and Posner argue that leadership is something that can be learned rather than something which we are born with. By exploring the personality characteristics of an individual they can suggest different ways in which different types of people can be developed into successful leaders. If we add the **individual–situational debate** to the discussion at this point, we could also argue that it should be possible to develop someone into the most successful type of leader based not only on their existing personality type and attitudes but also on the situation (group) which they are going to lead. Interestingly Kelley shifts the focus from leaders to followers although does not directly address the question of whether followership qualities are born or made. We might assume that he would suggest

> **ISSUES AND DEBATES (continued)**
>
> that the follower types are based on innate qualities of an individual but it is likely that the follower qualities discussed prior to the follower types are qualities that could be developed. As with many of the other theories that we have examined in this chapter, Kelley's work highlights the importance of the relationship between the leader and the situation; in this case the type of followers that the leader must lead. Increasing our understanding of these relationships is clearly useful for organisations and can be applied in a variety of ways. The work of Danserau helps further by explaining the stages through which the leader–group member relationship follows.

> **SELF-ASSESSMENT QUESTIONS**
>
> **5** Explain the difference between a 'task-oriented' leader and a 'relationship-oriented' leader.
>
> **6** In Scouller's 'Three levels of leadership model' which level did he suggest was the most important and why?
>
> **7** Explain what a low score would indicate in Fiedler's Least Preferred Co-worker Scale?
>
> **8** Identify the four qualities of effective followers, according to Kelley.

9.3 Group behaviour in organisations

Group development and roles
Group development

> **Reflection:** How does a group form? Think about some of the groups that you belong to. Were there stages of becoming a group?

Tuckman's stages of group development (1965) are well known. His proposal of a five stage group formation process (*forming – storming – norming – performing – adjourning*) has been applied to countless groups since its original proposal in 1965.

Forming

Team acquaints and establishes ground rules. Formalities are preserved and members are treated as strangers.

Storming

Members start to communicate their feelings but still view themselves as individuals rather than part of a team. They resist control by group leaders and show hostility.

Norming

People feel part of the team and realise that they can achieve work if they accept other viewpoints.

Performing

The team works in an open and trusting atmosphere where flexibility is the key and hierarchy is of little importance.

Adjourning

The team conducts an assessment of the year and implements a plan for transitioning roles and recognising members' contributions.

9.6 Tuckman's stages of group development

He proposes that all groups go through the same five stages during their formation and these are described in Figure 9.6.

Belbin's Theory of Team Roles

Belbin's Theory of Team Roles (1981) takes a slightly different approach to understanding group behaviour. Belbin proposes that an ideal team contains people who are prepared to take on different roles (see Table 9.4).

Action-oriented roles

Shapers are people who challenge the team to improve. They are dynamic and usually extroverted people who enjoy stimulating others, questioning established views and finding the best approaches for solving problems. Shapers tend to see obstacles as exciting challenges, although they may also be argumentative and upset colleagues. Implementers are the people who get things done. They turn the team's ideas and concepts into practical actions and plans. They tend to be people who work systematically and efficiently and are very well organised. However, they can be inflexible and resistant to change. Completer-finishers are the people who see that projects are completed thoroughly. They ensure there have been no mistakes and they pay attention to

Action-oriented roles	Shaper	Challenges the team to improve
	Implementer	Puts ideas into action
	Completer-finisher	Ensures thorough, timely completion
People-oriented roles	Coordinator	Acts as a chairperson
	Team worker	Encourages cooperation
	Resource investigator	Explores outside opportunities
Thought-oriented roles	Plant	Presents new ideas and approaches
	Monitor-evaluator	Analyses the options
	Specialist	Provides specialised skills

Table 9.4 A summary of the team roles proposed by Belbin

the smallest of details. They are very concerned with deadlines and will push the team to make sure the job is completed on time. They are described as perfectionists and may worry unnecessarily and find it hard to delegate.

People-oriented roles

Coordinators are the ones who take on the traditional team-leader role and guide the team to the objectives. They are often excellent listeners and they are naturally able to recognise the value that each team member brings to the table. They are calm and good-natured, and delegate tasks very effectively. Their potential weaknesses are that they may delegate too much personal responsibility, and may be manipulative. Team workers are the people who provide support and make sure that people within the team are working together effectively. These people are negotiators and are flexible, diplomatic and perceptive. These tend to be popular people who prioritise team cohesion and help people get along. They may be indecisive and struggle to commit to a position. Resource investigators are innovative and curious. They explore the available options, develop contacts and negotiate for resources on behalf of the team. They are enthusiastic team members, who identify and work with external stakeholders to help the team accomplish its objective. They are outgoing and people generally respond positively to them. However, they may lose enthusiasm quickly.

Thought-oriented roles

The plant is the creative person who comes up with new ideas. They thrive on praise but struggle to take criticism. Plants are often introverted and prefer to work on their own. Their ideas can sometimes be impractical and they may also be poor communicators. Monitor-evaluators are good at analysing and evaluating the ideas that other people propose. These people are shrewd, objective and strategic and they carefully weigh the pros and cons of all the options before coming to a decision. They can be seen as detached or unemotional. Specialists are people who have specialised knowledge that is needed to get the job done. They pride themselves on their skills and expertise but may sometimes focus on technicalities at the expense of the bigger picture.

Reflections: Which one of these role descriptions is most like you? Which one is least like you?

Measuring team roles

The Belbin Test is a test for assessing team roles. There are a number of these tests and you need to pay to access them. Paying to take the test produces a very detailed report of your skills and abilities in relation to the team roles already discussed such as advice on where you may be most comfortable, roles you may be best (or least) suited to and strategies for playing to your strengths.

Reflections: If there were no plants or team workers in a team what effect would this have on the team?

Evaluation

Tuckman's model of group formation is extremely useful in providing guidance on how groups form and in allowing organisations to see that these stages are part of the normal developmental processes. However, this model was originally proposed as an explanation of small groups and may not be as useful in helping to understand the development of larger groups. Tuckman does not provide guidance on timescales for moving from one stage to another and neither does he recognise that group formation is often cyclical rather than linear. Despite these and other criticisms his work has been extremely influential in understanding the stages that groups pass through. One final point is that he does not take account of the differing team roles that group members might have to adopt, which is where Belbin steps in. Rather than looking at the stages of group development, Belbin examines the type of people that are required in a group. This means that an important application of his work (and an important part of the development of a group) is to assess the preferred roles of each team member and to encourage all members to appreciate the characteristics and the strengths of the others. Of course, one problem when looking at Belbin's team roles is that many groups may be smaller than nine. Belbin recognised this himself and, in practice, group members in small groups will often take on more than one role. Unfortunately much of the research into Belbin's team roles suggests that many management teams have too many implementers and shapers and not enough plants and team workers. This is likely to mean that plans are formulated and given detail fairly quickly, but that they may lack creativity and may alienate some members (Arnold et al., 2005). However Belbin must be given credit for his focus on the need for diversity within teams and the value of different characteristics and skills.

Decision making

The decision making process

It is widely assumed that people make rational, reasonable and logical decisions. This assumption rests on a further assumption – that people making decisions have access to complete and accurate information and that they can process this without bias.

Wedley and Field (1984) describe the pre-planning stage of the decision making process and the decisions that are taken before beginning to solve a problem. These include deciding which type of leadership to use, whether to involve others, how to gather information, what people to contact and how to generate alternatives. These are not the end decisions but are important 'pre-decisions' that need to be considered. Wedley and Field suggest that once the decision making process has been started, it is difficult to stop and this may lead to poor decisions being taken. They propose that for greater flexibility, managers should be encouraged to pre-plan the decision making process.

They identify a set of problem-solving stages that is widely considered to be logical and rational (Table 9.5). However, it is unlikely that every decision making situation will fit this model: there may be time pressures, there may be information missing and so on. A decision support system (DSS) is a computer-based system that supports decision making activities.

Groupthink

Groupthink is defined as a psychological phenomenon that occurs within a group of people, in which the desire for harmony or conformity in the group results in an irrational or dysfunctional decision making outcome. In other words, the group creates a situation in which a decision is made which would not have been made by individuals.

> **Reflections:** Some famous examples of groupthink are the Bay of Pigs/Pearl Harbor. Research one of these and find out how groupthink resulted in poor decision making.

Janis (1971) identified eight different "symptoms" that indicate groupthink and these are:

1. Illusions of invulnerability. This means that members of the group believe that they can do no wrong and can never be in any sort of trouble. This can lead to overly optimistic thinking about likely outcomes and encourages risky decision making.

Stage	Decisions to make
Identify the problem or opportunity	What business problem will be solved? What market opportunity presents itself? Be sure to identify the problem or opportunity accurately.
Formulate your objective(s)	Faced with this problem or opportunity, what is the company's goal? What are the criteria that must be met before decision makers conclude that a good decision has been made?
Familiarise yourself with the problem	Learn all that you can about the problem, including its causes and effects.
Generate alternative solutions	What are the possible solutions to this problem? Collect data about the appropriateness of each alternative, including its potential outcomes and whether it can realistically be achieved.
Evaluate the alternatives	Which solutions meet the criteria established for an effective decision? How do these solutions compare in terms of costs and benefits?
Choose the best alternative	Which alternative best meets the company's goal?
Implement the alternative	Take action. Commit organisational resources.
Follow up with evaluation of the results	Did the action solve the problem or seize the opportunity? Compare the results obtained with the goals and criteria originally established.

Table 9.5 Stages of rational problem solving decision making

2 Unquestioned beliefs. A lack of questioning, particularly from a legal or moral standpoint, can prevent group members from considering all the possible consequences of their decisions.

3 Rationalising. This is where group members ignore warning signs and assume that everything will be alright.

4 Stereotyping. Group decision making can involve stereotypical views of those who raise issues or point out problems. This can mean that they are ignored or labelled as members of an 'out-group'.

5 Self-censorship. In a group situation we are less likely to listen to our own doubts or misgivings as it appears to us that no-one else has any doubts or misgivings. This is a little like the 'pluralistic ignorance' seen in bystanders to an accident when they assume that, since no-one else is responding, that there is no real emergency. In this way, everyone is convinced that there is nothing to worry about.

6 Mind guards. Janis described these as 'self-appointed censors to hide problematic information from the group'. We don't want the rest of the group to see that we are worried and so we hide this. Unfortunately, if everyone is feeling the same way and hiding their feelings, this can lead to some very risky decisions.

7 Illusions of unanimity. Groups behaving in the ways that we have just considered will produce the illusion of 'unanimity' or agreement.

8 Direct pressure to conform. Groups can place dissenters (those who disagree) or those who question under a great deal of pressure, in some cases making them appear as though they are being disloyal or traitorous by asking questions.

This means that groupthink can lead to extremely poor decision making. However groupthink can also have benefits. When working with a large number of people, it often allows the group to make decisions, complete tasks, and finish projects quickly and efficiently.

Groupthink is caused by a number of factors. It occurs more in situations where group members are very similar to one another and is more likely to take place if there is an extremely charismatic leader. High levels of stress or situations that are morally challenging also seem to increase the chances of groupthink occurring.

Strategies to reduce the risk of groupthink

To reduce the risk of groupthink, leaders need to give group members the opportunity to express their own ideas or argue against ideas that have already been proposed. Breaking up members into smaller independent teams can also be helpful. The leader should avoid stating their views too forcefully, especially at the start of the discussion, to ensure that people are able to develop their own views first. If someone is instructed to take the role of 'devil's advocate', that is to deliberately present the opposing view regardless of their own personal viewpoints, this can also reduce the likelihood of groupthink occurring and encourage the group members to take a critical perspective.

Cognitive limitations and errors

Individuals in a group decision making setting are often functioning under substantial cognitive demands. As a result, cognitive and motivational biases can often affect group decision-making adversely. Forsyth (2006) suggests that there are three categories of potential biases that may affect group decision making.

The first is called 'Sins of Commission' and refers to the misuse of information in the decision making process. This may involve the use of information in the decision making process that has already been shown to be inaccurate (belief perseverance). Alternatively, it may be shown by group members remaining committed to a plan because some investment of time or money has already been made even though this plan may now be obviously flawed (sunk cost bias). If a group chooses to use information despite having been told to ignore it then they are guilty of extra-evidentiary bias and, finally, falsely overestimating the importance of past knowledge or experience is termed hindsight bias.

The second category of bias is 'Sins of Omission' and this is overlooking key information. This can include base rate bias which would be overlooking very basic relevant information. The fundamental attribution error is made when members of a group make decisions based on inaccurate appraisals of an individual's behaviour.

The third category is 'Sins of Imprecision' and this involves relying too heavily on heuristics that over-simplify complex decisions. Heuristics include the availability heuristic (over-reliance on the information that is most easily and readily available), the conjunctive bias (failing to consider relationships between events) and the representativeness heuristic (where group members rely too heavily on decision making factors that may appear meaningful but are, in fact, misleading).

Evaluation

Understanding the process of decision making is clearly very useful and will have obvious applications to any organisation. Wedley and Field not only explain the process of decision making but identify several strategies to ensure that poor decisions are avoided. These include the use of pre-planning as well as the use of computer-based decision support systems. Janis's exploration of groupthink is also useful and can be applied in organisations to ensure that the negative outcomes of groupthink are avoided. It is important to remember that groupthink can sometimes be extremely useful, allowing for big decisions to be taken quickly and easily, but that there are also pitfalls. The strategies outlined above should be common practice in any organisation where decision making occurs regularly. Forsyth examines cognitive limitations and errors in even more detail and knowledge of these biases would be valuable information within an organisation that takes decisions frequently. Acknowledging and recognising the possibility of these errors will allow an organisation to take steps to reduce them.

Group conflict

Levels and causes of group conflict

There are several types of conflict that can occur in organisational contexts. These include:

- *Intra-group* conflict: when people within the same group are in conflict.
- *Inter-group* conflict: conflict between two groups within the same organisation.
- *Inter-individual* conflict: conflict between two or more individuals within a group.

All forms of conflict can interfere with the achievement of a goal and all organisations will attempt to keep conflicts to a minimum. Although there can be numerous causes of conflict within a group, Riggio (2009) suggested that these may be divided into two broad categories. These categories are organisational factors and interpersonal factors.

Organisational factors could be conflict over status or salary, or disagreements over how to achieve a goal. A lack of resources or space may also create conflict.

Interpersonal factors may be as simple as a personality clash between two people or that they do not work well together for some reason. If the interpersonal conflict is between leaders of different groups then this can produce increased conflict very easily.

> **Reflections:** You are part of a group that has been given responsibility for organising some sort of leaving event for your school year. Make a list of all the possible causes of conflict.

Positive and negative effects of conflict

Conflict can have both positive and negative effects. Some of the positive effects of conflict have been identified by Pruitt and Rubin (2003). They suggest that it is conflict which produces change and this may be particularly true of small organisations where change can be more easily implemented than in large organisations. The resolution of conflict may also strengthen group unity and commitment to organisational goals or to groups within the organisation (remember that the 'storming' phase of group formation was a necessary stage). Conflict can help to ensure that decisions are fully considered and explored and may prevent 'risky' decision making such as groupthink, and may also produce creative and innovative suggestions. Conflict can take the form of healthy competition such as sales staff competing for the highest sales of the month or the year and this can have positive effects on total revenue. However, management should be cautious about using competition as a means of increasing motivation as there are several possible negative effects that need to be considered.

Conflict can distract workers from their jobs, reducing overall productivity and can waste time, resources and money. Goals can become distorted as people become more focussed on the conflict than on their jobs. Conflict can have significant effects on the physical and psychological health of the people involved, increasing absenteeism and turnover and reducing staff satisfaction. If people feel that the conflict includes any behaviours that could be described as bullying or harassment, this would need to be referred to the Human Resources department and if made public, could have extremely negative effects on the public perception of the company.

The management of conflict is obviously extremely important for all organisations. Riggio offers a starting point in identifying that conflict may have individual or situational causes. Situational causes will be something to do with the organisation; the working conditions, salary levels, expectations and so on and being able to identify the causes may help in identifying a solution. However conflict may not be situational. It may simply be between two individuals and obviously very different strategies will be needed to manage this.

However it is also useful to recognise that conflict can also be positive and organisations need to recognise the potential positive outcomes from allowing some conflict to continue. Disagreement is not conflict and one problem for organisations may be to establish the level of conflict that ensures good decision making (all aspects of the argument have been considered) and reduces the chances of groupthink while at the same time does not lead to the breakdown of good working relationships.

Having a range of strategies for managing conflict is obviously important for all organisations. When is it appropriate to allow the individuals concerned to continue to fight until one of them wins and when it is appropriate to step in and offer some sort of compromise solution? Strategies based on collaboration or the pursuit of a superordinate goal have their roots in the social psychology of prejudice and discrimination and the application of this understanding to the workplace is invaluable.

Managing group conflict

Thomas (1976) suggests five strategies that can be used to manage group conflict:

- *Competition*: individuals may persist in conflict until someone wins and someone loses. At this point, the conflict is over.
- *Accommodation*: here one individual will need to make a sacrifice in order to reduce the conflict. This can be extremely effective in reducing conflict and preventing further damage to the relationship.
- *Compromise*: each group or individual under conflict must make some compromise and give up something to reduce the conflict. This will be effective only if both sides lose comparable things.
- *Collaboration*: the group has to work together to overcome the conflict.
- *Avoidance*: avoidance involves suppressing the conflict or withdrawing from the conflict completely. This does not resolve the conflict which is still there and has not been addressed. This can be effective in creating a cooling-off period.

Another way to address conflict is to create a superordinate goal; a goal that both groups and individuals have to work together to achieve. This is similar to collaboration, above, although the group are working towards something other than overcoming the conflict.

Reflections: Research the study called the Robber's Cave study conducted by Sherif et al. (1961). Explain how Sherif used superordinate goals to reduce the prejudice that he had created.

SELF-ASSESSMENT QUESTIONS

9 Name Tuckman's stages of group formation and explain what happens in the 'norming' stage.

10 Explain what Belbin meant by 'people oriented roles'.

11 Explain what is meant by the term 'groupthink'.

12 Suggest two ways in which group conflict might be managed.

9.4 Organisational work conditions

Physical and psychological work conditions
Physical: The Hawthorne Studies

The Hawthorne effect is a well-known concept in organisational psychology which refers to the phenomena of behaviour changing simply because it is being investigated, rather than as a result of any of the variables that were being manipulated. Although this is a familiar concept in psychology, less is known about the original research that demonstrated this effect. An article by Wickstrom and Bendix (2000) describes the original Hawthorne studies and challenges the conclusions that were drawn.

The original Hawthorne Studies were conducted in 1924 at the Hawthorne Works in Cicero, Illinois, USA. The managers, working with Massachusetts Institute of Technology and Harvard University, examined the effects on productivity of lighting changes and work structure changes such as working hours and break times. In the first study, the effect of lighting on productivity was examined. An experimental group was exposed to decreasing levels of light while a control group received a constant level of light. Interestingly both groups steadily increased their performance on their tasks. It was not until the light was only as bright as moonlight that the experimental group showed any decrease in productivity. The researchers concluded that lighting level did not significantly affect productivity so long as it was sufficient for the job to be done.

A series of further experiments were conducted which explored the effect of several other variables. In each of these studies, the researchers were forced to conclude that the variable under examination was not responsible for the increased productivity and some other variable must be responsible. Initially the suggestion was made that the improved relationships between the workers and the management was the key. Wickstrom and Bendix (2000) argue that this initial suggestion 'evolved into a conclusion' (page 364). The workers who took part in the studies received a number of special privileges as a result of taking part.

However, there are other interpretations. For example the workers in one of the studies increasingly took the opportunity to alter their work roles. Kahn (1975) described this as a genuine transfer of power, as rather than being supervised as they had been before, the women in this study were consulted about each stage of the experiment and genuine efforts were made to create positive working environments. Greenwood (1983) interviewed some of these original participants 50 years after the study and concluded that the women had worked harder in the test rooms to avoid being sent back to the ordinary manufacturing rooms where the supervision was described as 'harsh'. The original experiments also lacked experimental rigour with many uncontrolled variables and changes of participants. It is also important to realise that the studies were conducted during the Depression, a time of economic hardship across the USA. Therefore the threat of losing one's job may also have contributed to the

work levels. Finally, the workers were being paid according to an incentive pay system based on the outcome of the experimental group rather than the workforce as a whole and this is likely to have improved productivity.

Wickstrom and Bendix conclude that reference to the Hawthorne effect should be avoided in attempting to explain the results of intervention studies as its use is likely to add more confusion than clarity.

Bullying at work

A key issue in considering organisational working conditions is bullying. Einarsen (1999) has produced a review article which identifies a number of different types of bullying at work. The term 'bullying' can refer to a wide range of behaviours but in this paper is defined as 'hostile and aggressive behaviour, either physical or non-physical, directed at one or more colleagues or subordinates'. Bullying causes humiliation, offence and distress and may also affect an individual's work performance and create a negative working environment.

Zapf (cited in Einarsen, 1999) suggests that there are five types of bullying behaviour. These are shown in Figure 9.7.

9.7 Zapf's five types of bullying behaviour

One of the key factors in workplace bullying is power. Einarsen claims that managers and supervisors are perceived as the bullies in the majority of cases and that bullying by a superior creates more psychological distress than bullying by a co-worker. Einarsen suggests that it is important to consider whether peer-bullying and leadership bullying are the same behaviours or whether they are different enough to warrant separate examination.

Bullying tends to develop gradually. Four stages of bullying are suggested in this article:

- aggressive behaviour
- bullying
- stigmatisation
- severe trauma.

Reflections: The stages of bullying reported here have many similarities with the stages of prejudice first described by Gordon Allport (1954). He identifies ' anti-location', 'avoidance', 'harassment' and finally physical attacks which he termed 'extermination'. Research this further and make notes on the similarity between these two behaviours.

Causes of bullying can be divided into two broad areas: individual or personality factors of the victim and of the bully and psycho-social or situational factors. One of the reported studies (Bjorkqvist et al., 1994) surveyed employees at a Finnish university and identified three main perceived reasons for bullying. These were competition concerning status and job position, envy and the aggressor being uncertain about their own abilities. A surprisingly high proportion felt that the personality of the victim was also a significant factor. Many other studies reported by Einarsen support these findings.

There is some evidence to support the notion that victims of bullying are different from their non-bullied colleagues. Studies have found that victims are more sensitive, suspicious and angry, tend to have lower self-esteem and be more anxious in social settings. However, these conclusions need to be considered carefully. Apart from leading to a state where we can blame the victim rather than the bully it is also highly likely that the personality differences identified are as result of the bullying and this can only be established through longitudinal research, which has not been conducted.

Other research has focused on the situational factors which may promote (or at least allow) bullying to take place. These include:

- deficiencies in work design
- deficiencies in leadership behaviour
- socially exposed position of the victim
- low morale in the department.

Finally, Einarsen concludes by discussing the need to identify different types of bullying. He argues that we need to move away from treating all bullying as one phenomenon and that we need to develop an understanding of the very many different types. Predatory bullying is where the victim has done nothing to trigger the bullying behaviour, but is 'accidentally' in a situation where a predator is demonstrating power over others. This would be what might be termed 'institutional harassment' where a culture of bullying and aggression is ingrained throughout the organisation. The victim may be a member of a certain group (the first woman in that role for example) and this may produce bullying behaviour against the individual as a representative of that group. Bullying may also occur when people are highly stressed or frustrated and are looking for someone to vent their frustration on. This is called scapegoating and has also been used as an explanation of prejudice. In many cases, the organisation effectively tolerates the bullying by not responding appropriately to it or by failing to have the correct policies and procedures in place.

Open plan offices

One key change in many office-based organisations is the move to open plan offices. Oldham and Brass (1979) have conducted a field study which shows that employee satisfaction ratings fell dramatically after the working environment was changed to an open plan one.

This research was conducted in a large newspaper office in the USA. At the start of the research, all the employees worked in a conventional 'multi-cellular' office (Figure 9.8). Each department was in a separate office and within each office desks or workstations were separated from each other by internal walls, or by filing cabinets and partitions. This meant that employees had their own space and that in order to interact with anyone, it was necessary to travel down corridors and around partitions.

9.8 Multi-cellular office

The management had been considering a change of office location for a number of reasons. Firstly the current office space was nowhere near a railway and this meant that papers had to be moved from the offices to the railway station by truck, creating additional expense as well as using up valuable time. Secondly, the current office had many practical problems; it lacked air conditioning, was difficult to heat and there was limited storage space. Finally the management also thought that the current layout of the offices was not conducive to good communication both between individuals and between departments. They believed that an open plan office would alleviate this problem and create a more positive working environment. All of these reasons meant that a move to new office premises was necessary.

The new office was purpose built and was located next to a railway line. It was constructed as a typical open plan design. There were no internal walls and no cabinets or partitions more than three feet (one metre) high. There were no private offices anywhere in the building although two meeting rooms were available. All members of a department were still grouped together as they had been in the old building and the amount of space was roughly equivalent in both old and new buildings. The only exception to this was staff working in the pressroom, who kept their working space as it had been. This was useful as these staff formed a type of naturally occurring **control group**.

RESEARCH METHODS
Why is it important to have a **control group** in psychological research?

Staff were fully informed at all stages of this process and data was collected at the beginning of the research which revealed that most staff were in agreement that the old building was no longer 'fit for purpose'. It is also important to note that the change in office was the only change – the move did not produce any other changes to people's working conditions, contracts, salaries or duties.

Data was all collected at the offices. The first set of data was collected approximately eight weeks before the move to the open plan office. The authors used the abbreviation T1 (time 1) for this. Data was then collected nine weeks after the move (T2) and then again 18 weeks after the move (T3).

Participants were told that this was a study designed to assess employees' reactions to their new office and to their work. Data was collected using a questionnaire which was given out to groups ranging from two to 12 people. Participants were asked to put their names on the questionnaires so that their

responses could be followed through the different stages of the study. However they were assured that their responses would be confidential. Management and staff were also questioned more informally to gather additional feedback about the move to the new office.

RESEARCH METHODS
Staff were asked to put their names on their questionnaires although they were assured that their responses would be confidential. What effect do you think asking staff to put their names on their questionnaires might have had?

All the full-time employees were invited to participate. This was a total of 140 people of whom 128 participated in some way. A total of 76 participated in all three stages of the study and the majority of the results presented by the authors are based on these 76 participants. Five members of the pressroom formed the control group. Although they completed the questionnaires at all three time periods, the fact that their working environment remained unchanged meant that little if any change over time was predicted for this group.

Briefly, the questionnaire measured the following:

- work satisfaction
- interpersonal satisfaction
- internal work motivation.

The experimenters predicted that there would be an increase in supervisor and co-worker feedback, friendship opportunities, intra-departmental and inter-departmental interaction.

Findings were that employees' internal motivation and satisfaction with work and colleagues actually decreased sharply after the move to the open plan office. The control group showed no such changes. The interview data revealed that workers felt that they were in a 'fishbowl', that it was difficult to concentrate and complete a task. It was also difficult to develop friendships and impossible to do something like invite someone for a drink after work without the whole office hearing. A supervisor also commented that it was difficult to provide feedback to a worker without moving to a private meeting room. All of this strongly suggests that it was the physical space itself rather than any other factors associated with the move that were responsible for these changes and although there are some weaknesses with the way that this study was designed these weaknesses do not contradict this conclusion.

One of the main themes in this section is the effect of working conditions, that is the situation in which you are working, and so the **individual–situational debate** is crucial here. All three studies demonstrate that situation, whether this be change, office layout or a culture of bullying, can have significant effects on the individuals who work in these situations. This is important for organisations and for organisational psychologists to recognise so that they can strive for the most effective and harmonious working environments.

Evaluation

RESEARCH METHODS

The Hawthorne studies discussed by Wickstrom and Bendix and the study into open plan offices by Oldham and Brass were both experimental studies. The Hawthorne studies can be described as a **field experiment** as the experimenters manipulated the variables that they were interested in but did this in a real working environment as opposed to a laboratory environment. This gives the research high levels of **ecological validity**, which means that the results can easily be applied to the real world. However, conducting research in this way also produces very low levels of control. As we saw earlier, there are a number of other variables that were not considered at the time of the research that might actually offer a better explanation of the findings than the explanations that were offered at the time. In a similar way, the study by Oldham and Brass also has high levels of ecological validity but low levels of control. This can be described as a **natural experiment**; the experimenters did not move the workers from one office environment to the other for the purposes of the research but took advantage of this naturally occurring change (**independent variable**) to investigate the effects. Unfortunately in this kind of study it is going to be almost impossible to control for every possible variable and this does mean there are weaknesses with the way that this study was conducted. The **control group** only contained five individuals, which makes comparisons difficult. The researchers were only able to collect data on worker motivation and worker satisfaction and it is possible that scores on productivity or efficiency for example may have shown significant benefits of moving to the open plan office. Finally it is also possible that the negative ratings would have been temporary and continuing to monitor the employees over a longer time period would have shown more positive results later.

Temporal conditions of work environments
Shiftwork

Temporal conditions refer to the time conditions under which people work. Many people work at night in a variety of organisations; manufacturing sometimes continues for 24 hours, health care needs to be available 24 hours a day and leisure and retail services are becoming increasingly available 24 hours a day. This means that increasing numbers of people work 'shifts', a term used to describe any working pattern that does not involve the same work pattern every week. To maintain 24 hour service many organisations run a rotation of three shifts a day. A day shift is typically 6 a.m. till 2 p.m., an afternoon (or twilight) shift would be 2 p.m. to 10 p.m. and a night shift 10 p.m. to 6 a.m.

It is important to manage shifts so that any negative effects can be reduced. Pheasant (1991) identifies two main approaches to the organisation of shift working and these are rapid rotation theory and slow rotation theory.

- Rapid rotation shifts are frequent shift changes that workers have to follow. Metropolitan rotas are where workers work two day shifts, then two afternoon shifts and then two night shifts. They then have two days off before the shift pattern starts all over again. Note that this is a total of eight days per rotation so that the weekly pattern shifts a day ahead each week. A continental rota is where workers complete two day shifts, two twilight shifts, three night shifts, then two days off work, two day shifts, three twilight shifts, two night shifts and then three days of work. After this the cycle begins again.
- Slow rotation shift changes are infrequent changes; for example working day shifts for several weeks and then night shifts for several weeks. It is suggested that this kind of slow rotation can allow circadian rhythms to adapt to one shift without being forced to change too rapidly and cause health problems.

The effects of shift work on health

In Knutsson's 2003 review of the effects of shift work, he brings together evidence on the relationship between working at night or on a shift work pattern and specific serious medical disorders. He begins by noting that there is no specific evidence that suggests that shift work actually affects longevity. Two studies are mentioned that have directly compared mortality rates between day workers and shift workers, one conducted in the UK and one conducted in Denmark. The UK study reported no significant difference and the Danish study reported a very tiny increase in relative death risk for shift workers. Knutsson then moves on to examine specific disorders and conditions:

- *Gastrointestinal disease*: this is significantly more common in shift workers than in day workers, most commonly constipation and diarrhoea experienced when working night shifts. There is also some evidence that peptic ulcers are more common in those who regularly work shifts, including taxi and truck drivers, factory workers, printers and night watchmen. The risk of duodenal ulcers is also reported to be doubled in shift workers.

- *Cardiovascular disease*: it is well known that working conditions can contribute to the risk of cardiovascular disease. This includes physical factors such as chemicals, noise and vibrations as well as psycho-social factors such as stress and the organisation of work schedules. Studies conducted in a range of different countries support the relationship between shift work and cardiovascular disease.

- *Cancer*: there has been some interest in this area and some research has revealed an increased risk of breast cancer in women who work night shifts. These studies have been conducted with nurses, flight attendants and radio and telegraph operators. However, increased exposure to other carcinogens in these occupations could not be controlled for. There has been some discussion about the role of low levels of melatonin but there is no conclusive evidence for the risk of cancer being increased by shift work.

- *Diabetes and other metabolic disturbances*: concentrations of certain substances in the body, including potassium, uric acid, glucose and cholesterol, are higher during night work which may be related to increased metabolic disturbances. Studies of weight and body mass index (BMI) have tended to be inconclusive, although some have shown higher BMIs in those working shift work. However there is evidence to support the increased chances of developing diabetes if you work shifts.

- *Pregnancy*: studies show relationships between shift work and low birth weight as well as shift work and premature birth. One paper has reported an increased risk of miscarriage among shift workers. Knutsson argues that this evidence is strong and that pregnant women would be well advised to avoid shift work.

- *Exacerbation of existing disorders*: many normal biological processes follow a circadian rhythm and this can be interrupted or interfered with by shift work. This means that taking medicines is more complex when

working shifts. Even taking the same dose at the same time can cause different effects due to the differences in the internal body clock. Sleep deprivation can also affect existing disorders such as the frequency of seizures experienced by epileptics and the frequency of asthma attacks.

Shift work and accidents

Gold et al. (1992) conducted a survey of Massachusetts nurses which asked about shift work, sleep and accidents. This study used a self-administered questionnaire and was handed out to 878 registered nurses between June and September 1986. They were asked whether they worked variable shifts or whether they always worked the same shift. The nurse was asked to give information relating to the current week, the previous two weeks and the following week on the number of day, evening or night shifts worked. They were also asked to record their sleep and wake times for all shifts and for days off.

The questionnaire also asked about:

- quality of sleep
- use of alcohol
- use of prescription or non-prescription medication
- sleeping aids
- times they had 'nodded off' (fallen asleep) at work (in the past week)
- times they had 'nodded off' while driving to and from work (in the past year)
- accidents, errors and 'near-miss' accidents in the past year: this included driving accidents, medication errors, job procedural errors and work related personal injuries that could be attributed to sleepiness.

They were divided into groups dependent on their work practices. Day and evening shift work was grouped together as the shift from day to evening work has not been shown to disrupt circadian rhythms. The other groups were those who worked night shifts only and 'rotators'; those who changed shift patterns frequently.

Of the 878 questionnaires given out, 687 were returned. The mean age of the sample was 33.9 years.

Results showed that rotators and night shift workers reported fewer hours of sleep than day/evening workers. The researchers used a concept of 'anchor sleep' (defined as having four or more hours sleep during the same clock hours every night).

The results showed that 92% of the day/evening nurses obtained regular anchor sleep but only 6.3% of the night nurses and none of the rotators obtained anchor sleep regularly throughout the month. Anchor sleep disruption was experienced by 49% of the day/evening workers, 94% of the rotators and 2.9% of the night nurses.

Night nurses were 1.8 times more likely to report poor quality sleep than the day/evening workers and rotators were 2.8 times more likely to report poor quality sleep than the day/evening workers. Night nurses and rotators were twice as likely to use medications to help them sleep.

Nodding off on the night shift occurred at least once a week in 35% of rotators, 32% of night nurses and 20% of day evening workers who worked the occasional night shift. In contrast, only 2.7% of day/evening nurses and 2.8% of rotators reported any incidences of nodding off on day or evening shifts.

When compared to day/evening nurses, rotators were 3.9 times as likely and night nurses 3.6 times as likely to nod off while driving to and from work in the previous year.

Although length of time working at the hospital, age and use of alcohol were factors that contributed to errors, even when these factors were taken into account, rotators reported twice as many accidents as day/evening nurses.

The results are consistent with laboratory demonstrations of the effects of sleep deprivation and the disruption of circadian rhythms, particularly in the sense of increased cognitive errors. The authors conclude that the application of circadian principles to the design of work schedules may produce improved health and safety for nurses and patients.

Evaluation

ISSUES AND DEBATES

It is possible to consider the material in this section in relation to the **nature versus nurture debate**. Shift work may interfere with the natural functioning of the body and this is likely to explain the many negative effects. We have a natural circadian (daily) rhythm and working constantly changing shifts may disrupt this. The effects identified by Knutsson are correlational, and those considered by Gold et al. rely heavily on self-reports, and this will be considered in the Research Methods section below. All of the research considered in this section has useful applications. By identifying the risks that shift working may pose, not only are individuals able to make informed decisions about their own working practices, but employers are able to establish procedures designed to minimise these risks.

RESEARCH METHODS

A correlation shows a relationship between something; for example a relationship between working shifts and an increased chance of gastrointestinal disorders. However, it does not show that working shifts causes an increase in gastrointestinal disorders even though it might seem to make sense to interpret the results in this way. To show a causal relationship we would need to have conducted an experiment. We would need to have carefully controlled for all possible extraneous variables and then randomly allocated similar participants to both the experimental and the control group. The experimental group would then work changing shifts for a period of time whilst the control group would work normal day shifts. If, at the end of the study, there was a significant difference in the incidence of gastrointestinal disorders, and we could show that we had controlled for all possible extraneous variables, we could conclude that working shifts causes gastrointestinal disorders. However, this type of research would raise many ethical issues and would be unlikely to be conducted. It is also difficult to draw causal conclusions from the research by Gold, although this can be described as **quasi-experimental** as he was able to compare two naturally occurring groups, thus creating an **independent variable**. However he was not able to randomly allocate participants to these different groups meaning that there may be many differences between them that might explain the results he found. However, the research findings are supported by laboratory experiments into short-term sleep deprivation and cognitive errors. Finally, there may be reporting biases in this study and a **longitudinal study** to track accidents and errors and to correlate these with shift work patterns might be more effective.

Health and safety
Accidents at work: errors and accidents in operator-machine systems

Technology has led to the development of machinery that largely replaces many of the tasks previously done by human workers. This leaves the human as the 'operator' of the machine and the interaction between the machine and its operator is sometimes extremely complex and the consequences of 'human error' can be catastrophic (Nagel, 1988).

A famous example of human error with near catastrophic consequences occurred at the Three Mile Island power plant in the USA in 1979. An employee shut down an alternate feedwater pipe and went off duty without turning this back on again. The reactor started to overheat and warning sirens began to sound but no one at the power plant knew what the problem was. It took two hours and 18 minutes to find the fault. It is not appropriate to simply blame the operator for his error. Nothing in the system had been designed to tell anyone that the pipe had been turned off and when a relief valve also failed to open, no warning system was in place. Later examination of the processes required to identify the fault revealed that the operators looking for the fault had to scan over 1600 gauges. For some reason, colours had been used differently in different systems and in some places a colour represented safety whereas in another part of the system it represented danger. It was clear that while there had been human errors there were also significant failings in the design of the systems as well as the safety procedures.

Since then we have seen the development of 'human factors' experts, who ensure that the design of machines reflect our knowledge and understanding not only of human cognition, but of the limitations of human cognition. This might involve making sure that display systems are clear and easy to interpret, that operators are not expected to maintain vigilance for too long without a break (such as the tasks performed by air traffic controllers) and that there are tried and tested emergency procedures.

Reducing accidents at work

The study by Fox et al. (1987) investigated the use of a token economy to reward workers for not having accidents or injuries for a specified amount of time. The study was conducted at two open pit mines and their associated product processing plants. Both mines were in the USA. Prior to the study, the number of days lost from work due to injuries on the job in one of the mines was over eight times the natural average for all mines and three times the national average at the other mine. In the five years preceding this study, two people had been killed and a third person had suffered a permanent disability.

> **Reflections:** Token economy has been considered in Chapters 6 and 8, and is an application of the behaviourist approach. It involves rewarding people for desirable behaviour such as remaining in the presence of a phobic object. Suggest how a token economy could be used to encourage someone who needs to overcome their fear of public speaking in order to try for a promotion in work.

The two settings were similar in many ways. They used the same mining procedures and were of similar sizes.

Injuries had occurred in all areas of both mines but were particularly associated with the use and maintenance of heavy equipment.

> **RESEARCH METHODS**
> Explain why it was important that the two settings were as similar as possible.

The participants in this study were the employees at the two mines, including office and clerical workers, engineers, managers, custodial, maintenance and production workers. The number of employees in the first mine was 197 when data collection began in 1970, rose to a high of 606 by 1979 and then decreased to 214 by 1983 due to the declining value of the uranium ore mined there. The second mine employed 450 staff in 1970 which had increased to 501 in 1983 and remained relatively stable from there.

Workers were divided into four groups based on the numbers of working days lost due to injury:

- Group 1 was workers in the least hazardous jobs, mainly office workers.
- Group 2 was made up of foremen, shift supervisors, technicians, engineers and surveyors.
- Group 3 included mechanics, labourers, maintenance workers and operators of bulldozers, front end loaders, shovel, dragline and truck operators.
- Group 4 was made up of the workers in the most hazardous jobs. These were the electricians, the scraper operators and the fuel and lube workers.

The token economy systems began in 1972 in the first mine and in 1975 in the second. Workers were given a specified number of 'trading stamps' with their pay envelope if they had not suffered a lost time injury or injury that required a doctor's attention during the month. The amount of trading stamps varied by the risk factors of each group, for example, in the first mine, Group 1 received 300 stamps, Group 2 received 400 stamps, Group 3 received 500 stamps and Group 4 received 700 stamps. In addition to these 'rewards' all workers managed by a common supervisor were given further stamps if the whole group of workers under that supervisor had avoided lost time or medically treated injuries. Further still, any safety suggestions that were subsequently adopted by the miner, any acts that prevented injury to others or damage to property could be rewarded with amounts ranging from 500 to 25 000 stamps.

However, a worker who missed one or two days of work due to injury would receive no stamps for one month. If three or four days of work were lost they would receive no stamps for two months and if five or six days were lost there would be no reward for three months, increasing like this up to a maximum of six months with no reward if more than ten days were lost. No one in the group would receive any of the group award if any time had been lost and anyone responsible for an accident that damaged equipment would lose their individual stamp reward for one month for every $2000 of damage up to a maximum of 12 months. All members of that worker's group would lose their group award for as many months as the individual lost his individual awards. Anyone failing to report an accident or injury would lose all of their individual awards for one month and their group would lose their group award for the same length of time.

Six weeks before this scheme was started, workers were given information about how this would work. One month before the start of the scheme, any worker who had not had an equipment-damaging accident or a lost time injury was given 1000 stamps.

Stamps could be 'spent' at local stores and could be exchanged for anything from a huge range of merchandise. In 1972, 3000 stamps would buy a spice rack, 7600 would buy a comforter for a full-size bed and 20 400 stamps would buy a gas-fired barbecue. No restrictions were placed on how the stamps could be spent and the authors report that casual conversations around the mines revealed a range of products being purchased including microwave ovens, cuckoo clocks and shotguns!

The miners had to keep careful safety data including the number of accidents (referred to as frequency rate) and total numbers of days lost (severity) were recorded. In addition, direct costs of these injuries and accidents were recorded under the headings of compensation insurance, medical care and repairing damaged equipment. The mines also kept data on the cost of the trading stamps. This allowed a benefit-to-cost ratio to be calculated to see if the dollars saved as a result of operating the token economy exceeded the cost of the token economy.

The results showed that there were significant decreases in number of days lost in both mines in the first years that the token economy was operating. Costs of accidents and injuries in the first mine declined from a baseline average

of $294 000 to an average of $29 000 for the years that the token economy was in effect. A similar decline was seen in the second mine, from a baseline average of $367 696 to an average of $38 972. Both declines were approximately 90%. The costs of the token economy scheme in the first mine never rose above $13 850 and the costs in the second mine was $21 940 in the first year but between $11 000 and $13 000? in subsequent years.

RESEARCH METHODS
How did Fox et al. measure the effectiveness of their token economy?

This would suggest that the use of a token economy apparently benefitted all parties. Days lost from work decreased, accidents and injuries decreased and no deaths or permanent disabilities occurred at either mine during the time that the token economy was in operation. Towards the end of the scheme the number of days lost was around a quarter of the national average in the first mine and one-twelfth the national average in the second mine. In addition to the much lowered risk of accident, workers also benefitted from the goods they were able to buy with their trading stamps. Although no direct measure of this was taken, anecdotal evidence suggests that these stamps were greatly appreciated by all workers even though they were sceptical to begin with. In fact one of the unions even requested that the programme be written into contracts and when stamps were left out of a small number of workers' pay envelopes the spouse of one called the mine to complain and the spouse of another drove 50 miles (80 km) to collect them!

Safety promotion campaigns

This is a report of a study conducted by Cowpe (1989). At the time this research was conducted, chip-pan fires were a major cause of domestic fires in the UK. Approximately one-third of all domestic fires were caused by chip-pans. In 1981, there were 21 deaths and 1372 injuries caused by 15 000 chippan fires in the UK. Not only this but chip-pan fires were a major cost to the taxpayer in terms of providing emergency fire crews and police and the associated costs to the National Health Service.

Cowpe considered two strategies for his advertising campaign. The first was the prevention strategy in which

305

the advert would tell people how to avoid a chip-pan fire starting (for example, don't overfill the pan with oil, don't leave the pan unattended). The second was the containment strategy in which people would be educated about the correct and the incorrect procedures to follow should a chip-pan catch fire. After considering these two options, the prevention strategy was rejected as the research team felt that the causes of fires such as leaving the pan unattended were often simply accidents or the results of misjudgements and telling people not to do this would not be successful. They also felt that, as most people tend to think, 'accidents only happen to other people'. They would not perceive a prevention-focussed advert to be aimed at them and would ignore it. This left them with the containment strategy; educating people about the correct procedures to follow in the event of a chip-pan fire. However, they quickly realised that an advert that showed someone actually tackling a fire would raise concerns in the viewer about their own abilities to do this and this would make them more receptive to messages about prevention. Cowpe also concludes that this is a more appropriate tone to set. Rather than saying 'Don't do this' (which is likely to be ignored) they could say 'Here's what to do if you're unlucky enough to have a chip-pan fire; putting it out isn't easy, so why not remember why it happens in the first place'.

The aim of this study was to test the effectiveness of an advertising campaign warning people about chip-pan fires. This can be understood as a quasi-experiment. Two 60 second advertisements were produced, both of which showed the initial cause of the fire (overfilling in one and inattendance in the other) and then the actions required to put this out. The advertisements were shown on television in ten UK regional television areas between 1976 and 1984.

The effectiveness of this advertising campaign was measured through the use of fire brigade statistics. Cowpe reports an overall 12% drop in fires (with drops between 7% and 25% in the different television areas in which the advert was shown) and also reports that high levels of awareness and recall of the adverts existed; not only during the times that they were shown but for a considerable time afterwards.

The conclusion was that the advertising proved effective as shown by the reduction in chip-pan fires. However what is not known is the extent to which the 'prevention' part of the advert was successful and fewer fires broke out and the extent to which the 'containment' part of

the advert was successful and people were able to deal appropriately with the fire and had no need to call the fire brigade. Cowpe suggests that the advert increased both knowledge and confidence of containment procedures but that it was the combined effect of the two strategies that created the success of the advertisement in reducing fires, saving money, and much more importantly, saving lives.

> **Reflections:** There are many causes of accidents. In some countries currently there are concerns about driving while using a cell (mobile) phone. Design a campaign which aims to highlight the dangers of driving and texting.

Evaluation

The study by Fox et al. demonstrates the effectiveness of the application of psychological principles to the workplace. The application of a token economy is a simple behaviourist technique which offers consistent and predictable rewards to desired behaviours. The usefulness of the token economy in this instance is obvious. The number of accidents was reduced significantly and worker safety was increased. Some critics of the behaviourist approach argue that such techniques are over-controlling and may be unethical. This is a judgement that you can make but in this instance the use of rewards proved highly effective and was not used instead of safety training but in addition to the safety training. Many organisations offer similar schemes where workers are rewarded in this way. The study by Fox et al. shows that the way the working environment (situation) is constructed can have significant effects on the way that individuals behave. All the workers had been trained in safety procedures and you would think, would be motivated to keep themselves out of danger, but the addition of small rewards had a powerful effect.

The study by Cowpe measures the effectiveness of a safety campaign designed to reduce chippan fires. It used an experimental approach in that the researchers were able to compare the incidences of chippan fires prior to the campaign with the incidence after the campaign although it would be very difficult to control **extraneous variables** in this study. However, this study is high in **ecological validity** as the participants were members of the general public who watched television adverts in their own homes.

Unfortunately it would not be possible to know who had watched this advert and whether it did specifically prevent a fire and there is some evidence to suggest that the over-use of media campaigns reduces effect and awareness as people become desensitised to the message.

9.5 Satisfaction at work

Theories of job satisfaction

Two-factor theory

The two-factor theory proposed by Frederick Herzberg (1959) states that job satisfaction and job dissatisfaction work independently of each other. In other words there are certain factors which cause satisfaction and there are other factors which cause dissatisfaction.

Herzberg begins by stating that workers are not satisfied with jobs or roles which simply meet their lower order needs (these would be the physiological and safety needs according to Maslow's hierarchy of needs). He proposes that individuals also look for the gratification of higher-level needs such as relatedness or self-esteem needs. These are likely to be met by the nature of the work itself (rather than the lower-level needs which may be met primarily through the fact that one is paid for the work that one does).

Although there are many obvious overlaps between this theory and Maslow's hierarchy of needs, Herzberg has added a further dimension to his theory by suggesting that one group of job characteristics leads to worker satisfaction whilst another, completely separate group of job characteristics leads to worker dissatisfaction. This is an interesting suggestion as it is likely that most people would assume that satisfaction and dissatisfaction are on a continuum, from satisfied to dissatisfied, rather than being completely separate entities.

Herzberg conducted over 200 interviews with engineers and accountants in the Pittsburgh area. He chose these professions as they were developing in importance in the business world at the time that he conducted his research. He asked them to describe periods in their lives when they were 'exceedingly happy' and 'exceedingly unhappy' with their jobs. Interviewees were asked to give as much information as they could, with specific focus on the changes that took place.

He found that factors related to the job itself could make people feel a sense of achievement and thus a sense of satisfaction. Interestingly, though, if the job did not have any of these gratifying characteristics this did not lead to dissatisfaction. Dissatisfaction results from very different factors, such as working conditions, technical problems and salary levels. This means that these two factors need to be considered separately – increasing satisfaction is not the same thing as decreasing dissatisfaction.

Finally, Herzberg's two-factor theory distinguishes between motivators and hygiene factors. Motivators are the factors that produce satisfaction such as challenging and rewarding work, responsibility and autonomy, recognition and the sense that one is doing something meaningful and important. Hygiene factors include things like job security, salary, working conditions, benefits such as paid holidays and insurance. These do not contribute to the feeling of satisfaction but their absence can contribute to a feeling of dissatisfaction.

RESEARCH METHODS
There have been several examples of psychometric tests in this section. Give one strength and one weakness of psychometric tests.

Therefore, in order to remove dissatisfaction in a work environment, these hygiene factors must be addressed. There are several ways that this can be done but some of the most important ways to decrease dissatisfaction would be to pay reasonable wages, ensure employee job security, and to create a positive culture in the workplace. However, eliminating dissatisfaction is only one-half of the task of the two-factor theory and increasing satisfaction can be done by improving on motivating factors.

Reflections: Imagine you are the manager of an organisation where research has shown that all the workers score highly on measures of dissatisfaction and low on measures of satisfaction. You improve their working conditions, give them salary increases and improve their holiday entitlements. Their dissatisfaction ratings are now much lower but their satisfaction ratings have not changed. What might you try next?

The two-factor theory produces four possible combinations of these two factors:

- High hygiene + high motivation = the ideal situation, where employees are highly motivated and have few complaints.
- High hygiene + low motivation = employees have few complaints but are not highly motivated. The job is viewed as a pay-packet.
- Low hygiene + high motivation = employees are motivated but have a lot of complaints. A situation where the job is exciting and challenging but salaries and work conditions are not up to par.
- Low hygiene + low motivation = this is the worst situation, where employees are not motivated and have many complaints.

Job Characteristics Theory

Job Characteristics Theory (Hackman and Oldham, 1976) is a theory that can be used to create jobs that appeal to workers and keep them motivated. Five key factors, described in the model as 'core job characteristics' are identified:

- *Skill variety*: A job that motivates workers should require different skills and utilise a range of the skills that the worker has.
- *Task identity*: A job that motivates workers should require the completion of a whole piece of work rather than a disjointed element.
- *Task significance*: The job should have an impact on other people, either inside or outside the organisation.
- *Autonomy*: The job should allow the worker some autonomy in planning, scheduling and carrying out their work. This will obviously be easier in some jobs than others but even a small level of autonomy can increase motivation for a low level job.
- *Feedback*: The job itself (rather than other people) should provide information on how well the worker is performing the job. This can increase motivation.

These produce three critical psychological states which collectively, are thought to impact three outcomes: motivation, satisfaction and work performance. This is shown in Figure 9.9.

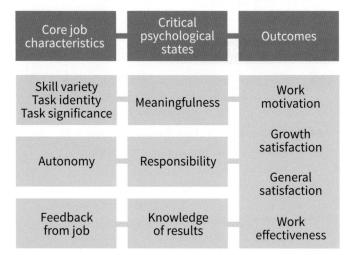

9.9 Hackman and Oldham's job characteristics model

Reflections: Suggest how Hackman and Oldham's five characteristics could be applied to one or more of the following jobs: shopworker, nurse, teacher, journalist, chef.

Techniques of job design

Three further techniques of job design can be used once a job has started that will also allow for increased satisfaction and motivation in workers. The first of these is job enrichment. Job enrichment involves giving workers a greater variety of tasks to perform which in turn, increases the level of skills and responsibility that they are working at. This gives workers a greater sense of control over their job and makes the job more interesting. In turn this will increase motivation and satisfaction. This is obviously easier to put into practice in some organisations than others.

Job rotation means that workers have regular changes of tasks within their normal role. For example in a kitchen, workers could rotate around all the different preparation areas; in a large supermarket, workers could rotate between departments and between tasks within these departments. This should again have the effect of producing variety and stopping workers from becoming too bored by one task. An additional benefit is the increased skills of the worker meaning that they can be placed in several places within the organisations dependent on need.

Job enlargement can be horizontal or vertical. Horizontal job enlargement involves giving workers more tasks to do but usually at the same level. This will increase variety. Vertical job enlargement involves the addition of further decision making responsibilities and/or higher level, more challenging tasks (Arnold et al., 2005). This will not only increase variety but also the workers' competence and sense of empowerment. For example, someone is not given a formal promotion or increase in status but they are given more freedom to do their job in the way that they see fit. Allowing teams to manage themselves is another example of vertical job enlargement.

Evaluation

The practical applications of Herzberg's models are that those in charge of organisations must focus on increasing those characteristics which produce worker satisfaction and on decreasing those factors that produce worker dissatisfaction rather than assuming that they are the same thing. Although this may seem obvious, Herzberg made a significant contribution to organisational psychology when he drew a clear distinction between factors which create satisfaction and factors which create dissatisfaction. If a manager wished to increase satisfaction, he or she should focus on factors related to the nature of the work itself, including the promotion prospects, opportunities for gaining responsibility or for working autonomously and, in Maslow's terms, achieving self-actualisation. If workers are dissatisfied, then the manager needs to focus on different factors, including policies, procedures, supervision and general working conditions. Obviously a focus on both would be ideal. Although this is a theoretical model, it is based on interviews with over 200 participants, which is a large enough sample to generalise from and enough data to support the predictions made in the model.

Hackman and Oldham's Job Characteristics Theory also has many useful applications. By identifying the core job characteristics that produce critical psychological states, which in turn affect motivation, satisfaction and work performance, we can begin to design jobs around these characteristics. Not surprisingly, this model has generated a great deal of research. It provides precise, testable hypotheses and there have been several studies which demonstrate that the core characteristics do correlate with motivation and satisfaction. However, Arnold et al. note that it is surprising that there have been very few attempts to experimentally manipulate jobs so that they have more of the core job characteristics. Of those that have been done, findings suggest that changes to job characteristics have

an impact on satisfaction and motivation rather than work performance. However, this clearly fits within an **individual – situational debate** as it makes it clear that even relatively small changes to the job characteristics (situation) can impact on the individual and their attitudes.

The final section on techniques of job design bring these two theories together as they demonstrate the very many ways in which jobs can be redesigned and the effects that this can have. Although this is not a report of a piece of research, it is clear that all of these techniques could be implemented in real-life situations and their effects measured. However, given that this research would be either a **field experiment** or a **quasi-experiment**, the researchers would need to take great care in interpreting their findings (see the Hawthorne effect, discussed in Section 9.4).

Measuring job satisfaction

Job Descriptive Index

The Job Descriptive Index (Smith et al., 1969) is one of the best known and most widely used measures of job satisfaction. It measures five aspects of job satisfaction:

- experience of the work
- salary
- promotion prospects
- experience of supervision
- experience of co-workers.

It is a very simple scale to which workers simply answer *yes*, *no* or *can't decide* in response to a series of statements about their job (Table 9.6).

This is an interesting example of a scale to study as the results are compared with standardised norms based on data from a large sample of people which is regularly updated. Any individual's score can be compared with normative scores in respect of age, gender, job level, education and 'community prosperity'. This means that rather than simply measuring the satisfaction of an individual, their satisfaction can be compared with these norms to see whether the individual is more or less satisfied with his or her job than other similar individuals. Some of the advantages of the Job Descriptive Index identified by Smith et al. include that it measures specific, objective areas of job satisfaction rather than satisfaction in general terms. It is relatively easy to read and does not use any complex language, which makes it suitable to use with a large variety of people.

Jobs in general
Think of your job in general. All in all, what is it like most of the time? In the space beside each word or phrase, write Y for 'yes' if it describes your job N for 'no' if it does not describe it ? for '?' if you cannot decide
Pleasant
Bad
Great
Waste of time
Good
Undesirable
Worthwhile
Worse than most
Acceptable
Superior
Better than most
Disagreeable
Makes me content
Inadequate
Excellent
Rotten
Enjoyable
Poor

Table 9.6 The Job Descriptive Index

The Minnesota Satisfaction Questionnaire

The Minnesota Satisfaction Questionnaire (MSQ) was designed by Weiss et al. (1967) and is designed to measure an employee's satisfaction with their job. There is a long version (100 items) and a shorter version (20 items). The MSQ measures satisfaction with a range of aspects of an employee's job including: company policies, scope for advancement, security, independence, recognition, responsibility, variety and working conditions.

It originally used the following five response choices:

- very satisfied
- satisfied
- 'N' (neither satisfied nor dissatisfied)
- dissatisfied
- very dissatisfied.

However, results using this set of response choices tended to be skewed and generally alternated between 'satisfied' and 'very satisfied'. A later version adjusted for this by using the following five response categories:

- not satisfied
- somewhat satisfied
- satisfied
- very satisfied
- extremely satisfied.

Results from this version tended to be more varied and although 'satisfied' was the most common response, responses were spread in both directions around this central point.

> **Reflections:** Write some questions measuring an employee's satisfaction with their working conditions. Which set of response choices would you use and why?

Quality of working life (QWL)

Quality of working life (QWL) is a term used commonly in organisational psychology although there does not appear to be one agreed definition. Heskett, Sasser and Schlesinger (1997) proposed that QWL could be described as the feelings that employees have towards their jobs, colleagues and companies and that these feelings would affect an organisation's growth and profitability. Others see QWL as a process by which an organisation responds to employee needs. For the purposes of this discussion we will consider the QWL in its broadest sense: a range of factors such as job security, reward systems, pay levels and opportunity for growth which determine our feelings about our working life.

Walton (1974) developed a typology which can be used to assess QWL and this consists of eight key components . They are described using different words in different texts but their core meanings are the same:

- Fair and adequate payment: In order to measure this the researcher could ask questions to determine whether the pay received by the worker is enough for them to live on or whether it is equivalent to the pay that other workers are receiving. They might also ask participants to rate their agreement with statements such as 'I am satisfied with the amount of money I earn'.
- Safe and healthy working conditions: Walton's typology can be used to assess a range of health and safety issues

which may contribute to QWL. For example, appropriate clothing and safety procedures may be in place as a result of employer concern, union action or legislation and whilst this may vary from culture to culture it is evident that this is required for QWL.

- Providing opportunities to use and develop skills: People will rate their QWL higher if they are given autonomy and independence to do their jobs and if there is scope to develop their skills.
- Opportunity for career growth and security: This is obviously related to the previous point in its focus on career growth but also refers to the sense of security that an employee feels in his or her employment. There has been a move away from permanent employment to fixed term or even 'zero-hours' contracts (with no guaranteed weekly hours) in some cultures recently and this will bring with it a drop in QWL.
- Positive social relationships/integration within the workplace: QWL is affected by the social context. Positive relationships at work will be of great benefit, not only raising worker productivity and satisfaction but decreasing stress, absenteeism and staff turnover. You could explain this in terms of the importance of social needs in Maslow's theory of motivation.
- The total life space: Western society often refers to this as the 'work-life balance'. Any assessment of QWL would need to measure the extent to which employees were able to maintain this balance. It may seem like a small gesture, but allowing someone an afternoon off to watch their child perform in a school play will significantly affect their ratings of their QWL.
- Constitutionalism (policies and procedures) in the workplace: Does the workplace have appropriate policies in place for dealing with bullying for example, or for managing dissent? To what extent do employees value the 'organisational culture' and to what extent is this culture a supportive one?
- Social relevance: Finally, QWL is enhanced when people can rate the social relevance of what they do (or what the organisation does) positively.

We have met many of these ideas already in the chapter and it is interesting to see them brought together under the heading of 'Quality of work(ing) life'.

Walton's typology has been used to develop a variety of techniques to measure QWL in a variety of organisations and cultures. However different these organisations and cultures are these same eight components of QWL will be valid.

Evaluation

The three areas covered here all involve some type of psychometric testing. We have considered the strengths and weaknesses of psychometric tests earlier in this chapter but briefly it is important to realise that although such tests can be relatively easy to administer and score, they are prone to **demand characteristics** and **social desirability bias**, and flaws in their construction can have serious effects on the outcomes.

The Job Description Index has many strengths in comparison with other similar tests. It is one of the most thoroughly tested and carefully validated tests and is based on standardised norms, which means that each individual's score can be compared to a bank of scores taken from a huge sample of participants in many different occupations. It is therefore possible to identify whether the individual is more or less satisfied than others of the same age, sex, occupation and so on. The Minnesota Satisfaction Questionnaire is also a well-validated test but the discussion above on the different response categories highlights one of the problems of psychometric tests. Offering respondents slightly different responses to choose from can have significant effects on the answers that they give which would clearly reduce both the reliability and the validity of the test. However, both tests are widely used and the results can be applied to improving aspects of the working environment in order to make workers more satisfied and hence more motivated and productive.

Finally, we examined quality of working life. This is a very useful, although very broad, concept whose application has generated a range of initiatives in many organisations from the development of workable policies for dealing with bullying, allowing for compassionate leave or the ability to work flexibly through to the provision of social activities designed to improve employees' quality of working life.

Attitudes to work
Workplace sabotage

Workplace sabotage describes behaviours that are designed to break the rules and deliberately try to stop work from taking place. These behaviours are most commonly the result of dissatisfaction and powerlessness.

In a study by Giacalone and Rosenfeld (1987), unionised workers at a factory were asked to rate a variety of reasons which would justify the use of sabotage in an organisation, as well as the justifiability of four general methods of sabotage (slowdowns, destructiveness, dishonesty and causing chaos). Results showed that compared with those who did not accept a wide variety of reasons for sabotage, those who accepted a variety of reasons would more readily justify all forms of sabotage except dishonesty.

The participants of this study were 38 unionised labourers working in an electrical factory. The questionnaire was constructed with the help of an ex-employee (with five years' service) who listed all the ways that were used by the employees to sabotage the company. This produced a total of 29 general sabotage methods which could be grouped into four general categories:

- Work slowdowns
- Destruction of machinery, premises or products
- Dishonesty
- Causing chaos.

A further list was created of all the reasons for sabotage:

- Self defence
- Revenge
- An eye for an eye
- Protect oneself from boss/company
- Protect one's job
- The foreman/company deserved it
- The foreman/company hurt me previously
- No one was hurt by the action
- Release of frustrations
- Just for fun.

Each participant was given the list of sabotage methods and the list of sabotage reasons and asked to rate them individually on a scale of 1 (not at all justifiable) to 7 (totally justifiable).

A **median** split was performed on the potential reasons for sabotage creating two groups – high-reason acceptors and low-reason acceptors.

RESEARCH METHODS

The **median** is the mid-point in a list which has been put in order from lowest to highest. A median split is where a group is split into two using the mid-point as the division.

Results included the following differences: High-reason acceptors justified production slowdowns more than low-reason acceptors. High-reason acceptors also justified destruction of machinery, premises or products more than low-reason acceptors. Unexpectedly, high-reason acceptors did not justify dishonesty more than low-reason acceptors but high-reason acceptors did justify causing chaos more than low-reason accepters.

The authors conclude that while acceptance seems to affect justification of sabotage in many forms, this is not the case for dishonesty. This is possibly seen as different from the other forms of sabotage. Work slowdowns, destruction and causing chaos may be aimed at hurting the company, but they do not represent potential monetary gains for the employee. This may make dishonesty a qualitatively different form of sabotage (justified for very different reasons such as poor salaries) and potentially interpreted in very different ways by management. If this type of sabotage was simply interpreted as self-serving, then it has not served the desired demonstrative function. It may also be that dishonesty threatens self-esteem in a way that the other forms of sabotage do not.

Absenteeism

Absenteeism is one of the major costs to employees. In the UK, the Confederation of Business and Industry found that workplace stress was one of the major causes of absenteeism. Absenteeism can be voluntary or involuntary. Involuntary absenteeism is when the worker has no choice but to be absent, usually due to illness. Organisations will expect some illnesses and should have policies in place to deal with this (for example a school may have a regular 'supply teacher' to cover for absences or may be able to phone a supply agency). Voluntary absenteeism is where the worker has chosen not to attend work and this may well be a measure of dissatisfaction but is a difficult factor to measure.

The paper by Blau and Boal (1987) uses the concepts of job involvement and organisational commitment to predict turnover and absenteeism. Job involvement can be high or low, and organisational commitment can also be high or low. This produces four possible situations:

- High job involvement and high organisational commitment
- High job involvement and low organisational commitment
- Low job involvement and high organisational commitment
- Low job involvement and low organisational commitment.

Each of these is predicted to have a different impact on turnover and absenteeism. The first group, high job involvement and high organisational commitment, describes individuals for whom work is important to their self-esteem. These individuals will exert a great deal of time and effort in their jobs. In addition, because they identify strongly with the organisation, it is predicted that they will also become highly involved with group activities that help to maintain the organisation. They can be seen to represent the most valued members of the organisation and are likely to move up through the organisation. It is expected that this group will show the lowest level of turnover and absenteeism although if members of this group were to be absent or leave this would have a greater impact on the organisation as they may be more difficult to replace.

The second group contains individuals who show a high level of job involvement and a low level of organisational commitment. Although their work is important to them, they do not identify with the organisation or with its goals. They are likely to show high levels of effort for individual tasks but a low level of effort for group tasks. If the first groups are the 'stars' of the organisation, then this group are the 'lone wolves'. Such people are highly sensitive to factors such as working conditions and pay. If better opportunities were to arise elsewhere these people would leave. The effect of turnover here would be different from the first group. Despite their high levels of individual effort, they do not integrate themselves within the organisation. This can breed resentment if others then need to pick up their group work tasks and perceived inequities can damage the cohesiveness of the group. The authors also argue that absenteeism among this group is likely to reflect them taking career enhancing opportunities – and being more willing to violate absenteeism policies if there is a conflict between a work goal and a personal goal.

The third group includes people who show a low level of job involvement but a high level of organisational commitment. Their work is not personally important to them but they do identify with the organisation and its goals. They may exert little effort on individual tasks but a great deal on group maintenance tasks. The authors describe these people as the corporate citizens of the organisation. Their absence can have a significant impact on others.

Finally the fourth group is those individuals who exhibit low levels of both job involvement and organisational commitment. Work is not viewed as being important to their self-image and so they do not put a great deal of effort into individual tasks and as the organisation is not strongly identified with, they do not contribute to group maintenance. These are the least valuable members of an organisation and are described as 'apathetic employees'.

Measuring organisational commitment

Organisational commitment is the attitude that workers have towards the organisation that they work for. Organisational commitment is defined as 'the relative strength of an individual's identification with and involvement in an organisation' (Mowday et al., 1979). Some authors discuss organisational commitment as having three forms; the desire to remain within the organisation, belief in and acceptance of the organisation's values and willingness to exert effort on behalf of the organisation. However, other authors such as Allen and Meyer (1990) identify three types of organisational commitment:

- *Continuance* commitment: where workers remain in their post (or in the organisation) as the costs and risks of leaving would be too great. This may be financial in the sense that people cannot give up a salary or other benefits but may also reflect the lack of suitable alternatives.
- *Affective* commitment: concerns an individual's emotional attachment to the organisation and is where workers remain because they strongly agree with the organisation's goals and overall beliefs and views. As long as these don't change, the workers choose to remain with the organisation.
- *Normative* commitment: where people stay because of pressure from others or a feeling of obligation.

Being able to measure commitment is useful as committed workers are much more likely to stay with an organisation and work for the good of the organisation. The study by Mowday et al. (1979) is one of the earliest attempts to develop a method for measuring organisational commitment. This is a 15-item questionnaire called the Organisational Commitment Questionnaire (OCQ) and consists of items such as:

> *I feel very little loyalty to this organisation*

> *I am willing to put in a great deal of effort beyond that normally expected in order to help this organisation be successful*

> *I really care about the fate of this organisation*

RESEARCH METHODS

Some of these items have been reversed. That is, some are positively written and some are negatively written. Explain why this is good practice when constructing this type of questionnaire.

Although this was originally designed as a measure of general organisational commitment, it is now understood to measure affective commitment.

The study by Mowday reports on the process of developing and validating this scale. To do this the scale was administered to 2563 people working in a large variety of jobs in nine different organisations in a number of separate studies. The jobs and organisations included public employees such as those working in a range of hospital, social services and health care related jobs and supervisory and administrative personnel, university employees, bank employees, telephone company employees, scientists and engineers and retail management trainees.

The study was designed to assess a number of aspects of reliability and validity of the scale as well as the scale's ability to discriminate. Mean scores ranged from a low 4 to a high 6.1, suggesting that the scale produces an acceptable level of discrimination.

No items stood out as producing odd results or being less related to the overall score than other items. Test–retest scores were good, suggesting high reliability. To measure validity, the results were compared with a number of other scales which measure similar affective responses. This is the standard way of assessing validity. Correlations were high suggesting good validity. A second way of determining the validity of this scale was to correlate this with the individual's intention to remain with the organisation. This single item measure was collected in five of the studies and all five revealed significant correlations. This provides good evidence as clearly a range of other variables, including personal ones, would also impact this relationship. Evidence was also found to support the discriminant validity of the scale. Finally predictive validity was checked by some studies which looked to see whether scores on the Organisational Commitment Questionnaire would predict how long an employee would stay/how quickly they would leave. This was supported in that individuals with low scores were more likely to leave the organisation. Significant

relationships were also found between low organisational commitment and absenteeism and to a lesser extent between commitment and performance.

This can all be used to support the use of the OCQ although the authors do identify several reasons to be cautious. One of these is that respondents may easily manipulate their answers to this scale as it is relatively easy to determine what is being measured. This is highly likely to happen if people feel that the results of any research may be used against them in some way. They also suggest that the shorter nine-item questionnaire may be an acceptable substitute for the 15-item questionnaire. They end by identifying several areas for further research, including the need to consider the relationship between behavioural and attitudinal commitment and some of the other factors (occupation, age, sex, etc.) that may influence organisational commitment.

Evaluation

Giacalone and Roseneld conducted a survey on sabotage. Surveys suffer from the same weaknesses as all self-report methods and probably the most important one here is **social desirability bias**. It may be that respondents were concerned about who would see their answers and this may have had an impact on what they were prepared to say. However, this study was also able to use a **quasi-experimental** approach when comparing the high-reason acceptors with the low-reason acceptors and this has yielded useful results. In particular the finding that both groups saw 'dishonesty' as qualitatively different from all other forms of sabotage is a useful one. This could allow employers to respond to dishonesty in a different way from how they might respond to other acts of sabotage. Someone who commits an act of sabotage may be sending a message to their employers about their working conditions or their quality of work life. This study clearly shows how the workplace environment (situation) can impact on the individual's behaviour.

The study by Blau is useful in bringing together the concepts of job involvement and organisational commitment. In allowing organisations to be able to predict potential staff turnover, they are able to plan for this or put measures in place to reduce this risk. Prediction, even if not 100% correct, is crucial for the effective running of large organisations.

In order to be able to predict, you need to be able to measure, and Mowday's measurement of organisational commitment has many useful applications to organisations. Clearly, these measures of commitment are **self-report** – that is the individual reports how committed they are. This obviously makes sense as the person is in the best position to know how they feel about the organisation that they work for. However we might be biased (or responding to demand characteristics) and it could be argued that perhaps others could provide a more objective measure of how committed we appear to be. Interestingly, a study conducted in 2001 by Goffin and Gellatly suggested that self-reported measures of commitment showed only a weak correlation with the reports made by others.

SELF-ASSESSMENT QUESTIONS

17 From Herzberg's two-factor theory of job satisfaction, give example of factors that affect job satisfaction and factors that affect job dissatisfaction.

18 Explain what is meant by 'job rotation'.

19 There have been several examples of psychometric tests in this section. Give one strength and one weakness of psychometric tests.

20 Explain what is meant by 'organisational commitment'.

Summary

This chapter has covered five major areas of organisational psychology. These have included well-established psychological theories that have been applied to the workplace as well as more contemporary research that has been conducted in a range of organisational environments.

We began by examining the topic of motivation. This included theories of motivation by **Maslow (1970)**, **Aldefer (1972)** and **McClelland (1965)** as well as cognitive theories such as goal setting theory (**Latham and Locke, 1984**), expectancy theory (**Vroom, 1964**) and equity theory (**Adams, 1964**). We also looked at intrinsic and extrinsic motivation and a variety of reward systems; both financial and non-financial. Our discussion of this largely centred around the application of these theoretical approaches to the workplace.

In the second topic on leadership and management, we examined traditional and modern theories of leadership including adaptive leadership (**Heifetz et al., 1997**) and **Scouller's (2011)** three levels of leadership. We then considered the importance of leadership style and the crucial relationship between leaders and followers. Once again, a key issue was the application of this work to an organisational setting but we also considered the important issues of individual differences and the roles of individual versus situational factors. We were also able to consider the nature versus nurture debate in relation to the question of whether leaders are 'born or made'.

We then moved on to consider group behaviour in organisations. We began by considering the development of groups (**Tuckman, 1965**) and the importance of different roles within the group (**Belbin, 1981**). We also examined the decision making process (**Wedley and Field, 1963**) and the dangers of groupthink (**Janis,**

1971) and cognitive limitations and errors (**Forsyth, 2006**). Finally, in this section we also considered the levels and causes of group conflict as well as strategies for the management of group conflict (**Thomas, 1976**). Applications to the workplace were key considerations in our evaluation of this area, with particular focus on the development of strategies to avoid groupthink and other cognitive errors as well as coping with conflict.

The importance of organisational work conditions was the next topic to be considered and this included a very wide range of research. We began with a consideration of the classic Hawthorne studies (**Wikstrom and Bendix, 2000**), the nature and effects of bullying at work (Einarsen, 1999) and the reactions of employees working on a newspaper to being moved to an open plan office (**Oldham and Brass, 1979**). We also examined the effects of shiftwork on health (**Knutsson, 2003**) and on accidents (**Gold et al. 1992**) and finally in this section, we considered a range of research related to health and safety. Here, for the first time, we were focussing on experimental research rather than theory and were able to consider a range of strengths and weaknesses of the research methods used.

The final section of this chapter focussed on satisfaction at work. We began by considering theories of job satisfaction including the two-factor theory (**Herzberg, 1959**) and job characteristics theory (**Hackman and Oldham, 1976**) before moving on to examine a number of techniques for measuring job satisfaction. Finally we examined some research into negative workplace behaviours including sabotage (**Giacolone and Rosenfeld, 1987**) and research into absenteeism (**Blau and Boal, 1987**). Our evaluation here focussed on applications but also considered the strengths and weaknesses of psychometric testing.

Exam-style questions

1   **a** Describe what is meant by 'shiftwork'. **[2 marks]**

     b Describe **one** study that has investigated the effects of shiftwork. **[4 marks]**

     c Discuss **one** strength and **one** weakness of the study you described in part (b). **[6 marks]**

2   **a** Describe what psychologists have found out about group development and roles. **[8 marks]**

     b Evaluate what psychologists have found out about group development and roles including a discussion of the practical applications. **[10 marks]**

3   **a** Design a study to investigate groupthink. **[10 marks]**

     b Explain the psychological and methodological evidence on which your study is based. **[8 marks]**

Answers to self-assessment questions

Chapter 1

1 a i Laboratory experiment; because there would be controls (such as how long they had to do the picture).

   ii Field experiment; because they are in the normal situation for the activity (they are doing art in an art class).

 b i Gender; males and females.

   ii Creativity; how well they reproduce the image.

 c Deception/informed consent; the students do not know that they are in an experiment about creativity and gender differences/do not know they are in an experiment at all (so cannot give consent).

 d Privacy; would be a problem in the art class because the participants could see each other's drawings; they could have each student on a separate desk (like a test);

   Confidentiality; could be a problem if the students wrote their names on their work; they would have to be given participant numbers.

2 a For example (example must match closed/open):

   closed: Tick any of the following that you are afraid of: the dark ☐, water ☐, slimy animals ☐ (offering the choices earns the second mark);
open: Describe when you first noticed your fear.

 b It will enable her to collect more detailed data; which could include why people have the phobias they do.

 c The participants might feel that they have to answer all the questions; which would be distressing; they might even find the questions frightening; the questions might invade the participant's privacy; they might not want to reveal the things they are afraid of/how scared they really are.

3 a Interview; questionnaire; observation.

 b i The participant might feel obliged to answer questions; as they are the only one/because they have developed a relationship with the researcher; this would be distressing; because the investigation is about emotions it might invade their privacy; they might not want to tell Damon/Inka how they feel.

   ii Feeling obliged: tell them they don't have to continue if they don't want to; this would help them to stop if they wanted to/gives them the right to withdraw;

   privacy: tell them they don't have to answer any question if they don't want to; this would help them to avoid being embarrassed if they wanted to keep something a secret/would prevent them becoming distressed about having to say things/about lying if they didn't want to say.

 c Probably not because it is only a case study so is only of one person; and different people's emotional reactions might differ;

   Because people often have phobias to different things; so their reactions might be not be the same.

4 a naturalistic = Debra; controlled = Jin

 b Covert; because she plans to hide in a tree.

 c Unstructured: because it is important to see all the different behaviours that the animals produce; otherwise there may be important aspects of the animals' responses that are missed;

   Structured: because it is important to have a set of behaviours to record to make the study reliable; otherwise the recordings for different animals won't be comparable; because Debra and Jin would have higher inter-observer reliability if they had a set of definitions to follow.

5 a Because they are measuring both variables; it is impossible to manipulate the number of dreams a person has/it might be unethical to manipulate the amount of coffee people drink.

 b A positive correlation because drinking more coffee may be linked to having more dreams; a negative correlation because drinking more coffee may be linked to having fewer dreams (no marks for saying drinking coffee will *cause* more/fewer dreams).

 c i For example: how many cups they have a day; how many litres they drink a day.

   ii How many cups they have a day: the cup size might vary; this would make the measure unreliable.

How many litres they drink a day: measuring the coffee might draw their attention to their coffee drinking; this might make the findings less valid (because they might worry about their coffee consumption/drink more or less coffee than normal).

6 a Species; cat or dog.

   b Intelligence/time taken to find the food; measured in seconds.

   c For example, 'There will be a difference in intelligence between cats and dogs'.

   d There will be no difference in intelligence between cats and dogs / Any difference in intelligence between cats and dogs is due to chance.

   e Opportunity sampling; because the animals used were readily available because they were pets.

   f The mean; because time is continuous data and it is the most informative.

   g Validity is about being certain you are testing what you claim to test; if the food-search task measured ability to smell it would not be testing intelligence/ if the animals differed in their sense of smell it would not be testing intelligence.

7 a Volunteer/self-selected sampling; because the participants responded to an advert.

   b Gender bias because more females; and women's sleep might be affected differently from men's sleep by the recording.

   c Deception; because some participants were misinformed about the effects of the recording; distress/harm/protection; because the participants might not sleep well (because they were misinformed) which might upset or harm them.

   d The timing; because people might feel they have not slept well even if they did.

Chapter 2

1 Brain scanners are unfamiliar environments so the participants' emotional behaviour may have been affected, making the measure of the DV of emotional arousal unrealistic;

Although we do respond emotionally to static images, much of our emotional behaviour is in the context of interactions with moving, speaking people, so the participant's emotional arousal is likely to have been lower than it would be in real-life situations.

2 The images chosen were from standardised sets so were of known emotional valence;

The presentation time and interval were kept the same throughout;

Participants fixated on a cross so that they would all be looking in the right place so they wouldn't miss seeing the picture making the exposure shorter;

Head movement was minimised by using a bite-bar formed with each participant's dental impression.

3 a Ten right-handed healthy females.

   b *Ten* is quite a small number, although given that the study used an fMRI scanner, this is unsurprising;

Right-handed is unlikely to matter, although there could be differences, such as the effects of bullying of left handers or brain differences;

Healthy may be important as individuals with mental health problems often have emotional difficulties, so the findings may not apply to them;

Females are different from males in terms of the way they express and deal with emotions, so the findings are unlikely to generalize directly to males.

4 a Because Biyu wouldn't know whether each reported dream was real or not; reducing validity. [1]

   b Because it is unethical as it is deception because it is really about dreaming; which would mean people couldn't give informed consent; because they wouldn't know it was really a study about dreaming. [2]

5 a Because he is trying to draw a causal conclusion from a correlation, which is not possible; even if there is a correlation, he will not know whether the amount eaten is the cause of that relationship. [1]

   b Sleeping: estimation of the time spent asleep in minutes; Eating: the number of calories consumed / the number of meals and snacks eaten. [2]

6 The Two-Factor Theory says both physiology and cognition are important to emotions. These two factors were manipulated in the study, physiology by the injection of adrenalin and cognition by the use of the angry or euphoric stooge. The greatest influence on emotions was when these factors were *combined* i.e. when there was no other

(cognitive) interpretation for their physiological state i.e. in misinformed plus euphoric stooge and in ignorant plus angry stooge. This suggests we use cognitions to label physiological arousal.

7   The participants couldn't give *informed consent*, as they didn't know what would happen e.g. in terms of adrenalin injections;

The participants were *deceived*, as they were told it was a study on vitamins and vision when in fact it was about emotions;

There was a (small) *risk of harm*, both psychological, if the participants were distressed by the questionnaire or the angry stooge, and physical from the injection of adrenalin (although records had been checked with the student health centre).

8   Self-report; of how angry/euphoric they felt;

Observation; how susceptible they were to joining in with the stooge.

9   *Self-report:*

The participants may have reported feelings they thought they should have (demand characteristics);

They might have lied, e.g. saying they were not angry when they were because they thought this would be unacceptable (social desirability bias).

Observation:

The participants' behaviour may not have reflected how they felt, e.g. if they were 'well behaved' because they were in an unfamiliar place, even though they felt angry;

The observers may have misinterpreted behaviours, e.g. 'joining in' might have been due to demand characteristics rather than the participant's euphoria.

Chapter 3

1   It used static faces, and normally we see moving faces;

It only used the eyes, normally we can study the whole face, e.g. the mouth is expressive too.

2   The choices were too easy because there were only two and they were opposites, it was changed to four. The differences might have arisen due to lack of understanding of the words, so a glossary was added.

3   Made it full face/make it from films not just pictures.

4   a   Putting participants into different levels of the IV with an equal chance for each person that they could end up in any condition.

    b   Because there will be individual differences between participants, e.g. whether they really do like asparagus very much, and how susceptible they are to a false memory suggestion and it would be a confounding variable if similar people, e.g. easy to fool ones, were all in one level of the IV.

5   Give them false feedback about having liked a food they don't eat any more because it's made them sick, or some different ones they never liked eating anyway, and that should make them believe that those foods are worth eating.

319

Chapter 4

1

Sex of child									
	Boy					Girl			
Sex of model	Male		Male		No model	Female		Female		No model
Action of model	agg	non-agg	agg	non-agg		agg	non-agg	agg	non-agg	
	6	6	6	6	12	6	6	6	6	12

2   Any two from:

Boys are more likely than girls to copy physical aggression;

Girls are more likely than boys to copy verbal aggression (although not significantly so);

Girls played more with dolls;

Girls played more with tea sets;

Boys engaged in more exploratory play;

Boys engaged in more gun play.

3   To find out whether exposure therapy, based on classical conditioning, could help a young boy with a phobia

of buttons by reducing the disgust and distress he experienced.

4   Exposure therapy is successful. It can change the emotions and cognitions relating to disgust about the phobic stimulus, in this case buttons. Imagery exposure has long-term effects, reducing distress by removing negative evaluations.

5   To investigate whether a parrot could learn to understand the symbolic concepts of 'same' and 'different' and to use vocal category labels to reply to questions to demonstrate this understanding.

6 *Strengths:* In order to reduce the risk of experimenter bias caused by the person testing Alex knowing the answer to the question and unconsciously guiding his answer, the question order and materials were selected by a different person. Furthermore, Alex was not tested by the same person who trained him in the same/different task, the trainer was not the experimenter;

The data collected were quantitative – the number of correct responses to questions asking same/different. This is an objective measure of understanding abstract concepts as it does not rely on the experimenter interpreting the parrot's responses.

Weaknesses: As this was a case study it is hard to generalise the findings as they are based on a single individual, especially as it was a laboratory trained parrot. Wild parrots might respond differently;

Although the parrot was stimulated by the training and testing the study still raises ethical issues as parrots are quite an intelligent species so being limited to an artificial environment for a long time could have been a source of distress.

Chapter 5

1 *Quantitative finding*: 100% of participants administered 300 V, 65% gave maximum 450 V.

Qualitative finding: comments made by participants, e.g. 'I don't think I can go on with this' or behaviour exhibited by participants (nervous laughter, shaking, sweating).

2 Any two of:

Legitimacy of the setting at Yale University;

Authority conveyed by the experimenter's lab coat;

Perceived randomness of role selection;

Payment incentive increased sense of obligation;

Belief that learner had also volunteered and was free to leave.

3 A person is less likely to take action in an emergency situation where there are others there also able to help – the feeling of responsibility is shared or 'diffused'.

4 *Strength*: high ecological validity, participants will usually behave in a natural way;

Strength: use of experimental design means IV can be manipulated and DV can be measured to show cause and effect;

Weakness: low control over extraneous variables;

Weakness: may be ethical issues if participants are not aware they are taking part in the study.

5 Any two from:

One booth had a transparent panel;

One booth had an opaque panel;

Chimpanzees were seated in pairs, one each side;

The chimpanzee participant was presented with a tray of seven items;

There was a slot in the panel to allow items to be passed through;

Chimpanzees could stand and look over or around the panel at their partner.

6 *Can see condition*: transparent panel between chimpanzees;

Cannot see condition: opaque panel between chimpanzees.

Chapter 6

1 Using virtual reality to assess symptoms of disorders like schizophrenia measures a person's actual behaviour, rather than just what they chose to tell a clinician. The virtual environment can be controlled, meaning that the test is standardised and reliable, like a questionnaire.

2 PET scans expose patients to small doses of radiation. Whilst these may not be harmful if conducted occasionally, they could be risky for some vulnerable groups, so other scanning techniques might be used for children or pregnant women.

3 In the study, participants were assessed before the start of their treatment, at treatment completion) and at a nine-month follow-up. If those rating the participants were aware of the condition they had been allocated (CBT or befriending), it could have biased the results.

4 Long periods of euphoria: mania

Loss of interest in normal activities: depression

Sudden interest in new activities: mania

Fatigue or exhaustion: depression

Changes to usual sleep patterns: both mania and depression

5 The link between BDI and positivity of attribution was correlational, which means you can't establish from the experimental design a cause and effect relationship. For example, depression could be causing pessimistic attributions, or another factor such as life events or genetics could be responsible for both.

Chapter 7

1 Finlay et al. found that the 'Kranes' type casino (or the playground model), a design incorporating environmental elements such as sunlight, green space and moving water, were rated as much higher on measures of pleasure and restoration (relief from stress) than were the casinos based on the Freidman design where the machines were the dominant feature.

2 The dependent variable in this study was the amount of money spent per person. This was calculated separately for starters, main course, desserts, coffee, bar drinks and wine and was then added up to produce overall drinks bill, overall food bill and total spend. The researchers also measured the amount of time that each person spent in the restaurant.

3 The main strength of any field experiment is its real life setting and the study by Gueguen et al. was conducted at a real market stall at a real outdoor market giving it high ecological validity. The main weakness is the lack of control that this gives you over possible extraneous variables. For example, it is suggested that the unusual nature of music being played at an outdoor stall might have been one factor responsible for the attraction.

4 If the students were wearing perfume, this would create another variable and it would be impossible to say whether the perfume worn by them was affecting the results given by those they questioned. It also ensured that this variable was as consistent as possible across all the student interviewers.

5 The more crowded the shoppers perceived the shops to be, the more negatively they described their shopping experience.

6 They used a laboratory experiment in their first study and a field experiment in their second.

7 They led respondents to describe the food as more calorific and also as more appealing. They also made more positive comments about the food after eating.

8 Possible distress caused to the people in the queue who were not aware that they were taking part in an experiment. You could also identify lack of consent or lack of debriefing as an answer here.

9 'Satisficing' means that customers 'get approximately where they want to go' and then stop the decision making process. In other words, we stop when we have found something that is 'good enough'.

10 They were shown a product for four seconds and then the product with the price for four seconds and then a third screen which asked them to choose whether they wanted to purchase this item at this price. Their brains were being scanned with an fMRI scanner while they did this.

11 Choice blindness is when we are blind to our own choices and preferences so that we might not notice when we are given something that is not what we asked for.

12 Simply, because Bugs Bunny is not a Disney character and so could not ever have been at a Disney attraction!

13 Classical conditioning may influence our colour choices because we form associations between colour and emotions or preferences. The study by Grossman and Wisenblit demonstrated that when given the choice, people chose coloured objects that had been associated with pleasant music.

14 A 'product-focussed sale technique' is one that largely ignores the needs of the customers and focusses on producing or selling a high quality product.

15 The 'disrupt-then-reframe' technique is effective because it motivates customers to accept a reframed message and this aids cognitive closure.

16 The 4 'P's are product, place, price and promotion.

17 The aim of this study was to see if children would be more likely to choose a soft drink that they had seen in a movie clip before being asked to choose.

18 It was a board game with squares for all the categories of products (e.g. cereals, cigarettes). The children had to match the logo cards with the correct product.

19 A 'hard sell' approach uses a direct approach telling the customer what the benefits of the product are and focusses on product quality. A 'soft sell' approach is more indirect or subtle and creates positive associations with the product such as style or humour. This is a focus on product image.

Chapter 8

1 *Reason for*: this was shown to produce the greatest acceptability and this matters because it inspires confidence in the doctor.

Reason against: in the study there was no comparison of a female doctor in very formal clothing, and this might have scored even higher. This matters because some patients could find a white lab coat intimidating so it would have a detrimental effect.

2 Produce a checklist of behaviours relating to doctor-centred and patient-centred behaviours for the doctors (e.g. with items from Tables 8.3 and 8.4) to discover their own consultation style and encourage them to adopt a more patient-centred approach where appropriate.

3 He is often ill, sometimes with things that can't be readily explained, like strange rashes and wounds that won't heal. He attends the surgery often enough to be well known and is comforted by receiving a diagnosis. By rubbing dirt into his wounds he could be making the infection worse. He could also be producing the red rashes himself, or giving himself diarrhoea, although there is no evidence for this.

4 a programme

   b provider

   c patient

   d patient

5 For example, questions about:

   knowledge, e.g. 'Do you know what could happen if you exercise?'

321

barriers, e.g. 'Is there any aspect of the medication that you are worried about?'

perceived threat e.g. 'How serious do you think the consequences would be if you don't follow the special diet?'

motivation/predisposition, e.g. 'To what extent to you feel able to make yourself attend physiotherapy regularly?'

6   All measures are somewhat flawed, so two methods would give a better estimate. In self reports patients may lie, or forget and in research terms the sample of those who provide self reports may tend to include those with better adherence, pill counting and repeat prescriptions can be ticked by simply throwing drugs away rather than taking them. Even with electronic trackers this may be the case, although the timing of doses can be gauged. Biochemical tests are highly accurate but cannot (usually) assess adherence to diet, exercise or physiotherapy regimes.

7   Acute pain only lasts a short time, until the source of the pain has been resolved. Chronic pain lasts a long time, persisting after even after healing.

8   intensity: how much it hurts

duration: how long the pain lasts for

location: where the pain is felt

9   This is likely because all pain, even pain with an obvious physical cause, has a psychological component and this can be manipulated with cognitive strategies, for example by distraction closing the gate.

10 People tend not to report stress retrospectively very accurately, but if you set up a prospective study, knowing they are being tracked for stress might also affect reporting. Also, people may not want to report the causes, or symptoms, of stress. This potentially makes the measures unreliable and invalid, and although physiological measures are better in this respect as they are more objective, they cannot reflect the qualitative nature of the stress being experienced, only the quantitative effects of that stress.

11 One way is to compare a group of participants' stress levels before and after treatment. If it works, their stress levels should have reduced. However, you wouldn't know whether their stress levels would have fallen over time anyway. So, an alternative way is to compare two groups, one treated with the new stress management technique and one with an old technique or a placebo technique (e.g. just a 'talking' group, who receive contact with other people but no actual treatment) and measure their relative stress levels before and after treatment.

Chapter 9

1   Maslow described 'self-actualisation' as reaching your full potential or becoming 'the best that you can be'.

2   A strength of projective tests is that they allow the individual a completely free response (rather than giving them a choice of responses which may not contain the answer they want to give). The main weakness is that the interpretation of the response is subjective; one psychologist might interpret the answer as meaning one thing and another might interpret this in a completely different way.

3   The person might ask for a pay rise but they might also decide to decrease their work rate (output) as they might feel that they shouldn't have to work as hard as someone who is being paid more.

4   Internal motivation comes from within the person and includes factors such as a sense of motivation or a sense of satisfaction. External motivation comes from outside the person and includes factors such as money or status.

5   'Task-oriented' leaders focus specifically on the task to be completed and on the structure of targets and standards required to achieve this. 'Relationship-oriented' leaders are more focussed on the wellbeing of the workforce and will take time to understand relationships between individuals.

6   Scouller suggested that the innermost level (personal qualities) was the most important as these qualities were at the heart of the leader's ability to affect those around him.

7   A low score means that they have given relatively positive ratings even to their least preferred co-worker and this would indicate that they have a relationship-oriented leadership style.

8   The four qualities are self-management, commitment, competence and courage.

9   The five stages are forming, storming, norming, performing and adjourning. The 'norming' phase is the third phase and is where group norms are established and the individual members of the group begin to feel like a group.

10 'People oriented roles' are those roles that focus on relationships between the different group members. 'People oriented roles' include co-ordinators, team workers and resource investigators.

11 'Groupthink' is where groups make irrational or dysfunctional decisions due to the pressures for conformity and harmony within the group. Decisions made as a result of 'groupthink' would be highly unlikely to be made by an individual.

12 Thomas suggests five ways in which group conflict might be managed and these are:

Competition: individuals may persist in conflict until someone wins and someone loses. At this point, the conflict is over.

Accommodation: here one individual will need to make a sacrifice in order to reduce the conflict. This can be extremely effective in reducing conflict and preventing further damage to the relationship.

Compromise: each group or individual under conflict must make some compromise and give up something to reduce the conflict. This will be effective only if both sides lose comparable things.

Collaboration: the group has to work together to overcome the conflict.

Avoidance: avoidance involves suppressing the conflict or withdrawing from the conflict completely. This does not resolve the conflict which is still there and has not been addressed. This can be effective in creating a cooling-off period.

Another way to address conflict is to create a superordinate goal; a goal that both groups and individuals have to work together to achieve. This is similar to collaboration.

13 One strength of this study is that it was conducted in a real organisation and thus has high ecological validity (rather than being conducted in an artificial environment). One weakness is that it is impossible to control all the variables that might have affected the worker's responses.

14 There are several effects mentioned in the study by Knutsson. These include increased gastrointestinal diseases, higher risk of heart disease, increased risks of breast cancer and diabetes, increased incidences of obesity as well as low birth weight in babies born to mothers who worked shifts.

15 There were two measures; numbers of days lost due to accidents and the costs of accidents and injuries.

16 One conclusion is that the campaign was successful although Cowpe warned that the effectiveness would 'wear off' as time passed and also that there was a danger of overexposure to the campaign leading to a decrease in effectiveness.

17 Factors that affect job satisfaction include factors relating to the job such as a sense of achievement or a sense that one is doing something worthwhile. Factors that affect job dissatisfaction include working conditions and salary levels.

18 'Job rotation' is where workers have regular changes of tasks within their normal roles such as working in different areas of a supermarket.

19 Psychometric tests are easy to administer and generally are easy to score. However they are prone to social desirability bias and demand characteristics.

20 'Organisational commitment' is described as the attitude that workers have to their workplace/organisation.

Answers to exam-style questions
All answers have been written by the authors of the book

Chapter 1

1 a Directional; because it is predicting that one condition (adrenalin) will produce stronger emotions than the other (rather than simply that there will be a difference). **[1 mark]**

b There will be no difference in emotional response between people injected with adrenalin and saline. / Any difference in emotional response between people injected with adrenalin and saline is due to chance. **[2 marks]**

2 a *Advantage*: The participants would be less likely to be affected by Declan himself if it was a questionnaire as they could do it on their own; this might produce more honest answers from participants who think that people who claim they have phobias are making it up.

Disadvantage: If the participants were distressed by the questionnaire Declan wouldn't be able to return them to their previous state by reassuring them; which would be unethical because it fails to follow the ethical guideline of avoiding causing harm. **[4 marks]**

b For example:

Open: Describe how you would feel if someone in your office left the room because there was an insect flying around and they said they were afraid of it.

Closed: Do you know anyone with any of the following phobias: dogs/mice/birds/small spaces/the dark? **[2 marks]**

c Reliability; because he is concerned that he would not interpret similar answers in the same way each time. **[2 marks]**

3 a An experiment may include for example:
- whether it is a laboratory or field experiment (with an explanation);
- an IV (boys and girls), which should be stated;
- a DV (how much they doodle), which should be operationalised;
- a statement of the experimental design (independent measures);
- suitable controls;
- standardisation if appropriate;
- the sampling technique and how it will be employed. **[10 marks]**

Level 3 (8–10 marks)
- Response is described in sufficient detail to be replicable.
- Response may have a minor omission.
- Use of psychological terminology is accurate and comprehensive.

Level 2 (5–7 marks)
- Response is in some detail.
- Response has minor omission(s).
- Use of psychological terminology is mainly accurate.

Level 1 (1–4 marks)
- Response is basic in detail.
- Response has major omission(s).
- If response is impossible to conduct max. 2 marks.
- Use of psychological terminology is accurate.

Level 0 (0 marks): No response worthy of credit.

Major omissions are:
- what (definition of the DV)
- how (controls).

Minor omissions are:
- where (lab or field, actual location stated)
- who (sampling).

b Problems may, for example, be matters of:
- Validity
  - operationalisation;
  - difficulty with covertly observing doodling.
- Reliability
  - inter-rater consistency of 'more' doodling (e.g. amount versus complexity);

    If the problem was an obvious omission in (a), marks can be awarded here if the candidate refers to the omission. **[4 marks]**

Mark according to the levels of response criteria below:

Level 3 (3–4 marks)

- Appropriate problem identified.
- Appropriate solution is clearly described.

Level 2 (2 marks)

- Appropriate problem identified.
- Explanation of why it is a problem.

OR

- Solution is possible but ineffectual.

Level 1 (1 mark)

- Appropriate problem identified.
- Little or no justification.

Level 0 (0 marks): No response worthy of credit.

Chapter 2

1   **emotional intensity** of the scenes; (0=) not emotionally intense at all to (3=) extremely emotionally intense;

(an unexpected) **recognition test of scenes**; all 96 scenes and 48 new ones (foils) (which matched the original scenes in valence and arousal characteristics);

certainty was rated; (as 1, 2 or 3) "remember", "know" and forgotten;

brain scan/fMRI; to measure activation of the amygdala.
[6 marks]

2   The level of amygdala activation reflects the subjective experience of emotion that we feel / greater amygdala activation is related to more intense emotions;

The greater the brain/amygdala activation in an emotional experience, the better our memory.
[2 marks]

3   It collected quantitative/objective data; for example from the EEG;

It tested falsifiable hypotheses; such as that participants would remember more dreams from REM than nREM.
[2 marks]

4   **a**   For example:
Does dream recall differ between eye movement (**REM**) and quiescent (**nREM**) stages of sleep?

Is there a positive correlation between subjective estimates of dream duration and the length of the REM period before waking?

Are eye movement patterns related to dream content?
[1 mark]

b   Nearly 80% of the times participants were woken from REM they recalled a dream, so less than 20% of the time they didn't whereas when they were woken up from nREM they recalled a dream recall only 17% of the time and 93% of the awakenings they didn't.
[3 marks]

5   The biological approach focuses on the physiological causes of behaviour, for example Schachter and Singer looked at the role of the hormone adrenalin in emotions; whereas the learning approach focuses on the acquisition of behaviours;

The biological approach often studies physiology using brain scans/EEGs or by manipulating biological variables like Schachter and Singer did by injecting adrenalin; whereas the learning approach typically uses observation of behaviour/laboratory experiments;

The biological approach focuses on physiological processes *within* individuals, such as brain activity/the role of hormones like Schachter and Singer did by testing adrenalin; whereas the learning approach focuses on the behaviour of individuals.
[4 marks]

6   They were given the **right to withdraw** at the beginning; because they were told they would receive an injection; (after completing the questionnaire) the participants were **debriefed**; the experimenter explained the deception (in detail) and answered any questions from the participants;

To ensure **protection from harm**; all the potential participants were cleared with the student health service to ensure no harmful effects would arise from the injections.
[2 marks]

Chapter 3

1   **a**   Because generally we doodle 'freehand'; without the constraints of squares and circles the participants were given.
[2 marks]

b   (In a natural experiment participants are not allocated to conditions so) I would compare natural doodlers to non-doodlers;

I would do a pilot study to watch people to see who doodled most and least;

then use them as the two levels of the IV;

so I would have 'high doodlers' (who I had seen doodle at least 4 times in a week);

and 'non-doodlers' who I had never seen doodle;

so it would be an independent measures design;

I would measure the DV of concentration;

by seeing how well they could answer some questions after I'd read out a passage;

the passage would be about my pets and they would be asked questions about animals I do have and ones I'd like to have but don't have;

it would be difficult to control participant variables but I would control some situational variables like having the room quiet for everyone;

so that they would be able to concentrate the same amount;

so my sampling technique would be opportunity sampling. **[10 marks]**

2 So that there wasn't much to think about; so they would be more likely to doodle. **[2 marks]**

3 Because males and females may display emotions differently, so only one type of expression would be being measured;

Because males and females may respond differently to same and different gender examples of emotions. **[2 marks]**

4 Social and non-social. **[2 marks]**

5 People on the autistic spectrum have a lower social intelligence than non-autistics; but their non-social intelligence is unaffected;

Women have a slightly higher social intelligence than men; but these differences are not significant. **[4 marks]**

6 To test whether giving false feedback about childhood memories of eating asparagus would cause a false memory/belief OR To test whether a false memory about eating asparagus as a child would affect adult behaviour like buying it/eating it. **[2 marks]**

7 Because false feedback led to a false memory which made people more likely to say that they would eat asparagus/would pay more for it; which would be a change in their behaviour. **[2 marks]**

Chapter 4

1 Operant conditioning involves trial and error, i.e. producing a random range of behaviours which may or may not lead to reinforcement. This takes time. Also, even when the correct behaviour is produced and reinforced, it is not immediately part of the repertoire, it must be repeatedly reinforced. Finally, if the behaviour is complex, it may be necessary to learn it a step at a time (successive approximations). In imitation, repetition is also necessary, but the behaviour can be observed in its correct form, and in its entirety. **[2 marks]**

2 Participants would give informed consent, that is, agree on the basis of an understanding of the research.

However, as young children may not understand, their parents/guardians should give informed consent *in addition* to the children themselves being asked in a way that they will understand. **[3 marks]**

3 a Consequences affect the frequency of the behaviour they follow; so good consequences/rewards result in the behaviour becoming more frequent; this is called positive reinforcement; negative reinforcement also increases the frequency of a behaviour; by making nasty things stop; and punishment reduces the frequency of a behaviour; by making nasty things happen. **[3 marks]**

b Using contingency management, which means controlling the consequences of the desired behaviours/items on the exposure hierarchy; the mother gave the boy rewards/positive reinforcement every time he completed an item on the exposure hierarchy; so he was more likely to repeat the behaviour such as 'hugging mum when she wears large plastic buttons'. **[2 marks]**

4 a Nature: innate, controlled by biology/genes; nurture: acquired, controlled by the environment/experience. **[2 marks]**

b Because many species share it this suggests it has an evolutionary root; so it must be controlled genetically. **[2 marks]**

c Alex learned to respond to the shape/colour/material of objects (to tell 'same' or 'different'); this was acquired by experience/as a result of operant conditioning; because he was rewarded/was given the object/was positively reinforced for correct choices; which made him repeat the choice by strengthening the concept (of same or different) and punished for incorrect responses/was scolded/had the object taken away; and he had experience of social learning as two humans modelled responses; so he could imitate their behaviours. **[4 marks]**

Chapter 5

1 a *Protection of participants:* they shouldn't suffer any more physical or psychological risks than they would in their normal lives.

Debrief: explaining the aims and possible consequences of the study at the end and ensuring that the participants leave feeling at least as happy as at the start.

Right to withdraw: participants need to know they can leave the study whenever they like. **[2 marks]**

b *Protection of participants*: by asking psychology students and colleagues about what they thought would happen; and having the estimate that 97% of participants wouldn't deliver the maximum shock; he had good reason to believe it would not be such as stressful study.

Debrief: the participants (teachers) were (interviewed afterwards and) told the real aim, had the deception explained to them and were reassured that they had not really hurt the learner.

Right to withdraw: participants were told they could have the $4.50 for taking part and that it was not conditional on finishing the study, just for being willing to take part so it didn't matter when they left. **[4 marks]**

2 Diffusion of responsibility says that people are less likely to help when there are more people present;

Because the responsibility for helping is shared out/each person feels less need to help;

The results, however, showed that people (generally) helped very quickly, even though there were other people in the carriage;

In fact, in bigger groups the latency to help was shorter (which is the opposite of the prediction), e.g. seven person groups were faster to respond than three person groups;

And the model rarely needed to step in because people helped so quickly;

Nearly 80% of victims received spontaneous help (before model intervened or in a no-model condition);

And about 60% of victims were helped by more than one person. **[6 marks]**

3 To find out if chimpanzees can understand the needs of other chimpanzees.

This was supported because they responded by offering an object when another chimp was in need;

showing that they understood that the other chimpanzee needed help;

For example in the 'can see' condition, objects were offered in 91% of trials;

and in the 'cannot see' condition, at least one object was offered in 96% of trials;

although this was usually in response to a request (such as holding out a hand).

To find out whether chimpanzees can respond to the needs of other chimpanzees with appropriate help.

This was supported because they chose to offer tools (e.g. a stick or straw) rather than other things (such as a brush);

and offered the appropriate tool (stick or straw) in the 'can see' condition but not in the 'can't see' condition;

that is there was no significant difference in which tool was offered when they couldn't see which tool would be useful. **[6 marks]**

Chapter 6

1 a Agoraphobia is the extreme or irrational fear of being in public places, such as being in open spaces, standing in line or using public transport. These situations cause fear and anxiety in the person with agoraphobia so they may avoid being in public. This can impair their normal functioning, making it difficult to lead a normal life (as they find it hard to go shopping, meet friends or go out to work). **[2 marks]**

b One measure of obsessive-compulsive and related disorders is the known as the Blood-Injury Phobia Inventory (BIPI), developed by Mas et al, 2010. It is a way of measuring the specific phobia of blood using a standardised self-report method. The BIPI gives 18 different situations that involve blood and/or injections, such as seeing another person cut their finger or personally getting an injection. The individual has to consider how they would react to each hypothetical situation and state what their most likely response would be. This could be their thoughts, bodily reactions or behaviour. The frequency of each item is also rated on a scale of 0-3, with 0 being never and 3 being always. Once all items are completed, the test produces an overall score of the severity of a person's blood phobia, as a quantitative measurement. **[4 marks]**

c One strength of Watson's theory that phobias are acquired through classical conditioning is that it is based on laboratory-based research. In the case study of Little Albert, Watson and Rayner demonstrate that Albert learned his fear of rats through a training schedule. Observations of Albert's behaviour were taken before classical conditioning took place, then after exposure to the unconditioned stimulus (loud noise) was paired with the neutral stimulus (white rat). This allowed them to demonstrate an observable change in behaviour, which had taken place within a controlled environment. It therefore suggests that the research supporting Watson's theory has a high level of validity in this context.

One weakness of this theory, however, is that it relies on research that was conducted in an artificial environment. In real life, people acquire phobias in much less structured ways. In contrast, research by DiNardo et al. suggests that individuals with specific phobias (i.e. dogs) often have no memory or explanation of negative events which may have caused them to learn their phobias. Or, in some cases, individuals who have had traumatic or painful experiences such as dog bites do not rate highly on anxiety relating to dogs. This means that in outside of the laboratory setting, classical conditioning may not be able to explain how phobias are acquired, and that other theories, such as those from the cognitive approach might be better supported by empirical evidence. **[6 marks]**

Chapter 7

1 **a** The independent variable is whether the clip contained Pepsi or not. The dependent variable is whether the children chose Pepsi or Coca-Cola when given the choice. **[2 marks]**

b The children could have been asked to play a game of shops. The experimenter could have arranged for a range of items to have been available for the children (rather than just two) and then they could have observed to see if more children in the experimental group put Pepsi in their shopping basket than children in the control group. **[4 marks]**

c One strength of the way this study was conducted was that giving the children a choice of drinks would have seemed quite natural and not necessarily as if it were part of the study. This means that is highly unlikely that the children would have realised that this was the important question and would have answered naturally. One weakness is that it would be impossible to control for individual differences such as whether the children always had Pepsi rather than Coca-Cola at home which may have affected their choices. It would also be impossible to control for individual differences in terms of who had seen the film before and how many times and although the researchers measured this they might have been better making their own film clip so that no one would have seen it before. **[4 marks]**

d There are several advantages and disadvantages to using children in psychology experiments. One important advantage is that using children allows us to see the development of children's abilities or understanding. If we used children of different ages in studies in consumer psychology we might be able to suggest that different marketing strategies would be effective with different age groups. Alternatively,

the use of longitudinal studies in psychology would allow us to measure changes over time. Another advantage is that children are less likely to respond to demand characteristics, especially if they are not aware that they are taking part in experimental research. For example the children in this study were probably not able to guess that the researchers expected them to choose Pepsi rather than Coca-Cola and it is likely that an adult group would have worked this out. However the fact that children may not be aware that they are in an experiment brings us to the disadvantages; children cannot give their own consent to take part in a study, this has to be given by a parent or guardian and this means that the parent needs to trust the researcher to withdraw the child if they appear distressed as they are unlikely to be able to tell you this. Their lack of language skills may also mean that it might be difficult to get the information that you need. **[5 marks]**

Chapter 8

1 **a** Fear arousal and providing information. **[2 marks]**

b Fear arousal is good because it has an impact. Janis and Feshbach (1953) found that 76% of participants who had seen a scary film about teeth were worried by it but only 46% of the low-fear group were affected. This shows that fear arousal affects people because many more of the scary film group changed their view. However, when it comes to changing behaviour, fear is not so effective. In the same study, only 28% of the high-fear group changed their teeth-cleaning habits, but half of the low-fear group did, showing this was much more effective in the long run. **[4 marks]**

c One factor that affects whether an individual will change their health beliefs is whether their hope is realistic or not. Weinstein (1980) called the mistakes people make in believing they are not at risk from accidents or illness 'unrealistic optimism'. These optimists' biased thinking results from the way they as an individual perceive events. Their cognition is faulty – they believe bad things happen more often to other people than to them. This thinking becomes even more biased because the worse the possible consequence is, the more they believe they are not at risk, and they think the reverse for positive things, they believe these are more likely to happen to them. Their beliefs about the likelihood of an event happening to them make matters worse. If they think the probability of a health problem is high, or they have personal experience of it, they also believe that their own chances of avoiding it are better than average. So if they believed being fat puts you at risk of heart attacks, they will think they won't have a heart attack and that because one could kill you, it definitely won't happen to them. **[4 marks]**

d Campaigns for health are good because they give people information to make good health decisions, which helps to improve their wellbeing. This is especially so if they encourage healthy living, so influence people before they damage their health. For example, Janis and Feshbach's dental films helped the low-fear group to brush their teeth better, so they would protect them from decay.

Tapper's Food Dudes campaign showed that education had a long-term effect on children's health. The Food Dudes helped the children to make healthy choices for lunch at school and their eating habits changed. The exposure to a range of fruit and vegetables and healthy eating models, plus rewards for tasting new foods and eating a whole portion, led to better eating habits even a month later.

It is also good to use campaigns because it is cheaper to prevent than to treat. Lewin showed that a campaign to encourage exercise made heart attack patients less depressed and they saw their doctors less than a placebo group, which means they put less demand on the health service.

However, we need to change behaviour rather than just beliefs. Just knowing something is unhealthy won't necessarily stop people doing it. We know this from Weinstein's idea of unrealistic optimism – people can convince themselves they aren't at risk even when they are, so they may ignore information in campaigns. For example, the people in Farquar's Five City Project probably already knew what they should do to cut their risk of heart disease, they just didn't do it. In fact, even though the project worked, in a long-term follow-up they found that men were less likely than women to have reduced saturated fat intake and that the people at greatest risk used preventative interventions the least.

Finally, the effects need to be long term, but this isn't always measured, for example Janis and Feshbach only retested behaviour after a week. However, Fox et al. used a safety campaign in a mine and, after the token economy, the miners were still working carefully ten years later.

2 a I would do a field experiment to compare people who were supposed to be taking the same dose of the same medication, such as Mesalazine for bowel disease. I would use patients with the same condition from three different health centres, and make sure they all received the same instructions on how and when to take the tablets. These would be my controls. To compare methods I would use pill counting as a physical measure and a questionnaire as a self report method. The patients would fill in my questionnaire every Sunday, asking the closed question 'How many tablets have you taken this week? 0/1-4/5-10/11-15/20-25/25-30'. This will indicate whether they are taking the right amount, too many or not enough. I would also ask them to bring all their remaining tablets and empty boxes with them to the clinic so I could count how many were left compared to the week before. These are the two levels of the independent variable. As each patient uses both methods, it is a repeated measures design.

I would then test how true each measure was by comparing it to a urine test to detect whether they had really been taking the tablets. The difference between how much they had actually taken shown by their urine test and the results of each of the other methods would tell me how good each method was. This is the dependent variable. If they are effective measures of adherence, the difference from the urinalysis data will be small. To ensure my study is ethical, I will have to get their informed consent to collect data, including the urinalysis, and they would have to know what my study was about. **[10 marks]**

b Riekart and Droter found that patients with better adherence were more likely to be the ones who volunteered for their research into adherence. This isn't all that surprising as social desirability will play a part in people's responses. It suggests that all research on adherence to medication that is based on self-reports is biased as the sample will be more compliant than average.

There might be several reasons for people's non-adherence. Bulpitt suggests it is a rational choice, with patients weighing up the benefits, such as potentially getting better, and the costs, such as the cost of the prescription. When the benefits exceed the costs they will act healthily. The compliance model suggested by Becker says that these positives and negatives do matter, but so do beliefs, e.g. in how well the treatment will work, and modifying factors, such as whether they have been exposed

329

to a cue to act, e.g. exposure to someone who is suffering from the same thing.

Pill counting should therefore be more objective as it would be less affected by the subjectivity of people's worries (costs according to Bulpitt) and motives (according to Becker). Chung and Naya used tablets in special bottles that recorded when, and the number of times, they were opened. As a physical method this will be more accurate than my simple counting, as it records when the pills were removed from the pot. My participants could have taken them any time of day. However, in either case they could just get the tablets out and throw them away. Then the tablet count would suggest they had taken more than they really had.

Even so, any of the methods might be useful as an indicator of when patients are refusing or forgetting to take medication. They can help practitioners to find out why, such as if they are confused or have memory problems or if the drug is causing side effects. A self-report might be better for this as they could ask extra open questions about the problems. **[8 marks]**

For a top band answer to part (a), the essay must include an appropriate, detailed, coherent and accurately described design, which includes four or five methodological features. These can include the research method, experimental design (if appropriate), sampling, ethics, controls, measures (e.g., DV, questions, response categories) and analysis as well as general procedural matters.

Chapter 9

1 **a** 'Shiftwork' is any working pattern that does not involve the same work pattern every week. Typically shift workers move between day, evening and night shifts. **[2 marks]**

b One study that investigated the effect of shiftwork was Gold. He conducted a survey of more than 600 nurses who either worked fixed shift patterns (always days or always nights) or those who 'rotated' between days and nights. He asked them to complete a questionnaire which asked about their shift patterns and also asked about quality of sleep, use of alcohol, how many times they had fallen asleep at work or in the car driving to and from work in the last year and the numbers of accidents, errors or 'near-misses' that could be attributed to sleepiness also in the last year. He found that rotators had poorer sleep patterns, that

falling asleep was common among rotators and that accidents were twice as common in the rotators group than the day shift group. **[4 marks]**

c One strength is the fact that Gold was able to collect so much data; not only was the data collected from a large sample of nurses, the data also gave information on a whole range of factors associated with shift work. One weakness is the fact that the data was self-report and may have been subject to demand characteristics or social desirability bias as well as being inaccurate due to not being able to remember properly. For example, they were asked to report the number of accidents, errors or near misses that had occurred in the previous year. It is highly unlikely that someone would be able to give a completely accurate answer to this question. **[6 marks]**

2 **a** Tuckman proposed that there were five stages to the development of a group. He called these stages 'forming, storming, norming, performing and adjourning'. Forming is where the group members get to know each other, storming is where conflicts may occur as the leader tries to gain control and norming is where the group becomes an established group, with its own norms and values. The fourth stage, performing, is where the group works on the tasks that it has been set and once these are complete they move into the adjourning stage. In this stage they can either move onto a new task or the group may naturally come to an end and new groups, for new tasks, will be formed and the process will start all over again.

Belbin studied group roles and suggested that the ideal group consisted of people who would take on different roles. He divided these roles into three categories each containing three different roles. The first were the action oriented roles; Belbin identified the shaper, the implementer and the completer-finisher as roles that were all focussed on action. The next group were the people-oriented roles and these include the coordinator, the team worker and the resource investigator. These are all roles that involve a focus on the relationship between people in the group. Finally he identified the thought oriented roles called the plant, the monitor-evaluator and the specialist. These are the thinkers. Belbin suggested that everyone fits one of these roles more than the others and his Team Inventory is designed to determine which role you are best suited to. **[8 marks]**

b Tuckman's model of group formation has obvious practical applications to the workplace. For example, it is useful for managers to recognise that these stages are a normal part of group development so they should not be concerned with the 'storming' phase but allow it to happen. However it is important to recognise that this model was initially designed to explain group formation in small groups rather than larger more permanent groups and so it may not be applicable to every group. Tuckman also fails to provide suggestions for timescales – how long should a group be in the 'storming' phase for example before a manager might decide to step in and take control? There are also critics that suggest that group formation is cyclical rather than linear – in other words, groups may go back to the beginning of these stages with every new task or every change in working conditions. All of these criticisms might reduce the usefulness of this model. Belbin takes a different view of teams and it may be that another criticism of Tuckman is that he doesn't examine different team roles. Belbin does and again this has many practical applications, especially in conjunction with the Team Inventory. Not only does the theory help an organisation to recognise that they need different people to fulfil different roles within the team, they also have the tools required to identify the people that best fit these roles. However, there are also problems with Belbin's theory, particularly in terms of the need for so many people to fill the different roles. In practical terms, it is highly likely that people will have to take on more than one role within a team. The theory does show us clearly that there are many different skills involved in teams and that they are all equally important. **[10 marks]**

3 a I would design a questionnaire study to be completed anonymously and online to collect data about the frequency of bullying behaviours within an organisation. I would design the questionnaire to collect the following information:

Details about the person: age, sex, job role and how long they had worked for the organisation;

Experience of being bullying: who by, how often and what form this took;

How the person dealt with the bullying;

How the organisation dealt with the bullying;

Knowledge of any bullying directed at any other members of staff and how they/the organisation responded to this;

Knowledge and understanding of the company policies on bullying;

I would also include details of where people could obtain help or guidance after completing the questionnaire in case this has upset them in any way.

I would request permission to email all employees including a link to my questionnaire which could then be completed in their own time. I would also leave leaflets/posters around the organisation so that people could access the questionnaire without following the link from their email in case they were worried that this would mean that they could be identified. I would stress that this was entirely confidential. I could also add to my study by interviewing a smaller sample of people and perhaps by a participant observation method where I could gain employment in the organisation in order to observe bullying behaviour for myself. **[10 marks]**

b My study is largely based on the review conducted by Einarsen who identified five different types of bullying behaviour; work related (such as making the person's job more and more difficult), social isolation, personal attacks or ridicule, verbal threats and physical violence. Einarsen linked bullying with power and suggested that bullying by a superior is more distressing than bullying by a peer. This is why it is important that my questionnaire asks about who is doing the bullying as bullying by a boss is going to be a very different experience than bullying by a co-worker. However this is also important for other reasons. If someone is being bullied by a superior then they may be far less likely to respond to the questionnaire if they have any doubts about the confidentiality of their response or if they believe that their superior might see their answers. Bullying by a peer or co-worker might be much easier to reveal, especially if the individual's manager is sympathetic and is dealing with the issue. This is why also collecting data through interviews and by participant observation would help. **[8 marks]**

Glossary

Abnormality: behaviour, thinking or emotions that depart from the norm. This may be states or behaviours that are rarely seen in most people (e.g. hallucinations), states or behaviours that are not considered normal in a particular society, or that distress or harm the individual or those around them.

Adherence: sticking. 'Adherence to medical advice' means following advice given by a medical practitioner.

Adrenalin: a hormone released from the adrenal glands in response to stress or excitement. It is also known as epinephrine, and is a medication, hormone and neurotransmitter. Common side effects include shakiness, anxiety, sweating; a fast heart rate and high blood pressure may occur. Strong emotions such as fear or anger can cause adrenalin to be released into the bloodstream.

Affect: a person's feelings or emotions. A 'flat' affect can refer to a lack of visible response such as a frown or smile.

Affective: relating to mental disorders in which disturbance of mood is the primary symptom.

Alternative hypothesis: the testable statement which predicts a difference or relationship between variables in a particular investigation.

Altruistic: acting helpfully towards others without obvious benefit to oneself, e.g. chasing after a stranger in order to return their wallet, which involves no guarantee of reward.

Amplitude: the 'height' of waves, e.g. on an EEG (indicating voltage).

Amygdala: part of the brain involved in emotional responses.

Anaesthesia: a temporary state of induced loss of sensation or consciousness which is used to relieve pain and suffering. It should be used where appropriate to ensure that animal studies are ethical.

Analgesia: pain relief. This should be used in animal studies when pain is caused that is not essential to the study.

Application to everyday life: the practical use of a theory, or the findings of a study, to help to improve processes or people's lives, for example, in terms of bettering physical or mental health, safety, production at work or sales by a company.

Arterial spin-labelling perfusion MRI: arterial blood (coming away from the heart) is labelled or tagged with a radioactive compound and, after a delay, moves into the imaging plane or volume, during which time there is decay of the label or tag. Images are acquired in labelled and control conditions and subtracted and the difference produces an image that illustrates cerebral blood flow to areas of the brain.

Attention: the concentration of mental effort on a particular stimulus. It may be focused or divided.

Attribution: the cognitive process by which individuals explain the causes of behaviour and events. Our attributions may be faulty or biased; tending to always look to specific causes for behaviour on the basis of our previous life experience.

Autism (or autistic spectrum disorder, ASD): developmental disorders characterised by difficulty in social, communicative and imaginative areas. They are also associated with repetitive physical behaviours.

Autism Spectrum Quotient Test (AQ): a self-report questionnaire with scores ranging from 0 to 50. A higher score suggests that the person completing it has more autistic traits.

Aversive stimuli: unpleasant stimuli that an individual would choose to avoid. They should not generally be used in animal studies.

Bar chart: a graph used for data in discrete categories and total or average scores. There are gaps between each bar that is plotted on the graph because the columns are not related in a linear way.

Basic emotions: Ekman (1992) said there are six basic emotions that are recognised universally by adults and even very young children developing normally. These emotions are happiness, sadness, anger, surprise, fear and disgust.

Behavioural categories: the activities recorded in an observation. They should be operationalised and should break a continuous stream of activity into discrete recordable events. They must be observable actions rather than inferred states.

Behavioural therapy: a key influence on behaviour is the previous learning process, so behavioural therapy aims to produce a new set of more desirable behaviours.

Bias: differences in behaviour (responses), feelings or cognition that are caused by an extraneous factor rather than the variable under investigation. See also response bias, social desirability bias.

Bystander: a person who is present at, but may not be directly involved in, a particular situation. 'Bystander apathy' or the 'bystander effect' refers to the actions of bystanders who don't help others in the event of an emergency.

Case study: a detailed investigation of one instance, usually a single person (but alternatively a single family, company or event). These may be rare or instances that could not be created artificially but can provide useful information. It uses a range of techniques such as interviewing, observation and testing.

Causal relationship: (cause and effect relationship) A relationship between two variables in which a change in one variable is responsible for a change in the other variable (the effect). This is seen in experiments, in which the IV causes changes in the DV but not in correlations.

Cause and effect: see causal relationship.

Ceiling effect: this occurs when a test is too easy and all participants in a condition score the top score. This is problematic as it does not allow the research to differentiate between participants.

Choice blindness: ways in which people are unaware of their own choices and preferences. People often do not notice when they are presented with something which was not what they asked for.

Chronic: something that occurs for a long time or is on-going. It can be used to refer to a mental or physical disorder, or to a course of treatment.

Classical conditioning: learning through association, studied in both humans and animals. A new stimulus, which initially has no effect (the neutral stimulus, NS), becomes associated with another stimulus (the unconditioned stimulus, UCS). The UCS already produces a response (the unconditioned response, UCR), which is often an innate (instinctive) reaction. Following pairing of the UCS and NS, the NS will produce a response similar to the UCR, so the NS becomes known as the conditioned stimulus (CS) and the newly learned response, the conditioned response (CR).

Closed questions: questionnaire, interview or test items that produce quantitative data. They have only a few, stated alternative responses and no opportunity to expand on answers.

Cognitive map: an internal representation of an external geographical reality or 'a mental representation of one's physical environment'. Asking someone to draw a map of their environment is one way of exploring what the important features of the environment are for them.

Cognitive therapy: a key influence on behaviour is how a person thinks about a situation, so cognitive therapy aims to change maladaptive or unwanted thoughts and feelings.

Concordance: the presence of a particular observable trait or disorder in both individuals within a set of twins.

Concurrent validity: a way to judge validity by comparing measures of the same phenomenon in different ways at the *same time* to show that they produce similar results in the same circumstances.

Confederate: someone who is playing a role in a piece of research and has been instructed as to how to behave by the researcher.

Confidentiality: an ethical guideline stating that participants' results and personal information should be kept safely and not released to anyone outside the study.

Confounding variables: extraneous factors that affect the performance of participants. In an experiment they would therefore affect scores on the DV, and so could obscure the effect of the IV.

Conspecific: member of the same species.

Continuous reinforcement: when a learner receives a reward each time they perform a desirable behaviour. It is one of several possible schedules of reinforcement.

Control: a way to keep a potential extraneous variable constant. In an experiment this would prevent the variable from affecting the DV in addition to or instead of the IV. This makes the study more valid because it means the experimenter would be more likely to be able to find a cause and effect relationship.

Control condition: a level of the IV in an experiment from which the IV is absent. It is compared to one or more experimental condition(s).

Control group: often used in experiments, this group does not receive the manipulation of the independent variable and can be used for comparison with the experimental group or groups.

Controlled observation: a study conducted by watching the participants' behaviour in a situation in which the social or physical environment has been manipulated by the researchers. It can be conducted in either the participants' normal environment or in an artificial situation.

Coronary heart disease (CHD): Coronary heart disease (CHD) occurs where a waxy substance called plaque builds up inside the coronary arteries. These arteries supply oxygen-rich blood to your heart muscle. Hardened plaque narrows the coronary arteries and reduces the flow of oxygen-rich blood to the heart.

Correlation coefficient: a number between –1 and 1 which shows the strength of a relationship between two variables. A coefficient of –1 means there is a perfect negative correlation and a coefficient of 1 means there is a perfect positive correlation.

Correlation: a research method which looks for a relationship between two measured variables. A change in one variable is related to a change in the other (although these changes cannot be assumed to be causal).

Cost–benefit model: a decision making process in which a person weighs up the advantages and disadvantages of helping. If it seems beneficial to help, then the person is more likely to do so; if the risks are too great, they may not help.

Counterbalancing: a technique used to overcome order effects in a repeated measures design. Each possible order of levels of the IV is performed by a different sub-group of participants. This can be described as an ABBA design, as half the participants do condition A then B, and half do B then A.

Covert observer: where the role of the person collecting data in an observation is not obvious to the participants, e.g. because they are hidden or disguised.

Cross-sectional study: a way to investigate developmental changes by comparing separate groups of participants of different ages.

Crowding: The subjective experience of density.

Daydreaming: a mildly altered state of consciousness in which we experience a sense of being 'lost in our thoughts', typically positive ones, and a detachment from our environment.

Debriefing: an ethical procedure giving participants a full explanation of the aims and potential consequences of the study at the end of a study so that they leave in at least as positive a condition as they arrived.

Deception: an ethical issue as participants should not be deliberately misinformed (lied to) about the aim or procedure of the study. If this is unavoidable, the study should be planned to minimise the risk of distress, and participants should be thoroughly debriefed.

Demand characteristics: features of the experimental situation which give away the aims. They can cause participants to try to change their behaviour, e.g. to fit with their beliefs about what is supposed to happen, which reduces the validity of the study.

Density: the number of people in a given space.

Dependent variable: the factor in an experiment which is measured and is expected to change under the influence of the independent variable.

Destructive obedience: obedience that involves direct or indirect harm towards an individual, through carrying out orders from a figure of authority.

Determinism: the extent to which a psychological phenomenon, such as a feature of our emotions, thinking or behaviour, is governed by processes that are beyond our control. A 'deterministic' view suggests that we have little free will to choose how we feel, think or behave and that we are the product of biological, social or other environmental influences.

Deterministic: see Determinism.

Diagnosis: the process of understanding which mental disorder can best explain an individual's symptoms. Like diagnosing physical problems, it involves looking for particular signs that meet the criteria for known illnesses.

Diagnostic and Statistical Manual (DSM): published by the American Psychiatric Association, it is used as a classification and diagnostic tool by doctors, psychiatrists and psychologists across the globe.

Diffusion of responsibility: the lowered likelihood of a person to take action in an emergency where there are others there also able to help. In a large group, the perceived sense of individual responsibility towards those in need is 'diffused' or reduced to the extent that people feel little obligation to intervene. An explanation for the bystander effect.

Directional (one-tailed) hypothesis: a statement predicting the direction of a relationship between variables, e.g. in an experiment whether the levels of the IV will produce an increase or a decrease in the DV or in a correlation whether an increase in one variable will be linked to an increase or a decrease in another variable.

Divided attention: the ability to split mental effort between two or more simultaneous tasks (called 'dual tasks'), e.g. driving a car and talking to a passenger. Divided attention is easier when the tasks involved are simple, well practised and automatic.

Double blind technique: an experimental procedure such that neither the participant nor the researcher are aware of which condition the participant is in to prevent demand characteristics and act as a control to improve the validity of any data collected.

Duration: length of time, e.g. how long the individual experiences the symptoms or illness.

Ecological validity: the extent to which the findings of research in one situation would generalise to other situations. This is influenced by whether the situation (e.g. a laboratory) represents the real world effectively and whether the task is relevant to real life (has *mundane realism*).

Electroencephalograph (EEG): a machine used to detect and record electrical activity in nerve and muscle cells when many are active at the same time. It uses macroelectrodes, which are large electrodes stuck to the skin or scalp (note they are *recording* electrodes – they cannot give the participant an electric shock!).

Ethical guidelines: pieces of advice that guide psychologists to consider the welfare of participants and wider society.

Euthanasia: intentionally ending the life of an individual. If unavoidable, this should be used as a procedure to reduce enduring suffering in animal studies to ensure they are ethical.

Ethical issues: problems in research that raise concerns about the welfare of participants (or have the potential for a wider negative impact on society).

Evaluative learning: a form of classical conditioning in which attitudes to stimuli are considered to be the product of complex thought processes and emotions which lead an individual to perceive or evaluate a previously neutral stimulus negatively.

Evolution: the process of natural selection of offspring which have inherited characteristics that make them most likely to survive.

Experiment: an investigation looking for a causal relationship in which an independent variable is manipulated and is expected to be responsible for changes in the dependent variable.

Experimental condition: one or more of the situations in an experiment which represent different levels of the IV and are compared (or compared to a control condition).

Experimental design: the way in which participants are allocated to levels of the IV.

Extraneous variable: a variable which either acts randomly, affecting the DV in all levels of the IV or systematically, i.e. on one level of the IV (called a confounding variable) so can obscure the effect of the IV, making the results difficult to interpret.

Eye movement desensitisation and reprocessing (EDMR) exercises: a therapy in which the individual recalls problem behaviour or memories while the therapist directs their eye movement in one of several patterns, using their hands or other stimuli.

Eyes test: a test of the ability to detect other people's emotions used as a measure of 'theory of mind' by Baron-Cohen et al. (1997).

Face validity: a simple measure of validity indicating whether a measure appears to test what it claims to, i.e. whether it does so at 'face value'.

False memory: an implanted piece of information that is recalled by an individual as if it had really happened to them.

Fatigue effect: a situation where participants' performance declines because they have experienced an experimental task more than once, e.g. due to boredom or tiredness.

Field experiment: an investigation looking for a causal relationship in which an independent variable is manipulated and is expected to be responsible for changes in the dependent variable. It is conducted in the normal environment for the participants for the behaviour being investigated.

Filler questions: items put into a questionnaire, interview or test to disguise the aim of the study by hiding the important questions among irrelevant ones so that participants are less likely to alter their behaviour by working out the aims.

Focused attention: the picking out of a particular input from a mass of information, such as an array or a continuous stream, for example, listening to a conversation over the sound of loud music.

Foil: an unknown or unseen object that is used as a control when testing a participant's memory.

Frequency: the number of events per fixed period of time, e.g. the number of eye movements per minute (approximately 60/minute in REM sleep) or the number of brain waves (cycles) per second or Hertz (Hz), e.g. 13–30 Hz for beta waves.

Generalisability: how widely findings apply, e.g. to other settings and populations.

Genes: inherited instructions that are passed on from parents to children that control our development and influence some aspects of our thinking, behaviour and emotions, such as our personality and intelligence. One way this can happen is by affecting brain function.

Good Samaritan: a helper or altruist. The term originates from the New Testament in the Bible. It refers to a story of a Samaritan (person originating from ancient Samaria) who stops to offer help to an injured stranger.

Habituated: when a person becomes accustomed to something, such as when someone is frequently exposed to a certain stimulus.

Heuristics: mental shortcuts that help us make decisions and judgements quickly without having to spend a lot of time researching and analysing information.

Histogram: a graph used to illustrate continuous data, e.g. to show the distribution of a set of scores. It has a bar for each score value, or group of scores, along the x-axis. The y-axis has the frequency of each category.

Holistic: the explanation of a psychological phenomenon, such as features of our emotions, thinking or behaviour, using higher level concepts than just the most basic elements. In addition to neurotransmitters and genes, other factors such as cognition and social influences are considered. It is the opposite of reductionist.

Homeostasis: the control of internal conditions, e.g. temperature, specific blood conditions or other variables within living organisms.

Hormones: chemicals that are released from glands and travel around the body in the blood to communicate messages between organs.

Hypothesis (plural: hypotheses): a testable statement predicting a difference between variables (in an experiment) or a relationship between variables (in a correlation).

Imitative (social) learning: the learning of a new behaviour which is observed in a role model and imitated later in the absence of that model.

In vitro: instances where exposure is imagined, such as through a visualisation exercise. For example as used with phobic stimuli.

In vivo: instances where exposure to a stimulus is direct, such as when an individual is exposed to a phobic stimulus in real life.

Independent measures design: an experimental design in which a different group of participants is used for each level of the IV (condition).

Independent samples t-test: a statistical test comparing two groups of subjects and which requires interval data.

Independent variable: the factor under investigation in an experiment which is manipulated to create two or more conditions (levels) and is expected to be responsible for changes in the dependent variable.

In-depth: detailed, often descriptive e.g. investigation or information, such as that collected in a case study.

Individual–situational debate: the extent to which a person's beliefs or behaviour are controlled by factors, such as their personality or physiology, that are unique to them (individual) or by factors in the setting, such as the people or the place (situational).

Informed consent: an ethical guideline stating that participants should know enough about a study to decide whether they want to agree to participate.

Inhibit: to hinder or prevent. In neuropsychology, inhibition occurs when a chemical or chemical process is reduced or stopped.

Insula: another name given to the area of the brain known as the insular cortex, the tissue surrounding the largest portion of the brain. It has a number of roles including perception, self-awareness and cognition.

Internal validity: how well an experiment controls for confounding variables. If an experiment has internal validity the researcher is confident that it is only the IV that is affecting the DV and no confounding variables are having an impact on the results.

International Classification of Disorders (ICD): a tool for classifying disorders published by the World Health Organization (WHO). It is similar to the DSM, but has a wider scope and covers all health-related conditions, not only mental health and psychological conditions.

Interpersonal skills: 'inter' and 'personal' mean 'between people'; the abilities we have (or don't have) that allow us to communicate effectively with others.

Inter-rater/observer reliability: the extent to which two researchers interpreting qualitative responses in a questionnaire (or interview) will produce the same records from the same raw data.

Interview: a research method that uses verbal questions asked directly, e.g. face-to-face or on the telephone.

IQ: a measure of intelligence that produces a score representing a person's mental age. The average range of IQ is between 85 and 115.

Laboratory experiment: a research method in which there is an IV, a DV and strict controls. It looks for a causal relationship and is conducted in a setting that is not in the usual environment for the participants with regard to the behaviour they are performing.

Longitudinal study: research which follows up the same participants at intervals over time to track their development. (see also cross-sectional study).

Matched pairs design: an experimental design in which participants are arranged into pairs. Each pair is similar in ways that are important to the study and one member of each pair performs in a different level of the IV.

Maturity: level of development, for example the capacity to set high but attainable goals, willingness and ability to take responsibility for the task, and relevant education and/or experience of an individual or a group for the task.

Mean: the measure of central tendency calculated by adding up all the scores and dividing by the number of scores in the data set.

Measure of central tendency: a mathematical way to find the typical or average score from a data set, using the mode, median or mean.

Measure of spread: a mathematical way to describe the variation or dispersion within a data set.

Median: the measure of central tendency that identifies the middle score of a data set which is in rank order (smallest to largest). If there are two numbers in the middle they are added together and divided by two.

Mesial frontal cortex: the mesial frontal cortex plays a role in planning, decision making and complex cognitive behaviours.

Milieu therapy: a type of treatment which involves the use of a therapeutic community. Patients live collectively in a clinic or treatment centre and are encouraged to look after both themselves and each other, to promote social engagement and relationship building.

Mode: the measure of central tendency that identifies the most frequent score(s) in a data set.

Morbidity: the incidence of a disease across a population and/or geographic location during a predefined timeframe.

Mortality: the rate of death in a population.

Multi-dimensional scaling: a statistical technique that can take a range of responses (such as preferences and perceptions) from respondents and present them visually.

Mundane realism: the extent to which a task represents a real-world situation. For example, whether the test used in an experiment is like an actual behaviour that we would do in everyday life.

Muscle relaxation: a technique used in therapies to relieve tension from within the body and mind. It can be induced using medication, visualisation exercises or repetition of calming phrases. Progressive muscle relaxation is achieved through systematically tensing and relaxing the muscles of the body in turn, for example from head to toe.

Natural experiment: an investigation looking for a causal relationship in which the independent variable cannot be directly manipulated by the experimenter. Instead they study the effect of an existing difference or change. Since the researcher cannot manipulate the levels of the IV it is not a true experiment.

Naturalistic observation: a study conducted by watching the participants' behaviour in their normal environment without interference from the researchers in either the social or physical environment.

Nature–nurture debate: the extent to which behaviour, feelings or thinking result from innate, genetic factors (nature) or from environmental influences such as learning and other people (nurture).

Need for cognitive closure (NFCC): (sometimes just referred to as need for closure) a dislike of ambiguity and uncertainty and a preference for definitive answers to questions.

Negative correlation: a relationship between two variables in which an increase in one accompanies a decrease in the other, i.e. higher scores on one variable correspond with lower scores on the other.

Nervous system: the brain, spinal cord and all the nerve cells in the body that communicate to control our thinking, behaviour and emotions.

Neuroendocrine mechanisms: the system by which the hypothalamus maintains homeostasis, regulating reproduction, metabolism, eating and drinking behaviour, energy utilisation and blood pressure.

Neuron: a nerve cell.

Neurotransmitter: a chemical that sends messages between nerve cells (neurons).

Nociception: the encoding and processing of harmful stimuli in the nervous system, and, therefore, the ability of a body to sense potential harm.

Non-adherence to medication: this occurs when a patient goes against a physician's instructions for drug dosage, for instance by stopping taking their medication.

Non-clinical population: a term used in the study of health which refers to a group who are not specifically targeted in contrast to a clinical population which is a group of particular interest, such as those with a medical or mental health disorder.

Non-directional (two-tailed) hypothesis: a statement predicting only that one variable will be related to another, e.g. that there will be a difference in the DV between levels of the IV in an experiment or that there will be a relationship between the measured variables in a correlation.

Non-participant observer: a researcher who does not become involved in the situation being studied, e.g. by watching through one way glass or by keeping apart from the social group of the participants.

Non-rapid eye movement sleep (nREM): the stages of sleep (1 to 4) in which our eyes are still. It is also called quiescent (quiet) sleep. This is not associated with dreaming.

Normal distribution: an even spread of a variable that is symmetrical about the mean, median and mode. The graph showing this distribution is sometimes called a 'bell curve' because of its shape. The graph of the frequency of each score or value rises gradually and symmetrically to a maximum at the point of the mean, median and mode.

Noxious: harmful, poisonous, or very unpleasant.

Nucleus accumbens: (NAc or NAccis) a region in the basal forebrain thought to play an important role in reward, pleasure and addiction.

Null hypothesis: a testable statement saying that any difference or correlation in the results is due to chance, i.e. that no pattern in the results has arisen because of the variables being studied.

Obedience: following a direct order from a person or people in authority.

Objectivity: an unbiased external viewpoint that is not affected by an individual's feelings, beliefs or experiences, so should be consistent between different researchers.

Observation: a research method used when watching human or animal participants directly, to gather data about their behaviour.

Open questions: questionnaire, interview or test items that produce qualitative data. Participants give full and detailed answers in their own words, i.e. no categories or choices are given.

Operationalisation: the definition of variables so that they can be accurately manipulated, measured or quantified and replicated. This includes the IV and DV in experiments and the two measured variables in correlations and observational categories.

Opiates: a group of powerful drugs which have historically been used as painkillers. Many opiates are considered high risk for drug abuse (heroin is one type of opiate).

Opportunity sampling: a technique for obtaining participants which chooses participants because they are available, e.g. university students are selected because they are present at the university where the research is taking place.

Order effects: practice and fatigue effects are the consequences of participating in a study more than once, e.g. in a repeated measures design. They cause changes in performance between conditions that are not due to the IV, so can obscure the effect on the DV.

Overt observer: the role of the observer is obvious to the participants.

Panic disorder: a recognised mental health disorder characterised by spontaneous and unexpected panic attacks. The attacks may range in frequency from several per day to only a few per year.

Participant observer: a researcher who watches the participants from the perspective of being part of the social setting.

Participant variables: individual differences between participants (such as age, personality and intelligence) that could affect their behaviour in a study. For example, they could hide or exaggerate differences between levels of the IV.

Persecutory ideation: the process of forming an idea that one is at risk of being ill-treated or harmed by others.

Phobia: the irrational, persistent fear of an object or event which poses little real danger but creates anxiety and avoidance in the sufferer.

Physical harm: see Protection of participants.

Physiological: to do with the biological processes in the body, e.g. hormones.

Pilot study: a small-scale trial run of the design of a study to identify and resolve any problems with the procedure.

Placebo: a substance administered to people that has no actual effect. In experiments a placebo condition may be used as a control. For research into the therapeutic use of drugs, a placebo is a therapeutically ineffective treatment for a physical illness or other mental health disorder. It is given to deceive the patient so that they believe it should improve or relieve their condition. Use of placebo trials is crucial in testing the effectiveness of medication.

Planogram: a diagram that shows how and where specific retail products should be placed on retail shelves or displays in order to increase customer purchases. *Planogramming* is a skill used in merchandising and retail space planning.

Polymorphism: a variation in a gene or genes. Whereas mutation means a a unique change, polymorphism refers to the different expressions that may be present in a normal population, even if that expression occurs infrequently.

Population: the group, sharing one or more characteristics, from which a sample is drawn.

Positive correlation: a relationship between two variables in which an increase in one accompanies an increase in the other, i.e. the two variables increase together.

Positive reinforcement: a consequence in operant conditioning. A reward which follows a behaviour and encourages it to be repeated. For example, chocolate tastes nice and this consequence positively reinforces the tendency to eat more of it.

Positron emission tomography (PET) scanning: a technique which uses gamma cameras to detect the breakdown of radioactive tracers such as glucose which have been injected into the blood. The tracer builds up in areas of high activity during the scan, allowing it to become visible for analysis.

Practice effect: a situation where participants' performance improves because they experience the experimental task more than once, e.g. due to familiarity or learning the task.

Presumptive consent: gaining agreement to participate, in principle, from a group of people similar to the intended participants. They are asked if they would object to the procedure. It is used when gaining informed consent from the participants themselves would lead to their working out the aim of the study.

Privacy: an ethical guideline relating to avoiding the invasion of participants' emotions and physical space. For example, participants should not be observed in situations or places where they would not expect to be seen.

Projective test: a personality test that uses ambiguous stimuli such an ink blots or Thematic Apperception Test images. The response given to the stimuli is thought to reveal hidden emotions and conflicts which the individual projects onto the image.

Protection of participants: participants should not be exposed to any greater physical or psychological risk than they would expect in their day-to-day life.

Psychiatrist: a doctor with specialised medical training to deal with the diagnosis and treatment of disorders. (Most psychologists are not doctors.)

Psychological harm: see Protection of participants.

Qualitative data: descriptive, in-depth results indicating the *quality* of a psychological characteristic, such as responses to open questions in self-reports or case studies and detailed observations.

Quantitative data: numerical results about the *quantity* of a psychological measure such as pulse rate or a score on an intelligence test.

Quasi-experiment: quasi means 'almost', and refers to the fact that these experiments often have lots of control over the procedure, but not over how participants are allocated to conditions within the study.

Questionnaire: a research method that uses written questions.

Random allocation: a way to reduce the effect of confounding variables such as individual differences. Participants are put in each level of the IV such that each has an equal chance of being in any condition.

Random sampling: a technique for obtaining participants such that all members of the population (i.e. possible participants) are allocated numbers and a fixed amount of these are selected in a unbiased way, e.g. by taking numbers from a hat.

Range: A measure of spread found by working out the difference between the biggest and smallest values in the data set plus one.

Rapid eye movement sleep (REM): a stage of sleep in which our eyes move rapidly under the lids, which is associated with vivid, visual dreams.

Rational: based on or in accordance with reason or logic.

Reconstructive memory: a theory of memory recall which suggests that the act of remembering is influenced by various other factors such as cultural beliefs, expectations and stereotyping.

Reinforcers: something that encourages the replication of a desired behaviour. This could be external (money), internal (a positive feeling) or vicarious (by observing other people).

Reductionism: the extent to which a psychological phenomenon, such as a feature of our emotions, thinking or behaviour, can be explained by a theory or concept in terms of its most basic elements. These basic elements are usually biological factors such as the actions of neurotransmitters or genes. In a wider sense it can be used to refer to considering only some of many elements that are important in explaining a phenomenon, such as looking only at cognitive factors (to do with the way we think) and excluding biological or social ones. It is the opposite of holism.

Reliability: the extent to which a procedure, task or measure is consistent, for example that it would produce the same results with the same people on each occasion.

Repeated measures design: an experimental design in which each participant performs in every level of the IV.

Replicable: capable of being done again, e.g. a study which can be repeated using the same procedure.

Representative: situations or findings which are typical of another setting or group of people, such as when an experimental setting is like the real world or the results from a large sample of participants would generalise to the wider population.

Researcher bias: an unconscious tendency of the researcher to act in ways that alter the results, often in the expected direction.

Response bias: the tendency of a participant to prefer one choice or another in the way that they react in a study. For example, the way they reply on a questionnaire or their reaction on a measure of the DV in an experiment: they may tend towards one end of a scale in a questionnaire or to always press the left hand button in a task.

Retroactive interference: where new information interferes with the memory of old information. For example, learning your new phone number interferes with the memory of the previous one.

Right to withdraw: an ethical guideline relating to ensuring that participants know that they can remove themselves, and their data, from the study at any time.

Sample: the group of people selected to represent the population in a study.

Sampling technique: the method used to obtain the participants for a study from the population.

Scatter graph: a way to display data from a correlational study. Each point on the graph represents the point where one participant's score on each scale for the two measured variables cross.

Schemas: units of knowledge about the world, which help us to categorise new experiences and details. Our individual systems of schema underlie virtually all cognition, such as reasoning, memory and perception.

Self-control: a form of cognitive behavioural therapy. It involves using 'self-talk'; the individual is taught to recognise difficult situations, acknowledge troubling thoughts and consider alternative, positive thoughts.

Self-selecting sampling: see volunteer sampling.

Self-report: a research method, such as a questionnaire or interview, which obtains data by asking participants to provide information about themselves.

Semi-structured interview: an interview with a fixed list of open and closed questions. The interviewer can add more questions if necessary.

Severity: the intensity with which the individual experiences the symptoms or illness.

Sex-typed behaviour: actions that are typically performed by one particular gender and are seen in society as more appropriate for that gender. For example, aggression is seen as a masculine-type behaviour.

Sexually dimorphic: differences between males and females of any species which are not just differences in organs or genitalia. These differences are caused by inheriting either male or female patterns of genetic material.

Situational variable: a confounding variable caused by an aspect of the environment, e.g. the amount of light or noise.

Social cognition: the study of how people process social information and how this processing might affect how a person behaves towards or around other people.

Socially desirable: responding to a question in a way that you feel is expected by the researcher or socially accepted.

Social desirability bias: trying to present oneself in the best light by determining what a test is asking.

Social learning: see imitative learning.

Space syntax: a science-based, human-focused approach that investigates relationships between spatial layout and a range of social, economic and environmental phenomena.

Standard deviation: a measure of spread which calculates the average difference between each score in the data set and the mean. Bigger values indicate greater variation (a measure of spread).

Standardisation: keeping the procedure for each participant in an experiment (or interview) exactly the same to ensure that any differences between participants or conditions are due to the variables under investigation rather than differences in the way they were treated.

Standardised procedure: see standardisation.

Statistical analysis: involves the use of statistical tests which measure the likelihood of differences or relationships in data being due to chance.

Stooge: a person who appears to be another participant or someone not related to the study, but who is in fact working on behalf of the researcher. They are also sometimes known as 'confederates' and may be used to mislead real participants within the study.

Structured interview: an interview with questions in a fixed order which may be scripted. Consistency might also be required for the interviewer's posture, voice, etc. so they are standardised.

Structured observation: a study in which the observer records only a limited range of behaviours.

Subjectivity: a personal viewpoint, which may be biased by one's feelings, beliefs or experiences, so may differ between individual researchers. Unlike objectivity it is dependent on the situation.

Sympathetic arousal: the activation of the sympathetic nervous system which causes the pupils to dilate, the heart rate to increase, digestive activity to slow down and glucose to be released by the liver for extra energy. It is a response to alarm, stress or excitement.

Sympathetic division of the autonomic nervous system: the autonomic nervous system is an automatic control of the body's internal environment and has a role in our emotional experience to external situations. The sympathetic division responds to emergencies such as stress or injury and controls the 'fight or flight' response.

Synergistic: leading to the interaction of more than one condition which creates a combined effect greater than the sum of either of their effects separately.

Target population: the group from which a sample is drawn. See also population.

Test–retest: a way to measure the consistency of a test or task. The test is used twice and if the participants' two sets of scores are similar, i.e. correlate well, it has good reliability.

Two-factor theory: an explanation of emotion that says it depends on both physiological and cognitive factors (tested by Schachter and Singer, 1962).

Twin study: a type of investigation which compares sets of twins to analyse similarities and differences. This may include concordance for intelligence or mental disorders. Both monozygotic (MZ) and dizygotic (DZ) twins are studied, as well as twins who have been raised together or separately (i.e. adoption studies).

Uncontrolled variable: a confounding variable that may not have been identified and eliminated in an experiment, which can confuse the results. It may be a feature of the participants or the situation.

Unstructured interview: an interview in which most questions (after the first one) depend on the respondent's answers. A list of topics may be given to the interviewer.

Unstructured observation: a study in which the observer records the whole range of possible behaviours, which is usually confined to a pilot stage at the beginning of a study to refine the behavioural categories to be observed.

Valence: when discussing emotions this refers to the attractiveness (positive valence) or aversiveness (negative valence) of an event, object or situation.

Validity: the extent to which the researcher is testing what they claim to be testing.

Volunteer (self-selected) sampling: a technique for obtaining participants by inviting them to participate, e.g. through advertisements via email or notices. Those who reply become the sample.

White collar workers: refers to individuals who work in professional occupations, as compared to 'blue collar' workers which refers to those who perform manual work.

Working memory model: A model of memory which suggests that two different types of current or 'working' memory can be used at the same time, one is visuo-spatial and the other auditory. These are governed by an overall 'central executive'.

References

Abramowitz, J. S., Deacon, B. J., Olatunji, B. O., Wheaton, M. G., Berman, N. C., Losardo, D., and Hale, L. R. (2010). Assessment of obsessive-compulsive symptom dimensions: Development and evaluation of the Dimensional Obsessive-Compulsive Scale. *Psychological Assessment*, *22*(1), 180.

Adams, J. S. (1965). Inequity in social exchange. In L. Berkowitz (Ed.), *Advances in experimental social psychology* (pages 267–299). New York: Academic Press.

Agras, W. S. (1967). Transfer during systematic desensitization therapy. *Behaviour Research and Therapy*, *5*(3), 193–199.

Ajzen, I. (1991). The theory of planned behavior. *Organizational Behavior and Human Decision Processes 50* (2): 179–211.

Alderfer, C. P., (1972) *Existence, Relatedness, and Growth; Human Needs in Organizational Settings*, New York: Free Press.

Aleem, A., and Ajarim, D. S. (1995), 'Munchausen Syndrome – Presenting as Immunodeficiency: A Case Report and Review of Literature', in *Annals of Saudi Medicine*, vol. 15, no. 4, [online], pages 404–406.

Allen, N., and Meyer, J. P. (1990). Organizational Socialization Tactics: A Longitudinal Analysis of Links to Newcomers' Commitment and Role Orientation. *Academy of Management Journal* December 1, 1990 33:4847–858.

Allport, G. (1954) *The nature of prejudice*. Addison-Wesley.

Andrade, J. (2010). What does doodling do? *Applied Cognitive Psychology*, *24*(1), 100–106.

Atalay, A. S., Bodur, H. O., and Rasolofoarison, D. (2012). Shining in the center: Central gaze cascade effect on product choice. *Journal of Consumer Research*, *39*(4), 848–866.

Areni, C. S., and Kim, D. (1993). The influence of background music on shopping behaviour: Classical versus top-forty music in a wine store. *Advances in Consumer Research*, *20*, 336– 340.

Arnold, A. with Silvester, J., Patterson, F., Robertson, I., Cooper, C. and Burnes, B., (2005). *Work Psychology: Understanding behaviour in the real world*. Harlow: Pearson Educational.

Aserinsky, E., and Kleitman, N. (1955). Two types of ocular motility occurring in sleep. *Journal of Applied Physiology*, *8*, 1–10.

Atreja, A., Bellam, N., and Levy, S. R. (2005). Strategies to enhance patient adherence: making it simple. *Medscape General Medicine, 7*(1), 4. Chicago.

Auty, S. G., and Lewis, C. (2004). Exploring children's choice: the reminder effect of product placement. *Psychology and Marketing*, *21*(9), 697–713.

Bandura, A. (1977). *Social learning theory*. Englewood Cliffs, NJ: Prentice Hall.

Bandura, A., Ross, D., and Ross, S. A. (1961). Transmission of aggression through imitation of aggressive models. *Journal of Abnormal and Social Psychology*, *63*(3), 575–582.

Barlow, D., and Durand, V. (2011), *Abnormal psychology: An integrative approach*. Belmont, CA: Wadsworth Publishing.

Baron-Cohen, S., Jollife, T., Mortimore, C., and Robertson, M. (1997). Another advanced test of theory of mind: Evidence from very high functioning adults with autism or Asperger syndrome. *Journal of Child Psychology and Psychiatry*, *38*, 813–822.

Baron-Cohen, S., Wheelwright, J., Hill, J., Raste, Y., and Plumb, I. (2001). The 'Reading the Mind in the Eyes' Test revised version: A study with normal adults, and adults with Asperger Syndrome or High-functioning Autism. *Journal of Child Psychology and Psychiatry*, *42*(2), 241–251.

Bateson, P. (1986). When to experiment on animals. *New Scientist*, *1496*, 30–32.

Beck, A. T. (Ed.). (1979). *Cognitive therapy of depression*. New York: Guilford Press.

Becker, M. H. (1974), 'The Health Belief Model and sick role behavior', in Becker, M. H. (Ed.), *The Health Belief Model and Personal Health Behaviour,* Thorofare, New Jersey: Charles S. Black, Inc., pages 82–92.

Belbin, M. (1981). *Management Teams*. London: Heinemann.

Belfield, R. and Marsden, D. (2003), Performance pay, monitoring environments, and establishment performance, *International Journal of Manpower*, *24*, 4: 452-471

Bernstein, D.M., Laney, C., Morris, E.K., and Loftus, E.F. (2005). False memories about food can lead to food avoidance. *Social Cognition, 23*(1), 11–34.

Betancur, C. (2014). *El vendedor Halcón: sus estrategias. El poder de la venta consultiva para ganar más clientes satisfechos*. Medellín: Colombia.

Bjorkqvist, K., Osterman, K. and Hjelt-Back, M. (1994a), Aggression among university employees. *Aggressive Behavior*, *20*, pages 173–84.

Black, D. W., and Grant, J. E. (2014). *DSM-5® Guidebook: The Essential Companion to the Diagnostic and Statistical Manual of Mental Disorders*. Washington: American Psychiatric Publications.

Blau, G. J., and Boal, K. B. (1987). Conceptualizing how job involvement and organizational commitment affect turnover and absenteeism. *Academy of Management Review*, 288–300.

Blaszczynski, A., and Nower, L. (2003). Imaginal desensitisation: A relaxation-based technique for impulse control disorders. *Journal of Clinical Activities, Assignments and Handouts in Psychotherapy Practice, 2*(4), 1–14.

Bloom, M. (1999), The performance effects of pay dispersion on individuals and organizations, *Academy of Management Journal, 42*, 1: 25-40

Boush, D. M. (1993), How advertising slogans can prime evaluations of brand extensions. *Psychology and Marketing 10:* 67–78. doi: 10.1002/mar.4220100106

Boyd-Jansson, C. (2010). *Consumer Psychology.* Maidenhead: Open University Press.

Braun, K.A., Ellis, R., and Loftus, E.F. (2002). Make my memory: How advertising can change our memories of the past. *Psychology and Marketing, 19*(1), 1–23.

Braun-LaTour, K. A., LaTour, M. S., Pickrell, J. E., and Loftus, E. F., (2004). How and when advertising can influence memory for consumer experience. *Journal of Advertising, 33*(4), 7–25.

Bridge, L. R., Benson, P., Pietroni, P. C., and Priest, R. G. (1988), 'Relaxation and imagery in the treatment of breast cancer', in *BMJ*, vol. 297, [online], pages 1169–1172.

British Psychological Society (2009) *Code of Ethics and Conduct.* BPS.

British Psychological Society (2012) *Guidance for psychologists working with animals.* BPS.

Budzynski, T. H., and Stoyva, J. M. (1969), An Instrument for Producing Deep Muscle Relaxation by Means of Analog Information Feedback, *Journal of Applied Behavior Analysis, 2*, no. 4, [online], pages 231–237.

Bulpitt, C. J. (1994), 'Risks and benefits of drug treatment of hypertension in the elderly', in *Journal of the Royal Society of Medicine, 87*, suppl. 23, pages 16–18.

Burton, P. R., McNiel, D. E., and Binder, R. L. (2012). Firesetting, arson, pyromania, and the forensic mental health expert. *Journal of the American Academy of Psychiatry and the Law Online, 40*(3), 355–365.

Byrne, P. S., and Long, B. E. (1976), *Doctors talking to patients. A study of the verbal behaviour of general practitioners consulting in their surgeries.* London: HMSO.

Canli T., Zhao Z., Desmond J.E., Glover G., Gabrieli J.D.E. (1999). fMRI identifies a network of structures correlated with retention of positive and negative emotional memory. *Psychobiology 27:* 441– 452.

Canli, T., Zhao, Z., Brewer, J., Gabrieli, J. D. E., and Cahill, L. (2000). Event-related activation in the human amygdala associates with later memory for individual emotional experience. *Journal of Neuroscience, 20*, 1–5.

Cave, S. (1998) *Applying Psychology to the Environment.* London: Hodder and Stoughton.

Chandola, T., Britton, A., Brunner, E., Hemingway, H., Malik, M., Kumari, M., Bradrick, E., Kivimaki, M., and Marmot, M. (2008), Work stress and coronary heart disease: what are the mechanisms? *European Heart Journal, 29*, no. 5, [online], pages 640–648.

Chebat, J. C., and Michon, R. (2003). Impact of ambient odors on mall shoppers' emotions, cognition, and spending: A test of competitive causal theories. *Journal of Business Research, 56*(7), 529–539.

Chung, K. F., and Naya, I. (2000), Compliance with an oral asthma medication: a pilot study using an electronic monitoring device *Respiratory medicine, 94*, no. 9, [online], pages 852–858.

Comings, D. E., and Blum, K. (2000). Reward deficiency syndrome: genetic aspects of behavioral disorders. *Progress in brain research, 126*, 325-341.

Cowpe, C. (1989) Chip pan fire prevention 1976–1988, in C. Channer (ed.) *Television Advertising Case Histories*, 2nd edn, London: Cassell).

Dansereau, F., Graen, G. and Haga, W. J. (1975). A vertical dyad linkage approach to leadership. within formal organizations, *Organizational Behavior and Human Performance, 13*, 46–78.

Dansereau, F., Yammarino, F. J., Markham, S. E., Alutto, J. A., Newman, J., Dumas, M., and Keller, T. (1995). Individualized leadership: A new multiple-level approach. *The Leadership Quarterly, 6*(3), 413–450.

Darley, J. M., and Latané, B. (1968). Bystander intervention in emergencies: diffusion of responsibility. *Journal of Personality and Social Psychology, 8*(4), 377–383.

Davis, Barbara Price and Eric S. Knowles (1999), A Disrupt then-Reframe Technique of Social Influence, *Journal of Personality and Social Psychology, 76* (2), 192–99.

Dayan, E., and Bar-Hillel, M. (2011). Nudge to nobesity II: Menu positions influence food orders. *Judgment and Decision Making, 6*(4), 333–342.

De Jong, P. J., Andrea, H., and Muris, P. (1997). Spider phobia in children: Disgust and fear before and after treatment. *Behaviour Research and Therapy, 35*, 559–562.

de Waal and Jansen (2011) The bonus as hygiene factor: the role of reward systems in the high performance organization *Presented during the 3rd European Reward Management*

Conference 2011, 1-2 December 2011 http://www.hpocenter.nl/wp-content/uploads/2013/07/The-bonus-as-hygiene-factor-the-role-of-reward-systems-in-the-high-performance-organization.pdf

Dement, W., and Kleitman, N. (1957). The relation of eye movements during sleep to dream activity: an objective method for the study of dreaming. *Journal of Experimental Psychology, 53,* 339–346.

Di Nardo, P. A., Guzy, L. T., and Bak, R. M. (1988). Anxiety response patterns and etiological factors in dog-fearful and non-fearful subjects. *Behaviour Research and Therapy, 26*(3), 245–251.

Dierckx, B., Heijnen, W. T., van den Broek, W. W., and Birkenhäger, T. K. (2012). Efficacy of electroconvulsive therapy in bipolar versus unipolar major depression: A meta-analysis. *Bipolar Disorders, 14*(2), 146–150.

Do, S. L., and Schallert, D. L. (2004). Emotions and classroom talk: Toward a model of the role of affect in students' experiences of classroom discussions. *Journal of Educational Psychology, 96,* 619–634.

Driscoll, J. W., and Bateson, P. (1988). Animals in behavioural research. *Animal Behaviour, 3,* 1569–1574.

Duffhues, P. and Kabir, R. (2008), Is the pay–performance relationship always positive?: Evidence from the Netherlands, *Journal of Multinational Financial Management, 18,* 1: 45-60.

Einarsen, S. (1999). The nature and causes of bullying at work. *International journal of manpower, 20*(1/2), 16–27.

Ekman, P. (1992). An argument for basic emotions, *Cognition and Emotion, 6*(3/4), 169–200.

Ellis, A. (1962). *Reason and emotion in psychotherapy.* Lyle Stuart.

Engel, J., Blackwell, D. and Kollat, R. (1968) *Consumer Behaviour.* New York: Holt, Rinehart, and Winston.

Erdogan, B., Bauer, T. N., and Walter, J. (2015). Deeds that Help and Words that Hurt: Helping and Gossip as Moderators of the Relationship Between Leader–Member Exchange and Advice Network Centrality. *Personnel Psychology, 68*(1), 185-214.

Esfahani, S., Motaghipour, Y., Kamkari, K., Zahiredin, A., and Janbozorgi, M. (2012). Reliability and Validity of the Persian Version of the Yale-Brown Obsessive-Compulsive Scale (Y-BOCS). (English). *Iranian Journal Of Psychiatry and Clinical Psychology, 17*(4), 297-303.

Evans, G. W., and Wener, R. E. (2007), Crowding and personal space invasion on the train: Please don't make me sit in the middle, *Journal of Environmental Psychology, 27,* no. 1, [online], pages 90–94.

Fattorusso, J., Skovoroda, R., Buck, T. and Bruce, A. (2007), UK executive bonuses and transparency - A research note, *British Journal of Industrial Relations, 45*: 518–536.

Farquhar, J. W., Fortmann, S. P., Maccoby, N., Haskell, W. L., Williams, P. T., Flora, J. A., Taylor, C. B., Brown, B. W. Jr., Solomon, D. S., and Hulley, S. B. (1985), The Stanford Five-City Project: design and methods, in American Journal of Epidemiology, vol. 122, no. 2, [online], pages 323–334.

Felipe, N.J. and Somner, R. (1966) Invasions of personal space. *Social Problems, 14*(2), 206–214.

Fennis, Bob M., Enny H. H. J. Das, and Ad Th. H. Pruyn (2004), 'If You Can't Dazzle Them with Brilliance, Baffle Them with Nonsense': Extending the Impact of the Disrupt-Then-Reframe technique of Social Influence, *Journal of Consumer Psychology, 14*(3), 280–90.

Fiedler, F. E. (1967) *A Theory of Leadership Effectiveness,* New York: McGraw-Hill.

Finlay, K., Kanetkar, V., Londerville, J., and Marmurek, H. H. (2006). The physical and psychological measurement of gambling environments. *Environment and Behavior, 38*(4), 570–581.

Fischer, P. M., Schwartz, M. P., Richards, J. W., Goldstein, A. O., and Rojas, T. H. (1991). Brand logo recognition by children aged 3 to 6 years: Mickey Mouse and Old Joe the Camel. *JAMA, 266*(22), 3145–3148.

Forsyth, D. R. (2006). Decision making. In Forsyth, D. R., *Group Dynamics* (5th Ed.) (page 317–349) Belmont: CA, Wadsworth, Cengage Learning.

Fournier, J. C., DeRubeis, R. J., Hollon, S. D., Dimidjian, S., Amsterdam, J. D., Shelton, R. C., and Fawcett, J. (2010). Antidepressant drug effects and depression severity: a patient-level meta-analysis. *JAMA, 303*(1), 47–53.

Fox, D. K., Hopkins, B. L., and Anger, W. K. (1987), 'The Long-term Effects of a Token Economy in Safety Performance in Open Pit Mining', *Journal of Applied Behavior Analysis, 20,* no. 3, [online], pages 215–224.

Freeman, D. (2008). Studying and treating schizophrenia using virtual reality: A new paradigm. *Schizophrenia Bulletin, 34*(4), 605–610.

Freud, S. (1909). Analysis of a phobia in a five-year-old boy. *The Standard Edition of the Complete Psychological Works of Sigmund Freud, 10(3).* Hogarth Press.

Friedman, B. (2000). *Designing casinos to dominate the competition.* Reno, NV: Institute for the Study of Gambling and Commercial Gaming.

Friedman, M., and Rosenman, R. H. (1974), *Type A Behavior and Your Heart.* New York: Alfred A Knopf / Random House.

Frith, C. D. (1992). *The cognitive neuropsychology of schizophrenia.* Psychology Press.

Garra, G., Singer, A. J., Taira, B. R., Chohan, J., Cardoz, H., Chisena, E., and Thode, H. C. (2010). Validation of the Wong-Baker FACES pain rating scale in pediatric emergency department patients. *Academic Emergency Medicine*, *17*(1), 50–54.

Giacalone, R. A., and Rosenfeld, P. (1987). Reasons for employee sabotage in the workplace. *Journal of Business and Psychology*, *1*(4), 367–378.

Gil, J., Tobari, E., Lemlij, M., Rose, A., and Penn, A. R. (2009). The differentiating behaviour of shoppers: clustering of individual movement traces in a supermarket. In: Koch, D. and Marcus, L. and Steen, J., (eds.) *Proceedings of the 7th International Space Syntax Symposium.* Royal Institute of Technology (KTH): Stockholm, Sweden.

Glover, J. H. (2011). A case of kleptomania treated by covert sensitization. *British Journal of Clinical Psychology*, *24*(3), 213–214.

Goffin, R. D., and Gellatly, I. R. (2001). A Multi rater assessment of organizational commitment: Are self-report measures biased? *Journal of Organizational Behavior, 22*, 437-451.

Gold, D. R., Rogacz, S., Bock, N., Tosteson, T. D., Baum, T. M., Speizer, F. E., and Czeisler, C. A. (1992). Rotating shift work, sleep, and accidents related to sleepiness in hospital nurses. *American Journal of Public Health*, *82*(7), 1011–1014.

Goodman, W. K., Price, L. H., Rasmussen, S. A., Mazure, C., Fleischmann, R. L., Hill, C. L., and Charney, D. S. (1989). The Yale-Brown obsessive compulsive scale: I. Development, use, and reliability. *Archives of General Psychiatry*, *46*(11), 1006–1011.

Gottesman, I. I., and Shields, J. (1972). *Schizophrenia and genetics: A twin study vantage point.* Academic Press.

Grant, J. E., Kim, S. W., Hollander, E., and Potenza, M. N. (2008). Predicting response to opiate antagonists and placebo in the treatment of pathological gambling. *Psychopharmacology*, *200*(4), 521–527.

Greenwood, R., Bolton, A., Greenwood, R. (1983) Hawthorne a half century later: relay assembly participants remember. *Journal of Management 9*:217–31.

Griffiths, M. (2005). A 'components' model of addiction within a biopsychosocial framework. *Journal of Substance Use*, *10*(4), 191–197.

Grossman, R., and Wisenblit, J. Z. (1999). What we know about consumers' color choices. *Journal of marketing practice: Applied marketing science, 5*(3), 78-88.

Gueguen, N., Jacob, C., Lourel, M., and Le Guellec, H. (2007). Effect of Background Music on Consumer's Behavior: A Field Experiment in a Open-Air Market. *European Journal of Scientific Research*, *16*(2), 268–272.

Hackman, J. R., and Oldham, G. R. (1976). Motivation through the design of work: Test of a theory. *Organizational behavior and human performance*, *16*(2), 250–279.

Hall, L., Johansson, P., Tärning, B., Sikström, S., and Deutgen, T. (2010). Magic at the marketplace: Choice blindness for the taste of jam and the smell of tea. *Cognition*, *117*(1), 54–61.

Hansen, F., Smith, M. and Hansen, R. (2002) Reward and recognition in employee motivation. *Compensation and Benefits Review*, October Issue, pages 64-71

Hayward, S., (1996) *Applying Psychology to Organisations.* London: Hodder and Stoughton.

Heifetz, R.A., Grashow, A., Linsky, M (2009) *The Practice of Adaptive Leadership.* Boston: Harvard Business Press.

Heifetz, R.A. and Linsky. M. (2002) *Leadership on the Line.* Boston: Harvard Business School Press.

Heifetz, R.A and Laurie, D.L., (1997) *The Work of Leadership.* Harvard Business Review.

Hepburn, T., and Page, A. C. (1999). Effects of images about fear and disgust upon responses to blood-injury phobic stimuli. *Behavior Therapy*, *30*(1), 63–77.

Hersey, P. and Blanchard, K.H. (1988). *Management of Organizational Behavior* (5th ed.), pages 169–201. Englewood Cliffs, NJ: Prentice Hall.

Herzberg, Frederick; Mausner, Bernard; Snyderman, Barbara B. (1959). *The Motivation to Work* (2nd ed.). New York: John Wiley.

Heskett, J., W. E. Sasser Jr., and L. Schlesinger. (1997) *The Service Profit Chain: How Leading Companies Link Profit and Growth to Loyalty, Satisfaction, and Value.* New York: Free Press.

Hodgson, R. J., and Rachman, S. (1977). Obsessional-compulsive complaints. *Behaviour Research and Therapy*, *15*(5), 389–395.

Hofmann, S. G., Asnaani, A., and Hinton, D. E. (2010). Cultural aspects in social anxiety and social anxiety disorder. *Depression and Anxiety*, *27*(12), 1117–1127.

Hollowell, B. (2005), An empirical examination of executive compensation, *Bank Accounting and Finance, 18*, 1: 45–47

Holmes, T. H., and Rahe, R. H. (1967), 'The social readjustment rating scale', *Journal of Psychosomatic Research*, vol. 11, no. 2, [online], pages 213–218.

Howard, Daniel J. (1992). Gift-Wrapping Effects on Product Attitudes: A Mood-Biasing Explanation. *Journal of Consumer Psychology 1* (3), 197–223.

345

Iftene, F., Predescu, E., Stefan, S., and David, D. (2015). Rational-emotive and cognitive-behavior therapy (REBT/CBT) versus pharmacotherapy versus REBT/CBT plus pharmacotherapy in the treatment of major depressive disorder in youth; a randomized clinical trial. *Psychiatry Research*, *225*(3), 687–694.

Janis, I. L. (1971). Groupthink. *Psychology Today*, *5*(6), 43–46.

Janis, I. L., and Feshbach, S. (1953), 'Effects of fear-arousing communications', *The Journal of Abnormal and Social Psychology*, vol. 48, no. 1, [online], pages 78–92.

Jelovac, A., Kolshus, E., and McLoughlin, D. M. (2013). Relapse following successful electroconvulsive therapy for major depression: a meta-analysis. *Neuropsychopharmacology*, *38*(12), 2467–2474.

Kahn R. In search of the Hawthorne effect. In: Cass E.L., Zimmer F.G, editors. *Man and work in society*. New York(NY): Van Nostrand Reinhold, 1975:49–63.

Khan, R.J., McNair, D.M., Limpan, R.S., Covi, L., (1986) Imipramine and chlordiazepoxide in depressive and anxiety disorders. *American Journal of Psychiatry*, 43:79–85.

Kahneman, D. (2011). *Thinking, fast and slow*. New York: Farrar, Straus and Giroux.

Kahneman, D., Tversky, A. (1979). Prospect Theory: An Analysis of Decision under Risk *Econometrica 47* (2): 263. doi:10.2307/1914185. ISSN 0012-9682.

Kardes, F. R., Fennis, B. M., Hirt, E. R., Tormala, Z. L., and Bullington, B. (2007). The Role of the Need for Cognitive Closure in the Effectiveness of the Disrupt-Then-Reframe Influence Technique. *Journal of Consumer Research*, *34*(3), 377–385.

Katz, P (1937) *Animals and Men*. New York: Longman.

Kelley, R. E. (1988) In praise of followers. *Harvard Business Review*, 66, 142–148.

Kimble, G. A. (1961). *Hilgard and Marquis' Conditioning and Learning*. Appleton-Century-Crofts.

Kimura, H. K., Kennedy, T. D., and Rhodes, L. E. (1972). Recurring assessment of changes in phobic behavior during the course of systematic desensitization. *Behaviour Research and Therapy*, *10*(3), 279–282.

Knutson, B., Rick, S., Wimmer, G. E., Prelec, D., and Loewenstein, G. (2007). Neural predictors of purchases. *Neuron*, *53*(1), 147–156.

Knutsson, A. (2003). Health disorders of shift workers. *Occupational Medicine*, *53*(2), 103–108.

Kohli, C., Leuthesser, L., and Suri, R. (2007). Got slogan? Guidelines for creating effective slogans. *Business Horizons*, *50*(5), 415–422.

Kouzes, J.M. and Posner, B.Z. (1987) Leadership practices inventory: LPI. Available from http://www.leadershipchallenge.com/UserFiles/English_LPI4eSampleReport.pdf

Kranes, D. (1995). Playgrounds. *Journal of Gambling Studies*, *11*, 91–102.

Kutlu, R., Manav, B., and Lanc, R. K. (2013). Retail Design: Color-Light Influence on Brand Identity-Image Perception. *World Applied Sciences Journal 23* (5): 598–606, 2013

LaBar, K .S., and Phelps, E. A. (1998). Arousal-mediated memory consolidation: Role of the medial temporal lobe in humans. *Psychological Science, 9*(6), 490–493.

Lagerwerf, l (2002) Deliberate ambiguity in slogans: recognition and appreciation. *Document design, 3* (3). pages 245–260. ISSN 1388–8951.

Laney, C., Morris, E., Bernstein, D., Wakefield, B., and Loftus, E. (2008). Asparagus, a love story. Healthier eating could be just a false memory away. *Experimental Psychology*, *55*(5), 291–300.

Lau, R. R., Quadrel, M. J., and Hartman, K. A. (1990), 'Development and Change of Young Adults' Preventive Health Beliefs and Behavior: Influence from Parents and Peers', in *Journal of Health and Social Behavior*, vol. 31, n0. 3, [online], pages 240–259.

Lauterborn, B. (1990). New Marketing Litany: Four Ps Passé: C-Words Take Over. Advertising Age, 61(41), 26.

Lavidge, R.J. and Steiner, G.A. (1961) . A model for predictive measurements of advertising effectiveness. *Journal of Marketing*. 25(October), 59–62.

Lazarus, R. (1966) *Psychological stress and the coping process*. New York: McGraw Hill.

Leckman, J. F., Goodman, W. K., North, W. G., Chappell, P. B., Price, L. H., Pauls, D. L., and Cohen, D. J. (1994). The role of central oxytocin in obsessive compulsive disorder and related normal behavior. *Psychoneuroendocrinology*, *19*(8), 723–749.

Lehmkuhl, H. D., Storch, E. A., Bodfish, J. W., and Geffken, G. R. (2008). Brief report: Exposure and response prevention for obsessive compulsive disorder in a 12-year-old with autism. *Journal of Autism and Developmental Disorders*, *38*(5), 977–981.

Leventhal, H., Watts, J. C., and Pagano, F. (1967). Effects of fear and instructions on how to cope with danger. *Journal of Personality and Social Psychology, 6*(3), 313.

Lewin, B., Robertson, I. R., Cay, E. L., Irving, J. B., and Campbell, M. (1992). Effects of self-help post-myocardial-infarction rehabilitation on psychological adjustment and use of health services. *The Lancet, 339*(8800), 1036-1040.

Lewin, R. J. P., Furze, G., Robinson, J., Griffith, K., Wiseman, S., Pye, M., and Boyle, R. (2002), 'A randomised controlled trial of a self-management plan for patients with newly diagnosed angina', in *British Journal of General Practice*, vol. 52, [online], pages 194–201.

Ley, P. (1988), *Communicating with patients: Improving communication, satisfaction and compliance*. New York: Croom Helm.

Lindström, L. H., Gefvert, O., Hagberg, G., Lundberg, T., Bergström, M., Hartvig, P., and Långström, B. (1999). Increased dopamine synthesis rate in medial prefrontal cortex and striatum in schizophrenia indicated by L-(β-11 C) DOPA and PET. *Biological Psychiatry, 46*(5), 681–688.

Locke, E. (1981) Goal setting and task performance; 1969-1980, *Psychological Bulletin, 90*(1) 125-152.

Locke, E. A. and Latham, G. P. (1984). *Goal setting: A motivational technique that works!* Englewood Cliffs, NJ: Prentice Hall.

Loftus, E. F., and Palmer, J. C. (1974). Reconstruction of auto-mobile destruction: An example of the interaction between language and memory. *Journal of Verbal Learning and Verbal Behavior*, 13, 585–589.

Lovell, K., Cox, D., Haddock, G., Jones, C., Raines, D., Garvey, R., and Hadley, S. (2006). Telephone administered cognitive behaviour therapy for treatment of obsessive compulsive disorder: Randomised controlled non-inferiority trial. *British Medical Journal, 333*(7574), 883.

Lyons, L. C., and Woods, P. J. (1991). The efficacy of rational-emotive therapy: A quantitative review of the outcome research. *Clinical Psychology Review, 11*(4), 357–369.

Machleit, K. A., Eroglu, S. A., and Mantel, S. P. (2000). Perceived retail crowding and shopping satisfaction: what modifies this relationship?. *Journal of Consumer Psychology, 9*(1), 29–42.

Mackay, D. B., and Olshavsky, R. W. (1975). Cognitive maps of retail locations: an investigation of some basic issues. *Journal of Consumer Research*, 197–205.

Martin, J. and Peterson, M. (1987) Two-tier wage structures: implications for equity theory. *Academy of Management Journal, 30*(2) 297–315.

Mas, M. B., Jiménez, A. M. L., and San Gregorio, M. Á. P. (2010). Blood-Injection Phobia Inventory (BIPI): Development, reliability and validity. *Anales de Psicología, 26*(1), 58–71.

Maslow, A. (1970) *Motivation and Personality*, 2nd ed., Harper and Row: New York.

Maslow, A. (1943). A Theory of Human Motivation. *Psychological Review, 50*(4), 370–96.

Mattheisen, M., Samuels, J. F., Wang, Y., Greenberg, B. D., Fyer, A. J., McCracken, J. T., and Riddle, M. A. (2015). OCD and related disorders: Diagnosis to treatment. *Abstracts: Obsessive-Compulsive and Related Disorders*, 13(2).

McCarthy, Jerome E. (1960). *Basic Marketing. A Managerial Approach*. Homewood, IL: Richard D. Irwin.

McClelland, D.C. (1965) Toward a theory of motive acquisition. *American Psychologist*, Vol 20(5), May 1965, 321–333.

McKenna, E., (2012) *Business Psychology and Organizational Behaviour*. Hove: Psychology Press.

McKinlay, J. B. (1975), 'Who is Really Ignorant–Physician or Patient?', in *Journal of Health and Social Behavior*, vol. 16, no. 1, [online], pages 3–11.

McKinstry, B., and Wang, J. X. (1991), 'Putting on the style: what patients think of the way their doctor dresses', in *British Journal of General Practice*, vol. 41, no. 348, [online], pages 270, 275–278.

Mehrabian, A., and Russell, J. (1974), *An Approach to Environmental Psychology*, Cambridge, Mass.: MIT Press.

Melzack, R., and Wall, P. D. (1965), 'Pain mechanisms: a new theory', in *Science, New Series,* vol. 150, no. 3699, pages 971–979.

Meichenbaum, D. H., and Deffenbacher, J. L. (1988), 'Stress inoculation training', in *The Counseling Psychologist*, vol. 16, no. 1, [online], pages 69–90.

Middlemist, R. D., Knowles, E. S. and Matter, C. F. (1976) Personal space invasions in the lavatory: suggestive evidence for arousal. *Journal of Personality and Social Psychology*, 33, 541–546.

Milgram, S. (1963). Behavioural study of obedience. *Journal of Abnormal and Social Psychology, 67*, 371–378.

Milgram, S. (1974). *Obedience to authority: An experimental view.* Harper Collins.

Milgram, S., Liberty, H. J., Toledo, R., and Wackenhut, J. (1986). Response to intrusion into waiting lines. *Journal of Personality and Social Psychology, 51*(4), 683.

Miller, R. (2010). The feeling-state theory of impulse-control disorders and the Impulse-Control Disorder Protocol. *Traumatology, 16*(3), 2.

Morley, S., Shapiro, D., Biggs, J., (2004) Developing a treatment manual for attention management in chronic pain, *Cognitive Behaviour Therapy*. Vol. 33, Iss. 1, 2004.

Mowday, R. T., Steers, R. M., and Porter, L. W. (1979). The measurement of organizational commitment. *Journal of Vocational Behavior, 14*(2), 224–247.

Muczyk, J. P., and Reimann, B. C. (1987). The case for directive leadership. *The Academy of Management Executive, 1*(4), 301–311.

Nagel, D. C. (1988) Human error in aviation operations. In E. L. W. and D. C. Nagel (Eds) *Human Factors in Aviation*. New York: Academic Press Inc.

Nestler, E. J. (1997). Schizophrenia–An emerging pathophysiology. *Nature, 385*(6617), 578–579.

Neumann, J., Morgenstern, O. (1944) *Theory of Games and Economic Behaviour*. Princeton University Press.

NICE. (2015). Guidance on the use of electroconvulsive therapy. Retrieved from https://www.nice.org.uk/guidance/ta59.

North, A. C., Shilcock, A., and Hargreaves, D. J. (2003). The effect of musical style on restaurant customers' spending. *Environment and Behavior, 35*(5), 712–718.

North, A. C., and Hargreaves, D. J. (1998). The effect of music on atmosphere and purchase intentions in a cafeteria. *Journal of Applied Social Psychology, 28*(24), 2254-2273.

Oldham, G. R., and Brass, D. J. (1979). Employee reactions to an open-plan office: A naturally occurring quasi-experiment. *Administrative Science Quarterly*, 267–284.

Oruc, L., Verheyen, G. R., Furac, I., Jakovljević, M., Ivezić, S., Raeymaekers, P., and Van Broeckhoven, C. (1997). Association analysis of the 5-HT2C receptor and 5-HT transporter genes in bipolar disorder. *American Journal of Medical Genetics, 74*(5), 504–506.

Öst, L. G. (1992). Blood and injection phobia: Background and cognitive, physiological, and behavioral variables. *Journal of Abnormal Psychology, 101*(1), 68.

Öst, L. G., Sterner, U., and Fellenius, J. (1989). Applied tension, applied relaxation, and the combination in the treatment of blood phobia. *Behaviour Research and Therapy, 27*(2), 109–121.

Öst, L. G., and Westling, B. E. (1995). Applied relaxation vs cognitive behavior therapy in the treatment of panic disorder. *Behaviour Research and Therapy, 33*(2), 145–158.

Pampaloni, I., Sivakumaran, T., Hawley, C. J., Al Allaq, A., Farrow, J., Nelson, S., and Fineberg, N. A. (2009). High-dose selective serotonin reuptake inhibitors in OCD: a systematic retrospective case notes survey. *Journal of Psychopharmacology, 28,* 596–602.

Paul, G. L., and Lentz, R. J. (1977). *Psychosocial treatment of chronic mental patients: Milieu versus social-learning programs.* Harvard University Press.

Pavesic, D. (2005). The Psychology of Menu Design: Reinvent Your 'Silent Salesperson' to Increase Check Averages and Guest Loyalty. Hospitality Faculty Publications. Paper 5.

Pepperberg, I. M. (1987). Acquisition of the same/different concept by an African Grey parrot (*Psittacus erithacus*): Learning with respect to categories of color, shape, and material. *Animal Learning and Behavior, 15*(4), 423–432.

Pfeffer, J. (1998) Six dangerous myths about pay. *Harvard Business Review*, May–June.

Piliavin, I. M., Rodin, J., and Piliavin, J. (1969). Good Samaritanism: An underground phenomenon? *Journal of Personality and Social Psychology, 13*(4), 289–299.

Pheasant, S. (1991) *Ergonomics, Work and Health*, Macmillan Academic and Professional Ltd. London.

Porublev, E., Brace-Govan, J., Minahan, S., and Dubelaar, C. (2009, January). To wrap or not to wrap? What is expected? Some initial findings from a study of gift wrapping. In *ANZMAC 2009: Sustainable management and marketing conference* (pages 1–8). Monash University.

Prochaska, J. O., and Velicer, W. F. (1997), 'The Transtheoretical Model of Health Behavior Change', in *American Journal of Health Promotion*, vol. 12, no. 1, [online], pages 38–48.

Pruitt, D. G. and Rubin, J. Z. (2003) *Social Conflict: Escalation, Stalemate and Settlement*. New York: McGraw-Hill

Rahe, R. H., Mahan, J. L., and Arthur, R. J. (1970). Prediction of near-future health change from subjects' preceding life changes. *Journal of Psychosomatic Research, 14*(4), 401–406.

Ramachandran, V. S., Blakeslee, S., and Sacks, O. W. (1998). *Phantoms in the brain: Probing the mysteries of the human mind*. New York: William Morrow.

Rapoport, J. L. (1989). *The boy who couldn't stop washing: The experience and treatment of obsessive-compulsive disorder.* Penguin.

Richarme, (2005). Consumer decision making models, strategies and theories; Oh My! *Decision Analyst*. http://www.decisionanalyst.com/Downloads/ConsumerDecisionMaking.pdf

Riekert, K. A., and Drotar, D. (1999), 'Who Participates in Research on Adherence to Treatment in Insulin-dependent

Diabetes Mellitus? Implications and Recommendations for Research', in *Journal of Pediatric Psychology*, vol. 24, no. 3, [online], pages 253–258.

Riggio, R. (2009). *Introduction to Industrial/Organizational Psychology*. New Jersey: Pearson Prentice Hall.

Roberts, G. E. (1994). Maximising performance appraisal systems effectiveness: Perspectives from municipal government personnel administrators. *Public Personnel Management, 23, 525–549.*

Robinson, R., and West, R. (1992), 'A comparison of computer and questionnaire methods of history-taking in a genito-urinary clinic', in *Psychology and Health*, vol. 6, no. 1–2, [online], pages 77–84.

Robson, S. K., Kimes, S. E., Becker, F. D., and Evans, G. W. (2011). Consumers' responses to table spacing in restaurants. *Cornell Hospitality Quarterly, 52*(3), 253–264.

Roedder, D. L. (1981). Age differences in children's responses to television advertising: An information processing approach. *Journal of Consumer Research*, 8(2) 144–153.

Rose, M. (1998), *Performance related pay in schools: an assessment of the Green papers*. NUT London.

Roth, H. P., and Caron, H. S. (1978), 'Accuracy of doctors' estimates and patients' statements on adherence to a drug regimen', in *Clinical Pharmacology and Therapeutics*, vol. 23, no. 3, [online], pages 361–370.

Ryan, T. A. (1970). *Intentional Behavior*. New York: Ronald Press.

Saavedra, L. M., and Silverman, W. K. (2002). Case Study: Disgust and a specific phobia of buttons. *Journal of the American Academy of Child and Adolescent Psychiatry, 41*(11), 1376–1379.

Safer, M. A., Tharps, Q. J., Jackson, T. C., and Leventhal, H. (1979), 'Determinants of Three Stages of Delay in Seeking Care at a Medical Clinic', in *Medical Care*, vol. 17, no. 1, [online], page 11.

Savage, R., and Armstrong, D. (1990), 'Effect of a general practitioner's consulting style on patients' satisfaction: a controlled study', in *BMJ: British Medical Journal*, vol. 301, no. 6758, [online], page. 968–970.

Schachter, S., and Singer, J. E. (1962). Cognitive, social and physiological determinants of emotional state. *Psychological Review, 69*, 379–399.

Schopler, J., and Matthews, M. W. (1965). The influence of the perceived causal locus of partner's dependence on the use of interpersonal power. *Journal of Personality and Social Psychology, 2*(4), 609.

Scouller, J. (2011). *The Three Levels of Leadership: How to Develop Your Leadership Presence, Knowhow and Skill*. Cirencester: Management Books.

Seaberg, A. (1971) *Menu Design: Merchandising and Marketing*. Wiley.

Seligman, M. E., Castellon, C., Cacciola, J., Schulman, P., Luborsky, L., Ollove, M., and Downing, R. (1988). Explanatory style change during cognitive therapy for unipolar depression. *Journal of Abnormal Psychology, 97*(1), 13.

H. Selye, (1936) *Stress without Distress*. New York, Philadelphia: Lippincott.

Sensky, T., Turkington, D., Kingdon, D., Scott, J. L., Scott, J., Siddle, R., and Barnes, T. R. (2000). A randomized controlled trial of cognitive-behavioral therapy for persistent symptoms in schizophrenia resistant to medication. *Archives of General Psychiatry, 57*(2), 165–172.

Sherif, M., Harvey, O. J., White, B. J., Hood, W. R., and Sherif, C. W. (1961). *Intergroup conflict and cooperation: The Robbers Cave experiment (Vol. 10)*. Norman, OK: University of Oklahoma Book Exchange.

Sherman, J., Hutson, A., Baumstein, S., and Hendeles, L. (2000), 'Telephoning the patient's pharmacy to assess adherence with asthma medications by measuring refill rate for prescriptions', in *The Journal of Pediatrics*, vol. 136, no. 4, [online], pages 532–536.

Shleifer, A. (2012). Psychologists at the Gate: A Review of Daniel Kahneman's "Thinking, Fast and Slow". *Journal of Economic Literature*, 1080–1091.

Simon, H. A. (1956). "Rational Choice and the Structure of the Environment". *Psychological Review*. 1956; 63(2): 129–138.

Kinner, B. F. 1938 *The Behavior of Organisms: An Experimental Analysis*, New York: Appleton-Century-Crofts.

Smith, P. C., Kendall, L. M., and Hulin, C. L. (1969). *Measurement of satisfaction in work and retirement*. Chicago: Rand McNally.

Snyder, M., and DeBono, K. G. (1985). Appeals to image and claims about quality: Understanding the psychology of advertising. *Journal of Personality and Social Psychology, 49*(3), 586.

Somner, R. (1969*) Personal Space*. Englewood Cliffs, NJ: Prentice Hall. Study of Gambling and Commercial Gaming.

Soomro, G. M., Altman, D., Rajagopal, S., and Oakley-Browne, M. (2008). Selective serotonin re-uptake inhibitors (SSRIs) versus placebo for obsessive compulsive disorder (OCD). *Cochrane Database of Systemic Reviews, 1*(1).

Spitzer, R. L., Kroenke, K., Williams, J. B., and Löwe, B. (2006). A brief measure for assessing generalized anxiety disorder: the GAD-7. *Archives of Internal Medicine, 166*(10), 1092–1097.

Stamp-Dawkins, M. (1998). *Through our eyes only? The search for animal consciousness*. Oxford University Press.

Stogdill, R.M., Coons, A.E. (eds), *Leader behavior: Its description and measurement*. Columbus, OH: Bureau of Buisness Research, Ohio State University.

Svetlova, M., Nichols, S., and Brownwell, C. (2010). Toddlers' prosocial behaviour: From instrumental to empathetic to altruistic helping. *Child Development, 81*, 1814–1827.

Taj, M. J. R., Viswanath, B., Purushottam, M., Kandavel, T., Janardhan Reddy, Y. C., and Jain, S. (2013). DRD4 gene and obsessive compulsive disorder: Do symptom dimensions have specific genetic correlates? *Progress in Neuropsychopharmacology and Biological Psychiatry, 41*, 18–23.

Tapper, K., Horne, P. J., and Lowe, C. F. (2003), 'The Food Dudes to the rescue', in *Psychologist*, vol. 16, no. 1, [online], pages 18–21.

Thomas, K. W. (1976). Conflict and conflict management. In M. D. Dunnette (Ed.), *Handbook of industrial and organizational psychology* (pages 889–935).

Tuckman, B. W. (1965). Developmental sequence in small groups. *Psychological bulletin, 63*(6), 384.

Turley, L. W., and Milliman, R. E. (2000). Atmospheric effects on shopping behavior: a review of the experimental evidence. *Journal of Business Research, 49*(2), 193–211.

Varni, J. W., Thompson, K. L., and Hanson, V. (1987), 'The Varni/Thompson Pediatric Pain Questionnaire. I. Chronic musculoskeletal pain in juvenile rheumatoid arthritis', in *Pain, The Journal of the International Association for the Study of Pain*, vol. 28 no 1, pages 27–38.

Vrechopoulos, A. P., O'Keefe, R. M., Doukidis, G. I., and Siomkos, G. J. (2004). Virtual store layout: an experimental comparison in the context of grocery retail. *Journal of Retailing, 80*(1), 13–22.

Vroom, V. H. (1964). *Work and Motivation*. New York: Wiley.

Walton, R. E. (1973). Quality of work life. *Sloan Management Review, 15*(1): 11–12.

Walton, R. E. (1974). QWL indicators: prospects and problems. In Portigal, A. H. (Eds.). *Measuring the quality of working life. A symposium on Social Indicators of Working Life*. Ottawa, March, 19–20.

Wang, J., Rao, H., Wetmore, G. S., Furlan, P. M., Korczykowski, M., Dinges, D. F., and Detre, J. A. (2005), 'Perfusion functional MRI reveals cerebral blood flow pattern under psychological stress', *Proceedings of the National Academy of Sciences of the United States of America*, vol. 102, no. 49, [online], pages 17804–17809

Wansink, B., Kent, R. J., and Hoch, S. (1998). An anchoring and adjustment model of purchase quantity decisions. *Journal of Marketing Research, 1998*, 71–81.

Wansink, B., Van Ittersum, K., and Painter, J. E. (2005). How descriptive food names bias sensory perceptions in restaurants. *Food Quality and Preference, 16*(5), 393–400.

Warwick, H. M., and Salkovskis, P. M. (1990), Hypochondriasis. *Behaviour Research Therapy, 28*, 105–117.

Watson, J. B., and Rayner, R. (1920). Conditioned emotional reactions. *Journal of Experimental Psychology, 3*(1), 1.

Watt, P. M., Clements, B., Devadason, S. G., and Chaney, G. M. (2003), 'Funhaler spacer: improving adherence without compromising delivery', in *Archives of Disease in Childhood*, vol. 88, no. 7, [online], pages 579–581.

Wedley, W. C., and Field, R. H. (1984). A predecision support system. *Academy of Management Review, 9*(4), 696–703.

Weinstein, N. D. (1980), 'Unrealistic Optimism About Future Life Events', in *Journal of Personality and Social Psychology*, vol. 36, no. 5, [online], pages 806–820.

Weiss, D. J. , Dawis, R. V. England, G. W. and Lofquist, L. H. (1967), Manual for the Minnesota Satisfaction Questionnaire. Vol. 22, *Minnesota Studies in Vocational Rehabilitation*, Minneapolis: University of Minnesota, Industrial Relations Center.

Wickström, G., and Bendix, T. (2000). The "Hawthorne effect"—what did the original Hawthorne studies actually show? *Scandinavian Journal of Work, Environment and Health*, 363–367.

Wiles, N., Thomas, L., Abel, A., Ridgway, N., Turner, N., Campbell, J. and Lewis, G. (2013). Cognitive behavioural therapy as an adjunct to pharmacotherapy for primary care based patients with treatment resistant depression: Results of the CoBalT randomised controlled trial. *The Lancet, 381*(9864), 375–384.

Wilson, T., and Brekke, N. (1994). Cited in Boyd-Jansson, C. (2010). *Consumer Psychology*. Maidenhead: Open University Press.

Wilson, K., and Korn, J. H. (2007). Attention during lectures: Beyond ten minutes. *Teaching of Psychology, 34*, 85–99.

Wise, C. D., Baden, M. M., and Stein, L. (1974). Post-mortem measurement of enzymes in human brain: evidence of a central noradrenergic deficit in schizophrenia. *Journal of Psychiatric Research, 11*, 185–198.

Wolpe, J. (1958). *Psychotherapy by reciprocal inhibition*. Stanford University Press.

Wong, D. L., and Baker, C. M. (1988), 'Pain in Children: Comparison of Assessment Scales', in *Pediatric Nursing*, vo. 14, no. 1, [online], pages 9–17.

Woods, F. A. (1913). *The Influence of Monarchs: Steps in a New Science of History*. New York, NY: Macmillan.

Woods, A. T., Poliakoff, E., Lloyd, D. M., Kuenzel, J., Hodson, R., Gonda, H., and Thomas, A. (2011). Effect of background noise on food perception. *Food Quality and Preference*, *22*(1), 42–47.

Yalch, R. F. (1981) Memory in a Jingle Jungle: Music as a Mnemonic Device in Communicating Advertising Slogans, *Journal of Applied Psychology* 76 (April), page 268–275

Yamamoto, S., Humle, T., and Tanaka, M. (2012). Chimpanzees' flexible targeted helping based on an understanding of conspecifics' goals. *Proceedings of the National Academy of Sciences*, *109*(9), 3588–3592.

Yao, S. (1997), Profit sharing, bonus payment, and productivity: a case study of Chinese state-owned enterprises, *Journal Of Comparative Economics*, *24*: 281–296.

Yokley, J. M., and Glenwick, D. S. (1984), 'Increasing the immunization of preschool children; an evaluation of applied community interventions', in *Journal of Applied Behavior Analysis*, vol. 17, no. 3, [online], pages 313–325.

Zajonc, R. B. and Markus, H. (1984), 'Affect and cognition: the hard interface'. In: Izard, C.E., Kagan, J. and Zajonc, R. B. (Eds.), *Emotions, Cognition, and Behavior*, Cambridge: Cambridge University Press, 63–103.

Index

Acknowledgements

p. 1: Imagemore Co, Ltd/Getty; p. 2 (T): Kues/Shutterstock; p. 2 (B): BraunS/Getty; p. 5: Flirt/Alamy; p. 6: photosindia/Getty; p. 11: RosalreneBetancourt 4/Alamy; p. 16: Maskot/Getty; p. 17: VladTeodor/Getty; p. 19: 2016 Quizlet Inc; p. 21: CaiaImage/Getty; p. 24: Granger, NYC/Alamy; p. 35: Ezra Bailey/Getty; p. 43: Jonathan Selig/Getty; p. 45: Miguel Medina/Stringer/Getty; p. 46: Dr P. Marazzi/Science Photo Library; p. 56: KidStock/Getty; p. 57: Fuse/Getty; p. 63: Jo karen/Shutterstock; p. 71: BJI/Lane Oatey/Getty; p. 75 (T): Rafael Ben-Ari/Alamy; p. 75 (B): Ullamaija Hanninen/Getty; p. 79: Civil/Shutterstock; p. 83: DoubleBubble/Shutterstock; p. 85: CaiaImage/Getty; p. 86: Courtesy of Albert Bandura; p. 95 (L): Bettman/Getty; p. 95 (R): Mikael Damkier/Shutterstock; p. 97: Cyril Ruoso/ Minden Pictures/Getty; p. 99: Anurak Pongpatimet/Shutterstock; p. 101: Djem/Shutterstock; p. 102: Bruno De Hogues/Getty; p. 104 (T): Milgram, S. from the film "Obedience"; p. 104 (B): Magnolia Pictures/BB Film Productions/FJ Productions/Kobal; p. 107: New York Daily News/Getty; p. 110: valdis torms/Shutterstock; p. 112 (T): Janine Wiedel Photolibrary/Alamy; p. 112 (B): Visuals Unlimited, Inc/Fiona Rogers/Getty; p. 115: Gerry Ellis/Getty; p. 119: Imuse/Getty; p. 122: Oxford Cognitive Approaches to Psychosis, University of Oxford; p. 123: Michal Krakowiak/ Getty; p. 125: Sovereign, ISM/Science Photo Library; p. 127: David Cooper/Getty; p. 137: Christian Thomas/Getty; p. 138: Westend61/Getty; p. 142: BSIP/Getty; p. 144: Peter Dazeley/ Getty; p. 145: JGI/Jamie Grill/Getty; p. 146: Archives of the History of American Psychology, The Drs. Nicholas and Dorothy Cummings Center for the History of Psychology, The university of Akron; p. 147 (T): DEA/B. Langrish/Getty; p. 147 (B): jannoon028/Shutterstock; p. 152: WR Publishing/ Alamy; p. 155 (T): Subbotina Anna/Shutterstock; p. 155 (B): images by Tang Ming Tung/Getty; p. 156: Alliance/Shutterstock; p. 159: Rob Atkins/Getty; p. 162 (T): Leonid Serebrennikov/ Alamy; p. 162 (C): Martin Carlsson/Alamy; p. 162 (B): I. Pilon/ Shutterstock; p. 170: David Ramos/Getty; p. 172: Jorge Gil, Eime Tobari, Maia Lemlij, Anna Rose, Alan Penn/Space Syntax; p. 174: Marchie/Shutterstock; p. 178: David R. Frazier Photolibrary, Inc/ Alamy; p. 190 (T): Stefanie Grewel/Getty; p. 190 (B): Bloomberg/ Getty; p. 199: Art Directors & TRIP/Alamy; p. 205: dpa picture alliance/American Broadcasting Companies, Inc/Alamy; p. 211: Peter Dazeley/Getty; p. 213: Brian McKinstry and Ji'xiang Wang; p. 220: Bob Pardue/Medical Lifestyle/Alamy; p. 237: Allergy Medical Store; p. 241 (TL): Media for Medical/Getty; p. 241 (TR): BSIP/Universal Images Group/Getty; p. 241 (B): Blend_Images/ Getty; p. 245: 1983 Wong-Baker FACES Foundation, originally published in Whaley & Wong's Nursing care of Infants and Children. (c) Elsevier Inc; p. 248: Andrey_Popov/Shutterstock; p. 249: Radharc Images/Alamy; p. 255: Miguel Medina/Stringer/ Getty; p. 260: Subbotina Anna/Shutterstock; p. 266: Bangor University (2000). All rights reserved; p. 274: istock/johavel/ iStock; p. 277: AF archive/Alamy; p. 285: Ian Cumming/Getty; p. 299: Corbis Super RF/Alamy.

Illustration acknowledgments
p. 55: Derek Easterby
All other illustrations by emc Design

361